*An Eyewitness Account
of the American Revolution
and New England Life*

Recent Titles in
Contributions in Military Studies

The Culture of War: Invention and Early Development
Richard A. Gabriel

Prisoners, Diplomats, and the Great War: A Study in the Diplomacy of Captivity
Richard Berry Speed III

Military Crisis Management: U.S. Intervention in the Dominican Republic, 1965
Herbert G. Schoonmaker

The Persian Gulf War: Lessons for Strategy, Law, and Diplomacy
Christopher C. Joyner, editor

Where Eagles Land: Planning and Development of U.S. Army Airfields,
1910-1941
Jerold E. Brown

First Strike Stability: Deterrence after Containment
Stephen J. Cimbala

Legitimacy and Commitment in the Military
Thomas C. Wyatt and Reuven Gal, editors

The Army's Nuclear Power Program: The Evolution of a Support Agency
Lawrence H. Suid

Russian Imperial Military Doctrine and Education, 1832-1914
Carl Van Dyke

The Eagle and the Dragon: The United States Military in China, 1901-1937
Dennis L. Noble

An Eyewitness Account of the American Revolution and New England Life

The Journal of J.F. Wasmus,
German Company Surgeon,
1776–1783

Translated by HELGA DOBLIN

Edited and Introduction by MARY C. LYNN

Contributions in Military Studies, Number 106

GREENWOOD PRESS
New York • Westport, Connecticut • London

Library of Congress Cataloging-in-Publication Data

Wasmus, J.F.
　　An eyewitness account of the American Revolution and New England
life : the journal of J.F. Wasmus, German company surgeon, 1776-1783
/ translated by Helga Doblin ; edited and introduction by Mary C.
Lynn.
　　　p.　　cm. — (Contributions in military studies, ISSN 0883-6884
; no. 106)
　　Includes bibliographical references (p.　) and indexes.
　　ISBN 0-313-27355-3 (lib. bdg. : alk. paper)
　　1. Wasmus, J.F.—Diaries.　2. United States—History—Revolution,
1775-1783—German mercenaries.　3. United States—History—
Revolution, 1775-1783—Personal narratives, German.　4. New
England—History—Revolution, 1775-1783—Personal narratives,
German.　5. Germans—New England—Diaries.
6. Physicians—New England—Diaries.　I. Doblin,
Helga.　II. Lynn, Mary C.　III. Title.　IV. Series.
E268.W2　1990
973.3'8—dc20　　　90-3631

British Library Cataloguing in Publication Data is available.

Library of Congress Catalog Card Number: 90-3631
ISBN: 0-313-27355-3
ISSN: 0883-6884

First published in 1990

Greenwood Press, 88 Post Road West, Westport, CT 06881
An imprint of Greenwood Publishing Group, Inc.

Printed in the United States of America

The paper used in this book complies with the
Permanent Paper Standard issued by the National
Information Standards Organization (Z39.48-1984).

10 9 8 7 6 5 4 3 2 1

Contents

Preface

The Journal of J.F. Wasmus, 1776-1783, was one of two journals kept by a Braunschweig surgeon to record his experiences in the Seven Years War and the American Revolution. The journal of Wasmus' Revolutionary experiences was kept for many years in the confidential archives of the Prussian military in Berlin, Germany. Its location there was noted by Marion Learned of the University of Pennsylvania, who in the early twentieth century searched many European archives for material relevant to the American Revolution, all of which was listed in his bibliography published in 1911. The journal was one of several such journals, which, along with letters, log books, and muster rolls were microfilmed under a special Library of Congress program which used the then-new technology of microfilm to copy all identifiable material in European archives bearing on the American Revolution between 1929 and 1931.

These microfilms were placed in the Library of Congress but received little attention until 1976, when, as part of the celebration of the Bicentennial of the American Revolution the Library of Congress published a bibliography (entitled Manuscripts and Sources in the Library of Congress for Research on the American Revolution, Washington, D.C., 1976) to encourage further scholarly work on the Revolutionary War. Inspired by this publication, the historians at the Saratoga National Historical Park, with the support of the late superintendent Glen Gray, secured microfilm copies of the texts which included information related to the Northern campaign and the Battle of Saratoga. I was hired by the Park Service in 1981 to translate them into English.

These German documents were written in Gothic characters, the so-called fraktur, while names, foreign words, French phrases and Latin expressions appear in Roman letters. Some of the text is illegible because of the poor condition of the original manuscripts, which were often written in haste during the campaign. Abbreviations and symbols, such as titles, dates, months, currency, weights, and measures present special problems, since many of these terms are archaic and their meanings are difficult to discover.

The journal of Company Surgeon J. F. Wasmus includes a number of Latin terms reflecting Wasmus' medical training, as well as French, which was the military language of the period. To assure that the translation is faithful to the original, I have translated the text as literally as possible, and have retained his underlinings, punctuation (including parentheses) and abbreviations. I have spelled geographical designations as they appear on modern maps and texts; personal names are spelled according to the individual's own signature whenever possible. Except for the St. Lawrence River, I have rendered all

Canadian place names north of Cumberland Head on Lake Champlain in French; those south of that border use the English spelling. I have also chosen to refer to Braunschweig and Hannover in the original German to differentiate them from the 11 Brunswicks and 15 Hanovers located in the United States.

Words appearing in brackets [ ] explain or translate the original text, e.g., "they [the men] are silent." Italics, appearing in brackets, have been added to make the sentence in question clearer, e.g., "Rice [*costs*] two piasters a pound." Wasmus' translations from the Revolutionary press are rendered in a different typeface, to set them apart. The names of ships are italicized, except for those which appear in the translations; these are underlined. Latin words are written in capital letters, and words from French, Spanish, and Italian are not underlined. Punctuation marks are set according to modern American usage.

Using the resources of the American Antiquarian Society in Worcester, Massachusetts, which include files of all the pertinent newspapers, either in the original or on micro-fiche, I have rated Wasmus translations of articles in the American press, which begin late in 1778 and continue through March, 1781, as accurate (accurate translations of the English original); summary (compressed versions of the English original); or selective (partial versions of the English original). The accurate passages render the sense of the original in detail; as these have undergone two translations, they rarely are verbatim replicas of the original. These newspaper translations have been printed in a distinctive typeface to distinguish them from, Wasmus' own comments, which sometimes occur inserted into the text of his translation. Whenever the discrepancy between Wasmus' translation and the original text became problematic, I have included the original version in brackets.

Helga Doblin
Stillwater, New York
January, 1990

Acknowledgments

Since the beginning of this project in 1981, we have been given generous assistance from many sources. Paul Okie and other historians of the Saratoga National Historical Park have been most helpful at all stages of the project. The reference staff of the Lucy Skidmore Library at Skidmore College made significant contributions. The translation was supported in part by a grant from the National Endowment for the Humanities, an independent federal agency, and preparation of the manuscript for publication was aided by a Skidmore College faculty research grant.

In Germany, Herr Arnoldt and the staff of the Niedersächsisches Archiv at Wolfenbüttel provided access to the original Wasmus journal and information about the Braunschweig contingent in America. The staff of the Kirchenamt in Braunschweig and Dr. Joachim Fischer, retired archivist for Frankfurt am Main, provided assistance, as did Dr. Kurt Hoffmann in Wolfenbüttel.

The staff at the American Antiquarian Society in Worcester, were helpful in providing access to the eighteenth-century newspapers Wasmus used to provide some perspective on the events of the war while he was a prisoner. Mrs. Helene J. Lindblad of the Brimfield, Massachusetts library was a source of useful information. Mme. Céline Villeneuve of the Archives Cartographiques at Québec and Dr. Robert Morgan of the University of Cape Breton, Nova Scotia, both helped us find pertinent maps and illustrations of the eighteenth century; so did Mr. Eugene Kosche, historian at the Bennington Museum, who was most resourceful and knowledgeable in providing us with historical material, as was Mr. Charles Westbrook of Fort Ticonderoga. (A brief selection from the journal covering Wasmus' visit to Halifax was published in the spring/summer 1990 issue of the Nova Scotia Historical Review.)

Typing and preparation of the manuscript were aided by the work of Libby Abel at Saratoga National Historical Park and by Nancy Osberg. Sue Stein's expertise and enthusiasm aided in the final and most cumbersome stages, for which two students Alexandra Tolan, and Caroline Hewitt provided considerable assistance. The transformation of the manuscript into camera-ready copy was immeasurably helped by Leo Geoffrion, Kevin Vaughn, and the staff of the Skidmore Computer Center. John Danison, of the Computer Center, was extraordinarily generous with his time, his Macintosh, and his advice; in addition he used his considerable artistic skills to simplify and edit the maps. Our editor, Mildred Vasan, and the staff at Greenwood Press were very helpful in providing direction and advice as we struggled through the final stages of readying the journal for publication.

x   Acknowledgments

We particularly thank President David Porter of Skidmore College for his active encouragement and we are thankful for all those who helped us complete what seems in retrospect to have been a dauntingly ambitious task.   Finally, we are grateful to our families for supporting this project in many ways too numerous to mention.

Introduction

The writing of history has recently been criticized for overspecialization and for the replacement of traditional narrative by the overly intensive study of narrow aspects of society. Yet one could also argue that history has been transformed positively by the work of the last twenty years which has led to a considerable amount of cross-fertilization between different areas of inquiry. The new military history provides us with a perfect example of this breakdown of barriers between specialized fields. Although military history is clearly the oldest, and for a very long time the most important kind of history, the study of command and campaign has suffered from a lack of prestige within the profession in the twentieth century, especially since World War I. Perhaps because of the participation of large numbers of passionate amateurs, or perhaps because of the practical or vocational attributes of military history as taught to aspiring officers, and certainly because of the increasing numbers of academics who have come to question the necessity or validity of war as an instrument of national policy (whether as part of the isolationism of the thirties or of the antiwar movement of the Vietnam period), military history has lost its former importance in many American graduate programs.

And yet much of the military history written in the last twenty years has not only been very good history indeed, but it has also been interdisciplinary, and at least some of its practitioners have been open to the insights and techniques of other historical specialties to a degree that one could wish was more common in the profession as a whole. Sadly, this important work has not received the attention it deserves from the profession.

Like all history, military history has been enormously changed by the impact of the revolution in social history, which began twenty years ago. Heavily influenced by French and British historians anxious to recover the experience of the past through the intensive use of local records, the new social history emphasized the lives of ordinary people rather than the heroic figures with which traditional history had been concerned. Women, workers, peasants, slaves, and children began to emerge as legitimate subjects for historical inquiry as town and church records, census material, and the correspondence of individuals previously considered unimportant began to be used, often in remarkably imaginative ways, to shed light on the history of the inarticulate.

Military history until the 1960's was dominated by the analyses of great commanders and crucial battles, just as mainstream history was dominated by the study of powerful leaders and national crises. But under the influence of the changes in focus and methodology of social history, military historians have developed what is rightly called "the new military history," a history which also emphasizes the role of those who had been hidden from the historian's analysis in the past.   Professor Fred Anderson, a leading exponent of the new military history, whose important 1984 study of Massachusetts soldiers in the Seven Years War, A People's Army,[1] has defined the new military history as "the history of warfare and military service recounted within a larger cultural and social context."[2]   Although this new kind of military history is being written for all American history, the military history of the American Revolution has proved to be a particularly fertile area for the application of this new method of analysis.

In some ways, the new military history is also social history, focusing on the lives and experiences of ordinary soldiers, but it clearly differs because those experiences take place in a strictly limited frame of time rather than over decades or even centuries.   New techniques and interests have allowed military historians to enliven the consideration of what were traditionally considered dull aspects of war and to write readable and interesting studies, for example Wayne Carp's To Starve the Army at Pleasure, a 1984 examination of the way in which the Continental Army was supplied (or not supplied.)[3]

For the past two decades, military historians have transformed the history of the American Revolution in a series of books and essays, such as Jesse Lemisch's path-breaking article on the experiences of American prisoners of the British in 1969;[4] Charles Royster's penetrating analysis of the Continental Army and the American character, A Revolutionary People at War;[5] and the works of Karp and Anderson cited above.   Robert Gross' important study of the Minutemen and of the communities of Lexington and Concord, The Minutemen and Their World,[6] belongs in a separate category, for it is social history which provides a specific context for military history with its study of the community of Concord based on vital records, tax records, wills, deeds, town meeting minutes, and genealogy.

As military history has become broader and more interdisciplinary, a number of important bibliographical essays have both catalogued these developments and directed scholars to work which still remains to be done.   In 1971 Peter Paret characterized American military historians as working in "two way...disciplinary isolation,"[7]   Paret mourned the failure of military historians to take advantage of new approaches that were being developed in other branches of history, and the failure of non-military historians to read and recognize what was happening in military history.   Several years later Martin K. Gordon, in an essay on "American Military Studies"[8] saw some evidence that this isolation still existed, but he also catalogued some of the new interdisciplinary work which was beginning to break down the barriers, including the work of John Shy.[9]   But Gordon seemed to be primarily concerned with "increased cooperation among all those interested in American military studies" and with the possibilities of an American Studies approach to military affairs.[10]

Even more explicit about the advantages of interdisciplinary cooperation was Peter Karsten, whose 1984 review essay on "The New American Military History" highlighted the impact of this growing interdisciplinarity as he chronicled the writing of studies of what he called the "rest of military history," by which he meant history which went beyond the study of "campaigns, leaders, strategy, tactics, weapons, logistics."[11]   The new military history was the history of "the recruitment, training and socialization of personnel, combat motivation, the effect of service and war on the individual soldier, the veteran, the internal dynamics of military institutions, inter- and intra-service tensions, civil-military relations, and the relationship between military systems and the greater society."[12]   By combining this somewhat limited definition with the larger concept suggested by Professor Anderson, which includes the social and cultural context in which these military activities take place, we can produce a clearer description of what has happened to military history since the 1960's.

As the new military history begins to transform the way we write the history of the American Revolution, it is also transforming the kinds of sources that we draw on for that record. Local vital statistics join muster rolls and orderly books when critical sources as new military historians record the experience of the Minutemen; the experiences of individual staff officers engaged in supplying the army become more important as the historians write the history of its supply operations; and the experiences of individual prisoners of war can become a window into the society and culture of the Revolutionary period, providing a resource for a variety of future studies.

This translation should provide another helpful resource for the new, interdisciplinary military history.   Julius Friedrich Wasmus was a Braunschweig company surgeon, a member of the auxiliary troops from Germany, who participated in General John Burgoyne's invasion of New York in 1777.   Captured at Bennington, a battle about which he gives a riveting description, the most complete description available from German sources, Wasmus went on to spend three years as a prisoner of war.   While the journal provides useful information for the historian interested in campaigns, issues of leadership, and battles, it is even more valuable for the new military historian, who can use it to explore the culture and organization of the British/Braunschweig army, as well as the society and culture of Revolutionary Massachusetts and British Canada.

The American Revolution was in many ways a world war; land and naval battles were ranging from Ceylon to Gibraltar, in addition to the better remembered conflicts in the West Indies and on the North American continent.   The force that the British assembled to subdue their rebellious colonies was an international one, an aspect of the war that has frequently been over-simplified by referring to the presence of the "Hessian mercenaries," who were hired by the King to do what British troops apparently would or could not do.   Yet the American enemy in the Revolution was no more a British-Hessian force than the Revolution was a war fought within the boundaries of the thirteen colonies. The British Commanders-in-Chief led a complex, international army, which included soldiers from England, Scotland, Ireland, six German principalities and duchies, native Americans, Canadians, and various American loyalist units--truly an international force. Perceiving the Revolution as an international conflict provides us with a far more complex and complete view of both the Revolution itself and of the culture and society of the thirteen colonies as they transformed themselves into a nation.   Individual accounts of ordinary soldiers and officers have assumed much greater importance because of the impact of social history on military history, so that we might expect that important resources for that international perception are the accounts of the auxiliary troops hired by the British crown: the letters, journals, and autobiographical fragments of the men, mostly German, who saw America for the first time as an invading army, as part of an occupation force, or as prisoners.

These Germans, who had come to America as a result of treaties by which the British paid the various German reigning dukes and princes to hire their armies to assist the hard-pressed British in maintaining their colonial empire while putting down the rebellion in America, included men of considerable education and experience. Even some of the ordinary soldiers were literate since compulsory education had been introduced into some of the German states in the early eighteenth century.[13] As professional soldiers, the Germans were committed, but they fought without the desperate fervor of the Americans and the Tories whose hearts and family futures were fully engaged. Some Germans seem to have been surprisingly objective about America and not without sympathy for its inhabitants and even for their cause. Their realistic descriptions of what they found here are invaluable sources for the historian and fascinating documents for all interested in what it was like to be in America at the time.

Auxiliary troops (as opposed to mercenaries, who hold individual contracts) had been commonplace in Europe for several hundred years.   Italians, Germans, even the Swiss fought in the wars of other nations; the British had made use of such forces on several occasions earlier in the eighteenth century.   The auxiliaries hired by the British in 1776 came from German states whose natural resources were so limited that their rulers exported soldiers as a source of income.   The Margrave of Ansbach Bayreuth sent 2,353 men, the Principality of Waldeck sent 1,225, the Count of Hesse-Hanau sent 2,422, while the Landgrave of Hesse Kassel sent 16,992, the Principality of Anhalt Zerbst 1,152 and the Duchy of Braunschweig and Lüneburg 5,723. Duke Carl of Braunschweig, who was married to Philippine Charlotte, sister of Frederick the Great of Prussia, was a logical source for King George III of England to approach for troops: King George's elder sister Augusta was married to Duke Carl's heir, the Hereditary Prince Karl Wilhelm Ferdinand.

Among the troops sent from Braunschweig to America in 1776 was Company Surgeon Julius Friedrich Wasmus, a veteran of the Seven Years War, an educated man, who was in the habit of keeping a diary. Both his diary from the Seven Years War and the journal of his experiences in the Revolution have survived and provide a fascinating portrait not only of life inside an eighteenth-century army on the move, but also of Revolutionary society and culture. Perhaps because Wasmus was a surgeon and not engaged in direct combat, some historians have not considered his journal as important as the accounts of some of his fellow auxiliaries in the American war. The diary may also have been neglected because of Wasmus' inclusion of his own translations of newspaper articles, (difficult to check for authenticity) which make up the bulk of the entries during two of the four years Wasmus spent as a prisoner of war in Massachusetts.

Wasmus, on his title page, calls his journal a "compilation" to distinguish it from a simple diary. Although the majority of his entries are in fact the daily record of his experiences, Wasmus, like other diarists of the period, was accustomed to adding additional information to his own first-hand account.[14] He seems to have had access to some sort of guidebook or traveller's account, particularly when he wrote his descriptions of Boston, Québec, Halifax, and Canada.[15] These descriptions are not especially different in language or style from the rest of the journal, but the tone is quite a new one, and the remarkable detail, which includes history, geography, and natural history suggests that he was using something more than conversations with the inhabitants as a source of information. In addition, Wasmus sometimes interviewed travellers or fellow officers to provide a richer account of a particular event. The best example of this occurs in August 1778 when he includes a very lengthy description of General John Sullivan's siege of the British garrison at Newport, Rhode Island, and the related naval battles to supplement a relatively brief newspaper account.[16] Wasmus records the source of his extraordinarily detailed information as "an English deserter," but the account reads like a high-level military report on both English and French actions off Newport. A careful reading of the full journal also reveals it a rich source of information from a cosmopolitan perspective on New England culture and on the workings of the British-German force as it invaded New York in 1776 and 1777.

Julius Friedrich Wasmus was born in Lichtenberg, a town in northern Bavaria near Bamberg, on October 11, 1739. According to his own account in the 1758 diary, his father was Carl Andreas Wasmus, who was surveyor and bailiff at the ducal court of Lichtenberg. His mother, Elisabeth Eleonora Stolzen was a doctor's daughter from Klein Lafferde. His sister was married to a surgeon in Salzgitter and one of his grandfathers was a solicitor, Justus Friedrich Mackensen.[17]

Young Wasmus was confirmed in the Lutheran church at the age of thirteen in 1752 and entered the Hochschule at Wolfenbüttel the same year. Two years later, after his father's death, Wasmus was apprenticed to City Surgeon Dreyer in Wolfenbüttel for a period of two and a half years, for which his family paid 100 gulden tuition. His studies were successful, since he passed the examination set for him by the Wolfenbüttel City Physician Dr. Kortum in 1757, and in September of that year he went to work for City Surgeon Raab in Wolfenbüttel. At that time Wolfenbüttel was occupied by the French, who, after the defeat of the Duke of Cumberland's army of Hannoverians, Hessians, and Braunschweigers at the Battle of Hastenbeck, July 26, 1757, marched into Braunschweig and Wolfenbüttel in August. The citizenry were disarmed and ordered to quarter the French heavy cavalry and infantry regiments. By the middle of September, Wolfenbüttel had become the French headquarters. After Frederic the Great's victory over the French at Rossbach on November 5, the French army was weakened and eventually evacuated Wolfenbüttel in February 1758.

In 1758 Wasmus had a difficult and dangerous encounter when he was on the verge of taking over his aging supervisor's role as surgeon to the Leib regiment of Braunschweig, the Duke's personal guard. On the evening of December 18, 1758, he and a fellow surgeon, Dr. Müller became involved in a street quarrel with an actor, a member of the troupe of the renowned and very popular Nicolini. According to Wasmus' diary, the actor was first to draw his sword, but the young surgeon landed a blow on his opponent's head. Müller was arrested and demoted to musketeer for taking part in the fracas. Wasmus escaped capture, fleeing to his mother in Lichtenberg and then to his brother-in-law in Salzgitter. The Duke's warrant pursued him, and the unlucky Wasmus gave himself up at his mother's insistence on January 26, 1759 and was taken into custody by the court bailiff and some farmers.

Wasmus' family furnished his bail, and he began to negotiate the settlement of his difficulties. Having heard rumors that the Duke would accept his enlistment into the army, Wasmus tried to enlist as a company surgeon, but was initially disappointed; he joined and petitioned his colonel, Lt. Colonel Stisser, to secure the position, persisting in his efforts to practice his profession. The Duke transferred him to the Leib Regiment in February, and after a summer furlough and repeated apologies Wasmus was formally pardoned on November 11. Thereafter Wasmus took up his interrupted career, passed the appropriate examination at the local medical college and was appointed company surgeon in the Leib Regiment.

Wasmus continued to serve the Duke throughout the Braunschweig campaigns in the Seven Years War, maintaining the diary he had begun when the French occupied Wolfenbüttel.[18]   That diary ends in February 1763 when the Braunschweig troops returned home. Wasmus settled in the house of the mill clerk Spangenberg while he served the Wolfenbüttel garrison, and he married the next year. Peace had come to Braunschweig, but Wasmus' adventures were hardly over.

When King George III of England negotiated a treaty in 1776 with Duke Karl of Braunschweig to hire auxiliary troops to send to the rebellious American colonies, Wasmus was among them even though he had two children, a son and a daughter. He was still a company surgeon and still a diarist, promising one of his friends, Chancery Administrator Werner, to send him a running account of his adventures. Wasmus apparently jotted down quick notes after each event and then later reworked those accounts into a complete account of his activities, making successive copies, which he forwarded to Werner in order to have as many chances as possible for his record to survive the vagaries of the transatlantic crossing; indeed, the copy in the archives is remarkably complete. The journal covers the period from February 1776, when Wasmus and the Braunschweigers left Wolfenbüttel, to October 1783, when they finally returned home and he was reunited with his wife and children.

The Braunschweigers marched to the coast and sailed for Portsmouth where troop convoys were assembled for the sometimes perilous trip across the Atlantic. Wasmus faithfully recorded the events of the trip, on board the ship, on land, and even on the surrounding seas, as he and the other 2,400 men of the first Braunschweig contingent traveled to Canada. Once they arrived in the New World, Wasmus described the inhabitants of Canada, both the recently conquered French, the original native American inhabitants, and the more recent English settlers, and the local flora and fauna, especially the rattlesnakes, which fascinated him.

Battle had already taken place in Canada before Wasmus arrived; the American invasion under Benedict Arnold and Richard Montgomery had penetrated to the walls of Québec before being driven back at the start of 1776. American troops under General William Thompson attacked Trois-Rivières in June, not knowing that Burgoyne's troops, including Wasmus, had just been quartered at that site with predictably disastrous results. Burgoyne pursued the rebels south on his first invasion of New York that summer, with the Braunschweigers forming a substantial component of his invasion force.   But Benedict Arnold was successful in slowing the British attack at the battle of Valcour Island in October, and the British and their German auxiliaries returned to winter quarters in Canada.

Burgoyne spent the winter in London, while our diarist settled in for the winter at Trois-Rivières, returning to Canada in the spring to displace General Sir Guy Carleton with his new strategy.   A second invasion of New York along the route provided by Lake Champlain and the Hudson River was planned to split off rebellious New England from the rest of the colonies.   Burgoyne replaced Carleton in command and began his march south in late June 1777.   The combined British and German force arrived at Crown Point on June 27 and captured Ticonderoga from a weak American garrison on July 5. Wasmus provides a detailed account of the invasion army's progress and of the successful strategy used at Ticonderoga, as well as of the subsequent conflicts with the Americans at Hubbardton and Skenesborough (the modern Whitehall).   Instead of proceeding south from Ticonderoga by way of Lake George, Burgoyne elected to proceed along Wood Creek to Fort Edward, a route which was to prove disastrously slow, allowing the Americans under General Philip Schuyler and eventually General Horatio Gates sufficient time to assemble the men and supplies necessary to block the British invasion.   (At one point, the British took 22 days to march 20 miles.)   Burgoyne's supply lines were stretched thin, and horses, fodder, and food were scarce in the wilderness that surrounded them.   At the end of July, Burgoyne directed General Friedrich Adolphus von Riedesel, commander of the Braunschweig forces, to plan a raid eastward into the Connecticut Valley to acquire horses and supplies and to recruit Tory volunteers.   Riedesel was uncomfortable with Burgoyne's ambitious plan and with his choice of Lt. Col. Friedrich Baum as commander of the operation and protested, but the raid went forth nonetheless with about 800 men, half of them Germans, under the leadership of Baum, who marched east from the Hudson River on August 6.   As one of the company surgeons in the Dragoon Regiment, Wasmus went along to Bennington, where Baum had his fatal encounter with the Americans under John Stark and Seth Warner.   The doctor's graphic description of attending the wounded, sheltered from flying bullets behind an oak tree, is a compelling one.   Because Baum and many in his force were killed and the rest were captured, Wasmus' account is the only surviving account of the Bennington battle from the German point of view.   Since Baum's force was half German (only fifty British regulars and three hundred Canadians, Tories and Indians accompanied the expedition, and the Indians fled early in the course of the battle), the diary provides an important perspective on the American victory.

Wasmus was captured in a dramatic encounter at bayonet point and then spent four years in captivity.   His status as a surgeon earned him the respect of the Americans; indeed he dined with Stark and Warner (whose name he rendered politely as von Werner) the night after the battle.   Eventually he was marched to Brimfield, Massachusetts with other German prisoners.   Wasmus and his fellow officers were treated kindly; they were boarded with local families and allowed to move freely about the area (first within a radius of one mile, eventually in a larger territory).   He stayed with the family of Joseph Hitchcock for the year, providing medical services to Braunschweig prisoners and to the local inhabitants.   He learned of Burgoyne's surrender at Saratoga, on October 17, 1777. Although initially he got his information on the war and the fate of the rest of Riedesel's troops from rumors reaching the local inhabitants, he soon began to read the patriot press.

The Wasmus diary is also a useful source of information on medical practice of the period.   With the Dragoon Regiment, he treated major and minor injuries, from frostbite to bullet wounds and amputations, and performed meticulous autopsies.   In Massachusetts he treated both his fellow Braunschweigers and local inhabitants, for a wide variety of ailments, broken bones, jaundice, severe burns, and festering sores.   In the diary Wasmus is quite specific about his methods, usually listing the various medicines he administered and describing the course of his treatment and the patient's outcome.

Wasmus was slow to learn English, convinced that his exchange was imminent, but his medical skills transcended the language barrier.   The Braunschweig prisoners were popular dinner guests in Brimfield and were often invited to local celebrations.   The diary provides fascinating descriptions of everyday life in the wartime colonies and local records confirm many accounts.   His diary records that "old and young were crying in the house" when he left the place where he and Pastor Melzheimer had "enjoyed...much friendship."

In late September 1778, Wasmus was sent to Westminster, in Worcester County, close to the small town of Rutland, Massachusetts, and he assumed that German prisoners were being assembled for exchange.   However, he had been sent there at Riedesel's request to provide medical care for German officers remaining in the area after the Convention Army (Burgoyne's troops from Saratoga) marched south to Virginia.   In February 1779, Wasmus was ordered to Rutland where he lodged with the local minister, Joseph Buckminster, who proved to be another agreeable host.

1779 was a difficult year for Wasmus.   Still not fluent in English, he at times seems to have despaired of being exchanged, and the diary entries, with one exception, are either very brief or consist of German translations of American newspaper articles from Boston, Worcester, and Hartford papers.   These articles prove to be quite interesting: Wasmus included some 369 such translations between 1778 and 1781, 90% of which we have been able to compare with the originals.   Wasmus was quite accurate, although he was often wrong in rendering numbers from English into German.

The press that Wasmus depended on as a connection to the wider world was highly partisan.   Although Benjamin Franklin had argued that "Printers are educated in this Belief, that when men differ in Opinion, both sides ought equally to have the Advantage of being heard by the Publick," in 1731,[19] the crisis of the American Revolution had eliminated neutrality as an option for American printers.   Stephen Botein has shown that although eighteenth-century printers attempted to hold themselves apart from local disputes in order to protect their circulation, when the feelings of a community became "polarized," the printers had to choose one faction to support to avoid antagonizing all of them.[20]   The majority of American printers were patriots, and Wasmus was right to be skeptical of the accuracy of their news.[21]

Printers published newspapers as part of a wider spectrum of activities that could include the publication of books, pamphlets, government documents, tickets, forms, and bills.   During the Revolution a few, like George Goodwin of the Hartford Courant, began to identify themselves as the "editors" of their papers.[22]   They derived much of their information from other newspapers (Paul Langford refers to plagiarism as the "fundamental basis" of all eighteenth-century journalism)[23], from passing travellers (ships' captains were a useful source of information) and from anonymous correspondence, some of dubious veracity.   Wasmus' translations thus describe naval battles which never happened and other bits of misinformation or propaganda, as well as actual events.

The American newspapers that Wasmus translated and quoted in the diary included the Independent Ledger, the Continental Journal, and the Independent Chronicle, all published in Boston, the Massachusetts Spy published in Worcester, the Connecticut Courant and the Hartford Post of Hartford, and Rivington's New York Gazette of New York.   In Québec, he read the Québec Gazette.   He often disagreed with the opinions of the editors, providing information which contradicted their views.

The paper that Wasmus quoted most frequently during his sojourn in Rutland was the Massachusetts Spy, which Isaiah Thomas began to publish in Worcester in 1775.

Thomas, born in poverty in Boston in 1749 and apprenticed as a child to a printer, had established the Massachusetts Spy in Boston in 1770. One historian has commented on his "clever facility for combining editorial comment with news,"[24] which was certainly still in use at the time Wasmus read his paper. Financed in part by John Hancock, Thomas supported the patriots, printing the Sons of Liberty's handbills in secret by 1773. In 1774, perhaps fearful of his future in Boston, he established a third press in Worcester (he had expanded to Newburyport in 1773) and took the Massachusetts Spy to that town shortly after the events at Lexington and Concord, publishing the Massachusetts Spy or American Oracle of Liberty, the "first thing ever printed in Worcester" in May 1775.[25] Forced to leave Worcester for a time, Thomas returned to the city in 1779 and "began anew."[26] Wasmus often argued with "Brother Thomas." He found the content of Rivington's New-York Gazette somewhat more palatable. James Rivington had begun to publish his Gazetteer in 1773 in New York, fled to England at the outset of hostilities, but then returned to British-occupied New York as the King's Printer. According to Stephen Botein, he might have been acting as a double agent by 1781, providing information to the Americans as a way of protecting his future should the British lose the war.[27]

The articles provide some insight into Wasmus' view of the Revolutionary War. First, the pieces he chose to translate were often relatively obscure, not the leading articles in the particular newspaper he was reading. Second, they offered a rather cosmopolitan perspective on the conflict; not only did they contain accounts of battles and events in North America, but they also emphasized the importance of the West Indian naval theater and the global nature of the conflict, giving information on the siege of Gibraltar and on various engagements between the British and French in India and Ceylon. Finally, Wasmus' imaginary conversations with the American journalists, especially Isaiah Thomas, the publisher of the Massachusetts Spy and American Oracle of Liberty, illustrate his distrust of newspaper information (which was frequently based on the vaguest of rumors) and his growing, if grudging, respect for the Americans and their cause.

By the beginning of 1780, Wasmus had been away from his friends and family in Wolfenbüttel for nearly four years and sometimes despaired of ever seeing them again. One entry, in the summer of 1779, is written in the form of a letter to his friends and family in Germany, detailing his isolation and melancholy and questioning why he has received no letters at all since September 1776. In March, he received a three-year-old letter from a Wolfenbüttel physician, who informed him that his family was alive and well, or at least had been when the letter was written. The 1780 diary records Wasmus' treatment of several difficult and interesting patients and more rumors of a pending prisoner exchange, as well as more translations of American newspaper articles. Finally, in August 1780, anxieties about his family were somewhat relieved when he received a letter from his wife written the preceding January, assuring him that she and the children were in good health. His mother had died in 1779, and Wasmus recorded his belated grief over the news.

At the end of 1780, Wasmus' fellow officers were exchanged. He was not exchanged, however, because his name was not on the list of officers of the Dragoon Regiment. Despite Wasmus' explanation that he was a surgeon and would not have been listed with the other officers, the American Commissary of Prisoners, Major Hopkins remained adamant against his exchange. Captain Heinrich Christian von Fricke, who seems to have resented Wasmus' popularity with the Americans, had slandered him, arguing that he was merely a barber and thus ranked lower than a corporal. Wasmus' other colleagues argued with Hopkins on his behalf, but some apparently turned against him, suggesting that he had arranged the contretemps with Hopkins because he did not really want to be exchanged. Hopkins left, offering to arrange an exchange with a captured American doctor, and Wasmus wrote a pleading letter to Riedesel, imploring his intervention.

1781 found Wasmus still a paroled prisoner in Rutland, treating American patients; the husband of one wrote a poem praising his skill. Due to the growth of his practice, he noted in April that he no longer had time to read and translate the papers, and the diary returns to a record of his daily activities.   Several days a week he rode to the nearby town of Hardwick, where he saw patients in his own room at Major General [Jonathan?] Warner's house.   He also maintained a small pharmacy and practice in the town of Holden at the house of John Child, an attorney, who, like the Warners, provided him a rent-free room for his patients.   Finally, in June, he received a certificate exchanging him for an American doctor from Virginia, named Skinner.

Wasmus' friends and patients in Massachusetts were sad to see him leave; he himself seems to have considered staying in Massachusetts but was reluctant to have himself branded a deserter.   And he feared that his wife could not make the dangerous and difficult journey to America to join him should he desert and settle there.   So he began preparations to rejoin his regiment, collecting the substantial monies due him for his professional practice.   While making his plans to travel to New York to join the Braunschweig troops there, he received word that the Germans were en route to Canada, forcing him to rejoin them by the "dreadful journey" across the Gulf of St. Lawrence and along the river to Québec.   He prepared for the journey to Boston where in September he found a cartel ship ready to sail to Halifax.

When Wasmus arrived in Halifax on September 21, he discovered it was late in the year to begin a journey to Sorel where his regiment was stationed.   Because no ships were left to make the journey, the Lieutenant Governor of the colony, Sir Andrew Hamond, arranged for a captured American ship to be bought at auction and put under the command of the cartel ship captain for the voyage to Québec.   Against the advice of friends in Halifax, Wasmus embarked on October 6, on the dangerous journey.   The ship was threatened by American privateers and bad weather, eventually going aground on the rocks off Cacouna, from which, having lost everything, Wasmus was rescued by local Indians.   Once again the doctor was impoverished; instead of returning to his duties well supplied with money and medicine, he was left penniless, forced to appeal to his superiors for some compensation for his losses.   Wasmus was able, however, to deny the vicious rumors of some of his fellow officers that he had deserted.

Wasmus spent the next two years in Québec, functioning as company surgeon to the dragoons and general practitioner to the Canadian inhabitants in his vicinity.   He faithfully recorded his reactions to Canada and its inhabitants.   He finally returned home in the fall of 1783, sailing, as he had come, in the company of General von Riedesel.   He records his meeting with his wife in remarkably matter-of-fact terms and closes the diary with an account of his continued appointment as company surgeon and assignment to the garrison at Braunschweig where he settled in with his wife and family.

Braunschweig records indicate that Wasmus served as Regimental Surgeon with the Artillery in 1788 and von Riedesel's correspondence mentions him as Regimental Surgeon with the Regiment von Riedesel in 1795.   Wasmus' son became a company surgeon, following in his father's footsteps.   The diaries from the Seven Years War and from the Revolution are now in the archives at Wolfenbüttel; his other work that we know of, a treatise on the medicinal plants of New England, was lost in transit to Wolfenbüttel.

Only a company surgeon, not rising to the more prestigious position of regimental surgeon until after he returned to Braunschweig, Wasmus seems to have made friends with a number of the influential figures whom he encountered in his travels.   He traveled to America in the suite of General von Riedesel, who remembered him when the time came to return to Germany and insisted that he join the headquarters party for the voyage home.   In Massachusetts he was acquainted with General Timothy Danielson and his family, as well as with General Warner, whose daughters, Amity, Constance and Unity, seem to have made him an honorary family member.   On his arduous journey to Canada in 1781 he was befriended by the Fillis and Achincloss families, loyalist refugees, who beseeched him to stay with them instead of proceeding up the St. Lawrence in winter. Even in his account of the Seven Years War, he includes descriptions of humorous interchanges he had with such august personages as Duke Carl and Prince Ferdinand. He seems to have been quick-witted and articulate, commending himself to those he met as dedicated and well-educated, well worth cultivation.

The prime fascination of the Wasmus diary is its version of one man's odyssey through the war-wracked colonies. Again and again Wasmus loses all his possessions and is left with only the shirt on his back to call his own. First at Bennington and then on the rocks at Cacouna the doctor is shipwrecked and forced to rebuild his life and livelihood. Only rarely did he lament his fate; instead he reestablished himself as soon as possible. No matter how he was tempted by the prospect of a new and prosperous life in an America that he had come to love, he had kept his honor and met his obligations by returning to Braunschweig.

Wasmus' journal can logically be compared with that of the well-known journal of Johann Ewald, the Hessian officer who later rose to fame as a general in the service of the Danish crown, and whose journal, ably translated and edited by Joseph Tustin, was published by Yale University Press in 1979.[28] Yet there are very significant differences between them. Ewald was a combat officer, whose diary is almost wholly concerned with his military activities. Except for nine rather touching love letters to Miss Jeannette Van Horne, the diary is not particularly introspective. Ewald occasionally commented on the individual Americans he met, but clearly his central purpose was to give a record of his military activity. Ewald kept the diary on a daily basis during his time in America, then edited it, and had it copied in 1791. He certainly hoped that others would benefit from the military lessons it contained, and military activities completely dominate the text. In contrast, Wasmus was a surgeon, who was less concerned with leading troops into battle than he was with safeguarding the health of his patients. His journal entries were dispatched, in the form of letters, to an audience consisting of family and friends in Braunschweig, an audience he assumed was interested not only in their distant friend's experience, but also in the new society and the new land.

In contrast to other Braunschweig accounts (both General Riedesel and his wife's journals have been published) Wasmus' journal chronicles the time and gives a very different perspective that is closer to the ranks. Wasmus' somewhat ambiguous status proves to be an advantage for the historian interested in the whole experience of the army rather than just that of those in command. An educated man with some professional training, a thirty-seven-year-old veteran of another war, who seems to have spent much of his time with officers and with the staff, Wasmus was not, technically, an officer. He walked with the troops, rather than riding to Bennington. He certainly spent much of his time tending ordinary soldiers. In this way Wasmus, unlike Ewald, is able to give us a picture of the army from both the bottom and the top. He traveled back and forth to America in the retinue of General von Riedesel, and yet he did not enjoy all of the privileges of rank and was familiar with the hazards of a soldier's life.

Wasmus' odyssey from Braunschweig to America and back to Braunschweig tells us much about America and Germany in the late eighteenth century. It is the story of an unusual man who gave intelligent notice to a new country and a new culture.

Mary C. Lynn
Saratoga Springs, New York
January, 1990

NOTES

1. Fred Anderson, A People's Army, Chapel Hill and London: University of North Carolina Press, 1984.

2. Review of E. Wayne Carp, To Starve the Army at Pleasure: Continental Army Administration and American Political Culture, 1775-1783, in The Virginia Magazine of History and Biography, vol. 93, April, 1985, pp. 214-216.

3. Wayne Carp, To Starve the Army at Pleasure, Chapel Hill and London: University of North Carolina Press, 1984.

4. Jesse Lemisch, "Listening to the Inarticulate: William Widger's Dream and the Loyalties of American Revolutionary Seamen in British Prisons," Journal of Social History, 3, 1969.

5. Charles Royster, A Revolutionary People at War, Chapel Hill and London: University of North Carolina Press, 1979.

6. Robert A. Gross. The Minutemen and Their World, New York: Hill & Wang, 1976.

7. Peter Paret, "The History of War," Daedalus: The History and the World of the Twentieth Century. 100 (Spring, 1971): 376-396.

8. Martin K. Gordon, "American Military Studies," in Jefferson B. Kellogg and Robert H. Walker, Sources for American Studies, Westport, Ct.: Greenwood Press, 1983, pp. 273-294.

9. John Shy, A People Numerous and Armed: Reflections on the Military Struggle for American Independence, New York: Oxford University Press, 1976.

10. Gordon, p. 281.

11. Peter Karsten, "The New Military History," American Quarterly, 36, no. 3 (bibliography 1984), pp. 389-418.

12. Ibid.

13. One example is the translation by Helga Doblin of "A Brunswick Grenadier With Burgoyne: The Journal of Johann Bense, 1776-1783," New York History, October, 1985, pp. 421-444.

14. Captain Johann Ewald, of the Hessian Field Jägers(see below) included others' reports of actions in which he had not himself participated, reports which his editor had to eliminate due to the length of his diary; Thomas Anburey, a British officer, whose epistolary account was published in 1789 as Travels Through the Interior Parts of North America, included many long passages from the Annual Register of Events and other sources, stating in his preface that "Every thing the Reader may meet with will not appear strictly nouvelle." (London, 1789, p. vi.).

15. June 6, 1776 (p. 33), the 1777 "Remarks About Canada," (pp. 45-48 and 80-82), September 11, 1781, and July 31, 1783.

16. August 1778, p. 120.

17. This biographical material is derived from W. Wagner's account, based on the 1758-1763 diary, "Erinnerungen eines Braunschweigers aus dem Siebenjahrigen Kriege," which appeared in the Braunschweigisches Magazin, vol. 20, 7 October, 1900, pp. 153-159.

18. The original is in the archives at Wolfenbüttel; an edited version was published by the Braunschweigisches Magazin in October 1900, and in 1907 Wasmus' great-grandson, Kurt, who was then a factory owner in Braunschweig, placed both journals in the county archives of Braunschweig.

19. Pennsylvania Gazette, June 10, 1731.

20. Stephen Botein, "Printers and the American Revolution," in Bernard Bailyn and John B. Hench, eds. The Press and the American Revolution, Worcester: American Antiquarian Society, 1980, pp. 21-22.

21. According to Botein, Sidney Kobre in The Development of the Colonial Newspaper (Pittsburgh: Colonial Press, 1944, pp. 147-148) characterized 38 Revolutionary papers as patriot and 19 as Tory. (Ibid., p. 32.)

22. Ibid., p. 48.

23. Paul Langford, "British Correspondence in the Colonial Press," in Bailyn and Hench, p. 274.

24. Marcus A. McCorison, "Foreword," in Bailyn and Hench, p. 5.

25. Ibid., p. 8.

26. Ibid., p. 9.

27. Ibid., p. 46.

28. Captain Johann Ewald, <u>Diary of the American War</u>, translated and edited by Joseph P. Tustin, New Haven and London: Yale University Press, 1979.

Facsimile of a page of the original text.

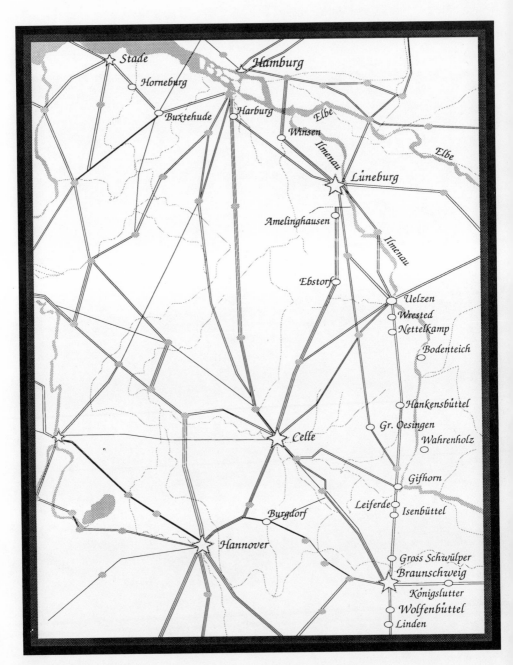

Map of northwest Germany showing route from Wolfenbüttel to Stade (based on a 1784 postal route map).

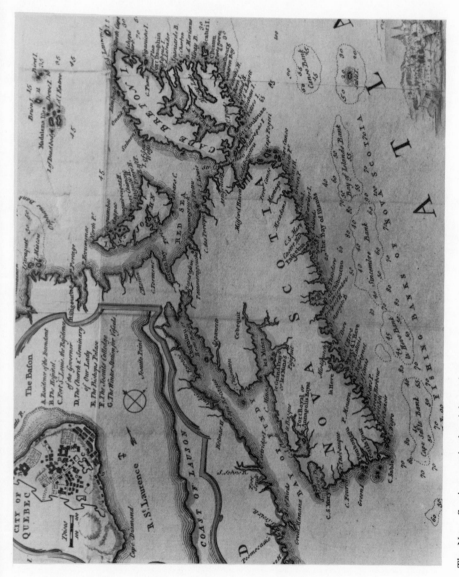

The Nova Scotia coast in the eighteenth century.

The St. Lawrence Gulf and River, 1774. Courtesy of the Archives nationales du Québec à Québec; P600-4/A-990—Canada—1774.

The city of Québec in the eighteenth century. Courtesy of the Archives nationales du Québec à Québec; P600-5/GH-573-46.

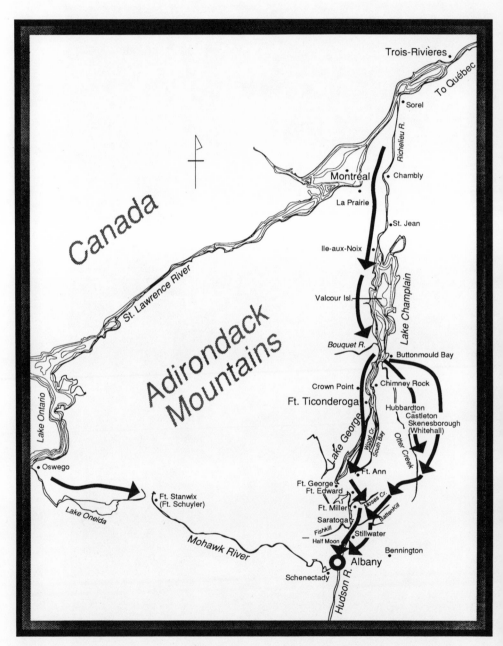

Map of Burgoyne's northeastern campaign route. Courtesy of the Saratoga National Historical Park.

Original drawing of a Braunschweig Dragoon by Knoetel. Courtesy of the Bennington Museum, Bennington, Vermont.

Jäger-Corps (Braunschweig).
1776-1783
Bennington.

Original Drawing of a Braunschweig Grenadier by Knoetel. Courtesy of the Bennington Museum, Bennington, Vermont.

Exterior of the Meeting House in Bennington (before 1805). Courtesy of the Bennington Museum, Bennington, Vermont.

Interior of the Meeting House in Bennington. Courtesy of the Bennington Museum, Bennington, Vermont.

1789 map of Ticonderoga [Thomas Jeffreys]. Courtesy of the Fort Ticonderoga Museum.

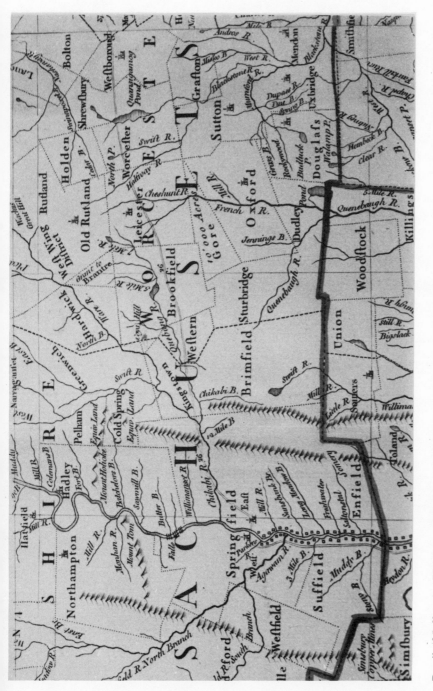

Detail of Jeffreys's 1774 "Map of the Most Inhabited Part of New England." Courtesy of the Bennington Museum, Bennington, Vermont.

*An Eyewitness Account
of the American Revolution
and New England Life*

Chancery Administrator

Werner
Wolfenbüttel
ex folio 221

Address Dedication

To my dear friend, Mr. C. W.[1] in Wolfenbüttel

Dear Friend,

I am taking the liberty of sending you the journal of my voyage to America. I am aware that various accounts of this journey have already appeared in Braunschweig[2] and Wolfenbüttel, which without a doubt have been better composed and also written in a better style than mine. I am writing the present account for no other reason than to fulfill the promise I have given you. It may not be to the taste of the learned world but what does that matter to me. It is enough that I have told the truth and that it adequately fulfills the purpose of letting my children know of the perilous situations their father had to face when he was roaming about in America. The computation of miles in latitude and longitude is correct; I have copied them day by day from the captain's logbook. If at times I have written of terror, [*the whole experience*] has actually been even more terrible than that and [*my account*] gives but a poor idea of the long sea voyage.

Read this, dear friend, and what I shall send you in future, and in doing so honor me with thoughts of friendship, which no period of absence however long can change; I, on my part, shall be your friend forever.

J. F. Wasmus

La Prairie in Canada
opposite Montréal
September 24, 1776

1776

22nd   It was today that the First Division of the illustrious Braunschweig troops marched out of Wolfenbüttel under the command of Colonel von Riedesel and consisted of:

1.)	The Dragoon Regiment, which Lieut. Colonel Baum commanded	276 men
2.)	The Regiment Prinz Friedrich, commanded by Lieut. Colonel Prätorius	680 men
3.)	The Regiment von Riedesel, commanded by Lieut. Col. von Speth[3]	680 men
4.)	The General Staff	22 men
5.)	The Combined Grenadier Battalion, which Lieut. Colonel Breymann commanded and which marched out of Braunschweig[4]	564 men
	Total	2,222 men

At 6 o'clock this morning, the general order was beaten and at 6:30 assembly. The Dragoon Regiment assembled on the broad Herzogstrasse; the Regiment von Riedesel had assembled on the Holzmarkt. It was past 7 o'clock when we marched off to the right. Colonel von Riedesel, who commanded the Dragoon Regiment himself, had all the regiments march past him. The march proceeded by way of the Herzogstor. The baggage had been driven to the market and followed the regiments in the order in which they marched; that of the General Staff formed the tête. The rearguard consisted of 1 officer, 3 noncommissioned officers and 30 men. These formed the tail end behind the baggage and had orders to arrest anything [sic] getting out of line. All the sick that could possibly be transported were taken along on wagons; we had 13 men who had to be driven. We marched through small towns on the old Braunschweig road to Melverode. The road was very bad since it had rained a great deal. After Melverode, we wheeled toward the right, toward Heid Mountain,[5] because the terrain was dry there. We marched through and between the Schliestedt[6] Gardens and the gardens of the great Braunschweig military road and came onto the glacis at the August Gate before Braunschweig; from there the march proceeded between the gardens of the Stein and Fallersleben Gates toward the drill ground. At this point, Our Serene Highness Duke Carl took a last sublime look at us while having the entire corps march past him. From there, we marched toward the Wendish Towers[7] where the quarters for the regiments were distributed. Colonel von Riedesel's headquarters were at Leiferde where the

Dragoon Regiment was also quartered. The Dragoon Squadron of Colonel von Riedesel went to Gross Schwülper for night quarters. The march commissaries also arrived in Leiferde; they were Major von Malorty[8] from the Engl. side, von Mueller from the Hannover Dragoon Regiment; Magistrate Meyer and his clerk from Winsen on the Luhe and Colonel von Hoym from the Braunschweig side. Colonel von Riedesel's promotion to major general was made public tonight.

23rd   We marched to Isenbüttel in the District of Gifhorn; general headquarters were in Gifhorn.

24th   We marched through Gifhorn to Wahrenholz; the Drag. Regiment von Bremer is stationed in garrison at Gifhorn. Headquarters were in Hankensbüttel today.

25th   We had a day of rest in Wahrenholz.

26th   We marched to Nettelkamp in the District of Bodenteich; headquarters were in Wrestedt.

27th   We marched near the city of Uelzen to Linden in the district of Ebstorf; headquarters were in Ebstorf.

28th   We marched to Amelinghausen where we had a day of rest on the 29th; headquarters were also here.

Month of March 1776

1st   On our march today, we saw the city of Lüneburg about 2 hours [march] to our right.[9] Our quarters were at the chapter house of Ramselsloh; headquarters were also here.

2nd   We marched to quarters at Harburg. There, I visited the castle that had been bombarded in 1758, as well as the barracks. Lieut. Gen. Braun is garrisoned here; our General Staff was also here.

3rd   We marched to Buxtehude. Because foot and mouth disease was rampant in this district, all baggage had to be reloaded in front of the city.

4th   We had a day of rest. General von Baehr is garrisoned here with a part of his cavalry regiment. Major General von Riedesel went to Stade this morning and returned this evening.

5th   We marched through the city of Horneburg to Stade. We entered by the High Gate past the English Colonel Fawcett[10] and marched onto the big square in front of the arsenal. Here, the men were assigned to their quarters. The Regiment Prinz Friedrich marched into cantonment quarters in Buxtehude and the Regiment von Riedesel to theirs in Horneburg. I was quartered with the burgher Peter Dietrich Kolster. As a matter of courtesy, every burgher offered a meal to those quartered in his house because the provisions had been discontinued. We received bread for 3 days, quite good rye bread, not army bread [Kommissbrot]. Since the departure from Wolfenbüttel, 2 groschen per day were deducted from the allowance of each noncommissioned officer and each private, which amounted in 12 days to 1 piaster Casson money[11] for each man. For that, the farmers were to give us 2 or 3 meals a day, both food and drink. Except for one noncommissioned officer at each gate to prevent desertions, no guard is furnished here by our regiments or by the Grenadier Battalion. The local garrison consists of 2 battalions von Bock and one battalion von Kielmansegge; these stay in the barracks and the battalion Claushaar is quartered with the burghers. Stade is a very good place but although the walls are covered with cannon, it is not a strong fortress. It has 4 gates and 3 principal churches, also a rather beautiful arsenal. The Elbe [River] flows for about an hour's march below Stade. One of its tributaries, which is called the Schwinge, comes up here to the center of Stade. At flood tide, the vessels ride on it to the middle of the market with fish and many other kinds of victuals. At ebb tide, after the water has run off, one can walk in the ditch as it is then completely dry. Foodstuffs are very reasonable here but particularly so are all kinds of live fish; codfish, haddock, and many other types of fish are very inexpensive.

6th   Orders were given for tomorrow's review. General Count Kielmansegge,[12] Commander of Stade, arrived here this morning.

7th   We were reviewed by Colonel Fawcett on the great square in front of the arsenal, which is called Auf dem Sande [on the sand]. Each man's name was read, each one had to go past Colonel Fawcett and answer in a loud voice. Thereafter, each regiment had to form a circle on the opposite side of the square and swear [the oath of] loyalty to the King of England; after that we went back to our quarters.

8th   Maj. Gen. von Riedesel, Colonels Fawcett and [von] Hoym went to Horneburg and Buxtehude, where other reviews were held.

9th   The delivery of the troops was signed by Maj. Gen. von Riedesel and Colonel Fawcett today and sent to London and Braunschweig.

11th   It was reported to Colonel Fawcett that ships have been sighted near Cuxhaven. I went in a boat with my host to Braunshausen, a village situated on the Elbe. We inspected a large three-masted ship, called the *Kronenschiff*, which is keeping watch here. It is a very beautiful ship and carries 60 cannon.

12th   A naval officer, by the name of Hill, reported to Colonel Fawcett this morning that 7 transport ships had arrived: the *Pallas*, *Minerva*, *James and John*, *Union*, *Apollo*, *Laury*, and *Royal Briton*. Because of tomorrow's embarkation, orders are being given as early as this afternoon so that the Regiments Prinz Friedrich and von Riedesel, that are supposed to march here tomorrow, can do so.

13th   At 8 o'clock this morning, all men had to be in front of their chiefs' quarters. At 9 o'clock, the companies marched to the Fish Market and filed onto the vessels. After all baggage had been loaded, we rode down the Schwinge Canal toward the Elbe River with the full band playing. I believe very few people stayed in their houses, going instead to the Fish Market to see our embarkation and departure. Not only the windows but also the roofs on both sides of the canal were full of people who shouted farewell and bon voyage. We reached the Elbe and the transport ship *Pallas,* on which the General Staff and the squadron of the general embarked. We boarded the ship under continual beating of the field march. When I came on deck, I was happy with its cleanliness and soon learned that the sailors had to wash the ship's deck every morning. Our *Pallas* carries 344 tons of ballast, goes 13 feet deep into the water, has 3 masts and is a merchant vessel. The captain's name is Bell. He is going to America for the 11th time, but to Canada for the first time. In addition to the captain, there are on the ship a first and second helmsman, a carpenter, a dispenser, a cook, 20 sailors and 2 cabin boys, who answer to the captain. At the stern is the cabin, which is furnished like a parlor. On the sides are the bunks, one on top of another; all space is made use of and 2 large windows render it very bright. Major General von Riedesel and the other officers have taken this cabin. Next to it is the cabin in which the ship's captain is lodging and next to that are a few cubicles for the helmsmen and carpenter. Then follows the room for the sailors where bunks are put up all around; some also sleep in hammocks. These are beds that hang from ropes. Then follows the room for the dragoons, which contains 3 rows of bunks; each is 7 feet square, in which 3 and no more than 4 men lie. Our ship carries the smallest number [of troops], i.e., only 110 men, including the officers. Enough space is left in between these rows of bunks to walk through. Each man receives one mattress, 3 woolen blankets, among them white and colored ones, as well as a pillow filled with hair and this is all. In addition, each man receives a wooden bowl and dish. Underneath this room is the room where the water barrels, provisions and ammunition are stored, for we have 6 cannon on board; the anchor cables are also brought into this room. Underneath this room is still a third room [the bilge], about 3 feet high, where water gathers which is frequently pumped out, but yet not more than once every 3 days. Instead of ballast, this room is filled with stones, balls and cartridges. Besides me, there is no other CHIRURGUS [surgeon] on this ship. Our ship's provisions are the same for officers and privates; each one has 3 pence deducted per day for his ration, that is about 21 pfennig in Convention money.[13] We receive 4 pounds of ship biscuit per 6 men each day. On other ships, 6 men receive 4 stübchen[14] [liquid measure] of Engl. malt beer; a barrel of this beer is set on the foredeck of our ship and each one can drink as he pleases and as much as he wants. The bitters, which are largely brewed in London and other cities, are quite good. In addition, 6 men receive each day the following:

Sunday	- 4 pounds of salted pork and yellow peas
Monday	- sufficient oatmeal; each man 3 ounces of butter and 3 ounces of cheese
Tuesday	- 2 pounds of beef, 3 lbs. of fine flour, 1 lb. of raisins, from which a pudding is made
Wednesday	- like Monday
Thursday	- like Sunday
Friday	- peas, oatmeal, butter and cheese
Saturday	- like Tuesday.

"When the beer is gone," our ship's captain said, "we will get rum, a strong drink." The best rum is distilled in Jamaica, in the West Indies. Would that we do not stay so long on the ship that the beer is finished. We gladly do without the rum, as the beer is very good for us. Everything is cooked with coal on our ship. Since the wind is blowing from the SW, the ships that are still missing will soon arrive.

14th   Three other transport vessels arrived today and cast anchor near us; these were the *Polly, Harmony* and *Elizabeth*. The wind continues to be SWW. All our men are happy about their good appetite; the reason must be that we are staying on water. I myself was not able to eat as much during the entire day in Wolfenbüttel as I eat on the ship for breakfast. The High Bailiff of Harzburg and the Bailiff of Luntenberg and Salder drove past us to the *James and John* today to visit their brother, Lieut. Colonel Breymann.

15th   Four companies of the Regiment von Riedesel embarked on the transport ships that arrived here yesterday. On the advice of our ship's captain, I provided myself with all kinds of victuals, particularly with bread, surgical spirit [rubbing alcohol], coffee, sugar, tea, lemons and tobacco. I had already brought such items as hams, sausages etc. along from Wolfenbüttel. As a nightcap and before going to bed, we drink a good punch. We are enjoying our life on the Elbe and I have wished many times that we could be done with our journey to America right here on the Elbe. Every day we have visitors from all walks of life not only from Stade but also from Hamburg and other cities. Colonel Fawcett also visited us today and inquired whether everything was all right with us and whether we were satisfied. Major General von Riedesel also came on board today with his brother, Lieut. Colonel von Riedesel. The latter offered to take letters back to shore; each one was to have his ready one day before our departure.

16th   The ships that had been missing thus far, arrived today; *Prince of Wales, Providence, Lord Sandwich, Nancy, Peggy* and *Martha*; and tomorrow everybody is to embark. There was a violent windstorm from SWW today and we were able to notice the ship's motion, a strange sensation indeed.

17th   According to yesterday's order, everybody is embarked.

18th   Our Major General von Riedesel and all the officers belonging to the General Staff embarked on board our *Pallas*. All the horses of the First and Second Divisions were taken on board the *Martha* and hoisted up. There were 32 in number. The English officers, i.e., Captain Foy, the commissary of our division, and Captain Haynes, agent and Commodore of our fleet, embarked. Lieut. Colonel von Riedesel departed today without saying goodbye and without taking the letters along. The letters will go off by mail today. A pilot, who is to guide us to the North Sea, came on board; up to that point, he will rule and command our ship and our sailors. He is a farmer from the country, who was born not far from Stade. Every ship must have such a pilot. He must be responsible for the ship and if the ship gets lost through his negligence, or inexperience, capsizing against cliffs or on sandbanks, he is to pay with his life. For this, he gets 1.) for each foot the ship draws, 2 shillings; that means our pilot gets 26 shillings. He must share the money with the Hamburg Admiralty because he is bound to them by oath and duty; 2.) on Royal ships he gets one additional shilling per day. Recruits, levied by the Hannoverian Colonel Scheiter,[15] embarked on 2 Hamburg ships today. They are being taken to England to complete the English regiments destined for America. I must mention that here in Stade I met a neighbor from Wolfenbüttel, by the name of Hogreve, who had failed to pay his debts in Wolfenbüttel. He had enlisted with one of the Scheiter Corps. I spoke with him in Stade several times and am almost certain that he embarked on one of the Hamburg ships. I wished him luck on the journey. These Hamburg ships and 10 of ours will set sail today.

19th   With contrary winds, we are still calmly riding at anchor.

20th   Since the wind has not yet changed to our advantage, we are

21st   at rest. Last night, the wind turned to ENE. We weighed anchor and set sail with music and drum beating, passed the pleasant countryside, which is settled on both banks, and also the Danish fortress of Glückstadt. Since the wind became weaker, we were hardly able to reach Freiburg this evening, where we cast anchor. Here we came upon the ships that had departed on the 18th. For the benefit of large ships, the shallow ford of the Elbe is marked off with barrels [buoys], which on the Hannover side are red and on the Danish side white. The miles, indicated here in the future are Engl. miles; 4 1/4 [Engl. miles] equal one German mile and 3 Engl. miles 1 lieue or league. From Stade up to here we sailed[16] --16

22nd   Since the wind was blowing more strongly from the NE this morning, we weighed anchor and sailed to Cuxhaven and cast anchor near the village of Ritzebüttel. Up to here, we advanced --28

23rd   At 6 o'clock this morning, we set sail with a SSE wind. At about 8 o'clock we passed the big red barrel, which indicates the end of the Elbe. Here our pilot left us. He as well as the pilots from the other ships returned on a ship from Hamburg. We had now reached the near ocean. At 10 o'clock we saw the red cliffs of the Island of Helgoland; at 12 o'clock we were opposite this island. We had sailed ----------------------32 We took a westward course and since our ship had our Maj. Gen. von Riedesel on board, she was considered the Commodore's ship and on orders of our Capt. Haynes we hoisted flags and pennants. No ship was allowed to go ahead of ours. In the afternoon the wind grew weaker and we advanced very little. The weather is pleasant this evening and we continued seeing the lanterns of Helgoland. We saw large quantities of big fish that often rolled on the water in half bows. The English call them porpoises; they are not edible but produce a good train oil [whale oil]. Several small fishing vessels came to us today and sold us plaice, shellfish, codfish etc., all alive. Smoke and vapor rose from the sea this evening.

24th   With strong SSW wind, a heavy fog sprang up this morning. Small arms were fired almost continually from all ships in order to warn them not to collide with each other. We continued our westward course. Toward 10 o'clock, the wind started to blow so furiously and the ship moved so violently that no one could keep his footing. Since the waves often swept across the ship, no one could stand it on deck and each looked for his bed.

Total --76

The ship's motion became increasingly more violent and the sea showed nothing but high mountains and horrible abysses so that everyone believed the waves would devour us at any moment. Nevertheless, I did not think that we were in any great danger because the sailors were laughing at us, especially since our men were becoming seasick. All now became sick and lay in bed. Of all the Germans on our ship, Maj. Gen. von Riedesel and Gen. von Witzleben were the only ones who did not get seasick. We advanced -------57

25th   The violent SW wind is continuing. The sea shows nothing but horrible abysses; everybody is in bed and seasick. In the past hours we advanced ------------------102

26th   The wind changed to WNW. Our course is westward. Since the weather is growing bright and clear, our sick begin to get better. I am able to smoke my pipe on deck again. About noon, the wind turned very favorable since it changed to ESE and we sail with far less motion of the ship. In the last 24 hours, we have come closer to England by --114

27th   With this continuous good weather, no one is seasick this morning. I must also be well again since I was able to eat a slice of Schlackwurst[17] after the coffee. Since all were eager to see land, everyone was on the ship's foredeck. We saw the French coast and also the fortress of Calais at a distance of about 2 Engl. miles to our left. At a greater distance, we saw the English coast. In front of us were South and North Foreland, whose high shores were white due to their chalk edges and pleasantly caught our eye. We passed them at about 10 o'clock and had the city of Dover to our right at a distance of one Engl. mile. We had now advanced in the English channel until noon ----102
The English commissary Foy went in a boat from here to Dover in order to continue his journey to London on land and to report our arrival to the King. We passed by many other beautiful places in the Engl. Channel including the cities of Dungeness, Folkstone, Rumley etc.

28th   At 9 o'clock this morning, we reached the roadside of Spithead and cast anchor. We saw the fortress of Portsmouth one mile away from us. A great number of ships were lying here. Until noon, we advanced ---96

Total   --547

Our Major General von Riedesel went in a boat to Portsmouth and left behind the order that only reliable people were to be allowed to go on land. On the left side, we saw a city, called Gosport, which is separated from Portsmouth by the Portsmouth Channel. Portsmouth is a very beautiful city and, with its suburbs, is bigger than Braunschweig. Most of the shipbuilding in England is going on here, and it has one of the most beautiful harbors. Because of the citadel and other fortifications, it is considered the strongest fortress in all of England. The fair sex [das zweite Geschlecht] are very beautiful here and so unrestrained [frei] as to accost us on almost every street; and the beaux were soon found. ------ We had been warned, but --------- many did not wish to be warned. This contemptible sort were wearing such elegant dress in the English style that everyone thought them to be distinguished ladies. Many a man who was carried away by all the beauty and seductiveness was to regret it greatly at a later date.

29th   I went to Portsmouth with Captain Bell. He was so kind as to drive me to two warships; the *Britannia* with 110 cannon was not quite completed. This will be the largest ship ever built in England. Although there were several ships in England carrying 110 cannon, they were not as large. From here, we also saw the *Barfleur*[18] of 90 cannon. How surprised I was to see such structures and the splendor inside. The entire crew of the former amounts to 1,000 and that of the *Barfleur* to 750 men. It was quite late when we returned on board the *Pallas*.

30th   On the left side not far from Gosport, we saw a magnificent building which had the appearance of a very large and beautiful castle. It was a hospital for sailors. I asked to be put ashore and looked at that world renowned hospital. Two thousand five hundred sick can be admitted here. The chief surgeon of the hospital took pains to show me everything worth seeing; the pharmacy, the church and the waterworks that carry fresh water into all the rooms.[19] This afternoon the Hesse-Hanau Regiment of the Erbprinz [heir to the throne] of Hesse-Cassel arrived here in 4 ships and cast anchor near us. This regiment, which is 668 men strong, is commanded by Colonel von Gall. The ships were the *Content, Three Sisters, Stark* and *Margaretha Martha*. Six other ships with English Artillery and Scotsmen cast anchor near us together with 4 ships loaded with provisions. These ships were the *Rosseau, Fall, Charming, Nancy, Prince George, British Queen, Woodlands, Devonshire, Lilly, Charlotte* and *Jupiter;* almost all of them were new and very handsome. Next to these, two other frigates, *Juno* and *Blonde*, each one of 32 cannon, were riding at anchor. These are to accompany us as escort to America. The former is to lead and command the fleet. She will in future transmit her orders through cannon shots, flags and pennants and at night through lanterns; each ship's captain has been instructed about the meaning of each signal. Otherwise, there are many other small ships riding at anchor here with 50, 60, 64, 74, 80, 90, 98, 100 and 110 cannon. No one can imagine a more glorious sight, the roadstead of Spithead seems a floating city. Tonight, carpenters and cabinet makers came and worked on board.

31st   Forty-five men were taken from our ship onto other ships today because a portion of our room was partitioned off to make a [*new*] room for the sailors. A combination of cabin and dining room was made out of the former sailors' room, for the great number of officers did not have enough space in the one cabin. The regular cabin [salon] was now occupied by our Major General von Riedesel, the English agent Captain Haynes, the English commissary Captain Foy and the Adjutant General Captain Edmonstone, who had been sent by the King to our Major General von Riedesel. Captain of the Cavalry Fricke, Quartermaster General Captain Gerlach, Adjutant General Lieutenant Cleve,[20] First Field Paymaster Gödecke and Secretary Langemeyer were assigned to the second cabin. This was the cabin that also served as dining room. Five English doctors or CHIRURGI[21] had also been sent from London, who were to go to America with us. None of them came on board our ship, however, as they were distributed among other ships of our fleet. Everything was very expensive in Portsmouth. One pound of roasted coffee cost 6 shillings, that is more than 42 groschen, 6 pfennig. Unroasted coffee may not be sold at retail here or anywhere else in England under penalty of 50 pounds sterling. Thus, none of us was able to buy any coffee. -- One pound of sugar cost 7 groschen, one pound of tobacco 10 groschen 8 pfennig. One bottle of Port cost 2 shillings; thus, everything was very expensive.

End of this Month

Month of April 1776

1st   Captain Foy came back on board.

2nd   Boats again go to Portsmouth very frequently; there is talk of our imminent departure. Money was disbursed among the men. All subaltern officers received one guinea, noncommissioned officers five shillings, privates two and a half shillings sterling. It was also announced that all letters home were to go now post paid; each letter had to have an envelope. To try it out, I quickly wrote to my wife.[22]

3rd   I again went to Portsmouth. At 2 o'clock in the afternoon, 13 cannon shots from the frigate *Juno* were heard: that was the signal for our departure -- and I was still in Portsmouth! What anguish! Our *Pallas* had already set sail. Finally a boat was found that took me across, and luckily I did get on board. The fleet cast anchor near St. Helens on the Isle of Wight. Up to there we advanced --6

4th   Major General von Riedesel returned on board our ship this morning. Lieutenant General Burgoyne, Paymaster General Dramond with Adjutant General Gambier went on board the frigate *Juno*. This one is commanded by Captain Dalrymple and, as I have mentioned before, she will lead the fleet at the tête. No ship is allowed to go ahead of her. Major General Phillips,[23] commander of the English Artillery, went on board the *Blonde*. This frigate is commanded by Captain Pownal and forms the rearguard of our fleet. After the signal of 13 cannon shots from the *Blonde*, the anchors were weighed and our fleet, consisting of 16 Braunschweig, 4 Hessian, 10 English ships as well as 2 frigates, set sail. The weather was fair and the NE wind favorable; many cannon were fired, music resounded and drums were beaten. We drove past the famous Isle of Wight, but lost sight of it during the afternoon. Tonight, a lantern burned at the stern of the frigate *Juno*. Our course went westward.

5th   With a continual weak NW wind, we sailed until noon. --------------------------62
At that time, we passed the high mountains of Portland[24] and were at 50° 39' latitude on a westward course. The wind, having turned to NW, became contrary in the afternoon and we had to tack. At 9 o'clock tonight, a cannon shot was fired from the *Juno* and 3 lanterns were seen burning on that ship. Thereupon, a lantern was quickly lit on each ship. The obvious reason was that the ships would be better able to see each other in the dark of night and, while tacking in the stormy contrary wind, avoid colliding.

6th   During the past 24 hours, we did not sail more than ------------------------------42

Total--657

Latitude 50° 28'. Westward course. We passed a high rock, rising out of the sea, which is called Edenstone;[25] on top of it stands a lighthouse. The wind continues to be contrary, that is NW, and we have to keep on tacking. This is dangerous work.--

7th   At 5 o'clock this morning, the wind changed to southeast. We passed Star Point and Bamhead and from afar saw the harbors of Plymouth. Today, we saw another huge number of porpoises, rolling about on the water. Until noon, we advanced but ------60
Latitude 50° 9' westward course. In the afternoon, we passed the harbors of Plymouth. Fishermen, who came here on boats to us, took our letters along; they were to be sent to Germany; I likewise wrote a few lines to my friend. Seven transport ships with the 21st Engl. Regiment on board joined us here; they also were to sail with us to America. The ships' names were *Katy, Walter, St. Helena, Lively, Friendship, Prince Royal* and *Neptune* and together with these, our fleet consisted of 39 sailing ships. The wind is NNW and contrary, the sea is terribly agitated.

8th   This morning we passed the harbors of Falmouth. The wind continues to be NNW. According to the calculation of our captain, we advanced till noon [only] ----------43
Latitude 49° 50'. Westward course. We passed Cape Cornwall. The wind changed to east in the afternoon and raged so violently that everything not clinched and riveted or tied down with ropes fell pell-mell all about. We reached the tip of Britannia, called Land's End; everybody on board ship became seasick and this night we believed that the waves, which every few minutes were sweeping across the ship with terrible noise, would bury us in the unfathomable ocean. No one was able to sleep for, through the ship's violent motion, we were forever being thrown on top of each other. I was looking forward to daybreak with great anticipation,

9th   and although the storm from the NE continued with the same violence [as yesterday], it [the day] did strengthen my confidence. I went or rather crept onto the foredeck to get some fresh air. We advanced very far, up to noon covering -------------133 Latitude 48° 30', longitude 2° 23'. This longitude has been calculated from Cape Lizard on, from where our captain will daily determine the latitude. The wind changed to ENE tonight. Although still quite sick, I lasted a good hour on the foredeck tonight. I saw with amazement how the ship was cutting through the waves and how through the friction and the sea's violent motion, fiery sparks emanated as big as walnuts and even bigger. These occurred in such quantity that one believed the sea to be on fire.[26] The waves that were continuously sweeping across the ship compelled me to look for my bed; during the night I slept a little. As the ship kept her rather violent motions, I had myself tied to my bed.

10th   Up to noon, we came nearer to America by ---------------------------------------101

Total --893

Latitude 47° 50', longitude 47° 53'. We continue having east wind but no longer that strong. All the sick are improving. I myself also feel a little better today. The wind changed again to ENE tonight.

11th   Until noon, we advanced --79 Latitude 47° 38', longitude 6° 48'. Westward course. The sea keeps on rising terribly high; nevertheless, I am smoking my pipe on the foredeck tonight and observe the artificial machine [sic] as well as the large fiery sparks on the sea. The wind is blowing stronger from the NE again and the waves are often marching [sic] across the foredeck.

12th   The wind changed to ESE and with it we advanced till noon --------------------113 Latitude 47° 21' and longitude 9° 36'. Westward course.

13th   With continual ESE wind, we advanced in 24 hours -----------------------------87 Latitude 47° 15', longitude 11° 44'. The weather is pleasant. Since several ships are missing, we have to go slow. We again saw very many porpoises rolling on the water. When I see these gentlemen, I grow anxious because they hardly ever fail to announce bad weather.

14th   With a SSE wind, we advanced till noon -------------------------------------96 and found the elevation of the pole to be 47° 6'; and the change 14° 2'. With this SE wind, so favorable for us, we could have advanced much further but because some of our ships were missing, we had to furl the sails and go slowly; they had fallen behind or had been driven off their course. The weather was so pleasant this afternoon that we danced a quadrille on the foredeck.

15th   Tonight, we had a strong east wind again. With this, we moved closer to America in the past 24 hours by --114 Latitude 46° 30', longitude 17° 16'. Westward course. Today the wind again began to rage terribly, even more violently than on April 8. Toward evening, the large sail at the mainmast tore apart and the sailors had to put on a new sail. As the ship was often lying so far on the side that the tips of the masts frequently touched the waves, this turned out to be a horrible task. The wind and the sea made such a noise that the captain was forced to speak through his speaking trumpet if the sailors were to understand his orders. At nightfall, the wind changed to an adverse NW wind. This was another horrible night. Many of us became sick; so did I.

16th   Last night, the wind changed to SSW and with this, we advanced --------------109

Total --1,592

Latitude 46° 6', longitude 19° 8', westward course. The number of sick is increasing, the sea rises unusually high and our ship is like a ball tossed from one wave to the next.

17th   As of noon, we have come closer to America by ----------------------------------77
Latitude 45° 10', longitude 20° 30'. Snow and hail fell in the afternoon.

18th   With SE wind we advanced in the past 24 hours------------------------------------79
Latitude 44° 45', longitude 21° 56'. The sea is getting a little calmer.

19th   In complete calm, we advanced but --21
Latitude 44° 36', longitude 22° 28'. Almost all of our seasick have improved. We have seen a fleet of 40 ships about 4 miles behind us but do not know as yet what kind of ships they are; probably Engl. ships. Always calm, i.e., no wind during the afternoon. The sea is like a mirror, the wind comes from SSW.

20th   With this, we advanced till noon ---43
Latitude 44° 47', longitude 23° 20'. Westward course. The fleet we saw yesterday came closer today and we recognized it as being an Irish fleet having Engl., Irish and Scottish troops on board. It was following the same course as we were and was also destined for Canada; it was protected by 2 frigates: the frigate *Pearl*, commanded by Capt. O'Hara and the frigate *Carysford*, that Capt. Fanshave commanded. Each carried 32 cannon. Our fleet is quite respectable now and incl. the frigates consists of 79 sailing ships, all of them 3-masted: a truly beautiful sight similar to a glimmering city.

21st   With a continual SWS wind, we advanced until noon ----------------------------55
Latitude 45°, longitude 24° 40'. Westward course. It is too bad that the strong SW wind is not favorable for us. We could speedily advance and not have such agitation on board. But as we have to sail against the waves, they also frequently march [sic] across our ship putting her in very violent motion. Seeing many and various kinds of birds today, our dragoons believe that we must definitely be close to land. We also saw many types of marine life that no one could identify. It is getting colder by the day.

22nd   We have lost sight of the Irish fleet and advanced till noon -----------------------75
Latitude 45° 30', longitude 26° 13'. Westward course.

23rd   With an agitated sea and NW wind we advanced till noon -----------------------78
Latitude 44° 40', longitude 27° 41'. Course always westward.

Total   ---2,020

We again saw several ships from the Irish fleet. Paymaster General Dramond died on the frigate *Juno* and was buried at sea.

24th   The wind changed to SSW. With this, we advanced till noon----------------------63
Latitude 44° 45', longitude 29°. We passed a packet boat, which came from America and sailed to England.

25th   After a very stormy night, we have come closer to America by -------------------71
Latitude 44° 53', longitude 30° 11'. It is getting colder by the day.

26th   With a SSW wind, the ship's motions were so strong last night that we, in our beds, alternately stood on our heads and on our feet and sometimes rolled around sideways. Oh, what a miserable life this is! In the last 24 hours, we advanced but --------40
Latitude 44° 55', longitude 31° 26'. The Irish fleet has left us again. Last night, we also lost sight of the frigate *Blonde* and 10 transport ships from our fleet. The continual SWS

wind was freezing. It was so cold that the sail on the foremast iced up. Every few minutes, the waves swept across the ship.

27th   This morning, the wind changed to ENE. With this, we advanced till noon ----80 Latitude 44° 44', longitude 33° 6'. Westward course. Several of our lost ships have been found again. In spite of the pleasant sunshine, it is very cold today and it seems to get colder and colder by the day.

28th   With continual east wind, we advanced till noon --------------------------------114 Latitude 44° 37', longitude 35° 15'. Westward course. The wind again changed to NNW and raged violently, increasing the severe cold. Through the negligence of the sailors we almost met with disaster tonight. When the ship was changing course while tacking, the sailors did not move the sail around quickly enough; thereby the ship almost capsized. On one side, she was almost underneath the water and we stood on our heads although we were tacking.

29th   In the past 24 hours we advanced as much as -------------------------------------74 Latitude 44° 13', longitude 36° 29'. Westward course. In spite of bright sunshine, it was so terribly cold that one could not stand on the foredeck long enough to smoke a pipe of tobacco to the end. The severe cold probably comes from the New World to which we are getting closer by the day.

30th   With continual NNW wind we advanced till noon --------------------------------61 Latitude 43° 36', longitude 37° 30'. Early this morning, we saw a ship at a distance of 6 or 7 English miles, which our captain took to be an American ship.

Total   --- 2,523

Through a signal shot and a flag hoisted from the frigate *Juno*, the captain of the frigate *Blonde* quickly got orders to reconnoiter with his ship. The *Blonde*, sailing very speedily, quickly gave chase to the alleged Rebel[27] ship and would have overtaken it for sure. Through a cannon shot, however, the *Juno* gave orders to the fleet to turn the ships tacking all the while. The *Blonde* took this cannon shot for an order to discontinue the chase. We changed our course very often today, now to the east, now to the south, then again to the west. No one knows the reason for it. The cold grows more severe by the day. Today is the last day of April and we ardently wished we would see land very soon.

End of this Month

Month of May 1776

Oh, the pleasant first of May! Yes, what a pleasant day in Germany! Just about everyone is looking forward to this day. Oh, you lucky Germans! You see the pleasant, the green and gentle side of nature! You hear the enchanting tones of the nightingale! And what do we hear? As if locked in a horrible prison, we hear nothing but the nerve-racking noise of the waves up from the bottomless ocean which, with their frightening roar, are threatening our ruin. -- It is calm and foggy today so that one cannot even see 5 paces [*ahead*]; that is why small arms are continually fired and the drummers must continually drum. Until noon we only covered --22 Latitude 43° 49', longitude 38° 9'. The fog disappeared tonight and there was bright moonlight; but it was also very cold.

2nd   This morning, the fog reappeared and although a strong wind was blowing from WNW, it could not disperse the fog. Until noon, we advanced ------------------------55

Latitude 44° 6', longitude 39° 16', westward course. Our Captain Bell assured us that because of the severe cold and the almost constant fog, we ought to be very close to Terre Neuve [Newfoundland].[28] He had the plummet cast and found no bottom at 150 fathoms and 6 feet.

3rd   Until noon, we moved closer to America by --82

Total --2,682

This morning, our ship's captain measured a depth of 40 fathoms. Thus we had reached the great fish bank of the New World (Terre Neuve). This bank is a mountain 100 Engl. mile long, lying beneath the water. We found 2 French ships here, whose sailors were fishing. According to today's calculation the polar height is 44° 30' and the length 41° 46'. Our course is continually toward the west. As the fog lifted during the afternoon, a heavy rainshower came down. This did not hinder us from entertaining ourselves with fishing and we caught 9 of those fish the English call codfish and we Kabeljau. This is the fish that when salted and dried is called Klippfisch or Stockfisch [dried cod]. Those which our sailors caught today weighed between 20 and 30 pounds; they were very tasty and, according to the English, are often caught weighing 40 pounds and more. As there is an incredible quantity of these fish around, one finds [*people from*] all nations and parts of the world here to fish. Actually no nation may do so without permission from the English but because the English do not care enough, millions and millions [*of fish*] are taken by other nations. They all are caught by fishing rod and one person can catch up to 400 in one day. The profit from this fishery used to bring the King of England 800,000 pounds sterling per year; before the present war, the city of Boston alone sold [*fish valued at*] 400,000 pounds sterling. One estimates that the inhabitants of Terre Neuve - in English, Newfoundland - number 12,000 souls, who mostly live on St. John's Island. Their main business is fishing but they are also engaged in very profitable fur trading with the Savages.[29] Placentia is Terre Neuve's principal city. Today we are having a strong SE wind but it still cannot disperse the fog. And the cold, alas! It is so severe that, when out of bed, one can hardly stay alive. Orders were given by Major General von Riedesel to all our ships and those approaching us that every night a watch was to be kept on the foredeck by 8 men with loaded guns. This was done because St. John's Island probably continued to be occupied by the Rebels, and we had to pass by it. Terre Neuve lies to our right, while St. John's is to our left close to Cap Breton. Since almost all the ships sailed near ours today, we learned that our men were in the best of health and that so far no more than 4 men had been buried at sea. Our captain found a depth of 30 fathoms this afternoon. One noncommissioned officer and 8 men kept watch on the foredeck tonight. Some of our transport ships are missing again.

4th   The favorable SE wind has advanced us until noon by --------------------------107

Total --2,789

Latitude 49° 11', longitude 46° 6', westward course. Although it is quite foggy, we saw a great number of all kinds of birds. It is colder today than it was last January in Wolfenbüttel. This afternoon, the wind became contrary again, i.e., SSW.

5th   Because of it, we did not advance any farther till noon than ----------------------42
Latitude 44° 11', longitude 46° 56'. Today is real April weather: now rain, now sunshine, now snow, now hail. We saw 3 whales that made a loud noise in the water. Whenever they got above water with the upper part of their bodies, they sprayed the water like a fountain high into the air, which then fell down like dust or smoke. It could be mistaken for the smoke of a fired cannon. Tonight the wind again is blowing strongly from NW and we are tacking. The drummers must continually drum since the fog is so dense. With still prevailing contrary NW wind and tacking,

6th   we advanced till noon --44

Latitude 44° 50', longitude 47° 40'. The weather is good today, the

7th,   but it is terribly cold. In the afternoon again dense fog. With still prevailing NNW wind and tacking we advanced until noon --49
Latitude 44° 56', longitude 48° 34'; westward course. It is snowing and raining and the waves are extremely high.

8th   During last night's turbulence we again lost sight of 5 ships of our fleet and since a Hessian ship has been missing since April 15, 6 ships have been driven off their course. Last night, 4 ships from the Irish fleet that had lost contact with their own fleet came to us. Yesterday we passed the so-called whale bank. With prevailing contrary NWN wind we did not advance in 24 hours any farther than --------------------------------35
Latitude 45° 16', longitude 49°. We again saw a whale very close to our ship today. Every day, a great deal of grass and many weeds and all kinds of things, even wood, come floating on the water so that one should think us close to the land. Here I remember the voyage of Columbus, who also reported that he had seen such things every day.

9th   With still prevailing NNW wind and tacking we advanced till noon --------------49

Total --2,959

Latitude 45° 34', longitude 49° 40'. Westward course. To recuperate, we stayed in bed the whole day. We met a French ship that wanted to fish on the banks of Terre Neuve. The frigate *Juno* fired a cannon shot; the French ship quickly sailed to the frigate, lowered her sails and showed her passports. In this same manner, all the nations have to acknowledge the naval supremacy of the English at sea. Every day we see a great deal of grass and weeds floating at sea toward us; I keep thinking of Columbus.

10th   With prevailing contrary NNW wind, we have come closer to America during the past 24 hours by --59
Latitude 45° 58', longitude 50° 21'. The cold appears to be getting more severe and it is so bitter that it begins to annoy us. How could we help it! Did we not have to suffer through a very cold winter in Germany this year? But over there, we could get warm near a hot stove and now we have to endure another winter at sea and have no stoves --- that is reason enough for us to be wishing ourselves back in Germany.---

11th   Last night the wind changed to SSW and we advanced ----------------------------87
Latitude 46° 3', longitude 51° 45'. Last night we again had to suffer greatly; we could not lie down, stand or walk. Because it was very dark, our drummers had to beat their drums continually; and in spite of it, we almost collided with the *Minerva*. [*This*] could have easily shattered both ships. Although we were so close that we could have stepped from one ship to the other, at the very last moment, we were able to turn aside. Several ships, among them the frigate *Juno*, suffered some damage to the masts and sails last night; on our ship, the large sail on the large or mainmast was also torn, and in the most impenetrable darkness the sailors had to climb up quickly and fasten a new sail.

12th   The wind is again blowing from NW and until noon we have come closer to Canada by ---68
Latitude 46° 59', longitude 52° 56'. We have our work cut out for us today in trying to guard ourselves from head injuries. The sea rises so high that the masts of the ships often touch the waves with their tips. We also saw many birds which nobody could identify; some were beautifully marked.

13th   This morning, I was awakened very early by hearing the sailors' shouts. The helmsman had discovered America from the crow's nest. The joy and curiosity to see this continent drove everybody on the foredeck, me included, and we saw the mountains of Cap Breton a little to our left; to us they appeared to be clouds. Until noon we advanced   ---63

Total ---3,285

Latitude 47° 16', longitude 53° 48'. Westward course. Shortly before nightfall, we very distinctly saw the Ile St. Paul and Cap du Nord on Cap Breton.

14th   We reached the St. Lawrence Gulf last night and today saw both shores alternately, i.e., Terre Neuve to the right and Cap Breton to the left. N.B. because we were tacking. Otherwise one cannot see either shore when in the center, for the gulf is 40 German miles wide here. We saw the shores covered with ice and the high mountains with snow. The main fortress of Cap Breton is Louisbourg,[30] which, while being captured from the French, was demolished by the English. Cap Breton is very famous for coal, which is found particularly on the banks of the Spanish [Sydney] River,[31] and many cargoes of it are taken to Québec, Halifax, New York etc. every year. We passed the Birds' Islands or Iles-de-la-Madeleine as well as St. John's Island to our left. With SW and NE winds we advanced --79
Latitude 47° 55', longitude 55°. We again saw many birds.

15th   With NE wind, we approached Canada in the past 24 hours by ------------------81
Latitude 48° 58', longitude 56° 9'. Since yesterday we have not seen any land again. The cold seems to get worse every day. We saw many strange specimens of marine life (Seetiere). Our captain said those were cows, pigs, dogs, wolves etc. but who knows? Who has really observed them scientifically? Certainly not our captain.

16th   Until noon, we moved further ahead toward Québec by --------------------------59
NNW course. We passed Bonaventure and Cap de Gaspé, the first mainland of Canada, and reached the St. Lawrence River, which is still at least 20 German miles wide here. In this region, there is almost continual NW wind and the water is quite agitated. It is therefore rather difficult to enter the St. Lawrence River; in addition, ebb and flood tides cause a very strong current and many a ship had to keep tacking for 4, 5 or even 6 weeks without being able to enter the St. Lawrence River. We were lucky to have entered so quickly. Tonight, we saw the Northern Lights, larger than any of us had ever seen before. Our captain said we would see many more like them in Canada. Were such Northern Lights to be seen in Germany, what horrible prognostications would result from them![32]

17th   With NW winds and tacking, we did not advance any further than --------------32
As there was a clear sky this morning, Capt. Bell observed the sun at noon and found that we were under the 49° 10' northern latitude. In the afternoon, we saw on our right the Ile d'Anticosti, which we likewise found covered with snow and whose shores were full of ice. This island is 100 miles long and 12 miles wide, has unproductive soil and has not been inhabited since Canada was taken away from the French.

18th   Until noon we advanced --33

Total ---3,568

Latitude 49° 45'. In the afternoon, it was clouding up and began to snow; within the period of one hour, the snow lay one foot deep on the deck of our ship. As our [drinking] water was stinking, snow was now collected and boiled for making coffee. As carefully as the snow was gathered in the vessels, our effort was badly rewarded: the coffee tasted worse by far than that [made] of our ship's water which, through continual boiling, had by now lost much of its smell. Our beer had also been consumed and today every 6 men will receive one quart of rum which will give the foul water a better flavor.

This is a good healthy spirit and is made from sugar and syrup. The best rum comes from Jamaica in the West Indies. There is heavy frost on our ship today.

19th   With continual NW wind we did not advance any further till noon than ---------31 Latitude 49° 54'. W and NW course. With continual tacking, we alternately saw Cap-des-Rosiers and Anticosti, the former to the south, the latter to the north. Every day, we saw a great number of seals.

20th   Last night, the wind changed to SSW; we advanced until noon -------------------56 Not all of our ships have joined up with us as yet. We encountered a merchant ship today that came from Québec and wanted to go to Halifax in New Scotland. We learned from them that the Governor General Sir Guy Carleton had defended the fortress of Québec against all attacks by the Rebels and that, upon the arrival of the *Isis* on the 7th of this month with 50 cannon and 14 transport ships, the enemy had taken to flight toward Trois-Rivières and Montréal.

21st   Last night, the wind shifted to ENE; we advanced --------------------------------87 We met the frigate *Neger*, which was sailing to Halifax to be repaired; they confirmed the news from yesterday. We passed Cap Chat[33] and found the shores still covered with snow and ice.

22nd   With contrary WNW wind and continual tacking, we advanced till noon -------26 We saw Cap Chat all day. The still prevailing NW wind did not

23rd   take us any farther in the past 24 hours than--18 The weather continues to be turbulent and disagreeable.

24th   In weak SE wind we advanced till noon   ---27 We passed Mont Camille. With a weak NE wind, it is raining

25th   and very cold. At 3 o'clock we finally reached the ardently desired Ile-de-St. Barnabé. The *Juno* gave orders to cast anchors and the fleet did do so. Through hoisted flags, the captains of all the ships were at the same time ordered to go to the frigate *Juno*. She lay about half a mile from us at Cap-à-l'Orignal. On account of the sunken rocks and sand banks which are found here and there in the St. Lawrence River, we are not able to sail ahead without a pilot. The frigate *Surprise* was riding here at anchor. When our captain returned from the *Juno,* we learned that the Irish fleet had sailed through yesterday morning and had taken all the pilots along; but Capt. Dalrymple had decided, if the wind remained favorable, to continue his course to Québec without a pilot. We sailed to the Ile-du-Bic --29

Total   --3,842

I have managed pretty well, that is to say, I have not consumed everything I had. The anchor was cast today for the first time again and as tomorrow will be the first day of Pentecost, I and several of my friends pooled all our last resources and made a good punch. At this time, we remembered all our friends and relatives in Germany. There was a violent storm tonight but what should I care? We are riding at anchor and -- I have drunk punch. The wind shifted to WNW and was blowing terribly hard. We were at rest today. Major General von Riedesel went on board the frigate *Juno* with his suite to pay a visit to Lieut. General Burgoyne; from there he went to the Ile-du-Bic. On this island lived but one man, the captain of the pilots, who has to provide approaching vessels with pilots. The island was uncultivated, overgrown with woods and brush. The shores were beset with cliffs and rocks. Lieut. Gen. Burgoyne went ahead to Québec today on the frigate *Surprise*. He was saluted by the *Surprise* with 13 cannon shots. This evening, the weather was very pleasant with bright moonlight and as the wind shifted to NEN at midnight, having given the signal, we weighed anchor and sailed through the remainder of the night.

27th   At daybreak, we had lost sight of the Ile-du-Bic and had the Ile Verte on our left. The shore behind the Ile Verte was settled and we saw the first houses on the mainland. As we had been used to seeing nothing but sky and water for a long time, this sight gave us great joy and we could not get enough of it. The right or northern shore was not settled at all. In the afternoon we reached the Rock Islands, also called Iles-des-Pélerins, to our left. We cast anchor and had the village of Kamouraska on our left. With NE wind, we advanced up to here --79

28th   With still prevailing NE wind, the anchors were weighed at 5 o'clock this evening and we set sail. We saw many porpoises rolling on the water but these were very different from those we saw at sea. They were white as snow and 20 to 30 or more feet long. They do not leave the St. Lawrence River. The Canadians use their skins instead of leather for straps for their dogs; their flesh produces very good train oil. Today we found both banks, the one to the right and the one to the left, very well settled. It was 4 o'clock in the afternoon when we reached the Ile-aux-Coudres. This place was designated as rendezvous for our fleet in case ships should go astray or be driven off course. We got closer to Québec by ---56
The river was full of rocks and boulders here. We almost ran aground on one; we also just missed colliding with the *Apollo*. We cast anchor very close to the Ile-aux-Coudres. A pilot came from this island onto our ship who quickly had us weigh anchor to cast it again some 100 paces further ahead. In pleasant weather, Maj. Gen. von Riedesel went on the island with his suite. The circumference of it is 21 Engl. miles; it supports 300 souls, who live in 66 houses. The owner of this island is the Bishop of Québec. Each inhabitant pays him one shilling sterling fee-farm rent for each morgen [2.116 acres] of land, which is about 7 groschen 1 1/2 pfennig in our Convention money. These are Frenchmen of the Roman Catholic faith, who first settled here 80 years ago. The clothing of these men is said to be very similar to that of the Indians and consists of a short woolen jacket and smock made out of a kind of white material (kersey). Over it, they have a multi-colored sash with fringes. On the legs, they wear a kind of leggings [Stiefeletten], which serving them as shoes they call Demitas [dimity]. They tie them with multi-colored fringes and ribbons below the knee; some also go above the knee. Their shoes are called moccasins and are the proper shoes of the Savages, which cannot be adequately described. The fair sex is dressed in French fashion; their houses are the worst I have ever seen in a city. Whoever saw them from the outside would certainly have lost all desire to live inside. I have seen grains and garden fruit of all kinds here, also fowl. I have also seen maple trees, from which the inhabitants draw sugar; likewise a type of fir tree, called épinette [spruce], from which they boil glue. The inhabitants have everything in great abundance, which they sell in Québec, which is but 45 Engl. miles away from here. I was most interested in getting some bread and for one shill. sterl. bought a loaf weighing 4 pounds. I think that expensive; it was white bread somewhat like French army bread [Kommissbrot] in the Seven Years War. But what joy! to eat bread which can be cut with a knife! We had not been treated to that for a long time. Since the flood tide came toward midnight, the pilot had the anchor weighed and we sailed to the north side of the island with great effort and cast anchor there.

29th   We had contrary wind and lay quiet today. An officer came to us from Québec, through whom we learned that the British army under General Howe[34] had left Boston on March 17 and moved to Halifax. Since the wind did not seem to turn favorable for us, we weighed anchor at 11 o'clock tonight in order to ride with the tide, but were soon being tossed about again.

Total ---3,977

30th   Toward noon we got a favorable wind but it was weak. We rode through the so-called new dams [breakwaters]; several ships of our fleet rode through the old dams. Around 8 o'clock this evening, we reached the eastern tip of the Ile-d'Orléans and cast anchor there after having come closer to Québec by ---18

31st   At the dot of midnight, the anchors were weighed. Because of contrary wind, we had to tack the entire day and cast anchor at 7 o'clock in the evening. We sailed -------12 We are riding here at anchor between Pointe St. Jean and Pointe Dauphin near the Ile-d'Orléans. This island is quite attractively settled; anyway, the houses appear to be better than on the Ile-aux-Coudres. It is 36 miles long; the southwest tip almost touches Québec and it has 8 parishes. Capt. Bell assures us that we will be off Québec tomorrow. This makes us very happy at the end of this month.

Month of June 1776

1st   At midnight the anchors were weighed again; although the wind continued to be contrary, we went with the flood tide. At 6 o'clock this morning, we cast anchors again near the Ile-d'Orléans. In the afternoon, we again set sail with the flood tide and since we had reached the SW tip of the Ile-d'Orléans, we had the famous falls of Montmorency on our right. They are indescribably beautiful with the water plunging down from a height of 240 feet. They make a noise that can be heard at a great distance. At 6 o'clock this evening, we finally reached Québec with great effort and continual tacking. Up to here we sailed --15 Québec is located below the 46° 55' degree of northern latitude. Our Major General von Riedesel immediately went to Québec to report the arrival of our First Division to Governor General Sir Guy Carleton,[35] who himself had only yesterday returned to Québec and given the command of the army over to Lieut. General Burgoyne. Today the report came that Captain Forster from the 8th Regiment had taken 400 Rebels prisoner in Fort Cèdres.[36]

2nd   We are riding here at anchor in the St. Lawrence River between Québec and Pointe Lévi.[37] Québec is a strong fortress [made] almost invincible by nature itself because on the east and south sides is fortified by the St. Lawrence River, on the west and north sides by very high walls, rocks and cliffs. It actually consists of two cities, the lower city and the upper city. Most of the inhabitants are French; several Englishmen and Germans, also many German Jews, are [living] here. Together both cities have about 880 houses, which for the most part are two stories high and covered with shingles or at times with fir tree boards. The streets are not paved and in bad weather very filthy. I also climbed to the Plains of Abraham where, in 1759, the two Generals Wolfe and Montcalm,[38] the commanders of both armies, were shot; the former by the English and the latter by the French army. What a wonderful view one had from here and especially onto Cap Diamant! The terrific height lets one see for quite some distance around; ships sailing to and fro on the St. Lawrence River, the exceedingly beautiful falls of Montmorency and both banks of the St. Lawrence River, which are built up with houses; all these seem rather to be pleasure gardens. Since we have to provide ourselves again with necessities, I was shocked [upon learning] that 1 lb. of coffee costs 2, and 1 lb. of sugar 1 shilling. Rice [costs] 1 shilling per pound. There is some talk of disembarking.

Total of Engl. miles from Stade to Québec ------------------------------------4,022

3rd   Today the order came that our Dragoon Regiment and the Regiment Prinz Friedrich are to disembark and stay in Québec as occupation [forces]. The dragoons were taken from our ship onto the ship *Peggy* whereupon as many musketeers from the Regiment von Riedesel came onto our ship. Several hundred Americans are in Québec as prisoners; they are very shabby and do not look like soldiers. When I returned on board our *Pallas* tonight, I got orders from Major Gen. von Riedesel that I was to remain as surgeon of the General Staff in future. My baggage, that had already been taken on board the *Peggy,* had to be brought back to our ship immediately. The following ships are riding at anchor in Québec: the *Isis* with 50 cannon, the frigates *Juno, Blonde, Pearl,*

Carysfort, Surprise and *Triton*, each with 32 cannon; as well as more than 100 transport and merchant vessels.

4th   Today, Major General von Riedesel went on board the *Isis* and was saluted with 13 cannon shots. Since the birthday of the King of Great Britain was celebrated today, a great feast was organized in Québec; cannon were fired from the fortress as well as from all the ships! Twenty-one shots were fired from each ship and from each battery: that is the Royal Salute.

5th   Both regiments disembarked and moved into the barracks.

6th   Today the Feast of Corpus Christi was celebrated and that was done in the same manner as in the Catholic cities in Germany. Ever since we have been riding here at anchor, I have had the opportunity of making the acquaintance of several German inhabitants of Québec. One of them told me a great deal about last winter's siege. The city had been surrounded for 7 months and since he had been continually on guard or picket duty, he had not slept in his own bed for 30 nights at that time. The Rebels had not, however, gotten into the Lower City; when the St. Lawrence River had frozen over, they had gone across on the ice. On Dec. 31, 1775, they had assaulted the city in a terrible snow storm during the night . The name of the general and commander of this expedition was Montgomery,[39] and after he had climbed across the first barrier underneath Cap Diamant, he was killed in front of the second by grapeshot. His aide-de-camp and all those around him were killed along with him. The command was given to Benedict Arnold,[40] who had likewise been wounded, and who had earned immortal glory through his march through the wilderness into Canada. He had had the command on the other side of Québec and had already climbed across the large battery at St. Rogues when he was wounded and led back. His corps kept advancing since they did not know about the fate of their General Montgomery, and defended themselves against the whole garrison in sheer desperation for more than 3 hours. Finally, they had to surrender and become prisoners of war; these were the same prisoners of whom I wrote on the 3rd of this month. The Provincials or Rebels, as the English call them, have made 2 expeditions against Canada: one under General Montgomery, who invaded upper Canada towards Montréal; the second was undertaken against lower Canada towards Québec, an expedition that has had no equal on this earth. The latter was undertaken by Colonel Benedict Arnold who, in mid-September 1775, set out from his camp at Boston with two infantry regiments consisting of about 1,500 men, and marched to Newburyport where the Merrimack River empties into the sea. Here his troops with provisions, ammunition and baggages embarked and sailed about 130 miles across the sea to the Kennebec River in New Hampshire [now in Maine] where they arrived on September 20. At Gardiner on the Kennebec River he had his troops embark in about 200 batteaux. Riding up the Kennebec, he found a fast flowing river in which there were many huge boulders and sandbanks. They frequently came upon waterfalls and places where they not only had to unload everything they had with them but also had to carry it along on land upon their shoulders. In addition, their batteaux had to be transported [*in the same way*]. The terrain was impassable, a wilderness that no man had ever passed through as long as the forest had been in existence. When they got back on the river, the batteaux either filled up with water or capsized and soon they had to be loaded and unloaded anew. One of those places where everything had to be transported on [*the men's*] shoulders was more than 12 miles long. Moreover, they had first to clear a road for many miles through the wilderness, cross swamps and then climb across dangerous mountains and cliffs with the greatest difficulty. All this not only caused the march to proceed very slowly but many in the corps became ill because their provisions were near the end; so they ate all the dogs they had with them and lived off weeds and roots. When they finally reached the end of the Kennebec River, Arnold sent his sick men back; with these, a colonel deserted with one third of the corps, claiming that the lack of victuals was driving them back.[41] This happened without Arnold as commander-in-chief knowing anything about it. Although the corps was much weakened by it, Arnold continued his steadfast march and finally arrived at the source of the Rivière Chaudière. This one flows in the opposite direction from the Kennebec River into the St. Lawrence River near Québec, while the Kennebec River empties into the sea at Gardiner; thus the one flows to the north and the other to the south. When Arnold had reached this river, his greatest difficulties were over. He sent several of his men ahead down the river who returned on Nov. 3 bringing some provisions along. Not long afterwards, they came to a house; this was the first in 43 days, a period during which they had not come upon anything human. The Canadians received this corps here with the same kindness and friendship with which the corps under General Montgomery had been welcomed in the vicinity of Montréal. Arnold published an address to the people of Canada that had been signed by General Washington. In it, the Canadians were invited to unite with the rest of the colonies as inseparable and to join under the flag of freedom. He also averred that they had not come to Canada to plunder but to protect the Canadians against a tyrannical regime. Therefore they should consider the Americans their best friends and not flee from their houses but provide support with victuals that would immediately be all paid for in cash. The fortress of Québec was very sparsely occupied, and the inhabitants were very dissatisfied with the Engl. government on account of a certain act,[42] and because petitions they had sent to London had not been answered yet. For this reason, the Canadians believed that both the English and the French looked at them with eyes full of suspicion and mistrust. Since the local troops had been sent to Montréal to ward off the Rebels, the settlers had been asking for arms and ammunition to defend themselves for a long time; but all this was rejected. Thus no one else was in Québec now but a few unarmed Emigrants[43] under Colonel MacLean, who had arrived in Québec from Sorel. Arnold appeared at Pointe Lévi on November 9. Fortunately, the St. Lawrence River was between him and Québec with its batteaux, otherwise Arnold would have taken the fortress without resistance during the first confusion. This defect was quickly repaired by the Canadians inasmuch as they ferried Arnold's Corps across in small canoes; in spite of the vigilance of frigates and warships, he crossed the river with his corps in the dark of night. This enraged the discontented inhabitants of Québec, the English as well as the French. As soon as they saw the danger threatening them and their estates, they assembled in a first alarm [sic] and demanded to be armed. Their wishes were quickly fulfilled and they immediately occupied the fortress as best they could. All the sailors came ashore from their ships in order to be used as gunners and now the garrison was quite a bit stronger than the corps under Arnold. Since he did not have any artillery, he could not undertake anything further but blocked all the entrances. Thus he cut the communication between the fortress and the countryside and awaiting Montgomery's arrival, cut off the supplies that were brought into town. Arnold paraded on the hills around Québec for several days, sending a flag to the inhabitants several times to surrender the fortress, but none was accepted. In fact, they (the flags) were shot at each time, whereupon Arnold had his corps go into their own quarters to recuperate somewhat. Around this time, Governor General Carleton arrived in Québec. His first order read that anyone unwilling or unable to bear arms should quickly move out of the city. The garrison consisted of 1,500 serviceable men in addition to 450 sailors. But these could only occupy the fortifications sparsely. On Dec. 5, General Montgomery also arrived before Québec. In order to prevent the bloodshed that an assault would produce, his first order of business was to write to General Carleton asking him immediately to surrender the city etc. He greatly exaggerated his power against which the weak garrison, without hope of reinforcement or rescue, could not long offer any resistance. But this appeal did not fare any better than the first [sent] by Arnold: as soon as they approached, they were shot at and any communication was strictly forbidden by General Carleton. Thereupon Montgomery began to besiege and bombard the city, but his artillery was too light and his corps too weak to be really effective. The siege lasted until Dec. 31 when, as I said before, Montgomery's brave life was ended. Yet, I still have to tell more about him. Richard Montgomery was a gentleman from an excellent family in the northern part of Ireland. His brother Alexander Montgomery is the present knight of the county of Donogal. These two brothers served their King in the last war under General Wolfe and on every occasion showed their knowledge in military matters.[44] In the year 1763, Richard Montgomery resigned his commission because he felt offended that a young officer had been given preference over him. His excellent character and naturally good qualities were admired and honored by everyone who set eyes on him, and on either side there certainly was no one involved in this war whose loss would be more mourned in England and America; he is described as a zealous worshipper of freedom. He married a beautiful young woman, bought an estate in the Province of New York, and so considered himself an American.[45] He was so carried away by his love for freedom that he rejected the delights that - considering his charming young wife and his great wealth - life was able to offer him. He exposed himself to all the misery and dangers that are inevitable in any war and more particularly in this unfortunate one. He doubtless had great knowledge of military matters and that was the reason that he was appointed major general at the very beginning of the war and made chief of the unfortunate and useless expedition against Canada. --   In short, in America he is considered a martyr, who sacrificed himself for freedom, slain in the prime of life, a man of excellent character, - who had deserved a better lot. -   But what is even more noteworthy, is that the greatest orators[46] in the British Parliament took pains to praise his virtues, to make eulogies and - to mourn his unfortunate fate. All the enmity against this brave general disappeared with his life - and on orders of Lieut. General and Governor Sir Guy Carleton, his body received every sign of reverence from his conquerors. He was brought into Québec on the first day of the year 1776 with all the military honors due to a brave soldier, and buried with great pomp.

7th   Since everybody still wanted to buy something, the batteaux frequently went to Québec this morning. Here I saw the first American Savages from the tribes of the Huron and Iroquois. They had come to offer their services to the King. Most of them were all naked and only some had wrapped white woolen blankets around themselves; many, however, were completely naked. Some had silver or tin plates hanging on their chests and around their arms. The outer rims of their ears were severed at the upper rounding and hung down to their shoulders; in these hangings, which had the thickness of a pipe's shank, they had rings hanging, [made] of all kinds of material; some also had scalps hanging from their ears, others on their chests. They had painted their faces with cinnabar; except for a tuft remaining on the crown of the head, the hair on their head was shorn off and the head itself painted with cinnabar. In the remaining tuft of hair, they had fastened red, white and green feathers and several tentacles. But what was most striking were the rings they wore in the septum between the nostrils. From these rings, additional small pins were hanging down to their mouths [Mäuler 'maws']. Their [skin] color was brownish-yellow, not quite chestnut brown. Their women were of smaller stature, also almost naked; they looked most disgusting. The men were all well-built, big and strong. The feet of both men and women turned inward as if they continually used the shoemaker's strap, but this was caused by their use of snowshoes. I was still in Québec when at 2 o'clock in the afternoon the signal shots were fired from the warship *Isis* that the fleet was to weigh anchor and set sail. We departed in a favorable NE wind with music and drum beating. The frigate *Triton* sailed at the tête and our beautiful *Blonde* formed the rear. We saw many settlements on both banks. As the wind calmed down toward evening, our pilot, whom we had gotten from Québec today, had the anchors cast and we were riding very calmly.

8th   At 7 o'clock in the morning, we weighed anchor but at 11 o'clock they were cast again.

9th   This morning we had a strong NE wind but it became weaker when we set sail. Some Englishmen disembarked at Cap Santé on the right bank. At 12 o'clock, we saw a 3-masted ship that had been stranded on a sandbank to our right; to our left [was] a waterfall. The church at Cap Santé has 4 towers. At 9 o'clock in the evening, we cast anchor not far from the town of Trois-Rivières, Québec; up to here we sailed --------------90

10th   Early this morning we weighed anchor but soon cast it again. We are floating straight across from Trois-Rivières. This town got its name from a river that because of 2 islands, splits into 3 rivers and then empties into the St. Lawrence River. Here the Irish fleet was riding at anchor. We also found those ships here that had been missing on the great ocean ever since April 26. All the troops of this fleet had disembarked at their arrival and driven off the rearguard of Colonel Arnold's Corps, which had taken its stand at this place. The enemy Brigadier General Thompson[47] had been captured here, together with several officers and privates, and taken to Québec. The troops re-embarked here. From Québec to Trois-Rivières we passed the following parishes on the banks of the St. Lawrence River: on the right, St. Augustin, Pointe-aux-Trembles, La Croix, St. Jean, Cap Santé, Deschambault, Grondines, Ste. Anne, Batiscan, Champlain, Cap-de-la-Madeleine; on the left, Pointe Lévi, St. Nicolas, St. Antoine, Ste. Croix, Lotbinière, St. Jean, St. Pierre le petit and Bécancour.

11th   This morning the anchors were weighed but because the wind became too weak, they were recast immediately. Also, since the ebb and flood failed to appear at all, we could not possibly move ahead without wind. The weather is beautiful but we also have a heat wave.

12th   We have beautiful weather but no wind whatsoever. Our Maj. Gen. von Riedesel, who has his headquarters there, went to Trois-Rivières to Governor General Carleton today. Rumor has it that all are to disembark at the Godefrey River. It was 5 o'clock when our general came back on board. Two Canadian officers accompanied him, with whom he went ashore on the left bank together with the Brigade Major, Capt. von Pöllniz[48] and Capt. Gerlach. From the *Elizabeth*, 24 men from the Regiment von Riedesel disembarked at the left bank as pickets.

13th   At 4 o'clock this morning, our general returned on board ship but went immediately to Governor General Carleton in Trois-Rivières. The rumor continues today that all are to disembark at the Godefrey River. It was 8 o'clock when our general returned on board and a cannon shot was immediately fired from our *Pallas* and from the *Rosseau* as a signal to weigh anchor as of that moment. We set sail in favorable NE wind; not far from Trois-Rivières we were saluted by a battery with 13 cannon shots. About 2 Engl. miles farther on, the *Elizabeth*, riding to the left of us, had to approach the left bank to take Capt. Gerlach and the 24 men back on board. Toward 12 o'clock we reached Lac St. Pierre, which is 24 miles long and 12 miles wide. Our fleet, 67 big ships in all, appeared on this small lake; it was exceedingly beautiful. In the afternoon, the wind calmed, and as we had almost crossed the lake, we cast anchor. Not even today did we disembark.

14th   In a weak NE wind we set sail as early as 3 o'clock this morning and cast anchor at 10 o'clock. At noon we set sail again and recast anchor at 1 o'clock. Many Savages rode in between our fleet in their canots d'écorce (small boats made from birch bark). Since we are supposed to disembark today, provisions for 2 days were given out and every soldier received 30 cartridges. Thus the affair seems to be getting serious. At 8 o'clock everybody had to go on deck with bag and baggage and the signal shot for disembarkation was fired. Nevertheless, only a few English regiments disembarked. This evening, the river became very agitated.

15th   We set sail as early as 4 o'clock but almost immediately cast anchor. At noon we set out again and toward evening cast anchor not far from Sorel. Sorel lies to our left and consists of a little church, a windmill and several wretched houses standing very close to the river. The Rebels had left Sorel only yesterday and we could still see the entrenchments. Here the Rivière Richelieu empties into the St. Lawrence River. Most of the Irish fleet entered the Rivière Richelieu and their troops disembarked very close to Sorel. These immediately continued their march toward Chambly. We set sail again but soon cast anchor with Sorel behind us. We had sailed 45 miles up to Sorel and had passed the following parishes and villages at the banks of the St. Lawrence River: on the right, Pointe-du-Lac, Grand Yamachiche, Petit Yamachiche, [La Seigneurie de la] Rivière-du-Loup, Maskinongé, and Berthier; on the left, Nicolet, La Baie, St. François, La Baie de Yamaska and Sorel.

16th   At 4 o'clock this morning, we weighed anchor in a favorable NNE wind but since the wind became contrary, we cast anchor at 10 o'clock. The weather was quite pleasant. Our Captain von Tunderfeldt,[49] Brigade Major of Governor Gen. Carleton, came to us with orders that all the troops should disembark today. At noon, another round of signal shots was fired for disembarking and provisions for 2 days were immediately given out. Thus we had 4 days supply. All the baggage was to remain on the ships. Three distinguished Savages came on board to pay a visit to our general. The one ----- had brought his wife along, a woman of very charming appearance. If the people in Braunschweig got a glimpse of her, they would no longer be so eager to hang witches. -- The Savage was so generous as to leave her to Major Gen. von Riedesel as a companion - for several days or weeks - and this caused much laughter. -- This evening at 5 o'clock, Major Gen. von Riedesel went to the left bank with his suite and now everyone disembarked and we got ashore at the parish of Contrecoeur. There were calashes for our general and his suite; thus I and Chief Clerk Senf sat together in one. At one o'clock that night we reached Verchéres, where we took up quarters. Thus I was finally rid of the ship *Pallas,* that had served as my abode for 96 days and carried me across the terrible ocean. Up to Montréal the following settlements lay on our right: Lanoraie, Lavaltrie, St. Sulpice, Repentigny, Pointe-aux-Trembles, La longue Pointe and Montréal on the Ile-de-Montréal; on our left: Grand St. Ours and Contrecoeur.

17th   As late as 1 o'clock this afternoon, the Regiments von Riedesel, Hesse-Hanau and Brigadier Breymann's Battalion arrived here. Since it had rained the whole night and the men were not used to marching, especially carrying 4 days supplies, the first march was difficult for them. This was also the reason that some already deserted on this first march. His Excellency Gov. Gen. Carleton went ashore at Verchéres and proceeded from there on land; also a comp. of English Artillery joined us. We marched 18 miles today.

18th   At 5 o'clock this morning we marched away from here, then through the village of Varennes to Boucherville. Here, we were quartered after having marched 15 miles.

19th   At 5 o'clock this morning, we set out and marched through Longueuil to La Prairie; up to here we had covered 16 miles. On our march today, we saw the city of Montréal lying on an island of the same name in the St. Lawrence River, along whose banks we had continuously been marching. A number of citizens provided with guns came out of this city over to us offering their services to Gov. Gen. Carleton to pursue the Rebels. But they knew quite well that the Rebels had already abandoned Chambly and St. Jean and withdrawn across Lake Champlain. The regiments were placed in cantonment quarters here but so close together that the Grenadier Comp. of Lieut. Colonel Breymann was quartered in one [*single*] house - but this was the largest house that I have seen in the whole of Canada. It belonged to a German who had gone away with the Rebels. Here were the headquarters of Gov. Gen. Carleton, Maj. Gen. von Riedesel and Brigadier General Gordon.

21st   His Excel., Gov. Gen. Carleton, took up headquarters in Montréal today. The supplies that are furnished here are more like those on board ship and are the same for officers and privates. Every man receives 1 1/2 lbs. of good white bread, 1 1/2 lbs. of fresh beef, butter and whatever else we got aboard ship.

22nd   Orders came from Gov. Gen. Carleton, that all the baggage was to be taken from the ships because the transports were to sail back to England. All the heavy baggage was to be moved to Québec, Sorel and Montréal, and as Gen. Carleton intends to send an officer to England, all the letters were sent to Montréal today. I sent letters to my friend C.W. in Wolfenbüttel, to my wife, mother, brothers and sister. Between here, Chambly, St. Jean and La Savanne lie 15 regiments distributed among 5 brigades, i.e., the brigade of Maj. Gen. von Riedesel, the brigades of Generals Fraser, Gordon, Nesbitt and Powell together with several comp. of Engl. Artillery.

23rd   Major General von Riedesel went to Montréal with a large suite today to attend the induction ceremony of the Savages there and since Gen. Carleton wanted this to be a rather solemn event, all the officers in the army, from capt. on up, were invited to it.   At 5 o'clock in the afternoon, the 5 Iroquois nations, namely the Onontars, Anugutais, Enyouguais, Nontaquahugnes and Canistota[50] were assembled in the former Jesuit church, that had previously been prepared for this ceremony.   In the center of the high choir was an armchair for Gen. Carleton and at the sides were chairs and benches for the remaining generals and officers.   About 300 [men] were present from the 5 nations; these were sitting on benches around the church smoking tobacco.   At these events, Gen. Carleton always had his hat on his head; behind him at a table sat the 2 Adjutant Gens., Capt. Carleton, the general's brother, and Capt. Foy, who performed the duties of secretaries.   Each nation had a superior or premier represent them, and an interpreter said the following to Gen. Carleton in French; "Since the Rebels have revolted against the Engl. nation, we have come to offer the King our services and will love and obey Gen. Carleton, who has been quashing the enemies' assaults."   Gen. Carleton then reproached the Savages from Sault St. Louis, of whom some were present and living but 9 miles from La Prairie, that they had been neutral up to now and had not joined the King at the beginning of the war.   They alleged as excuse that it had been the fault of their oldest leader, who was 80 years old but not present. Hereupon the Savages were taken into the service of the King for one year; they would get further directions as to where they were to be placed.   Then all the Savages shook hands with Gen. Carleton and all the other officers and offered Gen. Carleton and Gen. Burgoyne several scalps they had brought along as presents. (N.B. the scalp is the skin which covers the head bones. The Savages cut this skin above the ears all around [the head] down to the skull and tear it off. Therefore, everyone who is being scalped must either die immediately or bleed to death etc. The Savages desiccate these scalps and adorn themselves with them. Most prisoners who have the misfortune to fall into the power of the Savages are scalped; but if they [the Savages] feel too much offended, they will also eat them.[51])

Montréal lies in a plain and is built like Québec; the streets are not paved either; it is surrounded by a wall and has a strong blockhouse at the NE corner.   It is not a well established place and contains 1,000 houses at the most.   The ships come so close to the docks that one steps from the ships [directly] into the city.   The St. Lawrence River is very wide here, having a width of 9 miles between La Prairie and Montréal, but because of rocks and boulders, it is not navigable for large ships beyond Montréal.   The Engl. commissary Curtis, whose acquaintance I have made today, must take the blame for my late arrival at La Prairie.

24th   Those commanded to it went to the ships to get our baggage.

25th   Our men started drilling.   I go botanizing every day, have found many herbs I know and many I do not know.   I shall give a special report on them as well as on the diseases, as much as I understand of them.   I have already been called to several Canadian patients.

27th   Maj. Gen. von Riedesel drove to Gov. Gen Carleton in Chambly where he [Carleton] has moved his headquarters.   Chambly is 9 miles away from La Prairie and lies on the Rivière Richelieu.   The Rebels have burned Fort Chambly down to the walls.

28th   I received the first letter from Wolfenbüttel through Maj. Gen. von Riedesel, dated the 28th of March.   It was from my wife and had been enclosed in a letter from Mrs. von Riedesel.   In the entire corps no one else has received a letter.   I cannot expect another one soon.   All the baggage from the ships arrived here today.   On orders of our Maj. Gen. von Riedesel, spruce beer is being brewed here from fir sprigs, (épinette rouge), toasted bread and syrup.   This is a very healthy beverage, an anti-scorbutic, and tastes very much like resin.

30th   This Sunday a great procession and communion was held by all the German regiments.

Month of July 1776

1st   Our General von Riedesel went to Little Prairie for drill this morning.

2nd   This morning, I was called to some sick people in St. Pierre, 15 miles from here.

3rd   A musketeer from the Hesse-Hanau regiment was buried with the usual ceremonies; the English and Canadians were astounded by the magnificent burial; letters were again sent to Germany via England.

7th   There was a great procession and communion.

9th   I went to St. Philippe to visit the sick there.

10th   I also learned from headquarters at Chambly that General Howe has taken New York, and since I was going to Montréal today, I had the opportunity to get further information there.[52] The Island of Montréal is 30 miles long and 12 miles wide; in addition to the city of Montréal, 9 parishes are on this island. On the other side of Montréal, in the St. Lawrence River, lies another island called Jésus which, although settled, is not as large as Montréal. In the city of Montréal, there are 4 principal Catholic churches; of these the Jesuit Church has been dissolved. The fur trade with the Savages on the St. Lawrence River, on the lakes and on Hudson Bay is quite considerable. English and Canadians go there at certain seasons, not singly but in caravans; they give the Savages coarse pieces of cloth, dimity, woolen blankets, cinnabar, with which the Savages paint themselves; salt, silver or silver-plated bracelets, brass rings, small mirrors, enamel-work and other insignificant trinkets, with which the Savages adorn and embellish themselves. Under the French government, a fair was held in Montréal which went on for 3 months. Tradesmen came from more than 100 miles away to this fair. Montréal lies 45° 95' of Northern Latitude.

11th   The Savages have done some patrolling on Crown Point[53] of Lake Champlain and taken 5 Rebels prisoner, who have been brought to St. Jean today. Since an Engl. officer and several Canadians had been with the Savages, they had not been allowed to scalp anyone. One of these prisoners stated that the Rebels had made all kinds of advance preparations to abandon Crown Point. Would that this be true so that we will not need to cross Lake Champlain. There was also a report from headquarters that the frigate *Tartar* arrived in Québec from England on the 7th of this month, bringing along letters for the Hesse-Hanau Reg. This frigate has also brought 10 batteaux for our army, which can be put together without much effort; each one is said to carry one 16 lb. cannon. They are destined for Lake Champlain.

12th   Several of these batteaux are also being built at St. Jean. Today, Capt. Haynes visited us, who believes that most of the transport ships will sail back to Europe this year. Shipbuilding is continuing at St. Jean with the greatest diligence. A fleet is being built there as, according to all reports, the Rebels continue to have 15 or 16 warships on Lake Champlain; they are small, however, with but 10, 14, 16, 20 and 24 cannon. The ships on this lake have been built on its shores and therefore have to remain there, for the rapids of Lac St. Pierre have neither entrance nor exit. Large ships coming from Québec and Montréal cannot go further than Chambly on the Rivière Richelieu because at this point there are many rapids, boulders and dangerous rocks through which no batteau can pass, much less a ship. Many batteaux are also being built on which the army is to cross Lake Champlain.

15th   Many are sick in our army. The main illness is bloody flux, but no dysentery. Ipecacuanha and rhubarb are the most beneficial remedies but unfortunately these are so rare and expensive here that one pound of rhubarb costs 10 shill. We now have 60 sick men from the Reg. von Riedesel, from our Grenadier Battalion, and the Hesse-Hanau Regiment in the hospital at Montréal and 150 sick in the quarters. The heat is extraordinarily intense and the many insects, mosquitoes etc. make life disagreeable.

24th   Brigadier Gen. Gordon was wounded not far from St. Jean by two bullets out of the bushes; one bullet went through his shoulder and the second shattered his arm above the elbow.[54] Since one suspects that it was done by Rebels still hidden in the woods and bushes, the Savages were sent into the forest today to find the culprit if possible. In spite of the great heat, there is drill every day.

25th   Today, many Savages were again sent into the woods to catch the one who shot Brig. Gen. Gordon. He is supposed to be a Rebel lieut. but who knows; he may well be a Canadian, they are our fanatical enemies; the brigadier is in imminent danger of dying.

26th   The Savages and Canadians have taken 3 officers and 33 privates from the American army prisoner and taken them to St. Jean whereby one Savage was shot and one Canadian wounded. We now know for sure that the Americans have a fleet of 16 warships on Lake Champlain, that there is a garrison of 500 at Crown Point and 1,000 or 2,000 men at Ticonderoga or Carillon.[55] The latter is very well fortified and provided with adequate artillery. The enemy force at Ticonderoga used to be 6,000 men [strong], but when the enemy there received the news that 150 transport ships with Hessians on board had arrived in New York, 4,000 men were detached there. One hundred specie (piasters) were promised to those who captured the man who had shot Brig. Gen. Gordon. There are fewer mosquitoes now but instead, huge numbers of flies and smaller insects have come. There are few swallows here, neither are there any other birds that live off insects. But what I do not like at all are the many snakes here. The Canadians call these couleuvres[56] and aver that they do no harm to humans, but I am very much afraid of them. They have very beautiful markings and, as soon as one comes too close to them, their eyes will glitter like a cat's eyes in the dark, and they will hiss and stretch out their tongue, red as fire. Every Canadian has a small house near his residence where he keeps his milk in the summer; inside and next to these houses, one can always find couleuvres. Rattlesnakes, however, do not exist in Canada.

27th   The Spanish possessions in South America are called New Spain. Our men often talk with one another about this part of the world and firmly believe that Spain borders on America. They confuse the European Spain with the American and think it possible to get from Spain to France and then further to Germany by land. This erroneous belief tempted some to desert but they could not even get out of Canada. Because no bridges had been built across the rivers they found in the wilderness, they either had to starve to death in the wilderness or be brought back by the Savages or Canadians that had been sent after them. For each deserter, a prize of one portuguese, i.e., 10 shill. 16 groschen in Convention money, has been allowed, which has indeed been paid out by Governor General Carleton each time.

29th   Today 6 deserters had to run the gauntlet, tomorrow 3 others are to run and many are still locked up.

31st   Brigadier General Gordon died of his wounds today. Since the sun rises here 5 hours later than in Braunschweig, nothing could be seen here of the eclipse of the moon, which was visible in Germany last night.

Month of August 1776

1st   The birthday of our Serene Highness, the Duke, was celebrated with all ceremony by Maj. Gen. von Riedesel; the English officers were present at the fête in the evening.

2nd   The deceased Brig. Gen. Gordon was taken to Montréal through here.

3rd   I am sick and suffering from the rampant, bloody flux; nobody is spared. As Brig. Gen. Gordon is to be buried in Montréal today, all the officers of the army have been invited. At 3 o'clock in the afternoon, our general also went with his men to Montréal. My illness lasted with the same vehemence from the 4th [3rd] to the 10th. The infantry has to practice target shooting; he who hits the bull's eye receives 2 piasters from Governor Carleton.

12th   Today I am as sick as I have ever been before. My friends, the Regimental Surgeons Henckel and Heidelbach, the former from our Grenadier Battalion and the latter from the Hesse-Hanau Regiment, as well as colleague Müller are visiting me very faithfully and are most interested in speeding my recovery. Today, however, they almost made me angry because they said I should not think so much of my family and relatives in Germany. I saw and read it in their faces that they believed I was homesick and - soon I should believe it too.

13th   Having taken my fourth emetic yesterday, I am a little better today and thus all those sick in this way must vomit three or four times until they get better. Two Canadians were knouted today because they had taken pieces of regimentals from our deserters, and 4 of our deserters had to run the gauntlet; one of our Grenadier Battalion, by the name of Heidenbach, had to run 8 times; he died 8 hours later. Although it had been carried out in accordance with the "taste" of the Commander, Lieut. Col. B. [Breymann], this provoked many into thinking deeply about it [the punishment]. Gov. Gen. Carleton had gone to Québec in the early morning.

14th   On orders of our Maj. Gen. von Riedesel, the grenadier who died yesterday was dissected today. The intercostal muscles had been cut through and he had died of mortification. The VISUM REPERTUM [certificate of findings] of the Regimental Surgeon Henckel, however, did not say one word about this; he [the dead grenadier] had so many other defects that running the gauntlet had only been an incidental cause of his death. Whether this was right or wrong, I shall not examine here, but whoever has known his [Henckel's] chief, Lieut. Col. B.[Breymann], will somehow pardon him [Henckel]. I am a little better today and have been out of bed almost the entire day.

18th   Our Major General von Riedesel is going to Montréal today and will continue his trip to Québec from there by land tomorrow. The detachment of 170 men under the command of Lieut. Colonel von Speth has gone to St. Jean on the 10th of this month and shall be relieved there every 7th day. My illness has almost been conquered now.

21st   Gov. Gen. Carleton has returned to Chambly today.

23rd   Although not yet fully recovered, I have to go again to St. Philippe to [visit] the sick; the Canadians will not leave me alone. On orders of His Excellency Gov. Gen. Carleton, the brigade of Brigadier Gen. Gordon, which consisted of the 21st, 29th and 62nd Regiments, has been distributed among the other English brigades.

24th   Today, I went to Longueuil to visit sick Canadians. Since the restive Canadians below Québec do not yet want to submit to the Engl. government but continue to resist it, a detachment was sent to Kamouraska from Québec [*consisting*] of men from our Dragoon Regiment and the Reg. Prinz Friedrich under the command of Lieut. Colonel Prätorius. Similar detachments are going to the villages (parishes) of St. Charles, St. Pierre, St. François, Berthier and Ste. Anne to keep the restive Canadians in line.

26th   Our Maj. Gen. von Riedesel came back again. How fast one can drive in Canada from one posthouse to the next can be deduced from the fact that our general journeyed to Montréal from Québec, i.e., 60 leagues or 180 Engl. miles, in 27 hours. If I figure 5 Engl. equal one German mile, this amounts to 36 German miles. Every 3 leagues or 9 Engl. miles is a posthouse. The Canadians eat their salad with vinegar but without olive oil; they eat cucumbers raw. They neither know our beautiful lettuce nor do they eat it even if ever so well prepared. I have tried this more than once. There are a great many watermelons here, also all kinds of beautiful garden melons.

27th   Each brigade has been sent a certain number of batteaux and our men must learn how to row on the St. Lawrence River in order to be able to take themselves across Lake Champlain. In St. Jean, shipbuilding is continuing very actively, but since, according to the assertion by the Canadians, winter comes here early, nothing will come of the expedition this year.

29th   Today it was ordered that 100 ball-cartridges should be ready for each man in the army; this is why there is talk of early marching. There also came a report of the arrival of our Second Division. An Artillery ship that has arrived in Québec, having a company of Hesse-Hanau Artillerymen with 6 cannon on board, is said to have brought the news. Today, Colonel von Gall was made Brigadier Gen. in the army, and Major Carleton, the Governor's brother, was named Lieut. Colonel and Commander of the 29th Regt. to replace the late Brigadier Gen. Gordon.

31st   Capt. Päusch, Commander of the Hesse-Hanau Artillery Company,[57] arrived here today to make the report to Brigadier von Gall that the Artillery Comp. is on the march and has already passed Trois-Rivières. And we now received reliable news that this Artillery ship had indeed departed from England with our 2nd Division but on the second day after the departure had immediately been separated from it and since then not been seen again; thus the first report had been wrong. Today, a detachment of Canadians and Savages left St. Jean for the shores of Lake Champlain under the command of the Canadian officer, Monsieur Lorimier, to reconnoiter.

Month of September 1776

1st   I went with Madame Duprès, daughter of the captain of the militia, Monsieur Rouville, to St. Pierre to visit the little damsel Duprès, who is 9 months old. Most Canadians give their newborn children to wet nurses or to women who nurse children in the countryside. This was also the case here. This little child had whooping cough, which threatened to suffocate her. I gave a solution of TARTAR EMETICO by teaspoonfuls until she had thrown up 4 times. But how those present did begin to howl and to cry upon seeing that I had given the child an emetic! They all fell to their knees and prayed, believing the child had to die. Thereupon I gave her some purgative juices and she was rid of her cough. Our Quartermaster General Capt. Gerlach went from here today to meet our 2nd Division in order to take them to the army.

2nd   Our troops had to prepare for tomorrow's maneuvers.

3rd   This morning, His Excell. Gov. Gen. Carleton, Lieut. Gen. Burgoyne and Maj. Gen. Phillips came here and saw our troops maneuver in army fashion. There also came the news that the enemy was advancing.

4th   Our Maj. Gen. von Riedesel went to Montréal himself intending to ride down the St. Lawrence River to Québec in a bark canoe to lead our 2nd Division to the army; Gov. Gen. Carleton had given him permission for this. On the way, he learned from a messenger from Lieut. Gen. Burgoyne going to Gov. Gen. Carleton that on the other side of the Ile-aux-Noix 50 Rebel batteaux had been observed on the west side of the Rivière Richelieu. Maj. Gen. Phillips immediately departed from Montréal and proceeded to his post in St. Jean. Two English regiments also advanced toward St. Jean under the command of Lieut. Colonel Hamilton in case the Rebels should try to land north of St. Jean and attack our flank. The parishes of Chambly and St. Thérèse, which the English regiments have left, are to be occupied by Canadians and the German brigade today.

5th   Last night, the report came that 8,000 Rebels on 400 batteaux had passed Rivière LaColle and had already landed on the Ile-aux-Noix. Thus we got orders to set out immediately and move into a camp at La Savanne; our Maj. Gen. von Riedesel went ahead immediately to establish our place of encampment. It was 3 o'clock in the afternoon when he moved ahead with the quartermasters and scouts. As many vehicles were needed for the regiments, we could not set out before 6 o'clock and did not arrive at La Savanne until 11 o'clock at night. In order to extend it, our encampment was set up with a depth of only two tents. From La Savanne to here, we moved 9 miles farther.

6th   Our Maj. Gen. von Riedesel went to Gov. Gen. Carleton, where the report of the enemy was no longer so terrifying; it is said that only 40 batteaux have been seen but no one had disembarked. The brigade of Brigadier Gen. Fraser,[58] however, had been standing to its arms for 3 nights while the Savages had been sent to reconnoiter in the woods. Not only is shipbuilding actively proceeding in St. Jean but this place is also being increasingly cleared and fortified.

7th   The Breymann Battalion marched to St. Jean. Not far from the Ile-aux-Noix, the Savages have attacked a Rebel detachment that had been sent out; of the 18 men, 14 were killed whereupon the nearby Rebel fleet shot many cannon balls into the woods but without [causing] any harm. From the 4 prisoners, we learned that 1,000 Rebels had reconnoitered on 60 batteaux but only 18 disembarked. Our camp here at La Savanne is being entrenched.

8th   Four Engl. cannon with Hesse-Hanau Artillerymen were moved to the front line of our camp; the same number goes to the Breymann Battalion in St. Jean.

9th   Many bark canoes are passing through here [on their way] to St. Jean.

10th   Capt. Carleton, second brother of the Gov. Gen., passed our camp with 400 Savages today and continued his march to St. Jean.[59] Grenadier Bärtling from our Grenadier Battalion has been condemned to death because of desertion and insubordination to his noncommissioned officer and was to be shot today. Having lived through the agony of death, he was pardoned by Maj. Gen. von Riedesel.[60]

11th   Orders came that from each company throughout the army, 7 batteaux were to cross Lake Champlain, i.e., from the German brigade 42 officers and 1,200 noncommissioned officers and privates. During our absence those remaining will keep our post occupied under the command of Colonel MacLean. All the sick will be taken to the Jesuit Church in Montréal. Each Engl. regiment will receive 26 batteaux, our Grenadier Battalion 23, our von Riedesel and Hesse-Hanau Regiments 32 each. The Hesse-Hanau Artillery will proceed to St. Jean today. We received the report from headquarters that our 2nd Division has arrived at the Ile-du-Bic.

12th   Since the medicines I had brought along from Wolfenbüttel were almost gone, Maj. Gen. von Riedesel spoke to Gov. Gen. Carleton about it. He in turn gave the order that I was to be consigned the items needed against cash payment from the hospital in Montréal. The Surgeon General of the English army in Canada, by the name of Kennedy,[61] was to take care of it; he was at headquarters at Chambly. Maj. Gen. von Riedesel gave me a letter for Doctor Kennedy and this morning I rode to Chambly via Ste. Thérèse in the company of the Engl. commissary Curtis; he rode along as a favor because I did not know the way. I met Doctor Kennedy at Lieut. Gen. Burgoyne's and gave him the letter. He told me with much politeness that I should make a list of what I needed, which I immediately did in his tent. He looked it over and told me to come to Montréal the following day when I would receive the medicines; he would wait for me in the hospital pharmacy. I rode to my friend Curtis, who was to take care of the midday meal in the meantime. In the afternoon, we rode to La Prairie but I could not sleep at the commissary's because his wife had come from Montréal to visit him. I, therefore, lodged with my old landlord, Monsieur Rochez.

13th   Early this morning I rode to Longueuil in order to cross the St. Lawrence River there. When I was just about to climb into the batteau, Doctor Kennedy came back from Montréal telling me that they could not spare any medicine at Montréal; he would send me the requested medicine from the dispensary tent at Ste. Thérèse. Thus, I returned to La Prairie and as the weather was bad, I stayed here.

14th   Around noon I returned to the camp at La Savanne. The most recent [development] was that the Rebels had placed themselves 30 miles behind the Ile-aux-Noix. Captain Fraser [62] had been ordered to the Rivière LaColle with a detachment to reconnoiter the enemy, if possible. Our Dragoon Regiment and the Regiment Prinz Friedrich have received orders to join the army promptly; this will be disagreeable news to them and they will be very sorry to leave Québec.

18th   Our Major General von Riedesel has gone to headquarters at Chambly each day for 3 consecutive days; all the large baggage from the army will go to Montréal.

19th   I was at St. Jean and had the opportunity to see the radeau or Floating Battery. She carries 6-24 pound cannon on the lower deck and 10-12 pounders as well as 2 mortars on the upper deck.[63] The ships *Carleton* and *Maria*, the latter being named after the Governor Gen.'s wife, have been built here and lie ready to sail; the former carries 12, the latter 14 cannon. A frigate and other small ships are still lying in framework but are to be used in the next expedition. Ten large batteaux are also lying here of which I have [already] written on p. 25. There are many workers of all types about and the camp of the English and Germans makes this desolate place very lively. Gov. Gen. Carleton was given the message today that the Engl. frigate *Amazon* arrived in Québec. Together with the frigate *Garland*, she had led our 2nd Division, about which we will soon receive more information.

20th   Lieut. Scott from the 24th Reg.,[64] who had been sent out to reconnoiter with 24 Savages and 2 Canadians, has returned. He reported that a few leagues behind the Rivière LaColle, [they had seen] five Rebel ships, 1, 2 and 3-masted ones with cannon. They were about to set sail when the 2 Canadians went to the bank and called to the Rebels to take them along: they were deserters. Thereupon the Rebels immediately lowered a boat with 10 men and rowed toward the bank. The Savages sneaked through the bushes close to the bank to receive the Rebels at their landing. The Rebels, however, might have noticed something as they turned their boat around and went in the other direction. At that moment, the Savages shot at them, and 8 Rebels fell from their thwarts backwards into the water. The other 2 applied all their strength to get back to the ships. Now the Rebels poured whole volleys into the woods and fired for more than an hour but could not harm anything but trees, for Lieut. Scott was already safe.

21st   The ships *Carleton* and *Maria* set sail today. We returned to La Savanne and found at our arrival that Capt. O'Connell from our Second Division had gotten in; they had reached Bic on the 17th of this month. One of the ships, by the name of *Vriesland* of

800 tons, on which 2 1/2 companies of the Regiment Specht had embarked, had been missing for 7 weeks. Our 2nd Division consists of the

Regiment Specht, commanded by Colonel Specht ---------------------------------------680 men
Regiment von Rhetz, commanded by Lieut. Colonel von Ehrenkrook, ----------------680 "
of the Light Infantry Regiment von Bärner ---564 "
and of one company of ducal jägers, whom Capt. Schottelius commands. ------------120 "
According to p. 2, our First Division has a strength of -------------------------------2,222 "
thus our Braunschweig Corps in America has a strength of -------------------------4,266 "

This Second Division did not suffer more than 8 dead on its journey from Europe.[65]

22nd   Maj. Gen. von Riedesel went to headquarters to present his 3rd aide-de-camp, Capt. O'Connell, to Gov. Gen. Carleton. It is certain that the army is to push forward in a few days.

26th   Orders came today that we are to set out tomorrow. There are many bears and wolves in this region. I have seen several; they are not as big as the European bears.

27th   It was 8 o'clock this morning when we left our camp at La Savanne and marched 9 miles in order to move into a new one at St. Jean.

28th   Today a detachment went to the Ile-aux-Noix. In this camp here, the snakes visit us in our tents at night. Because of this, as well as the grumbling of the bears and the howling of the wolves, one cannot sleep.

29th   At 10 o'clock this morning, the frigate *Inflexible* was launched. It was beautiful to see how she had been set on a sled-like machine, which had been rendered slippery with tallow and soap. With much effort, the ship got into motion but went into the water with great speed and cast anchor in the Rivière Richelieu. And now there sounded a cry of hurrah, done 3 times by the sailors and workmen. Before winter, barracks are to be built here. The snakes visiting us come for bread.

Month of October 1776

1st   We received the dismaying order to set out tomorrow; tonight, most of the baggage was taken onto the batteaux at the Rivière Richelieu.

2nd   At 9 o'clock this morning, we embarked together with the German brigade: 18 to 22 men on each batteau. The General Staff of Maj. Gen. von Riedesel formed the tête. On account of the many swamps, there is impassable, dense wilderness on both banks. It was 4 o'clock in the afternoon when we disembarked on the Ile-aux-Noix. The island lies in the middle of the Richelieu, and is almost one mile long and half a mile wide. We pitched camp on the worst spot where the ground is swampy. The 3 Engl. regiments had taken up the best place that was still somewhat dry. Straw cannot be found here at all and because of the daily rain, we had to lie most miserably in this swamp and water. In addition, there are many large mice about running over everything. As no wood is left on this island, it must be brought from the other side of the river in batteaux. Four ships are riding at anchor here. From St. Jean up to here is 12 miles.

4th   Our fleet sailed to Lake Champlain today together with 20 large cannon batteaux. Gov. Gen. Carleton stayed on board the *Maria*. The air is damp and cold. There are but 2 houses and one barn here [Ile-aux-Noix]; the one has been built for Gov. General Carleton, the other is inhabited by a Frenchman engaged in farming. The Engl. have driven the Rebels off this island whereby 7 Engl. soldiers had been shot, who lie buried here. On each grave, a board has been placed with an epitaph and the name of the dead. On one board, I read the following epitaph: "Do not lament nor me deplore, I am not lost but gone before."

5th   The frigate *Inflexible* sailed past here today to join the fleet; she was built in 28 days.

6th   Today the TE DEUM was sung and a thanksgiving service was held because our Serene Highness, Duke Carl, had been restored from a grave illness last month. During the church service we heard a violent cannonade on Lake Champlain. If we continue to stay on this island, most of us will be buried here. Half of the men have dysentery; the sole reason for it is the wet camp. The misery on this island is indescribable.

7th   Fraser's brigade rowed from here to Rivière LaColle today, and the 20th and 62nd Regiments moved in again.

8th   Our Gen. Staff moved into another camp near a house on the left shore of the island because the ground is dry there.

9th   God be praised! Tonight, our baggage from the Gen. Staff will be taken onto the batteaux.

10th   Our Dragoon Regiment and Light Infantry Regiment von Bärner moved into a camp at St. Jean.

11th   Sad prospects! Our baggage lies on the batteaux and we have no marching orders as yet.

12th   A batteau arrived on which there were an Engl. officer, 8 Engl. soldiers and one Hesse-Hanau Artilleryman. They all had been wounded in an action on Lake Champlain. They were [*operated on*] in the field hospital here; one arm and 2 legs were amputated. Otherwise, we have not heard anything of the recent action; we have no marching orders yet; everyone wishes to be off this unfortunate island as soon as possible. Today, Major von Bärner[66] came here with our Jäger Company. I got 2 letters from Wolfenbüttel, old letters that had, in my opinion, been dated the 14th and arrived here on the 15th [sic].

13th   The wounded were sent to the hospital in Montréal. We still have no marching orders.

14th   Toward evening, Colonel Anstruther, Commander of the 62nd Regiment, arrived here in a batteau with music and drum beating and brought a letter to Maj. Gen. von Riedesel from Gov. Gen. Carleton. In it, Carleton told that the Rebel fleet had been beaten and destroyed on Lake Champlain by the Engl. fleet; that the Americans had burned 6 of their own ships; that 12 had been sunk and 2 been taken by the Engl.; only 3 had escaped and thus been saved. On this occasion, the American General Benedict Arnold has shown that he was equally able as admiral in command of a fleet. This is the more to be admired since before this war he had been a horse trader, who went from New England to Canada buying and selling horses. The following is a detailed [*description*] of the action on Lake (Lac) Champlain: When His Excellency Gov. Gen. Carleton advanced with the fleet on the 11th of this month to look for the enemy, he discovered the enemy fleet in battle array between Valcour Island and the western shore so positioned that they could defend the entrance very well. They had hidden behind the island in such a way that only by chance could they be discovered; thus the Royal ships had almost sailed past them, leaving them behind, which could have had bad consequences. No opinion is offered on whether it is true that the enemy, seeing the Engl. fleet and a 3-masted ship on this lake, has fled in astonishment alarmed by the sheer force of the English . One should much rather believe that the building of big ships, undertaken at St. Jean, could not be kept secret for very long. For - be that as it may - a vehement cannonade now began from both sides, which lasted for several hours. The wind, continuing to be unfavorable for the Engl. fleet, prevented the big ship *Inflexible* and the rest of the ships from getting near the enemy and bringing about something of importance. The whole burden, therefore, fell upon the ship *Carleton* and the cannon batteaux, whose crews showed the greatest courage here. Both officers and privates deserve the highest praise but neither can the enemy be denied the glory of a brave defense. Two of the biggest American ships were sunk. When night fell, Captain Pringle, who commanded the fleet under His Excellency, saw how necessary it was to cut off the enemy's retreat. Through signals, he ordered the ships that had been engaged to pull back; then the fleet formed a line in the entrance riding at anchor as closely to each other as possible. Now, it seemed almost impossible for the enemy to escape and yet they did succeed in getting away under cover of the very dark night. For they intended to reach Crown Point where they believed themselves to be safer than here where they saw themselves locked in by a superior power. Here again, Arnold showed his zeal. Since, at the tête of the American army, he had already done wonders with his march through the wilderness, he wanted to show the world that he was also an experienced seaman, and Fortune was so kind to him that at daybreak he had lost sight of the Engl. fleet. As soon as the Engl. fleet had become aware of the enemy's flight, it immediately set sail and gave chase to them. Wind and other circumstances peculiar to the navigation on this lake, that so far had been advantageous to the Americans, now became favorable to the English. Thus the American fleet was overtaken on the 13th of this month around noon when they were but a few hours away from Crown Point. The first ships escaped through flight yet most of them were overtaken and a major engagement ensued and lasted for some time. The ship *Washington*, which had on board Brigadier General Waterbury,[67] the 2nd-in-command, as well as the ship *Trumbull*, reefed their sails and surrendered. Seeing that his enemies were superior to him and that he was not properly supported by the captains of his other ships, Arnold decided to inform his people of their imminent capture, put them ashore and burn his ships so that these would not fall into enemy hands. He retreated with the same resolution with which he had fought. He went with the ship *Congress*, on which he was riding, and with 5 other ships so near the shore that he could see his men on shore and his ships on fire without the English being able to prevent it. Here Arnold's fame rose among his countrymen as they saw him rescuing them with so much intelligence when each had already considered himself lost. But that which raised [*the reputation of*] his character still further aloft was that he did not abandon his ship any sooner than when she was everywhere ablaze. Thus, he wished to prevent any of the English coming aboard and lowering the American flag, that remained hoisted until the ship was consumed by the flames. In this engagement, another 2 enemy ships were sunk and 3 took to flight.[68]

Thus, Lake Champlain was free again as most of the enemy fleet had been transformed into nothing. Having set fire to and demolished everything, the enemy left Crown Point and moved back to their army in Ticonderoga or Carillon. Gov. Gen. Carleton then took possession of the ruins at Crown Point. Lieutenant Dacres[69], who in the action had commanded the ship *Carleton*, is going through here to Québec. He will be sent to England by His Excellency, Gov. Gen. Carleton, to give the King a personal report of the victory achieved.

15th   We embarked onto our batteaux together with the German brigade and rowed 9 miles further to the Rivière LaColle where we pitched camp. This is a pleasant place inhabited by just one Canadian. The water of the Rivière LaColle looked brown and all who drank from it got a violent stomach ache and diarrhea. The Canadian said that the water was poisonous and showed us some good spring water.

16th   We embarked again and rowed 9 miles further up to Pointe-au-Fer [Rouses Point] and pitched camp. Here is the Canadian border, and the district of Albania [Albany], which belongs to the Province of New Hampshire, starts here.[70] Lake Champlain begins at this point. There is but one house in this place, which has been burned down to the stone walls by the Rebels. It had been a pleasure and hunting lodge, which Colonel Christie in Montréal had ordered built for himself. The region had been given to him as a present by the King; it is extraordinarily beautiful.[71]

18th   Although we keep thinking that the army will move ahead to Crown Point, it is not probable because the Hesse-Hanau Regiment is returning to the Rivière LaColle today; so we too will surely go back. It is already getting very cold here.

19th   An English captain, by the name of MacKay, an Engl. surgeon and 3 Engl. soldiers came to us. They had been taken prisoner at St. Jean by the American army under Gen. Montgomery on Nov. 3, 1775 and sent to New England. Having had much freedom there, they had made use of it, had deserted, gone through the wilderness and arrived here on the 25th day of their travels. They had befriended a few dogs before [engaging in] their long trip and taken them along. They had eaten 2 of them on their trip; the rest being hungry had run back. Never have I seen men so misshapen. They had lived off herbs and roots and were so emaciated that they looked pitiful. Maj. Gen. von Riedesel had them fed out of his [own] kitchen.

20th   The captured ship Washington cast anchor today. She had Lieut. Gen. Burgoyne on board, who went ashore here and intends to go to England before winter [sets in].[72] He visited our general and we learned that His Excellency, Gov. Gen. Carleton, had actually intended to make an attempt on Fort Carillon. Therefore, as soon as the Advance Guard of the army had arrived at Crown Point, detachments were at hand and ships sent out on the water to reconnoiter the distance up to Carillon, to examine the channel and the depth of the water. However, the big fortifications there and the difficulties of getting near them, the steadfastness and uncertain number of the enemy, the long distance from Canada from where such necessities as ammunition, supplies and other war needs had to be transported across Lake Champlain as well as the fast approaching Canadian winter and other important considerations were [the reasons] that brought this plan to naught for this year. We received the order to set out tomorrow and to go to Trois-Rivières into winter quarters. Maj. Gen. von Riedesel intends to ride to Crown Point tomorrow.

21st   Maj. Gen. von Riedesel went on board the Washington early this morning, which immediately weighed anchor and set sail for Crown Point. We had not quite lost sight of her when we, the General Staff and the regiments, embarked on the batteaux and took course toward St. Jean. As the wind was against us, the men had to work hard rowing against the waves. We passed the Rivière LaColle and the Ile-aux-Noix and reached the coast of St. Jean with much effort by 9 o'clock at night. Since our batteaux were heavily loaded with the general's baggage, we could not row like the other batteaux and therefore were the last. We were but a gunshot away from St. Jean when we ran aground on a boulder. We took great trouble and made every effort to get free, but to no avail. We saw many fires burn on the shore as well as many men to whom we called to help us; that we had run aground, that we belonged to the German Corps and other such things. It was the Hesse-Hanau Regiment who refused to help us, however. Finally, some of our General Staff, who had already disembarked, heard us, came and took us in; we got ashore at 11 o'clock.

22nd   Our Dragoon Regiment, that was encamped here, set out this morning to go into winter quarters at Trois-Rivières and the adjacent villages; the Free Battalion von Bärner remained. We could not immediately embark here again because the batteaux had first to be taken over the rapids and boulders. The baggage was loaded on carts, driven below the rapids and reloaded on the batteaux. It was 4 o'clock in the afternoon before we were done, and we were still supposed to row to Chambly today. We set ourselves in motion and were not yet 2 miles away from St. Jean when we again ran aground on a boulder. We worked for two hours but could not get loose, for we could not find any solid ground around the boulder with the oars. Canadians were passing not far from us to whom we called for help; but in order not to hear our calls, the Canadians started to sing. They did not want to help us for we are cats, mind you, German dogs, so the

Canadians say. We, therefore, had to be patient and await our fate. Together with 8 servants of the general, there were also 8 persons on our batteau, who were to row.

23rd   Last night, we had endured much cold; at daybreak, the water became troubled and a favorable gust of wind threw our batteau off the boulder. As soon as we were free, we rowed toward Ste. Thérèse; yet before reaching this village, we came to an uninhabited island. The question now was whether we should let the island lie to our right or to our left. I argued very ardently that, seeing Ste. Thérèse located on the left bank we should keep meticulously close to the left bank and leave the island at our right but the others said that, the river being very wide, we had to pass the island on our left. I was outvoted and - what else could I do against so many? -- let them row. No sooner had we reached the tip of the island, than our batteau was moving very swiftly without our rowing, then more so and finally as fast as a bird flies. It went toward the right bank because the river made a curve here. We were pushed against the bank with great force so that we all fell down in the batteau. Through the power of the water and with the same vehemence, we were pushed against the bank another 4 or 5 times and the batteau came close to being shattered. If the bank had not been so high, I would have ventured to jump. But when, through the rustling of the water, we became aware of a waterfall in front of us, all hope left us. Everyone in the batteau panicked and let go of the oars. Although I too was somewhat bewildered, I did ask the men to direct the batteau with the oars so that it would go straight and not be swept sideways into the waterfall; otherwise we would be lost. I helped diligently and we were lucky enough that the bow went straight down the fall. Now, I thought we would sink down into an abyss but our batteau rose up and emerged out of the gorge. It then knocked with great force more than 10 times against the rocks lying underneath; these knocks threatened our ruin at any moment. Through vigorous rowing, we finally came closer to the left bank and cast anchor. This did not catch, however, and we continued to be driven off. As I saw the bottom about 3 feet down, I ventured to jump into the water and safely reached the bank about 12 paces away. I went all the way to Chambly on foot and how happy I was using my feet. We met all our batteaux again, which were to be taken from here to Chambly. There are many other rapids and cascades about which are dangerous to pass. Thus, in order to move on rapidly, orders came to load the baggage on carts and drive them below Chambly. The batteaux of all the regiments were to be taken one by one through the rapids by 4 soldiers and one Canadian. But that was really dangerous work! For lack of vehicles, much baggage had to remain in the batteaux whereby much got lost. The batteaux crashed against the rocks so that the men were scarcely able to save their lives. Of the Hesse-Hanau Regiment, one batteau perished with all the baggage. As soon as the batteaux arrived below Chambly, they were loaded. It was past 4 o'clock when all batteaux were reloaded and we, i.e., 6 batteaux of the General Staff, received the order from the Brigade [Major] Captain von Pöllniz to ride on this same day across the little lake near Chambly, which is about 3 miles long and wide. We could have the best quarters on that side, so they said, because here all was full of English [troops] . We set ourselves in motion but had unfortunately not taken any Canadian along as pilot. In the middle of this lake, a windstorm overtook us and in the deep darkness we thought that the waves, filling our batteau with water, would swallow us at any moment. Rowing was useless; so that we would not sink, everybody had to work with shovels, hats etc. to bail the water out of the batteau. We gave ourselves to the waves that threw us onto a desolate island one hour later. Imagine, dear reader, how a man feels who twice in one day escaped the greatest danger to his life. None of us had anything to eat, not one morsel of bread but we made a big fire to guard against the cold and were all in good spirits.

24th   At daybreak we climbed into our batteau and rowed to St. Charles in calm water.

25th   We rode to the parish of Sorel.

26th   This morning, we rowed to Fort Sorel where we arrived by 8 o'clock and received supplies. Around noon a heavy thunderstorm broke out whereby the water grew so troubled that we did not want to venture onto the St. Lawrence River today. The Hesse-Hanau Regiment was in the middle of the St. Lawrence River during the thunderstorm and, because of the violent motions of the water, they could neither go back nor forth. From a distance it appeared that the waves would swallow the whole regiment at any moment. I have already stated that the Rivière Richelieu flows into the St. Lawrence River at Sorel. At this spot in the Richelieu, several transport ships that had come from Europe with us were still riding at anchor and were to spend the winter here. The *Pallas* was also still around and I seized the opportunity to pay my respects to Captain Bell and take a glimpse of my old quarters.   Since the water remained troubled the whole day long, and all the houses in Sorel were occupied either by Englishmen or our Dragoon Regiment, we rowed across to the other side of the Richelieu and took quarters there.

27th   After we had embarked very early in the morning, we departed, entered the St. Lawrence River and arrived in Berthier this same morning. Here we took a pilot from the captain of the militia and reached St. Peter's Lake (Lac St. Pierre) in the afternoon. The lake became so troubled that we were no longer quite masters of our batteaux. Nevertheless, we were able to enter [La Seigneurie de la] Rivière-du-Loup before nightfall where we took quarters.

28th   As we first had to receive our provisions here, we could not leave the Rivière Richelieu before 11 o'clock in the morning and again came to Lac St. Pierre. Here, however, it began to blow so hard by 1 o'clock that the waves surged up and into our batteau, filling it with water; we had to work hard to get it out. Just as we were about to start panicking again, our pilot led us over to the left side, and we finally arrived at Grand Yamachiche. The Regiments von Rhetz and Specht were stationed here and we had to make the best of a miserable situation that night.

29th   The regiments marched on but since the lake continued to be troubled, we took a complete rest today.

30th   Since the lake was still stormy, the general's baggage was transported on carts today and we reached Pointe-du-Lac. But in order to stop travelling by boat once and for all, I took a horse and rode to Trois-Rivières, where I arrived around midnight.

31st   The general's baggage arrived here as well as our Regiment's Quartermaster, Captain of the Cavalry Fricke. This day was spent with assigning quarters. The Dragoon Regiment is cantoning at Pointe-du-Lac. Thus, we have successfully ended the first campaign.

Month of November 1776

1st   Our Dragoon Regiment arrived here today but none except the general's squadron and the Leib Company[73] of the Regiment von Riedesel stayed on; the other squadrons and companies of both regiments were moved to the adjacent villages. I got my lodging at Monsieur Arnvi's and my cousin [Vetter][74] is staying here with me. Trois-Rivières is the oldest city in Canada, has about 200 houses, a monastery [convent], and 2 churches. It lies on the St. Lawrence River and has gotten its name from the Rivière Noire [Black River], which separates into 3 rivers forming 2 islands. It empties into the St. Lawrence River where one can see the current [in the St. Lawrence River] black as ink for a long time. A detachment of the Dragoon Regiment and the Regiment von Riedesel has been placed in the barracks here and is supposed to be relieved every 4 weeks. The detachment is to be on guard duty.   Last night our Major General von

Riedesel also arrived here. Among the enemy cannon found at Crown Point, one came upon several cannon quite carefully inscribed AUGUST WILHELM H.Z.B.U.L. and the rest.[75] How did those ever get here?

10th   On orders of Maj. Gen. von Riedesel, Lieut. Freyenhagen from the Regiment von Riedesel, who died at Pointe-du-Lac, was dissected today and that in the presence of the Regimental Surgeons Pralle and Vorbrodt. I and my colleague Müller performed the autopsy. My VISUM REPERTUM [findings] was as follows: After the lower abdomen was opened, I found the OMENTUM inflamed, the GLANDULA MESERAICA [lymph glands, nodes, of the mesentery] very obstructed, the intestines normal. In the stomach were no traces of food and its substance very thin; also the TUNICA VELOSA [skin?] was inflamed; the liver was very healthy and its substance full of blood and of extraordinary size; the gall bladder was filled with bile of dark color; the spleen and both kidneys were full of black, coagulated blood; otherwise nothing abnormal could be discovered in this cavity about these or the other viscera. Opening the chest, we found both LOBI PULMONALES [lung lobes] adhered to the PLEURA but more so on the right side. They were not only very small in substance but also very inflamed on the outside and when they were cut open, we found them full of a black, bloody liquid, especially on the right side. On this lobe on the outside hung a cyst full of 4 to 5 tablespoons of pus; both lobes were full of small abcesses; in the PERICARDIO was about one tablespoon of a LIQUORIS SEROSI [serous liquor] - pericardial fluid. In the heart itself, the right ventricle was not only filled with black blood but we also found a polyp in it, thick like a little finger and 5 inches long; the left, however, was empty, and neither could we notice anything of the polyp in the adjacent large blood vessels. Otherwise everything in the chest was normal.[76]

12th   About 2 feet of snow have fallen but the cold is still bearable.

15th   Since His Excellency, Governor Carleton, is expected here, the garrison (the dragoons in boots) has been in motion the whole day; but he did not come today. Governor General Carleton has gone past here on a ship to Québec. The army has returned to Canada and gone into winter quarters. The outermost post of our army is on the Ile-aux-Noix; they will have the enemy there.

24th   It is becoming increasingly cold but it still is like that in Germany: bearable. We are now receiving nothing but salt supplies and ship's zwieback, i.e., biscuit, peas, butter and cheese; fresh meat can be had here for money. Thus, everybody lives as well as he can.

Month of December 1776

10th   The snow is now more than 3 feet deep. In my opinion it is quite cold, yet not colder than the recent month of January in Wolfenbüttel. Gov. Gen. Carleton has ordered that each man in the army be provided with a pair of snowshoes (raquets). He is to practice so as to be able to walk on them in case an expedition should be undertaken during the winter. With these raquets, that are made of a piece of wood, oval and curved, and interwoven with straps, one can walk through the snow. They are tied to the feet and legs.

31st   Our Major General von Riedesel traveled to Québec and today a thanksgiving was celebrated in the army; for one year ago today, the enemy was beaten in Québec, and Canada is now completely free from enemies. N.B. the Canadians excluded; they are our greatest enemies and would like to do away with us if they only could. The priests would also like to absolve them from all the sins; such fanaticism reigns here among the devout Canadians. As I said before, they call us the German dogs. At the conclusion of this year, I wish with all my heart that we will soon get out of Canada for it can rightfully be called the American Siberia, and how disagreeable it is to live among such, such a -- nation.

NOTES

1. Wasmus's friend was Chancery Administrator Werner, in the city of Wolfenbüttel.

2. Braunschweig, Engl., Brunswick, was a sovereign duchy in North Central Germany which consisted of nine distinct pieces of territory. The principal, or northern part of Braunschweig, in which was located the capital, Braunschweig, and the older capital, Wolfenbüttel, was located between the provinces of Hannover and Saxony. Henry the Proud, Duke of Saxony and Bavaria, inherited Braunschweig in the 12th century, and it, along with the neighboring duchy of Lüneburg, was among the few possessions left to his son, Henry the Lion, when the Saxon duchy was dismembered in 1181. During the ensuing 500 years, Braunschweig and Lüneburg were alternately united and divided between Henry's successors, a process which also involved the founding of what became the house of Hannover from the Lüneburg-Celle line in 1569. Duke Carl I (1713-1780) married Philippine Charlotte, sister of Frederick the Great and ascended the Braunschweig-Wolfenbüttel throne in 1735. His brother, Duke Ferdinand of Braunschweig and Lüneburg (1721-1792), was a Prussian field marshal and the hero of the Battle of Minden (1759). The hereditary prince, Carl Wilhelm Ferdinand (1735-1806), was married in 1764 to Augusta, elder sister of George III of England. In 1753, Carl I moved the capital from Wolfenbüttel to Braunschweig, a city which was said to have been founded in 861 A.D. by Bruno, son of Duke Ludolf of Saxony. Wolfenbüttel, the capital between 1671 and 1753, was seven miles south of the City of Braunschweig, what is today Lower Saxony. ("Brunswick," Encyclopedia Britannica, 13th ed. N.Y., 1926, v.3-4, p.690.)

3. The chief of a regiment, who literally owned the regiment and for whom it was named, was not necessarily its field commander. Hence the Regiment von Riedesel was commanded by Lt. Col. von Speth.

4. Lt. Col. Friedrich Baum, b. 1727, was the son of a forester who began his military career as a corporal in 1753. He fought in the Seven Years War, entering the Braunschweig Regiment as a major, and in 1776 was given the command of the Dragoon Regiment. He was wounded in the Battle of Bennington and died two days later, August 18, 1777; Bückeburg records indicate that he was "captured and roasted by the savages," (Mahnecke Genealogischer Schauplatz, Mss. Prov. Library, Hannover, V1.II, p. 9R) but there is no evidence that this was the case.
     Lt. Col. Prätorius, b. 1721, retired 1783 with a pension of 240 talers per year, d. April 10, 1794, in Holzminden. (Otto Elster, Geschichte der stehenden Truppen im Herzogtum Braunschweig-Wolfenbüttel, vol. II, 1714-1806, Leipzig: Heinsius Verlag, 1901, p. 452.)
     Lt. Col. Ernst Ludwig Wilhelm von Speth, b. Jan. 12, 1728; made Col. in 1780, died October 27, 1800 as Major General and Commander of Braunschweig in Wolfenbüttel.
     Lt. Col. Heinrich Christoph Breymann, d.1777, when Arnold overran his redoubt at the Battle of Saratoga. (Elster, p.378, p. 404.)

5. The Heidberg, a small elevation (85 meters), is now incorporated as a district in the city of Braunschweig.

6. The Schliestedt Gardens surrounded the castle of the same name. Built in 1760 on the foundation of an earlier structure, the "little castle" [Schlösschen] still stands in Braunschweig and is used as a retirement home.

7. The Wendish Towers, or the Wendentürme, protected the entrance to the Hamburg military road; but according to the Niedersächsisches Archiv the name is thought to refer not to the Wends, or the Wenden countryside (named for the Wends, or Sorbs, a Slavic people whose territory in medieval times extended from Prussia into West Saxony), but to a town first mentioned A.D. 1031 as "Guinitthun," or fenced-in terrain.

8. Du Roi mentions a Major von Malorty or Malorti as one of the commissaries who supplied the Braunschweig troops on their route through Hannover; von Riedesel, in a letter to his wife, mentions a "Malatti," who may be the same individual. (In Marvin L. Brown, Jr., Baroness von Riedesel and the American Revolution: Journal and Correspondence of a Tour of Duty, 1776-1783. Chapel Hill, 1965, p. 151.)

9. Two hours march was approximately 8 kilometers, at the typical rate of 4 km per hour; at quick march, they would cover 6 km per hour.

10. Col. William Fawcett (or Faucitt; 1728-1804), born in Yorkshire and educated at Lancaster, fought with the British at Minden in 1759 and had, according to Professor Alan Valentine, been made a Lieutenant Colonel in 1760 after bringing the news of a victory at Warburg to George II in German. He was the British representative in Stade who negotiated the auxiliary troop contracts and inspected the levies raised, rejecting those who were unfit for military service. Promoted to Major General in 1777, he was made a Knight of the Bath in 1786, and a privy councillor in 1799. (The British Establishment, 1760-1784. Oklahoma , 1970, I, p. 310.)

11. These were funds from the military chest, administered by Chief Paymaster Johann Conrad Gödecke, ?-1782.

12. General Kielmansegge's sister Sophie was the mother of Admiral Howe and General Howe, both of whom would be important figures in the British effort to suppress the American rebellion.

13. Convention money was coined according to the Vienna standard, set by a convention between several states of the Holy Roman Empire of the German Nation.

14. A stübchen was a liquid measure of between 3 and 4 liters.

15. Col. Albrecht von Scheiter was one of the last of the private military enterprisers who recruited troops by offering bounties, uniforms, and adventurous employment and then hired them out to various rulers and governments for a specific price per head. Scheiter was a Hannoverian veteran of the Seven Years War, who had undertaken in 1775 to raise 2,000 men for the British at £10 a head, and to raise a further 2,000 if he was successful; due to the competition from German princes like the Duke of Braunschweig, Scheiter had difficulty finding soldiers acceptable to Col. Fawcett, and according to Professor Rodney Atwood, "was unable to make a worthwhile profit."(The Hessians: Mercenaries from Hessen-Kassel in the American Revolution. Cambridge, 1980, p. 10.)

16. From this point on, Wasmus records his daily mileage, running totals at the end of each stage of his journey.

17. Schlackwurst is a kind of bloodsausage, made with tiny bits of raw meat and lard.

18. The *Barfleur* is recorded as carrying 98 cannon; it had been built at Chatham and served as a guardship at Portsmouth.

19. This was the Haslar hospital for sailors.

20. Heinrich Christian Fricke (1729-1808) as a retired Major in Königslutter; after his return in 1783, he became Captain of the Cavalry (and oldest officer, at 54) in the Dragoon Regiment. (Elster, p. 454, p. 459.)
Captain Heinrich Daniel Gerlach, Quartermaster General (?-1798); at his death he was Lt. Col. and Commander of the Artillery of Braunschweig. (Elster, p. 454.)
Lieutenant Friedrich Christ. Cleve, at that time adjutant to Riedesel, not to be confused with his brother, Heinrich Urban Cleve, who later shuttled between London and Braunschweig at Riedesel's behest; returning to Canada with recruits, was sent to Penobscot, over his protests. After the war Heinrich Urban Cleve became War Councillor at the War Treasury in Braunschweig. (Elster, pp. 453-454.)

21. Surgeons; Wasmus apparently refers to surgeons as CHIRURGI to emphasize their higher level of education and professional training and to distinguish them from common feldschers and barber surgeons.

22. Soldiers and officers could send mail home on open half sheets turned in by regiment, shipped to London in bulk, and then, via Amsterdam to Braunschweig, where the recipients were charged 12 groschen per letter.

23. Major General William Phillips, of the Royal Artillery; Burgoyne's second-in-command in America, ca.1731-81. Phillips had led the British Artillery at the Battle of Minden and later served as a Member of Parliament between 1775 and 1780, although fighting or a prisoner in America during most of that period.

24. The Isle of Portland is actually a peninsula of the Dorset coast. Its shores are generally precipitous, and the highest point is Verne Hill, 500 ft.

25. This was no doubt the Eddystone light, which had been completed in 1759 at a cost of 40,000 pounds. This was the third such structure at Eddystone. Built by John Smeaton, its masonry tower marked rocks which were submerged by spring tides about 14 miles off Plymouth. The structure Wasmus saw was replaced in 1878, but the base of Smeaton's tower still stands.

26. This phosphorescence is not an uncommon phenomenon and is caused by marine algae.

27. The British typically referred to the Americans as the Rebels, but as time went on, and the Americans earned the grudging respect of their enemies, this often changed to the Continentals (as they called themselves) or even the Americans. Loyalist units were called "Provincials."

28. John Cabot sighted Newfoundland in 1497 and claimed it for England. By the time of Hakluyt's voyage in 1578, the rich fishing off its coast was attracting upwards of 400 European ships each year, one-quarter of them English. In the early 17th century, several permanent settlements were founded by English settlers, but they were harassed by the French who also coveted the territory for its fishing. The hostilities were ended by the Treaty of Utrecht in 1713, which, while asserting British sovereignty over Newfoundland, allowed the French the right to use the northern and western coasts for drying fish, thus closing those areas to settlement. The 1775 census recorded a permanent population of 12,438.

29. Like most Europeans, Wasmus refers to the native Americans as Savages, literally Wilde.

30. The fortress of Louisbourg, a French stronghold, had been captured by General James Wolfe and Lord Jeffery Amherst in July 1758, marking England's first major success in the Seven Years War.

31. What is now called the Sydney River was originally the Spanish River, so named because Spanish ships fishing off the Grand Banks stopped there to take on fresh water.

32. This was the aurora borealis, which occurs when charged particles from the sun strike the earth's upper atmosphere near the poles. By the 18th century the aurora had begun to be studied scientifically by, among others, Benjamin Franklin, who shared the prevailing notion that it was in some way related to lightning and electricity, and noted that sightings increased in frequency during periods of sunspot activity. Since the European auroral zone is generally limited to Northern Sweden, Norway, and the Siberian coast, the North American zone, which extends south to Labrador and the central Hudson's Bay region, would provide Wasmus with the kind of novel spectacle he mentions here.

33. Cap Chat on the Gaspé Peninsula.

34. General Sir William Howe (1729-1814), 5th Viscount Howe and Member of Parliament for Nottingham from 1758 to 1780, had led Wolfe's attack on Quebec in 1759 and took command of the British army at Boston in 1775. Howe had evacuated Boston on March 17, 1776, following General George Washington's fortification of the Dorchester Heights. About 1,000 loyalists sailed with Howe and the British army to Halifax.

35. Guy Carleton, first Baron Dorchester (1724-1808). Carleton, born into an Anglo-Irish family, served with distinction in the Seven Years War and was Governor-General of Canada from 1766-1778. At the end of the Revolution, Carleton was made Governor of all the American colonies to oversee the transition to independence, and, incidentally, to protect loyalists who remained in the colonies. He served again as Governor-General of Canada from 1786 to 1796.

36. On May 19, 1776, Captain George Forster of the 8th Foot had come down from Oswegatchie (Ogdensburg) with 126 soldiers and 120 Indians and captured 430 Americans at Fort Cèdres, 30 miles upstream from Montreal.

37. Pointe Lévi, named for Joseph Lévi, an early settler, is now called Levis.

38. After a secret night scaling of the Heights of Abraham at Quebec, General James Wolfe, commander of the British forces, defeated the Marquis de Montcalm's French army on the Plains of Abraham, but both commanders were killed in the battle.

39. After sixteen years in the British Army, Richard Montgomery (1738-1775) settled in Dutchess County in 1772. He had served under Amherst at Louisbourg and had participated in the capture of Crown Point and Ticonderoga in New York during the Seven Years War. The New York provincial congress made him a major general in the Continental Army in 1775, and he led the American expedition to Canada in the fall of that year.

40. Benedict Arnold (1741-1801) was a patriot before he was a traitor. Born in Connecticut, he served in the Seven Years War as a fourteen year old runaway, participating in the Champlain campaign before he deserted. Once grown, he was a druggist and bookseller, and prospered in the West India trade; he also did business as a horse trader, which took him to Canada. At the outbreak of war he was a captain in the colonial militia, but his aggressive conduct on the Ticonderoga expedition in 1775 and in the invasion of Canada earned him a Congressional promotion to Brigadier General in January 1776.

41. This was Col. Enos, Arnold's second-in-command; in a subsequent court-martial, his actions were justified since he had believed himself to be saving his men from certain death on the march.

42. The "certain act" was the Quebec Act, passed in 1774, which denied the Canadians an elected assembly, established the Catholic Church, and restored the French civil code, thus angering Canadians of British origin, while the act's retention of the English criminal code angered the French Canadians.

43. These were the "Royal Emigrants," mostly Scots, who had fought in the Seven Years War and had been compensated with land along the New York frontier, raised as His Majesty's Royal Highland Regiment of Emigrants in 1775, subsequently the 84th Foot.

44. According to one source, Alexander Montgomery had executed French Canadian prisoners at Château Riche during Wolfe's Quebec campaign, justifying his actions because the Canadians had been disguised as Indians. (William Wood, The Passing of New France, Toronto, 1922, p. 118.)

45. The beautiful young woman was Janet Livingston, of the powerful New York family, who had first met Montgomery at the age of 16 during his military service in America. He married her in 1772.

46. Edmund Burke, Isaac Barre, and Charles Fox all eulogized Montgomery in the House of Commons on March 3, 1776.

47. Brigadier General William Thompson of Pennsylvania had brought some 2,000 men to relieve the retreating Americans; he had assaulted Trois-Rivières without realizing that two-thirds of Burgoyne's force had recently disembarked there.

48. Julius Ludwig August von Pöllniz (?-1805). After his return in 1783, he was promoted to major and transferred to the Dragoons; at his death, he was a major general and commander in Wolfenbüttel. According to Boyd (Papers of Thomas Jefferson, VIII, p. 525), he was married to the daughter of the Earl of Bute.

49. Captain Carl August Heinrich von Tunderfeldt became Chamberlain at Court in 1783 and died in Braunschweig in 1802. (Elster, p. 450, 452.)

50. The Iroquois in 1776 comprised the Mohawk, Seneca, Onondaga, Oneida, Cayuga, and Tuscarora; the Six Nations were deeply divided over the war, with some factions of the Mohawks, Cayugas, Senecas, and Onondagas supporting the British.

51. The tortures and ritual cannibalism the Indians inflicted upon their captives had considerable religious significance. A brave captive who remained silent during torture inspired his captors to gain some of his courage by eating his heart. One historian of Indians in the Revolution compares Indian torture of captives to European practices such as burning heretics at the stake and forcing traitors to be drawn and quartered. (Barbara Graymont, The Iroquois in the American Revolution, Syracuse, 1972, p. 19.)

52. Howe had arrived in New York harbor on the 25th of June, landing on Staten Island on the 30th. His forces did not actually occupy New York until September, after defeating the Americans at Long Island on August 27, 1776.

53. Americans led by Ethan Allen had captured Fort Ticonderoga (Carillon) and Crown Point from the British in May 1775; neither was strongly defended by the Americans in the spring of 1776.

54. Gordon had been ambushed by the American Captain Benjamin Whitcomb, who successfully eluded capture.

55. In 1731, the French built Fort St. Frédéric near the southern end of Lake Champlain and in 1756 erected Fort Carillon several miles to the South. Carillon dominated the narrows where Lake George flows into Lake Champlain, and was unsuccessfully attacked by General Abercrombie in 1758. Lord Jeffrey Amherst captured the fort in 1759, renaming it Ticonderoga and renaming Fort St. Frédéric as Crown Point. The French had burned the fort during Amherst's attack, and it had been partially repaired, first by the British, then, after 1775, by the Americans. General Philip Schuyler, commanding the Continental forces in New York, believed that only a force of 10,000 men could defend Ticonderoga successfully; by July the fort was receiving reinforcements, and by October, Horatio Gates, who became Schuyler's successor after exerting considerable political pressure on Congress, had about 12,000 men in the fort.

56. Couleuvre is the French term applying to a number of harmless viviparous snakes; the scientific term is colubriformes, and includes the common garter snake. According to herpetologist William S. Brown, the original range of the timber rattlesnake, CROTALUS HORRIDUS HORRIDUS, extended into the territory north of Lake Champlain.

57. The Hesse-Hanau Artillery company was commanded by Captain George Päusch, whose journal, in a translation by the 19th century American historian William L. Stone, has been reprinted by Arno Press.

58. Brigadier-General Simon Fraser (1729-1777) of Scottish ancestry, had served in the Seven Years War, fighting at Louisbourg, Cape Breton, Quebec and in Germany; promoted to Lt. Col. in Ireland in 1768, he travelled with his regiment (the 24th Foot) to Canada in 1776.

59. This was Captain Christopher Carleton, Guy Carleton's nephew and brother-in-law (?-1787). The second son of Guy Carleton's elder brother William, Christopher Carleton was commissioned lieutenant in the 31st Foot in 1763, married in 1770 to a daughter of the Earl of Effingham (whose sister subsequently married Guy Carleton), and made a captain in 1772. Guy's younger brother Thomas was Quartermaster-General of the British forces in Canada.

60. See Helga Doblin's article on military discipline and punishment: "The Case of the Musketeer Andreas Hasselmann," Military Affairs, v. 51, no. 2 (April, 1987), pp. 73-74.

61. Surgeon-General Kennedy; Dr. Hugh Alexander Kennedy treated the von Riedesels' youngest daughter Canada, who died in infancy in Sorel, and travelled with his own family along with the Riedesels on their voyage back to Europe in 1783.

62. Captain Alexander Fraser of the 34th Regiment was the nephew of General Simon Fraser; he headed a special unit of marksmen, Canadians, and Indians used for scouting and irregular work.

63. This floating battery, the *Thunderer*, carried a crew of 300. The *Carleton* and the *Maria* were schooners, and the British had dismantled the frigate *Inflexible* in Quebec and carried it overland to be reassembled on Lake Champlain.

64. This may have been Captain Thomas Scott, later sent with Burgoyne's messages to General Clinton.

65. Actually, Captain Jacobs reported on September 24, 1776, that 28 had died, mainly of scurvy. (Edward Curtis, The Organization of the British Army in the American Revolution, New Haven: 1926, pp. 125-126.)

66. Major Ferdinand Albrecht von Bärner (?-1797) of the Braunschweig Chasseur and Jäger Regiment; after his return to Braunschweig in 1783, von Bärner became Lt. Col. in the newly formed Prinz Friedrich Regiment, and Commander of the Grenadiers. (Elster, p. 454.)

67. General David Waterbury (1722-1801); Waterbury and the Washington's crew of 110 were immediately paroled and released by Carleton.

68. The major significance of the battle is that Arnold's tiny navy was able to delay Carleton until the season was too far advanced for further campaigning. Instead of pressing his advantage and capturing Ticonderoga, Carleton was forced to withdraw to the north for the winter.

69. Dacres, 1749-1810, had narrowly escaped being left for dead after the battle because of his serious wounds. As he was about to be consigned to the lake, one of his fellows intervened to save him. Once he had recovered, he was sent to England with dispatches which commended his courage. His subsequent career was brilliant, culminating in his appointment as vice-admiral of the White in 1805. (James Phinney Baxter, The British Invasion From the North, Albany, 1887, pp. 139-140.)

70. New York, New Hampshire, and Massachusetts all claimed what is now Vermont.

71. Col. Gabriel Christie (1722-1789) had served at the siege of Quebec during the Seven Years War, and was deputy quartermaster-general in 1764-65. At the close of the war he had purchased seigneuries at L'Islet de Portage, Bleury, Sabrevou, Noyan, all in 1764, at La Colle in 1765, and at Lery in 1777. He had extensive holdings on the shores of Lake Champlain before the Revolution.

72. Burgoyne had leave to return to England to attend to family matters (his wife had died). While there, he took advantage of Germain's impatience with Carleton to secure his own position as leader of the 1777 campaign. Carleton would stay behind in Canada while Burgoyne, aided by a diversion from the west led by Col. Barry St. Leger, would push south from Fort St. Jean to Albany, where he would place himself under Howe's command, thus splitting rebellious New England from the rest of the colonies.

73. The Leib company was the Duke's own company, responsible for guarding his life.

74. Actually his nephew, Heinrich Wasmus.

75. Braunschweig troops had fought against the French in Europe during the Seven Years War, as allies of the British; it is possible that these cannon had been captured by the French and later installed at Fort St. Frédéric. The inscription refers to August Wilhelm (1715-1781), the Duke of Braunschweig-Bevern, one of the outstanding soldiers in the army of Frederick the Great. (Herzog zu Braunschweig und Lüneburg).

76. According to Paul Formel, M.D., cardiologist (Albany N.Y.), Lt. Freyenhagen must have died from bacterial endocarditis, complicated by metastic lung abscesses and empyema.

1777

Month of January 1777

1st   The Canadians greet each other with kissing today.--

12th   Maj. Gen. von Riedesel returned from Québec again.

18th   Today, the Queen's birthday was celebrated; Maj. Gen. von Riedesel gave a magnificent ball.

27th   There was another ball at our general's today. The weather continues to be fair and cold. One often engages in sleigh rides in Canada which - I think - are as pleasant as can be: [(They have)] light sleighs that are fitted on the bottom with iron. Two people can comfortably sit on this and a horse is harnessed to it. Every farmer has one or two bear skins in his sleigh, in which one wraps legs and feet. If one is dressed warmly and pulls a busby over the ears, he can always stand it for a few hours.

Month of February 1777

1st   Also today was a ball at our Maj. Gen. von Riedesel's and

4th   since Maj. Gen. Phillips arrived today, our general gave another ball.

Month of March 1777

6th   Gov. Gen. Carleton arrived today.

7th   Today was review. Gov. Gen. Carleton went to Montréal and our general with him; but the latter returned by the

10th.   The weather continues to be quite fair.

Month of April 1777

The fair weather persists. Although the nights are as yet very cold, there is sunshine during the day. Since the month of Nov., the weather has been almost continuously fair. During all this time, the snow never melted nor did the ice break up in the rivers. Now the sun is melting away a great deal of the snow and in a few spots the bare ground can be seen.

18th   Soon the snow will be gone; one sees water on the ice, so the sleigh rides become dangerous.

25th   Today the ice has been breaking up on the St. Lawrence River with terrible noise.

28th   The first ship, coming from Montréal, passed by here with full sails. She was armed and saluted Trois-Rivières as the German headquarters with 13 cannon shots.[1] In these days, one can observe the arrival of a type of bird which in color and size resembles the Krammetsvogel [fieldfare] in Germany. It is a migratory bird here, which the Canadians call merles [blackbirds] and the English robins;[2] they do not taste good.

Month of May 1777

1st   This day is not as pleasant here as it frequently is in Germany where the delightful nightingale with its magic charm announces the all enlivening spring and all is green. No green can be seen here as yet, nor are there any nightingales about; [there are] very few swallows, no storks, no sparrows, no cuckoo; instead, various kinds of small birds of very beautiful colors.

11th   A kind of wild root grows here which looks yellowish, almost like a carrot, and which is very poisonous. Yesterday, a drummer of the Regiment von Riedesel ate a little of it and before one hour had elapsed, he died with violent convulsions. On orders of Maj. Gen. von Riedesel, an autopsy was performed on him today. We found a small portion of the consumed root in his stomach; hardly a quarter of it had been digested. Everything was as it should be, all the parts were healthy and not the slightest infection could be noticed either in the stomach or in the adjacent parts. That is proof that it must be an odd substance for, in case of poisoning, the stomach is always infected etc. The Canadians use this root as emetic with their horses and cows when these are sick. It has this effect on all the animals; I have also tried it on dogs. The root is called CAROTTE A MOREAU [spotted cowbane; water hemlock].[3] This noon, I heard the noise of marching in the street and I saw many local people running toward the woods with guns. When I inquired after the reason, they said that the wild pigeons were coming; we saw millions and millions of them in the air.[4] When there is a flight of birds in Canada, there often are so many of them together that the sky darkens.

A FEW REMARKS ABOUT CANADA

Indisputably, Canada is the largest of the provinces England possesses in America. It constitutes the outermost frontiers of the northern and northwestern parts of America. Probably not even the twentieth part of Canada is as yet inhabited, but no one knows for sure because the western borders of this province have not even been discovered; it comprises much wilderness. Among the many rivers which cut through Canada, the St. Lawrence River is the largest. So far no one has been able to discover its source. Although several Englishmen have ventured out with the help of Canadians and Savages and travelled more than 6,000 Engl. miles upstream - after all, the King had promised a substantial prize -, all these toilsome journeys have nevertheless not only been futile, but many of the explorers have never returned; they might have perished for lack of victuals or been killed in the wilderness by the Savages or by wild beasts. The St. Lawrence River loses itself in the Great Lakes, in which the St. Lawrence Rivers are; of these lakes, those known to us are Lakes Ontario, Erie, Huron, Michigan, Superior, Lake of the Woods etc. After all these have been travelled through one by one, the St. Lawrence will be there again, but yet its source cannot be found.[5] These lakes as well as all the rivers abound in fish. Of the many kinds of fish, the trout, which is only caught in small and stony rivers, tastes best. In general, the fish are not as tasty as those in Germany's rivers. A particular type of fishing is done in the Rivière Noire at Trois-Rivières. In the months of Jan. and Febr., the ice is cut through and then the Canadians catch a type of fish with poles wrapped in rags. As for their taste, they are very similar to fresh smelt in Stade and Hamburg, but they have bigger heads than smelt. The Canadians catch this fish in such great quantities that people cannot eat one percent thereof and feed cows and pigs with them; some - but not all - horses also eat this fish.

Winter is very severe in Canada; in general, it starts as early as November and lasts until April. The inhabitants assert that it gets so cold at times that the people have to wear masks on their faces. Last winter was not colder here than I have often experienced in Germany but the difference is that the cold lasts longer and that, with continual sunshine, the weather is always beautiful. The oldest people in Canada cannot remember a winter as mild as the recent one. In summer, the Canadians ride in light carriages, in winter in sleighs, in which they drive their wives to church. In order to make the land arable, the Canadians make the greatest effort to clear their forests. They go about it with so much waste, however, that if they continue cutting everything down, they will feel a great shortage [of wood] within a period of 6 years. Several kinds of wood are variants of those in Germany, but other species like the red and the white cedar, the maple tree, from which the Canadians draw sugar, the sassafras tree etc., do not grow in Germany. The wood is solid throughout and very good for ship building; much of it is exported to England.

As severe as the winter is in Canada, so great is the heat in summer, which in June, July and August is at times unbearable; this [heat] is rendered even more intolerable through the multitude of insects. The principal cities are Québec, Montréal, as well as such beautiful places as Trois-Rivières, L'Assumption and La Prairie. Both the Canadians and the Savages are greatly involved in hunting and fishing. They shoot and catch buffalo, moose, bear, wolves, foxes, wildcats, rats, and hare, which are snow-white in winter and regain their gray color in summer; [in addition] beavers, martens, turkeys and many other animals whose fur is good. The wildcats are very big and have good skins. Last winter every man in the army received a very fine cap made of cat furs; also rat [muskrat?] furs are used for making caps. The Canadians know nothing of venison. It must be too cold for that [deer]; the Canadian hare are very tasty. Bear meat is said to taste good; particularly the paws are praised as something extraordinary because they taste better than ox tongues. I have never tasted them myself, much less have I been able to try moose meat. Here in Trois-Rivières is a tame moose, who suffers a few times daily from epilepsy. They grow very tall, 18 to 20 hands high.[6] A beaver is a small animal not as big as a wildcat; it has shorter legs and the skin is brownish black and very beautiful. The beavers have big heads, a pointed snout and pointed teeth. The beaver is one of the smartest animals and very difficult to catch. The front feet are split claws, the ones in back are like goose feet [webbed feet]. According to the Linnean system,[7] they belong to the mammals and not to the amphibians; they live in the water and on land, their tail is their rudder and is broad, scaly, and hairless in appearance, similar to that of the water rat. The Canadians pull the tails off the beavers and smoke them because they consider them as tasty as bear paws. Beaver meat is also said to taste very good, but I have never tried it - the mere thought of it deprives me of all appetite. I know this is [pure] imagination, but how can I help it! - The Canadians and Savages shoot and catch most beavers at the time when these get out of the water to look for wood. When they fell the trees, which they saw off with their pointed teeth, they take the wind direction into consideration so that the trees fall into the water where the beavers are about to build their abodes. It is averred that when a beaver starts biting, he will not stop before he hears the noise of bones.

Canada is divided into parishes; each parish has a captain, a lieutenant and a sergeant, and 2 or 3 parishes often have a colonel or seigneur; for the most part, these constitute the ruling body. Every Canadian has a good gun and is bound to take the field in case of need.

Their grain is sown in the month of May and consists of wheat, rye, barley, oats, peas, maize and flax. They eat mostly white bread and also plant very many potatoes, carrots, white and red beets, white cabbage, various kinds of melons, garden and field berries. Cucumbers are eaten raw without olive oil and vinegar. Their cultivation of flax is bad because they either do not know how or are too lazy to cultivate it properly. Nothing is scarcer with the Canadians than linen; they are provided with few shirts. They also plant much tobacco, but it is bad because they do not know how to prepare it well. The dwellings in the villages are usually built very far apart from each other because each inhabitant has his land and woods around [*his house*]. All the farmers' houses are but 1 story high and are plastered with dirt and lime both inside and out. In the winter, each one has a stove in the living room, but one always finds walls and beds full of bedbugs; the Canadians are not very clean in general. - When winter has arrived, the Canadians slaughter their livestock for the whole winter at one time, i.e., oxen, pigs, geese, turkeys and chickens. The fowl has its neck wrung, it is not drawn but thrown on the ground, and so [*they do*] with all the meat which they want to eat fresh and unsalted; it will freeze as hard as stone. Whenever they want to cook or sell some, they cut a slice. Thus, without slaughtering [more than once], the Canadians have fresh meat throughout the winter. Pork, however, is mostly salted. They understand nothing at all about sausage making. Whenever the dogs cannot eat all of the intestines, the Canadians bury the rest. They beat their pigs to death, put them as straight as possible on their [the pigs'!] knees, cover them with much straw and burn the hair off so that the skins look as black as coal. Then they wash the pigs again with hot water; frequently, only half of the hair is off but nothing is done about it. They let the blood run into the ground. To be sure, every farmer has his land and yard fenced in, but because their barns and stables are very badly [*built*], they keep big dogs. So that their cattle will not be devoured by wild beasts, each farmer must keep good watch himself. Canadian cattle belong to a small species, but because the pasture is good, the cows give much milk, and this is the Canadians' principal food. They make little butter and hardly any cheese at all. The Canadians also sell much milk, which they take to the market in sacks during the winter. The milk is poured into big wooden bowls, freezes and looks like a tallow bottom. They throw it on the ground and whenever they need any or want to sell some, they chop or cut off a piece and melt it. The milk is very creamy and does not lose any of its taste through the freezing. The Canadian horses are some of the sturdiest one can imagine, of medium size, mostly blunted head and with short, bent neck. In summer they eat nothing but grass, and in winter nothing but hay and straw, but they are always ready to work. They run very fast and one can ride 50, 60, 70 and more Engl. miles in a sleigh with but one horse on one day, that is, on the ice of the St. Lawrence River.

On the Ile-aux-Coudres, men and women dress alike in every way, but in the cities, they are distinct from each other and dress very beautifully in Engl. or French fashion. This, however, is only true of the fair sex. The men are the women's slaves inasmuch as they have to do all the work. In summer, the women leave their rooms but a few times and in winter almost never except when they drive to church on Sundays. At that time, one sees the farmers' wives [*looking*] like high-ranking ladies with their husbands, who drive them like servants or harlequins in multicolored attire. Throughout, the women are in command of the house and the husbands obey them. They [the husbands] have their daily hours for working and for making love, for as soon as they enter the room, they are embraced. The Canadian men generally have strong, healthy constitutions; the women all look pale and sickly. They marry young, about 14 to 16 years old and one frequently finds women, 34 or 35 years old, who have as many as 15 or 16 children. As soon as the children are born, they are given to wet nurses who nurse them. An unmarried girl will rarely engage in intimacies with a young man unless she knows for sure that he wants to marry her. When we first arrived in Canada, the priests preached a great deal about us, describing us as the most dangerous heretics who are wont to seduce females; the latter should by all means avoid the company of these heretics. If females were so unfortunate as to become pregnant from such heretics, they would bring all such types of animals into this world as wolves, dogs, cats and the like. This rendered the fair children very shy in the beginning and they did not let themselves be touched by any of us. But as the fair sex likes to live in friendly surroundings, they could not bring themselves to resist here either for a long time (whether it just was out of curiosity or something else, cannot be determined), and hardly a year had passed that several of them brought fair little boys and girls into this world and the priests exposed themselves to frightful ridicule. - They hated us but for the sake of religion because they were convinced that, according to their creed, we would not be saved.

The greatest number of people in Canada are Savages. One counts more than 50 nations there, that almost all have particular languages and very rarely understand each other; that is, with the exception of the 5 Iroquois nations that live closest to Engl. possessions and only differ a little in regard to pronunciation. Many of them profess the Roman [*Catholic*] religion and have Franciscan Mendicant Friars as their priests, who have come from France. Could the American Savages perhaps be the tribes of the Jews that were lost in ancient times and whose whereabouts our Jews do not know? In their ceremonies, positions and gestures, the Savages certainly have much that is very similar to the Jews'. Their dwellings are nothing but huts, half built into the ground. In the center, they maintain a fire day and night, around which they lie. Some cultivate potatoes and maize, but, as I have mentioned before, they generally live off fishing and hunting. The oldest [*member*] is their chief, whom they honor and obey as their king. The fur trade is the only business in which they are engaged with other nations. They often change their dwellings, particularly when the smallpox appear among them; then they move on and let those inflicted with the pox lie until they are well again or have died. Since they allow old people, women and children to shift for themselves, the pox are wont to cause great devastation among them. The Savages never have any beards; as soon as the hair grows, they tear it out from all parts of their body besides their head; the fair sex does the same. -

30th   Lieut. Gen. Burgoyne arrived in Québec from England on board the *Isis*, and so did the fleet with the provisions. Lieut. Gen. Burgoyne, who in the future campaign will command the army as general-in-chief, sent orders for the army to Maj. Gen. von Riedesel tonight; they will be made known tomorrow.

At the conclusion of the last campaign, Gov. Gen. Sir Guy Carleton had sent a plan to the King and Parliament for the opening of this year's campaign and asked for reinforcements. But instead, he was sent a completely new plan through Lieut. Gen. Burgoyne, and the command over the army was taken from him and given to Lieut. Gen. Burgoyne; that was an insult, especially [*the fact*] that he was not even informed as to which and how many troops were to stay behind for the defense of Canada. I have already mentioned that under the good orders of Gov. Gen. Carleton, not only the Province of Canada had been freed from the enemy, but that this general had also ordered a fleet built at St. Jean in a very short time. With it, he completely destroyed the enemy fleet of the Americans on Lake Champlain and conquered Crown Point; only the late season restrained him from taking Carillon and from advancing toward the south. I had mentioned that as early as Oct. 20 of last year, and it can be looked up again on page 34.

A detachment from our German Corps will stay behind in Canada, consisting of several captains, subalterns, noncommissioned officers and 560 men; Lieut. Colonel von Ehrenkrook will command it.

Month of June 1777

Beginning of the Second Campaign

1st   After having spent 7 months in winter quarters in Trois-Rivières, we received orders this noon to march the day after tomorrow, which will be the 3rd. The army will be divided into 2 parts, the larger of which will march along the Rivière Richelieu via St. Jean under the command of Lieut. Gen. Burgoyne. This part consists of 7,173 men, i.e., 3,956 Engl. and 3,217 Braunschw. and Hesse-Hanau troops. The Royalists, Canadians and Savages are not included because I cannot ascertain their number. According to credible reports, there are more than 4,000 of them, i.e., 2,000 Canadians and 2,000 Savages. Since their number is daily increasing, the Royalists are difficult to count. In addition, there are 2,000 Canadians ordered to repair the defenses at Sorel, St. Jean and on the Ile-aux-Noix. But what is most disturbing to the Canadians is that they had to release 2,000 men at planting time when they sow their maize, rye, barley and oats. [*It was at that very time*] that they had to transport provisions, ammunition and baggage for the army across rivers and lakes, on water and on land, to St. Jean. This has lasted the entire month of May and will continue throughout the summer. Moreover, they had to furnish the necessary number of horses and carts. This is what I can at present report about our little army, that shows the greatest spirit and courage: it is richly provided with all necessities and its members - and that is the most admirable - are unusually healthy.

The 2nd part of the army is commanded by Colonel St. Leger[8] and consists of about 800 men of regular troops, the newly organized New York Regiment under Sir John Johnson,[9] a detachment of the 8th and 34th English Regiments, a strong comp. of Canadians and a comp. of newly organized Rangers, the Hesse-Hanau Jäger Regiment 800 men strong, and more than 2,000 Savages, Mohawks, Iroquois, Foxes, Ottawas etc. This army corps will march along the St. Lawrence River via Montréal toward the Mohawk River, and while dispersing the enemy in those regions wherever possible, will join our army in the vicinity of Albany where the Mohawk River runs into the Hudson River. The entire corps remaining in Canada consists of about 3,000 men incl. Canadians and Savages.

2nd   The Leib Comp. of the Regiment von Riedesel set out from here on batteaux and joined the regiment that was assembled in Grand Yamachiche. One comp. of the Regiment Specht had to relieve the detachment in the barracks. As I was saying goodbye to several inhabitants, they voiced their opinion, stating that we would surely take up winter quarters again in Canada next winter. They considered it impossible for us to drive the Bostonian Rebels from Crown Point, Carillon and Fort St. George, for there were insurmountable defenses at Carillon and large fortifications at all three places; moreover, [*the Rebels had*] an army of 60,000 men not counting their fleet on Lake Champlain. Terrible news! If all this is true, our small army will have very little effect and not get very far. As our departure is drawing near, the inhabitants of Trois-Rivières seem increasingly displeased. One must not, however, attribute this to their friendship or love for us, but to their greed and love for our money; after all, they have had great advantages through our money. As long as Trois-Rivières has been in existence, there never circulated as much money as in the period in which we have been here. Before our arrival in Canada, the inhabitants had rarely had the chance to see any money whatsoever, and there were many Canadians who had never seen a big French dollar in their lives. Men enlisted in the 33rd Regiment were marching through here; among them were many Germans recruited in Stade. I inquired about Hogreve and learned that he had been paroled due to his short arm and would perhaps be sent back to Europe.

3rd   It was 9 o'clock this morning when we and the Dragoon Squadron of Maj. Gen. von Riedesel embarked in our batteaux on the St. Lawrence River. Several Frenchmen expressed their displeasure at our departure and alas! the fair sex, who, as a whole, are a little soft-hearted in Canada, shed floods of tears whereby they disfigured their pale faces quite pitifully. One of these beautiful creatures, a married woman, even seemed ready to die. Her husband called me back from the batteau and pleaded that I should very quickly perform some blood-letting on his wife; she had suddenly fallen ill. She lay on her bed and made a frightful face. I quickly performed the operation and he who was the cause of her illness was catching the blood, anxiously asking whether his woman was in danger. It was our good A. Th. [Auditeur Thomas?] and I told him the illness would not disappear very fast but only gradually. He even wanted to know the name of the illness, but the batteaux were already being pushed off and I had to hurry. With drums beating we rowed upstream on the terrible St. Lawrence and were at Pointe-du-Lac at 12 o'clock. From here, we reached Lac St. Pierre, that became very rough in the afternoon because it was raining hard. It was 5 o'clock when we arrived at Grand Yamachiche and moved into our quarters. One part of the Regiment Prinz Friedrich and one part of the Regiment von Riedesel had held their winter quarters here and in the parish of Petit Yamachiche and had set out yesterday. In Grand Yamachiche, more than 100 new batteaux were built last winter. We moved 18 English miles today. ---------------18

4th   After embarkation, we came again onto Lac St. Pierre at 11 o'clock; it was so agitated that we had to exert every effort rowing against the high waves, for the wind was strong and contrary. It was already past 5 o'clock when we arrived at [La Seigneurie de la] Rivière-du-Loup and took quarters. Here, Lieut. Colonel Prätorius had been stationed with part of the Regiment Prinz Friedrich during the winter and had departed the day before yesterday. The rest of the squadrons have rejoined us yesterday and today, and the regiment is now complete. So far we have advanced --9

5th   At 6 o'clock this morning we embarked, running out of the Rivière-du-Loup and reached the Lac St. Pierre, which was very calm today. We had crossed this lake by noon. Because of the pilot's ignorance and also because several batteaux had gone ahead of our commander's batteau, we entered the wrong river and had to go back again. Lieut. Colonel Baum, our commander, repeated his previous order to the Adjutant, Lieut. Breva, with the [following] wording, "If a batteau goes ahead of my batteau, its commander shall be arrested even if he is a Captain of the Cavalry." We had reached the parish of Berthier at 4 o'clock when a thundershower and a strong wind forced us onto the banks but without doing us any harm. We could continue our course after 6 minutes and soon reached the church at Berthier. The Hesse-Hanau Regiment had been stationed here and in the parish of Maskinongé during the winter. It was 6 o'clock when we moved into our quarters. We advanced today. ---18

6th   We set out this morning at 8 o'clock and rowed in continual stormy weather to Sorel, which we reached at about 10 o'clock. We entered the Rivière Richelieu and hurried on land because we were to receive several batteaux and ammunition here. We did get 7 batteaux and now the regiment has 20. As for the ammunition, we will have to wait until Chambly or St. Jean. Near Sorel, several 3-masted transport ships are riding at anchor in the Richelieu: the *Lucretia, Canceaux, Lord North, Nancy, Laury, Sarah, Mary, Jane* and *Woodlands*. We continued our course at 11 o'clock, rode another league on the Rivière Richelieu and then moved into our quarters in the parish of Sorel. Because of contrary winds, we could not get very far today and advanced but -----------------------6

7th   This morning, we were moving around very early and soon embarked; on account of contrary winds, we could scarcely reach St. Ours. We advanced ----------------9

8th   We embarked as early as 8 o'clock this morning, passed the parish of St. Antoine on the right and St. Denis on the left on calmer waters, and arrived at St. Charles at 4 o'clock in the afternoon. We advanced ---12

9th   We started at 6 o'clock this morning and rowed to Beloeil where we took up quarters. The Regiment von Riedesel had been here last night and had pitched camp close by today. We advanced today --9

10th   We embarked this morning and took our course toward Chambly; the desert island where I had slept so soundly last year on the 24th of October lay on our left and we passed it. I again thanked my maker quietly for his gracious deliverance from that great danger. At our arrival in Chambly, the Regiment Prinz Friedrich departed for Ste. Thérèse and we moved into their barns; our squadron received one barn and one pigsty. We advanced ---9

11th   Today, we are at rest; we received supplies and ammunition. The Regiment von Riedesel, that had camped here behind the fort, set out to Ste. Thérèse, and the Regiments von Riedesel and Specht moved into the camping place. Our batteaux were being put on wagons and driven to Ste. Thérèse because they are not suited for crossing the rapids.

12th   We set out this morning and marched on land to Ste. Thérèse; I remembered the spot where I marched through the water onto shore last year and although I could not quite see the waterfall, I was again experiencing a little of that fear. ---- The 23rd of Oct.

will forever stay in my memory - yet, we have survived it; who knows what other dangers will be in store for us. We pitched our first camp at Ste. Thérèse. Our batteaux will be pulled up here by a detachment that we have left behind on our march today; for they [the batteaux] had been taken back onto the Richelieu between Chambly and Ste. Thérèse. The rapids are no less than 2 Engl. miles long. We had not even been in the camp for one hour when a violent rainstorm erupted, which lasted 20 hours. We advanced ---9

Total Transport Engl. Miles --99

13th   This morning at 5 o'clock, we climbed into our batteaux and took our course toward St. Jean; at 8 o'clock, we were in the vicinity of the place where I had spent a night on the boulders in the middle of the Richelieu last fall. At 9 o'clock, we reached the bank of St. Jean; here the batteaux had to be pulled across the rapids. This proved to be very difficult and dangerous work because the batteaux had to be pulled through many rocks and boulders. It was noon when we pitched camp at St. Jean. The neighborhood had changed quite a bit and where about 7 or 8 houses had stood last fall, we now counted 80 houses. All is very lively here and the defenses are also greatly improved. The radeau or Floating Battery, which I described last year, is still here and has even grown taller by one story. It now transports 14 24-pound and several 12-pound cannon; also 4 mortars. The 3-masted frigate *Royal George* has likewise been remodeled this spring and now carries 36 cannon. [*In addition, there are*] 20 large batteaux, each of them carrying 12- and 24-pound cannon, which are destined for the Hesse-Hanau Constables [Artillery]. The Regiment Prinz Friedrich set out today and went in batteaux to the beautiful Ile-aux-Noix. We advanced ---9

Total ---108

14th   We are at rest. The Regiment von Riedesel also set out from here to go to the Ile-aux-Noix. Generals Carleton, Burgoyne, Phillips and Riedesel are staying in this fort.

Last night, our Maj. General von Riedesel received a dispatch that Mrs. von Riedesel had arrived in Québec with her children and would continue her journey to meet her husband.[10] Our general went back to Chambly today to await his wife there. The 21st Engl. Regiment had their winter quarters here at St. Jean and was reviewed by Lieut. General Burgoyne today. Since this general had not seen our regiment, we too had to get out and pass in review and when the Regiments von Rhetz and Specht arrived at 10 o'clock, they in turn had to march up in parade and pass in review. Thereafter, they pitched their tents here.

Since we will not find any more convenient place for it [this procedure] in future, all our batteaux were inspected and repaired today. We received supplies for 2 weeks, i.e., ship rations, salted meat, that is to say pork, and ship zwieback, i.e., biscuit, quite nice and hard.

15th   We embarked at 5 o'clock this morning; we set course toward Lake Champlain and reached the beautiful Nut Island, i.e., Ile-aux-Noix, at 11 o'clock. Just like St. Jean, this had changed very much since last fall. Barracks and 70 to 80 houses had been built here. The 20th English Regiment was quartered on this deserted island during the winter and held the army's farthest outpost. With music and drums beating, we passed this island on its left side, letting it lie to our right. The ship *Maria* was riding at anchor here. We continued our course always keeping close to the right bank. As was ordered last year, all the batteaux must keep near the right bank and let all the islands lie to the left. Two armed ships coming from Lake Champlain went past us. It was 4 o'clock in the afternoon when we reached the Rivière LaColle, disembarked and pitched tents. I described this place last year and know the danger of drinking water from the Rivière LaColle. Since nobody else from our regiment had been here before, I reported this to our commander, Lieut. Colonel Baum. He quickly ordered that no water be taken from this river, but since the little [*amount of*] spring water available did not suffice for so many, the men should rather get the necessary water from the Richelieu. Nothing has been built up here as yet; the Canadians living here last fall are gone. The flies and mosquitoes [marenguens] have almost devoured us; everybody has bumps on hands and face from their poisonous stings. The faces of several of our men are so swollen from the stings of these little canaille that one cannot recognize them. There are wild pigeons in great quantity about, so bold that when they hear a shot, they do not even fly from one tree to another. We have seen various birds here, and the bullfrog, that lows like an ox, lets his voice be heard on the river. We advanced ---21

16th   By 5 o'clock this morning, we had already left the Rivière LaColle and reached Pointe-au-Fer as early as 10 o'clock; here we landed. A group of one noncommissioned officer and 13 dragoons was detached here from our regiment to relieve the detachment from the Regiment von Riedesel. The first regiment coming after us will have to relieve our detachment and so forth until all the regiments will have passed through. This detachment will remain here for security because a few provisions are still stored here. Up to Pointe-au-Fer we covered ---9

Total --138

On this bank lay 200 Iroquois Savages in 28 bark canoes; these are boats made from birch bark. They [the Savages] are being led to the army by Capt. Fraser, brother [nephew] of Brig. Gen. Fraser of our army. We pushed our batteaux off again and, after Pointe-au-Fer, left the Province of Canada and the Richelieu and reached Lake Champlain. This lake is 120 miles long and 30 miles wide at its broadest. We rode near its right shore. We were supposed to pitch tents on the Ile La Motte today where our Jäger Comp. had been.

We came to this large, wild island, which lies in the middle of Lake Champlain. Our commander went ashore, but as this island is covered throughout with woods and brush, he could not find the spot meant for the camp. We therefore continued and in the afternoon reached that part of the lake where the shores are so covered with cliffs and rocks that no one is able to land. About 4 o'clock, the Savages came in their canoes just when the water was becoming very agitated because of a thundershower. We did not know where to go, but in the end, Capt. Fraser found us a safe bay, which we entered; we slept this night on rocks and boulders. Notwithstanding the stormy waters, the Savages continued on their course. The place where we were was called Pointe-la-Rouge by the French. From Pointe-au-Fer up to here we covered -------------------------------15

17th   We left our bay at 6 o'clock this morning; the lake was very agitated. We kept to the right shore as much as possible, but nevertheless had to row straight across for a distance of 4 Engl. miles. During the last war, 30 batteaux with 4 French regiments in them capsized in this vicinity and all the men drowned. We fortunately got across and reached Cumberland Head by 10 o'clock. This miserable place was designated as assembly point and rendezvous for the army. We disembarked by the left wing of the army and pitched camp in the wilderness and on swampy ground where the regiment had previously cleared a camping place in these dense woods. Our batteaux were unloaded and pulled ashore. I do not know the reason why the ship *Maria*, with Lieut. Gen. Burgoyne on board, cast anchor not far from shore in the afternoon. It is very hot. We advanced ---9

Total --162

18th   Counting from the right wing, [*the following units*] camped here: The brigade of Brig. General Powell,[11] consisting of the 9th, 47th, and 53rd Engl. Regiments, our Jäger Comp., our Light Infantry Regiment von Bärner, our General Staff, our Grenadier Battalion Breymann, the Hesse-Hanau Regiment, the Regiments Prinz Friedrich, von Riedesel and the Dragoon Regiment; the Regiments von Rhetz and Specht, which arrived today, formed the left wing. Like us, these first had to clear a camping place in the dense woods so that they could pitch their tents. The forest consists of oak trees, beech, cedar, maple trees and the like, all unusually broad [in diameter] and tall; of known herbs, I found here VERONICA [speedwell], HEDERA TERRESTRIS [ground ivy], [tuss orlay], CAPIL. VENER. [CAPILLUS VENERIS, maidenhair fern], SCABIOSA [fleabane]; I also came upon many unknown herbs growing here in abundance. Our men drank nothing but tea made of VERONICA and maidenhair. There were a great number of squirrels about but fewer mosquitoes than at the Rivière LaColle. On the other hand, we had other kinds of insects that were far worse than those: one type had black and white wings and was as big as a flea; the other was entirely black and even smaller than a flea so that one could hardly see it with naked eyes. The French call them brûlies [no-see-ums]. They creep on the ground on their bare body and their sting produces a blister as if [the skin were] burned. [Upon] going to sleep, one has to cover his face and hands. Although we saw buffalo, moose, bears, wolves, foxes, beavers, wildcats, rats and Canadian hare, we have not yet seen any deer at all in America. Neither did we see any rattlesnakes, although there are said to be some; but we did see enough common couleuvres [snakes] on our journey, but these are not dangerous.

19th   Lieut. Gen. Burgoyne, who continues to stay on the ship *Maria*, passed our camp today and inspected those regiments he had not seen this year. This noon, orders came for us to depart tomorrow; we had not expected that. We had just been making ovens for baking and the Hesse-Hanau Regiment had already finished theirs - again, a futile enterprise. Beside the ship *Maria*, the 20-cannon batteau previously mentioned [the radeau] was riding at anchor. Every man was given 10 ball-cartridges; thus, the affair is becoming serious. --

20th   At 4 o'clock this morning, instead of reveille, the order for general march was beaten and immediately thereafter, that for assembly. The army then embarked on their batteaux and rowed out of Cumberland Bay up to the entrance of Lake Champlain. In accordance with yesterday's orders, the army assembled here at the first cannon shot from the ship *Maria*; at the 2nd shot, they set out in the following order: the armed batteaux formed the tête; then Major von Bärner followed with the Jäger Comp., then our Light Infantry Regiment von Bärner, the Grenadier Battalion Breymann, our Dragoon Regiment, Powell's brigade, the Hesse-Hanau Regiment and the Regiments Prinz Friedrich, von Riedesel, Specht and [von] Rhetz. After these, the batteaux moved in files of 4, and the ship *Maria* also weighed anchor; she accompanied us, always keeping to her right. The tenders and batteaux rode behind and next to her so that the necessary orders could be transmitted from Lieut. General Burgoyne to the regiments. Thus, the progress of the 11 regiments, together with the General Staff and the Jäger Comp., continued in favorable wind. Although the waves rose once more to the level of the batteaux today, no water got in because we were riding with the wind. Who in all the world ever saw anything more unusual than a small army riding in more than 300 batteaux, each one with a spread sail, through the waves of stormy weather? -- The beauty of this sight is beyond description but I do know how I felt every time a bold wave drenched me and threatened to devour us with a terrible noise. -- It was 10 o'clock in the forenoon when our escort *Maria* fired the signal gun for the army to go ashore. We rowed to the right shore and disembarked at Ligonier Bay. From afar, this shore resembles a very high, white battery. Close by, we climbed the bank and, having cleared a camping place in dense woods, mostly spruce, we pitched our tents on the top of the mountain. Here, we again waged war against the mosquitoes, which not being used to such plenty were stinging us unmercifully. Wild pigeons were also about in great numbers. Deer are likewise said to have been seen here and that was true. - In the afternoon, Lieut. Gen. Burgoyne's tent was pitched next to our regiment and a guard from our regiment was posted in front; but the general remained on the ship. Our regiment has been designated to cover headquarters throughout this campaign. The army followed the same order here in the camp as on water today: the Jäger Comp. formed the right wing and the Reg. von Rhetz the left one. Our Maj. Gen. von Riedesel returned today. He had met his wife in Chambly from where she has gone back to Trois-Rivières. In the afternoon, two other armed ships of our fleet arrived here.

Our *Maria* set sail with the *Royal George* and the *Inflexible* and we soon lost sight of them. Lake Champlain is said to be at its widest in this vicinity, but since this lake is sown with islands, as it were, one very seldom can see the opposite shore. Up to here we advanced --18

21st   Various instructions were given to the army by Lieut. Gen. Burgoyne today; the articles of war were read to our regiment, something which is supposed to be done more frequently in the future. Brig. Gen. Fraser commands the Advance Guard of the army, has Canadians and Savages in his corps and has already advanced to the Bouquet River.

Total ---180

22nd   Masons and bakers were selected from our regiment and sent ahead. The army is to set out tomorrow. The rest of the salted pork and the ship's biscuit, that we had taken along from St. Jean, was given out to our regiments today. The other regiments had not wanted any biscuit and have been without bread for several days. They had taken flour instead in order to bake some [of their own] bread; but they had not considered that in this wilderness, where no people were dwelling, there would not be any baker's ovens either. The soldiers made dough and put it on flat, glowing stones and baked it; it turned out to be very poor bread, however. There were many turtles in Ligonier Bay; near the 47th Regiment, I saw one that weighed more than 80 lbs. The English assert that it was very delicate food but although I had the opportunity, I have never been able to try it. The Savages eat them raw; no Englishman would do that. The Savages shot a big, black eagle here today. From the regiments of the left wing, a detachment was sent into the woods in the afternoon because horse tracks were seen there. I do not believe it; where should the horse come from? These may have been moose tracks. One sees very high mountain ranges on both shores but we cannot see the smaller ranges as yet; these mountains are said to stretch down to South Carolina and are 1,500 miles long.

23rd   At 3 o'clock this morning, instead of reveille, the order for general march was beaten. Although there was so violent a storm that the water swept over our batteaux standing on shore, the regimental quartermasters' foragers and the sharpshooters of the army embarked and departed. Our camp was struck but no order came to embark. The waters became increasingly terrifying. The drummers stood in front of the line and waited for the wind [to abate] in order to beat the order for assembly. Everybody looked at the lake with fearful glances hoping we would not have to depart today and pitied the men who had already gone; for it seemed almost impossible that they could get through all right. They said, "Perhaps we will never see them again." The forenoon was spent between fear and hope. In the afternoon, our Maj. Gen. von Riedesel sent his first aide-de-camp, Captain Edmonstone,[12] in a small sloop to the entrance of the bay to see if it was possible to depart. Since Lieut. General Burgoyne had gone ahead on the frigate *Royal George*, our general had the command over the army. When Captain Edmonstone came back, the army was given orders to pitch tents and to set out tomorrow at the same early hour as today.

24th   The camp was quietly struck this morning at 3 o'clock; we left this high mountain, embarked and set ourselves in motion. We had not yet moved out of our bay when a shower with severe thunder and lightning forced us to stop. There was heavy rain, but since there was no wind accompanying it, we could continue rowing for half an hour. It was almost 5 o'clock when we moved out of our bay.

We continuously kept to the right shore and wished with all our hearts that the waters would remain calm the more so as the right shore showed nothing but horrible cliffs where nobody could ever land. We continued having calm waters until 10 o'clock, but then a dense fog came from the land, that obscured our vision; a strong wind followed with heavy torrential rains. To our great satisfaction our regiment was at the corner of a woods and although this was rather far off, it nevertheless gave us a little protection, for the wind was blowing from the land. Several regiments were driven far out on the lake and although the rain lasted only 10 minutes, the wind did not entirely abate afterward. At noon, we passed to our left the 4 islands, called Four Brothers, which lay in a square in the middle of the lake; each one was about 3/4 of an Engl. mile in diameter. A little further ahead lay Valcour Island, behind which the Rebel fleet had hidden last year. At 1 o'clock, we reached the ship *Maria*, which was riding at anchor to our left; at 2 o'clock, we disembarked at the Bouquet River and had to climb a mountain just as high as the one we had just left. If we were to pitch our tents here, we would first have to clear a camping place in this immense and dense forest. The Fraser Corps had made a breastwork of big trees; they had set out from here this morning and taken their course toward Crown Point. They had driven off a detachment of Rebels from here whereby one Savage had been shot dead. The Savages had captured 6 Rebels and scalped all of them alive. After having endured a great deal in the storm, our foragers and sharpshooters arrived here safely yesterday. There are again very many mosquitoes at this place and although having left Canada by now, we have not seen swallows as yet nor any other birds that live off insects. Orders were issued to the army that no one should take his clothes off at night so that all may quickly appear at the front should there be any noise; for a detachment of 800 Rebels is said to be in the wilderness here. We also found the masons and bakers who had been detached the day before yesterday; they had built a baker's oven in the meantime and bread will be baked tomorrow. What joy! After all, we have not eaten anything but biscuit that was hard as rock. About 3 miles up the Bouquet River, there is a waterfall and below it are the ruins of a mill; there also stood a few houses whose inhabitants surely have moved on with the Rebels; now their houses have been burned down. Since the lake is not as wide around here, we also saw some dwellings on the opposite shore; these are the first inhabitants [sic] we have seen since Ste. Thérèse in Canada. The brigade of Brig. Gen. Hamilton, consisting of the 20th, 21st and 62nd Regiments of Engl. infantry, also arrived here this afternoon and pitched tent at the right wing. We are making fascines of wood and are 14 regiments now. Advanced till now ---21

Total --201

At this place, Lieut. General Burgoyne himself spoke to the Savages yesterday admonishing them in most urgent terms and ordering them not to scalp anybody anymore. On the other hand, they will get a gratuity for every prisoner they deliver alive but nothing at all for the scalps. This made them ill-disposed toward us for they used to get two piasters for every scalp.

25th   At 2 o'clock this afternoon, the order for general march was beaten and immediately thereafter, that for assembly. At 3 o'clock, we had embarked and were rowing in good weather and calm waters for 6 miles all along the right shore. We found the shore to consist of one solid rock, as it were, and so high that it was impossible to climb. Various kinds of trees and brush grew out of this rock and in about the middle of this precipice we saw an opening through the rock, called Split Rock, where 4 men abreast could march through. Through this opening, we observed a very large body of water and the opposite shore built up with several respectable houses. Close by to our left we came upon the ship *Maria*, which, for want of wind, was being towed by many sailors rowing in 3 boats. When Lieut Gen. Burgoyne appeared on the foredeck of this ship with his suite, he was saluted by us with drums beating and shouts of hurrah. Soon thereafter, that ship made use of a favorable wind and sailed away to our right. We saw several settlements on the left shore. The lake gets increasingly narrow at this point but bigger and smaller islands can still be found here and there. The reg. quartermasters, foragers and the army's sharpshooters formed the tête. It was dark night by now and the water quite agitated; no one knew where to go because the rocky shores made it impossible to land anywhere. At 10 o'clock at night, we approached the left shore and disembarked at Button Mould Bay. That night, we slept on rocks and cliffs. The regiments of the left wing did not get ashore before midnight. From the Fraser Corps that camped before us at Grand Point, we heard the retreat shot tonight. At the arrival of the

Fraser Corps, a detachment of Rebels, about 1,000 men strong, had left Crown Point with their fleet and cannon batteaux and withdrawn to Carillon. Today we advanced -----19

Total --220

26th   At 5 o'clock this morning, we climbed into our batteaux and rowed up to Grand Point, which lies to the left of Crown Point. Here we had the rendezvous. It was 8 o'clock when we disembarked. We had seen Crown Point from the middle of the lake for more than an hour; having had to tack continually, our escort *Maria* finally arrived and cast anchor next to the fleet. Ahead of us at Grand Point stood the Fraser Corps that was to leave its camp at 9 o'clock to advance further toward Carillon on the left shore; it was 15 Engl. miles from Crown Point to Carillon. At 11 o'clock, we alone, i.e., the Dragoon Regiment, set out, rowed to our right toward Crown Point, disembarked in the Bay of Crown Point and pitched our tents behind the fort all the while facing Carillon. Powell's brigade moved into our camp at the left wing and besides these, no other troops were around here. Between us and the English regiments were the headquarters of Lieut. Gen. Burgoyne, who was camping in a tent. Behind our front, Maj. Gen. Phillips was lodging in the house of a German. The guards for the quarters of both generals were from our regiment. When I learned that a German was living here, I visited him this morning. He was quite indifferent about seeing his countrymen and spoke with contempt of the German nation and of Germany. He was a Saxon by birth and probably a Rebel.

We all were very happy when we found a German who had settled here in the wilderness but could not understand why all these Germans met their countrymen with so much contempt. But when I considered that such a man might perhaps have committed many crimes and that the fear of punishment might have driven him to the desperate decision of going to America, then my admiration ceased and contempt took the place of friendship. The main body of the army continues to stay in Grand Point, which is the headquarters of our Major Gen. von Riedesel. This place received its name Crown Point from the English; the French call it Fort Frédéric. Likewise the name Carillon comes from the French, for the English call it Ticonderoga and so shall I call it in the future. That which is called Crown Point is a neck of land formed by Lake Champlain and the Bay of Crown Point. It is a rather pleasant place and while it was all built up, it was bigger than the city of Braunschweig.[13] Individual houses are still standing here and there, but the largest and best part has been burned down. The fort also was demolished by the enemy; it must have been very beautiful. Inside the fort are 3 more houses whose wooden parts have all been burned. They had been erected with building stones, two stories high and had probably been barracks. The longest had 36 window openings, the 2nd 24, and the 3rd 21 downstairs as well as upstairs. In between these houses is a square on which there are still 10 spiked iron cannon. We are in the midst of a heat wave and moreover day and night we are tortured by insects. Up to here, advanced ---------------9

27th   Last night we had very severe thunderstorms with lightning and heavy thunder such as I had never experienced in Germany. Today, Lieut. Gen. Burgoyne gave the regiments orders to entrench themselves. Our fleet and the cannon batteaux set sail toward Ticonderoga today while the ship *Washington* of 20 cannon arrived from St. Jean, loaded with provisions. A detachment of our regiment had to unload the provisions and take them ashore. Wine, rum, Engl. beer, coffee, sugar etc. continue to be sold to the regiments for twice as much as in Canada. But there is no tobacco to be had anywhere; I am happy to be amply provided with Canadian canaster [coarse tobacco].

28th   Orders were given today that all regiments hold 100 cartridges ready for each man; also, that after 4 cannon shots from the right and left wings, the army be always prepared to set out at once with the greatest of speed, be it night or day.

In that case, the army will let its tents stand; but after 2 cannon shots from both wings, the army will quickly embark on its batteaux. The baggage will then remain in the camp with a detachment. Moreover, all the regiments are to build baker's ovens at Crown Point.

29th   A little to the left of our line, there lies a demolished redoubt. A black snake, about 7 feet long, was killed behind our line today; rattlesnakes are supposed to be around but we have not seen any as yet. We have discovered as many adders as in Canada, and there were many in all the camps, but nobody has ever been harmed by them. Nevertheless, our men have frequently given them a sound thrashing, for nobody wishes to accept them as guests. I cannot describe how afraid, even terrified, I have been of them. They are after bread.

30th   Last night and even today, we have been hearing many cannon shots from the direction of Ticonderoga. Our Jäger Comp., our Light Infantry Regiment von Bärner and our Grenadier Battalion, which comprise the Breymann Corps, are setting out today to advance on batteaux toward Ticonderoga. Since Canada, we have not seen a single church. We have come upon many known and unknown herbs again.-
By now, we have safely crossed Lake Champlain. Would that we soon had Fort Ticonderoga behind us! Would that we soon will have news about peace! --

Total --229

End of this Month

Month of July 1777

1st   At 4 o'clock this morning, instead of reveille, the general march order was beaten and immediately thereafter, assembly. We embarked and rowed from Crown Point out of the Bay and reached Lake Champlain, but had to stop for almost an hour until the army had embarked. We then continued our journey to Ticonderoga. Our regiment formed the tête today. We went along the shore to our right and passed the 2nd redoubt of Crown Point that also had been demolished. Since the lake is becoming increasingly narrow here, we could observe that both shores continue to be beset by rocks. There is nothing left of the fleet at Crown Point but the Floating Battery. Of all the regiments, one detachment remained at Crown Point. At 8 o'clock, we saw many batteaux on the left shore and a camp on the height above: that was the Breymann Corps; at 9 o'clock, we saw a camp ahead on the right shore: that was the Fraser Corps. The cannon batteaux were on the lake in a straight line with this corps about one short [less than, but not quite a full one] mile from Ticonderoga. Behind these batteaux, our fleet was riding at anchor. We disembarked on the right bank behind the Fraser Corps at Three Mile Point and marched for half a mile onto a height in the woods. After the regiment had worked for 4 hours clearing a camping place, we pitched camp in this wilderness. I have never seen such a forest and such beautiful trunk wood. We heard many cannon shots from Ticonderoga on our trip today and while we were disembarking, the cannonade became very heavy from the enemy side; no shot has been fired as yet from our side. The Savages today took 2 Rebels away from the advanced post and scalped them. It is so very hot here that the bodies of some of our men who had taken off their clothes have been badly burned; large blisters developed on their skin. The unprotected arms and legs of many of our dragoons have also been burned. About 50 paces from here, Powell's brigade pitched camp. From Crown Point to Ticonderoga, we advanced --15

Total --244

2nd   A work detachment of 100 men went out from Powell's brigade today to clear a road through the dense forest toward Ticonderoga. None of our German troops are on this side; all stand on the left shore of the lake; in the camp across from us are the headquarters of our Maj. Gen. von Riedesel. Lieut. Gen. Burgoyne is aboard the *Royal George*. In this camp, we are again waging war against the flies that are torturing us during the day; at night, the snakes (adders) visit us in the tents. At 3 o'clock in the afternoon, a detachment from Powell's brigade set out in the direction of Ticonderoga and at 4 o'clock, we heard firing of cannon and small arms. A picket went out from our regiment this evening.

3rd   Last night, there were frequent shots from cannon and small arms. Several of the English have been seriously wounded and the officer who had been wounded yesterday died last night. The English field hospital consists of very large tents and is about 1,000 paces away from our line near the water. Prisoners and deserters, who are daily increasing in numbers, are being taken onto the frigates. The Rebels have Savages and Blacks in their army, who are, however, very much afraid of our Savages. Orders were given today that no sutler was to sell rum to the Savages. Whoever sells rum to the Savages will receive corporal punishment and be chased from the army. Every informer will receive 10 piasters. This is very good, for when the Savages are drunk, they scalp both friend and foe. Although batteries have been set up in the woods here and there and provided with cannon, they are still covered, and no shot has as yet been fired from our side against the enemy. All preparations have been made for a formal siege. It is said that the fort will be attacked from the water and on land on the 6th. The enemy has hoisted a red flag on the fort to express that they would rather lose their lives than their freedom.
Toward the fleet and on the Citadel Independence, they hoisted a white flag with 13 stars and 13 red stripes; the 13 stars signify the 13 Provinces.[14] Tonight, our bakers arrived from Crown Point with 400 [*one*] pound [*loaves of*] bread for our regiment; it is wheat bread and white like a roll.

4th   The English are very busy taking cannon and ammunition closer to the fort on the newly cleared roads; for want of horses, everything is being pulled by soldiers. Some English have been wounded both yesterday and today. The Savages have captured horses, oxen and cows. Last night, the brigade of Brig. Gen. von Gall, consisting of our Reg. Prinz Friedrich and the Hesse-Hanau Reg., moved from that side to this side. They reached the place that the Fraser Corps had left last night because these in turn had taken a position further to the right toward Ticonderoga. While I was walking on the lake shore today, a muscat rat (so called by the English) [muskrat] was killed there. They [the muskrats] are as large as cats and smell of muscat; their tail is hairless like a beaver's; they are gray in color, have a good pelt, live in the water and on land like the beaver and belong to the lower mammals. The English eat these rats and assert that they taste very good.[15] There are also many bullfrogs on the shore there; I have seen my first today. They are green and formed like other frogs but bigger than a large cat's head, have feet like duck feet [webbed feet] and low like oxen. On account of the calm, the radeau or Floating Battery has not yet been able to advance, but is supposed to be used in the siege of Ticonderoga. This afternoon, with rowing and casting anchor, they have moved it further ahead. The anchor is taken ahead in a batteau of common width for quite a distance, then cast and wound up again; for all the ships pull themselves toward the anchor when it is being wound. This afternoon, I went to the frigate *Royal George* and from there to the headquarters of our Major General von Riedesel. From here one could overlook all the fortifications of Ticonderoga, for the headquarters lie to the side of where we are camping. At the Citadel Independence, Lake Champlain is so narrow that the Americans can cannonade our Breymann Corps that stands right across from the citadel. From Ticonderoga, they [the Americans] can likewise reach this corps with cannon from a few entrenchments. Therefore, the Breymann Corps had to move and pitch their tents back in the woods again. One could recognize several entrenchments from here. The occupation [troops] seemed to consist of 3 rows [Tressen]. On our side, we and several English regiments that are positioned around Ticonderoga to the right would be exposed to the cannon fire from various retrenchments,[16] and not covered from them by woods and brush. From Ticonderoga to Fort Independence, a communicating bridge has been built and the passage underneath this has been blocked for large ships by means of large, joined beams; on that side of the fort, they still have some warships. This afternoon, we were supposed to advance closer to Ticonderoga. We embarked at 4 o'clock but hardly had we departed than we received orders not to advance before tomorrow morning. We returned to the old camp and camped that night without tents.

5th   At 5 o'clock this morning, we embarked and rowed toward the height where von Gall's brigade was camped. We climbed ashore and left our batteaux with a guard. Each one took the most necessary [*items*] of his baggage along, as much as he could carry, and continued marching on the road through the wilderness that Fraser's and Powell's brigades had cleared. We passed the lines of Powell's and Hamilton's brigades as well as Ticonderoga itself about half a mile to our left. We went there through a valley where we were even closer to the enemy so that their cannon could well have reached us; but we were covered by brush. We came to a long, well built bridge that spanned a wide river and beyond this bridge onto a smooth main road leading to Lake St. Sacrement or St. George, which begins not far from here. After continuing our march through a deep valley, we climbed 2 high elevations, one after the other. We reached our camping place and pitched our tents, which the dragoons had had to carry. We were facing Ticonderoga, being about one Engl. mile away from it. Next to us on our left stood the Fraser Corps in entrenched positions, which are called "the French lines" because they had been laid out by the French in the Seven Years War. In front of our right was a very high mountain, called Sugar Loaf (or Zuckerberg) [Mount Defiance]. From this mountain, Ticonderoga could be shot at and I cannot understand why it had not been occupied by the enemy. Last night, it was occupied by us with a detachment; on orders of Maj. Gen. Phillips, cannon were also taken onto this high mountain today with surprising preparations and much effort. This afternoon, we saw several enemy ships and batteaux sail along the shores of Ticonderoga; one ship fired on our pickets, but without effect. This evening, we saw many fires in Ticonderoga as if houses and cottages were burning. The enemy had also removed their flags before nightfall.

6th   This morning at daybreak, we became aware that the enemy had abandoned Ticonderoga and Independence. The frigates *Royal George* and *Inflexible*, the warships *Carleton*, *Maria*, *Washington* and the armed batteaux weighed anchor but could not get through the passage that was blocked by beams. Carpenters and laborers opened it as quickly as possible and as the wind was favorable, they [the ships] pursued the enemy. When I went to our batteaux this morning, all the regiments of our army were in motion hurrying onto their batteaux. They had left tents and baggage behind. At the Hesse-Hanau Reg., I found a deserter, a German, who said that the enemy was about 9,000 or 10,000 men strong[17]; they had been utterly surprised, however, upon seeing the powerful forces with which we had come. (That is ridiculous.) When the two generals St. Clair[18] and Schuyler had seen yesterday that we had occupied the Sugar Loaf Mountain, they quickly held a council of war and decided not to wait for our attack but to take flight the following night. Who could have thought or imagined that the enemy would abandon such an advantageous position! Our army has not fired a single shot against the fort, but it is said--that Lieut. Gen. Burgoyne had "shot" with guns [artillery] instead of cartridges and the Generals St. Clair and Schuyler had not been able to withstand such heavy fire - the Reg. Prinz Friedrich and the 62nd Engl. Reg. moved into Ticonderoga and occupied it. It is beyond description how much the enemy has left behind in ammunition, provisions and such victuals as wine, rum, sugar, coffee, chocolate, butter, cheese etc. The army is pursuing the enemy but we are still at rest and have no marching orders as yet. Carillon or Ticonderoga consists of 10 fortifications, of which the smallest holds 4 cannon, and each may mount up to 10 cannon. Independence is a high mountain, which nature itself has made insurmountable; it is cut off from Ticonderoga by a curve of Lake Champlain. At the foot of this mountain lies a retrenchment of 29 cannon in gun emplacements [Schiessgittern]. Above this line on a beautiful height stand 5 cannon in an entrenchment above the bank. One hundred and fifty paces further up lies an octagonal, star-shaped, palisaded fort where there are cannon and about 8 barracks en queue ['in a line']. Here and there, one finds other palisades provided with cannon, especially in those places where they could have expected an attack. All in all, the enemy left 140 cannon in Ticonderoga and Independence. Both forts had been wilderness places and the fortifications had first been laid out by the French in the Seven Years War. We have moved our batteaux closer to both forts.

7th   At 4 o'clock this morning, without any marching orders, general march was beaten and immediately thereafter assembly. We embarked and rowed underneath the bridge previously mentioned. We left Ticonderoga behind on our left and although we passed close by it, we could not recognize anything because of the dense fog that obscured the sky this morning. We reached Lake Champlain and found that both shores were nothing but rocks and rocky elevations of extraordinary height, but out of which all kinds of individual trees and bushes grow. On our entire journey, we have not seen any cliff or rocky elevation of such height as on this shore. At noon we encountered a batteau on which an officer, who had been shot through his abdomen, was lying. At 1 o'clock we came to the tip of Lake Champlain, which here forms a bay called La Belle [South Bay]; our fleet lay in this bay. We rowed to our left up a river and after half an hour, we came on the right bank upon the batteaux of our army. The regiments were marching on land pursuing the enemy. Two captured ships were also riding at anchor here that had been on their way to the Bay La Belle and carried 24 and 16 cannon respectively. Here and there were enemy batteaux, which had either been burned or demolished, and a few one-masted ships that were filled with provisions, ammunition and all sorts of necessary things; these had also been captured here. Nobody knew where our general and the regiments were. We had been assembling for about 2 hours when we received orders from Lieut. Gen. Burgoyne to set out and, in going back, cover all the batteaux of the army. Just before that, Lieut. Colonel Baum had been strongly reprimanded by Lieut. Gen. Burgoyne because he had left his post without orders etc. We rowed until [we came] into the Bay La Belle, where we arrived at 3 o'clock. All batteaux pushed ashore here and we made our camping place in the woods. Although we did not pitch camp, a camping place had nevertheless to be cleared where the tents could have been pitched. We had not seen any herring in America as yet but tonight I happened to eat a delicious herring salad and drink gin at Madame Aschholtz's; I was happy that we had ended the awful trip across Lake Champlain so well and so safely.

8th   The ship *Carleton* set sail for St. Jean today to get provisions from there. At 3 o'clock in the afternoon, we got marching orders. We embarked and along with all the other batteaux, rowed ahead up to the portage. Here we saw that the enemy had not been able to advance any further on account of rapids and waterfalls. The enemy had burned a 2-masted ship here; it had sunk but the masts could still be seen. A burned battery had also sunk near the bank but a little of it could still be seen; on it lay a very large mortar, many bombs and cartridges. Most of the more than 200 batteaux had been burned, a great deal of ammunition, provisions and other items had been thrown into the water. The enemy had caused great devastation here and except for one stone house, in which Lieut. Gen. Burgoyne was lodging, all the houses had been burned down. This was done out of hatred for Colonel Skene,[19] who owned this region and who was with our army. All sorts of mills had been burned for this same reason. Among the ruins, one saw large houses, half roasted beef and pork, Turkish wheat [maize] and other wheat; fruit, cannonballs and other things were also lying around. We left our batteaux in front and marched over the portage. On the height, we came upon another palisaded redoubt where 2 houses had been burned down. We marched up in front of the line of the Engl. camp and pitched our camp at the right wing on a rocky mountain. As usual, a camping place had first to be cleared. This place is called: At the Camp in Skenesborough. The army will assemble here again. So far we advanced --21

9th   This morning, we learned that our Maj. Gen. von Riedesel had returned on foot with his adjutant, Capt. Edmonstone, at 4 o'clock in the morning and then gone to the batteau. The 9th Regiment had taken some baggage from an enemy batteau, as booty: one trunk full of paper money, 2 taffeta regimental flags and 2 similar nautical flags. The flags could be seen in front of the 9th Regiment: the one of blue taffeta [had] on top a wreath of white and red stripes, in the middle a golden wreath and in a golden circle was written: "In Honor of Our Freedom;" underneath the intertwining letters: "United States of America" (die Vereinigten Staaten von Amerika). The 2nd had yellow taffeta and in the corner likewise 13 stripes; in the middle were 13 intertwining circles which together were again forming a circle. These were the 13 Provinces; on each circle stood the name of a Province in golden letters such as New Hampshire, Massachusetts Bay, Connecticut, Rhode Island, New York, New Jersey, Pennsylvania, Delaware, Maryland, Virginia, North Carolina, South Carolina, Georgia. In the center of this large circle was a golden sun, on which these words could be read: "we are one" or 'wir sind eins'. Around these words was written: "Congress American" [sic]. By the way, they were of the same type as the Engl. flags. We learned today that our Maj. Gen. von Riedesel had supported Brig. Gen. Fraser at Hubbardton with a detachment of jägers and grenadiers whereby the enemy had suffered considerable losses and been compelled to take to flight. Of our jägers, 2 were shot and 7 wounded; among the latter was Lieut. Cruse with 4 bullets in his face; he was only slightly wounded, however, for those were all grazing shots, a fortunate happenstance indeed. On the whole, our army has already suffered considerable losses of dead and wounded, among whom are a major and 4 officers from the Engl. grenadiers. The advanced regiments have now returned and pitched their camp at the left wing. Because we are lacking bread, baker's ovens are being built at the portage. Today a dragoon killed a black snake that was 6 feet long and had a white and scaly belly.

10th   The Regiments von Rhetz and Specht have gone from here on batteaux in order to move to a camp at Castleton. Lieut. Gen. Burgoyne had the following information given to the army: on the 6th, the Rebels had abandoned Ticonderoga and were driven away by nothing but the mere presence of the army. They ran on the one side till Hubbardton, on the other till Skenesborough. They left their entire artillery behind, all their ships, much ammunition, provisions and all their baggage.

Total ---265

[On the] 7th - With half of his brigade and without any artillery, Brig. Gen. Fraser came upon 2,000 heavily entrenched Rebels, attacked them and drove them off. Their officers lost 200 dead and 200 more were taken prisoner. To support Brig. Gen. Fraser, Maj. Gen. von Riedesel arrived in time with the Advance Guard, that consisted of the Jäger Comp., 80 grenadiers and light infantry. Through his well-timed and circumspect commands and the brave manner in which these were executed, he as well as his troops have received a large share of the honor of victory.

[On the] 8th - Lieut. Colonel Hill, commander of the 9th Regiment, was attacked at Fort Ann by the Rebels, who were 6 times as strong as he. After standing under continual fire for 3 hours, however, he drove them off with heavy losses.[20] Following this affair, the Rebels left Fort Ann, after having set it afire. A detachment of our army is now in possession [of the territory] on that side of the fort. This swift departure, for which one cannot thank God enough, accrues very much to our troops' honor, particularly the Fraser and Riedesel Corps. These, who through the bravery of both officers and soldiers have rendered the greatest service to the King and increased the reputation of the military profession, deserve most credit. These corps even merit additional praise because they had to endure great fatigue, bad weather, a lack of bread - and suffered all without grumbling. Next Sunday, a celebration of thanksgiving will be held at sunset and a feu de joie will be made with cannon and small arms in Carillon, Crown Point, Skenesborough, Castleton and also at the Corps of Lieut. Colonel Breymann. Major General von Riedesel will see to it that orders concerning these events are sent to the detached corps of the left wing. Brig. Gen. Hamilton, Commander of Ticonderoga, shall send them to Crown Point. A list will also be dispatched [with the information] as to how many wounded have been taken to the hospital in Ticonderoga. The Engl. and German brigades of the Advance Corps as well as the dragoons shall fill up their 100 cartridges per man. A list will be sent to Maj. Gen. Phillips tomorrow morning as to how much powder, bullets and papers are lacking to fill the needed amount. Since it is difficult [to assure] that the ammunition gets [to a given place] as fast as the army with their forced marches, there is no doubt that each regiment will conserve their ammunition as best they can. Among the captured as well as dead Rebels, there were many so-called riflemen (Scharfschützen) whose regimentals are white linen frocks with fringes, which are shorter than those our teamsters wear.

11th   All the captured Rebels, who already amount to more than 400, are being transported to Ticonderoga today.

12th   The General Staff of our Maj. Gen. von Riedesel set out this morning and went in batteaux to the camp in Castleton. Our general had our regiment informed today that Gen. Burgoyne had ordered our regiment to be mounted. Although nobody knows where the horses are supposed to come from, this news gave the dragoons much pleasure.

13th   Today a feast of thanksgiving was held; the TE DEUM was sung and at sunset, a feu de joie was made. The Hesse-Hanau Regiment also advanced to Castleton today. Here we saw a type of snake that looked like copper and was called copper snake [copperhead]; its bite is said to be lethal. A smooth road to Fort Ann begins at our lines. There also flows a small river, called Wood Creek, that is navigable for batteaux. The Rebels have barred both river and road with big, thick, felled trees, so that they are impassable and have to be cleared with much effort and toil. Last night, 29 deserters came to us and asserted that many more were roaming around in the woods, who had actually deserted. They would like to join us but abstained for fear of the Savages. The English are taking their batteaux over the portage today. Lieut. Gen. Burgoyne ordered it to be announced that a provost general had been appointed for the army. Our regiment was to provide a 2-man guard per company for him; in 10 days they would be relieved by another regiment.

15th   All the wounded of the army as well as wounded Rebels were carried onto batteaux and taken to the hospital in Ticonderoga. Many Canadian horses, designated for the artillery in our army and as pack horses, arrived here. The first rattlesnake was killed in front of our line today; it was almost 4 feet long and had 7 bells [rattles] at its tail. Before biting, it first makes a noise with the bells so that everyone coming too close can take heed. It was brownish black on the back, beautifully decorated in various colors and with an unusual pattern of scales. It was yellowish-white under the belly and shone as if a ring had grown here against and on top of it [sic]. As beautiful as its body was, its head and eyes were terrible. The head was broad and similar to that of a large toad, the teeth very sharp, crooked and pointed like fishhooks, with which it can do harm when it jumps [on its victims]. Under the tongue, it has a small cyst as big as a hazelnut in which it carries the poison; its flesh is said to have a very delicate taste. Whoever wants to kill a rattlesnake and use the meat must immediately take ahold of the head; for as soon as the snake becomes aware that it is in danger, it will bite itself and die in less than 2 minutes and thus be poisonous. It is very strange that a man who has the misfortune of being bitten by a rattlesnake will - before one hour has passed - fall into a coma, never to wake up again. Within a period of 24 hours, his dead body will have taken on the color of the snake; this proves that it is a very particular poison.[21]

16th   For each squadron of our regiment, 2 batteaux are being taken over the portage so that we can transport the baggage on them; for in the future, we are to march on land. The rest of the batteaux will go back to Ticonderoga. We are here in the district of Albany, which belongs to the Province of New York. Last night, a few more deserters came to us also asserting that many Royalists are staying in the wilderness, who, for fear of falling into the hands of the Savages, are in hiding. A tall and handsome young man, 19 years old, whose home is in Albany, also wanted to change over to us. He fell into the hands of the Savages, who took him in front of the army where they had their huts at some distance. Here, they bound the young man hand and foot and wanted to scalp him; some Englishmen present wanted to witness this spectacle. The Savages, of whom more and more had gathered, were all ready to start the dance customary at this operation. Just as they were about to begin, a few Germans from the Engl. regiments happened to come by and were so horrified at this cruelty that, with the help of the

Englishmen present, they liberated this unfortunate [*young man*], who was half dead by then. He was taken to Lieut. Gen. Burgoyne, who again reiterated his orders against scalping [captives], which he had given more than a few times before. As previously stated, we have Lake George to our right, and are happy that we did not have to cross it.

17th   At about 8 o'clock this morning, just when the guard was standing in front of the line, we heard three volleys of small arms fire toward the portage. Thereupon 4 cannon shots were immediately fired in front of our line not far from headquarters. The army quickly set out in front of the line without striking the camp. The shooting stopped and we soon learned that another 1,800 Savages had arrived, who belonged to the nations of the Mohawks, Ortoguais, Cayugas, Foxes, Onondagas, Senecas, Tuscaroras, Missaragois[22] and Chippewas. They had saluted our camp with their shots, and soon afterwards, we heard their horrible cries. These Savages, particularly the Mohawks, are very warlike and also the most dangerous of all the Savage nations. While the Iroquois have their bodies bedecked with beautiful material, these walk about completely naked and are chestnut brown. It is their custom not only to scalp the enemies that fall into their hand but also to eat them. The other Savages, who had been with our army, stepped aside in fear while looking at them [the Mohawks] with frightened eyes. We learned from our left wing that they had not seen anything of the enemy since the affair at Hubbardton.

19th   This morning, a detachment from the 9th Regiment, as the oldest of the army, went to the Savages' camp as guards to Lieut. Gen. Burgoyne. The detachment consisted of one officer and 50 men with their flag. The newly arrived Savages were to be taken into the service of the King today. They awaited Lieut. Gen. Burgoyne in their camp where they had placed themselves in two rows opposite each other. He arrived accompanied by generals and officers who had been invited to this ceremony. At his arrival, he was saluted by a feu de joie from the Savages and received by their given commander M. de St. Luc, a Frenchman and Chevalier of the Order of St. Louis.[23] He led him [Burgoyne] through the rows to a large arbor that they had made for him, wherein a chair was set. On both sides of the arbor, the Savages had felled large trees, on which the officers took their seats. The Savages lay down in 2 rows at the ends of the trees, on cut branches and twigs; they were smoking tobacco. When everything was quiet, the oldest of the Savages, whom these follow and respect as their superior or king, went to Lieut. Gen. Burgoyne, shook hands with him and talked to him in his Savage tongue; the Chevalier de S. Luc interpreted for Lieut. Gen. Burgoyne in French as follows:

"We have been called by Governor General Carleton to go to war against the enemies of the King, our father. As soon as the season, snow and ice permitted, we did not lose any time and set out in order to show our willingness and loyalty. Since we have inherited the tenet from our fathers to be loyal to our allies, we left our houses, wives and children, starting as early as the 11th of March. Most of us have covered 1,000 leagues, that is 3,000 Engl. miles, in this time. We comprise different nations, to be sure, but are all friends and allies and are of one mind, one mouth and one language, i.e., firmly resolved to serve our King. You see us all here in front of you, say what is your will. Speak, and we shall obey."

Hereupon Lieut. Gen. Burgoyne replied in French:

"In the name of the King our father, I thank you for the loyalty and obedience you have shown toward the orders given in his name.

I likewise thank you and praise the zeal and speed with which you have made every effort to come to us. There are some disloyal and unfaithful subjects who have revolted against the laws and started a rebellion. They have engulfed several provinces in war where peace and quiet used to reign. This is why the brave Mohawks and other nations have been called on to act in concert and to lead these monsters back to obedience. But listen to the will of the common father of us all: He wants to chastise, not destroy them, regard them as children and not as strangers, not extirpate them but offer them clemency. For this reason, it may be permissible that you scalp those whom you have killed in battle and treat them as you are wont. But in the name of my King, I forbid you to practice this on any prisoner or wounded; wherefore you shall have a gratuity for every prisoner you will bring. You ought to regard all old people, women and children as holy and do them no harm. Your wishes and all reasonable demands shall be granted you and I shall take care of you as of my children."[24]

After all this had been explained to the Savages, the oldest Savage, to show his joy and satisfaction, began a war song and while singing, danced past the other Savages. These showed their approval by emitting a sound with all their strength from their chests that is as indescribable as it is inimitable. Hereupon, they passed in review in a fashion just as uncommon. The commander M. de St. Luc came first in a green dress, which was trimmed on the seams with silver fringe; he danced in front of the general with much pleasing deportment in the Savages' fashion while singing a war song in the Savage tongue. Then followed the oldest and all the rest of the Savages according to their rank, all singing and dancing. Since this day was a feast for them, it was being spent with dancing and singing especially since they had been presented with a barrel of rum by Lieut. Gen. Burgoyne. The Savages love to excess all the strong drinks, especially rum. They drink without stopping as long as they are able to and have something to drink; their feasts usually end in bloodshed. Their singing is partly harmonious and rhythmical; at times, however, it resembles the howling of wolves or dogs. They make their music on a round vessel made of tin or wood over which a hide has been stretched; one of them hits the vessel on top with sticks, a few on the side. They carry this type of drum around the circle along with a horn on which they blow while having clubs and wooden swords in their hands. A large knife hangs from their chest [*suspended*] on a ribbon around their neck. They have various dances and their music is somewhat sad and frightening. They only dance on solemn occasions; while dancing, their bodies are bent and faces and bodies are directed toward the ground. Their expressions are very serious and they become angry whenever one laughs at them. It is very strange that, after having been drunk, they do not sober up for 2 or 3 days.

20th   Again today, 46 men, all provided with muskets, have come over from the Americans to us. They are all from the province around Albany. Among them are Germans [sic], whose fathers had been Germans. They assert that if we came to Albany, all the inhabitants would come to us and change over to the King's side. We would find a completely different type of countryside there; they had not believed that there existed such a terrible land as this here in the world; yes, indeed, but perhaps it could be even worse.

21st   All the Savages and a detachment of Canadians departed from here.

22nd   Orders came from Maj. Gen. von Riedesel that 1 officer and 1 noncommissioned officer from each regiment should be sent to Trois-Rivières to take charge of recruits, who had arrived from our homeland; they should also take the large baggage along to the army.

23rd   The Fraser Corps set out toward Ste. Anne [Fort Ann] on land; their baggage was transported on batteaux. The report that our regiment was to be mounted was reconfirmed today.

24th   On their march away from here, the Savages have lost 2 men who had been shot by the Rebels hiding out in the woods. This has rendered them so furious that they complained to Lieut. Gen. Burgoyne about it and asked to be permitted that, of the first captured Rebels falling into their power, they could take three. Of these, they wanted to roast and eat 2; after the third had witnessed it, they would send him back to the Rebels. The answer they got has not been made known. I pity the first Americans that fall into their power; it will be a horrible feast for them, they [the Americans] will not get away without being scalped. The Savage resembles a tiger that is only moved by blood and prey. --

25th   After having taken our baggage onto the batteaux which can go up Wood Creek to Fort Ann, we left our camp at 4 o'clock this morning. We took the tête of the army on the road leading to Fort Ann and had Wood Creek on our left. At 5 o'clock, we started marching with the army behind us. The march went over mountains and valleys, over terrible cliffs and rocky mountains to Jamestown [?], where we moved into our camp. Since the river, on which the batteaux were being pulled by our sick and weary dragoons, is very shallow, these [batteaux] will not reach us today and we had the honor of camping without tents. The campsite, where the tents could have been pitched, would have had to be cleared before. We found a blockhouse here in which an Englishman was living with his family, who had a large stock farm with oxen, cows, sheep, pigs and fowl. In his garden, we saw every possible kind of garden fruit. Those from the 9th Engl. Regiment as well as from the Americans [Rebels] who were killed in action, lie buried here. Since we are not used to marching, our march today has been very painful for us, and many of our men wished themselves back on the batteaux. Even so, we advanced   --10

26th   At 4 o'clock this morning, we set out in the same way as the day before, over rocks and rocky mountains, and reached Fort Ann ,that lies on the other side of the river, at 8 o'clock. We marched across the repaired bridge, passed the fort on our left, and moved into our camp in front of it. Our batteaux carrying our tents could not even reach us today and we camped without tents. Since it had been raining hard this afternoon, it turned out to be a sad night that we were to spend in a miserable state without even the most necessary things. So far advanced   --8

Total --283

27th   Powell's and Hamilton's brigades are camping behind us. The enemy completely burned down Fort Ann. The place is barren and at least 3,000 morgen[25] may have been cleared. One house is still standing, which is inhabited by several women. The men must have departed with the Rebels. There are some good gardens here with all kinds of fruit, and fields with wheat, rye, barley, Turkish wheat [maize] etc. One also sees almost every kind of animal. The cattle are much bigger than in Canada. Although a detachment has been stationed here since the 8th of this month, the dead have not yet been buried. The English dead were burned by a detachment today because the ground was very wet. The American dead remained lying there; this caused a disgusting odor; some of them had been scalped. This noon, our batteaux arrived and we pitched our tents. Because we had no further use for them, the batteaux, being unloaded, were taken back to Ticonderoga by a detachment.

28th   An Englishman killed a rattlesnake today, which he wanted to eat for lunch. I have never seen more beautiful colors. It had 11 rattles on its tail, which means that it was 15 years old; at 4 years, it grows the first.

29th   At 4 o'clock this morning, the army set out; our regiment formed the tête. On today's march we had the pleasure of seeing the first rye fields in America; they almost were like those in Germany. We passed several settlements, whose inhabitants had all fled. The houses were built in German style and covered with shingles. The farther we advanced, the more pleasant was the countryside; the one today was the most beautiful we have yet seen in America. The main road seemed to be quite passable. We have not been used to marching on such a road; we had gotten accustomed to climb nothing but terrible mountains and cliffs in this wilderness.[26] On this journey, I often thought of Charles XII.[27] His march through the Ukraine with his army could not have been worse [than this]. At 9 o'clock, we reached the headquarters of Lieut. Gen. Burgoyne, who was lodging in Jones' House under the cover of the 21st Regiment and the Hesse-Hanau Artillery. About a mile further to our right, there was a wide river, called Hudson or North River, which has a 5 mile portage here so that it is not navigable for the batteaux. Other beautiful houses were standing here as well as a mill in good condition. We also saw many maple trees from which they had drawn sugar in the spring. At about 11 o'clock, we reached the Fraser Corps; we chose our camping place behind them and built huts; yet first, a camping place had to be cleared and leveled. We advanced ------------------15

Total ---298

30th   Last night, our tents arrived. We set out very early. The Fraser Corps had already begun marching before us and, according to yesterday's order, was to occupy the heights at Fort Edward along with our regiment. To the baggage of the Fraser Corps, we attached all the Tories (American Royalists) who were bound to us by oath; we marched ahead along with the Savages. Because it was very foggy this morning, we established a rendezvous. In the woods to our left lay a dead American officer in brown regimentals, red facings and turnbacks. He had been scalped by the Savages and his soles had been detached. I do not know, however, whether these inhuman operations had been performed on him dead or alive, probably alive --- . We continued our march at 7 o'clock and at 9 o'clock reached Fort Edward, which had been demolished by the enemy. Here stood two well-built houses, both 2 stories high, that were painted red and yellow. The first we reached was taken as headquarters by Maj. Gen. Phillips and the second by Lieut. Gen. Burgoyne. Not far from them, we pitched our camp in a ripe rye field. The guards from our regiment lay down in front of the quarters of each of the two generals. The Rebels had camped here; they had abandoned the huts, which they had made of boards and brushwood, and burned them. At 4 o'clock, we had to strike our camp and occupy a mountain lying in front of our line and pitch our camp [there]. To the left of our line, a military road led into the woods; it was said to lead to Boston, which was more than 200 miles away from here. On this road, a picket from our regiment lay down this evening. We advanced --9

Total--307

31st   Today, several inhabitants came out of the woods with women and children and had a great number of cattle with them. One farmer alone had more than 60 head of horned cattle with him. Our Braunschweig regiments continue to be stationed at Fort Ann. All our baggage also continues to be stalled there since we have not yet been able to get it here for lack of necessary vehicles. In the house where Maj. Gen. Phillips is lodging, the English have discovered a cellar with barrels of wine and rum. This evening, 2 cannon went to the Fraser Corps. For additional coverage of headquarters, a picket of 1 officer, 1 noncommissioned officer and 24 men went out from our regiment tonight. By the way, we hear nothing of peace. We are living here quietly and well because we cannot possibly have any want of delectable meat. The woods are full of cattle which the inhabitants, for fear of us, had driven there.

Month of August 1777

1st   Out of the woods, on the road to the left, 56 Volunteers (Royalists, Tories) came today, among whom were many who spoke German because their fathers had been German. They were all provided with guns and wanted to serve the King since, on orders of Lieut. Gen. Burgoyne, they would then be bound by oath [sic]. The order given at Crown Point that, following the signal of cannon shots, the army was to move, was reiterated today. It is to be valid throughout the campaign. Because the enemy is roving near here in the woods, no one is to leave the camp. The Savages have already mistaken an Englishman, who had strayed too far, for a deserter and shot him. Every hour, our men are to submit to a roll call. The Savages have scalped a beautiful young woman, Miss McCrea;[28] she did not live far from here and came from a very good family. Her father, [Mr.] McCrea, was a Royalist. An English captain, who had made her acquaintance here, wanted to marry her and take her [home] with him; tomorrow they were to have been married. This misfortune caused quite an uproar in the army; everyone mourned the fate of this fine young woman. She was not even 19 years old. What cruelty! ---

2nd   Since several of the horses which the Savages had taken as booty or stolen had been bought by our regiment for transporting some of the baggage, the order came today that no one was to buy a horse from the Savages. In the afternoon, we heard small arms fire from the lines of the Fraser Corps and had to make ready to march out. Afterwards, we were informed that it was nothing more than the Savages amusing themselves a little. The General Staff of our Maj. Gen. von Riedesel arrived behind our line at the Hudson River and pitched camp. The general, however, is not expected before tomorrow and will move into the house that Maj. General Phillips left today. Oxen, cows and herds of sheep are on the increase as cattle continue coming out of the woods to us every day. Pork (salted meat from the pig) will be given out again today. They are building a baker's oven in front of our lines.

3rd   This afternoon, the Breymann Corps arrived here and pitched camp on our right wing. An officer and 2 men also came out of the woods on horseback this afternoon. This officer came from New York and had been sent to Lt. Gen. Burgoyne from General Howe.[29] We hope to get some information about our main army.

4th   We do not yet know anything of what the officer from New York has brought us from General Howe except that our main army stands both in and around New York. Our regiments moved their camp to Jones' House.

5th   Even today, nothing else is learned about the dispatch of General Howe except that the officer brought a small, hollow, silver bullet[30] in which were messages for Lieut. Gen. Burgoyne. We have learned that the enemy has abandoned Fort Miller. Two cannon of the Hesse-Hanau Artillery were moved in front of the line of the Breymann Corps.

6th   Many prisoners were taken to Fort St. George. Many batteaux and cannon batteaux have been taken to Lake St. George from Ticonderoga because the Rebels had demolished a great deal there.

7th   The Provincials (Tories) arriving here day after day assure us that the enemy is encamped 30 Engl. miles from here and that the American army is assembling under the command of Maj. Gen. Gates[31] in Stillwater and Halfmoon,[32] where they are heavily entrenched. On account of our continual lack of provisions, we cannot continue our march as yet. Our Maj. Gen. von Riedesel has himself informed the regiment today that it is to be mounted, that is to say, the regiment should mount itself and get the horses, but where? -- It is very hot during the day and the nights are cold and foggy. We saw some swallows here and fewer insects. Since Canada, we have not seen any churches. The inhabitants living here and around Lake Champlain profess the Calvinist doctrine. For lack of churches and ministers, they are neither baptized nor do they take communion. When a couple of young people want to get married, they take each other's hands in the presence of their parents and friends, thus asserting their faithfulness; and that is all. Parents instruct their children in religion as far as they themselves have been taught, expounding its tenets as they know them. Be that as it may, they are people of very friendly disposition who prove through their actions that they are Christians. Most of them are English, but some also Scottish and Irish. The Savages brought some prisoners today, among whom was a colonel.

8th   A detachment, chosen from all the German regiments except for ours, went to Fort George. Our regiment is to keep itself ready to march and so be able to set out at the first order.

9th   At midnight, the standards of our regiment were taken to the headquarters of our general; this is an indication that we are to be assigned to an important expedition. Leaving tents and baggage behind, we set out at 5 o'clock this morning, marched to our left through the camp of the Breymann Corps and attached ourselves to the baggage of the Fraser Corps, that had likewise set out on the march; our march continued along the Hudson River. We found both banks of this river settled with rather well-built houses in German style, which were all empty; the families had fled into the wilderness with all their belongings just for fear of the Germans. The beautiful wheat and rye fields were going to ruin; they were all ripe. We passed several bridges and places where the enemy had camped. We also saw grapes, although not ripe, as well as many bilberries, raspberries and blackberries on both sides of the well laid-out military road. It was noon when we entered the camp at Fort Miller. Here, we composed the right wing of the Fraser Corps and, facing Albany, camped close by the Hudson River, which was flowing on our right. On a height on our left, one saw a magnificent building, several respectable houses, as well as various sawmills and gristmills, which were all empty. We made huts with boards which were lying about in large quantities near the sawmills. We advanced ---18

Total ---325

10th   Today was a day of rest. The Hudson River here again requires a portage of 5 or 6 miles and is therefore not navigable for batteaux. I looked at the beautiful building previously mentioned, which could be called a small castle, and wondered what such a beautiful building was doing in this wilderness. The owner of this house had taken flight to Philadelphia.[33] Brig. Gen. Fraser has moved into this house. Around the house was a plain of more than 2,000 morgen of land, which was nearly all cultivated. The harvest was ripe but had not been gathered. Last night, 2 Hesse-Hanau cannon came to us and were placed in front of our regiment's lines. Lieut. Bach commanded them. Our Major General von Riedesel came to us this morning and had a long conversation with our Lieut. Colonel Baum and at his departure, he left our Captain O'Connell and the English Engineer Lieut. Durnford behind. Among the Volunteers, we also had Colonel Skene with us, who owns Skenesborough, Colonel Förster[34] [Pfister] (a Braunschweiger by birth), and Capt. MacKay.[35] These have been assigned to Lieut. Colonel Baum either as aides or because they knew the countryside around here and could understand several languages, especially English, French and the language of the Savages. Since Lieut. Colonel Baum understood none of all these languages, those men were very necessary for him. This evening, they sent us flour on horseback, from which bread is to be baked tonight. Our corps is designated to advance to Bennington in New Hampshire,[36] destroy the magazine there, and take horses and oxen etc. away from the inhabitants living on the way there as well as in the adjacent countryside. N.B. after we have driven off the scattered corps of the Americans, who are at Bennington. --

11th   This morning, beef and bread were given out. Brigadier Gen. Fraser came a few times this forenoon and talked with our Lieut. Colonel Baum. We set out at noon and our corps, which Lieut. Colonel Baum commanded, consisted of our Dragoon Regiment, not quite 200 men strong; 100 Tories, 100 Savage Mohawks, 100 Canadians and 50 Englishmen from Powell's brigade, that formed the tête of our regiment and were commanded by Capt. Fraser. The Savages were commanded by Capt. Lanaudière,[37] Adjutant of Gov. Gen. Carleton, the Tories by Colonel Förster, and the Canadians by Canadian officers. The two 3-pound cannon were being drawn along in front of our regiment. This was the corps designated for the expedition; the Fraser Corps remained quietly in the camp. We also passed quite a pleasant region, which was cultivated on both sides of the Hudson River. We came to a traverse whose river emptied into the Hudson.[38] For lack of a bridge, the corps had to walk up to their waists through the water, which was a most unpleasant and dangerous undertaking; for the current was so fast that one could hardly keep one's balance. To offset this discomfort, the corps had the delight of seeing the first church since Canada, which lay on the opposite side of the Hudson River. Near the church was a large manor with many respectable buildings, which belonged to Gen. Schuyler. He has been summoned by the Congress in Philadelphia to defend himself together with Gen. St. Clair as to why they had abandoned Ticonderoga so quickly. Not far from this large manor were 5 large barracks of identical construction wherein the workmen of this general were living.

The parish is called Saratoga.[39] We kept the Hudson River on our right and moved into a camp across from the church next to 2 beautiful houses. Some of the corn [grain] had been harvested and stored in the houses, some was overripe and being crushed. They had also started drawing the flax, but had run off. Their enmity against the King of England and the fear of the Germans had driven them away. They were probably roaming around in the woods, for their cattle returned to the house in the evening, but were treated in an overly aggressive manner by us strange, hungry guests. -- They cultivate much Turkish wheat [maize] here and many pumpkins have been planted in between. The gardens are full of fruit [*and vegetables*] especially potatoes, from which one can conclude that we are enjoying ourselves very much. -- Today, Musketeer Fasselabend is to be shot. He had deserted last year, had served under the Americans and had been caught in Ticonderoga. Whether the execution has actually been carried out, I do not know as yet. We advanced --16

Total---341

12th   Last night, another detachment of 50 men came to us; they were from our corps and under the command of Captain Dommes. We set out at 6 o'clock in the morning and marched up a mountain on our left and into the woods. We had hardly covered one mile in the woods when we went back again and made our camp one mile behind the place where we camped last night. The reason for this was a false report stating that the enemy, a few thousand men strong, had occupied a post not far from us. This afternoon, Generals Burgoyne and Phillips came to us, talked a long time with our Lieut. Colonel Baum, and returned to the army.

13th   At 5 o'clock this morning, we set out, marched along yesterday's road and reached the borders of New England at noon. The first village we came to was called New Cambridge[40] in the Province of New Hampshire. Here we took the first horses and captured 6 Rebels, one of whom deserted again. These had been sent out as patrols. We had lost the Hudson River, passed through the wilderness on a rough road, which only last year had been cleared by the Rebels. At 4 o'clock in the afternoon, we moved our camp into this village near a beautiful house. The house stood empty; the owner had taken to flight with his family this morning. Here we came upon a detachment of Rebels that were driven back. Thereby, one Tory was shot through his leg, which I bandaged. This evening, we heard the retreat shot of the American army very far away on our right. We gathered a booty of 15 horses today. This village is large and scattered and was first settled 12 years ago. Our herd of cattle has increased because we came upon some oxen at all the houses we passed. They allowed themselves to be tied and came with us. -- A report arrived that Colonel St. Leger has won a victory over the Americans; I had written about that on June 1. Without a doubt, this is only being spread to inspire our men with courage, for who would want to bring us this news here in the wilderness? We have advanced further toward Bennington by --23

Total --364

14th   We set out at 5 o'clock this morning, reached the parish of Sancoick[41] at 7 o'clock and made a rendezvous near a beautiful house, which the owner had left this very morning. There was little household furniture left in the house but what there was was being destroyed by the Savages. These also discovered a beautiful Engl. clock, several portuguese [coins] and guineas in a chest. The owner of this house, son of a Dutchman by birth, is called Van Rensselaer.[42] He had a gristmill with a sluice near his house. The mill was full of flour and the floor full of wheat and rye; we also found several barrels of salt here. Our têtes [Teten] had driven off the Rebel detachment that was standing in front of the bridge. Thereby one of the Savages was wounded, whom I had to bandage on orders of our commander. At this house, the enemy had just slaughtered an ox; it had not yet been completely skinned. We set out again and marched across the bridge at the mill; at the houses we were passing, we came across some more horses, which we took along. At noon, we arrived at the Walloon [Walloomsac] Creek just before the bridge across the river. We made our camp in the gardens of two houses here. The inhabitants had loaded 2 wagons full of furniture and put 6 oxen to them. They were just about to depart and take flight in the wilderness. But now they had to unload and our commander placed a guard in front of both houses so that nobody could take anything from them. They could safely remain there, for none of our men would take anything from them. Every one of us was happy enough if he could manage all that his shoulders were already forced to carry. But it was the habit of the Savages to scalp and demolish everything.

On the other side of the river stood another two houses at which the Savages, the Tories and the Canadians had taken up their posts. On our left, we had a very high mountain, which extended quite far. The oldest of all Savage Mohawks, whom they venerate as their king, was shot on our arrival at the bridge today. He had ventured out too far, perhaps to take some booty. The Savages were very grieved and sad about this incident. They made a kind of coffin, laid the dead man in it and carried him to a grave 4 feet deep. Carrying his musket to the grave, a detachment of 16 dragoons from our regiment followed. When the coffin had been lowered and covered with a little dirt, the detachment fired 3 volleys. The Savages appeared to be very satisfied with that. On the other hand, the enemy seemed to be alarmed. An enemy corps of some 1,900 men stood about half an Engl. mile in front of us behind a height. Since they had heard the bullets whistle at the burial shooting - the dragoons had loaded with balls --, they probably thought we were attacking them. They appeared on the height and attacked our patrols positioned there. We, the dragoons, quickly took possession of the mountain on our left and our 2 cannon were taken up that mountain. The enemy, still behind trees, however, focused their attack on our right and left wings at the foot of the mountain. On this side of the river stood our jägers and light infantry, namely the detachment that had come to us under the command of Capt. Dommes on the 12th. The enemy sneaked behind a house that stood on the other side of the river, where they loaded their guns and shot at our left wing. One cannon was being directed against this house and fired. As the 2nd shot went through the house, the enemy came out at full speed and ran away. On our right wing, they were likewise driven back and our cannon on the mountain pursued the enemy by the bridge, cannonading them on their retreat. We have seen today how the enemy attacks: either lying on the ground or standing behind trees, they load their guns and shoot. They run from one tree to another and then forward as circumstances demand, and the Savages do likewise. The house across from our left wing, behind which the enemy had hidden, was set afire. On our side nothing [sic] was killed or wounded, but in this affair the Savages had one killed and 2 wounded. I bandaged one of them, who had a bullet in his arm. When I had to cut it out, the Savage behaved rather shockingly and if I had been alone with him, I believe he would have scalped me; N.B. if he could indeed have overpowered me. -- The Savages were so enraged about this loss that they wanted to depart for Canada tonight. Perhaps they thought themselves rich enough for they had collected much money among themselves, also stolen some and sold many horses to officers in the army; almost every one of them had a horse laden with all kinds of stolen goods. The affair had not quite ended when another detachment of 50 men from our regiments came to us; they joined Capt. Dommes. Captain MacKay was very dissatisfied that the enemy had not been attacked and pursued with vigor. "Now they will become bold," he said, "we leave them too much time, for they will gather by the thousands during the night." "I cannot understand," he added, "how one can entrust a detachment to such a man as Lieut. Colonel Baum, who has no military expertise at all, cannot take proper measures, particularly here in the wilderness, and who has no knowledge at all of foreign languages." "How is it possible," he exclaimed, "that General Riedesel could entrust such a ----- man with such an important expedition, who is so coarse and rude and also despises the counsel of those who had been sent along for guidance, assistance and advice..." He said much more which I have forgotten.

Muskeeter Fasselabend of the Regiment von Riedesel has actually been shot by a firing squad at Fort Edward on the 11th of this month. Tonight, everything was quiet. The men were posted behind trees. It has forever remained incomprehensible to us why no picket or even a guard had been posted before the line of our regiment. No sentinel had been posted, -- I thought of Capt. MacKay. Up to here we advanced --------------------9

Total--373

15th   This morning, the attack upon the right wing started again. Under the command and direction of Capt. Fraser, the Tories and a few Englishmen had to lay out a small entrenchment with big trees at our left wing. The squadron of Maj. Gen. von Riedesel occupied it under the command of Captain of the Cavalry Fricke and Cornet Stutzer. A report came that the Breymann Corps was on its way to help us. Would that this be true or that we would withdraw but to the bridge at the mill in Sancoick. We would be much safer there than here where every 40 paces a man is standing behind a tree. The inhabitants living around here come and go through our camp; they will surely give the enemy information of our weakness. Soon I am afraid they will no longer be deterred by our 3-pound cannon but take them and all the rest of us. The Savages are all lying behind the baggage, dispirited; they do not want to go forward. The attack continues the whole day. Also today, we have neither dead nor wounded; the Tories and Canadians, however, have had losses both yesterday and today. We have more than 180 oxen, also the horses are on the increase; the officers have all they need. On our left wing it has been completely quiet today. Every 2 hours, patrols were sent out who have not seen anything in particular up to tonight.

16th   This morning, 100 oxen were sent to our army. Everything is quiet; we neither see nor hear anything of the enemy and the patrols that were sent out have not seen anything of the enemy as far as one hour's march away.

This morning, we took possession of many other horses. All noncommissioned officers of the regiment and several dragoons in each squadron have horses. If this continues, the regiment will soon be mounted. The 2nd patrol that had been sent out from our left wing brought the news that some of the enemy has appeared not far from us in the woods and in the brush. This was immediately reported to our commander. He sent Capt. O'Connell to reconnoiter, who indeed saw men in front of our line in the brush. After he had gone, it became increasingly lively in the brush in front of our line, [a fact] which was also reported by our Major von Meibom. A cannon was therefore requested, which was sent with the reminder: one should not consider a few individuals to be a line or a regiment. The strangest of all was that our commander did not know where we were standing. He had not visited us in these last 3 days and as Adjutant Lieut. Breva had to keep running from one wing to the other, the orders were transmitted through our Auditeur Thomas. -- All the Savages came onto our mountain, lay down behind the trees and refused to go forward against the enemy. Now came the news that the Breymann Corps was very near and would soon arrive. Everyone wished they were here already. The enemy is marching in force against our right wing and it appears that they want to encircle us. There is also some shooting on our right wing. After 12 o'clock, a patrol was sent out from our lines and was driven off by the enemy, who fired at them. Half an hour later, a violent volley of fire erupted against the entrenchment that was occupied by 35 dragoons. Our dragoons fired up volleys on the enemy in cold blood and with much courage, and it did not take them long to load their carbines behind the breastworks. But as soon as they rose up to take aim, bullets went through their heads. They fell backwards and no longer moved a finger. Thus, in a short time, our tallest and best dragoons were sent into eternity. The [German] cannon shot balls and grapeshot sometimes to the right, sometimes to the left and then again forward into the brush. The Savages made terrible faces and ran from one tree to the next. I had chosen a very big oak tree close behind our entrenchment, behind which I dressed the wounded. The Savages also came behind this tree and 4 or 5 of them lying down on top of me almost crushed me to death. From the enemy side, the fire became increasingly heavy and they [the enemy] pressed harder. When the Savages saw that, one of them, probably the oldest, emitted a strange cry, which cannot be described; whereupon they all ran down the mountain toward the baggage. The cannon in our entrenchment was quiet because the sergeant artificer, who commanded it, had been shot; the 8 men at the cannon were either shot or wounded. At the bridge, where our Lieut. Colonel Baum was standing, the cannon and volley fire had ceased. Capt. Dommes, who was covering our left flank and rear, was driven back with his few men and captured; we could see this quite well from our mountain. We were thus completely encircled. We too withdrew now with great speed while I was still busy dressing wounds. Then, following the regiment in a great hurry, I stumbled over a big, fallen tree about 300 paces from our entrenchment. When I got up, the enemy came rushing over our entrenchment and 3 quickly took aim and fired at me. I again fell to the ground behind the tree and the bullets were dreadful, whistling over and beyond me. I remained lying on the ground until the enemy urged me rather impolitely to get up. One grabbed me by the arm and another said he should kill me, whereupon he placed the bayonet of his gun with tightened trigger on my chest. He asked whether I was a Britisher or a Hessian. I told him I was a Braunschweig surgeon, shook hands with him, and called him my friend and brother; for what does one not do when in trouble. I was happy they understood me (Freund und Bruder) for that helped so much that he withdrew his gun. But he now took my watch, looked at it, held it to his ear and put it away [in his pocket]. After this, he made a friendly face and was so human that he urged me to take a drink from his wooden flask. He handed me over to his comrades, who started anew to search my pockets. One of them took nothing but my purse in which, however, were only 14 piasters (specie). He continued eagerly looking for money but then left, whereupon the third began searching my pockets. This one took all my small items as my knife, my paper, my lighter, but he did not find the best; they were so dumb that they did not see the pocket in my overcoat. Thus, I saved my Noble [sic] pipe. If I had put my watch and moneybag into this pocket, I would not have lost anything. Now, they made me sit down on the ground. There was still some shooting down near the bridge and I was terribly worried because I believed myself to be the only prisoner. I blamed myself in my mind for not having retreated earlier and faster, but as some other prisoners were brought to this spot, I was soon rid of my anxiety. These assured me that they all were prisoners and so I calmed down. It is surely true that a man likes to have company in his misfortune, -- and would a man in misery not fall into a kind of despair if he were persuaded to be the only miserable one of his kind! -- When one of the enemy heard that I was a CHIRURGUS [surgeon], he led me behind our entrenchment to dress the wound of his son, who had been shot through the thigh. Now I saw what effect our cannon and musket fire had had, since the enemy had suffered great losses here. General Stark,[43] who in attire and posture was very similar to the tailor Müller in Wolfenbüttel, had commanded the corps of the Americans against us. As he now saw me dressing the wounds of the first, he ordered me to bandage several others of the enemy, but I hurried toward our entrenchment because there were dragoons and Hesse-Hanau Artillerymen in need of my help. But the Americans did not allow me any time but pulled me along by force. We went past the trusty tree that had warded off so many bullets from me. Here I found some of my instruments and bandages etc. in a case. Putting all of it in a bag, I wanted to take it along, but my guide took it away from me and urged me to drink some strong rum with him. All the enemy were very well provided with it and I noticed that almost all of them were drunk. Each one had a wooden flask filled with rum hanging from his neck; they all were in shirt-sleeves, had nothing [to cover] their bodies but shirts, vests and long linen trousers, which reached down to their shoes; no stockings; [in addition] a powder horn, a bullet bag, a flask with rum and a gun - that was all they had on them. They all were well-shaped men of very healthy appearance and well-grown; better than the Canadians. -- We came to the bridge where Lieut. Colonel Baum had stood; our men had taken this route for their retreat and some of them had run through the water. Many had been killed or wounded in their flight; all the rest had been taken prisoner. They [the Rebels] did not capture one single Savage; it is incomprehensible to me how they [the Savages] got through. The unfortunate Tories (Royalist Americans) who were not killed also fell into the hands of their countrymen. Like cattle, they were tied to each other with cords and ropes and led away; it is presumed that they will be hanged.[44] Some of our men who had been wounded were still lying here and there; they will be taken to the houses at the bridge. These scenes can not really be described ---- reading this, the best will perhaps be moved, but it is actually not possible to feel the horror of these scenes. A thought that makes your flesh creep! To see a friend or fellow creature lie bleeding on the ground who has been cruelly wounded by the murderous lead and approaches his death shaking - crying for help, and then not be able, not be allowed to help him, is that not cruel? -- It was past 5 o'clock when we heard cannon and volley firing in the direction of Sancoik. This was the Breymann Corps that had been designated for our aid but unfortunately had now arrived too late. All the enemy ran there from the battlefield and all the prisoners who had assembled here at the bridge were quickly led away. It was 4 o'clock when I was made prisoner; this means we had continually been under fire since 1 o'clock, that is 3 hours. The dragoons had shot their 100 cartridges; in the artillery coffer lay another 3 shots of 174 [sic], that is to say one ball and 2 cartridge shots. We now were on the road to Bennington; my guide kept holding me tight by the arm, particularly when he was noticed by his countrymen. On this road, we came past Lieut. Col. Baum, who was lying completely naked on a cart. He was shot through the abdomen and was crying and begging that the cart should go slow but the men did not understand our language. Consequently, crying and begging were of no use. They speedily went to the parish of Bennington where the cart stopped at a house. We helped him from the cart, took him into the house where we had to lay him on the dirt floor. Since the Reg. Surgeon Vorbrodt also came by, it was the lieut. col.'s order that he or I, one of us, should stay with him. The time had come, however, that his orders were no longer allowed to be followed. The guard took us from him by force. Shaking hands with us, he said goodbye and still charged me and the Reg. Surgeon with several messages for our Gen. Riedesel and also for a person in the homeland. -- We were taken further, and on the way, Capt. O'Connell came to us, who was without regimentals and in nothing but shirt-sleeves. We went past one of our 12-lb. cannon; near it, instead of balls lay a pile of stones because they [the German artillerymen] had been out of balls. After darkness, we were taken into a house where we were to stay overnight. Another 8 wounded dragoons and several wounded Americans were also brought in, all of whose wounds I dressed. To my great sorrow, I learned that my cousin[45] had also been wounded on the retreat but no one could tell me where he was. About one hour later, Capt. von Bärtling sen. as well as the Lieuts. Gebhard and Meyer from our Grenadier Battalion came in and we learned that the Breymann Corps had suffered the same fate as we inasmuch as half of them were fatally wounded or captured.[46] If Lieut. Col. Breymann had hurried more to get to us, not as many men would have had to be sacrificed - and who knows what other unfortunate consequences this calamitous affair may have. - The Americans used to consider us invincible and did not believe they could capture our regular troops, but what will they now say about us! -- Will they keep on running away from us in the future? -- I thought of Capt. MacKay --. From our Dragoon Regiment, Captain of the Cavalry Reinking was shot dead. [The following] have been wounded: Lieut. Col. Baum, shot through the abdomen; Lieut. Adjutant Breva, shot through the joint of his right shoulder; Pastor Melzheimer, shot through the right arm; Cornet Stutzer, shot through his abdomen and leg. The remaining officers from the regiment have all been taken prisoner except for Captain of the Cavalry von Schlagenteuffel, who had remained in Fort Edward, Lieut. Bornemann, who had been commanded to the baggage, and Lieut. von Sommerlatte, who had been sent to Trois-Rivières for our heavy baggage. From the Breymann Corps, Capt. von Schick, Lieutenants Bode and Mühlenfeldt as well as Ensign Hagemann were shot; Lieut. Col. Breymann, Major von Bärner, Capt. von Gleissenberg were wounded but not captured; Lieut. Gebhard and Ensign Specht were wounded and taken prisoner; Captains von Bärtling sen., O'Connell and Dommes, Lieutenants Meyer, Burghoff, d'Aniers and Ensign Andrée were taken prisoner; Lieut. Bach from the Hesse-Hanau Artillery, the Engl. Engineer Lieut. Durnford and Ensign Baron von Salans were wounded and taken prisoner. An enemy major, a very handsome man, who had the command over us, was wearing a Braunschweiger Grenadier's cap on his head, had Ensign Andrée's gorget hanging on his chest and the long straight sword [Pallasch] of our dragoons on his side; with these he was showing off. One can well get an idea of the simplemindedness of these creatures. -- Capt. O'Connell spoke to this major in English, told him how my guide had taken possession of my things, and one quarter of an hour later my guide came and presented me with my things in a most polite manner; they were not embarrassed at all. -- As I still had one pound of ground coffee in there, this was most welcome to me. Otherwise, I was very poor, had no money and no prospect of getting any. [I had] my worst shirt on, the worst articles of clothing. As they had told us we would soon return, each one took his worst stuff along, but now! -- The future frightens me. To all appearances, we live here under a nation extremely enraged, whose language none of us understands; each one is asking what will become of us. -- But we were cheered up a little when we were regaled tonight with beef, pork, potatoes and punch; we were greatly pleased. "Well," everybody said, "I am satisfied if we will not be treated any better or worse during our imprisonment." While we were still sitting at dinner, a man entered the room who sat down at my side and joined us at dinner. This was the American Colonel Warner.[47] After the meal, he took out a small metal box from his pocket, which belonged to me. It contained lancets,[48] that he contemplated with great curiosity. Capt. O'Connell asked him in my name to return them to me. He gave me 6 pieces and the remaining 6 he wanted to keep as something very peculiar. He also had this journal of mine, which he returned to me together with my receipt book. I had someone inquire after the other items that had been in my coat folds, but he assured me that he had not seen the portmanteau. A soldier had given him the box and the papers. Van Rensselaer joined this gathering, whom I have already mentioned on the 14th of this month. He was a captain and, like the others, behaved with extreme politeness and civility toward us, but we could not understand each other. Up to here we advanced ---3

Total ---376

17th   This morning General Stark came and assured us that as much [*of our possessions*] as possible would be brought here and that we would get our lost things back. Gen. Stark had commanded the right wing while Colonel Warner had commanded the left wing against us. We set out and, accompanied by a heavy guard, went up to Bennington. On this road, at least 800 to 1,000 men came past us; mostly on horseback and provided with guns, they went to join General Gates' army. In Bennington, we came upon all our prisoners. All the officers were in the tavern,[49] in a room on the second floor, with a heavy guard in front of the door. The privates were locked in the church and as 480 men were in there already, it was quite crowded. We were also taken to the tavern in the room upstairs. Lieut. Col. Baum is supposed to be very sick and Colonel Förster is also lying in the same house; Lieut. Breva lies mortally wounded in a farmhouse while all the other wounded officers are lying in the tavern. We got fresh beef this noon, which was put in big chunks in a trough placed upon the table together with Turkish wheat [maize] bread. They did not give us any knives or forks and since all knives had been taken away from the prisoners, the meat was torn apart with our hands and devoured by our hungry stomachs; this was a remarkable scene. A vessel with water was placed in the room and each could drink as he pleased. The inhabitants of this province were said to be the worst Rebels; they made disagreeable faces and perhaps did not wish to express themselves in overly refined terms toward us; but to our comfort, we could not understand them anyway. There was no one among us proficient in the English language except Capt. O'Connell and the Engl. officers. Today the following calamitous incident occurred in the church. As the prisoners did not all have room enough for standing, sitting or lying, boards had been laid above the pulpit; the captured Canadians lay on these boards. They may have moved too forcefully whereupon one board broke. Afraid that the Canadians might fall down on their heads, the prisoners pressed towards the door. The guards standing in front of the church and hearing the noise and the uproar, believed that the prisoners wanted to break out. Since they did not understand each other, the guard shot into the church door whereby 5 men were wounded and 2 killed. I and my colleague Sandhagen had been asked for dinner by the enemy's doctor to another house belonging to a capt.; as we were just about to sit down at the table, the noise started. No one knew the reason for this uproar. The people all ran out of the house leaving us alone. Since we did not think we were safe, we wanted to go to our quarters. On the way, we came upon a detachment, which Pastor Allen[50] of Pittsfield was leading with his naked sword in hand. He first started to strike and push us, the detachment cocked their triggers and wanted to shoot. While the pastor was abusing my colleague, someone embraced me from the back and spoke to the detachment. Thereupon the men calmed down and did not shoot. Of his speech, I understood nothing but the word doctor. It was the major, who last night had guarded us not far from Bennington. He saved my colleague from the hands of the barbaric pastor after he [the pastor] had given him 40 or 50 blows with his naked sword. He then led us into the church where, after having tended to those unfortunate wounds, we stayed overnight. If the major had not recognized me in the dark, we would have been out of luck. I have never seen a man so enraged as this noble pastor. Another detachment came into the church tonight, inspected the pockets of all the prisoners and took all bread and other knives that they found away from them; so fearful were these Americans. In spite of everything, our dinner was not lost. The doctor called on us and we ate on the pulpit, [consuming] what he had brought us with great appetite. We also slept there, yet not without chagrin, for my colleague quarrelled with me and was annoyed that I had not, like him, been abused and beaten up by the pastor - another proof that a man likes to have company in his misfortune! -- The pastor's skill had been so extraordinary that all blows had fallen flat in the dark, for my colleague's coat showed no hole, but -- up to Bennington we advanced --4

Total---380

18th   This morning, I again went to the tavern, for we surgeons had yesterday gotten permission to look after the wounded. Last night, there had been another great alarm here. More wounded arrived today but my cousin was not among them. I learned, however, that he lay in the same house where Lieut. Colonel Baum and Colonel Förster were, who both have died of their wounds today. This Förster, born a Braunschweiger, had beautiful estates in the vicinity of Albany. -- One of the enemy doctors was a Mecklenburger, born in Gustrow; he had trained with Municipal CHIRURGUS Fricke in Braunschweig. He said his monthly salary amounted to 60 piasters in paper money; he wanted to persuade me to accept these. I no longer remember what I answered him because I was annoyed. He regaled us with Madeira wine, we became high-spirited, remembered the martial pastor and made a few more remarks about him and his huge wig. The major previously mentioned, who had recognized me in the dark, was again showing off today with the grenadier's cap, a gorget and the short, straight sword of a dragoon. All the Americans who saw him gazed at him in astonishment. -- Several of our officers got some of their baggage back today. General Stark had much captured baggage unloaded on a place near the church in Bennington and each could pick out his own, but nothing of mine could be found. Ensign Andrée had his watch returned; General Stark had sent it thinking it was mine. All the healthy, captured privates were taken away under heavy guard today. One can see that the Americans nourish great hatred against the English inasmuch as they treat them with much more contempt than us. I learned from the German doctor that at our arrival at the Walloon's Creek, the enemy had been no more than 1,500 men strong and we could have advanced up to Bennington without great resistance on the first day. They, in fact, had believed nothing else but that we were 1,500 men strong[51] and had 4 cannon with us. But the fact that we stopped at Walloon's Creek and did not go any further made them think that we were not as strong. This was indeed reported to Gen. Stark by the inhabitants who were going back and forth. Immediately upon our arrival, this general had sent out a summons to this province and the neighboring ones, whereupon the men were slowly assembling. By the 16th at noon, the general had, by reliable report, more than 6,000 men. -- Thus, they could have easily encircled and captured us. Our landlord had 5 sons in that action, of whom 2 were shot dead. All in the house were very sad and our presence was probably very disagreeable to these people. Capts. Fraser, Lanaudière, and MacKay are not here; I hope they are alive, well and safe. Not even one of the Savages has been captured; I cannot comprehend how they got through. Several volunteers from the American coast were also here; very handsome young men.

19th   Several other wounded came today but my cousin was not among them; that worries me a great deal. Generals Stark, Lincoln and Fellows[52] held a meeting here at the tavern this morning together with the Committee from Bennington. The officers and we too had to sign the parole that we would not desert nor talk in any way about the affairs of the war with the inhabitants of the country. More baggage was unloaded, and each one could pick out what was his, but there was nothing of mine there. I was so conscientious that I did not even take a shirt; mind you, I wore my worst shirt and had none besides that. -- Bennington is a village that had been settled but 18 years ago. The church has neither spires nor altar. The inhabitants profess the Calvinist doctrine; they are Presbyterians. We finally set out at noon; most of us, particularly the wounded officers, received riding horses. We had a new captain by the name of Johnson, and a few men on horseback with us who are all under the command of Gen. Fellows, who will accompany us up to Boston. Lieut. Breva remains in Bennington; Lieuts. Gebhard, Durnford, and Bach, Pastor Melzheimer, Cornet Stutzer and Ensign Specht, all 6 of whom had been wounded, went along. Although I was previously to stay in the hospital at Bennington, -- [as it was] my turn and I would have liked to remain there for my cousin's sake, I was ordered to go with the wounded officers. As I cannot stay with him, I warmly recommended my cousin to my colleagues Sandhagen, Radloff and Meyer, who were staying behind in Bennington, and I have full confidence that they will do everything possible for him. Our march went through the parish of Pownal to Williamstown. We were no longer treated as prisoners on our march. We rode and went as we pleased. In front of all the houses that we passed stood people who looked at us with the same intense curiosity as the people in Germany when the first rhinoceros arrived there. We understood no English but they treated us like friends, spontaneously offering us milk and beer. At all the houses there were orchards with trees full of fruit, which although not yet ripe, the inhabitants, especially the children, were eating. Wine and rum were very expensive in this region, each of these cost 3 specie or 3 piasters a quart. Most of us had no money and but one shirt. If this were ever to be washed, we would have to go without a shirt for that period of time. Is that not regrettable? No money and no hope for getting anything, what will become of us? -- Williamstown is a pleasant village and lies in a beautiful valley in between mountains that are called the Green Mountains. We all were quartered here in the inn and received very good food, wine and punch. Gen. Fellows asked the officers to request whatever they wished to have. If it could be provided, they would get it. With this kind of treatment, we could easily have forgotten we were prisoners, but our miserable equipage reminded us of it every moment. Everyone was surprised by the beauty of the fair sex and their dresses in the Engl. style, and with all that, they were but farmers' servants. One noticed but few men or none at all. At most houses, one saw black slaves and many children. We advanced toward Boston --18

20th   At 9 o'clock this morning, we set out and had a bad road ahead and many high mountains to climb. We did not have as many horses today as yesterday and arrived in Lanesborough after a troublesome march at 8 o'clock at night. We advanced ------------23

Total --422
[sic]

Besides the servants, we were 25 men and were quartered here in 5 houses. We received very good food and drink. On our march today, we had seen the first Savages again, disgusting creatures; they were from the Wolf Clan. Our landlady had a child, 9 months old, that she was carefully hiding. I was curious to know the reason and asked Capt. O'Connell to question the woman as to the cause. I was very much humiliated by my curiosity, however, because the landlady said she had heard the Germans were cannibals, slaughtering children etc. When we expressed our astonishment about that, she asked whether we had churches in our country and whether we also prayed! Whether we believed that God was our creator and Christ our Saviour! She had been reliably assured that we were the Savages of Germany. This had been told to the inhabitants to inculcate hatred against us. -- At 6 o'clock this morning we set out, passed through beautiful country, assembled in the village of Pittsfield and had breakfast there. Many fair women and girls came on horseback to take a look at us. They rode like hussars, riding sidesaddle [Engl. woman saddle]. Since Bennington, we have not seen any Germans. Here lived one who spoke German; his father had been Swiss. He was astonished that the King of England [hired] Germans who had to wage war against them [the Americans]; he spoke in an insulting, vile manner - and added that even if the King of England sent another 200,000 men to America, they [the Americans] would kill them all. In good hussar fashion, this man should get 50 blows. -- We continued our march through the parish of Lenox to Stockbridge. We were all placed in a house here. There still are many Savages in this region who do not, however, look as terrifying as the Mohawks etc. But not far from here is a Reformed Church and a preacher. We advanced toward Boston --24

Total--446

22nd   Everyone not wounded is marching to Great Barrington today. Lieut. Bach and Ensign Specht have only been slightly wounded and went along with the Reg. Surgeon Vorbrodt. The other 4 officers, whose wounds had not been as light and who had contracted a little fever on the strenuous marches in the great heat, stayed behind until they would be able to continue. The 5 Engl. officers also remained here. Gen. Fellows had promised that we would be invited to private homes. The preacher from Stockbridge called for our Pastor Melzheimer[53] and Auditeur Thomas and took them into his house. An enemy major by the name of Goodridge had been imprisoned in Québec last year and Cornet Stutzer had treated him there very amicably. For that reason, the major now took him into his house, treated him like his friend and thus paid off his debt. In what wondrous ways men can meet! -- Lieut. Gebhard and I remained all alone; no one took any notice of us. It was already past noon. A group of local people were still drinking some cold punch as seemed to be the custom in this country. One of them gave me the punch bowl, urged me to drink and asked whether the two of us wanted to stay with him; if yes, we should come along. We accepted the offer and immediately went with him. He was a man of 23 years, and his wife was 18 years old. They were very good people who took us in and treated us like brothers. At 3 o'clock, we had dinner that consisted of potatoes and mutton; after that, some raw cucumbers with pepper. We also ate some bread with butter and cheese and drank some punch that had been made of water, rum, milk, and sugar. Our landlord's name is Timothy Wenchel [Winchell]. Stockbridge lies in Berkshire County.

23rd   Our breakfast today was tea, and with it we had some toast (these are slices of white bread, roasted on coals and again made tender with butter); raw cucumber, roasted mutton, butter and cheese. At 3 o'clock, dinner was served and supper was like breakfast.

24th   Today was Sunday. After breakfast was eaten, my landlord urged me to go to church with him. The service began at 10 o'clock. In this church there was no altar either.[54] The preacher had his seat on the pulpit, stepped immediately forward and offered a long prayer during which he did not open his eyes. The whole congregation stood during the prayer. Most people had their backs turned toward the preacher and seemed to leave the devotion to the preacher alone. After the prayer, a psalm was sung by some young women. This was very beautiful music. -- After that, the pastor preached for about half an hour, whereupon another prayer followed and another psalm was sung; with that the service finally ended. But, how uncomfortable I was! It was Sunday, and I wore a dirty shirt. I could not put on a clean shirt because I did not have one.

25th   Since we now are without a guard, we go wherever we want to escape boredom. Our landlord and landlady become increasingly more sociable and amicable; it is only lamentable that we cannot talk to these good people; they would so much like to speak with us. Since I had my shirt washed today, I had to go without a shirt for that time. My landlady noticed this, wept and brought me a shirt that I was to put on; I cannot describe what I felt. Our landlord brought the news that Colonel St. Leger had been beaten at Fort Schuyler [Ft. Stanwix]. One thousand riflemen came through here today who together with many Savages and Blacks, were going to Gen. Gates' army.[55]

26th   My landlord sold me the loaned shirt for one guinea today but it did have to be mended. One guinea is 6 piasters 8 groschen Conv. money. Nothing is more scarce in America and Canada than linen and articles of clothing in general. This is very understandable since for the duration of the war, the communication with England and consequently the import of necessities has been discontinued. The Americans, however, know very well how to help themselves; as they have an abundance of flax, wool etc., they spin and weave their wool themselves; one finds looms etc. in all the houses.

27th   Today when the marching orders came, our landlord did not want to let us go. We should stay 4 more days with him and he would then take us with his horses to Springfield. He urged me specifically to say that the wounded officers were not able to continue their march; but I had already reported that they could quite well ride to Springfield. Thus, we set out at noon and rode to Tyringham. We had so far covered the most abominable road over mountains and cliffs and across forests. We came upon the rest of our officers here, who had arrived from Great Barrington and continued their march at our arrival. We first ate bread with butter and cheese, drank rum punch and then kept on riding. It became very dark, and we had to proceed on the most horrible road through a forest in the most impenetrable darkness. Because of the many cliffs and tree stumps, the horses frequently fell down. We advanced very slowly and arrived at Sandisfield at 11 o'clock at night, where we stayed overnight. On our march today, we saw our first cider presses. We advanced towards Boston -----------------------------------25

28th   This morning we set out again, passed through the villages of London and Glasgow and came to Blandford at 10 o'clock, where we had a good breakfast. At 10 [sic] o'clock we set out again and found open country as we had not seen in America as yet. We came to Westfield, a beautifully settled town of 500 houses. Here we saw the first church with towers and heard the first bell ringing. On orders of General Fellows, I remained here with the wounded officers; the rest continued for 2 more miles. In spite of our having here and there to contend with annoyed faces, we always were given good food and drink. Up to here, we advanced --26

29th   We set out early and three quarters of an hour later, we reached the house where the rest of our officers had lodged last night. We found them at breakfast, which was also quite welcome to us. From our lodging up to here, we had continually ridden among fruit trees. The fruit was beginning to ripen and we ate a great deal of it. After 2 hours, we finally reached the Connecticut River and came to Springfield, where we were quartered at the inn. Gen. Fellows also arrived and ordered the wounded officers, Lieut. Gebhard, Cornet Stutzer, Pastor Melzheimer and me to remain here until further notice. The rest of the officers were to continue their journey to Boston with him tomorrow, up to where they could reckon another 100 miles. We have passed through quite a Garden of Eden today and seen much fruit. From Westfield to Springfield, we advanced -----------7

Total --504

30th   This morning Gen. Fellows came for a visit and again assured us that he would do everything in his power to ease our imprisonment. So far, we cannot praise his kindly attitude toward us enough. Today, all the prisoners arrived here except our dragoons whose whereabouts no one knew. The prisoners will remain here and will not have to be distributed. Each inhabitant took home as many as he had room for. The English remained seated for a long time; in the beginning nobody wanted to take them; they are also being watched and not treated as well as our men. An Artillery officer, a Frenchman, came to our lodging and said he had been in Germany in the last war. Now the King of France had sent him with much artillery to help the Americans. Since he told us such bold lies, he was treated quite contemptuously by our officers. However, who can say for sure that he had not told the truth? -- Such people are probably also among the Americans through whom we have received artillery and ammunition. The Americans could have bought the artillery from France. How did the Braunschweig cannon get to Crown Point? The Americans must have bought these too.

31st   This morning all the officers and privates went from here to Boston. I wished we would remain in our quarters. Our landlord Mr. Stebbens [Stebbins] is such a good man and very obliging. I believe these people can gather from our faces what we want. They never had to ask what we wanted to have, eat or drink. -

Some Germans from Boston visited us and became acquainted with us. They were Rebels and we were not allowed to answer their remarks, which were really very insulting. They worked in the local arsenal and made cartridges day in and day out. Each one received 20 piasters in paper money per month; of rolled gold or silver, little or none. Springfield is a nicely settled town although not very regular [*in its layout*]; yet in between there are beautiful houses. South and West Springfield are separated by the Connecticut River; both sections are 15 miles long and have 4 churches. The Connecticut River is surely twice as wide as the Weser River at Holzminden in Germany, but on account of the many boulders and sandbanks, it is not navigable in these parts for big ships; it is extremely rich in fish and enters the sound not far from New London. From Springfield to Boston are---100

Thus from Trois-Rivières in Canada up to Boston ---604

Month of September 1777

1st   After I had eaten breakfast, a captain by the name of Morgan came in, and because we were to live with him, he took us to his house. This did not suit us at all. Our landlady, Mrs. Stebbins, may have sensed that we did not like leaving her house. She apologized saying that Gen. Fellows had done it because her house was actually the posthouse, but that we should often come for a visit as we had but a little less than a mile to walk to Capt. Morgan's House. We got a room on the second floor where two beds were standing, which were big enough for 4 people. Our midday meal consisted of beef with potatoes, string beans, gourd vegetable [squash], butter and cheese as well as apple wine (cider) to drink.

2nd   Our breakfast today consisted of cold milk, into which pieces of white bread had been cut, apple pie, raw cucumbers, raw onions, no coffee, no tea, nothing fried as at Madame Stebbins; we wished we were back there especially as it did not seem to be as clean as at the Stebbins'.

4th   Captain of the Artillery Sander visited us today and said he would go to the army with 10 cannon one of these days. We daily go into the woods near our house to eat bilberries, which grow here abundantly; we also enjoy eating fruit and drinking cider. The inhabitants do not know of pears, plums or prunes; this kind of fruit is unfamiliar to them. Nobody takes notice of us any longer, we go wherever we want to and do not give much thought to being prisoners. Eating, drinking and sleeping are our daily occupations; the officers as well as the Rev. Pastor Melzheimer are learning some English every day. I do not want to submit to that as yet because I hope that we will be exchanged before winter. Almost daily, people come from distant places to look at us. They are quite surprised that we are in form just like American men but regret that we had come to America for killing them and their children and for making them slaves. Our landlord complained today that although he was in his 60th year, he still had to go to the army. How many children our landlord has, we do not know as yet; we see more every day, big and small and, almost daily, some we have not seen before.

7th   Today, we had the honor of having breakfast with our entire lovely host family. Our little darlings were desperately trying to make friendly and sweet faces. Capt. Morgan has 2 grown-up daughters.

8th   Our former landlady, Mrs. Stebbins, visited us today and reprimanded us for not having visited her immediately as we had promised.

She advised Mrs. Morgan to treat us well since we were upright and good gentlemen. She asked us whether we were satisfied with our food and drink and so on. It is customary that all the meat they cook is put into one pot together with the vegetables, turnips, potatoes, cabbage and other such things, and that the pigs receive the broth; they have never heard of soup. The buttermilk, left over after the cream has been used for making butter, is also fed to the pigs. Their cheese is very good, almost as good as the English cheese, and is made from fresh milk.

10th   The wounded officers are improving and will be well in 2 weeks. One of the Germans, a Hesse-Darmstädter by birth, visited us today and said we should - if possible - stay here. We had it here a thousand times better than in Boston where everything is very expensive. Here, we are getting vegetables for nothing and in Boston, we would have to buy them. He assured us that our men would all be taken onto prison ships in the harbor; the Hessian Jägers, having been made prisoner at sea, were still on board the ships and had to live on miserable provisions. Those were troublesome reports and although I have often wished to see the city of Boston, of which I had heard and read so much in Germany, I now wish to remain here until our exchange; for life on board ship is no good.

11th   Last night, Gen. Fellows returned from Boston. He visited us this morning and told us that all the prisoners, Engl. as well as German, had been taken onto the prison ships off Boston and that all our officers had spent 8 days there. They had now been taken on land to Westminster, 55 miles away from Boston. As soon as our officers were able to start marching, - these were the orders - we should move 24 miles farther to Brimfield into quarters assigned to us. Here, the officers, Pastor Melzheimer and I had again to give our word of honor and sign a writ that none of us could read. Gen. Fellows said the contents read that none of us should remove himself farther than one mile from his quarters but that we could go to church even if it were 3 miles away; moreover, no one should talk in any shape or manner with the inhabitants of the country about the affairs of the war or other matters relating to the war; not get involved in any correspondence and otherwise behave so as it behooves men of our character, being gentlemen. All the servants will be excluded from sustenance and either have to look for work to earn their own bread or their masters have to pay for them. Gen. Fellows rode to Northampton, 17 miles from here, and since some dragoons were there, Cornet Stutzer rode along. The general further told us that on one of these days, it would come to a battle between the American army and ours.

12th   Last night, Cornet Stutzer returned from Northampton. He had much to tell of that town and also about 44 dragoons and 24 of our jägers who were living and very happily working there with the inhabitants. Gen. Fellows had selected 15 dragoons and taken them along to his estates at Sheffield; the inhabitants [of Northampton] did not at all like having to give them up.

Today, we received the reliable report that Colonel St. Leger returned to Canada without having been able either to join up with Lieut. Gen. Burgoyne or reach Albany. The details of this unfortunate expedition are as follows:

Colonel St. Leger had laid a formal siege to Fort Stanwix or Fort Schuyler, as it is now called by the Americans, and its trenches.[56] His artillery, however, was too light to be really effective. The American Governor, Colonel Gansevoort, who commanded the fort, defended his post like a brave soldier.[57] Col. St. Leger received a report that an American general by the name of Herkimer[58] was on his way with 900 militia men from Tryon County;[59] they were said to have much provision to help and relieve the fort. Foreseeing that it would be dangerous if he let himself be attacked in his trenches, St. Leger detached Sir John Johnson with his regiment, some regular troops and most of the Savages, who kept themselves hidden on both sides of the road, and awaited the enemy. One can hardly believe that such an experienced man as Gen. Herkimer should not have known in what manner the Savages waged war or their particular technique in going against the enemy in the woods and in the wilderness. However, without reconnoitering his terrain or sending patrols ahead or to the sides, he blindly went into the trap that had been set for his ruin. All of a sudden, they [his troops] were attacked from in front, from behind and almost all sides with a violent trained fire [Marqueten] and with the first shot, the Savages attacked these unfortunate men with their spears, axes and knives and delivered them a decisive defeat. Notwithstanding this horrible assault, some of the militia men still had enough strength to call to their brothers to retreat whereupon they withdrew onto a height. Almost one third of the corps saved themselves by fleeing during the heat of battle; 400 men were killed, 200 taken prisoner. This successful event was the more flattering to Col. St. Leger because he believed that most of the Rebels in this county had now been put out of the way; there was great joy. Only the Savages had to pay dearly for this victory since they counted 33 dead and 29 wounded. Among their dead were some of their chiefs and greatest warriors, which not only rendered them most unhappy but also so bloodthirsty and furious that the prisoners became unfortunate victims of their savage frenzy. Without their commander being able to prevent it, they murdered and tore them to pieces in barbarous fashion. Not only the Savages had suffered, also the other troops counted losses, both dead and wounded. On the very same day on which the cruel battle took place, the garrison had received news of the aid and decided to distract the enemy in order to help their approaching brothers. Under the direction of Colonel Willet,[60] who was 2nd-in-command, they planned to attempt a well devised sally. He carried out his task so well that they not only caused great destruction in the English camp but also seized various badges of honor and other items much needed in the fort. They also took a few prisoners along and all this without any significant loss. The successful outcome made them so bold that Col. Willet and several officers undertook a far more dangerous feat. With a few troops, he went right through the English camp and trenches under the protection of a dark night, disdaining all the danger threatening him if he should fall into the power of the cruel Savages. In order to call upon the inhabitants of the neighboring regions to relieve the fort and free the brothers, they walked for more than 100 miles through pathless, swampy wilderness where no human had ever set foot. Such an undertaking is deserving of praise even if done by the enemy. Colonel St. Leger did not leave a stone unturned to make the most of the victory described above. He kept addressing Governor Gansevoort [of the fort] in both oral and written form, admonishing him to surrender the fort, promising that he and his men would be safe from the hands of the Savages, assuring him that there was no more hope of receiving help from his countrymen since the entire reinforcement, designed to help him, had been massacred by the Savages. [*St. Leger also asserted that*] Lieut. Gen. Burgoyne was in Albany with his army and had received submission from all the subjects whose territory he had crossed on his march. Then exaggerating his own power, he threatened that unless the fort would immediately surrender, he could no longer keep the temper of the Savages in line. Not only the garrison but all the people, women and children in the environs, would then be massacred by the Savages; but now, they would enjoy all the benefits they could expect from a generous and magnanimous enemy. Colonel Gansevoort answered that he had been entrusted with the command by the United States of America in order to defend this post; he wanted to prove that he earned that trust and defend his post to the utmost without paying the least attention to what eventualities might threaten him and his people. This was what he owed as duty to his country, the United States, as well as to his honor. This was the more remarkable as this fort lay so many miles away and therefore was helpless in the wilderness. Colonel St. Leger got into the greatest difficulty since the fort was better fortified and better defended than he and everyone else would have thought. Being convinced that his artillery was too light to be effective, he tried to offset this shortcoming and decided to move his artillery so close that it had to be effective. Day and night, work was now done again on the trenches etc. The Savages were still unhappy, partly on account of their recent losses, partly because they had not gotten any booty as yet. They had murdered, slaughtered and torn men to pieces, but they had not yet plundered, and the hope and prospect of doing so grew less every day. The character of the Savages is such that as long as they move ahead, i.e., as long as they encounter a state of war where they can plunder, as long as they have no losses, as long as they can murder and scalp, they will be steadfast, alert at their posts and on their guard, showing the greatest courage on every occasion. But as soon as the opposite becomes evident, they will be unstable and fearful to the highest degree. While Colonel St. Leger mustered his greatest effort to move his trenches closer so that they became a real threat to his enemies, the Savages got the news that General Arnold was approaching with 1,000 men to bring relief to the fort. Colonel St. Leger took great pains to dispel their fears and assured the Savages that he would not only lead them in person against the enemy but also take the remainder of his best troops into battle.   In case some enemies should approach, he would show them and their commanders the terrain where they would receive and beat the enemies. He kept on making every effort to calm their spirits when the news spread again among the Savages that an enemy army of several thousand men was on the march with Gen. Arnold. It was also reported that Lieut. Gen. Burgoyne and his army had been massacred. Thereupon, Colonel St. Leger had all the superiors in the camp called together to a war council and particularly those who made the most impression on the Savages, like Sir John Johnson and their chief commanders, Colonels Claus, Brant and Butler,[61] but all was in vain. One part of the Savages left the camp during the time the war council was meeting, and the rest threatened to march unless he [St. Leger] left his camp that very moment and retreated.

Thus the retreat took place very quickly on Aug. 22; it was actually more like an escape whose disagreeable consequences could not be avoided. Tents, artillery and other such items fell into enemy hands and it is quite certain that Col. St. Leger was in greater danger from the Savages and had to fear more terrible scenes from these furies than from the Rebels themselves.   At the departure, one of these Savage nations, the Missaraquois[62] [?], who live in the extreme western regions, were already in the process of pillaging the batteaux that belonged to the army. Both English and American reports correspond in averring that immediately after the retreat, the Savages pillaged the officers' baggage and took everything they wanted. Just a few miles away from the fort, no one wishing to preserve his life would dare to distance himself but a few paces from the army. All Provincial soldiers, as well as Engl. and Germans that were discovered away from their corps, were quickly robbed of their guns and cruelly killed with their own bayonets. As for the succor and the news the Savages were getting, their vigilance was extremely efficient and functioned like that of any civilized nation on the face of the earth. As long as the siege lasted, the Savages always got the most reliable news from each other. Thus, it was quite certain that General Arnold was advancing from Halfmoon up the Mohawk River toward the besieged fort with 2,000 men. To bring help more quickly, Arnold left his corps and made forced marches with 900 volunteers so that he actually arrived at the fort on the 24th, 2 days after Colonel St. Leger had fled. It is therefore solely due to the Savages' watchfulness that this [St. Leger's] corps was not also completely lost. This misfortune and our own near Bennington are proclaimed great victories in America. There is nothing like the Americans' joy and the confidence they set in Providence. "You will see," so they say, "that God is helping us, God is on our side." Gansevoort and Willet, who defended the fort, Gen. Stark and Colonel Warner, who commanded at Bennington, are called the Alexanders and saviors of their country. Every American soldier (they are all farmers) now is proud and has lost all sense of distinction between himself and a professional soldier. Gen. Burgoyne and his army, of whom they had been so afraid, are now not only considered in indifferent or contemptuous terms, but even regarded as conquered. I am annoyed at all these prognostications that I am daily hearing from everybody; "Soon we will also have captured Burgoyne and his army."

13th   The Comp. Surgeon Radloff arrived here from Bennington with 18 slightly wounded and I learned to my sorrow that my cousin [sic], my brother's son, has died of his wound in Bennington on Aug. 27. He had been shot through the abdomen - and has embraced eternity.

14th   Since the wounded, who have recently arrived here, have not all recovered as yet, the local doctors today offered to take care of them in case I have to leave.

16th   The wounded have all been accommodated except for 2 Englishmen, whom nobody wants to take. Comp. Surgeon Radloff departed for Boston with them today.

Our landlord, Captain Morgan, also went away to General Gates' army, which is encamped at Stillwater. I was invited for dinner at the local pastor's. He was a good man; it was regrettable that we could not talk to each other. This was a different man from the martial Pastor Allen in Bennington.

17th   The French Artillery captain departed for General Gates' army with 10 cannon. A grenadier, born in Braunschweig, broke his right leg when his horse fell; I put on the bandage.

18th   The grenadier's leg is very swollen. This day was intended for our departure, but we had to remain here.

19th   The grenadier's leg is not as swollen. In the house where he lies are 3 daughters who constantly wait for his orders and put compresses on his leg. We have been in our quarters for 2 weeks and still do not know how many children are in the house.

20th   At 9 o'clock in the morning, we finally set out. Everyone in the house was crying when we took leave. We went past our first quarters and said goodbye to the Stebbins family. From there, we proceeded to the house where the grenadier who had broken his leg lay. I took off the bandage, the leg was in good condition. I left him in the care of a Doctor Brawer residing in Springfield, who happened to be present and saw how I put the bandage on again. The people in the house were very unhappy about my departure. "Our doctors," so they said, "do not know how to treat such an injury as well as the doctors in Germany. My father of blessed memory used to tell me that." I should stay until my countryman would be well again. These were good people. The grenadier had not worked on these people's farm but on their neighbor's. Since that house was small, they believed he would not get the necessary space, care or food there and therefore took him into their own house and gave him a room and a beautiful bed. During the whole time, one of the family has always sat up with him, particularly the host's 3 daughters. They got up every 2 hours at night and saw to it that the compresses would surely be renewed and asked the grenadier most tenderly if he cared for some tea or wanted anything else. -- Take note, you Germans, and learn to treat your friends as well as the inhabitants of New England treat their enemies! --
When we were taking leave, the woman said we should not forget that we had come to America to kill her and her children or to make them slaves. But we were human. Consequently, they too had to treat us as human, for God wanted that we should love and bless our enemies. "It is punishment enough for you," the woman said, "that you have had to leave father, mother, brother, sister, wife and children and cross the big ocean in order to wage war against a people that has never wronged you. But God is just and our cause must also be just, for God has delivered you into our power. How unhappy we would be if we had fallen into your power." -- I did not take exception.
Thereupon crossing the Connecticut River, we left West Springfield and came to South Springfield, which we thought much more beautifully laid-out. On the local church, I saw the most beautiful doors I have seen in America; also a gallery and the hand of the clock. The houses were 2 or 3 stories high; there were lightning rods on the house tops for which - so they said - they had Doctor Franklin to thank. Since then, all the thunderstorms had been passing them by; before the lightning rods had been put on, a few houses had burned down due to lightning every year, but now the lightning went down along the iron rods whenever a thunderstorm moved over the city. Farther ahead, it looked more like war. Here was a large arsenal, some other houses and numerous forges where many craftsmen manufactured arms needed for the army. On the height behind Springfield stood 24 12-pound cannon on their French carriages; the Rebels had a guard there. About 2 miles farther on, we came upon a pyramidal stone on which was engraved: 96 miles to Boston. Thus, we must have been on the road to Boston since at every Engl. mile of our further marches, we found stones indicating the number of miles to Boston. We arrived at our quarters in Palmer at 7 o'clock; having covered 17 miles, the march had fatigued us quite a bit.

In front of our houses stood a milestone: 83 miles to Boston. For dinner, we had chocolate, bread, butter and cheese. The chocolate was eaten with spoons, everyone got a full basin [Spülkumpen] of it; pieces of white bread had been put into the chocolate.

21st   This morning, we had the same for breakfast as last night for dinner and paid 18 paper shillings, which were here equal to those in gold and silver. These 18 shillings amounted to 4 piasters according to our Convention money. This was enough for 4 people but rather expensive. We started marching and came to milestone 81. Here we left the road to Boston, went across a river on our right and arrived in Brimfield at 1 o'clock. It was Sunday and many people had gathered to go to church. We went to the inn of Major Danielson and the whole crowd followed us. Here we again had the odious pleasure of having ourselves stared at. They viewed us with great curiosity but nothing elicited greater amazement than Cornet Stutzer's big hat. Finally the church service began and we could breathe freely. Brigadier General Danielson,[63] a brother of the major where we were stopped and who also lived here, had informed the inhabitants before church of the reason for our coming, he had intimated that, on orders of Congress, we were to be stationed in this village. General Fellows had written this to the brigadier - so he said - and asked him to take good care of us. The brigadier welcomed us with a punch bowl in his brother's house and drank with us and then took us along to his own house. He was a very civilized man, had studied in New Haven and was a member of the senate in Boston. Although he was no theologian, he like all jurists and doctors in this country could perform marriage ceremonies. After church, the Village Committee (something like a Bauverweser[64]) came to the brigadier and discussed our meals; but since it was Sunday, nothing could be decided today. The brigadier kept Pastor Melzheimer, a Lieut. Thompson took Lieut. Gebhard and Cornet Stutzer and another by the name of Mr. Charman [Sherman?] took me into his house and gave me something to eat and to drink. On this occasion, I had to let myself again be inspected by young and old and by all the neighbors until 10 o'clock at night.

22nd   This afternoon at 2 o'clock, we had to return to Danielson's Inn where the whole community had gathered. But they could not quite agree on who should take which one of us, for it depended on their willing kindness. -- Finally they cast lots. A man, advanced in years, took me and Pastor Melzheimer. My future host, who looked very barbaric and kept viewing me from the side up and down with wide open nostrils, went with me to the brig. gen.'s house to call for Pastor Melzheimer. Here, the brigadier's father and mother spoke with my host and urged him to treat us well since we were good people and Christians. We had been compelled to leave our country and families, which we had surely not done voluntarily. Weeping uncontrollably, the old woman further said to our landlord that he should consider how unhappy we were to be prisoners, and how, through their good treatment of us, his family ought to make our fate easier to bear. God would reward him and his family with blessings. The old man was a nail maker, a native of Ireland, 84 years old, and his wife was 79 years old. Night fell and we still had to march a mile to our future lodging. After half an hour, we finally arrived. As soon as we entered the house, a little girl, almost 5 years old, started to scream frightfully because she thought we were Savages. They had told the people beforehand, especially the children, that we were cannibals, Savages from Germany etc. Yet, before we went to bed, we had already made friends with this little darling. We had cold milk tonight, into which pieces of bread and fried apple had been cut, and then went to bed. Before, kneeling at a prayer desk, our host spoke a loud prayer. All were standing during the prayer with their backs turned toward the father. They did not know the custom of folding hands. -- Our host was called Joseph Hitchcock; the two officers were in the house of my closest neighbor, the Artillery Captain Nicolson [Nichols], half a mile away.[65]

23rd   It was 8 o'clock when we got out of bed, for we had much too good a bed. While still in bed, Pastor Melzheimer had wished for some good coffee but his wish was not to be fulfilled. Our host had already waited for us with his morning prayers. First, he read a chapter from the Bible, then a prayer followed. After the prayer, we were called to breakfast, which again consisted of cold milk, bread and baked apples. What a sad face Pastor Melzheimer pulled! I liked the food rather well and finally it also tasted good to our Rev. Pastor. For the midday meal, we had pudding made of Turkish wheat [maize] flour, which was very hard, but everybody softened his piece on his plate with good fresh butter. That tasted quite delicious. With it, we had beef and pork, potatoes and applesauce, which had been cooked in cider, delicious rye bread and quite good cider to drink.

On Sept. 18th, the Hartford newspaper wrote the following: *'Kingston, Sept. 1. We are credibly informed that Burgoyne, Chief and Director of the King of Great Britain's band of thieves, robbers, cutthroats, scalpers, murderers of every denomination now infesting the northern and western frontiers of several of the American United States, has not only discontinued the reward he had offered and given to the Savages, Tories, Indians, Britons, Hessians, Braunschweigers, Waldeckers and other profligate scum of the human race now in his service, for the scalps they brought him from the murdered and half-murdered inhabitants, but also strictly prohibited the practice of scalping. It must not, however, be supposed that this chief of the ruffian bands was so weak as to be in the least influenced in this prohibition, by any motives of compassion or humanity. -- -- His inducements were purely political; he has found by experience that his rewards lessened the number of his emissaries, -- who not only scalped some of his Tory friends, concealed among the inhabitants, but also scalped one another. A scalping party of a lieutenant and about 30 men, whom he had lately sent out with a large number of Indians, were by the latter all killed and scalped; none of the party has been since seen or heard of, and the lieutenant's hair was known as being remarkably full, bushy and red. We had intelligence from several persons that Burgoyne had laid aside his usual practice of scalping and strictly forbidden it for the future - but we did not know his reason for the prohibition. It is not improbable that he might be apprehensive that some of the dextrous hands about him might take the opportunity at one time or other to slip off his own night cap.'*
[Here follows a translation of the preceding paragraph into German.]

My landlord is 58 and my landlady 47 years old; they have produced 15 children, 9 sons and 6 daughters, who are all still alive. Five of their sons are married and have already begotten 18 children. Their names were almost all taken from the Bible: Joseph, Obed, Nathanael, Elisa, Peter, Heli, Medad, Aron, Zedoc; the daughters' names are Sarah, Ruth, Mary, Bathsheba, Phebe, Junes [sic].[66] Neither our hosts nor their 15 children have had smallpox so far. One finds this [disease] everywhere, while the natural pox [sic] are unknown here; one should be inoculated against it, but people are afraid of it. There is talk of a battle having occurred between our army and the one of General Gates on Sept. 19.[67] It was not clear who had won since both armies had maintained their positions. --

25th   In order to get more information, curiosity drove us to Danielson's Inn today where there was much talk of bloodshed. The Hartford paper in Connecticut reports that Gen. Washington's army was beaten at Brandywine Hill on the 11th of this month and that that army had lost 1,000 killed and wounded as well as 7 cannon; that Gen. Howe was 5 miles from Philadelphia.[68] In an old Boston paper from 1775, I read that the 13 United Provinces had established [*the following*] battalions: New Hampshire 3, Massachusetts Bay 15, Rhode Island 2, Connecticut 8, New York 4, New Jersey 4, Pennsylvania 12, Delaware 1, Maryland 3, Virginia 15, North Carolina 9, South Carolina 6, Georgia 1; all in all 83 battalions, each 650 men strong. Congress promises [*the following number of morgen of land*] after the end of the war: to a colonel 500, a lieut. colonel 450, a major 400, a captain 300, a lieut. 200, an ensign 150, every noncommissioned officer and private 100. The land is now covered with good, standing timber but could be cultivated. We received the very unpleasant news today that Forts St.

George and Ticonderoga were in American hands again. It surely is hard to believe because if so, our baggage would be lost.[69] -- Since dysentery is raging here and a 10 year old girl, a friend of our landlord, has died from it and is to be buried today, we 4 prisoners also had to attend the funeral. We went to the house where the body was laid out. The people surrounded us and, as usual, they looked at us with great curiosity. As always on these occasions, we made very serious faces. The village pastor, Mr. Williams, a man of 26 years, came to us, was very courteous and urged us to visit him.[70] He thereafter spoke to the inhabitants [admonishing them] to treat us politely for we came from a country famous for its good manners. -- People lived there according to Christian principles and our EXERCITIUM RELIGIONIS [religious exercise] was essentially the same as theirs. It could really not be assumed that we had undertaken such a long voyage across the great ocean of our own free will. -- Thereupon, the pastor urged us to come into the house and here we encountered even more people, all dressed in their everyday clothes. The pastor knelt at his prayer desk and said a long prayer; then, the troubled people went outside and looked at the dead child, who only now was put into the coffin. This was a coffin of boards nailed together in the same way the Jews do it. Then the coffin was taken in front of the door, nailed shut, placed on a plain bier and carried away. All the people present, at least 100 in number, and the preacher followed the body either on horseback or on foot; all wore their everyday clothes; only the preacher had put a black coat over his white working outfit. We came past a merchant's house and the merchant joined in behind the bier in his multicolored lounging robe. The child's parents also followed in their everyday attire. We came to the churchyard, the coffin was quietly interred but, as I noticed, not before having stopped at every grave. These people do not know of mourning clothes; since these are unnecessary and superfluous, I wished someone would initiate this custom in Germany; after all, I am well aware that many a family faces the greatest embarrassment when one of them has died. -- However, much may have changed during our absence. -- Our breakfast and evening meals always consist of milk, bread and a baked apple, which surely is a delicate meal.

28th   We went to church with our landlord. The service was the same as in Stockbridge and Springfield; they call themselves Calvinists or Presbyterians. -- They sent us some baggage from our army today; the wagon had departed from Saratoga on the 9th. People were again summoned to military service; they were to be sent to Gen. Gates' army. My landlord already has 2 sons in Gen. Washington's army and has to give up another.

29th   Those levied departed for the army; like all the others, my landlord's son Medad went for one month.[71]

30th   During the day, the weather is almost always fair and warm, but the nights are quite cold. But after all, tomorrow will be the 1st of Oct.! -- We went on a very high and rocky hill today, a good mile from our lodging, and had an extremely beautiful view from up there. We could look far around us and I believe we could see the mountain range near Albany etc.[72] I cannot imagine mountain ranges on any continent like those in North America. Brimfield and Springfield lie in the County of Hampshire in the Province of Massachusetts Bay in New England. That which is called New England consists of 4 provinces: New Hampshire, Massachusetts Bay, Connecticut, and Rhode Island. Boston is the capital of these; in addition, each of these 4 provinces has its own capital.

The local inhabitants tell us that the Americans have taken 160 prisoners at Fort St. George....is this true? As it now begins to get colder, we are becoming increasingly anxious as we are very badly supplied with clothing. The houses are very well constructed according to salutary tenets: the wind can blow through on all sides; there are fireplaces but no stoves! I wished we were through the winter at the end of this month.

Month of October 1777

Our landlord has very many apples and makes cider from most of them; the inhabitants do not know pears, plums, prunes etc. My landlord has more than 500 morgen of land incl. his garden and his woods. From these he scarcely gets as much produce as he needs for his consumption; the land is being badly cultivated. They are raising much Turkish wheat [maize] here, which is mixed with rye flour to bake bread. They have all kinds of field and garden fruit and vegetables but do not know lentils or broad beans. We do not know what to do to pass the time. If only I had the books I left behind! Now I am sitting and sweating over English books - I am without a grammar, a dictionary etc. The Engl. language is so difficult, it is so hard to learn; the pronunciation in particular is very difficult. Nevertheless, we are put in a situation where we do have to learn it so that we can speak with the people. We were asked for dinner at Mr. Williams' today; we were well entertained and he urged us to visit him more often. Weather permitting, we will surely do so although he lives about a mile away from us. He is a very kind man and looks very much like the Jew Moses Grünhut in Wolfenbüttel.

3rd   The Hartford newspapers reported today that a battle had taken place between our army and that of General Gates. Our army had thereby suffered very heavily but the Americans had not lost more than 50 men and remained masters of the battlefield.[73] [They furthermore reported] that the Americans had reconquered Forts Miller, Edward, Ann, St. George and Skenesborough, as well as reoccupying the French lines at Ticonderoga. If this is true, then Lieut. Gen. Burgoyne has lost his communication with Canada.[74] In beautiful weather, we climbed today on the same mountain [that we had climbed on Sept. 30].

5th   Today again as almost everyday, somebody dies of dysentery here. Nothing is more surprising in this country than the great harmony between parents and children, and this is also the case in my lodging. They do not even know what quarrelling is. The oldest daughter gives a command to the youngest and she does it; this one in turn gives an order to the oldest and, without a frown, she does what she is told. In the morning after everybody had gotten up and at night before they go to bed, the whole family of the house, to which we belong, gathers. As I have mentioned before, the father then reads a chapter from the Bible and afterwards says a beautiful prayer aloud. The entire Sunday is spent by young and old in reading and praying. Buying and selling or travelling on Sunday is considered a sin by the inhabitants unless it is a situation of dire necessity. In that case, the traveller has to have a license from the Village Committee, otherwise he will be arrested. For there is a warden in every village that arrests any traveller who is caught without a license. He takes him to church and, after charging him with some contribution for the poor, lets him resume his journey on Monday morning. On the other hand, physicians are allowed to travel in order to visit the sick. Nor will anyone go to the village inn for a drink on Sundays. Card playing as well as all games are considered sinful; if anyone plays cards, curses or swears on a Sunday, he will have to pay penance in public. In spite of all this, going to church seems to be a mere habit for most of them, for they neither sing nor pray. Eight or 10 men and women do the singing, the rest look at each other. All those not living near the church come on horseback, men and women; often 2 sit on one horse, the woman behind the man. The women usually ride sidesaddle. The horses are in small or large stables, many of which have been built there [by the church] for this purpose. Those living far away generally stay in church in summer until both services are over and then eat a piece of bread and cheese in the church. The Hartford newspapers report as certain that General Lincoln as well as Colonels Brown, Johnson and Woodbury have been detached [from Gates' forces] with 500 men. They had arrived on the upper end of Lake George on Sept. 17, made a surprise attack on 4 English and 6 Canadian companies and taken them prisoner. In addition, they had captured an armed sloop, some cannon batteaux and 200 other batteaux together with seamen, sailors and others that had been ordered there. They had then taken all the cannon out of the sloop and the batteaux and fired them against Ticonderoga; subsequently, they camped in the French lines and invited Ticonderoga [to surrender].

They had gotten nothing but a contemptuous reply from the commander Brig. Gen. Powell, whereupon they had attacked and stormed Ticonderoga and Fort Independence for 4 days in succession. They had been beaten back every time with some losses and since they were lacking all the necessities to undertake a formal siege, they have given up hope of reconquering this fortress this year. Everyday, the reports from our army are getting more unpleasant.[75] --

8th   Capt. Nicolson's [Nichols'] son has written a letter from the French lines before Ticonderoga on Oct. 1, in which the above report is reconfirmed. Since the troops are completely useless there, they daily wait for the order to withdraw. I have some hope therefore that our baggage has not been totally lost.

9th   Two reports came today, one good and one very bad. The first, that General Howe has taken Philadelphia and made very many prisoners, caused us much enjoyment.[76] The second was brought to us by a man from Gen. Gates' army, who assured us that Gen. Burgoyne and his army were surrounded and since he [Burgoyne] was lacking supplies, his army would soon have to surrender. That General Burgoyne does not have abundant supplies is quite probable, but how could this general have ventured so far that his communication with Canada was cut off! --
Everything has become very expensive here; a himten [2/3 bushel] of salt e.g. was sold here for 3 shillings, i.e., 18 groschen Conv. money before the war; now one himten costs 20 piasters or 120 shillings and so everything is very expensive. The reason is probably the paper money: one gets 3 piasters for one silver piaster. We see many kinds of paper money [but only] one kind of Continental money. One 3 piaster bill carries an emblem, which I wish to describe briefly: a heron is flying in the air and a hawk is swooping down on it for a kill but the heron turns about in the air and on its back tries to bite the hawk with its beak. The heading is EXITUS IN DUBIO EST (the outcome is in doubt). Thus every bill has its emblem, and many of them have been very well thought out and are very appropriate.
The Connecticut papers say that the American Congress has left Philadelphia and gone to Yorktown in the Province of New Jersey. This assures us that Philadelphia is in possession of the English.

12th   Today, my landlord received a letter from his son, who is in General Gates' army, dated Stillwater, Oct. 2. This now gave us the absolute certainty that Gen. Burgoyne and his army have been surrounded and that there is a great want of supplies; that an action occurred on Sept. 19 without either of the two armies changing its position, and that Gen. Howe has beaten Gen. Washington; again, good and bad news. As I was walking about in the garden, taking a leaf to my mouth and whistling on it, the whole household, old and young, surrounded me, amazed about the leaf music. The neighbors learned of it and came over to hear me whistle. They call it leaf singing - if only the news will not spread.

13th   Brig. Gen. Danielson lost his wife and 2 daughters from dysentery. Going for a walk today, I was called into some houses to "sing on the leaf" and I had to comply. Lieut. Gebhard, Cornet Stutzer and Pastor Melzheimer have now recovered. Lieut. Gebhard continues to have the bullet in his body.

14th   Today, the news arrived that a very bloody battle has been fought between our army and that of Gen. Gates on the 7th of this month. The outcome has been in doubt but our army is surely surrounded and my landlord has assured me that they would soon capture Gen. Burgoyne and his army.[77] The good man! Would that he lied this time! --

15th   Today, all 4 of us were again at Mr. Williams, who entertained us very nicely. He said he had heard that we sang so well and - we had to perform for him. We are everywhere being pestered with singing; this will soon be a big burden for us, for the inhabitants are travelling for many miles to hear us sing. There are not only young and fair maidens among them, but also old men and women, some of them looking at us through their eyeglasses.

16th   Today turned out to be a perilous day for me. Pastor Melzheimer wanted to take a walk after the meal when we were suddenly attacked by a number of boys who, making a circle around me and giving me leaves, forced me to sing. Soon, I shall have to stay home if I do not want to expose myself to that type of peril. -- Like all the New England villages, Brimfield consists of 7 square miles, has 200 inhabitants at present, who multiply every year. There are very many sweet chestnut trees in the woods here that seem extraordinarily heavy-laden and ripe, so that one could easily collect several himten underneath a tree; most of these, however, are immediately eaten by gray squirrels or pushed by them into their nests for the winter.

17th   The Hartford paper says that Brig. Gen. Fraser has been killed and aide-de-camp Clerke has been wounded and made prisoner of war.[78]

19th   Tonight, we received the sad news that our army has been captured at Saratoga. Therefore, they made a feu de joie with cannon in Springfield.

22nd   It has been confirmed that the army under Gen. Burgoyne has been captured and the Convention[79] with its 13 articles concluded: these facts are no longer in doubt.

23rd   Moreover, my landlord's son Medad has returned home tonight and told everything in great detail; how retreating from Freeman's Farm to Saratoga, Gen. Burgoyne had ordered tents and baggage burned and he (Medad) believed that much of it has been submerged in the Hudson River. The news is spreading that our captured army is to march to Boston and, according to the Convention, is to embark there and return to Europe.

29th   News comes from everywhere that our army is expected in Springfield.

30th   Today came the report that our army will arrive in Brookfield tomorrow. Since this is only 10 miles away from here, I left here the

31st   on horseback at 8 o'clock this morning but learned on the way that the German troops were expected in Brookfield but 2 days hence; thus, I rode back again.
From the Boston newspaper of Oct. 25, I have translated the following from the English: *One can justly compare the Americans to sheep, the English to dogs, the French to foxes, the Spanish to wolves and the Germans to bears. The naiveté and innocence of sheep makes a fair allusion to Americans just as the English in their wildness are likened to a pack of dogs. -- These do not protect the innocent out of magnanimous instincts or duty but, bloodthirsty with their barking, summon their murderous neighbors, the Hessian goats with their long hair and long, stinking beards, the Braunschweig, Waldeck, Hannover and Ansbach bears. All these are rapacious beasts, over whom avaricious and cruel instincts have great power; they have been hired by the British dogs to devour the herd and take part in the mangling. -- Yet, oh miracle under the sun, these impudent Engl. dogs and even more arrogant German fools have been captured by the lambs and a small number of sheep are taking an army of them* (dogs) *to Albany.*

Month of November 1777

1st   We learned today that our troops will spend tonight in Palmer and march to Brookfield tomorrow.

2nd   In pleasant weather, I rode to Brookfield this morning and on the road to Boston, I came upon a few stragglers from the Regiment von Riedesel, who told me that our General von Riedesel was about half an hour's march ahead; I soon caught up with him. The general was surprised to see me since the news had been spread in the camp at Fort Edward that I had been shot dead at Walloomsac Creek; but this had been my unfortunate cousin. I expressed the wish to return to Europe in case the army was to embark in Boston and set sail from there. The general replied that I had to have patience until the prisoner exchange, - we were prisoners according to the Convention and it was not certain when we would leave America. Yet, this could soon change. I also learned that our baggage has been sent back to Canada and that Captains MacKay and Fraser were still alive. On orders of our general I had to stay in Brookfield tonight. Our corps also remained there and camped in open air in the woods. I further learned that General Schuyler's estate at Saratoga had been destroyed and all the buildings burned;[80] that at the affair at Freeman's Farm on Oct. 7, where Brig. Gen. Fraser had been shot, Lieut. Colonel Breymann had also been killed; that Lieut. Colonel von Speth, Lieut. Häberlin and Ensign Denicke had likewise been taken prisoner that day; also that Corporal Voges from the Reg. von Riedesel had been scalped by hostile Savages on that same day. All the officers of our Jäger Company were present [in Brookfield] but not more than 9 privates. Of our Light Infantry Regiment von Bärner, there were only 3 officers, namely Lieuts. von Gladen, Fricke and Rhenius and about 100 privates; the Grenadier Battalion had 160 men. The sick and those detached from the Dragoon Regiment and left behind at Fort Edward, had been mounted; the remainder of the regiments, i.e., von Riedesel, [von] Rhetz, Specht, and Hesse-Hanau, were in good condition and although not complete, they were in rather good spirits etc. --

3rd   I rode back to Brimfield today; we read the following in the Boston newspaper:

Articles of the Convention between Lieut. Gen. Burgoyne and Maj. Gen. Gates:

Art. 1   The troops under Lieut. Gen. Burgoyne will march out of their camp with Honneur de Guerre [with honor of war, i.e., in all honors] and [move] the artillery out of its retrenchment up to the river where the old fort used to stand; there, on orders of their officers, they will pile up their guns.

Art. 2   The army under Gen. Burgoyne will be given free passage under the condition that as long as the present war lasts, they will not serve in North America; Boston harbor is assigned for entry of the transport ships, which General Howe will send.

Art. 3   Should there be a cartel at which Gen. Burgoyne could exchange a part of his army, then the above art. will be null and void as far as the exchange is concerned.

Art. 4   The Burgoyne army will march on the shortest and best way to Massachusetts Bay; in order that the troops' marching not be delayed and, when the transport ships arrive, the army can depart immediately, they are to be quartered around Boston as closely and properly as possible.

Art. 5   As long as they are on the march and in their quarters, the troops will be provided, on General Gates' orders, with the same type of provision that his own troops receive; the officers will be furnished with as much forage as is necessary for their horses and cattle according to the usual ration.

Art. 6   All the officers are permitted to take along their vehicles, packhorses and other animals; no baggage shall be stopped or searched. Gen. Burgoyne gives his word of honor that no war implements will be enclosed. Gen. Gates will take care that this article will be duly followed. Should some vehicles be needed on the march to transport the officers' baggage, they will be provided if at all possible and in accordance with the authorized rate.

Art. 7   On the march and during the troops' stay in Massachusetts Bay, as far as circumstances allow, the officers will not be separated from their men and quartered according to their rank; they shall not be hindered from coming together with their soldiers for roll call and other routines connected with regular services.

Art. 8   All the corps in Gen. Burgoyne's army, be they sailors, batteaux men, laborers, [Schatzgräber 'treasure-diggers'], drivers, independent companies and other followers of the army, wherever they may be, shall also be considered British subjects and included in these art. in every respect.

Art. 9 All the Canadians and all such persons belonging to the Canadian staff regiments as sailors, batteaux men, laborers, drivers, independent companies and other followers of the army, who do not fit under any particular art., are permitted to return to Canada and will be taken on the shortest way to the first Engl. post on Lake George as soon as possible. They will be provided with the same supplies as the other troops and are duty bound not to serve in the present war anymore.

Art. 10 Passports shall immediately be granted to 3 officers whose rank may not exceed that of captain, whom Lieut. Gen. Burgoyne is to appoint himself, to take dispatches to Gen. Howe, Gen. Carleton and via New York to England; General Gates promises by public trust and international law that these shall not be arrested. After recovering the dispatches, these officers will be able to depart immediately and travel on the shortest route and in great comfort.

Art. 11 As long as the troops stay in Massachusetts Bay, the officers will go out on parole and bear their side arms.

Art. 12 Should the army under Gen. Burgoyne find it necessary to send to Canada for clothing and baggage, that will be granted in the best possible way as will the passports.

Art. 13 These art. will be signed by both parties and exchanged at 9 o'clock tomorrow morning; the troops will march from their camp at 3 o'clock in the afternoon. Saratoga, Oct. 16, 1777. Lieut. General Burgoyne. Maj. General Gates.

5th   We hear from Ticonderoga that Gen. Carleton has arrived there with a few trains [artillery or supplies] and men in order to defend these posts; another report states that Colonel St. Leger has thrown himself with his corps in.[81] The *Invincible* was 3 times beaten back in a storm.

7th   Having inspected our troops, Lieut. Gebhard returned home today and we learned that they would not depart for Europe this year but be quartered in the barracks on the so-called Winter Hill near Cambridge, 3 miles from Boston, until next spring; one also presumes that a general exchange will be brought about this winter and that we will then all return to Europe.

Each inhabitant slaughters his own animals, yet they let all the blood run into the ground and know nothing of wurst making. They make a kind of fried sausage [Bratwurst]. The meat for these sausages is cut and not chopped; they are neither familiar with blood sausage nor with liverwurst; to eat blood would anyway be a sin. The Germans eat blood; so the inhabitants say: that is why they are so cruel. -- Nor do the inhabitants know that sheep can be milked. They are surprised that in Germany people make cheese and butter from sheep milk; the cheese they make of cow milk is good yet not as good as the Eng. cheese. All the cheese is made from fresh milk here while the sour milk, from whose cream they had made the butter, is given to the pigs, which also get all the meat broth. Since soups are not eaten here, one often finds oversized piglets weighing 150 lbs., that are not even one year old. The pigs are fed and fattened with Turkish wheat [maize], which is much cultivated here.

9th   In the local church, holy communion was celebrated without any ceremony today; my landlord is church warden and sent many pewter tankards partly with, partly without lids to the church this morning; the white bread that my landlady baked yesterday was cut into pieces and put into bowls. Below the pulpit was the church warden's pew; close by was a folding table with hinges that was opened up and served as altar. Tankards and bowls were set on this folding table. After the sermon, the pastor came down from the pulpit to the church warden's chair, offered a short prayer and filled the tankards with wine. The 2 elders took the bread and offered it to everyone, whereupon each one broke off a piece and ate it. Women, who had their children with them, also shared some with them. After that, the elders carried the tankards around to the pews and all drank to one another. The minister then offered another prayer and at the end, they sang a psalm.

10th   From the Hartford newspaper on Tuesday, Nov. 4: *'In the northern part of America, we took the following prisoners this year: six generals namely Lieut. Gen. Burgoyne, Maj. Gen. von Riedesel, Maj. Gen. Phillips, Brig. Gens. Hamilton, von Gall, Specht, together with 6 members of Parliament, who were in the suite of Gen. Burgoyne: among those surrendering were 2,442 British officers and soldiers; 2,189 Germans: 1,100 Canadians, Tories and so on, sent to Canada; 598 sick, 528 wounded; 400 [who had been made] prisoners before the surrender, 1,220 men captured and killed near Bennington; 600 men killed between Sept. 17 and Oct. 16; 415 men taken prisoner at Ticonderoga, 300 men at Fort Schuyler and at General Herkimer's action - 9,792 men all together. Furthermore, 37 metal [sic] cannon with all their appurtenances, 5,000 guns, 400 saddles with all the accessories, a good supply of ammunition, wagons and harnesses; 6 field cannon captured near Bennington, 6 of the same at Fort Schuyler.'*

N.B. Here are some inaccuracies, for the army has never been as strong without the Savages; at Bennington, they did not capture more than 4 cannon, i.e., 2 from us and 2 from the Breymann Corps. Besides, nearly 10,000 prisoners and only 5,000 guns? That would be strange indeed! After all, every man carried a gun, didn't he?

According to the report submitted to Gen. Burgoyne, his army has lost the following as prisoners of war, wounded or killed in the last unfortunate campaign before the surrender at Saratoga: 36 officers killed, 63 wounded and 47 captured; 1 regimental surgeon and 7 company surgeons captured; 27 sergeants and noncommissioned officers killed, 61 wounded and 73 captured; 4 drummers killed, 13 wounded and 24 captured; 426 privates killed, 474 wounded and 1,024 captured - 2,280 men all together.

It is getting cold; if we only had a simple German stove made from Dutch tiles! --

12th   From the Worcester newspaper we learned that a corps of English soldiers and Hessian Jägers, 2,400 men strong, had sailed up the Hudson River in 32 transport ships under the command of Lieut. Gen. Sir Henry Clinton to join up with Gen. Burgoyne. They took Fort Montgomery on Oct. 6, demolished it and crossed from there over to the other side of the Hudson River, burning down the beautiful city of Esopus [Kingston] so that not one single house remained intact. Before that, they had taken Forts Clinton and Constitution and demolished them; they burned down the newly built city of Continental Village [3 miles north of Peekskill], and although being only 40 miles away from Albany, they embarked and sailed downstream to New York again.[82] Nobody can give the reason why this corps did not advance to Albany and bring help to Lieut. Gen. Burgoyne, who was so ardently hoping for rescue; and this the more so as they [Clinton's force] had seapower with them, e.g,. several frigates under the command of Sir James Wallace. From the 3 demolished forts, the English took 67 cannon, much ammunition and many supplies. The fleet also burst through the large chain that had been manufactured by the Americans with great toil and a cost of 70,000 pounds sterling[83] and took parts of it away. This chain had been drawn across the Hudson River to block the passage to Albany. Sailing on a frigate, to which a kind of saw was attached, Sir James Wallace burst this chain when he went in strong wind and in full sail against it. This expedition under Lieut. Gen. Sir Henry Clinton has caused great, sheer indescribable destruction on both sides of the Hudson River. Posterity will be terrified and shudder [*seeing it*].

My landlord complained today that General Washington had sent an army corps to take Rhode Island and New York, but that this expedition had been unsuccessful. The cost for it has amounted to 30,000 piasters a day and nothing had come of it. He was scratching himself behind his ears [sic] because he knew that he had to contribute to it. -- The continual NW wind renders everything very cold. None of the animals, cows, sheep, pigs etc., are put into a shed but have to roam around in the snow day and night.

That keeps the animals healthy. Nobody in this country knows anything of cattle disease or the fact that sheep can get pox.

17th   Pastor Melzheimer and I were asked to a wedding today. A relative of my landlord wanted to get married on the day of public repentance, which will be celebrated on the 20th of this month. The days of public repentance are made known in the newspapers every year. They usually celebrate the day of public repentance but once a year and that after the harvest. Persons wishing to get married are not proclaimed from the pulpit, but both names are written on a slip of paper and nailed on the church door, where they remain for 2 Sundays. The Connecticut papers say that the English have left Ticonderoga and withdrawn to Canada. Before [*the withdrawal*] they demolished all the fortifications, burned all the houses and barracks; they have taken all the cannon and ships along. The Boston papers say that the Americans have captured an Engl. merchant vessel, which had merchandise on board, valued at 20,000 pounds sterling, and which was en route to Halifax in Nova Scotia. Furthermore: Letters from Germany report that customs officials of His Majesty the King of Prussia stopped some ducal troops destined for America and demanded from them the same passage money that has to be paid for all the cattle about to be sold.

20th   Everywhere, thanksgiving was celebrated for the harvest, and Congress had sent orders to all the ministers to give particular thanks for the victories that had been won. Mr. Williams especially mentioned in both his prayer and his sermon that the American troops had captured an entire army - he should have added, that 50,000 men had captured 5,000.[84] Nevertheless, he prayed at the same time for the King of England that God may preserve this King and his empire from downfall. A big dinner was served in my quarters today; three kinds of roasts were set on the table, spring chicken pies and all kinds of pastry. This was more than could be expected from a farmer. This day, called Thanksgiving in the English language, is the only feast day in the entire year. In the evening at sunset, we went to the wedding. The young men who were invited had to call for the invited young women; the bridegroom had decided beforehand which young man should call for which young woman. Each one came on horseback and had his girl behind him on his horse. We went to call on Pastor Williams and found Major Morgan and Merchant Hitchcock there, with whom we set out on foot to the wedding house. Mr. Williams got into the light carriage with his wife and drove. We were received by Lieut. Hook, the bride's father, who seemed to be highly pleased by our presence; so were all the others, and each one shook hands with us. Although the house was rather big, there was scarcely enough room for so many people. The married people were in one room, the unmarried in the other. Bride and bridegroom were with the unmarried. We were with the married couples, and the wedding ceremony took place in our room. They entered the room in the following order: the first to enter was a young woman, behind her came the bride and behind her the bridegroom; then followed all the young people. The bridegroom took the bride on his right side, a young woman stepped to her right side and a young man next to the groom. The preacher then asked both parents whether they gave their consent to the marriage. When these had answered in the affirmative, the minster knelt on a chair and asked God in a prayer for His blessing on this act. After the prayer, bride and bridegroom extended their right hands to each other and the minister spoke briefly to the bridegroom. He more or less said he should love his wife, be faithful to her, honor her and bear her weaknesses with patience; he said the same to the bride. Both had to reply in the affirmative. Thereupon the minister again said a short prayer and at the conclusion, they all sang Psalm 128. Bride and bridegroom had to shake hands again and kiss each other, after which they accepted congratulations from everybody. Mr. Williams and his wife were first, we followed and then all the rest of those present. Everyone had to kiss the bride, which I did with the greatest reluctance. -- After that, the young couple, the bridegroom first, went to the other room where the dancing was about to start. We were treated to cider, bread and cheese. Whoever wants to go to a wedding in this country should fill up at home beforehand. It may be different in big cities like Boston. We then were urged by the bride's father to watch the dancing. We entered the other room where they were dancing to [*the music of*] one single violin.

Since they had never heard anything better in their lives, they considered this music pleasant. It was similar to rustic music in Germany but I must confess that never in my life have I seen more beautiful Engl. dancing. After everyone had danced once with the bride and once with his own partner, they all rode to the bridegroom's house for more dancing; that is the custom. I liked the simplicity best of the whole ceremony. Bride and bridegroom as well as all invited guests were in their Sunday attire. There was hardly any expense; they served something to drink and bread and cheese to eat for anyone who wanted some. They accepted no presents; also the preacher did not get anything for his effort. Since he received a yearly salary, he did not get anything for baptisms or funerals either. We departed with Mr. Williams and went to his house where we had to partake of the evening meal; we returned home by 12 o'clock. Marriage customs are curious indeed among young people in this country. When a young man sees a young woman he likes, he goes to her house and asks for her company at night. Then they sit the whole night together or lie down on the bed. It is important to them that before going to bed, they do not take off their underclothes. They call this bundling and the parents are not asked [*permission*] for this freedom nor would they ever pay any attention to it. The young woman has the freedom to do it if she likes the young man. Neither are there any hard feelings if, after the period of one year or even sooner, the young man tells the young woman or vice-versa, "Our characters and temperaments, our likes and dislikes are so different that we would not be able to have a happy married life together. It will be best for us to separate." -- And the matter is settled.[85]

They generally bundle once a week. One would think this freedom would give rise to fornication but it happens very rarely that a young woman becomes pregnant; if that happens, however, the young man will have to marry her or leave the region, for in no way can he get away with it; his objections are not heeded. In accordance with Engl. law, the young woman swears an oath that the one she names is the father of the child. She has to take the oath before she gives birth, and the young man will be sentenced to marry her. If he has money to buy her off and she allows herself to be bought off, it is all right. By the way, men are not permitted to take an oath. Moreover, if a young married woman has a child 7 months or earlier after the wedding, then both have to pay penance the first time the wife is able to go to church. Then both stand in the middle of the church opposite the pulpit and the preacher deals in his sermon with the wrong they have done his congregation. At the same time, he asks these to forgive the young people because they in turn wish to make good their failing with them by doing good works in the future. [*He adds*]; "As a sign that you have forgiven them and will no longer think of it, raise your right hands," whereupon one sees all the right hands rise. Should an inhabitant by chance forget himself in a public inn or after a drink and curse using God's name in vain, he may not enter the church before being willing to pay public penance. But for one month previous to it, he must go to the preacher 2 or 3 times a week, who, in the presence of the church wardens, is to explain his shameful deed to him. When he [the culprit] comes to church the first time, he must place himself in the middle of the room opposite the preacher, who will preach on the tenet that cursing is forbidden and say, "Dear brethren, here is our brother John (or whatever his name is), who has sinned against the commandment; he is sorry and has very sincerely repented during the past 4 weeks; he has frequently been in my house in the presence of the church wardens, who are also present here. Through Christian conduct, he promises to make good the failing committed against you in the future. He is human like the rest of us and subject to weakness; we must be patient with human frailty; forgive him as I am asking you in his name for forgiveness. And as proof that you have forgiven him and do not think of it any longer, raise your right hands;" whereupon each one raises his right hand. At the close of the service, the congregation surrounds him in front of the church; everyone passes near him to be the first to shake hands with him and it is as if a lost sheep has been found again. These people consider lying one of the greatest vices. They say that a liar is capable of succumbing to every other vice. From this, one can conclude that they hold their yes and no sacred; this must only be mentioned with praise in the English colonies and in New England. The Canadians, in contrast, are more vicious; they do not call us by any other name but "the German dogs." They are a very unclean, bestial nation and deserve contempt. The German inhabitants of North America have also treated most of us quite shamefully in their utterances, even refused us entrance into their homes and closed their doors. The English colonists, on the other hand, whom we called Rebels, and whom we were supposed to subjugate, opened their doors to us and called us their brothers etc. But the Germans said, "Have your beggar dukes sold you sixpence apiece to the Tyrant King of England?" and "How long have you been in prison?" "I bet you are happy that in this way you have escaped the scourge and the gallows!" The Americans had generally been told that all the soldiers sent to America were uncouth or people who had been staying in prison for some crime, the King of England had bought them. It was those same Germans, however, who in order to escape punishment for their crimes had fled to America, that sought to make us unpopular with the rest of the population through that kind of talk. For during the period in which these people and their fathers had gone to America, nobody in Germany would have dared to make such a journey over the great ocean if he was not guilty of some crime and could have honestly earned his bread in Germany. But now enough of that. --

21st   When the young couple came to our house today, the remainder of the roasts was eaten.

20th [sic]   My landlord's son Heli [Eli] arrived home from the army today and said that some of our officers were still in Albany. Capt. Morgan also visited us from Springfield. Mr. Williams treated us to a delicious meal tonight.

30th   Brig. Gen. Danielson came home from Boston and brought orders for the local Committee that we should be permitted to walk around the whole village. Major Danielson, brother of Brig. Gen. Danielson, came home from the prison in Springfield. He had killed Capt. Nicolson's [Nichol's] brother here. He is now on parole until the month of April. Because the case will then be investigated and decided, he will have to return to prison in Springfield at that time.

End of this Month

Month of December 1777

1st   I have been sick with rheumatic fever [sic] for a few days and since I was not seen in church yesterday, many inhabitants came today to visit me, including the 2 local doctors, Mr. Movet [Mofitt] and Mr. Tresk [Trask].

2nd   I had many visitors, both men and women, who affectionately commiserated with me and who inquired whether I was satisfied with my lot; they consoled me and offered their help and support. -- You inhabitants of Germany, did you ever go out of your way to receive and treat a stranger with so much human kindness and friendship who fell as prisoner into your hands and had the misfortune of becoming sick? -- In spite of bright sunshine, the cold has been severe through the NW [wind] since the beginning of this month. If only I had the clothing I left behind in Canada, and an old, decrepit wood stove with Dutch tiles from Germany. Even in bed at night, one is shivering from cold. The mattresses are quite good but eiderdown covers are not known by the inhabitants here; instead, they have woolen blankets. The inhabitants laugh about us, saying "Sleeping between two eiderdown comforters, the Germans are bound to be quite foolish people." --

5th   The Hartford newspaper writes of the war between England and France; the inhabitants seem to be very satisfied about it.

7th   Children are usually baptized on Sunday afternoon after the sermon. This afternoon, after the sermon had ended, a 9 month old child was baptized. The preacher said, "Bring the child that is to be baptized." Thereupon father and mother stepped forward and placed themselves across from the pulpit. The mother held the child in her arms, the minister pronounced a short prayer and then went down from the pulpit to the church warden's chair, which is underneath the pulpit. Here stood a pewter basin with water. The mother handed the child to the father, who in turn went to the minister. On being asked, he told the minister what the child's name should be. Thereupon the minister said, "I baptize the child, whose name is Joseph, in the name of the Father, the Son, and the Holy Ghost, Amen;" thereby he had a few drops of water run down the child's forehead. The minister then returned to the pulpit, thanked God for the grace He had shown to parents and child and asked God to keep this child in His Holy care for ever. The father handed the child back to the mother and at the conclusion of the prayer, they returned to their places. This is the act of baptism; godfathers are unknown. It is getting increasingly cold and yet the men had to clean the flax, which is men's work in this country. The womenfolk do nothing but spin it. Flax is not steeped in water. After it is drawn up, it is dried and thrashed on the ground and then spread apart again. This goes on until the weather has steeped it; then, the men will accept it.

14th   The preacher, Mr. Williams, announced from the pulpit that, on orders of the American Congress, another thanksgiving is to be celebrated in all American States on the 18th of this month when the preachers are to give thanks for all the victories won. We will have a fine dinner then etc. --

17th   Snow, 3 feet deep, fell last night and with the continuous NW wind, it is mighty cold. Great preparations are being made in my quarters for tomorrow's thanksgiving.

18th   Thanksgiving was celebrated today, and since we did not attend church, they all made gloomy faces or was it my imagination? When we were asked the reason at dinner, we answered without hesitation that we could not give thanks for the victories they had won. The dinner was delicious; we liked that.

19th   The rest was eaten today. We were 21 persons at table this noon, among whom were the landlord's sons and daughters. He observed this fact with some satisfaction.

20th   Because he had to announce a matter of some importance, Brig. Gen. Danielson had the community assemble in church today. Returning home, my landlord said that the Brimfield community had to pay 1,900 pounds for the defrayal of the year. "We would not have had to make so great a contribution to the King of England in 20 years if this unfortunate war had not broken out." I assured him that this was but the beginning, the best was yet to follow. Being thoroughly disturbed, he read a chapter from the Bible. --

21st   Lieut. Gebhard returned from Cambridge today and we learned that our troops continued to stay in the barracks on a hill near Boston, called Winter Hill. Nobody has permission to descend from the hill unless he carries a sword or a passport; the Americans have posted guards on this hill. Nor may anyone from our army go to Boston. General Howe has sent a ship from New York to Boston with regimentals and money for our army. We also learned that the Master-Clerk Senf, who was said to have been captured and deported before the surrender at Saratoga, has become a captain of engineers in the American Army. I received the forage and baggage money to the tune of 16 guineas, that I still had coming this year.

22nd   The army of General Howe has moved into their winter quarters in and around Philadelphia. We heard the following about Capt. O'Connell: when our officers and privates from the Baum and Breymann Corps were on the prison ship off Boston, a German preacher by the name of Johann Christoph Hartwick[86] came aboard and spoke very amicably with officers and privates saying that the men would probably like to hear a sermon again. As they had perhaps not heard a sermon for a long time, he would preach for them, which was granted him. He spoke a great deal about American freedom and Germany slavery, telling our men that it now was the right time to tear themselves away from slavery. They should use the opportunity and throw themselves onto the noble bosom of liberty; he would lead them to the promised land, Philadelphia. -- Capt. O'Connell did not allow him to continue; he pushed over the barrel on which his books were lying and warned him that unless he left the ship immediately, he would throw him into the water. He should not tempt his men to break the oath they had sworn both to their sovereign and the King of England. The preacher quickly went into his boat and departed without saying a word. In Boston, however, he loudly complained about it so that the next day, a commission from Boston came aboard to investigate this matter. Capt. O'Connell defended himself very well indeed and the matter was settled; thereupon, the officers were transferred to Westminster. Now the pastor came back on board ship and together with the abject Comp. Surgeon Radloff, tried to tempt the men to go to Pennsylvania where they were to establish a village; he would be their preacher and Radloff their physician and surgeon. They [Hartwick and Radloff] could not attain their final goal, however, and were rejected with contempt.

24th   The Americans intend to make an expedition to Canada this winter, conquer St. Jean and burn the English fleet there. Go slowly, don't hurry! --

30th   The Worcester papers say: General Howe has undertaken an expedition from Philadelphia to Germantown with great success;[87] since they are saying it themselves, it seems plausible. Sleigh-driving is by far not as good here as in Canada because the country is very mountainous here. The sleighs are also much heavier than those in Canada and must be pulled by 2 horses. It is so cold that one gets little sleep in his bed at night.

31st   My landlord's son Heli [Eli] has returned to the army.

End of this year

NOTES

1. Traditionally, ships at sea saluted each other with guns and by the striking of topsails; apparently, the frequency of such salutes and the numbers of shots fired led to a "severe wastage of gunpowder." To control such waste, in 1675 Samuel Pepys, then Secretary of the British Admiralty, established a system of salutes according to rank, ranging from three guns for the most junior admiral to nineteen guns for the admiral of the fleet, and twenty-one guns for royalty. Salutes used odd numbers because even numbers were reserved for naval funerals. (Peter Kemp, ed. The Oxford Companion to Ships and the Sea, London, 1976, p. 747.)

2. Wasmus, like some other diarists of the period, is sometimes confused by the difficulties of identifying flora and fauna new to him. The fieldfare is, like the American robin, a thrush, TURDUS PILARIS; it has grey and brown plumage.

3. Professor Harold H. Howard of Greenwich, New York provided this identification.

4. This bird may well have been the passenger pigeon, ECTOPISTES MIGRATORIUS, so abundant that its migration darkened the skies for hours, until a combination of farmers cutting down beech trees (beech nuts were a principal food) and overhunting by market-hunters exterminated the species in the late 19th century. The last passenger pigeon died in an Ohio zoo in the early 20th century.

5. Wasmus did not know the facts; modern geographers place the source of the St. Lawrence in the Great Lakes. This seems to have been a separate essay Wasmus intended for his friends in Germany; at any rate his description of Canadian life is written in a different tone than the rest of his entries.

6. The moose, ALCES ALCES, so astonished the early French explorers that they called it l'original, later l'orignal. Canadians did try to train moose as draft animals, and some have even been raced competitively.

7. Carl von Linné (1707-1778) (later Carolus Linnaeus), the Swedish botanist, established a system of nomenclature and taxonomic classification in 1735.

8. Barry St. Leger (1737-1789) had served at Louisbourg and Québec in the Seven Years War. In the Revolution he was placed in command of a diversionary effort to march eastward along the Mohawk Valley to link up with Burgoyne in Albany.

9. Sir John Johnson (1742-1830), the son of Sir William Johnson (1715-1774), British superintendent of Indian Affairs in New York, was a prominent Loyalist leader in the Mohawk Valley who fled to Canada early in 1776, returning to New York with St. Leger in 1777 and on border raids in 1778 and 1780.

10. Frederika Charlotte Luise von Massow, Baroness von Riedesel (1746-1808), with her three little girls, Augusta (b. 1771), Frederika (b.1774), and Caroline (b. 1776), later joined by America (b. 1780) and Canada (1782-83), had followed the general to America. A revised translation of her journal and letters with introduction and notes by Marvin L. Brown, Jr. has been published as Baroness von Riedesel and the American Revolution: Journal and Correspondence of a Tour of Duty, 1776-1783, by the Institute of Early American History and Culture (1965).

11. Brigadier Henry Watson Powell of the 53rd Regiment (1733- 1814) had come to Canada in 1776 in command of the 53rd Foot, was promoted to Brigadier General, and was left in command of Ticonderoga in 1777. He later commanded at Montréal, Niagara, and Québec, returning to England after the Revolution. (Encyclopedia of Canada, Toronto, 1936, V, p. 147.)

12. Captain Archibald Edmonstone, Riedesel's English aide-de-camp, had studied at the Caroline Collegium in Braunschweig before the Revolution. He came from a wealthy Scottish family.

13. Wasmus is referring to the area of Braunschweig, not its population.

14. There is considerable debate among historians as to the date and place the first Stars and Stripes were flown. The Americans at Bennington carried a flag with nine stripes and 11 stars curving over the numbers "76" in the field. Congress had passed the Flag Resolution on June 14, 1777, providing for a flag with 13 stripes of red and white and a blue field with 13 stars, but had not been more specific in the design, so that early flags were not uniform. (Mark Mayo Boatner, III, Encyclopedia of the American Revolution, New York, 1966, pp.369-370.)

15. The word muskrat actually derives from the Algonkian "musquash;" Wasmus is inventing an etymology of his own here.

16. Wasmus uses several technical terms here, including: entrenchment (trench and parapet), redoubt, (a small temporary enclosed defensive work, used especially on hilltops and passes), retrenchment (defensive work within an entrenchment, consisting usually of a parapet and a ditch), abatis (a defensive obstacle made of trees whose boughs, often sharpened, are directed toward the enemy) and breastwork (a parapet made of beams, a rampart raised above the main wall of a fortification.)

17. The American commander, General Philip Schuyler (1703-1804) was a member of New York's Dutch aristocracy. After fighting in the Seven Years War, he had inherited substantial estates in Saratoga and in the Mohawk Valley. In 1775, he was appointed Major General and given the command of the Northern Department, supplying Montgomery's invasion of Canada from Albany. Gates would replace him as commander in August 1777. Schuyler at this point had only about 2,500 men.

18. Arthur St. Clair (1736-1818) had resigned from the 60th Foot in 1762 and settled in Boston, marrying an American heiress. He eventually bought 4,000 acres of land in Pennsylvania and, as a Colonel in the Pennsylvania militia, participated in the invasion of Canada in 1775. He succeeded Gates as commander on Lake Champlain in early 1777; he and Schuyler were cleared of incompetence for abandoning Ticonderoga at a court-martial in 1778. St. Clair served Washington as an aide-de-camp later in the Revolution, was elected to Congress in 1785, and later became Governor of the Northwest Territory.

19. Colonel Philip Skene (1725-1810) had acquired 60,000 acres on the shores of Lake Champlain after his military service under General Howe and Lord Jeffrey Amherst in the Seven Years War, building sawmills, foundries, and a shipyard at Skenesborough, the modern Whitehall. He was

Burgoyne's most important Loyalist aide, encouraging the General to believe that Vermont was full of Loyalist supporters and supplies, which the expedition to Bennington was supposed to collect.

20. Hill had about 200 troops with him; a Yankee "deserter" reported that the Americans had over 1,000 men, while in fact there were no more than 500.

21. Rattlesnakes do not bite themselves to poison their meat, and Wasmus exaggerates the effect of rattlesnake bites, but otherwise this description is quite accurate.

22. These were the Mississauga Indians, originally a band near the Mississagi River in southern Ontario on the shore of Lake Huron. Later, the name, meaning "River with several outlets," referred to most of the Southeastern Ojibwa.

23. St. Luc de la Corne (1712-1784) is sometimes confused with his two elder brothers, Louis de Chapt, Sieur de Lacorne, the seigneur (1696-1762) and Louis François de Lacorne (1703-1761) who was also a soldier. St. Luc de la Corne served in the French Army during the Seven Years War, was a legislative councillor of Québec, and served in Burgoyne's campaign as commander of the Canadian and Indian forces. (The Encyclopedia of Canada, Toronto, 1936, vol. III. p. 369.)

24. Burgoyne's speech to the Indians provoked a storm of hostile commentary on both sides of the Atlantic. In the House of Commons, Edmund Burke compared Burgoyne to a menagerie keeper releasing wild animals into the street: "My gentle lions, my humane bears, my sentimental wolves, my tender-hearted hyenas, go forth: but I exhort ye as ye are Christians and members of a civilized society, to take care not to hurt man, woman, or child." (Boatner, p.143.)

25. The morgen was an archaic German land measure; literally the amount of land a farmer could work in a day (Tagewerk); the area of a morgen differed in the various regions of Germany: in Prussia it was 2.116 acres.

26. This was most likely the Crown Point Road, built from Springfield, Vermont (Fort Number Four) to Crown Point in 1760.

27. During the Great Northern War, in 1709, Charles XII of Sweden invading Russia, suffered greatly during the long Russian winter. His 20,000 troops faced 50,000 Russians at Poltava and were decisively defeated on July 8, 1709. Only 1,500 Swedes, including Charles, escaped.

28. Jane McCrea had remained behind in order to meet her fiancé, Captain David Jones, serving with one of Burgoyne's Loyalist regiments, when her family fled south away from Burgoyne's invading forces . Illustrating the way the Revolution split some American families, Jane's brother John McCrea was a patriot; her father had died. According to some accounts, two Indians quarreled over Jane, whom they had captured as she waited for Captain Jones near Fort Edward; in the ensuing struggle she was shot and subsequently scalped. Jane McCrea's murder is said to have had a significant effect in attracting recruits to the American cause, although this had been considerably exaggerated. (The discussion in John R. Elting, The Battles of Saratoga, New Jersey, 1977, pp. 40-41, makes this quite clear.)

29. Burgoyne's invasion of New York was designed to isolate unruly New England from the rest of the colonies. St. Leger's expedition along the Mohawk and some sort of support from Howe in New York were part of the original plan. (There is an excellent discussion of the plan in John Luzader, Decision on the Hudson, Washington, 1975, pp. 3-16.)

30. The silver bullet trick did not always work; later that year, in October, General Sir Henry Clinton sent Daniel Taylor to Burgoyne to report the capture of Fort Montgomery with dispatches, concealed in a hollow silver bullet. Taylor was captured by the American General George Clinton (1739-1812) later Governor of New York. As he had been seen to swallow something as he was captured, General Clinton ordered he be forced to take a dose of tartar emetic, which eventually produced the bullet. Taylor was tried as a spy and executed. (Boatner, p. 1009.)

31. Horatio Gates (1728-1806) born in England as the son of the Duke of Leeds' housekeeper, enlisted in the army as a young man and fought in the Seven Years War, retiring as a major in the 60th Regiment in 1765. He settled in Virginia as a neighbor of the Washington family. Appointed Brigadier General in June 1775, he was sent to the Northern Department to serve under Schuyler in May 1776. Although Congress apparently intended him to replace Schuyler in command in March 1777, this decision was reversed in May, after which Gates travelled to Philadelphia to lobby Congress. When the

British captured Ticonderoga, Gates was given the command of the Northern Department. Gates was chosen by Congress on August 4 and did not arrive in Albany until the 19th. This reference gives some indication that Wasmus revised his journal after he had written it, perhaps when he made the multiple copies he used to protect his account from the vagaries of war and the precarious postal system.

32. Schuyler withdrew from Fort Edward on July 24 and camped 5 miles south at Moses Creek; his force was reduced by militia who left as their terms of service expired. On the 31st, he moved further south to Fort Miller, reaching Stillwater on the 4th of August, where reinforcements began to arrive. On August 18, he reached the confluence of the Mohawk and Hudson rivers (the modern Cohoes) where the army remained until Gates marched it back north to Stillwater on September 8.

33. This might have been the Duer house; William Duer (1747-1799) born in England, was active in the timber export business, and had met Philip Schuyler in 1768, establishing sawmills at his suggestion at Fort Miller. He settled permanently in New York in about 1773, becoming a colonel in the local militia, a judge of the county court, and a member of the provincial congress. He represented New York in the Continental Congress in 1777-78 and was eventually Assistant Secretary of the Treasury under Alexander Hamilton.

34. Colonel Francis Pfister, a retired British officer, who brought 90 Loyalists to aid Baum, lived near Hoosick Corners.

35. Captain Samuel MacKay, whose unit was the "Loyal Volunteers." MacKay had served in America with the 60th Regiment of Foot during the Seven Years War, retiring as a Lieutenant in 1763. He aided in the defense of Canada during the American invasion of 1775, was captured and held in Connecticut until an unsuccessful escape in May of 1776 was followed by a more successful effort in September. By March of 1777, he had raised a company of Canadians and had attacked American recruits at Sabbathday Point (Lake George), killing four and taking all but two of the rest as prisoners. (H. C. Burleigh, Captain MacKay and the Loyal Volunteers, Bloomfield, Ontario: 1977.)

36. What is now Vermont was claimed in the 18th century by New Hampshire, New York and Massachusetts. After a brief period as an independent republic, Vermont was admitted to the Union in 1791.

37. Charles Louis Tarieu de Lanaudière, St. Luc de la Corne's son-in-law.

38. This was no doubt the Battenkill.

39. The Schuylers had purchased land where Fish Creek entered the Hudson from some Mohawk sachems in 1683, where a blockhouse was built during the Indian wars in 1689. By the early 18th century Johannes Schuyler had built a brick mansion and several mills on the property. A frontier fort was built at Saratoga in 1721 to defend the northern frontier of New York. During King George's War (the War of the Austrian Succession) in 1745, the French and Indians burned the whole village of Saratoga, which had grown up there, some 30 houses, 4 mills, and the Schuyler's brick house. The fort was rebuilt the following year and called Fort Clinton, was attacked in 1747 by the French and Indians led by St. Luc de la Corne, and was abandoned in October by its defenders. By 1777 the settlement had grown to include the rebuilt Schuyler house, military barracks, sawmills. gristmills, a flaxmill, a church, barns, storehouses, and various other houses and structures.

40. Now the village of Cambridge, New York.

41. This mill was variously known as Sancoick's, Saint Coick's (perhaps a corruption of St. Croix) and even Van Schaick's mill, on the Hoosic River.

42. The Van Rensselaer family were among the earliest settlers in the region, establishing the first successful patroonship of New Netherland in the 17th century under Killian Van Rensselaer, who was born in Holland in 1595 and died in 1644. The eighth patroon, Stephen Van Rensselaer (1764-1839), is referred to here; he had succeeded his father in 1769 at the age of five and in 1783 would marry Philip Schuyler's daughter Margaret. Three of his kinsmen, Robert, Nicolas, and Henry, played important roles in the defense of New York: Robert (1741-1802) was a general in the New York militia, Henry Killian, (1744-1816) commanded a New York regiment, and Nicolas (1754-1848) was a colonel, serving at Saratoga.

43. General John Stark had served as a captain in Roger's Rangers in the Seven Years War. He fought at Bunker Hill and as a Brigadier under George Washington in New Jersey, but, denied a promotion by Congress early in 1777, he had retired to Manchester. When New Hampshire raised a brigade to resist Burgoyne's invasion, Stark accepted the command.

44. In fact, some of the Loyalist prisoners were exiled, some sent to the prison mines at Simsbury, Connecticut, while others had their property confiscated and, according to at least one account, were forced to do road work for the republic of Vermont that winter. (Frederic F. Van de Water, The Reluctant Republic, New York, 1941, p. 216; Charles Miner Thompson, Independent Vermont, Cambridge, 1942, p. 319.)

45. This was apparently Wasmus' nephew, Heinrich Wasmus, who died in Bennington on August 27, 1777. (See below, page 82.)

46. Captain Ernst August von Bärtling (von Bärtling senior, as opposed to Captain Carl Friedrich von Bärtling, who fought at Saratoga and died during the return trip to Braunschweig, at Münster, in 1783.) Lieutenants Theodore Friedrich Gebhard and Johann Andreas Meyer, all of the Braunschweig Grenadier Regiment, survived their captivity, and on their return to Braunschweig became members of the new Riedesel Regiment. (Elster, p. 423,453; 453, 440, 423.)

47. Colonel Seth Warner (1743-1784) was chosen Colonel of the Vermont Continental Regiment, the "Green Mountain Boys," in July 1776, had aided in Montgomery's capture of Montréal, and had captured the ruins of Crown Point after his cousin, Ethan Allen, had seized Ticonderoga in 1775.

48. Lancets are surgical instruments which have a narrow double-edged blade and a lance-shaped point; they were used to open abscesses and for bloodletting.

49. This was most likely the Catamount Tavern in Bennington.

50. Reverend Thomas Allen, who had graduated from Harvard in 1762, was ordained in 1764 as Pittsfield's first minister. He had served from October 1775 to January 1776 as a voluntary chaplain to the American army at White Plains, and renewed his efforts at Ticonderoga in June and July of 1777. He accompanied the Pittsfield volunteers to Bennington and, according to some accounts, went towards the British forces just before the battle, demanding their surrender; when he was fired upon, he fired the first American shot in response. After the battle, Allen is reported to have caught the horse belonging to a Braunschweig surgeon (presumably not Wasmus, who was apparently on foot), on which were panniers filled with bottles of wine. Allen gave the wine to the wounded but carried two of the square glass bottles home as souvenirs of his campaign.

51. Stark had about 800 men.

52. General Benjamin Lincoln (1733-1810) was given command of the Massachusetts troops around Boston in August 1776, was appointed Major General at Washington's recommendation in February 1777, and sent to take command of the New England militia east of the Hudson, much to the resentment of Stark. Lincoln skillfully convinced Stark to co-operate in attacking Baum at Bennington.
General John Fellows (1733-1808), a native of Pomfret, Connecticut, had served in the Seven Years War. A member of the provincial congress in 1775, after the battle of Lexington, Fellows led a regiment of Minutemen to Boston; he later commanded a brigade at White Plains.

53. Friedrich Valentin (or Carl) Melzheimer, Chaplain of the Dragoon Regiment, was born in Negenborn in 1749. His journal of the voyage from Wolfenbüttel to Québec was published in 1891 by the Literary and Historical Society of Québec (the original is in the Stadtkirchenamt, Braunschweig.) After his captivity in Massachusetts (and later New York), he was sent to Bethlehem, Pennsylvania, exchanged, and allowed to travel. In 1779 Melzheimer resigned his commission, married, and became pastor of several Lancaster County congregations, and later in his life was elected to the American Philosophical Society because of his work in natural history. He died in Hanover, Pennsylvania in 1814. Charles H. Glatfelter, Pastors and People: German Lutheran and Reformed Churches in the Pennsylvania Field, 1717-1793. Breinigsville, Pa., 1980, vol. I, pp. 87-88.

54. Good Lutheran Wasmus was discovering the Puritan style of worship, which eschewed altars, seated the congregation on all four sides of the church, and emphasized the preaching of God's word from the pulpit.

55. Gates was gathering his forces at Saratoga to resist Burgoyne's invasion.

56. Fort Stanwix (on the site of the present Rome, New York) was located at the head of navigation on the Mohawk; it had been built by the British in 1758 near an earlier French fort. Rebuilt by the Americans in 1776, it was named Fort Schuyler, which caused some confusion with an earlier Fort Schuyler, at Utica, named for General Schuyler's uncle. (William W. Campbell, Annals of Tryon County, New York, 1924, pp. 59-60.)

57. Colonel Peter Gansevoort (1749-1812) had participated in Montgomery's invasion of Canada in 1775. His 3rd New York Continentals occupied Fort Stanwix in April 1777.

58. General Nicholas Herkimer (1728-1777), Brigadier General of the New York militia.

59. Tryon County, New York, comprised the Mohawk Valley west of Schenectady and much of the land to the north--the modern Montgomery, Fulton, Herkimer, Otsego, Oneida, Oswego, Jefferson, Lewis, St. Lawrence, and Hamilton counties. It had been split off from Albany County in 1772 and named for Governor William Tryon.

60. Colonel Marinus Willet (1740-1830), a wealthy New York merchant active in the Sons of Liberty, had participated in the invasion of Canada and was second-in-command to Gansevoort.

61. Colonel Daniel Claus was married to one of Sir William Johnson's daughters. He led a party of 150 Mississauga and Iroquois warriors.
Chief Joseph Brant (1742-1807), a Mohawk leader whose sister Molly had been Sir William Johnson's mistress, had fought under Johnson in the Seven Years War. An Anglican convert, Brant worked to get the Mohawks to support the British. On a visit to England, Brant was presented at Court and painted by Romney and West. He led the Indians on St. Leger's expedition, ambushing Herkimer at Oriskany, and later led border raids on the New York frontier.
Walter Butler (1752-1781), another Loyalist soldier, had defeated Ethan Allen at Montréal in 1775 and was eventually captured while holding a Loyalist rally in the course of St. Leger's expedition. Convicted of espionage, he was sentenced to be hanged, but was reprieved and eventually escaped to lead border raids on the frontier.

62. The Mississauga (see note 22, above).

63. Brigadier General Timothy Danielson (1733-1791), a Yale graduate, was a delegate to the Massachusetts provincial congress and commanded one of its 25 militia regiments in 1775, but spent much of the Revolution in the state legislature and constitutional convention.

64. The Bauverweser in Germany was the local building inspector, supervising the upkeep of existing structures and regulating new construction.

65. The red house at the end of Prospect Hill Road in Brimfield was built by Captain William Nichols in 1738 and was said to be the oldest house in Brimfield. Now destroyed, the house was believed to be the headquarters of "Hessian" prisoners whose names were carved on the mantelpiece.

66. According to Brimfield town records, Joseph Hitchcock was born in 1719, married his wife, Mary, in 1750, and fathered ten children: Basheba, Elisha, Heli, Mary, Medad, Peter, Phebe, Ruth, Sarah, and Zadoc. He died in 1788; Mary survived him until 1809.

67. This was the Battle of Freeman's Farm, September 19, 1777. Burgoyne, blocked from proceeding towards Albany by the American fortifications on the bluffs commanding the river road, tried to draw the Americans out of their camp at Bemis Heights by a three-column movement toward the Americans. Riedesel's Germans arrived just in time to support Burgoyne, and the British were left in possession of the field, but their progress towards Albany was decisively blocked.

68. This was the Battle of the Brandywine, September 11, 1777. Washington, trying to block Howe's advance towards Philadelphia, made a stand on the banks of the Brandywine Creek, where Howe's successful flank attack and Knyphausen's blow at the American center defeated the Americans but did not prevent their escape to the east.

69. On September 18, American forces led by Colonel John Brown of Massachusetts had attacked Powell at Ticonderoga, capturing the old French lines and besieging the main fort and Mount

Independence for four days, after which they moved to the south and attacked Diamond Island in Lake George on the 24th. Defeated by British resistance, Brown retreated to Skenesborough, which had been abandoned by the British. The British retained Ticonderoga until November 8 when, after Burgoyne's surrender, they burned and evacuated the fortifications and retreated north to Canada.

70. Nehemiah Williams (1749-1796) was the first pastor of the First Congregational Church in Brimfield. He was appointed on October 27, 1774, having graduated from Harvard in 1769. Williams had 10 children, and at his death his widow supplied the pulpit for four months, "the salary being paid to her and she making such arrangements as she chose for preaching." (Charles M. Hyde, Historical Celebration of the Town of Brimfield, 1876, pp. 95-6.)

71. The brevity of militia enlistments was a serious problem for the Americans throughout the Revolution; the militia were state troops, part-time soldiers, who were much less reliable then the Continentals, the American regulars. Vermont militia under Stark had left the field just before the Battle of Bemis Heights because their enlistments had expired. (Boatner, pp. 705-707.)

72. These were probably the Berkshires.

73. Burgoyne had lost about 600 men killed or wounded at the Battle of Freeman's Farm, while the Americans had lost 65 killed and 118 wounded, 36 missing. (Boatner, p. 974.)

74. Burgoyne's line of communications with Canada was 185 miles long, and had been effectively severed when he crossed the Hudson River. (Boatner, p. 138.)

75. Brown's raid was one of three attacks sent by General Lincoln from Pawlet, Vermont. Colonels Johnson and Brown were to attack Ticonderoga while Colonel Woodbridge took possession of Skenesborough.

76. Howe had marched into Philadelphia on September 26; Congress had fled to York, Pennsylvania.

77. The Battle of Bemis Heights, October 7, 1777, was Burgoyne's second effort at breaking through the American blockade of the route to Albany. Burgoyne ordered a reconnaissance in force to test the American left; Fraser's advance was met by a powerful American response, and Benedict Arnold's heroic and successful attacks on the two British redoubts made the British position impossible; Burgoyne began his slow retreat to Saratoga.

78. In fact, Burgoyne's aide-de-camp Sir Francis Clerke had been mortally wounded and captured at Bemis Heights.

79. Surrounded at Saratoga, Burgoyne negotiated a convention with Gates under which the Americans agreed that the British could return to England, promising not to fight in the war again. This convention, rather than a more typical surrender, was responsible for the special status of Burgoyne's troops as the "Convention Army" rather than ordinary prisoners of war, at least until Congress disclaimed the agreement on January 8, 1778.

80. Burgoyne had spent the night of October 9 in Schuyler's house as he retreated north after his failure to break through the American army at the Battle of Bemis Heights. The slow pace of his retreat allowed the Americans to cut off his route to the north and bombard his positions at Schuylerville. The Schuyler mansion, which stood on the south side of Fish Creek (Burgoyne's final camp was to the north), was burned to prevent its being used as cover for an attack by the Americans, according to Hoffman Nickerson. (Turning Point of the Revolution, Cambridge, 1928, p. 379.)

81. Actually, the fort was destroyed and evacuated on November 8, 1777.

82. After Howe left New York for Philadelphia, Clinton was left with only 7,000 troops, 4,000 of which were regulars, in New York City. When, in September, Burgoyne asked for help, Clinton agreed to a diversion to the north later in the month. On October 6, Clinton captured Forts Clinton and Montgomery, too late to save Burgoyne, who was defeated by the Americans the next day.

83. Forts Clinton and Montgomery, Clinton's objectives, were on the west bank of the Hudson, four miles north of Peekskill; a chevaux-de-frise with a log boom and iron chain stretched across the river from Anthony's Nose to Fort Montgomery.

84. In fact, 12,000 had captured half their number.

85. David Freeman Hawke in <u>Everyday Life in Early America</u> (New York, 1988, pp. 64-65), estimates bridal pregnancy figures of about 20%. My own unpublished study of the town of Sturbridge (1973) found that about 30% of the brides in 1790 gave birth to their first child less than seven months after their weddings.

86. This was Johann Christoph (later John Christopher) Hartwick, born in Saxe-Gotha in 1714, educated at Halle University and called to American congregations in 1746, naturalized in 1754, and preached in Pennsylvania, but did not lead a congregation until after the Revolution. One biographer describes him as "irritable and capricious," and indicates that he "preferred hunting and fishing to pastoral visitation," although he was an "engaging preacher." He died at Clermont, New York in 1796, leaving money in his will for the "establishment of a theological seminary," which later became Hartwick College. Glattfelter, vol I. p. 52.

87. After Howe captured Philadelphia, the Americans controlled two forts on the Delaware, which prevented Howe from being supplied by sea. To release troops to capture the forts, Howe evacuated Germantown on October 19, but the Hessian attack on October 21 on Fort Mercer, under von Donop, failed miserably. Bombardment forced the Americans to abandon the other fort, Fort Mifflin, in mid-November, and the threat of a second attack with 5,000 men under Cornwallis led to the surrender of Fort Mercer on November 20. In early December Howe sent a sortie out of the city and there was a brief skirmish known as the Battle of Edge Hill, after which Howe retreated to Germantown while Washington took up winter quarters at Valley Forge. (Craig L. Symonds, <u>A Battlefield Atlas of the American Revolution</u>, 1986, p. 59.)

1778

Month of January 1778

1st   We all went to Mr. Williams to wish him luck in the new year.

2nd   Cornet Stutzer wants to visit his brother in Springfield and I decided to accompany him.

3rd   Because tomorrow will be Sunday and no horses will be available, we could not start our journey to Springfield; moreover, the inhabitants consider it a sin to travel without a weighty cause on Sunday.

4th   Our trip is fixed for tomorrow. There are many people in this place, and perhaps everywhere, who have not been baptized and therefore do not take holy communion. Major Danielson has not been baptized, nor have his 2 daughters, both over 20 years old. Brig. Gen. Danielson was probably not baptized either.

5th   Last night it snowed heavily, and this morning the weather continues to be quite stormy. We rode away at 10 o'clock and were in Palmer at noon where we ate lunch in the same inn where we had eaten chocolate with a spoon on Sept. 20 of last year. We continued our trip at 1 o'clock and arrived at South Springfield at 4 o'clock where we crossed the Connecticut River in great danger. In West Springfield, we reached the house of Capt. Morgan where we spent the night.

6th   After eating breakfast, we rode back and stopped first at Mr. Stebbins, from where we visited the Country Squire Stutzer. More than 200 men from our Braunschweig corps were working in Springfield. They had rented themselves out to the farmers, lived well, worked as much as they wished to and were in good spirits. We rode back to Palmer.

7th   We set out early in the morning and were back in Brimfield at noon. On our march today, we rode with an aide-de-camp of Gen. Gates, who told us that when they left Ticonderoga, the English had to burn all the baggage; that was terrible news for us! -- Yet this kind gentleman has surely lied to us; after all, they [the English] had enough time to send their baggage etc. ahead to Canada. He also told us a great deal about the talents of our former Master Clerk Senf, and that he was captain of engineers in their army. I was pleased about that because he [Senf] is a good and righteous man who was, however, too harshly treated by us in spite of his work and ability. I will have more to say about that at another time.

9th   The news is spreading here that 50,000 Russians are going to come to America next spring. Although this has not been confirmed, the inhabitants are very much afraid and are anxiously asking whether it is true that the Russians are such a barbaric nation.[1] When you tell them, their fear increases; whenever he hears of the Russians, my landlord quickly reads a chapter from the Bible. --

10th   We occupy ourselves with hunting and for want of deer, we shoot squirrels. There are gray, black and red ones here; the gray and black are best to eat. They are very tasty and have beautiful pelts; they are far bigger than the Eichhörner [squirrels] in Germany. There are also gray, red and black foxes here. These and another animal, the raccoon, which is as big as a fox, have very beautiful pelts. In addition, there are many wildcats, which are bigger than the house cats and also have beautiful pelts; they kill sheep and are almost as dangerous as wolves. There is also a kind of animal, similar to our hamster, which is of reddish color and mostly stays underground like the hamster; it is called woodchuck by the English. Then there is an animal called a skunk, which is as big as a house cat, of black color with a white stripe across head and back and with 4 white feet; the tip of the long tail is white. My landlord's dog killed one and unless the dog had moved out because of the stench, we could not have stayed in the house. When this animal is attacked, it pisses [sic] in its long hairy tail and thus wards off the dogs. The urine of this animal causes a horrible stench from which one could easily suffocate; the dog did not lose the scent for 4 weeks. The skunk is also known in Canada.

11th   Mr. Williams baptized his little daughter of 15 months himself, his wife handed him the child and he baptized her.

12th   I have mentioned that Brig. Gen. Danielson's wife and 2 daughters died of dysentery; none of them was baptized, just as the brig. gen. is not baptized.

14th   Continual NW wind and fair but very cold weather. Cornet Stutzer and Pastor Melzheimer have gone to Cambridge on horseback today to visit our Maj. Gen. von Riedesel.

16th   The Hartford newspaper announced that the Americans have captured an Engl. ship on which were 9,000 regimentals and many other very valuable items.
    Since there is a great want of this type of clothing here, the Americans will be very pleased. They also took 50 pieces [sic] of officers' wives prisoner, who will certainly be ransomed at once. --

17th   The Worcester newspaper reported that the King of England never would permit an exchange of his troops with his rebellious subjects just as he will not ratify the Convention of Saratoga. Thus, there is no chance for any exchange as yet. I have become acquainted with a few married couples in this village, none of whom is baptized. They in turn have produced 4 children, who are not baptized either.

23rd   The stormy NW wind drove snow in my face at night while I lay in bed; the houses are so ingeniously built that the wind drives the snow through just about everywhere. On the level ground, the snow lies 3 feet deep.

25th   Pastor Melzheimer returned from Cambridge and said that the army of Gen. Burgoyne expected the transport ships, destined to take them back to Europe, in the month of February; that barracks were being built in Rutland, 24 miles from here, for all prisoners of war and that we too would have to move there shortly; that, if left alone, our troops would desert from Winter Hill; that, when the army chaplain from the Hesse-Hanau Reg. decided to journey to Canada and asked Congress for permission, they not only sent him the passport but also 180 pounds of paper money for the church; that the Engl. ship had arrived in Boston from Rhode Island, on which Gen. Howe had sent not only all kinds of necessities for our army such as pieces of clothing etc., but also 80,000 guineas. An excellent medicine.

26th   My landlord brought a piece of news home that almost caused him a stroke: 300 transport ships had arrived in Rhode Island with troops thought to be Russians. He had been told that the Russians neither give nor accept pardon; he who captures a Russian has to kill him at once. This news surely originates with Tories or Royalists and is manufactured lies; I just cannot believe that Russian troops have come to America, although they would be the best soldiers for this country.

In spite of the severe cold and the deep snow, the cattle are not put into stables. The 6 pigs my landlord has slaughtered weigh more than 1,400 lbs. and 2 over 1,480. All these are salted down; little or nothing is known about [*curing by*] smoking.

29th   When I asked him, my landlord said that unmarried people of both sexes were allowed to sleep together. I replied that it was impossible for me to believe this, but in order to make certain, I would ask his minister, Mr. Williams, about it. He did not seem to like that, however. -- In the Hartford newspaper, we read that the King of France had encouraged the Canadians to take advantage of the opportunity to tear themselves away from the Engl. yoke and throw themselves under the protection of the Congress of the 13 United Provinces. Thereupon, the Canadians quickly sent a delegation to Congress and asked for its protection. Coming, however, from a newspaper, this needs confirmation!

31st   The news is spreading that the Canadians have revolted, and the occupation forces have fled from all the posts via Québec up to the Ile-d'Orléans where they had taken hold of themselves again. If this is true, then our baggage will surely be lost; but this is certainly a lie, for Governor General Carleton knows the Canadians and consequently enforces good order so that they cannot do such things. Moreover, the Canadians are too fearful; we will soon hear that these were lies.

End of this Month

Month of February 1778

1st   When I asked Mr. Williams this morning whether it was lawful for unmarried people of both sexes to sleep together, he said it was just as lawful as if I wanted to sleep with his wife. "I am sorry," he said, "that you witness so many of the bad habits of the Americans; our country is young - and needs to be educated." Several sick people have come to me, but I have no medicines. In Worcester, 20 Engl. miles from here, is a pharmacy, but I have no money to go there and buy medicine.

3rd   Today, I had to visit sick people in the company of the local doctor and since we get good cider wherever we go, I like these trips rather well.

4th   I was again sent a horse with which to visit some sick persons. The annoying news of the Canadian rebellion is in the newspapers at present; also, that an American corps, 4,000 men strong, is about to undertake an expedition to Canada under the command and leadership of General Wayne and Colonel Warner in order to burn the English fleet at St. Jean and unite with the Canadians.[2] If this is true, I consider it bold and unreasonable, - since they lost so many men in their first expedition of 1775. I am also sure that they would be less well received, for the fortifications are in all the places in a good state of defense now, anyway better than at the beginning of the war.

5th   Pastor Williams' 16 month old little daughter has had her whole upper body burned by boiling water; she is in imminent danger of losing her life. Cornet Stutzer came back from Cambridge tonight and brought the news that we were very soon to move to Rutland where we and all the prisoners of war were to live in newly built barracks. Most disagreeable news! They were still talking about our exchange in Cambridge. That the news about the Canadian revolt was nothing but lies was most unpleasant to hear.

17th   With the NW wind, the severe cold seems to continue. In between we had some east winds, which came from the ocean. Such rain or snow never lasts longer than 24 hours; one can count on that. The oldest inhabitants vouch that this is so. The Worcester newspaper reports that Gen. Washington has recalled the troops that were designated to go to Canada.[3]

18th   Visiting the sick today, I was in danger of losing my nose and ears; I can state with absolute certainty that never in my life, not even in Canada, have I been exposed to such cold.

19th   We drove in a sled to Brookfield with Mr. Williams today to visit his mother-in-law, who had injured her arm. Mr. Williams drove himself and on the way back, he overturned us. We all fell into the snow together; Lieut. Gebhard landed on Cornet Stutzer and I on Mr. Williams.

28th   The news came that a few Engl. regiments had marched from Winter Hill to Rutland and moved into the barracks. Many barracks must have been built there.

End of this Month

Month of March 1778

1st   All the American soldiers had to go back to the army today.

5th   We had to sign another paper sent by Congress; it was identical with the one we had to sign in Springfield with the addition that we now have permission to walk about the whole village; the Committee should also allow us to travel to other places if we so desired.

12th   The Connecticut newspapers report that the King of Great Britain will send 22,000 troops to America among whom [there will be] 11,500 Germans, i.e., 3,000 Swabians, 2,500 Hessians, 3,000 Mecklenburgers, 1,000 Ansbachers, and 2,000 Sachse-Gothaers. The papers specify the day on which Colonel Fawcett was in each one of these places in Germany. Everywhere the inhabitants are laughing about the King of England that he still intends to send troops to America. "And if he sends us another 100,000 men, they will not be able to subdue us," they say. This is the more probable as America is very populous. To take just the Province of Massachusetts Bay as an example, in case of need, this Province will assemble 100,000 men in less than 4 weeks; both old and young men will immediately go. My landlord says, and so do they all, "If my sons should be killed, I shall be happy to go to war myself." This newspaper further reports: "Because Gen. Howe has treated the prisoners so cruelly and so inhumanely, Congress has ordered that the prisoners from the Engl. side be treated in the same way. Since Gen. Howe has allowed the [American] prisoners to starve to death, he should send victuals for the [British] prisoners or they [Congress] would also let them starve. The Americans had been compelled to send provisions to New York hoping to keep a few of their men alive but when the provisions arrived, most of them had already died. In this way, Gen. Howe had allowed the 1,800 captured at Fort Washington to perish in a most shameful, unheard of manner.[4] Furthermore, Congress ordered the following: Since Gen. Howe has discontinued the paper money, all the imprisoned officers in all the provinces are to pay 2 silver piasters weekly to their landlords for their subsistence, for which they had previously paid in paper money." This was calamitous news for us, for one received 4 paper shill. for one silver shill.

13th   According to all reports, the army of Gen. Washington is gathering in White Plains. General Howe continues to be in and around Philadelphia with his army. The inhabitants here are almost angry with their Gen. Washington that he does not take Gen. Howe prisoner with his army just as Gen. Gates has captured Gen. Burgoyne. Here, I thought of the political twaddlers who had designed the plan of operation for Gen. Daun at that time, as Rabener says.[5]--

17th   It is 2 years ago today that Gen. Howe left Boston and moved to Halifax.

20th   Today, I saw the first multicolored snake (couleuvre) this year, about 1 1/2 ells long; this is early; I should think that these creatures are still asleep. The NW wind is continuing. The weather is fair and the snow almost gone.

23rd   In the Boston papers we read that Congress does not wish to surrender the Burgoyne army before the King of England has ratified the Saratoga Convention.[6] The transport ships that Gen. Howe has sent to Boston in order to collect the army had to sail off empty. Little Peggy Williams is now cured of the terrible gangrene although all the doctors and - the old, old women were doubting it.--

End of this Month

Month of April 1778

1st   The Hartford papers say that 32,000 men from the Engl., Irish and Scottish troops will come to America this spring - without the Germans. -- We hear from Boston that many ships are cruising off the harbor; that they are thought to be Engl. ships; that they are much afraid of a surprise attack on Boston by the Engl. fleet.

6th   It is very changeable weather just like April weather in Germany and the air is cold to boot.

9th   Today is Maundy Thursday. The air is very cold and much snow has again been falling.

13th   As we were celebrating the second Easter holiday [Easter Monday], the people inquired as to its significance. We explained the importance of this day to them. My landlord said that would be quite all right but he wished he could observe Sundays as he should and as God had commanded them to be observed. -- Since man had instituted the other days, they [New Englanders] did not pay attention to them. Today, we saw millions of wild pigeons in the air, nobody knows whence they come nor whither they go. As I mentioned before, they are birds of passage here as well as in Canada.

18th   In the Boston paper we read that the Hessian Gen. Heister had returned to Germany last fall and died on the day of his arrival in Cassel.[7] I took 2 weeks leave of absence from the Committee here to travel to our troops in Cambridge. The inhabitants begin sowing wheat and turnips.

20th   In very good weather, I started my trip to Cambridge this morning. I rode off at 6 o'clock, passed through Weston around 7 o'clock, and at 7:30 o'clock, I reached the big Boston military road in Brookfield at the milestone [indicating] 66 miles to Boston; at 9 o'clock, I had put Spencer behind and came to Leicester. Here I stopped at a Jew's in order to exchange some silver money. This Jew, by the name of Lupes [Aaron Lopez], is Portuguese and has settled at this place. In a big store, he has all kinds of merchandise to sell and does his transactions together with his sons and sons-in-law. This Jew Lupes speaks English, Portuguese, Spanish, Italian and French. I had to take my breakfast with him and had to promise to stop again on my way back.[8] I then rode through Worcester and came to Shrewsbury where I ate lunch; I continued my trip at 1 o'clock. I came through Northborough, Sudbury, Weston, Watertown and arrived in Cambridge at 8 o'clock this evening at the house where Maj. Gen. von Riedesel was staying. I had ridden 72 Engl. miles today on a horse that had not eaten anything but hay and straw during the whole winter. I was so stiff and shaken up that I could not get off the horse. The general's men got me down and I could scarcely walk to the house where Captains von Pöllniz, Gerlach, O'Connell and Lieut. Cleve were staying. Here, I took my lodging and agreed to pay 10 shill. in paper money every 24 hours for my horse; yet the horse got nothing but hay for it.

21st   This morning, I was so stiff that I could hardly get out of bed; I had to be helped. Nevertheless, I went to Winter Hill where our regiments were in the barracks, and returned quite late. The news here is that 3 commissioners have arrived from England to make peace with the Colonies.

22nd   I went to Winter Hill again, from where I went with my friends Müller and Ramcke to Mystic, a very beautiful place on the other side of Winter Hill. Here we enjoyed some Port wine. This was a happy day for us; we recalled our families and friends in Germany, the Port wine inspired us, -- and soon we had forgotten that we were prisoners. --

23rd   Today I went once more to Winter Hill and from there to Prospect Hill, where the Engl. regiments were stationed in their barracks. This hill is situated closer to the city of Boston and we could see quite well this beautiful city located about one Engl. mile across the water. It is beautiful, in oblong fashion, and has 5 big towers and several small ones. From here, we again went to Mystic.

24th   I was at our Gen. von Riedesel's on account of money, and Captain Gerlach was ordered to pay the money due me. I received 40 guineas for Cornet Stutzer and myself and 20 guineas from Lieut. von Muzell for Lieut. Gebhard. Pastor Melzheimer had not written to the general asking for money as the other gentlemen had done and therefore he did not get anything. The reason for my trip was to receive my money and maybe letters from Germany. I inquired about letters and learned from our general that letters had been here for me but no one could tell where they had gone. To rid myself of my low spirits, I went to Mystic.

25th   Since Gen. Burgoyne has gone to England, Gen. Phillips has command of the Engl. troops and Gen. von Riedesel over the German troops. As I intend to depart tomorrow, I took leave of my friends today.

26th   Today was Monday and Gen. von Riedesel told me that if I wanted to hear a German sermon, I should remain till noon since Pastor Kohle would be preaching in his downstairs room. During the sermon, the general had an attack of apoplexy and would have fallen from his chair if he had not been caught by those close by. I immediately opened a blood-vessel on his arm and he soon recovered. I may not depart now and am staying at the general's house for the time being.

27th   I still had to remain here this forenoon but finally departed from Cambridge this afternoon to Marlborough, to the milestone [*indicating*] 25 miles to Boston, and spent the night here.

28th   At 7 o'clock in the morning, I rode to Worcester where I bought medicine for 70 piasters in paper money from the Docts. Dix and Greene.[9] In Cambridge, I had received 16 piasters in paper money for one guinea. From here I rode to Leicester to the Jew Lupes, where I arrived just in time for lunch. The Jew regaled me with a bottle of

Madeira wine and I had him change 12 guineas into silver money. I continued my travel to Brimfield where I arrived at 10 o'clock at night. For my horse, I had to pay 3 silver piasters for the whole trip; this was not expensive. I have had quite beautiful weather during these days; tonight, it began to rain.

30th   The rain is continuing today. This rendered my landlord discontented as he wanted to start planting corn [maize].

End of this Month

Month of May 1778

1st   The weather continues unsettled just as it is in Germany on the 1st of May. But one sees absolutely no greenery here as one does in Germany where everything is green at this time and where one enjoys the sweet warbling of the nightingale, which is completely unknown here. There are no songsters at all about.

4th   Congress gave orders that the Province of Massachusetts Bay is to supply 3,300 recruits, i.e., 2,000 men to the Continental army and 1,300 to Pittskill; from our village, 5 men are joining.

5th   With W and NW wind, the weather is fine; the trees are showing buds which are about to open.

9th   In this continuing warm weather the leaves are coming out. In Springfield 1,800 people, old and young, had themselves inoculated against smallpox; of these 3 died; being ill, they should not have been inoculated.

12th   With NW wind and in spite of sunshine, it has been very cold since yesterday. Although we have seen no birds during the winter, we now see several kinds, all unknown to us. The larks here are a little bigger than field fares and therefore much larger than the larks in Germany but almost homogeneous in color. Below the trunk, however, they show a beautiful yellow reaching up to the beak, but they do not sing. Black birds of the same size are coal black and have red wings. One kind, as large as the bullfinch, is of a very dark red as if covered with red velvet; they are very beautiful. Some are yellow like the canary birds, some are yellow and have black heads and wings. One sees several kinds of birds with strange colorings. There are very many quail about but [*they are*] very different from those in Germany; just like the larks here, they are not birds of passage.[10] There are several types of partridges and birds of prey but no nightingale, no stork, no cuckoo, no sparrows and very few swallows; nightingale, stork, cuckoo and all the songsters are unknown here.

13th   On our walk today, we killed a black snake, about 6 feet long.

In the last Boston paper [Continental Journal] from Saturday May 8 [April 23], I have translated the following: *Mr. Deane*[11] *was sent here from a French port to deliver the report that His Most Christian Majesty, the King of France Louis XVI, has recognized the independence of the 13 United American Provinces. Last Thursday he departed from the harbor here on the French frigate Sensible of 36 cannon with an important message to Congress. This provoked great joy in Boston and at festivities arranged at the American coffee house, toasts were pronounced to the following:*
1. The United States of America. 2. The Congress. 3. King Louis XVI [Lewis the 16th] of France. 4. General Washington. 5. The American army and navy. 6. The American Ambassador to [at the court of] France.[12] *7. The memory of the heroes*

who fell in defense of American freedom. 8. May Freedom and Independence [of America] continue till the last descendant. 9. Freedom with danger is preferable to servitude with safety. 10. In defense of their freedom, Americans ought to overcome all the despotic lawgivers so that no people will be subdued that is determined to be free. [May the glorious struggle that the Americans are making in defense of their liberties convince all the arbitrary rulers that there is no subjecting a people determined to be free.] 11. May the free and independent States of America be at all times a place of refuge for the oppressed in the 4 continents of the world [prove an asylum for the sons of oppression in all the quarters of the globe]. 12. May the infernal enemies of America never enjoy the sweets of liberty. 13. Union of the United States of America must remain united till the end of the world [till time shall be no more]. [accurate]

25th   The weather is quite beautiful, but we have heavy thunderstorms almost daily. In this village, almost 190 people have had themselves inoculated against smallpox,[13] of whom most are married. Every day, the doctors would like to speak with me but I am not allowed to get closer to them than 50 paces. They would like to have me along in the smallpox houses, for those inoculated against smallpox have all been separated in two remote houses; but I am not allowed to go there. My landlord says that if I do that, I cannot come back to his house; so great is the fear of all the people here of smallpox. Neither my landlord nor my landlady nor any of their 15 children have had smallpox as yet and they will not go [*for the inoculation*] on their own. Many thousands of people die in America every year who have not had smallpox and have reached a ripe old age. The Expedition of 1775, which the Americans had undertaken against Canada, is said to have brought on their fear of smallpox. Many had been smitten with the pox in Canada and most of them had died from it. Those that survived and returned to New England were so disfigured by smallpox that parents did not recognize their children nor women their husbands and many were unwilling to accept them [their loved ones] back. --

30th   Last night there was a hoarfrost causing the leaves on the trees to turn black. My landlord has prophesized that not much fruit would grow this year. That would not be good because we would not have cider and who knows whether we will have to stay in captivity another winter.

31st   Last night, with NW wind, there again has been a hoarfrost and it is very cold today. This is quite unusual on the first day of Pentecost both for us and the inhabitants. Tonight, east wind and rain.

End of this Month

Month of June 1778

1st   Lieut. Gebhard has gone to Cambridge.

9th   Of the 190 people having submitted to inoculation, two have died. Doctor Trask told me today that since these had never been well before, they should not have been inoculated [*in the first place*].

13th   It is very hot with violent thunderstorms. Lieut. Gebhard has not brought anything new back from Cambridge.

14th   A 40 year old woman was baptized today. Pastor Melzheimer wore a white vest and trousers underneath his black coat when he climbed up into the pulpit to preach.

The Boston paper says that Gen. Howe has returned to England last month and that Gen. Clinton has taken over the command of the army.[14]

22nd　　Today, five cannon passed through here which had come from Springfield because the Americans want to seize this island [sic]; for this task, five men from Brimfield were also taken into the army.

24th　　Today we had a total eclipse of the sun; the sun was almost completely darkened and only one streak, scarcely half a finger wide, could be seen. It was as dark as if in clear weather the sun had just set in the evening.

28th　　Today, the husband of the woman who had been baptized a fortnight ago was baptized together with their 7 children, 2 to 14 years of age.

29th　　The Hartford paper [Connecticut Courant, June 23, 1778]: *London, March 23: Yesterday a messenger came from The Hague with the news that the King of Prussia had invaded Imperial [Austrian] Silesia with 3 armies. The first army was commanded by the King himself, the 2nd by his brother Prinz Heinrich [Henry], and the third by the Crown Prince of Braunschweig, who is married to the [Engl.] Princess Augusta. When the dispatch was sent off, a skirmish was in progress with the Regiment Colloredo etc., whereby they [the Prussians] had captured 3 battalions [were made prisoner].* [15] [accurate]

This paper furthermore reports that the King of England has made peace proposals to the Americans through the 3 commissioners Lord Carlisle, Governor Johnston and Willian Eden Esq. [16] [summary]

This will not accomplish anything, however. If they had come a year ago before the Americans had entered into an alliance with France, peace could surely have been made. It is very hot here at present.

End of this month

Month of July 1778

1st　　As I mentioned before, it is very hot here and violent thunderstorms occur every day.

2nd　　This afternoon, we had a violent thunderstorm such as I have never experienced before; lightning and thunder always occurred simultaneously and one often saw flashes of lightning being perpendicularly driven out of the clouds into the ground.

3rd　　In Worcester, 3 men and a female were arrested today; the High Sheriff himself has to do the hanging. He also has to perform the floggings, but is permitted to hire someone for this work. Since he could not get anyone, he had to do it himself this time. The crime of those hanged was [*as follows*]: The woman had bribed these 3 fellows to kill her husband, with whom she had lived very unhappily; this was done. They were an Engl. sergeant, an English and an American soldier. The dead man, by the name of Spooner, was a resident of Brookfield, a coarse, ill-bred individual. His wife, who had been practically forced to marry him, was the daughter of Brig. Gen. Ruggles of the Engl. army on Long Island. She was a very well-bred person who had enjoyed a fine education and accordingly was unable to love that husband of hers. Brig. Gen. Ruggles was a native of Hardwick [Mass.] where he had owned beautiful estates; because he had emigrated, these were now confiscated.[17]

4th   The 9,000 regimentals captured by the Americans, of which I had written on the 16th of Jan. of this year, have been ordered by Congress to be dyed black and to be given to Gen. Washington's army.

5th   Today, the man and his wife went to Holy Communion for the first time. The man is 46 years old and his wife 40. (cf. June 28).

6th   I visited some sick people in Northampton, 42 miles away from Brimfield.

9th   I was called to some sick people in Hartford, in the

13th   Province of Connecticut, from where I returned today.

The newspaper [Connecticut Courant, July 7, 1778] tells of an action which is said to have occurred near Monmouth in New Jersey between the Engl. and American armies on June 28. [The Engl. army is said to have lost 3,000 men and taken flight to the ships; the Americans do not tell anything of their own losses.] [18] [summary]

18th   Four children were baptized, the oldest of whom was 7 years of age. This may partly be our doing because we tell the people on every occasion what we were also taught: he who does not believe and is not baptized cannot be saved. This affects the people very deeply every time. --

The Hartford paper writes that a French fleet, 211 sails strong, has arrived, among which are 47 ships of the line (putting it mildly) and that this fleet has cast anchor 2 miles away from the Engl. fleet. It is commanded by Lieut. Gen. and Admiral Comte d'Estaing, Knight of the Royal Order.[19]

25th   A young married couple had to do penance in church because the wife had given birth to a child 7 months after the wedding. Under these circumstances, many in Germany would have to do penance in church.

27th   The Hartford paper writes that the Engl. fleet, 180 ships strong, has arrived in New York. The inhabitants are beginning to cut wheat and rye, which they sow in April; thus it must have been very hot.

29th   This summer, 3 rattlesnakes have been killed in these villages, of which the largest had 9 bells [sic] on its tail. The doctors here recommend its flesh to the comsumptive sick. There are several old people around claiming they have seen a 2-headed rattlesnake. The Hartford paper writes that the French fleet has seized 8 Engl. transport ships, which were coming from Cork in Ireland loaded with provisions, and forced them to enter [the harbor of] Philadelphia; that a Spanish fleet had united with the French fleet;[20] that the Tories and the Savages had killed more than 2,000 inhabitants in Susquehanna and 7 other villages; among these there had been a Tory who had murdered his mother, brothers and sisters.[21] The papers always tell astonishing things about the Tories; they lie in order to kindle an even greater hatred in the inhabitants against them. In addition, the paper writes that all the prisoners of war in the Province of Connecticut are to be exchanged on the 16th of this month. Presumably we too will soon have to leave our captivity - just as we are beginning to enjoy being prisoners. --

End of this Month

Month of August 1778

1st   Much ammunition coming from Springfield goes through here to Providence.

The Hartford paper writes among other articles from London, March 13: *One of our friends from London gave us news about the baggage that the first commissioner to come to America to make peace, had taken along; and since it is [a little] peculiar, it shall be made known to the public: 6 dozen of the finest perfumed gloves; 12 bottles of rose essence; 12 bottles of lavender essence; 36 lbs. of red and white grain powder; 36 dozen of toothbrushes; 50 dozens of the best toothpicks; 90 containers with dresses; 100 pairs of shoes with red heels; 24 large muffs; a small treatise on American history written for children; treatise on games; instruction on how to play whist; 2 billiard tables; one box of pastry; Grotius' 'Treatise on War,' bound in calf leather; Lord Carlisle's 'Poetry;' a wooden horse to practice riding while on board ship; 3 Italian hunting dogs; one large bass fiddle and an escritoire.* -- [accurate]

9th   Ammunition and cannon continue coming through here; they come from Springfield and are taken to Providence.

12th   The Boston paper writes that the combined French and Spanish fleets have seized 15 Engl. ships. I have spoken with an American officer here who had been present at the battle of Monmouth, of which I wrote on July 12; he averred that Gen. Washington, having lost more than 2,000 men, withdrew in the night after the battle. Thereupon, Gen. Clinton quietly continued his march to Sandy Hook where he arrived on July 5. He then embarked with his army onto transport ships, which had come there out of the Delaware River the day before, and sailed to New York. Neither the army nor the fleet was aware of the danger menacing them on those days. Through a ship, Gen. Clinton received news that the French fleet under Comte d'Estaing had been seen off the coastline of Virginia. If this fleet had immediately taken its course to Sandy Hook instead of the Delaware, it would have seized the Engl. fleet, which was protected by only 2 warships; this army would then have suffered the same fate as the Burgoyne army at Saratoga. The American officers said further that Gen. Washington himself had called Gen. Clinton's march through New Jersey a masterstroke.

14th   On account of the stormy NW wind it is very cold today and one must sit near the open fire; seeing that the houses are so miserably constructed, as I have mentioned before, I fear our house will collapse in this strong wind at any moment.

16th   I have been a prisoner for one year today. How calmly and happily we have been spending this year! and we would have lived much more cheerfully if we had understood the English language from the beginning. We can now speak a little with them and with the help of these friendly, these Christian people, we know more English every day because they all take great pains teaching us.

17th   Five recruits from our village go to Providence where a corps is assembling, destined to be transferred from there to Rhode Island. Under the command of General Sullivan, they are to capture any of the possessions the English may have there - but not too swiftly, not rashly.[22]

23rd   Every day, there is a kind of haze like smoke or steam in the air, which even the strong NW wind cannot drive away; at the same time, it is very hot. We are also having very heavy thunderstorms daily, frequently following each other throughout the night. The inhabitants have a restful sleep just the same and never get out of bed.[23] -- I spoke to a deserter who had escaped from the English out of the city of Newport in Rhode Island. He said, "The garrison of Newport is 7,000 men strong, half English half

Hessians; these are provided with supplies for 3 months. Newport is very well fortified and the American army, under Gen. Sullivan, is 10,000 men strong. He had landed not far from Howland's Ferry on the 9th of this month, that is the same day on which the French fleet had departed from Rhode Island. The Americans had not expected this move but believed the French fleet under Admiral Comte d'Estaing was supposed to encircle the Fort of Newport while Gen. Sullivan would besiege it on land.[24] This French fleet, which - as I mentioned before - had taken its course toward the Delaware, appeared, wholly unexpected, in Sandy Hook 4 days after the report of its existence had arrived in New York. It consisted of 12 warships and 3 frigates. Among the former was one of 90, one of 80 and 6 of 74 cannon; according to the most precise information, this fleet had 11,000 men aboard. The Engl. fleet under Admiral Lord Howe consisted of 6-64, 3-50, and 2-44 cannon ships, several frigates and sloops. Most of these ships were old and in bad condition; moreover, the ships were not adequately manned. One must therefore conclude that there was great consternation in New York to have such a terrifying enemy fleet so close by, one so superior to the Engl. fleet. If the French admiral had risked forcing the harbor, it would have brought about the total ruin of the Engl. fleet and of more than 300 transport and merchant ships. Yet fearing not to find enough depth, Comte d'Estaing was not willing to risk going over the bar with his big ships. (N.B. a bar is a sandbank over which all ships have to sail that wish to enter the harbor.) Thus this fleet cast anchor off the coast of the Province of New Jersey about 4 Engl. miles from Sandy Hook in the vicinity of the town of Shrewsbury. This gave the Engl. fleet time to recover from its shock and place itself into a better state of defense. One thousand volunteers immediately went from the transport and merchant ships onto [the ships of] the fleet; the rest of the sailors could not be held back, they all wanted [to go] onto the warships. Many deserted on boats at night and the commanders could hardly retain enough to guard their ships. Even merchants and tradesmen in New York asked for assignments and took their seats on the warships near the cannon just like common sailors; many went to sea in small boats to observe the enemy's movements. One merchant showed in an especially gallant way how much he had his King's interest at heart, a way perhaps unheard of in history. He asked that his ship, displaying his whole happiness and wealth, be changed into a fire ship, which he himself wished to sail among the enemy fleet to set them all afire. With contempt, he rejected all fear of death and any reward offered to him. Such heroism was not only found among seamen and merchants. Although the infantry had not yet recovered from their horrible and tedious march and the wounds of many officers and privates would not heal for a long time, they all went most eagerly on board the warships in order to serve as marines or sea soldiers. None wanted to stay behind. But since a garrison had absolutely to be retained in New York, the commander was compelled to have them cast lots; in one word, the stouthearted conduct shown by everyone on this occasion was unfathomable. The French fleet was occupied with taking fresh water and fresh supplies on board for 11 days and this tarrying lessened the fear in New York. Since the Engl. fleet had now positioned itself in a very good state of defense, it was certain that the French fleet could no longer carry out their operation without provoking their own ruin. Meanwhile, the vexation of the English and their mortification at seeing themselves blockaded in their own harbor by an enemy fleet was horrendous. What increased their vexation was seeing ships under English flags sail toward New York being captured by the enemy fleet every single day. Every one wished Admiral Byron would come with his fleet.[25] On July 22, the French fleet finally weighed anchor in a favorable wind. As the high tide would occur on this day and the water rise more than 20 feet higher on the bar than usual, the Engl. Admiral Lord Howe thought that Comte d'Estaing would carry out his prepared plan and that on this day one of the hottest and most desperate battles would take place on sea and on land between two nations, that have been cultivating a natural hatred against each other. If this had happened, there would have been a shedding of blood as the world has perhaps never known. On the English side, everything was in the best order and state of defense, but Comte d'Estaing considered the experiment too dangerous, changed his course and was out of sight in a few hours.

Nothing would ever have been more disastrous than if the French fleet had stayed longer off Sandy Hook; it had set sail at a fortunate and proper time, otherwise all or at least part of Admiral Byron's fleet would have fallen into its power. This fleet had departed from England and, through terrible storms, incurred very heavy damage at sea; almost all the ships had lost some masts. In addition, this fleet had been badly equipped in England and not been manned with an appropriate crew; moreover, half of them had gotten sick on the voyage and therefore were in miserable condition. One by one they reached the coastline of America at different places. In the period from July 22, when Comte d'Estaing had left Sandy Hook, to July 30, there arrived the *Renown* with 50 cannon from the West Indies, the *Raisonable* and *Centurion* with 4 and 50 cannon from Halifax, and the *Cornwall* with 74 cannon from Byron's fleet; all these ships arrived separately at Sandy Hook. The joy at this reinforcement was exceedingly great in New York because the plan which the French ministers had made with the American delegate in Paris, i.e., to capture the Engl. fleet and army on the Delaware and its banks, had failed. It was now decided to seize Rhode Island. Comte d'Estaing arrived there and cast anchor at the various entrances to the harbor. It was therefore agreed to place the Engl. forces in Rhode Island, under the command of General Pigot,[26] between 2 fires: General Sullivan should land with an army of 10,000 men and all the ships in Rhode Island should be partly burned, partly sent to various harbor entrances. Among these were 6 beautiful frigates, the *Orpheus, Lark, Juno, Cerberus, Flora* and *Falcon*. On Aug. 8, when the wind was favorable, the French fleet entered the harbor and, passing by, cannonaded the fortifications of the city of Newport. This was answered in like manner without any appreciable damage being done to either side. As soon as Admiral Howe had learned that Comte d'Estaing was at Rhode Island, he set sail for that place. He arrived there on the 9th and as the wind turned that day and the enemy fleet had been informed of the arrival of the English, the enemy fleet departed from Rhode Island. It is highly probable that it would have come to an engagement between both fleets if one of the most terrible storms ever had not prevented it. Nevertheless, several Engl. ships had the advantage of frequently firing broadside into the enemy ships. In this storm, most of the enemy ships lost their masts and were so severely damaged that they had to go to Boston to have the damage repaired; they were accompanied by Lord Howe.[27] It is exceedingly hot, the strong NW wind cannot drive off the haze, which feels like smoke and steam in the air. Having been informed through a letter from Cambridge that Gen. von Riedesel has given several letters that had come from Germany to commissary general Mercereau[28] in Rutland to reach those prisoners that were scattered around in Canada, I decided to travel there as early as tomorrow; I wanted to see whether I perhaps was lucky enough to have received a letter from Germany.

26th   This morning, I rode off from here and arrived in Rutland at 1 o'clock, passed by the barracks where the English regiments were [staying] and came to a little house where several dragoons were quartered; they got daily provisions here. I went to commissary Mercereau and inquired after letters. He said he had received many letters from the gen. but also sent most to the prisoners around the region; he could not remember having read my name. He searched and found 2 letters, one for Lieut. Gebhard and one for Cornet Stutzer; this means I had again traveled in vain. I had to eat lunch with the commissary and since several Engl. officers were at the same table with us the conversation centered on Rhode Island but they had no reliable news. As I was short on medicine, I decided to ride from here to Worcester where I arrived at 8 o'clock at night.

27th   This evening, I came back to Brimfield and traveled on the

28th   road to Union in the Province of Connecticut to visit some sick people. On the way back, I visited my patients in Sturbridge and South Brimfield and came on the

31st   back to my lodging. Everywhere I had gone, Rhode Island was the topic of conversation. Everyone wished the French ill, some even cursed the whole alliance with France. -- As I mentioned before, the Americans had assembled an army that was to act in concert with the French fleet. -- To bring this army, its artillery, ammunition and provisions together and to ferry it across onto the Island of Rhode Island was connected with immense cost and no less toil and danger. On that very same day when this army with everything belonging to it had been ferried across, the French fleet left the harbor. Nevertheless, Gen. Sullivan advanced with his army to the front of Fort Newport where he made preparations for a formal siege. But since a large part of his army ran home and his forces grew smaller by the day, he withdrew with prudence and little loss and sent his army back to New England on the night of the 29th to the 30th, just when Gen. Clinton arrived in Rhode Island from New York with reinforcements.[29]

End of this Month

Month of September 1778

2nd   Pastor Melzheimer came home from Westminster and brought the news that we would get orders in the next few days to move to Westminster where all the officers were to stay. The order of Gen. von Riedesel reads that as many prisoners as possible should stay together in case it comes to an exchange.

3rd   Last night it was freezing and today it is very hot.

7th   The French fleet is still in Boston Harbor. The Engl. fleet reconnoiters this harbor very diligently.

15th   Cornet Stutzer rode to Westminster to get precise information as to whether we should change our quarters before winter. My landlord told me today that as late as 15 years ago, the community had gone to hunt rattlesnakes every spring in the month of April and that they had once killed more than 6 of these creatures on one forenoon. Among these there had been one with 22 bells [sic] on its tail and when it was killed, 99 offspring had come out of her throat. He furthermore asserted and so did all the inhabitants here, that when men approach, the young snakes creep into the old one's throat to hide in that fortification, as it were, and after the danger has passed, they will come out again. I believe this because, even for a goodly sum of money, my landlord will not tell a lie and as I have mentioned before, lying is anyway considered one of the greatest sins here. But I could not help asking why there had been 99 and not 100 and remarking that they could not possibly have counted them so exactly; even if they had killed 99 young ones, several could perhaps have crawled away; this seemed to embarrass him. -- The rattlesnakes come out at the end of March and the beginning of April and go back as early as September. Their winter quarters are caves in between cliffs and rocks where they sleep throughout the winter. Fifteen or more have been found in a cluster together.[30]

19th   Cornet Stutzer has returned again; he brought the order from commissary Mercereau to the Committee here that we should go from Brimfield to Lancaster and take our quarters there; that the Committee should show a receipt that we had paid our landlord everything and not owed him anything. I also learned from the cornet that Reg. Surgeon Henckel from our Grenad. Battalion had died in Cambridge.

20th   My landlord's entire family is unhappy about my departure. They all want us to stay a little longer. It is quite certain that the Engl. fleet is cruising off Boston harbor.

25th   We had fixed Monday as the day of our trip to Lancaster, but tonight a messenger came from Westminster bringing us the order from our Major von Meibom that we should make our appearance at commissary Mercereau's in Rutland this Sunday noon, the 27th of this month, in order to be exchanged. This is quite unexpected news for me. -- When I took leave today, on the

26th,   everyone in the village was sad. I was given many a godspeed.

27th   We rode off at 7 o'clock this morning. Old and young were crying in the house. Pastor Melzheimer and I had lived one year and 5 days with this family and enjoyed much friendship. We rode 10 miles in one hour and were in Brookfield as early as 8 o'clock, when we ate breakfast. At 9 o'clock, we continued our trip and were in Rutland at 1 o'clock. We met all our officers here who were to go to Providence for the exchange tomorrow, and from there be ferried across to Rhode Island. Since no privates would be exchanged, 6 officers, i.e., Captain of the Cavalry Fricke, Captain von Bärtling sen., Lieuts. Gebhard and von Bothmer, Cornet Schönewald and Ensign Specht, stayed behind; these had been assigned by Maj. Gen. von Riedesel to stay behind to assist the privates. They were to take their quarters in Westminster and since Reg. Surgeon Vorbrodt departed with the others, I was to stay behind and provide all the prisoners in need of care with internal and external medicine. I was to buy the medicine and give the bill to the Captain of the Cavalry Fricke and to Capt. von Bärtling, who were supposed to pay for it. Since I was also assigned to stay in Westminster, I departed this morning from Rutland for Princeton where I remained overnight.

28th   Early this morning I arrived in Westminster in good weather and took my lodging at Lieut. Heywood's. Here I pay 4 piasters in paper money a week for room, board, i.e., breakfast, lunch and dinner, as well as laundry. Westminster was settled only 35 years ago, is very rugged, hilly and full of rocks and half of it is still woods where foxes and even bears can be found. Like all the villages in New England, it is 7 square miles in size. The inhabitants, who do not seem to be nearly as polite and friendly as those in Brimfield, assert that there are no rattlesnakes at all around and this reassures me greatly.

End of this Month

Month of October 1778

4th   Pastor Melzheimer sent his horse back to me last night and I learned from him that our officers departed from Providence and sailed to Rhode Island on the 1st of this month. During the day it is still beautiful, warm weather; at night it freezes. We received news from Winter Hill that the following lampoon on Maj. Gen. Phillips, who is now in command,[31] has been made by the Bostonians:

Great in his body, little in his mind,
Even to brutal manners most inclin'd.
Not all the charms in the fair sex we find,
Ever would smooth the roughness of his mind.
Rude blundering, fraction, unpleasing without cause,
And always flying in the face of the laws.
Licentious, nought that's virtuous he adores,
Placing his whole delight in keeping whores.
He, who of none but bastard birth can boost,
Is now the leader of a British hoost.
Look here! the offspring of a British b---d,
Is the first fav'rite of a tyrant lord.
Proud and insulting to all but his lass,
Sure they are fools who trust to such an ass.

N.B. The first letters come out as General Phillips.

12th   Since Pastor Melzheimer intended his horse for Brimfield, I rode there today to deliver it.

15th   Because the apples did not turn out well this year and no cider was being made in Westminster, I bought 7 barrels of cider today, paid 20 piasters in paper money for each barrel and agreed with Medad Hitchcock that he would transport them to Westminster for 40 shill. in paper money; this is a bad road, 40 miles long.

20th   I departed from Brimfield and went via Brookfield, Oakham, Rutland, Princeton to Westminster, where I arrived at 5 o'clock.

22nd   In good weather, I rode to Princeton this morning where I expected Medad with the cider. He came at 1 o'clock and complained that his wagon had broken down and that his oxen were lame; he, therefore, had been compelled to store the cider with the innkeeper Wood in Rutland. I rode to Templeton with Medad.

23rd   I rode to Rutland where I found my cider but, however much I tried, I could not find a coachman to drive here and so being extremely disgusted, I rode back to Westminster. When I could not get any coachman here either, I again rode to Rutland, today the

26th,   but again could not get any coachman. Mr. Wood wished the cider removed from his house and so did I because the cider had grown considerably less in these days. I finally sold it at a loss.

28th   Since my landlord wanted to have 5 piasters every week, I moved from his house to that of David Sawine, where I also pay 5 piasters but have a much better room. We have learned that our troops are to march to Virginia from Winter Hill because such provisions as required by the troops as flour, rice etc. have to be transported on ships from the southern parts of North America to Boston. For some reason, Gen. Clinton does not want to have those ships pass through any longer. In the Boston papers, we read that the army of Gen. Clinton embarked on more than 200 transport ships and sailed from New York. They had earlier emptied their magazines in New York and sold everything very cheaply except salt, butter, cheese, coffee, sugar, wine, rum etc. They had taken horses, wagons, cannon and all the ammunition on board and presumably will soon evacuate this fort. The same is being said of Newport, namely that the garrison of this fort has sailed to the West Indies. The Worcester paper reports that the King of England and the Empress of Russia have entered into an alliance and that the Empress has given order to her fleet to set sail immediately against the enemies of England. Believe it or not!

At the close of this month the guinea is worth 24 piasters in paper money.[32]

Month of November 1778

1st   The Worcester paper reports that the French have seized Dominica.[33] I rode to Rutland to visit the sick among our men, that lie in their barracks there.

5th   Today, the first snow was falling; I rode to my patients in Rutland.

7th   The newspapers have announced that the usual Thanksgiving will be on the 26th of this month.[34]

9th   East wind and rain. The First Division of our German troops set out to Virginia from Winter Hill under the command of Brig. Gen. Specht. The Second

Division will march tomorrow and the Third the day thereafter. To go on a journey of 800 Engl. miles at this time of year is terrible.

10th   As I was in Rutland today, I saw the First Division of the Engl. troops march off. They also march in 3 divisions.

14th   Continually blowing east wind and rain. The Boston paper gives the following very important and reliable news: *New York, Sept. 24. We are now reliably informed that the ship, recently seized, has brought dispatches of the greatest importance to Comte d'Estaing. The first article of his instructions is to proclaim Louis XVI [King] in all the American Provinces and, as guarantee for the debts, take immediate possession of New England. In the 2nd article, the Comte is ordered to force all the members of Congress to swear the oath of allegiance to the Most Christian King Louis XVI; in case they refuse, they are immediately to be thrown into the bastille in Philadelphia. The same ship also brought an appreciable freight of such antiquities along as 250,000 missals, 200 torture instruments, 3 million consecrated wafers, 150,000 crucifixes, 6 million rosaries, 200,000 pair of wooden shoes, five cases full of rouge for the fair sex, 10,000 cases filled with pills against the French disease. We also know now for certain that the passengers on these ships had all been priests, disguised as hairdressers, dentists, musicians and dance masters. In one letter found on this ship, it says that Doctor Franklin has recanted the Protestant religion and been honored with the Medal of the Holy Cross of Jerusalem. --*

16th   I have already mentioned the wildcats on page 106. Last night, they killed a sheep of my landlord's brother and scratched the eyes out of another. These are dangerous animals. From a letter out of Cambridge I got the information that our baggage from Canada had actually been off Boston but as the Engl. ship had not been allowed to enter the harbor, it had sailed from there to Rhode Island. [*I also learned*] that the officers that had gone to Rutland for the exchange were still in Newport.

20th   Many English and Germans are almost daily deserting from the Burgoyne army.[35] The Americans intend to undertake an expedition to Canada this winter and since they [with the Engl.] took this region away from the French in the last war, [they plan] to return it to the King of France. Because the Canadians had to give up their arms, they want to take 30,000 guns along. General Sullivan is to command the corps designated for this expedition, but nothing will surely come of it. If, however, they should be so bold as to risk it, they will not be kindly received.

26th   Great preparations are made for the Thanksgiving Feast tomorrow. It can rightfully be called a day of gluttony [Fresstag].

At the close of this month the guinea is worth 28 piasters in paper money.

Month of December 1778

1st   One of the inhabitants here sent me a wild turkey that, ready to be butchered, weighed 28 pounds. They are very abundant here and can hardly be distinguished from the tame ones. They are very tasty.

2nd   Since Maj. Gen. von Riedesel was expected in Brookfield today; I rode there but on my arrival was told that he had passed through on his trip to Virginia yesterday.

3rd   Tonight there was a total eclipse of the moon.

4th   Early this morning, I rode to Worcester and this afternoon on to Holden.

5th   I returned to Westminster via Princeton.

11th   In S and SE wind, much snow has fallen in the past several days, which the storm has driven [into drifts] 12 to 15 feet high.

17th   The Most Honorable Congress has established another day of prayer and fasting: the 30th of this month. This is supposed to be a day of praying and fasting; the Worcester paper writes that for this reason, Gen. Phillips has gone to Virginia on the 14th! [sic]

21st   It is being announced in all the villages that whoever wants to march to Canada this winter should commit himself for 8 months; for that he will receive 1,000 piasters in paper as pocket money and every month 100 piasters in wages. Each one should procure a pair of snowshoes (Raqueten) for himself. In these 8 months, so they say or rather hope, Canada must be back under French rule, and what is more, -- I bet that nothing will come of it; the Expedition of 1775 cost too many lives. --
The Worcester paper from the 17th of this month writes that the prisons in Germany have been cleared of those whom His Great British and Satanic Majesty has bought and sent across to America in order to poison, slaughter humans, murder, burn and destroy -- and moreover, that 1,200 men from our great army were lying in the hospital in Rhode Island.

30th   The day of prayer was celebrated, but since nothing was allowed to be eaten before evening, I enjoyed the wild turkey that my landlord had shot and my landlady had roasted in her oven; every farmer has a baker's oven in his kitchen.

At the close of this year, the guinea is worth 30 piasters in paper money.

NOTES

1. British strategists had repeatedly hoped for Russian aid. In the summer of 1776, Carleton had been told to expect the first of 20,000 Russians in the fall, but Catherine the Great, on the advice of Frederick II of Prussia, rejected the idea. In December 1776, Lord Howe had suggested that Russian or Hannoverian troops be hired for a 35,000 man offensive in New York and New England. As late as 1779, Lord Sandwich was hoping for a Russian squadron to strengthen the Channel fleet.

2. General "Mad Anthony" Wayne (1745-1796) had been Colonel of the 4th Pennsylvania Battalion in the 1775-6 invasion of Canada, serving as commandant of Ticonderoga after its capture in 1775.

3. In January 1778, Lafayette had been chosen by Congress to lead an invasion of Canada despite lack of troops and inadequate supplies. Washington, who had not been kept informed, criticized the plan, and it was abandoned in mid-March.

4. Howe had captured Fort Washington, a crude fortification in Northern Manhattan, in November 1776, holding its 2,800 man garrison as prisoners of war. The British held prisoners of war on land and on prison ships (as did the Americans) where overcrowding, poor sanitation and inadequate food led to the deaths of many prisoners from disease and starvation.

5. Gottlieb Wilhelm Rabener (1714-1771) was a German satirist, who edited and contributed to the "Bremer Beiträge" of 1744, and whose essays were collected in "Sammlung satirischer Schriften" in 1751 and 1755.
Leopold, Count Daun (1705-1766) was the Austrian Field Marshal, who defeated Frederick the Great at Kolin in 1757 and at Hochkirch in 1758 and was criticized by some for not following up on his victories.

6. The troops Burgoyne surrendered at Saratoga were known as the "Convention Army" and were not, at the outset, ordinary prisoners of war. Although the Convention Burgoyne and Gates signed stipulated that the army would return to Europe, Congress objected to the Convention (which would have released other troops for American service) using, among other issues, Burgoyne's angry statement in the winter of 1777 that "the public faith is broke" (by American refusal to properly house and feed his army) to justify not ratifying the Convention. When the King ordered Clinton to ratify the Convention, Congress argued that the King's orders could have been forged and demanded a witness who had actually observed the King sign them. Howe, for his part, had apparently intended to break the Convention as well by diverting the Convention Army transports to New York once they had set sail. The Convention was never ratified, and the troops spent the remainder of the war as prisoners. (W.H. Dabney, After Saratoga, Albuquerque, 1954, is a history of the Convention Army.)

7. Lieutenant General Leopold von Heister (1716?-1777) Commander-in-Chief of the first Hessian division to go to America, had commanded one of the two divisions of Howe's army during the summer of 1777. Howe thought the Hessians were too slow, and further criticized Heister for allowing his troops to plunder as they marched through New Jersey. Heister was recalled in June 1777 and died of a sudden illness a month after reaching Cassel; his widow told Col. Fawcett that the true cause of death was the chagrin in his recall in the middle of his campaign. (She received an annual pension of 600 talers from the Landgraf and 200 pounds from the King.) (Atwood, p. 113.)

8. According to one local historian, a "colony" of about 70 Jews, including servants and slaves, had fled Newport, Rhode Island in 1777 and come to Leicester. They were of Portuguese descent, and apparently comprised a large extended family whose head was Aaron Lopez. After the Revolution, the Jews returned to Newport, and Aaron Lopez' house was purchased by local leaders and used for the first building of Leicester Academy. (Rev. Abijah P. Marvin, "Leicester," History of Worcester County, Mass. vol. I, pp. 625-628.)

9. According to Hyde, Dr. Greene was the "first physician's name to be found in the town books." "Historical Address," Historical Celebration of the Town of Brimfield, p. 171.

10. Wasmus is evidently referring to the meadowlark (STURNELLA), the red-winged blackbird (AGELAIUS PHOENICEUS), the cardinal (RICHMONDENA CARDINALIS), the goldfinch (SPINUS TRISTIS TRISTIS), the quail, (COLINUS VIRGINIANUS).

11. Silas Deane (1737-1789), a Connecticut lawyer, was elected to the Continental Congress in 1774 and sent to France to negotiate military assistance in April 1776, after having been defeated in the recent election. He had been joined in December by his co- commissioners, Benjamin Franklin and Arthur Lee (1740-1792). Their successful mission led to the French alliance, ratified by Congress on May 4, 1778, after which Deane was recalled to Washington because of charges made by Lee that he had made huge profits from the shipment of French supplies to America.

12. Franklin was treated by the French as the chief of the three American commissioners; he was appointed sole plenipotentiary in September 1778, after successfully negotiating the French alliance.

13. The Revolution included several smallpox epidemics, notably the 1775 outbreak, which so disastrously weakened the American army invading Canada. Vaccination was not yet known, so that the only protection against the dangerous disease was deliberately contracting a mild case through inoculation with matter from the pox of a smallpox victim (often with disastrous results); those inoculated were often confined to inoculation hospitals or houses to isolate them and protect the population from the uncontrolled spread of the disease.

14. Howe had asked to be relieved in October 1777; he was eventually replaced by General Sir Henry Clinton (1738-1795) in May 1778. Clinton, whose father had been Governor of New York and Newfoundland, had served in the Seven Years War, was elected to Parliament in 1772, and had been assigned as second-in-command to Howe in 1775.

15. Frederick II of Prussia invaded Bohemia via Silesia to counter the Austrian seizure of lower Bavaria; this was part of the War of the Bavarian Succession, the so-called "Potato War" (1777-1779).

16. The British were attempting to settle their dispute with the Americans before the French could join the conflict. Frederick Howard (1748-1825), Fifth Earl of Carlisle, a privy councillor and friend of Fox headed the commission, which also included William Eden (1744-1814), a member of the Board of Trade who was a close friend of Carlisle's, and George Johnstone (1730-1787), the former

Governor of West Florida, sympathetic to America but a hot-tempered politician prone to duels, including one with Germain in 1770. The mission was a fiasco and the commissioners returned to England in November, 1778.

17. General Timothy Ruggles (1711-1795), a loyalist of Hardwick, Massachusetts, had graduated from Harvard and followed a career as a lawyer and tavernkeeper. He was a Brigadier General in 1755 under Sir William Johnson, became a judge in 1757, and President of the Congress of Nine Colonies in 1765. He and James Otis led opposing political parties in Massachusetts, and he attempted to raise a loyalist corps in Boston after the outbreak of the Revolution. When the British left Boston, Ruggles was evacuated to Halifax and later organized loyalist militia in New York. His estates were confiscated in 1779 and he eventually settled in Nova Scotia. His daughter Bathsheba was convicted of hiring William Brooks and James Buchannan of the Convention Army, along with one Ezra Ross, to murder her husband, Joshua Spooner of Brookfield. All four were convicted in April 1778 and hanged in July.

18. This was the Battle of Monmouth, June 28, 1778. General Clinton had evacuated Philadelphia on June 18 and marched towards New York. On June 28, the Americans caught up with him. After an initial British success against the American vanguard led by General Charles Lee, Washington rallied the American forces and withstood successive British attacks, demonstrating that the Continental troops could stand up to British regulars.

19. Charles Hector Theodat, Comte d'Estaing (1729-1794), led naval operations against the British in India in the Seven Years War, was captured and imprisoned at Portsmouth, which imbued him with a life-long hatred of the English. Made Vice Admiral in 1777, he was given command of the French fleet sent to America to fight the British. Personally brave, he was notably unsuccessful as a naval leader; in 1794 he was guillotined, apparently because of his testimony on behalf of Marie Antoinette.

20. Cork served as a staging point for the supply convoys sent from Britain to America. A victualling depot had been opened there in 1776 to facilitate the shipment of Irish beef and butter. (Piers Mackesy, The War For America, Cambridge, 1964, p. 67.)

21. This was the Wyoming massacre on the 3rd and 4th of July near what is now Wilkes-Barre, Pennsylvania. The Susquehanna region had received many Tory refugees early in the Revolution, some of whom were rounded up by Patriot residents and imprisoned in the Connecticut mines. In June, Major John Butler, the Tory raider, and a party of some 1,100 whites and Indians, marched into the Wyoming Valley and, after a brief battle with local militia, killed some 300 people and burned 1,000 houses.

22. Brigadier General John Sullivan (1740-1795), a New Hampshire lawyer, was elected to the Continental Congress in 1774 and had commanded a brigade at Winter Hill during the siege of Boston. He assumed command of the American invasion of Canada in 1776 after the death of General Thomas and led the retreat to Lake Champlain. Captured at the Battle of Long Island, he was exchanged and fought at Trenton, Brandywine, and Germantown. He was made commander of the Continental Army in Rhode Island in 1778 (1,000 regulars at Providence), and led the combined operations against the British under General Robert Pigot at Newport in August. Although Sullivan had almost 10,000 men, and d'Estaing brought the French fleet and troops for land operations, Sullivan and d'Estaing could not cooperate. The British fleet arrived on August 9 in the middle of the combined operation. After a storm and an inconclusive naval engagement, the British returned to New York and d'Estaing sailed to Boston for repairs, abandoning Sullivan, many of whose troops deserted when they learned that the French had withdrawn. Sullivan himself began to withdraw on August 28.

23. As a precautionary measure in rural areas of Northern Germany, it has been the traditional custom to have the whole family fully dressed to wait out a thunderstorm downstairs in the house, especially at night. Thus Wasmus is astonished at the more casual approach to storms he finds in America.

24. Between the 10th and 12th of August, Howe, with a fleet 2/3 the size of d'Estaing's, began a naval engagement off Newport, which was interrupted by a violent gale which dispersed both fleets; the British returned to New York on the 14th, while d'Estaing sailed to Boston, both to refit unseaworthy ships.

25. Admiral John Byron (1723-1786), known as "Foul-Weather-Jack," was the grandfather of the poet. On his voyage around the world at the close of the Seven Years War, he claimed the Falkland Islands for England in 1765, naming the harbor Port Egmont. He served as Governor of Newfoundland from 1769-1772 and was made Rear Admiral in 1775.

26. General Robert Pigot (1720-1796) had commanded a regiment at Bunker Hill and was made Major General in 1777. He commanded British forces on land at Newport when Sullivan attacked in August 1778.

27. Although Sullivan expected support from the French naval force after the British had sailed back to New York after the storm, d'Estaing sailed for Boston on the 20th without landing the French troops he had taken onto his ships when the British fleet had appeared on August 9. Sullivan published a letter stating that d'Estaing's withdrawal and lack of support "stain the honor of France..." and were "an outrageous offense upon the alliance of the two nations." (Boatner, p. 793.)

28. Joshua Mercereau or Mersereau (called by Riedesel "Masserow") was one of the five Deputy Commissary Generals of Prisoners; Elias Boudinot was the Commissary General of Prisoners. One volume of Mercereau's account book, covering the period December 1777 to February 1779, is in the Library of Congress.

29. His siege unsuccessful, Sullivan's withdrawal was interrupted by General Pigot, who attacked on August 29 with the Hessians under von Lossberg. The Americans evacuated on the 31st just in time to escape Clinton, who arrived on September 1.

30. According to herpetologist William S.Brown, this is entirely accurate.

31. Since Burgoyne, on parole, had returned to England to defend himself before Parliament, Phillips was the senior officer of the Convention Army.

32. Since Congress was financing the war by printing more and more paper money, inflation became an increasingly serious problem, which Wasmus documents at the end of each month from here on.

33. The Marquis de Bouillé had captured Domenica, a British island entirely surrounded by French possessions, on September 8, 1778; his 2,000 men causing the 500 British defenders to surrender.

34. The early settlers frequently observed days of Thanksgiving not only in Plymouth, but in Maine, Massachusetts, Virginia, and even Florida. Colonial governments issued civil proclamations for days of prayer and thanksgiving in honor of victories, or to recognize the rain which ended drought, or the end of an epidemic. By the end of the seventeenth century, annual autumn Thanksgivings were a regular feature of life in Massachusetts, and during the Revolutionary era the authorities often included civil liberties among the items the people were to be thankful for. Congress proclaimed December 18, 1777 "a day of solemn Thanksgiving and praise" for the success of Saratoga; Washington proclaimed a special Thanksgiving in May 1778 to celebrate the news of the French alliance; and Congress declared December 30, 1778 a day of Thanksgiving to God for "disposing the heart of a powerful monarch to enter into an alliance with us and aid our cause." (See Wasmus's entry for December 17) Massachusetts celebrated twice that year, having already designated the 26th of November as Thanksgiving. (Diana Karter Applebaum, Thanksgiving: An American Holiday, An American History, New York, 1984, passim.)

35. The Convention Army had initially consisted of almost 5,000 men, just over 2,000 of whom were Germans. Boatner comments that by the end of the war, "their numbers had been reduced by death, desertion, paroles, and exchange to about half the original 5,000," (p. 276) and there were certainly several efforts at encouraging the troops to desert and join the Americans, including some which involved German-speaking Americans visiting the German troops and offering them land and jobs, should they desert.

1779

Month of January 1779

1st   Oh, my beloved Germans! Today, you are wishing each other happiness and luck. Full of gratitude you are thinking about the favors the Eternal has bestowed upon you during this past year and are now preparing to ask your gracious Lord for renewed blessings to begin in this coming year -- the Americans are not doing any such thing. -- Alas! This is the third New Year's Day on which I am making my wish to return to Germany! Would that it be fulfilled this year, would that I be so happy as to receive letters from my folks. My dear relatives, I wish you happiness in the new year, you, my wife, children, mother, brother, sister and all my friends. May God keep you once again in His Holy care during this year! Without a doubt, you will be happier on this day than I who have been spending this day - as so many in the past - in captivity, that is sighing, -- counting the sleepless nights and at present not knowing what to do to pass the time; for I have to do without my favorite pastime: reading letters. Nevertheless, I hope soon to set sail for Europe! -- Oh, you bottomless ocean! Your horrible noise will then no longer be able to frighten me! I shall be going to my country, to my beloved people, this thought that I will feel, -- in anticipation of seeing my relatives, so many friends together, -- these are the firm cliffs against which your terrible will, oh ocean, will be powerless. I know your tricks from experience, I am well acquainted with them; you will make me sick but do me no harm; I shall prepare myself as much as lies in my power and that which I shall still have to expect from your rage will be a real blessing. --It would save me the trouble of taking ipecacuanha!--

2nd   The Worcester paper says that after having presided over the government of Canada since Sept. 27, 1766, Lieut. Gen. Carleton has gone to England from Canada; Lieut. Gen. Haldimand, a Swiss by birth, has been appointed in his stead.[1] Lieut. General Carleton was best able to keep the unstable Canadians in order and faithful to their King. He had the clergy as friends; everyone knows what power these -- people have over the minds of the Canadians.[2] The Americans believe that the King of England will acknowledge their independence this winter rather than prepare for a new campaign. Capt. von Bärtling sen. departed for Boston today in order to take advantage of a passport to travel to Rhode Island so as to get money for us from there.

Worcester paper [Massachusetts Spy, Jan. 7]: *London, Sept. 19 [Boston, Dec. 28]. The Engl. and French fleets have lost 1,000 men each in their latest engagement. Ten Engl. warships were dealt with so harshly that they have to have new masts. The Engl. fleet was 39, and the French 36, warships strong.*[3] [selective]

10th   Last night, Capt. von Bärtling returned from Boston but had not been able to get a passport from General Gates because the latter had first to get permission for it from General Washington.

17th   Today came the unexpected report that the Dep. Commissary General Mercereau has returned to Rutland. During his absence, his wife is said to have departed for Virginia to see a lieutenant of the Artillery by the name of Smith, who had stayed at the home of the commissary at the time when the Convention troops had been in Rutland. Since the Americans called this Mercereau a Tory or Royalist, everybody believed that since he had been absent for more than 3 months, Congress had terminated his commission.

18th   Capt. von Bärtling, Capt. of the Cavalry Fricke, and I rode to commissary Mercereau in Rutland today. We learned from him that our officers, who had departed to Providence from Rutland for the exchange on Sept. 27, were in Easton in the Province of New Jersey [now Pennsylvania] without having been exchanged; that the commissaries have been ordered to move all the prisoners of war to Rutland from Westminster; that he [Mercereau] intended to give passports to two of our noncommissioned officers who were to go into the countryside to gather all of our men; for they were supposed to be moved into the barracks at Rutland. It could be, so the commissary said, that when all the prisoners of war are assembled, we would soon be recalled and possibly exchanged; or else perhaps moved to New Jersey or Pennsylvania because [most] supplies and provisions had to be brought up from there.[4] Since I stayed in Rutland today, I took care of the passports for the noncommissioned officers.

19th   Today I rode back to Westminster via Princeton.

From the Worcester paper [Massachusetts Spy, Jan. 21, 1779] I have translated the following:

London, Oct. 3, 1778. The Count of Anhalt, the favorite of the King of Prussia, has fallen out of favor and will soon be punished for his disobedience. He had been sent by the King with a detachment to join the Erbprinz [heir to the throne] of Braunschweig [Duke Ferdinand]; soon afterwards, the Prince ordered him and his corps to occupy a height, which the enemy threatened to seize. But the Count let the Prince know that he could not follow his orders because he was General and First Adjutant of the King and would first have to have positive orders from the King himself. Meanwhile the favorable moment had passed by and the enemy occupied the height. The Prince had the Count arrested and sent him with a strong guard to the King, who immediately ordered him locked up in the fortress [of N.] Everybody believes that he will lose his life for this misdeed; nobody suspected such behavior from this Count of Anhalt, who is known in the world as an excellent and gallant officer.[5] [accurate]

From Philadelphia, Jan. 2, in Congress:

The 13 United Provinces had to pay 15 million dollars this year and [will have to pay] *every year 6 million for 18 subsequent years in order to pay off these debts. The two Generals Clinton and Washington had commissioners convene at Amboy to negotiate the exchange of the prisoners of war; they could not, however, come to any other conclusion but that each should keep his own prisoners of war. Both generals now have all the officers on parole recalled, among whom is Lieut. Gen. Burgoyne.* {accurate{

At the end of this month, the guinea is worth 36 piasters in paper money.

Month of February 1779

1st   We will momentarily have to depart for Rutland.

2nd   Today, the 2 noncommissioned officers are going into the countryside to look for our men who are to be taken to the barracks in Rutland.

3rd   I rode to Rutland and rented lodging at Pastor Buckminster's.

5th   Lieut. Gebhard and Ensign Specht departed to Rutland from here.

The Boston paper [Continental Journal, Febr. 4] *reports that the Americans have captured a ship coming from Ireland and taken it into Boston harbor. Among other items, she had 800 [80] tons of butter on board. In addition, the paper says that the English have taken the Island of St. Lucia in the West Indies from the French.*[6] [selective]

9th   I went from Westminster to Rutland and moved into my lodging at Pastor Buckminster's. Before his departure to Boston, commissary Mercereau had firmly committed himself to getting a passport for one of our officers from Gen. Gates so that he [the officer] could go to Rhode Island to get money and our baggage there; but he [Mercereau] returned without a passport. We are all in need of money; some of our men have already arrived in the barracks. But if there is no money, they will soon leave again for nobody can live on the meager provision of just 3/4 of a portion. Everyone gets 10 ounces of bread and 10 ounces of salted meat a day or the same of dried cod and a little rice; the meat, however, is frequently rancid and therefore not edible.

The Boston paper from the 14th of this month reports that *the King of Spain has 4 warships and many frigates ready to sail but nobody knows their destination or which power Spain will join.*[7] *The paper writes further that several warships and frigates have departed from Brest in order to reinforce Comte d'Estaing, who then could seize all the British Islands in the West Indies.* [not found]

All! All at once? Why not!

21st   Commissary Mercereau has gone to New London and given Lieut. Gebhard a passport for Uxbridge. There, he will receive a passport from Major General Sullivan, sent him by the commissary, and thus go to Rhode Island. Sea turn is a heavy fog that the east wind drives from the sea onto the land. This forenoon, it was warm, the sun was shining and the air was calm. After 12 o'clock, a sea turn appeared that darkened the sky and it became very cold. At times, such a fog occurs on the hottest summer days when it darkens the sky and brings about a sharp chill so that one must sit by the fire; it will often last 20 to 24 hours.
    Again, nothing has come of the Canadian expedition and since it is now too late, nothing will come of it any more.

28th   Beside the infantry, 55 dragoons from our regiment are in the barracks now. My host, Pastor Buckminster and his family, are very good people. When he goes up into the pulpit, the pastor has not a single black piece of clothing on his body but is always dressed in blue. He is hated by the inhabitants because he never includes Congress in his prayers; he is a true Royalist.[8]

At the end of this month, a guinea is worth 40 piasters in paper money.

Month of March 1779

1st   Lieut. Gebhard went to Uxbridge from here.

Boston paper [Independent Ledger] from March 8: *St. Christopher, Jan. 9:*
Extract from a letter from Antigua. Wednesday morning. Last night, the Royal ship Ariadne (Capt. Pringle) arrived from the Engl. harbor of St. Lucia and brought the reliable report that the French had altogether left this island; that on Dec. 17, Comte d'Estaing with 4,000 men attacked Gen. Meadow, who had occupied the outworks with 1,500 men. For a quarter of an hour, the French made very violent charges but nothing was able to withstand the courage of our [British] troops. The gallant Gen. Meadow had shot the little ammunition he had and now had his men with fixed bayonets charge the enemy, who took to flight. We discovered 700 dead Frenchmen on the battlefield and counted more than 900 wounded and prisoners of war. Had Gen. Meadow been so fortunate as to have an adequate magazine, I certainly believe this affair would have ended in a complete defeat for the French army. After the remainder of Comte d'Estaing's troops had reembarked, he went around to Cul de Sac with his fleet where Admiral Barrington with his small fleet was riding at anchor in the harbor. The enemy made quite a lively attack here, but the fire from our fleet and from the 2 forts commanding the entrance into the harbor was expertly aimed and of such effect that the French fleet was overcome with confusion within a short time. The damage which the fleet incurred brought on their decision to set sail for Martinique as fast as they could. Our losses are very negligible on sea as well as on land. [accurate]
Philadelphia, Febr. 10. Last Saturday was the anniversary of the alliance between France and the United American States. The most honorable Congress gave a great public festival for His Excellency the Plenipotentiary Minister of His Most Christian Majesty and during the firing of many cannon, toasts were pronounced to
1) the duration of the alliance between France and the 13 United Provinces.
2) the United American States.
3) His Most Christian Majesty [King of France, Louis XVI].
4) the Queen of France.
5) His Catholic Majesty [King of Spain]
6) the Princes of the House of Bourbon.
7) favorable continuance of the war of the United Forces.
8) General Washington and the army.
9) the friends of Freedom in all the parts of the world.
10) the new alliance that it may reach the highest summit.
11) American victories that they may drive Great Britain to her senses.
12) the memory of the heroes who have sacrificed their lives for the Freedom and Independence of America.
13) a good and honorable peace.
The English have seized Savannah, capital of Georgia, from the Americans and are now advancing toward South Carolina with great force.[9] *Spain will join France and America.* [accurate]
In New York they are busy with the embarkation of troops but their destination continues to remain a secret. Yesterday came the news that the English have assembled boats at Billop's Point on Staten Island. This caused our militia to

assemble in Woodbridge and New Brunswick and, especially since our militia has assembled so quickly, it is to be hoped that this will quash the intentions that the enemy might have against these states. [accurate]

Baltimore, Febr. 9: More than 200 Engl. ships, frigates, armed ships, privateers[10] and letters of marque* [this is Wasmus' footnote symbol.] have much interrupted our actions, but we have seized quite a number of them and dispersed the rest. On good authority we know that there is much talk of peace in London and since England does not want to listen to France's proposals, Spain has declared that she would join the French side.

From New York: We have known it for a long time and also learned from all the deserters coming here from the Rebels that the supplies are unusually scarce in all the provinces and that almost nobody can buy anything for the paper money, which is made from old wives' chemises (Smoxtail money). Although people are sending all old wives' chemises they can do without to the paper mills, the money has almost lost its value. [accurate]

Boston paper [Independent Ledger] March 22: Philadelphia: Extract from a letter from Martinique:

Admirals Byron and Barrington have joined in St. Lucia[11] and together [their fleet] consists of 16 warships and 6 frigates. The health problems there continue and there are so many sick in the English fleet that 10 to 15 men die every day. Comte d'Estaing is at Fort Royal [Fort-de-France][12] at present; his fleet is in a very good position of defense and all his men are well. Every day, we expect Comte de Grasse,[13] who -as we know - set sail from France with 10 warships, 4 frigates and 60 transport ships 37 days ago. We presume that Comte d'Estaing will set sail to meet him. One of our frigates has seized 2 small English warships, the _Swift_ of 24 and the _Weazel_ of 16 cannon. We have enough provisions for some time now. The latest news from France states that the 3 ports, Dunkirk, St. Malo and Bayonne have sent out 130 capers[14] of 20, 10 and 36 cannon, which have already achieved miracles. When the letters bringing this news were sent off, there already were 7,000 prisoners of war, Engl. sailors and soldiers, in these 3 ports. In France, they are making great preparations; everyone is showing much spirit and courage, and - if needs be - all the merchants are resolved to give their all to the war [effort]. With France's help we are in a very good position to tarnish the pride of Great Brit., and to cleanse the slayings and shame with which the last peace has left us. There is no soldier in our army and no sailor in our fleet who does not eagerly wish to avenge our cruel peace and is at the same time resolved to die for the freedom and honor of his fatherland [motherland]. Now is the time when France's greatness is in the ascent, when she has every opportunity to get satisfaction for all the evil she had to suffer from England. The present King Louis XVI is rising to such glory and greatness as none ever before him and this monarch, who has so magnanimously offered his friendship and support to a free-born people, deserves to be the one to overcome all the tyrants in the whole world. [accurate]

Spain has offered to lend the American States 30 million piasters.

26th   The snow is more than 3 feet deep here in Rutland and one cannot walk without snowshoes. Today, Lieut. Gebhard returned from Rhode Island and brought us very good medicine, which we had all been very eagerly awaiting, i.e., 800 guineas. Our baggage had been off Newport for a long time but had finally been sent to Virginia 4 weeks ago.   An English fleet is riding at anchor off Newport and there are between

6,000 and 7,000 men in garrison in the fortress, half English and half Hessians. The cost of living is high there and in Boston there is apparently a great dearth of bread. Many families from that city have moved to the country just because of the lack of victuals. Two thirds of a bushel [a himten] of wheat costs 50 piasters, two thirds of a bushel of rye 40 piasters, and two thirds of a bushel of potatoes cost 20 piasters in paper money; all these prices are terribly high.

Our men are assembling in the barracks here. From our Dragoon Regiment, there are 80, from our Infantry 70, Hessian Jäger 40, and British troops 90 men.

At the end of this month, the guinea is worth 40 piasters in paper money.

*Letter of marque is a merchant ship that carries cannon and has the right of capture, i.e., to seize enemy ships.

Month of April 1779

Boston paper [Independent Ledger] from April 5: *Extract from a letter from St. Pierre on the Island of Martinique, Febr. 22:*
Since the expedition of St. Lucia, the French Admiral Comte d'Estaing has been riding at anchor at Fort Royal with 12 warships; five days ago, he received another 55 [54] warships and is now 17 [16] [sic] ships strong; we hourly expect another 4 warships together with several frigates and transport ships with another 5,000 troops on board. Admiral Byron is riding at anchor at St. Lucia; several warships that have come from England have joined him. We believe that we have 20 or 22 ships as well as 6 frigates and he hourly expects reinforcement of warships and troops. It seems that such great power will shortly assemble in these seas that nothing will be done on either side. It is presumed that the English will be stronger by sea and the French on land. Each power will defend her islands as much as they are able to. It is thought that the first attack will aim at recapturing Dominica. [accurate]
The London paper from Dec. 2 said that [no more than] *12,000 troops are to be sent to America* [from England] *early this spring.* [summary]

Boston [Independent Ledger], April 19:
There was great joy in our city last Friday when the American [Continental] frigate Warren *(Capt. Hopkins) [of 32 cannon] arrived. She had set sail several weeks ago and now returned with rich booty. This frigate sailed from here as a companion ship of the* Queen of France *[of 24 cannon] and the* Ranger *of 26 cannon. They first seized a war sloop of 14 cannon, which came from New York. Capt. Hopkins learned from her that a fleet has cleared the port of New York loaded with provisions and general merchandise destined for Georgia. Captain Hopkins cruised after them and was fortunate enough to discover them not far from Cape Henry and seized them after [encountering] very weak resistance. This fleet consisted of 9 ships, which, except for 2 small ones that were able to get away under the cover of darkness, were all captured. The ship* Jason *(Capt. Porterfield) had 1,800 tons of flour on board and carried 20 cannon;* Maria *of 16 cannon was loaded with salt, meat, wine and rum. The rest were small one-masted ships, loaded with general merchandise. Moreover, there were on these ships a complete equipage for a cavalry regiment and 24 officers of different ranks among whom [was]* [were a Hessian Colonel by the name of Köhler and] *an English Lieutenant Colonel by the name of Campbell.*[15] *The latter*

said himself that this loss would greatly embarrass the English army in Georgia. Our gallant men on board our ships have not only become rich themselves through these prizes but also rendered the greatest service to the states. The Jason has safely arrived in port here and the rest are hourly expected. [accurate]

And whose fault was this misfortune and loss? The crew of the English war sloop that was first seized by the Americans. These were the traitors who had divulged the departure of the English fleet; these should therefore be punished as traitors.

Last Saturday, a packet boat arrived here from France after a journey of 42 days; the dispatches were immediately sent to Congress. At the departure of this packet boat from Brest, no war had as yet been declared against England but the capers were very busy on both sides; many English privateers had already been brought into French ports. [16] [accurate]

Hartford [Connecticut Courant], April 6: *Extract from a letter from Philadelphia March 21 [28]:*
Holland has commissioned 37 warships. Denmark has offered to provide 6,000 sailors and jointly with Sweden has given England to understand that they value free trade with France, America and all the world [and they intend to defend it]. *Spain is ready for war as are many other European powers -- perhaps -- the moment may soon come when Great Britain is making overtures of peace to America.*[17] [accurate]

N.B. That may be, but not yet!

Rutland, April 26. Since it does not appear that we will be exchanged as yet and since the men are tired of living on such miserable provisions, commissary Mercereau is giving them passports to return to the farmers in the countryside; it will, however, not be too easy to bring them back again.

29th   Colonel Köhler, Lieut. Standenroth, and Ensign Pauli from the Hessian Corps, as well as Lieut. Colonel Campbell, 1 major, 5 captains, 5 subalterns and 50 naval officers and merchants, all Englishmen, arrived today.
Each one quartered himself as well as he could with the inhabitants.

At the end of this month, one guinea has the value of 40 piasters in paper money.

Month of May 1779

On the first of May, the weather shows itself rough and disagreeable; the earth is still covered with a lot of snow and at night we still have heavy frost.

Boston paper [Independent Ledger], from May 3: *Paris, Dec. 27.*
Since Nov. 20, 26 Engl. ships have been brought into Brest harbor. The fleet at Brest, which is supposed to be ready to set sail on May 15, consists of 38 warships. The fleet under Mr. de Fabry in Toulon consists of 12 warships and 6 frigates. At Gibraltar, the English have no more than 2 warships and 2 frigates as guards to protect the trade in the Mediterranean. The Royal Privateer Charlotte of 44 cannon, which had been sent out by the Queen of England, has immediately been seized. The French frigates and privateers have cleansed the sea as if it had been swept with a broom because all the Engl. capers have either been seized or have sailed home.

The Dutch, on the one hand, have declared themselves neutral but, on the other, have let it be understood that they would provide the French fleet with ropes and sails.

Through France as mediator, the King of Prussia and the German Emperor have finally made peace.[18] *The French frigate* Vogel *has been seized by the English frigate* Phoenix. *This is really strange that there still remained an English ship that could seize the* Vogel. *The broom with which the old ocean had been swept did not reach so far as to get the English frigate out of the way.* [not found]

Boston paper [Independent Ledger] from May 10: *From the Royalist Paper in New York. London, March 3.*

General Clinton has sent a letter to the Secretary of War, which he [Clinton] had received from General Washington. In it Washington demanded that General Burgoyne return together with all the officers, who, although on parole, had departed without their being exchanged. [not found]

Boston paper [Independent Ledger] from May 17: *From a letter from S. Eustatius we learn that the honorable Doctor Franklin has taken a loan of over 10 million guilders for the United American States and that France has given the security for their repayment.*

From the headquarters of General Washington we learn that about 2 weeks ago, the English have demolished the fortifications at Kingsbridge and withdrawn to Harlem Heights.[19] *From New York we received reliable news that a short time ago, a fleet has sailed from there with troops on board. It is hardly to be believed, however, that 7,000 men could have been there since that would amount to more than the enemy had in this fort a while ago. Admiral Gambier*[20] *is said to command the fleet and General Clinton marches in person at the head of the land forces. A few Hessians have remained as occupation. No one knows as yet for what this fleet is destined. They may want to capture the Convention troops in Virginia. Be this as it may, New York is surely not heavily guarded. Perhaps it will be a mistake to think this place safe and secure enough to withstand American power. From Albany on April 24, we learn that the Savages and Tories have made an attack on and caused great devastation in the settlements of Stone Arabia.*[21] [not found]

[Continental Journal, May 27] New London; May 20.
From Charleston, South Carolina we have the report that the British army [under the command of General Prevost], *7,000 men strong, is but 60 [50] Engl. miles away from this city; that this city is being heavily fortified by the inhabitants; that these are also resolved to defend it to the last man if the enemy should be so bold as to approach this city any further. General Lincoln's army is 5,000 [3,000] men strong and General Caswell's army 3,000 men strong.*[22] [summary]

London, Jan. 5. The Empress of Russia has given the order to have 18 warships, destined for the service of the King of England, sail into the roadstead at Spithead.[23] [not found]

This surely is a lie, for England has more ships than all the other European sea powers together.

London, Jan. 26. Two companies of Hannover Artillery will presumably be sent from Hannover to America next spring and join Gen. Clinton's army. [not found]

This too is surely a lie.

In a letter from Fort Pitt, much fuss is again made about the killing and burning by the Savages and Tories, but -- if it is true, I for my part do not believe it.[24]

At the end of this month, the guinea is worth 46 [piasters] in paper money.

Month of June 1779

Boston paper [Independent Ledger] from June 7: *Providence, May 29. Through a ship which arrived here from Cadiz last week, we have learned that the greatest warlike preparations are being made throughout all of Spain and that it is well known everywhere that an attack against Gibraltar will be made with the approval of everyone in this Kingdom; that 30 warships together with a number of frigates are ready and able to be put out to sea any day. When the ship departed there on April 9, 7,000 [70,000] men were ready to embark in the harbors of Cadiz, of Santa Maria and San Lucas; that the American capers [privateers] have been very successful in the European seas, that they are permitted to sell their booty in the Spanish ports and have their ships repaired there, and all that with the same freedom as in their own ports; that the French capers have seized a great number of Engl. ships and especially 2 in the English Channel with very rich cargoes, which they took to Malaga.* [accurate]

That is strange! Why did they not take them to one of the French [*ports*], which were so near them! These must again be lies!

Moreover, we have heard that the Spanish General O'Reilly[25] had a bridge built over the Guadalquivir River, not far from the Bay of Cadiz. When it was finished and supposed to be dedicated, many people assembled on this bridge to attend the inaugural ceremony. Unfortunately, this bridge collapsed and 1,500 people of those who fell into the river drowned. [summary]

That must certainly have been a miserable bridge!

Boston, June 7: According to the latest reports from New York, the last 3,000 troops who sailed away have safely arrived in Virginia. Several French ships have also arrived at Hampton in Virginia, which have brought the reliable report that the French have seized the Engl. fortress of Madras in East India. This is the most important place of all Engl. possessions in East India, on the shores of Coromandel. In addition to the natives, the occupation force generally consisted of 3,000 or 4,000 [300 or 400] men.[26] [accurate]

Rutland, June 15. Lieut. Colonel Campbell went to New York with several Engl. officers on parole this morning.

Continental Journal, June 17: *Extracts from a letter from Pennsylvania to a friend in Boston, May 31.*
With the greatest pleasure, I report to you that General von Riedesel from the Braunschweig troops has bought up lands in Virginia for 19,000 guineas and that he has sworn our states the oath of allegiance.[27] [accurate]

The Boston paper [Independent Ledger] from June 21 *says that the English army has twice been beaten by Generals Moultrie and Lincoln before Charleston in South Carolina so that they have taken to flight and lost all their artillery and baggage.*[28] *It is also reported from Fishkill that our enemy, the English, are fortifying Stony Point. Our forts at West Point etc. on the east and west side are in a very good state of defense. The following is a good estimate of the enemy forces at King's Ferry: on the east side of the river there are 19 comp. of grenadiers, 19 comp. of light infantry, the 33rd Reg., 4 comp. of Lord Cathcart's Legion of Foot, Robinson's Corps, 3 battalions of Hessian Grenadiers, [1 or] 2 comp. of Hessian Jägers and the Reg. Prinz Carl: on the west side of the river, the 17th, 63rd and 64th Reg.; the 42nd Reg.; the Irish Volunteers; one part of the King's Guard that had been exhausted from the hard march to Virginia has returned to New York.*

We have heard that our cruel enemy, the English, have raped and plundered all the inhabitants [of the place] where they had been camping, have taken 2,000 head of cattle and completely ruined [have otherwise distressed] the inhabitants. [summary]

Since Saturday, 21 deserters of the Engl. army have come to us. The German [Dutchess County] militia has joined us from several places and has united with us. High ranking gentlemen of the 1st character daily come to us. They have been driven from New York, Long Island and other places and now serve as privates [jealously] disposed to support their country's cause. [accurate]

In the Boston paper [Independent Ledger] from June 28, *we are again assured that the Engl. army under General Prevost has been totally defeated in the vicinity of Charleston. Fifteen hundred men were killed there and the rest taken prisoner. The entire loss of the Engl. army is said to be close to 10,000 men.* [selective]

That is a lot!   But if only the news report will not be retracted!

The subjects of His Most Christian Majesty, serving in South Carolina under the command of the French minister, Mr. Gérard,[29] *have proposed to Congress to establish a corps of volunteers to defend this province; but it should be commanded by officers of their own nation. Congress was very surprised and directed M. [the Marquis of] Britigny, who had proposed it, to the Governor of South Carolina as the only person who could command the corps.* [accurate]

Extract from a letter from the Highlands, June 10: Yesterday, 1 major, several officers and 160 privates deserted from the Engl. army to us; they were sent to reconnoiter. [accurate]

Another lie!

In Congress, May 21. It is resolved that the United Provinces are to pay 45 million piasters for the defrayal of the war budget; the 13th Province Georgia is at present occupied by the enemy and is to pay its portion later.

New Hampshire	1,500,000	Massachusetts Bay	6,000,000
Rhode Island	750,000	Connecticut	5,100,000
New York	2,400,000	New Jersey	2,400,000
Pennsylvania	5,700,000	Delaware	450,000
Maryland	4,680,000	Virginia	7,200,000
North Carolina	3,270,000	South Carolina	5,550,000

IN SUMMA 45 million. [accurate]

At the end of this month the guinea is worth 60 piasters in paper money.

Month of July 1779

The Boston paper [Independent Ledger] from July 5 *states that the Engl. and French fleets have been put out to sea; the former is commanded by the Admirals Byron and Barrington and has set sail from St. Lucia, the latter is commanded by Admiral Comte d'Estaing and has set sail from Martinique.* [accurate]

Philadelphia, extract from a letter from Port-au-Prince, May 16th:

Conditions that from time to time are very unfavorable for our enemy are coming to the fore and we [think] [can then flatter ourselves in the hope] *that this terrible war will not last very much longer. --America will secure her independence and her commerce. The inhabitants of the West Indies are in great need of victuals. I have been in the company of several gentlemen who have lately come from Jamaica and informed me [that they got no supplies and] that they wished heartily to conciliate relations with America. --But the deserved punishment will soon come down, very soon indeed, upon the heads of the destroyer.* [accurate]

Rutland: Through an order from Congress, it is strictly forbidden to give more for gold or silver coins, but since too much paper money is in circulation, it is difficult to attain order. Merchants, who have their merchandise come from the West Indies, from France or Holland, are compelled to exchange gold or silver because nobody would want to sell them anything in exchange for paper money. A huge amount of paper money is in circulation. As I am writing this, I have 2 bills lying on my table; one is a GS or piaster bill and carries the number 498381, printed on Febr. 26, 1778. The second is an 80 piaster bill No. 387839, printed on Jan. 14, 1779. The entire printed sheet carries the number; every bill on every printed sheet has numbers of one sort or another. The printed sheet with the first number has the value of 220 piasters, the printed sheet with the 2nd number has the value of 520 piasters; the bills are not of the same type; they usually begin with 3-6-10 piasters and stop at 60-80 piasters. The bills mentioned previously are only printed on 2 days within 2 years. The first was printed in 1775; in subsequent years, the printing was always done on different days. Presumably more than 1,000 million piasters are now in circulation; without these they could not wage war.

[Independent Ledger, July 5, 1779] *From an American Magazine: The Address of America's Genius to the People of the American World:* [In the following article, my translation of Wasmus' translation is given on the left, while the newspaper original appears on the right side. H.D.]

America is blooming like an open rose and rises like a splendid cedar; every morning, the sun shows the growing of her glory and every new day extends her power and adds a halo to her crown. Here flow rivers of affluence, here are tenderness and sensitivity in sciences and knowledge; stars of wisdom, the light of virtue and the sun of eternity. Everything that is splendid joins here in a circle of bliss, superabundance and beauty for the

America is blooming like an open rose and rises like a towering cedar; every morning, the sun shows her glory growing and each new day extends her power and adds new glories to her crown. Here flow streams of affluence, the beams of science and general knowledge. Stars of wisdom, the light of virtue and the sun of liberty will all unite their rays and form the sublime circle of beauty, splendor and felicity. Americans! Look toward the East and human race, as it were. Americans! Look toward the East and the West, toward the North and the South. The treasuries of the nation and the blessing of the universe are ready to share everything with you and pour itself over your happy country. The friendly ocean flows all around you and sheer innumerable harbors are open to the 4 winds of the sky. The heavenly sound of freedom rings from place to place and a swift-moving spirit drives it out of the city into the country and like a bolt of lightning through all parts of our mighty country. The time will come when the knees of all powerful kingdoms will bend before your might and greatness, opulence, superabundance and treasures that can be owned by no other majesty but your own. So walk, my sons, on the paths of virtue and religion. The honor shall be yours-and you shall be the surprise of the whole earth. The name of American will carry honor and majesty along with it. Everyone will seek to make use of this as a blessing and [remember] the present as a happy time. The general schools will bloom with distinguished teachers, laurels will crown them and these shining suns write something new as time passes: each one of the pages will remark on the brilliant time of the revolt and describe the duties performed by worthy patriots. FAMA [glory] will lend wings to this acquired honor and impart the immortal names of those who overcome to the whole world, to all the peoples of the earth. Moreover, drive the salute to freedom onward from the North Pole to the South Pole - and - a world will have arisen from slavery. Ye Immortals, hear! who inhabit other worlds, stand still and listen to the heroic deeds and the glory of America. FAMA joyfully beat her wings and the sounds of her spreading the news penetrated the air.

the West, toward the North and the South . The storm of nature and the blessing of the universe are ready to pour over your happy land. The friendly ocean flows round you and your countless harbors are open to the 4 winds of the heaven.

The inspiring voice of liberty echoes from state to state and her swift-moving spirit kindles from the city to the country and flashes like lightning through the distant regions of our vast continent. The time is coming when the knees of emperors and splendid kingdoms will bow to your greatness and supplicate favor and your liberty and powerless majesty. Go on, my sons, in the way of virtue and religion, and you shall be the astonishment of the whole earth. The name of American will carry honor and majesty in the world, and men esteem it a blessing to wear the venerable and commanding title. Seminaries will bloom with bright laurels of literature and those shining suns write something new at each hour as it flies and brightens every page of the revolving time with the patriot's glorious deeds!

Wings of fame will bear immortal names round the globe, kindle the spirit of freedom from pole to pole and rouse up a world of fares [?]. Now drive the salute to freedom onward from the North Pole to the South Pole - and - a world will have arisen from slavery. Hark ye, Immortals! who inhabit other worlds, stand still and with new, kindled rapture hear the glory of America. FAMA joyfully beat her wings and the sounds of her spreading the news penetrated the air.

[accurate]

Rutland is to send 5 recruits to the army. The community has hired 5 and gives each 1,000 piasters in paper money. For that, they have committed themselves for 9 months and will depart tomorrow.

[Continental Journal, July 8] *Williamsburg, Virginia, June 5:*
The surrender of Fort Sackville is reported from there and with it the Articles of the Capitulation. This fort is of no importance and on Febr. 24 was surrendered by Lieut. Governor Hamilton to Colonel Clarke, who had besieged it. [30] [summary]

Great ado was made over it as if a kingdom had been conquered: a fort which could in no way maintain itself.

Boston, July 12. From 3 persons who arrived at Newburyport last week from Penobscot [and that ran from the frigate LeBlanc], we have learned that the enemy forces there consist of 10 ships, partly frigates, schooners and 2 transport ships as well as 900 land forces who, under the command of Gen. Francis MacLean, [31] *have arrived there from Halifax; they have no artillery with them.* [summary]

But probably [it is] with their fleet!

A report has come here that a corps of our troops has attacked and seized St. Jean in Canada; we cannot tell as yet whether this report is well founded. [not found]

Oh yes, one can say that it is a lie.

Rutland, July 12. All the naval officers and all the merchants who had been captured on the way to Georgia from New York on April 7 went to Boston for their exchange today. I gave them some letters to take along to Germany and inside these sheets, some pages of my journal. The ship's captain, Mr. Hudson, promised on his word of honor not to hide these but to give them to the first English ship going to Europe. Furthermore, I gave a letter to the helmsman Mr. Armstrong. This letter was for the Chancery Administrator Werner, my friend in Wolfenbüttel, [*sent off*] on June 1. Would that it reaches Wolfenbüttel! This is the letter:

"Dear friend,
Should this paper come into your hands, I would wish with all my heart that you and your loved ones are alive and in good health. [*As for me*] I never was in better health than now, but since Aug. 16, 1777, I have been in American captivity. During this time I have written many letters to be sent off to Germany, but I have torn them all up, in part because I could not find any opportunity to send them. And whenever an uncertain opportunity was offered, all the letters had to be opened so that they could first be read by the Americans. In this condition I have now been living for more than 21 months and, as I mentioned before, written more than 20 letters and torn them all up again. I have sent two letters on the off-chance, the first to my wife, dated May 16, the second to my dear friend Anker, dated Sept. 26, 1778. I do not know, however, whether these letters did leave America. I hope that you, my wife, relatives and friends, will forgive me if you have not received more letters from me during this time. When you consider that such a long imprisonment brings many annoyances, every one of you will be more indulgent toward me. To live as prisoner of war in a faraway continent under a foreign nation, that is very much stirred up, whose language one does not understand, -- I keep on asking everyone of you whether that is not more disagreeable than drinking a pitcher of Braunschweig bock beer behind the worst Dutch tile stove in Germany. I cannot complain that I have received too many letters from Germany; the last I got was from you, my dear friend, dated Sept. 30, 1776. I would like to know the reason why I have not gotten a single letter from anybody; it is as if my wife, mother, brother, sisters and all

my friends have forgotten me. Letters have often arrived here from Germany, and many have come from Braunschweig and Wolfenbüttel to our prison; none can have been sent to me from there, otherwise I would have surely gotten it. Alas, my dear Germans, you do not understand what consolation a letter from family or friends brings to a German roving about in America. You are sitting behind your warm stoves and keep us sighing here in the wilderness by the fireplace. Even if America is a very beautiful country, I could never forget my fatherland, my family and friends. We Americans live and drink our rum and you Braunschweigers do not live as well and drink your Mum [strong Braunschweig ale].

But [*consider*] all the fear and deadly perils we have had to endure on this continent! However, as we have abandoned ourselves completely to the Lord's gracious providence, His powerful hand has protected us. Although thousands threatened to sink us, no terrible wave of the bottomless ocean was allowed to swallow us.[32] We stepped on land in Canada and there began the terrible hardships. Carl XII [of Sweden] went through the Ukraine with his army. The lack of victuals alone made his march difficult. We did not have to fear this but we went to New England from Canada in miserable batteaux across terrible lakes and through impassable wildernesses in order to suffer the same fate here that his army had at Poltava. Walloon's Creek in the Province of New Hampshire[33] was the place where our corps, 500 men strong, was killed, wounded or taken prisoner by more than 5,000 Americans; the Breymann Corps, designated for our support, arrived one hour late, -- and almost had the same fate at Sancoik.[34] Bennington was the place where those still living but wounded, as well as the prisoners of war, were gathered. The church in which all the prisoners of war were being kept had become too small and the wounded, whose number through a dreadful mistake had even grown, -- the Americans had killed and wounded a few more of our men inside the church[35] -- were taken into some of the houses. All those able to march had to set out on a march to Boston on Aug. 18. How our men were treated there and later on the guard ship in the harbor off the city of Boston, only those who have been there can tell. I, for my part, went with six wounded officers from Bennington and stayed in Springfield on the Connecticut River. Since that time we have been living in this Province of Massachusetts Bay, paying cash for our room and board. Since the inhabitants appeared very angry during the first days of our captivity and probably did not express themselves very politely toward us, it was our consolation that we did not understand their English language at the time. On the other hand, they later became much more courteous and amicable toward us especially when they learned that we are Christians and not Savages from Germany, as the inhabitants had been made to believe. All in all, the Americans have taken us in and not treated us as enemies but as friends; more in detail about that later. You can also read in my diary how Lieut. General Burgoyne's army later conceded at Saratoga. I have decided to send it over to you so that I will not lose it all again. It got lost at Walloon's Creek, and through the good offices of the American Colonel Warner, some of it found its way back into my hands.

At this time, our forces in America are very scattered: one part is in Canada, another in Massachusetts Bay, another in New York and one part even in Virginia. Would that all these be reunited one day! No, it will not be possible before Resurrection! We here are about in the middle. Québec is 500 Engl. miles and Virginia 800 Engl. miles from here. Our Maj. Gen. von Riedesel is in Virginia with the regiments that were part of the Convention of Saratoga; most of our Dragoon Regiment is in that Province. All the prisoners of war have to assemble here in Rutland; they will be transferred into the barracks and have to live on very scanty supplies. I have also arrived here from Westminster on Febr. 9 and am living in this village with the pastor, by the name of Buckminster. I am well taken care of. Since all the prisoners of war are assembling here, it stands to reason that we will be exchanged, but nothing certain has been said about that so far.

What do you think, dear friend, and what do they say about us in Germany? I am quite certain that when two or three friends come together, we are the topic of their conversation! "Alas! What are our countrymen in America doing! If we could only get one detailed report from there! -- Is he still alive? -- Alas, and that one, would that I knew how he is getting along -- he might be already dead, he has not written for so long, -- but how can he write when he is in captivity?" My beloved Germans, even if you have no relatives in America, do remember your countrymen with a feeling of tenderness and compassion. You well know that we deserve that even more than you can imagine. But you! You who accompany your father, brother or cousin in America with your sighs, you whose beating hearts yearn every day for being reunited with [us] your friends. But when will this happy moment of [fulfillment of] your wishes come to pass, friend? For many [of us], not in this world! -- In that better world, you will be reunited with those whom you now bemoan in vain, -- friends, dry your tears and stop needlessly frightening your hearts, -- implore your gracious God with quiet hearts for the fulfillment of your wishes and know that our lives are safe in His fatherly hands. He knows how many days we shall have, He knows what protects us, He sets the limits of our fates. I am feeling all that those suffering most among you will ever feel: in my God's Providence, I have left behind those that are dearest to me in this world. I know that God values them and will keep them. I wish I could see them again one more time! Shall I ever rejoice in this happiness? -- Lord! Thy will be done!

The most beloved of my friends in America, he who was even a blood relative [36] of mine and whose daily company often tore me away from all that disquieted my heart, is gone; a mad bullet cut his life's thread in the prime of youth; -- Bennington is the place where he gave his body to the elements! Oh, what grief I have suffered! And how terrible this notice must have been to you, my brother! -- Alas, I pity you, I commiserate with you and I only wish that this will reach you to ease your mind and that you should know, my dear brother, that as long as I was able to be with him, I did everything for your son that duty demands of a brother. My diary, which you will receive through the good offices of a worthy friend, will inform you of the terrible event with all the particulars. -- Yet it is time to think of ending this letter and asking your forgiveness for this lengthy epistle. When I am writing to you, it is as if I am conversing with you, and these moments are so sweet to me that I often become too long-winded. Please, send my regards to your dear family and tell mine that I am alive and well. Farewell, my dear friend, may God bless you with health and keep you forever in His care."

Several of our men who have been living with inhabitants in New England since their capture have been so unfortunate as to forget their mother tongue, and since they have learned but little or faulty English, they speak no language at all; it is an abominable mixture, half German and half English, that no one can understand.

The latest paper [Continental Journal, July 1] from Boston writes *that the Engl. army has been encircled near Charleston and will soon have to surrender. On the other hand, a newspaper from New York, June 26, writes: The position of the army under General Prevost at Stono not far from Charleston in South Carolina is totally secure against all the attacks which the Rebel army might plan to make.* [summary]

Boston, July 8. Last Thursday, a captured English ship arrived in the harbor here with 400 tons in ballast; after a very strong resistance, the privateer Harlequin of Salem seized it. She carried 18 cannon [six and nines] and had 5,400 tons of [beef and pork] *[provisions] on board, [of which] 1,300 tons were flour.* [accurate]

An important article for the Engl. army, therefore a great loss.

From a London newspaper. Advertisement: Items immediately in demand. About 30,000 good and strong men who know how to handle muskets for the service of the King of Great Britain in America. He who can serve or support the Government is asked at once to notify the licentious minister Frederick North at Downing Street in Westminster.[37] At the same time, no less than one dozen warships are required, each of 90 or 100 tons. Whosoever is able to procure these, can be sure of getting a good reward. --Lost by mistake: Thirteen Provinces in America with all appurtenances.

A fine, new commercial business with an annual worth of 2 million pounds of straw. More than 20,000 well-trained soldiers.
Our natural influence on European affairs.
The integrity of our ministers.
Freedom of the subjects and the virtue, justice and good sense of our King.
Anyone capable of producing these or knowing some means by which the afore-mentioned items can be restored as a whole or in part, should notify the Royal officers who are appointed [to watch] *over these items, which have by mistake been lost: their lodgings are on Cleveland Row. There, they should be promised a rich reward for said service.*[38]

The Boston paper [Continental Journal] from July 17 [15] *reports that an English fleet under the command of Commodore George Collier has had troops disembark which, under the command of Governor Tryon, have plundered and burned down the cities of New Haven and Fairfield. In the Province of Connecticut, a number* of *women have been bestially abused in the presence of their closest relatives.* [39] [accurate]

If that is true, it is abominable. But there is always much ill being said about the English.

Hartford paper [Connecticut Courant], July 18 [20]: *Extract from a letter from July 16:*
If before receiving this you have not heard anything about it, I assure you that Stony Point, a newly laid-out fort at King's Ferry on the North [Hudson] River, is in our hands with all its stored provisions, ammunition etc. [and about 500 men who composed the garrison]. [The English occupation force under the command of Col. Johnston of the 17th Regiment has been taken prisoner.] *[Col. Johnston of the 17th Regiment commanded the British fort.] Our General Wayne took the fort on the 15th at midnight. We have had 4 men killed and the general has been slightly wounded.*[40] [accurate]
Part of a letter from Col. Clarke, April 29, 1779.
Moreover, this paper writes that another 6 Savage nations are fighting against the Americans, that is, one part of the Shawnee, the Meandes, half of the Chippewas, the Ottawas, Tawnyans and Potawatime nations, who live near the [Great] *Lakes* [in Canada]. *The following nations have joined the Americans: those living near the Wabash River as there are the nations of the Peankishaw, the Kaskaskies, the Onaottinans. Such nations on the Mississippi and Illinois Rivers as the Rockackies, the Peorians, Mechiganies, Foxes, Serks, Opays, Illinois, Shoces, Poues and one part of the nation of the Chippewas have declared themselves neutral and are peaceful.*[41] *It is also reported that the nations of the Cherokees and Chickasaws have revolted against the Americans.* [An American army under the command of General Sullivan is marching toward Niagara; in their opinion this fort, which they call the Key to Canada, will soon be conquered.] [42] [selective]

N.B. If they only do not hasten too much.

In the Boston paper [Independent Ledger] from July 19, *they are writing from Charleston in South Carolina about some skirmishes that took place between the armies of General Prevost and General Lincoln; according to previous papers, the Engl. army under Gen. Prevost has been beaten, encircled, captured and the like.*

Extract from a letter of a field-officer in Wyoming, [Pennsylvania],
dated June 24: Our troops are quite well and amply provided with all necessities.
Most items in our magazine such as provisions and ammunition arrive here in
batteaux on the Susquehanna River. --Our army is very strong, consisting of good
soldiers and is commanded by 6 generals, namely, Maj. Gen. Sullivan, Commander-
in-Chief, Brig. Generals Clinton, Maxwell, Poor, Hand and Proctor as well as the
militia from Pennsylvania. All our forces are not assembled as yet. Clinton's and
Proctor's brigades have so far not joined up with us. A great number of warriors
from the nations of the Oneidas, Tuscaroras, and Stockbridge Savages will unite
with us; the Reverend Mr. Kirkland,[43] *a missionary of the Savages, is the interpreter*
with us. [accurate]

[Continental Journal, July 22]. *From Philadelphia [July 9] came the report that*
letters which have arrived from England are giving assurances that a great rebellion
has erupted in Ireland. The letters state that 15,000 Rebels are on the north side and
25,000 in the other parts of that Kingdom; the Rebels' Commanders are Charles
O'Neil, the Honorable Charles Conolly and the Earl of Clanrickard.[44] *Comte*
d'Estaing has been reinforced; his fleet consists of 22 warships and 24 frigates.
{accurate[

The French have taken the Islands of Jersey and Guernsey from the English.
Gibraltar has been besieged by a Spanish and Port Mahon by a French fleet. [45]
[accurate]

Surprising News! Is it really all true?

And another piece of news: *News from Philadelphia states that* [the King of]
Spain declared the American States independent on April 19 [11]. [accurate]

[Continental Journal, July 29. Hartford July 27]. *Baltimore, June 19. A few days*
ago, the April packet boat arrived in New York from England and brought the news
that Admiral Arbuthnot had set sail to America from England with his fleet and
many transports. This fleet has 9,000 men, land forces, on board. [accurate]

Boston paper [The Evening Post], July 24. *Extract from a letter from Fairfield,*
July 15 :
I am sitting down to describe to you some of the [sad and] horrible events which
have taken place in our beautiful and pleasant town, -- but now a sad place, a
devastated heap of ruins, horrible sight of a most terrible destruction. It was in the
beginning of wheat harvest, one of the best times of the year with joyous and merry
work, a time so good that our old folks could not remember ever having had any
better a time which promised us the greatest plenty. The British fleet and the army
with the [German and] American refugees [and foreigners], which had taken
possession of New Haven and plundered it, set sail from that distressed community
on the 6th of this month. About 4 o'clock of the following morning through the firing
of a gun from a [small] fort which lies south of us on Grover's Hill, we became
aware of the approaching fleet, but it appeared as if they intended to pass by. About
7 o'clock, we saw them sailing toward the west -- we thought -- to New York. A
heavy fog now setting in hid the fleet from our sight. Between 9 and 10 o'clock,
however, after the fog had lifted, we again saw them to our right below us on the
western shore. Several ships approached King's [Kinzie's] Point, cast their anchors
and were riding there until 4 o'clock in the afternoon. Then some troops began to

disembark to the east of King's [Kinzie's] Point. From there, the troops marched [along the beach until they came to a lane opposite] to the center of our town [through which they proceeded] and kept parading in 2 [three] divisions between church and city hall [the Meeting House and Court House] for a period of one hour. After that, they detached their guards, separated into small corps and began their hellish business. Their naval commander was Sir George Collier, and Generals Tryon and Garth were the commanders on land. Since the fleet had so quickly appeared, few of the militia could be summoned. As soon as the fog had lifted, the alarm guns were fired but there was no possible way of preventing the enemy from landing; our forces were much too weak. [accurate]   After having fired the field cannon with grapeshot and our small arms into them, the militia had to withdraw; the cannon fire from Grover's Hill also could not keep the enemy back. [summary]

Our city was almost bare of inhabitants. A few women, some of them ladies of the most respectable families, had lost too much time with a view of saving their most precious possessions; they might also have imagined that their sex and character would protect them. They even placed their confidence in the magnanimity of the enemy, who had previously been considered prudent and humane and [probably] still was. They [the ladies] thought that meeting them with kind and submissive demeanor would secure them against coarse behavior and a rough encounter, but they were badly mistaken and too late regretted the trust they had placed in the enemy's magnaminity. The Hessians were the first party that was let loose to plunder and destroy; these broke into the houses, brutalized friend and foe [Whig and Tory] without difference, broke open chests, trunks, closets and boxes and took everything of value. They robbed women of buckles, rings, bonnets, aprons and handkerchiefs; they did not only abuse them in the most disgusting language [but also (threatening their life) stepped on them with their feet] and put bayonets to their breasts. Pleading and wailing, accompanied by the most fervent tears, could not move these brutes to showing some regard for the female sex. They listened and looked around [wondering] how the mirrored furniture, china and porcelain and everything they set their eyes on could be smashed. A sucking infant was robbed of its clothing as a bayonet was set to the breast of the mother, [who held him in her arms] [Here, Wasmus left out a paragraph describing further brutalities. H.D.] The English came last and devastated the rest. Several of these officers seemed to feel sorry for us and for the misfortune of our country but it had to be done, it was one of the means of attaining power over us. --Some of the Engl. troops were particularly violent against the female sex, -- they insulted them and attempted their chastity, -- raping seemed not to be permitted but some [women] were forced to submit to the most indelicate and disgusting treatment -- some employed all their power and strength to defend their virtue and chastity against that brutal treatment. [Some still show the scars and bruises of the horrid conflict.] [accurate]

Shortly before sunset, the fire broke out. The women [weibliche Geschlecht] threw themselves at General Tryon's feet [begging] that some houses and particularly the churches be spared, but his heart was cruel; he refused it. A good Tory, whose house had also been completely plundered, was begging him at the same time, but nothing seemed to help. Finally came the order to spare Mr. Burr's house and the house of him who has written this letter; also the churches were to remain unharmed. General Garth, who had the command on the other side of town, was much more humane and granted much of what General Tryon refused. [summary]

On the next morning at sunrise, a considerable part of the town was still standing but before two hours had passed, the incendiaries had diligently kindled their *business and except for a few houses, the fire consumed the city. At about 8 o'clock, the enemy began to withdraw; the churches and a few houses were still standing. This gave us a little consolation amid the desolate scenery -- but then came the rear guard that consisted of the most savage band that has ever been let loose on humans. They set fire to everything that General Tryon had left standing; the big, magnificent church, the parsonage, Mr. Burr's and other houses, that had previously received protection, were destroyed by fire. --They tore Gen. Tryon's letters of safe conduct to pieces, cursed Gen. Tryon and his letters of safe conduct and abused the 2nd sex in the most despicable manner after which they ignominiously ran away.*

Fortunately some of our militia came and extinguished the fire in several houses so that we are not completely in ruins. The old English church has also been destroyed but I did not know by whom.

This rearguard, that acted so infamously, were mostly Germans, called Jägers; they carry short, drawn rifles and behave almost worse than the Savages. These Hessians can quite rightfully be called the sons of plunder, destruction and devastation.

Our fort is still standing, the enemy put a galley in front but could not silence it. Throughout the night, there was continual fire from both sides. The enemy made some attempts to capture it, but it was courageously defended by Lieut. Isaac Jarvis from Fairfield, who had no more than 23 men with him.

The militia pursued the bloody devastators up to the place of embarkation where they pressed them very hard. The embarkation was over by noon and the cruel mob set sail toward Long Island at 3 o'clock; several were killed on both sides. They also took several prisoners along, but no person of distinction. The report in the Hartford paper, according to which a man was cooked in brandy and later burned, is false; among all their godless tricks, there was none of that type of cruelty. [accurate]

Boston [Continental Journal, July 29]: *Last Monday, a cartel ship arrived here from New York with 114 Americans, [who afforded a shocking spectacle to humanity], who had been so fortunate as to be captured by the English; these had exercised their usual cruelty on them, which makes every feeling heart tremble. -- Most had lost their strength and were unable to stand on their feet. Alas, how unfortunate are they who get into the power of those brutes! How cruelly are they treated by our savage enemy! -- Several of our brethren had already died on the trip here from New York and many more of those who have arrived are about to die at any moment; very few of them seem likely to recover or reach their former state of health. -- Oh, you Englishmen, are you not blushing with shame? [Britain, where is thy blush?]* [accurate]

In a letter from Martinique from June 29 [?], it is reported that Comte d'Estaing has seized the Island of St. Vincent and is about to take Grenada. As General Clinton's reputation has so greatly suffered, Lord Cornwallis will relieve him. [selective]

We have learned from a gentleman who arrived here yesterday from Salem that last Tuesday several persons passing the border of Penobscot heard a heavy cannonade from 6 o'clock in the morning until sunset; we will soon get more information from there. [accurate]

Today, the 31st, Major Edwards came to Rutland from Providence. Since commissary Mercereau was still absent, he was given the command over the prisoners of war by General Gates. Edwards was Lieutenant in Colonel Jackson's Regiment and has conferred the title of Major on himself during the trip here. He took com. Mercereau's passports from all the prisoners and gave them others.

At the end of this month the guinea is worth 70 specie in paper money.

Month of August 1779

Worcester paper [Massachusetts Spy], Aug. 5: *Fishkill, July 29.*
Our gallant Light Infantry, who under the courageous and stout-hearted General Wayne has acquired immortal glory at the stormy seizure of Stony Point, was composed of drafts from each state of our Provincial soldiers. The manner in which they calmly marched up to the attack and seized the American Gibraltar, so called by our enemies, has never been carried out any better in the world neither in olden times nor in the present and cannot be praised enough. [The officers and men were even emulous to go upon the Forlorn Hope, which was decided by lot, when one gentleman, disappointed in that command by the lots favoring his neighbor, expressed himself as one child of misfortune from the cradle while the other bounded from the group with joy.] The officers and soldiers were equally courageous in that engagement and without having a bullet in their guns or a whisper in their mouths, they climbed over the abatis and then scrambled up the precipices. The enemy called to them, 'Come here, ye damn'd Rebels, come here!' Several of our gallant men very softly replied, 'Take it easy, fellows, we'll soon be with you!' And 20 minutes later, they began to fire from the fort and the parapets they had scaled and seized. According to a discovered orderly book, the enemy had been in readiness and an order had been given for the garrison that night at 9 o'clock to man the walls and lay on their arms. We stormed this fort with but 900 men, overcoming every obstruction and all the obstacles. The garrison was 600 men strong. If our men had wanted to take revenge on the enemy in the attack! -- but their conduct was as Christian as always and everybody can ascribe to their humane consideration and loving-kindness! -- which also are the inseparable characteristics of true courage. They pressed into the fort with the firm and fiery resolve to slaughter all the enemies since they remembered how these had often cruelly killed the Americans with the bayonet. Many of them had seen that and also held in recent memory how they had burned unarmed towns and villages with savage cruelty, insulted the female sex, who cannot defend themselves, abused them in a bestial manner -- raping them --, not protecting nor sparing the old folks and the children but robbing them and leaving them wretched. But now they are loudly crying, 'Mercy! mercy! dear Americans! Mercy! Quarter! Quarter! brave Americans! Forgive us!' This changed their [the Americans'] resolve and effected a change of heart in them so that the Engl. commandant, Colonel Johnson, did publicly confess that not a drop of blood was shed in vain. --Blush, oh Britain, blush! How low did you sink! [accurate] *Go and sigh about the infamous action you committed on your brethren in America! [Go on, make bonfires of the sacked villages, until full retaliation will open your eyes with a vengeance.] --Publicly confirm our independence, do justice to the leaders of this terrible, devilish war! --Then we can shake hands, -- for the sake of the virtuous who live among us and in memory of the country from which the tree of freedom has been transplanted here, let us then shake hands and you can thereafter amicably harvest the very wealth of our superabundance, which you cannot obtain by force.* [selective]

Worcester paper [Massachusetts Spy], Aug. 5:

Before this sheet left the press, we have learned from some gentlemen from Boston that in accordance with our wishes, our expedition to Penobscot is proceeding well. Last Friday, an enemy redoubt had been seized there in an assault. The enemies destroyed 2 of their frigates; the remainder of the ships fell into our hands with all the things on board. In the next paper, we hope to be able to give you a detailed report of this big and important affair.

The English army in South Carolina is also said to be totally beaten and ruined. [accurate]

Hartford paper [Connecticut Courant], Aug. 3: *Extract from a letter from Bennington, July 18.*

Last Tuesday, Major Wright Hopkins, commander at Fort St. George, sent a lieutenant [Lt. Michael Dunning] with a detachment across Lake George to reconnoiter whether he could discover any of the enemy. On the following day, Major Hopkins decided on a water excursion in a boat on the lake with several officers [and soldiers] and a few ladies. The weather was very pleasant and they assiduously rowed to meet up with the lieutenant, who had been sent out the day before. This did indeed happen a little north of the so-called 14 Mile Island. A contrary wind, however, that changed into a gale, forced them to remain on this island. They pulled their batteaux ashore and built huts to spend the night as comfortably as possible. They thought themselves safe because the dispatched lieutenant had not observed any trace of the enemy. But at daybreak, they were attacked by some Savages and Tories. Major Hopkins, two sergeants, three privates, and two ladies were shot dead and scalped; two captains, one lieutenant [Lt. Michael Dunning] and the rest were captured and led away. [accurate]

[Continental Journal, August 5] *Extract of a letter from France. Nancy, June 3.*

The Spanish ambassador left the Court of St. James [Engl. Court] without officially taking leave. It had been confirmed that our fleet will sail from Brest tomorrow; it consists of 28 warships, 9 frigates, 7 advice boats, and 3 fire ships. The other warships [the <u>Burgoyne</u> and the <u>Victory</u>], will join this fleet at sea [or at Cadiz]; the fleet has 10,000 land forces on board. One believes that it will join the Spanish fleet, which is 32 warships strong, and then attack Gibraltar and Minorca. [accurate]

Don't be too hotheaded!

Comte d'Estaing will keep Admiral Byron at bay, and the 10 Spanish warships riding at anchor at Havana will try to capture the Engl. islands in the West Indies or support the Americans on the continent. We know for certain that the Engl. fleet at Portsmouth cannot be ready before the end of this month; 8,000 sailors are wanted to complete it. [accurate]

Last Tuesday, a French frigate of 32 cannon from France entered the harbor here. On it, His Excel. the Chevalier de la Luzerne, Plenipotentiary of His Most Christian Majesty, came to the United American States. [accurate]

This newspaper reports from a letter from Majabagaduce that they [?] had a skirmish with the English whereby they gained some advantage; but they have not yet driven them out of Penobscot much less captured the army and the fleet.[46] [summary]

N.B. What will become of this! If these will also turn out to be lies? You journalists in America, you will overdraw your account with your countrymen if you are every now and then telling such big lies. The lies about South Carolina have much disgraced you; your own nation is angry about it. These things about Penobscot will again be lies; what other kind of lies will you finally bring forth to your defense?

Boston paper [Independent Ledger], Aug. 9: *From a letter from Amsterdam, March 29.*

Reports from there state that the recruits from Ansbach and Hanau are daily waiting for the transport ships to take them to England. The recruits from Hesse-Cassel and Waldeck are in Bremerlehe [Bremerhaven] and those from Braunschweig and Anhalt-Zerbst have embarked in Stade; all these troops are destined for America. [accurate]

Extract from a letter of the Royal Journalist, Mr. Rivington in New York.[47]

The Hessians, these coarse hirelings, who can never have enough, will soon put us in the embarrassing situation that nothing can be had any more for money. Mutton, an Englishman's favorite dish, can scarcely be seen in our markets. You are well enough acquainted with these fiendish gluttons, our companions in this type of food, that you can surely believe that everything will soon be scarce. If we would only be rid of them! [not found]

London, May 31: From Falmouth we have received the good news through a dispatch that the West Indian fleet has safely arrived there without any loss. [not found]

Extract from a letter from Torbay, May 29. Admiral Arbuthnot has joined the fleet under Admiral Darby[48] *and now commands 20 warships, 6 frigates, 2 fire ships and some other armed ships. The Admiral gave the fleet the signal to be ready to sail the following morning. The Empress of Russia has offered to support the King of England with 20 warships, 6 frigates and 20,000 land forces for 3 years.* [not found]

N.B. This is again a lie, England has a greater sea power than all the other European powers together.

The gallant Sir James Wallace is the Commodore Designate over 6 frigates in Georgian Waters.

London, June 1. The armed ship Hind arrived in Portsmouth from Stade with 20 transport ships. These have 5,000 German troops on board destined for America.

Our big fleet will not sail from Spithead before Admiral Darby's fleet returns. This one is accompanying the New York fleet up to a certain latitude. One presumes them to be back by the end of July. [not found]

Rutland, Aug. 14. Today, the news came that the American army has been beaten and completely dispersed at Penobscot; that, at the arrival of the Engl. fleet, their fleet has taken to flight upstream toward Penobscot and that they have burned their ships except for two that fell into the power of the English. Their fleet consisted of 48 sails.[49] This morning the order also came from commissary Mercereau to the deputy commissary Pape [?] to send the prisoners of war of the 71st Scots Regiment to New London for exchange.

Boston paper [Independent Ledger], Aug. 16: *Madrid, April 20.*

Our large fleet continues riding at anchor in the harbor of Cadiz, where great preparations are being made. What this fleet will finally be destined for continues to be a secret; there has not yet been an order to sail. The continual exchange of couriers between our and the French harbors indicates that important matters are on the carpet. [accurate]

Paris, May 7. The Marquis de Lafayette[50] *will return to America; fifteen hundred of the best officers will accompany him, who, upon their arrival, are to be distributed among the regiments of the United States. They are to make these [American regiments] as perfect as possible and to instruct and improve them to the utmost in all the military sciences.* [accurate]

London, May 18. Yesterday, Sir Charles Hardy[51] *had the large flag hoisted on board of the* Victory *of 100 cannon. He has been appointed Commander-in-Chief of the great fleet, which is riding at anchor at Spithead and St. Helens.* [accurate]

The King has taken pleasure in appointing Maj. Gen. James Robinson [52] *to take the place of Maj. Gen. Tryon as Captain General and Governor-in-Chief in the Royal Province of New York in North America.* [accurate]

Worcester paper [Massachusetts Spy], Aug. 19: *Boston, Aug. 16. Last Friday, the ship* Thames *arrived here from St. Eustatius. She sailed from there on July 22 and brings us the reliable information that the islands of St. Vincent and Grenada definitely are in French hands and that Comte d'Estaing won a victory over the English Admiral Byron, who lost 10 warships either taken or sunk. Several of the large ships having lost their masts went to St. Kitts with the help of some frigates. They are to be repaired but have been blockaded there by the French fleet. When the merchants and several inhabitants saw the Engl. fleet enter in such deplorable condition, they fled with all their belongings to St. Eustatius.*[53] [summary]

Providence, Aug. 19. The 3 ships that had sailed away from here some time ago have been captured by the English and taken to Antigua. Our men who were on board, officers as well as privates, were imprisoned, put in irons and very inhumanely treated.

Yesterday, a ship arrived from Savannah that had sailed from there 2 weeks ago. It brought the news that the Spanish Court has declared war on England on July 22, and that 40 warships are riding at anchor ready to sail. [not found]

N.B. Might this number not be reckoned too high?

Rutland, Aug. 23.   A rumor is spreading here that should apparently make us feel very good; a general exchange of all the prisoners of the warring powers has been agreed upon. Thus, we should shortly be exchanged. If this is supposed to happen before winter, it had better happen soon as long as the weather is good. But as much as we might wish for it, I still do not believe it.

Boston paper [Independent Ledger], Aug. 22 [23]: *From this city, a very detailed report is given of the sea battle between Comte d'Estaing and Admiral Byron, which is said to have occurred on July 6. This report is similar to the one mentioned before. The Engl. fleet had great losses--which is true. According to their own account, the French had 170 dead and 773 wounded. According to these reports, England will soon lose everything in the West Indies. In this paper, the Spanish*

Declaration of War as well as the answer to the King of England are written up. [summary]

Worcester paper [Massachusetts Spy], Aug. 26: *Basse Terre on the Island of St. Christopher in the West Indies, July 10 [Oct. 17].*
From here another report is given of the sea battle between Admiral Byron and Comte d'Estaing. The English suffered no more than 300 dead and wounded in their fleet, and since, according to their own report, the French had 943 dead and wounded, the affair has not been correctly told. [summary]

Rutland, Aug. 27.   The Scots of the 71st Regiment departed for New York to be exchanged. There were supposedly 60 men but only 16 men went; the others did not want to be exchanged. The inhabitants are happy that they wish to stay in this country. They are working on the farms and earn 8-10-12 perhaps even 16 specie in silver money for their labor.   The amount depends on how much they work and how well they know how to do farm work.   During the winter months, however, they earn not even half as much.

Boston paper [Independent Ledger], Aug. 30: *Boston. Last Friday, a cartel ship arrived at the harbor here which carried General MacLean from Penobscot with 60 prisoners of war; these had been captured in the 2 ships, Hunter and Hampden, that had fallen into English hands.* [accurate]

And how did all this happen? You have previously written in the Worcester paper, Aug. 5, that you had the Engl. fleet and army in your power and now everything is turned upside down.   That is fine!--It must be very painful, my dear journalist Thomas, when one must openly confess to have lied to the public. [54]

At the end of this month, the guinea is worth 80 specie in paper money.

Month of September 1779

Worcester paper [Massachusetts Spy], Sept. 2: *From Worcester:*
We have often seized the opportunity to write with contempt about our enemies in accusing them of making false statements about various affairs. In no way do we wish to grant our enemies the power of discovering our mistakes in the various incidents, -- but we have waited long enough to receive a detailed report of the expedition to Penobscot from Boston, which has been promised. But nobody knows as yet when it will come [from that quarter]. Among all the reports we have, this one is the most important and the most reliable: After having seized one of two redoubts from the enemy, our commanders at sea and on land spent their time with making observations until the enemies were reinforced by several big ships. As soon as this reinforcement appeared, two of our ships took to flight, two fell into the power of the enemy and the rest of the ships reached safety with the help of gun fire. Our irregular troops effected an irregular retreat [commanded] -- as we hear -- by an irregular brigadier general and a new-fangled commodore, without any loss excepting the entire fleet [saving two vessels] with all ammunition, provisions and the like. About 160 [70] men were taken prisoner, very few died. A small number perished [in the fatigue] in going through the wilderness. This was the end of the expedition to Penobscot as reported. The question now is who is to blame? Certainly not the noncommissioned officers and the privates. [accurate]

Boston, Monday paper [Independent Ledger] Sept. 6: *Philadelphia at the court-martial, July 26.*

We received the report from Colonel Bland, Commander of the Convention Barracks not far from Charlottesville in Virginia, that many of the Convention troops have deserted to rejoin the enemies. All the officers in the service of the United American States are hereby seriously admonished to be on the lookout for and immediately arrest all the deserters. All the civil officers and loyal subjects are likewise called upon to deliver all the British and German deserters, coming from the south and passing through the country, to the nearest commissary over prisoners or else to put them in jail. Many of these troops have passed themselves off for friends and sworn the oath of allegiance to the United States, whereupon they received passports to wander through the country. They only did this, however, to find an opportunity of joining our enemies. All the officers, judges and magistrates who have administered the oath of allegiance and given passports to those deserters are herewith seriously reminded that it is forbidden to do these very harmful deeds in the future. These conferred passports, with which they can more easily cross over to the enemy, are but a proof of their imposture; therefore, every one of these shall in future be considered a deserter and treated as such. Not all are wearing short linen smock frocks [they are generally clad in short linen coat or coatres [sic] and linen overalls] and like our riflemen, carry their regimental coats in knapsacks. The troops of the Convention of Saratoga comprise the 9th, 20th, 24th, 47th, [53rd] and 62nd Regiments; a detachment of the 33rd Regiment, Lord Balcarres' Corps and Royal British Artillery; several Braunschweig Dragoons as well as the Regiments von Riedesel, [von] Rhetz, [Specht], von Bärner, Hesse-Hanau, Hesse-Hanau Artillery and a Braunschweig Grenadier Battalion. The regiments and corps can be recognized by the regimentals and the names on the regimental buttons; these will make their desertion manifest. P. Scull, Secretary.[55] [accurate]

Hartford paper [Connecticut Courant], Sept. 7: *Philadelphia, Aug. 28th:*

Extract of a letter from [Maj.] Gen. Lincoln [to the President of Congress], dated Charleston, [South Carolina], July 3 [9, 1779].

The enemy has [completely] withdrawn from Stono Ferry and [on the main] has sent their sick to St. Augustine. They marched 90 miles down the shore and have devastated and plundered the richest settlements and the most distinguished inhabitants of the land [this state], almost completely ruining them. Among these are some who have lost 300 to 400 blackmen, more than 100 pounds of silver [1,600 ounces of plate], all their cattle and generally all their most valuable possessions. The enemy made no difference between friend and foe [Whig and Tory] and even if they had promised protection to this one or that one, he would still be stripped. Even the widows and orphans have lost everything. Many are completely stripped so that they cannot even dress [have not a second suit of clothes], in short they took everything. [accurate]

New York, Aug. 16 [26]. We reported in our last paper that the Royal ship <u>Russel</u> *has arrived at Sandy Hook. Last Tuesday, she came closer and cast anchor in the North or Hudson River. She is one of the most beautiful of 74 cannon ships in the English navy and has a copper bottom. She had 400,000 guineas [sterling] on board for the Royal army. Yesterday, Marrionet [Marriot] Arbuthnot Esq., Vice Admiral of the blue [flag] and Commander-in-Chief of His Majesty's fleet in North America, arrived here in the Royal ship* <u>Europe</u> *of 64 cannon, together with the first division of troops, which are to join the Royal army here.*[56] [accurate]

Rutland, Sept. 7.   Today, Captain of the Cavalry Fricke went to Rhode Island to get money for the prisoners of war.

Boston, Saturday's paper [Independent Ledger], Sept. 11 [13]: *Boston.*

Last Monday, the city was informed through signals from the small fort that several ships were sailing toward our harbor. We soon learned that they were 2 of our frigates, namely the Dearle and the Boston; the former is commanded by Capt. Nicholson and the latter by Capt. Tucker. They had two prizes with them, one packet boat that had been sent to England from New York, and the new sloop of war York of 14 cannon, which has a copper bottom. This one had been sent from England with dispatches to the Commander of New York from the English Government, wherein the troubles with Spain were reported. These two frigates have previously sent 8 prizes here. In the sloop of war, a painter has been taken prisoner who had plates, paper and antimony to counterfeit the most recent American paper money. Some of his accomplices are said to be men of high rank, who were doubtless living in the hope of making a big profit from this mischief. The English have made use of all the advantages of fraud just as they are practicing all kinds of cruelty on the Americans in this unfortunate war. But the steadfastness, courage, virtue and stoutheartedness of the inhabitants of the United American States do overcome everything and bring all their [the English] designs to naught. The following were taken prisoner in the packet boat: Lieut. Colonel Duncan MacPherson and Capt. Ross of the 73rd Reg., Major Gardner and family from the 16th Reg. and 3 ship captains travelling home. [selective]

Rutland, Sept. 17.   Captain of the Cavalry Fricke returned from Rhode Island and brought 1,200 guinea pieces along; this is the right medicine for us.

Boston [Continental Journal], Saturday's paper, Sept. 18 [16]: *Extract from a letter from Paris [May 25, 1779], to a gentleman in Philadelphia.*

I received the news from a friend in London today that the following troops have been sent to New York on the fleet of Admiral Arbuthnot: 4 warships, each of 74 cannon; the transports had the Glasgow Regiment with 1,168 [1,163] newly formed; the Edinburgh Regiment with 1,168 men [illeg. word] as well as 1,500 [500] German recruits, in all 3,836 [2,834] men. [accurate]

Worcester paper [Massachusetts Spy], Sept. 23: *Extract of a letter from London, June 26.*

The Spanish declaration has set many things in motion here. An act will pass next Tuesday to increase the militia to 15,000 men and to gain another 15,000 men in voluntary companies. Colonel Campbell himself will set up 2,000 men [in Scotland]; the 8,000 men there are to be doubled. This makes our power on this island for internal defense upwards of 100,000 [effective] men under arms; in Ireland there will be 30,000. Another act will pass on Wednesday. The Parliament says that this month another 15 to 20 warships will be launched and the necessary sailors pressed into service. On the 18th [4th] of this month, the fleet sailed from Brest and will join the Spanish fleet. This French fleet consists of 28 warships, 3 of 110 cannon, 3 of 90, 9 of 74, and 20 of 64 cannon [ships, chiefly old and indifferently manned and 12 of them 64's and only 3 first and second rates] and all are mounted with the requisite crews. Moreover, two warships of 74 cannon are at Brest and will soon follow the fleet. Spain has 60 warships but will probably not be able to man 30 with crews. Sir

Charles Hardy set sail on the 16th of this month and is pursuing the French fleet with 3 ships of 100 cannon, 6 [5] of 98 [90], 19 of 74, 3 of 64 cannon. Next Tuesday, these will be followed by one of 98 [90] cannon, 1 of 81 [80], 5 [3] of 74, and 1 of 64 cannon. In all, 39 warships and 36 frigates of 28 to 44 cannon. This is one of the most beautiful fleets the old ocean has ever carried. Twelve warships will soon be ready and will then join Admiral Hardy's fleet. A very serious war will be waged against France and Spain. It is quite probable that we will have many more than 100 battleships at sea this year and anyway many more than 400 [200] warships, which have more than 100,000 sailors on board. One hundred thousand men are on [this island], 30,000 in Ireland [at least], 60,000 men in India, and 80,000 [60,000] men in North America and the West Indies, all armed and in the service of the King of Great Britain. Yet, the government offices are at their wits' ends. Remember, it is an evil war, and you know it, poor [old] England must perish, -- the great financier Lord North seems to be prepared for the campaign with all possibilities -- and this is true. [accurate]

Boston, Sept. 16. Three thousand men, mostly Hessians, embarked on 36 transport ships and sailed from New York, covered by 2 warships. Nobody knows their true destination but it is believed that they sailed to Québec. [accurate]

Another embarkation of 7,000 to 8,000 men is said to happen shortly, who are destined to go either to the southward or to Boston. In New York, one apparently does not have any conception of the fact that M. d'Estaing could come there although it is well known that he has sailed through the passage of Puerto Rico! [accurate]

Worcester [Sept. 23]: News from Bilbao in Spain, which has been brought us by the privateer Gen. Stark, *states that the French and Spanish fleets, consisting of 130 warships, are invading Gibraltar and Minorca; these [places] are occupied by foreign troops. Supposedly they have already been subdued and seized.* [accurate]

N.B. You must only take your time and not hasten too much, my dear Thomas!

The following is an accurate list of the land and naval forces in and around Halifax in Nova Scotia, namely the Duke of Argyle's Scots Regiment of 1,000 men, the Duke of Hamilton's Regiment of 1,100 men, the Orange Rangers, a dirty Tory corps of 500 men, and a Hessian Regiment of 700 men. In the absence of Mr. MacLean, these are commanded by Lieut. Colonel Campbell. Naval forces: An old ship of 74 cannon, an old French frigate, a sloop of war and 3 privateers each of 20 cannon.

The Spaniards have discovered a new silver mine in Mexico of such immense wealth that if they wanted, they could deluge all of Europe with silver, and the silver would lose half its value.

Yesterday, the ship Capt. Coffin *[sic] arrived here from Amsterdam, which had departed from there 8 weeks ago. It brought the news that Admiral Hardy was closed in at Torbay with 39 [31] warships by the combined French and Spanish fleets, which without frigates are 54 warships strong. It is daily expected that 50,000 French troops will land in England [on some part of Great Britain]. In a proclamation, the King of England is said to have ordered his subjects for safety's sake to drive all the cattle from the coasts into the interior.*[57] [accurate]

N.B. My dear Thomas, a short time ago, it was written that the combined fleet is 130 warships strong and now you have reduced it to 54. What is one to believe? Most of your reports are nothing but false assertions.

Boston [Independent Chronicle], Thursday's paper, Sept. 23: *London, June 19.*

The rebellious Irish cause us much unrest. The Americans take the same measures, are happy and shake off the yoke that has oppressed them under a corrupt government; the gallant Lord George Minden* is to take over the command of the army with his forces [invade France and Spain], drive the Turks out of their country and destroy Mohammed's grave in Mecca. Furthermore, it is his plan to seize Persia and all the countries in the east -- and then the army is to march to America where all inhabitants will throw themselves to Lord [North's] *[M--] feet and get a kick on their behinds [to be kicked]. -- Nothing can be more advantageous for France and Spain than the continuation of the present ministry. Those who have performed such heroic deeds in small affairs will doubtless effect far more in the present epic situation. --*

*This is the same Lord G. Germain, former Lord Sackville, who commanded the English Cavalry in the last war in Germany and acted so badly in the battle of Minden, Aug. 1, 1759.[58]

The ministers themselves must now see the imprudence with which they treated the late Earl of Chatham when he proposed his plan for accommodation with America.[59] This plan would surely have been accepted because it had the approval of Congress and would have made America your friend and restored peace. This honorable man surely was great in the eyes of the world; no easy substitute will be found for him. It can truthfully be said that from the moment he left or rather was driven from the monarch's privy councils, the confusion started [decline of this Empire]. The toasts our enemies are now pronouncing are 'Long live North, Germain and Sandwich, the conquerors of America'.[60] -- The present unrest deserves an annotation in history. No such scene has occurred since Jan. 30, 1648 or since James II left the throne: the Kingdom of Great Britain is now shaken to its very core.[61] [accurate]

At the last transaction between Doctor Franklin and the French minister, the minister promised to support the Americans with 10,000 men in the event that Great Britain hired 20,000 Hannoverians or as many Russians [for the American war]. [accurate]

Philadelphia, Aug. 21. Last Saturday, 5 English officers arrived here -- the others being on parole elsewhere -- as well as 148 privates, who had been captured at Paulus Hook [within view of New York].[62] [accurate]

A week ago Tuesday, 82 transport ships from Cork, Ireland arrived in New York with provisions. With these ships came the news of a rebellion in Scotland and also that a French fleet would undertake a landing on the north side of Ireland with many troops. [not found]

Last Friday, 2 of our ships, each of 20 cannon, arrived here from Penobscot and we have learned that our fleet had been destroyed in Penobscot by our own men so that it would not fall into English hands. [not found]

From Marblehead and Hartford comes the report that Comte d'Estaing has arrived at Charleston, South Carolina; thus, we will soon get news from there. Captain Taylor has seized a transport ship with 350 Hessians.

From Rivington's Royal paper, New York City, Sept. 20 [15] [and New York Gazette and Weekly Mercury, Sept. 13].

Last Tuesday, the Royal ship <u>Blonde</u> *arrived here and brought news of the glorious progress of the Royal arms at Penobscot. -- On Friday, Aug. 31, the Royal fleet under the command of George Collier, consisting of the* <u>Raisonable</u> *of 64 cannon and* <u>Blonde</u> *of 32,* <u>Greyhound</u> *and* <u>Virginia</u>, *each of 28,* <u>North</u> *of 24,* <u>Galatea</u> *and* <u>Camilla</u>, *each of 20 cannon, arrived at the entrance of the Penobscot River. On the following morning, the Rebel fleet appeared riding at anchor in a line of battle. They sent out a boat to reconnoiter and on its return, the Rebels did not take time to weigh the anchors but cut them off and took to flight upstream. The Engl. fleet pursued them and was very near when they had to cast anchor because the Rebels had left a ship in the middle of the river and had set it on fire. That kept the Royal fleet from capturing the entire Rebel fleet although they were but one cannon shot away from them. But Sir George Collier immediately sent out a boat with sailors to pull the burning ship ashore so that the English fleet could safely pass by. As soon as the Rebels saw that, they set their entire fleet afire. The English officers and sailors were courageous enough and thrust forward so fast that they took from the Rebels 2 small warships, one ordinance ship with a few 18-pound Somerset cannon on board and 2 provision ships. Before the arrival of the Royal fleet, these had made three assaults against the Engl. fort at Penobscot but had always been beaten back with great losses. Nevertheless, this same day had been designated by them for undertaking a major assault, which, however, turned out very badly for their forces both at sea and on land. As long as the siege lasted, General MacLean thwarted all assaults by the Rebels with his gallant officers and brave soldiers and never did anyone conceive of the possibility that they could fall into the hands of the Rebels.*

A great number of Rebels found their grave in the river. When they tried to save themselves by fleeing in their boats, they were buried in the river by the cannon balls from the fort. The losses in this expedition were very large: more than fifty of their best ships were consumed by fire; more than 10,000 tons of different types of provisions, their entire artillery, ammunition and baggage belonging to their army were likewise lost. Their human losses amounted to more than 6,000 men. List of the Rebel fleet, destroyed or seized at Penobscot: the frigate <u>Warren</u> *of 32 cannon,* <u>Monmouth</u>, <u>Vengeance</u>, *each of 24;* <u>Putnam</u>, <u>Sally</u>, *each of 22;* <u>Hector</u> *of 20;* <u>Black Prince</u> *of 18;* <u>Sky Rocket</u> *of 16;* <u>Active</u> *of 16;* <u>Defense</u> *of 16;* <u>Hazard</u> *of 16;* <u>Diligent</u> *of 14;* <u>Tyrannicide</u> *of 14; a schooner of 12 cannon and more than 50 transport and provision ships were consumed by fire.*

The <u>Hampden</u> *of 20 and* <u>Hunter</u> *of 18 cannon were seized. The 17 ships mentioned above had 1,940 men on board.*[63] [selective]

Mr. Rivington asserts in his Royal Gazette in New York that 38 men had been lost at Paulus Hook.

Boston [Continental Journal], Sept. 23. *From a gentleman, coming here from Providence yesterday, we have learned that the Hon. General Gates has received a letter from His Excel. General Washington assuring him that Comte d'Estaing has arrived at Sandy Hook.* [accurate]

The same report has also come from New London. -- And I still do not believe it! -- From Amsterdam it has also been reported that the entire fleet has been closed in at Torbay. Also lies.

Boston, Saturday's paper, Sept. 25: *From Boston. Last Monday, three deserters from the Royal army came from Newport to the headquarters* [of Gen. Gates] *in*

Providence and on Tuesday, five others came. They all confirmed the report that the enemy presume that they will soon receive a visit from the fleet of His Most Christian Majesty under the gallant d'Estaing. They are preparing as best they can to offer obstinate resistance; they are repairing Tomming Hill and put up several fortifications nearby.[64] [accurate]

Boston, Monday's paper [Independent Ledger], Sept. 27: *From Boston.*
From a gentleman having come here from Cadiz in 46 days, we learn that the combined fleet, consisting of 70 warships and a great number of troops, are preparing for an important undertaking; that Gibraltar is occupied by 5,000 [Hannoverian] [foreign troops], who were totally hemmed in by 20,000 Spanish troops and that they have not gotten any supplies since the beginning [end] of June. Since it is known that they had provisions but for a few months, it seems possible that they have surrendered a long time ago. [accurate]
The latest news coming from England gives a picture of utter confusion. They are in particularly great want of sailors and none of their ships is manned with the required crew. France has captured 30,000 English sailors and has not yet allowed an exchange to take place. [accurate]

At the end of this month, a guinea has the value of 90 to 95 paper specie or Spanish piasters.

Month of October 1779

Worcester paper [Massachusetts Spy], Oct. 7: *Boston, Sept. 30.*
We have received reports from New York that 8,000 men are to be sent from there to Ireland for the safety of the Kingdom. For, in her own bad situation, England is not able to lend any support. [accurate]

In fact, the English expect a landing in their own country any day, and meanwhile the rebellion is continuing in Ireland.

One of our small privateers of 4 cannon has brought an Engl. ship of 6 cannon into Newbury, which among other rare items had 1,100 tons of butter on board. [accurate]
Yesterday, Capt. Benjamin arrived here from Cadiz in 54 days and brought the news that Gibraltar is being besieged by 20,000 Spaniards on land and 10 warships at sea; that Admiral Duff[65] *has been closed in at Gibraltar and that the French have seized the English frigate* <u>Montreal</u> *and immediately sent her back to sea against the English. A Portuguese ship has been seized on her way to take provisions to Gibraltar. When the English fleet in the Mediterranean heard of the war with Spain, it entered [the port of] Lisbon and is now closed in there.* [accurate]
Charleston, South Carolina, Aug. 6. We hear that the troops in Savannah are very sick and that 4 to 10 Hessians are dying every day. [accurate]
Philadelphia, Sept. 16. We have gotten a reliable report from New York that a corps of troops, between 5,000 and 8,000 men strong, embarked and departed from there but it is not known what course they have taken. [summary]
Seven hundred men of Admiral Arbuthnot's fleet have died at sea and 1,200 sick have arrived in New York. [accurate]

Again one of their famous lies but yet they [*the newspapers*] have let some of them stay alive.

Boston [Continental Journal], Friday [Thursday] paper, Oct. 8 [7]: *Extract from a letter from Hartford [dated Oct. 4].*

From the dispatches that the Governor has received from Congress, we are assured that Congress received dispatches on Sept. 25 that Comte d'Estaing arrived off Georgia with his fleet on Sept. 5. He immediately sent an express boat to Charleston, South Carolina to the Council and General Lincoln with a [detailed] *plan of how to attack and beat the enemy on Sept. 9. As soon as this is accomplished, he would proceed to New York. He would carry out the plan drawn up to attack and seize the city as soon as the* [French] *fleet arrives in New York* [we will be able to announce more good news about the fortunate progress of our undertakings]. [accurate]

N.B. If only it is not like the news that has become famous about the affairs at Penobscot.
General Sullivan's army destroyed and burned 14 villages of the Savages on his Western Expedition.
But here in Rutland, a rumor is secretly spreading that Gen. Sullivan has been beaten by the Savages and has been compelled to withdraw.

Boston [Continental Journal], Saturday [Thursday] paper, Oct. 9 [14]: *New London, Oct. 6.*
In this instant, we have received the pleasant news from Long Island that the French fleet under the gallant Comte d'Estaing arrived at Sandy Hook last Saturday [having left Georgia the 16th of last month]. [accurate]
Sept. 16: Moreover, we have learned that a fleet of 70 sails has sailed through Holling Gate. [accurate]

N.B. There we go again moving much too fast with this gallant Comte d'Estaing. If only we will not once more have reason to laugh about something!

Boston. The mail from Weston reports that another transport ship with 200 [300] Hessian troops has been seized. [selective]

[Continental Journal, Oct. 14]. *Last Wednesday, 3 Hessian deserters and one British [from the 2nd Regiment] came from Rhode Island to us from whom we learned that there is some movement among the enemy and that they will apparently evacuate that island.* [selective]

The Boston Tuesday Paper from Oct. 14 gives the reliable news that Comte d'Estaing is still in Georgia. [summary]

Nothing but contradictions.
Rutland, Oct. 16. The Province of Massachusetts Bay is to send 2,000 recruits to the army of General Washington to seize New York; Rutland is to furnish 1 lieut., 1 sergeant and 9 privates.

One of our correspondents has favored us with the following:
A gentleman who arrived here from New England last Tuesday told us that the devious skills of the High Council and Committee in Boston have succeeded to such a degree that the paper dollars have increased in value. When the Rebel fleet set sail for the expedition to Penobscot, one could not get more than 8 piasters for one silver

piaster but when the news of the burning of the Rebel fleet arrived and that their army had taken flight in the wilderness, they gave 70 dollars for one guinea and 3 days later, 30 dollars for one silver dollar. The Bostonian gentleman was very angry about the conduct of their dignified General Mr. Lowell, who before this war had shown the greatest erudition as village schoolmaster and instructed his subjects with such learning and great judgment that one could hope for the greatest talents both in the arts of war and in commanding an army as a great general.[66]

Mr. Saltonstall, Commodore of the late American Rebel fleet, was proclaimed JUSTITIARIUS in the Province of Connecticut, i.e., a great man of law, -- but all the degrees of his erudition were ineffective here and were no match for the courage of Sir George Collier.[67]

Reply from the above from Boston:

Mr. Rivington's correspondent is very mistaken in regard to the person of General Lowell. The person he mentions was never commander in our army, not even in the militia. For some time he has been a member of our Most Honorable Congress and we believe he still is a member of this lawful assembly.

Commander Saltonstall may have been a judge in the Province of Connecticut but let us not investigate here how far his erudition extended, -- we believe that any honest business does not render an honest man dishonest. [not found]

[Continental Journal, Oct. 21] *Extract from a letter from Nancy, Aug. 12.*

The present political affairs of Europe are oppressive and humiliating for England; not one single European power has declared in her favor. [In spite of the (England's) greatest efforts], *France and Spain are united against* [this Kingdom (her)]. *The British Ministry has not been able to set more than 40 warships [belonging to her united enemies]. Besides frigates and small warships the French and Spanish forces, that are united against England, amount to 100 [110] sails.* [accurate]

Sixty thousand men are assembling between Brest and Dunkirk, who are apparently supposed to land in England. [accurate]

There also is talk of peace because England has been driven to the utmost limit and is compelled to lend an ear to any possible solution. [accurate]

When this is read in England, there will be hearty laughter.

Extract of a letter from Lorient, Aug. 18. Sixty-six [sixty-four] warships, 47 frigates together with a number of smaller French and Spanish warships, are now in the Channel. Sixty thousand French troops have already embarked [and are to land in England]. Gibraltar has been closed in by 7 [Spanish] warships and a number of frigates by sea and by 30,000 Spaniards on land; because of lack of victuals, it cannot hold out much longer. England will soon offer us our independence. [accurate]

The King of Prussia has very emphatically given Holland to understand that she is to observe strict neutrality; Portugal will quite surely soon follow France and Spain [and join them]. England does not have more than 40 [36] warships [and 10 frigates] [riding at Torbay and St. Helens]. [They also have] a great number of militiamen on shore but are without help or allies; or such only as offer their mediation for peace. There will probably soon be peace. [accurate]

Boston, Oct. 16. Last Tuesday, Captain James Monroe, who recently commanded the privateer Saratoga, *arrived at Providence. He had been taken prisoner by the English and taken to New York, where he deserted from the guard ship together with a number of officers [other prisoners]. He left the ship on the 6th of this month, and brought us the reliable report that in New York, the enemy is in the greatest confusion because they are expecting Comte d'Estaing by the hour.*[68] *All inhabitants have to work daily on the fortifications and as soon as Comte d'Estaing appears, 11 large ships are prepared to sink in the narrows below the town and a large number of heavy cannon are placed in the South Battery and at Paulus Hook.*

The land force in and around New York is as follows:

Troops on Long Island	9,000 [5,000]	men
York Island	4,000	.
Staten Island	1,500	.
Paulus Hook	1,000	.
Total	15,000	men

Ships: Russel of 74 cannon with a [new] copper bottom; Raisonable and Europe, each of 64 cannon; Renown of 50 cannon; Roebuck of 44 cannon; 10 frigates, 10 gun ships, 2 warships and more than 800 transport and merchant ships etc. [accurate]

Extracts from a letter from Providence, Oct. 1 [14]:

It is absolutely certain that the Royal Pirate Army in Newport on Rhode Island is preparing soon to leave the fort; everything there is in the greatest confusion. I would wish from the bottom of my heart that all American warships would assemble off the harbor of Newport. You ask me why? It will redound to their honor and profit to hold all military birds [of prey] on the wing. [accurate]

New York City. Last Wednesday, the entire English and Irish fleet arrived here. Four hundred ships came here under the command of Sir Andrew Snape Hamond; after a short passage not one ship was missing in this fleet. [not found]

Rutland, Oct. 18. Today, the report came that the English have left Rhode Island.

Rutland, Oct. 21. Wholly unexpected, commissary Mercereau returned here today after a 5 month absence. His wife had deserted to Virginia during this time and followed an English Artillery Lieutenant named Smith, who had lived in their house.

Rutland, Oct. 22. Commissary Mercereau again took over the command of the prisoners of war and Mr. Edwards left. Our men are regaining more freedom.

Boston, Saturday paper, Oct. 23: Boston:

We have been informed that the enemy in Rhode Island is very busy with taking their cannon and the rest of the provisions on board ship, with raping and plundering the inhabitants there and robbing the churches of their bells and organs etc. They have demolished the North Battery and burned the lighthouse at Beaver Tail so that we will presumably be able to announce the departure of this gang of robbers (I mean to say) of these nice men. [not found]

Boston, Monday paper, Oct. 25: *London, Morning Post or Morning Paper, June 18.*

Sir Charles Hardy had all officers of the flag and the captains convene on board the Victory of 100 cannon before his departure. When they had all assembled in the big hall or cabin, he briefly addressed them as follows:

'Gentlemen! It is true that I have not been at sea for many years, but my previous knowledge of service at sea -- I am fully confident of this -- enables me to risk it one more time and give up everything in order to fulfill the duties which I owe my King and my country.

I believe that the fleet has been manned under my command with reasonable officers and I hope that everyone will be mindful of his duties. Should there be anyone, however, who to my displeasure does not obey my signs and signals, I shall not hesitate one moment to dismiss him from the service for which he had been hired etc.'

Boston, Thursday paper, Oct. 28:
Excerpt from a letter of an officer in the suite of Gen. Gates. Providence, Oct. 25.
Sir, Through a dispatch from His Excel. Gen. Washington to our Gen. Gates, we have gotten the report that the enemy army in the South has been seized. Our allies have paid dearly for the victory with their losses. Without [counting] the dead and wounded, 700 regular troops and 200 Tories have been made prisoners of war. One ship of 50 cannon, several frigates and 20 transport ships have been captured from the enemy. In consequence of this affair, the entire British Force in Georgia is bound to come into our power.

The position of General Lincoln has cut off his retreat to Pensacola and Comte d'Estaing is advancing toward Savannah.[69]

Boston, Friday paper, Oct. 29: Excerpt from a letter from Providence, Oct. 27.
Last Tuesday morning, the English left Newport and the Island of Rhode Island. The rascals left it in a deplorable condition. They plundered the city, having examined the wells, cellars and chimneys for anything hidden there. They tore down several previous buildings and insulted the inhabitants most shamefully.

Boston, Oct. 29. We had news from New York that 21 ships, mostly American, were lost on the shores of Martinique during the latest gale whereby most men have lost their lives. We were also informed that the German troops under Mr. Clinton have been very malcontented in New York and do not hesitate to state in public that they do not wish to fight any longer against the Americans. In the first assault General Washington would undertake against New York, they would rather cross over to him and join that army. [not found]

N.B. My dear journalists White and Adams! If you could give yourselves but the slightest idea of the German military caste, you would not allow the above to be printed. Moreover, there are termites in this paper: Mr. MacLean and his bandits continue devastating [the region] at Majabagaduce not far from Penobscot and oppressing the inhabitants there beyond measure, but it is to be hoped that they will soon leave that place; the 2 ships in our bay are designated to accompany them here.

N.B. Here, my good White and Adams, is another thing I would like to remind you of in regard to the expedition to Penobscot. It is the same MacLean over whom you could not prevail and who does not command bandits but fine soldiers. The 2 ships in your bay should render themselves as secure as they can so that they won't have the same fate as your large fleet under Judge Saltonstall.

Rutland, Oct. 30. The English Captain Rivers returned here from Rhode Island and we now know for sure that the English have left Rhode Island.

At the end of this month the guinea is worth 140 [*guineas? piasters? specie?*] in paper money.

Month of November 1779

Boston, Monday paper [Independent Ledger], Nov. 1: *From Boston.*
A letter from Providence, Oct. 28.
The enemy left Rhode Island and the city of Newport in better condition than we could assume; the report that they had robbed the churches of their organs etc, [and bells] *is false. --Some of their fortifications have been demolished, but all [most of] the barracks have remained in good condition and only through negligence did one burn down. They have left 300 fathom cords of wood for the inhabitants. The inhabitants have not been plundered; they* [the enemy] *have also left a large supply of hay. General Prescott left all furniture and household utensils in his home in the best order. Twenty-six Tories have left with the enemy. The conduct of these troops greatly changed at their departure if you remember how they behaved in other places; they did not take the least bit away from the inhabitants [not even a fowl from any of the farmers], not even from inside the homes. They have left some dry goods in the magazine houses and merchant ships, which our General Gates had ordered to be left alone and not to sell before the clothiers in our army were adequately supplied with woolen and linen cloth. Four thousand himten* [himten = 2/3 bushel] *salt have been found in the warehouses; an item of very great value for us. They also left behind a very large supply of corn [maize or wheat?]. They have left 1,400 tons of hay behind on this island and on the smaller Island of Conanicut. (One ton of hay is 2,000 pounds.) No one knows where the enemy has gone. As far as we can gather from the inhabitants in the city of Newport, they went to New York; but that is by no means certain. They said they would definitely come back in 3 months.* [accurate]

N.B. Mr. Deaper and Mr. Folsom are much more candid in their Monday paper than White and Adams in their Saturday paper; for they are writing the truth.
We have learned that Mr. MacLean and his bandits have left Majabagaduce.

Boston [Continental Journal], Friday paper, Nov. 5: *Basseterre, Sept. 22.*
Last Friday, the frigate <u>Maidstone</u> *sailed away from Barbados to go to England with Vice Admiral Byron on board. Admiral Peter Parker commands the English fleet in his stead.*[70] [accurate]
      Philadelphia, Oct. 21: Extract from a letter from Annapolis, Maryland, Oct. 15.
Mr. William Carr of Dumfries arrived with the news this morning that Comte d'Estaing had sent a dispatch to the High Council in Virginia demanding provision for the fleet and reporting that this fleet was off our coast with 3,000 English prisoners on board. [He also stated] *that the English had suffered 1,000 dead and wounded in the latest engagement and lost [one ship of 74], one ship of 50 cannon, several frigates and 30 transport ships.* [accurate]

Boston [Continental Journal] Saturday [Thursday] paper, *Nov. 6 [12]: Providence, Oct. 25 [Philadelphia, Oct. 26].*

Through a dispatch from His Excel. Gen. Washington to Gen. Gates, who was passing through here, (it happened to be the anniversary feast of the Most Gracious, Most Serene, Most Christian and Most Holy Majesty George the Third, Protector of the Faith, the Best of All Kings to the Thrones of Great Britain, France, Ireland, All of North America etc.) we have received the following very important news: The gallant Comte d'Estaing has completely disarmed Mr. Prevost's Royal British army, seized Beaufort with 1,200 men, among whom were 200 dirty Tories, and has taken the _Experiment_ of 50 cannon from the English. The latter was commanded by Sir James Wallace, who had been knighted by his most Gracious Master for the skill with which he has cannonaded and burned down the houses of our peaceful inhabitants in Bristol; he also cannonaded the Bay. Several frigates and transport ships with all kinds of provisions, ammunition etc. have been sunk. We also know that General Lincoln has taken up such a position with his gallant army that the scattered enemy from General Prevost's army cannot come to Pensacola or to St. Augustine but they will have to fall into his hands.[71] [selective]

Mr. James Rivington is now also using your highly officious style and writes: Thus ended the glorious expedition to Georgia and the Carolinas.

The Most Honorable Mr. Laurens Esq.[72] has reported to His Excel. Gen. Washington that Colonel Maitland has made his retreat to Savannah from Beaufort while leaving behind his hospital, magazine, and artillery; that Comte d'Estaing with 5,000 men was in sight of the enemy before Savannah with General Lincoln, who was on the other side in his rear. The latter is any day awaiting reinforcements from Generals McIntosh and Williamson, who have been detached to the outer frontiers of the province. On the 2nd of this month, they want to open their fortifications in front of Savannah with 38 heavy cannon and 8 mortars. Comte d'Estaing has seized the ship _Experiment_ of 50 cannon, which had been commanded by the infamous Wallace. On board that ship was General Vaughan together with several officers and the entire war chest of the army in the South. Moreover, the enemy lost the ships _Fowey_ and _Ariel_ as well as a sloop of war and all the transport ships in the South. These had 4,000 regimentals and a large supply of beef and pork, rum, butter, cheese and other things on board. All this fell into the hands of Comte d'Estaing. General Prevost thrice attacked but was every time beaten back with great losses. He asked for permission to send his wife and his service of plate etc. to New York, whereupon Comte d'Estaing answered that Mme. Prevost would certainly be treated with courtesy and compliance. But [in the meantime] he [Comte d'Estaing] has learned that Mr. Prevost had acquired the service of plate from the inhabitants of the country, our noble allies, in such a way that he could in no way make a rightful claim to it. [selective]

Worcester [Massachusetts Spy] paper, Nov. IX [11]. *The order is herewith issued by Congress that Thursday, Dec. 9, a general thanksgiving shall be celebrated in all the American states.*

Today, a sergeant was hanged in Worcester. [accurate]

The high sheriff had to perform the hanging himself. He was hanged for the rape of a girl. He had been taken prisoner in Saratoga and had been hired here in Worcester as a school teacher. He had seduced one of his pupils, an 11 year old girl; so strict are the laws here.

The Boston Monday paper [Independent Ledger], writes that on Sept. 14 [4] *a very bloody sea battle has taken place in the English Channel between the English and the combined [French and Spanish] fleet whereby the combined fleet won and seized 3 Engl. warships, among which was one of 100 cannon. This combined fleet also seized the Engl. warship Ardent of 64 cannon off Portsmouth.*

Moreover, they are writing from Philadelphia that in order to make his flight possible, Colonel Maitland had to flee through marshes and swampy land, which previously had not been attempted by any human but only by bears and wolves. {accurate{

Worcester [Massachusetts Spy], Nov. 18:
The last news from Europe states that France and Spain certainly intend making a landing on England [on some part of Great Britain] or Ireland. [accurate]
All reports from the South agree that our matters in the South look positive.[accurate]
In the Western States, they are betting high that the enemy will certainly leave New York before the month of March. Last Monday, General Gates was in Hartford with the troops he commands and is continuing his march to General Washington's headquarters. [accurate]
It is believed that the arrival of the French fleet under Comte d'Estaing has kept the British army from paying a visit to Boston. [accurate]
We have heard that one of our privateers has recently gone into the harbor of Huntington on Long Island close under the cannon of an enemy battery; having spiked all the battery cannon, they left again without having been discovered. The enemy has recently made a similar discovery in New York -- so we hear -- when all the cannon on one of their batteries on Governor's Island had been spiked by our men. [accurate]

N.B. My dear Thomas, by way of replying to the items above, let me remind you that with respect to the landing in England, you will find the answer in history. Philip the Second, King of Spain, wanted to send his unconquerable fleet across to England in order to conquer this island.[73] It had 24,000 soldiers on board who were to disembark, 10,000 sailors and 30,000 slaves for rowing. This terrible fleet, 150 capital ships strong, could most rightfully be called unconquerable. The old ocean had never seen such a spectacle. They had 100 bishops and prelates on board in addition to a huge number of priests who were continually reading mass and yet this fleet was too weak and could not reach the Engl. coasts because the fortunate Elizabeth had the great Director of all things to protect her. One of the most severe gales men have ever experienced demolished this great fleet. Forty-six ships returned without masts to Spain, the remaining 104 had either been seized by the English or lay buried in the ocean.

The news from the South that your affairs there are on safe grounds is certainly false, for you have too often retracted your statements.

The gentlemen who are betting that the English army will leave New York prior to next May, will certainly lose. This place will not be abandoned before England will have recognized your independence and one does not think that this will happen in this century.

General Gates went to General Washington's army from Rhode Island with the troops under his command, but why? If they wanted, the English could take Rhode Island back. General Gates knows that and in order not to be captured, he has asked permission to return to the army.

As for the visit to Boston, do have a little patience, things will soon change.

And it is now possible that a privateer can enter a harbor, which at its entrance is covered by a guardship, pass through a fleet, spike cannon that are covered by posts, and escape without being discovered. My dear Thomas! However good friends we may be, I have nevertheless to state that here you have -- lied -- too triflingly, too noticeably.

Boston, Monday paper [Independent Ledger], Nov. 22: *Charleston in South Carolina, Sept. 29.*

We have many news items from the American army under the command of Gen. Lincoln, that acts in consort with the army of His Most Christian Majesty, our great and powerful ally, which is commanded by His Excel. Comte d'Estaing. It seems very probable that the main attack [upon Savannah] cannot be undertaken before tomorrow or the day after. Bad weather, poor roads and so many difficulties in moving the heavy artillery, i.e., cannon, mortars etc. on such a long road have prolonged matters so that we will not be able to give the detailed reports from there earlier. [summary]

Boston. How the Americans multiply, one can conclude from the following: in Woodstock, which is under the jurisdiction of Windham, the 84 year old Mrs. Sanger went 2 Engl. miles to be together with her daughter, granddaughter, great granddaughter, and great great granddaughter. Said daughter was the mother of 19 children before she had reached her 40th year. [accurate]

Extract of a letter from the camp at Peekskill, Nov. 19 [9]. The late time of year and several and sundry difficulties seem to prevent Comte d'Estaing from paying New York a visit this year. Great preparations are here being made again. [accurate]

N.B. No one in New York is afraid of Comte d'Estaing any longer; he would not dare to sail there since he would certainly not be received very kindly. A little while ago, it was completely in his power to demolish the English fleet there.

London, Aug. 26. In case the enemy should dare to land in England, the King is firmly resolved to march into battle himself. [accurate]

London, Aug. 28. The Admiralty received the report that on the 19th of this month, our large fleet under the command of Sir Charles Hardy was cruising 18 sea miles west of Scilly and that it had joined the Ramillies, *the* Marlborough *[and the* Isis] *[each of 74, and the one of His Majesty] of 50 cannon. Therefore, the fleet is now 46 warships, 7 of 50 cannon, and* [30] *[a considerable number of] frigates strong.*

The Royal tent [marquee] is ready, very beautiful, not too big, and contains 12 apartments within. [accurate]

Hartford paper [Connecticut Courant], Nov. 22 [23]: *Fishkill, Nov. 16 [18].*

Comte d'Estaing mentioned to Gen. Lincoln at the beginning of last month that his time was limited and that he was committed shortly to sail back to the West Indies. Thereupon a council of war was held in which it was decided to storm the town of Savannah. Comte d'Estaing asked General Prevost beforehand to surrender the city. He asked for 24 hours time to see what he could do, which was granted. --In these 24 hours, he was reinforced by 600 men under the command of Colonel Maitland, a fact that gave his troops added courage. [He no longer wanted to consider any surrender]. *Comte d'Estaing and Gen. Lincoln thereupon attacked the city in 2 columns on Oct. 9 but were beaten back by General Prevost with great loss. Detailed reports have not come in as yet but we do know that more than 500 Frenchmen and Americans remained dead on the spot* [without (counting) the wounded]. *Enemy losses are said to be similar to ours but we do not know it for sure. General Comte Pulaski, [a Pole by birth] was fatally wounded while storming the citadel at the tête of his cavalry; he lived but 2 days afterwards.*[74] *Comte d'Estaing was slightly wounded in his arm and leg. [He kept the field four days after the attack and afterwards] his troops reembarked* [in great haste -- and probably set sail for the West Indies]. *This report has come to us from Major Clarkson, aide-de-camp of Gen. Lincoln.* [accurate]

Rutland, Nov. 27. Several captured officers arrived here today, namely Captains Wardlow and James, Lieuts. Skinner, Rose, and Davidson, Physician Goldson and the Master and Purser of the sloop of war *Thorn*, that the Americans had taken away from the English.

New York City, Oct. 30. Capt. Saltar came here from Québec in 21 days and assured us that 2 days before his departure, 2 warships and a number of transports that had an appreciable number of land forces on board were arriving there after a journey of 6 weeks. [not found]

The Boston paper [Massachusetts Spy, Dec. 2] from Nov. 29 *presents the news that Comte d'Orvilliers and Sir Charles Hardy had offered one of the bloodiest sea battles in the* [English] *Channel that anyone can remember.*[75] *The English lost 7 warships there, and the scattered English fleet entered various English harbors. One English flagship went down with full sails and all hands.* [accurate]

We have learned that the Engl. general who has been taken prisoner on board the ship Experiment, *is General Garth, who had excelled much in the expedition to Connecticut in burning down the defenseless cities of Fairfield and Norwalk. On board of this ship, one also found a total of 80,000 guineas to pay the troops in Georgia.*

We also learned that 2 weeks ago, a ship with a number of Engl. officers, who were coming from Georgia, entered Newport in Rhode Island. The ship cast anchor and no one [on board] *thought of the possibility that the Engl. troops had left this island. But they were soon disabused of their error and taken to safety.* [not found]

At the end of this month, the guinea is worth 160 piasters in paper money.

Month of December 1779

In the Boston Thursday paper, Dec. 2, they again give the assurance that the English will leave New York after this winter.

Boston Friday paper, Dec. 3: *Halifax, Sept. 21.*
From a letter from Limerick in Ireland, we learn that the Spanish Ambassador has received orders to leave England within 48 hours. The war with Spain has excited the English nations to such an extent that one hears of nothing else but equipping privateers. The Roman Catholics in Ireland are very favorably inclined toward the present government. Of these alone, 4,000 men were in and around Cork under arms to fight the French, when it was announced that they had landed in Bantry Bay but it happened to be our own fleet sailing under French flags. The militia is in all of Ireland under arms. Should the French attempt another landing, they will not take Ireland as easily as they might have perhaps imagined. [not found]

Boston Saturday paper, Dec. 4: Boston. *We have learned from New York that Admiral Rodney has arrived in the West Indies from England with 18 warships and several frigates in order to reinforce Admiral Parker. An English frigate, a brig, and a sloop have seized 2 French frigates after a very furious fight and taken them into Port Royal. Seeing the French frigates, the captain of the English frigate immediately gave firm orders to nail his flag* [to the mast] *since he was absolutely determined not to lower his flag, nor to surrender to his enemies; he wanted to be victorious or else perish.* [not found]

Extract from a letter from Dublin, July 15. -- The liberty England has given us to cultivate tobacco [in this Kingdom] shows that they are doubtful about their reconquest of the American Provinces [Colonies in America], especially those of Virginia and Maryland. They are afraid that this large line of business will be further expanded by the French and they will be totally out of it. Our tyrants are trembling at the thought that there could come a day when they had to receive these and other products out of the hands of their enemies. [accurate]

Boston, Monday paper [Independent Ledger], Dec. 6: *Philadelphia, Nov. [20].*
Since Seigneur Gérard, the French Minister here, has asked to be returned because of a weak physical constitution, the King of France has sent Chevalier de la Luzerne in his stead, who brought a letter to Congress, which reads:
My very dear and great friends and allies!
The bad physical condition of Seigneur Gérard, our Minister Plenipotentiary with you, has made it necessary for him to ask for his return. We have made a change and determined to place Chevalier de la Luzerne, colonel in our service, in his position. We have no doubt that he will meet with your approval and that you will put full trust in him. We are asking you to give full credence to that which he will tell you from us, especially whenever he will give you assurances of our sincerity and our wishes for your prosperity as well as the continual duration of our good intentions and friendship toward the United States in general and toward each person in particular. We pray God forever to keep you, our dear and great friends and allies, in His Holy care.
Written at Versailles, May 31, 1779. [Your good Friend and Ally] Louis.[76]
[accurate]

Worcester paper [Massachusetts Spy], Dec. 10: *Boston, Dec. 2. All news from Philadelphia confirms the unfortunate attempt on the British lines at Savannah, and that the conduct of the troops of our allies as well as of their leaders deserve the highest praise. They assure us that the most entire harmony has been reigning between Comte d'Estaing and Gen. Lincoln as well as between the French and the American officers and troops.* [accurate]

Everyone was sensible that, in view of the circumstances in the West Indies, it was impossible for Comte d'Estaing to wait so long as to be able to undertake a regular siege. He has given every proof of his warmest friendship and affection for the American cause as he has amply demonstrated. His courage cannot be praised enough since many a time he has greatly endangered his own life for our freedom -- even shed his blood. -- This must never be forgotten by us. Comte d'Estaing may now do for us that which was impossible in Georgia where his courage could not overcome the difficulties.

The recapture of all the Engl. islands in the West Indies will adequately compensate for that which has been lost in Georgia. [accurate]

We have the report that 2 privateers, one from Salem and one from Marblehead, have seized 7 ships in the Bay of Fundy, loaded with provisions, that had been destined to sail from Halifax to Penobscot.

The paper from Georgia of Nov. 4 presents the news of Colonel Maitland's death. He died of the wound he had received before Savannah on Oct. 9; he is everywhere being mourned. All the French and Rebel ships have quickly left the Savannah River.

Worcester paper [Massachusetts Spy], Dec. 16, *taken from the Hartford Post. The latest paper from Martinique states that a naval battle has raged between the combined and the English fleets in the Channel, that lasted 11 hours. It was one of the bloodiest battles that had ever been fought at sea. Three French and 2 Engl. warships were sunk; the combined fleet consisted of 52 warships and 30 frigates and the Engl. fleet of 47 warships and 20 frigates.*[77] [accurate]

N.B. If it is true that a naval battle has taken place, then the French have been beaten. Otherwise it would have been reported who has won the victory.

Boston [Continental Journal], Dec. 10. *Last Monday, the sentence was passed upon Robert Taylor, native of Philadelphia, by the High Court of this city. He had stolen 350 guinea pieces [lbs. in gold and silver] and 5,000 piasters in paper money [dollars in Continental currency] from Mr. John Ballard. His sentence read that he would receive 20 strokes on his bare back at the public market [whipping post], refund [to pay treble] the stolen money and pay for the expenses [cost of court]. In the event the stolen money could not be raised [but he being unable to comply with the latter], he was ordered to be sold as bondsman to a countryman for 30 years.* [accurate]

London, Sept. 2. Through Sir Joseph Yorke, news has been sent from the Hague that a number of ships have sailed to Boston from Holland, loaded with cannon, ammunition etc. Upon this news, orders were sent to Plymouth from the Admiralty for 2 frigates to sail immediately to intercept the Dutchmen. [accurate]

Boston, Saturday paper, Dec. 18. *We now know for sure that the Court of Versailles was given permission for dividing the Kingdom of Poland if the German powers will acknowledge the Independence of the American United States. -- This again is exerting pressure on Great Britain because it will restrain Russia from declaring herself for England.* [accurate]

N.B. All that nonsense that the Americans are writing in their papers! When the German potentates want to share in the partition of Poland, they will not ask France for permission. Just as it makes no difference to them if America is dependent on England or not.

[Massachusetts Spy] Chatham, Nov. 20 [30]. *Last week, Major Generals von Riedesel and Phillips went through Elizabethtown to New York on parole.*[78] *A packet boat, which General Washington had sent to Comte d'Estaing with dispatches, was seized and taken to New York.*[78] [accurate]

[Massachusetts Spy, Dec. 23] *Constantinople, Capital of the Turkish Empire, July 3.*

After a long dry period, we have been having rain for the past month. We, therefore, had the best prospect that the soil would bear good fruit. But [the locusts] [a multitude of devouring vermin (grasshoppers, locusts, etc.)] have taken away all hope. They have almost completely eaten the corn, grapes, herbs and all the vegetables, at first in Asia but later also in our regions; and have devastated a large part of our fields. Our prospects, therefore, are very bad and our most needed victuals will be disastrously sparse. In the last 2 weeks, many people have died, who for lack of victuals had gone to the seashore. There they had eaten a type of haddock through which they had caught an epidemic disease. Experiments have been made on dogs, cats and chickens, which, having eaten of this fish, died 15 minutes later. This is adequate proof that the fish has produced the contagious disease. The doctors have also proven that it was a poisonous fish and [in Greek and Armenian churches], in Greece and Armenia, they have prescribed remedies for the use of the inhabitants to check the epidemic. Nothing remains for us but to ask God to ward off this misfortune and grant us clean air which alone can prevent the total extinction of this city. [accurate]

A Russian major brought the ratification of the recently concluded peace between Russia and the Sublime Porte as well as appreciable presents for the Sultan and Grand Vizier.[79] [accurate]

Worcester paper [Massachusetts Spy], Dec. 30.

The latest news from New York assures us that they do not know anything there of a naval battle said to have been fought in the Channel. Our latest European news states that peace is very probable to be made between England on the one hand and France on the other. If this is true, England will have to recognize our independence. It is well known that the disputes will be settled before the time, that France will break her alliance with us or England will recognize our independence; these have so far been the issues. Now one believes, however, that England's sterling has fallen so much that, to her own advantage, she will hurry matters along. For if England recognizes our independence, she will open the door to our commerce for her own benefit and renew our friendship. [summary]

At the end of this year, one gets 170 piasters in paper money for one guinea.

NOTES

1. Sir Frederick Haldimand (1718-1791) was born in Switzerland, served in the Swiss Guards for the Dutch and became Lt. Col. of the 62nd Royal Americans during the Seven Years War, fighting at Ticonderoga, Oswego, and Montréal. After the conquest of Canada he became the military governor of Trois-Rivières and later was appointed commander of British forces in Florida. In 1777, he was appointed Governor and Commander-in-Chief in Canada, serving until Carlton's second term in 1786, but was only in the province between 1778 and 1784. Among his accomplishments as governor was the settling of Loyalist refugees in Ontario.

2. Wasmus is referring to the power of the Catholic clergy over the Canadians; one of the chief difficulties the British faced in administering Canada after the Seven Years War was the Catholicism of the population and the people's resistance to the Anglican church and to civil administration.

3. The only significant naval action between the French and the British in the summer of 1778 (except for a dramatic frigate action involving only a few ships in June) was the Battle of Ushant, July 27, 1778. The French, under Comte d'Orvilliers, concentrated their fire on the British masts and rigging, with the result that some of Admiral Lord Augustus Keppel's ships were disabled; by the time Keppel could re-form his line, it was too late to renew the action. Neither side lost a single vessel, and the defeat led to Keppel's court-martial, which exonerated him amidst vociferous demonstrations by his supporters.

4. The Convention Army was marched to Virginia, arriving in the middle of February 1779, because of fears that the British would rescue them as long as they were located near the coast and because feeding and fueling the army had also placed a considerable burden on Massachusetts.

5. According to at least one authority, the Revolution cost about $170,000,000; loans from the French and Spanish governments and from Dutch bankers amounted to $7,830,000. (Boatner, p. 367.)

Burgoyne had been paroled to return to Britain on March 3, 1778; eventually the British Government directed him to return to America, but he refused on grounds of ill-health. He was ultimately exchanged for 1047 enlisted men and officers in February 1782. (Rupert Furneaux, The Battle of Saratoga, New York, 1971, p. 290.)

6. English troops under General James Grant (1720-1806) had been landed by Admiral Samuel Barrington (1729-1800) on December 12, 1778, on St. Lucia in the Windward Islands, which was an important French naval base. d'Estaing's French squadron had arrived in the West Indies one day after Hotham's British force (Barrington took command on the 11th) and was much larger than the British; the French attacked at long range but did not close for a more decisive action, but d'Estaing did land troops to dislodge the British. Grant repulsed the French and d'Estaing withdrew to Martinique, providing the British with a naval base within range of the main French base at Fort Royal.

7. The Spanish had demanded Britain return Gibraltar as the price for their non-intervention in the conflict. They were refused and signed an alliance with France on April 12, 1779, finally declaring war against Britain June 21, 1779.

8. Joseph Buckminster (1719-1792) served for more than fifty years as the minister in Rutland. His "Thoughts for Sunday" were a regular feature of the Worcester newspaper. J. Warren Bigelow, writing the chapter on "Rutland" for the History of Worcester County, (Boston, 1879), commented that Rutland's "minister was not very zealous in taking up arms against the mother country." (Vol. II, p. 265.)

9. The British, under Lt. Col. Archibald Campbell, attacked Savannah, defended by 850 American militia under General Robert Howe. On December 29, 1778, with minimal casualties, the British defeated Howe and took the city.

10. The term privateer stems from "private man of war," a privately owned armed ship carrying a government letter of marque (see Wasmus's footnote, in the text) empowering it to make war. The American colonists had used privateers as early as King William's War, 1689-1797.

11. Admiral Barrington, commanding in the West Indies, was replaced by Byron on January 6, 1779.

12. Fort Royal, the main French base in the West Indies; now Fort-de-France, the capital of Martinique.

13. François-Joseph-Paul, Comte de Grasse (1722-1788), French Admiral, served in the French navy in the War of Jenkins' Ear, was a prisoner of war in England in 1747, served in India, the West Indies, and in the Mediterranean. He led a division at Ushant in 1778 and commanded a squadron off Grenada. He would play a crucial role at Yorktown.

14. Capers: an archaic term for privateers.

15. Lt. Col Campbell of the 71st Regiment had actually been captured in March 1776, when American vessels captured two ships carrying 450 men and 17 officers of the Scotch brigade sailing into Boston, unaware that Howe had evacuated the city. A prisoner for two years, he was exchanged for Ethan Allen in 1778. Later that year he led the capture of Savannah and Augusta and eventually commanded British forces in Georgia.

16. Although the Spanish were to sign a treaty of alliance with France later in the month, they would not enter the war until June 21.

17. Denmark and Sweden had profitted from the hostilities between Britain and France by increasing their share of international shipping. While the British tried to enforce a blockade of their enemies, the French tried to organize neutral powers against Britain's claim of belligerent rights formally recognizing that the property of belligerent nations was free on board neutral vessels (except for

contraband of war.) In 1780 Denmark and Sweden would join with Russia in "Armed Neutrality" to prevent the British from seizing their enemies' goods carried on neutral ships; eventually all the European seapowers joined and isolated the British until 1783.

18. This was Joseph II (1741-1790; eldest son of Maria Theresa) who had become Holy Roman Emperor of the German Nation in 1765 but had little real power until the death of his mother in 1780.

19. Kingsbridge was where the post road crossed the creek between Manhattan and the Bronx.

20. Admiral James Gambier (1723-1789) was of Huguenot descent, had served at Louisbourg and in the West Indies during the Seven Years War, and had been made second-in-command to Howe in 1778.

21. Stone Arabia, a Palatine settlement in the Mohawk Valley, was burned by Sir John Johnson in October 1780 in one of a series of raids operating out of Niagara, Oswego, and Canada in which Tory exiles (the Johnsons, the Butlers) and Mohawks under Joseph Brant laid waste American frontier settlements.

22. Charleston, after withstanding a British attack in 1776, was threatened by Clinton's Southern campaign in 1779; General Augustine Prevost (1723-1786) had threatened to expand the British beachhead at Savannah after Campbell's capture of Atlanta. Campbell's efforts at raising Loyalist resistance was thwarted by the patriot forces at the Battle of Kettle Creek on February 14. Campbell returned to Savannah to avoid General Benjamin Lincoln, who had marched from Charleston to maintain patriot control of South Carolina, defeating a small unit of patriots at the Battle of Briar Creek on March 2. In May, while Lincoln marched inland to liberate Augusta, Prevost marched to Charleston and demanded the surrender of the town; the Governor, John Rutledge, offered to make Charleston an open city instead. Prevost returned to Savannah after a brief engagement with Lincoln, who unsuccessfully attacked the British rear guard at Stono Ferry on June 20.

23. This Russian aid was, of course, never sent.

24. Pittsburgh was the American headquarters for operations in the West; frontier warfare was vicious and endemic in the region.

25. Alejandro O'Reilly (1725-1794), an Irish General in Spanish service.

26. In July 1778, when news of the French declaration of war reached India, British forces from Madras successfully besieged the French settlement at Pondichéry. The last French outpost in India, Mahe, surrendered in March 1779, although a French squadron under the Bailli de Suffren (Admiral Pierre André de Suffren de Saint Tropez, (1729-1788) captured Trincomalee (Ceylon) in 1781.

27. According to a letter that Major General von Riedesel wrote at Orange Court House on September 16, 1779, Riedesel had in fact rented the Collé plantation for his family and entourage, near Charlottesville, Virginia, from a Mr. Mazzei.

28. Prevost had marched to threaten Charleston in order to draw the Americans under Lincoln off from Augusta; Lincoln returned to Charleston in order to save it in May as General William Moultrie (1730-1805) organized the defense.

29. Conrad-Alexandre Gérard (1729-1790) was appointed Plenipotentiary Minister to the United States in March 1778.

30. Vincennes, Indiana, a French settlement on the Wabash was induced to shift allegiance to the Americans by Pierre Gibault, a Catholic missionary, and was occupied by a detachment of militia sent by George Rogers Clark (1752-1818). In December 1778, it was retaken by British Lt. Col. Henry Hamilton (?-1796) and renamed Fort Sackville. On February 24, 1779, Clark and a force of American and French volunteers retook the place; Hamilton, known as the "Hair Buyer" because of the scalp bounties he had paid, was sent as a prisoner to Virginia, and eventually paroled to New York.

31. General Francis MacLean was commander of the British Forces in Nova Scotia.

32. This is a reference to the 91st Psalm.

33. The Walloomsac River, site of the Battle of Bennington.

34. See above, 1777, note 40.

35. See above, entry for August 17, 1777.

36. Wasmus apparently expected his friend, Chancellor Werner, to pass this portion of the journal on to his brother, since Heinrich Wasmus had died of an abdominal wound on August 27, 1777.

37. Sir Frederick North (1732-1792) was known as Lord North until 1790 when he succeeded to his father's title as second Earl of Guilford. North served as a member of Parliament for 40 years, holding office as First Lord of the Treasury from 1759-1765, Chancellor of the Exchequer in 1767, and Prime Minister from 1770 to 1782. He had opposed the war at the outset and resigned after Yorktown.

38. Cleveland Row, St. James, in London, is the passage in front of St. James's Palace, forming the continuation westward of Pall Mall; Lord George Germain (1716-1785), the Secretary of State for American Colonies from 1775-1782, had rented Lord Waldegrave's house in Pall Mall; the Secretaries had their offices in Cleveland Row.

39. New Haven, East Haven, Green's Farms, Norwalk, and Fairfield, Connecticut were occupied, plundered, and burned by the British on July 8, 1779, as part of Clinton's punitive raid on the Connecticut coast in response to Connecticut attacks on British shipping on Long Island Sound and Connecticut supplies, which were reaching the Continentals.

40. On June 1, 1779, the British had captured Stony Point, securing King's Ferry and blocking American communications across the Hudson. Washington ordered Wayne to try to retake this crucial position; Wayne made a night attack on July 16 and captured Lt. Col. Henry Johnson, who had held the partially completed fortifications with the 17th Regiment. Washington was unable to defend the fort and so it was destroyed.

41. Some of these Indian tribes can be identified according to the synonymy index in volume 15 of The Handbook of North American Indians as follows: the Peankishaw were the Piankashaw, a tribe of the Miami group from what is now Indiana; the Kaskaskies were the Kaskaskia, a tribe of the Illinois confederacy; Onaottinans (on the Wabash) do not appear in the index, nor do the Rockackies; the Peorians (Peoria) and Mechiganies (Michigamea) were other tribes of the Illinois confederacy, while the Foxes and Serks (Sauks) were Wisconsin tribes; Opays are not found in the index; the Illinois were correctly named; the Shoces were possibly the Shawnee; the Poues were the Potawatomi, as abbreviated by the French; the Chippewas (on the Mississippi and Illinois), Cherokees and Chickasaws are well known. The letter Wasmus translates is apparently from George Rogers Clark (see above, note 30) and considerably exaggerates his success in detaching the Western Indian tribes from the British alliance.

42. In response to Tory and Indian raids from Canada and Fort Niagara, Washington directed Major General John Sullivan on a campaign to relieve the pressure on the frontier. Sullivan left Easton, Pennsylvania for a rendezvous with another force under General James Clinton (1733-1812), brother of New York's governor, who was marching south from the Mohawk Valley. Sullivan and Clinton made relatively slow progress, meeting at Tioga on August 19. The combined force then moved north and west, burning some 40 Indian villages, crops, and orchards, a blow from which the Six Nations never recovered.

43. Samuel Kirkland (1741-1808) was a missionary to the Oneida Indians for most of his life and had been instrumental in persuading the Six Nations to stay neutral at the outset of the Revolution. Barbara Graymont calls him "one of the Congress' most effective agents in the Indian country." He founded Hamilton College to educate both whites and Indians. (Graymont, p. 101.)

44. This was not a general rising, although R.B. McDowell states that agricultural discontent was "endemic" in Ireland, and there was considerable sympathy for the colonists. But the need for troops probably stemmed from the fear of a Spanish or French invasion, not from a large popular uprising. In 1779, however, the Irish economy, damaged by the wartime restrictions on trade, generated popular protests in favor of Irish free trade, which was enacted by Parliament in February 1780. ("Nationalism and the Winning of Parliamentary Independence 1760-1782," ch. VIII in A New History of Ireland, T.W. Moody and W.E. Vaughn, eds., vol. IV, 1691- 1800, Oxford, 1986, p. 202.)

45. After Spanish entry into the war, a combined Franco-Spanish fleet in the Channel threatened to invade England or Ireland; Gibraltar was besieged until the end of the war, saved by three separate relief expeditions; Port Mahon, on Minorca, was not so fortunate, falling to the French in December 1781.

46. In June 1779, General Francis MacLean and two regiments landed on the Bagaduce peninsula (near the modern Castine, Maine) in Penobscot Bay to establish an outpost for sending timber north to Nova Scotia, which could also be used as a refuge for Loyalists and a base for raiding the surrounding territory (then claimed by Massachusetts). The state of Massachusetts mounted an expedition led by Commodore Dudley Saltonstall (see 67n, below) and Brigadier Solomon Lovell (66n below), consisting of 3 ships from the Continental navy, 40 ships from Massachusetts (including part of the Massachusetts state "navy" and various private vessels) and 1,000 militia men.

47. James Rivington (1724-1802) was the King's Printer in New York City before the Revolution. Between 1777 and 1783 he published The Royal Gazette, which was the first American daily newspaper. Although Rivington secretly sent information to the patriots beginning in 1781, his paper was silenced by the Sons of Liberty in 1783.

48. Admiral George Darby (ca. 1720-1790) became a naval lieutenant in 1742, fought in the West Indies in the Seven Years War, was made Rear Admiral in 1778 and Vice Admiral in 1779.

49. At Penobscot, with Lt. Col. Paul Revere in command of the artillery (six field pieces), Saltonstall and Lovell were unable to co-operate, and several weeks were spent building fortifications and firing at the enemy. On August 11, a land attack failed when the Americans broke and ran, and on August 12, a British fleet sailed into the bay. The American fleet, attempting to escape up the river, was dispersed or ran aground, ships were burned, and the Americans fled into the woods. Saltonstall was court-martialled and dismissed because of the disaster, out of which not a single ship escaped.

50. Marie Joseph Paul Yves Roch Gilbert du Motier, Marquis de Lafayette (1757-1834) had entered the French army in 1771. His romantic ideas about the Revolution led him to approach Franklin in Paris, and, despite his family's opposition, to come to America in June 1777; he was given a Major General's commission in July.

51. Sir Charles Hardy (1716-1780) had entered the navy in 1731, becoming a captain in 1741. In 1744 he was court-martialled for loss of a convoy to Newfoundland, but was exonerated and in 1746 promoted to Rear Admiral. Knighted in 1755, he served as Governor of New York from 1755-1757, was made Admiral in 1770 and commanded the Channel fleet in 1779 and 1780.

52. Although the Independent Ledger and Wasmus both refer to "James Robinson," we believe this is a reference to James Robertson (1720?-1788), who became civil governor of New York in 1779 . Robertson was a military man who had been barrack-master in New York where he acquired a fortune by "peculation and extortion," paying for government supplies in "Robertsons," notes which circulated until the Chamber of Commerce declared them acceptable only at their intrinsic (paper) value.   He had profited from the evacuation of Boston in 1776. Back in England, he had intrigued against Howe and Tryon, which led to his 1779 appointment. His harsh rule in New York was notorious for the heavy taxes in kind on farmers and markets. (Appleton's Cyclopedia of American Biography, New York, 1888, vol. V, p. 278.)

53. D'Estaing had captured St. Vincent on June 16 and Grenada on July 4; Byron had delivered an indecisive British counterattack on July 6.

54. Wasmus is referring to Isaiah Thomas, the Boston-born printer who began to publish The Massachusetts Spy in 1770, and was forced to flee to Worcester in April of 1775 due to his paper's support of the American cause. In Worcester, he established the town's first paper, Thomas's Massachusetts Spy and American Oracle of Liberty, which was published by his successors from April 1776 to May 1781, when he again took control. (John Nelson, Worcester County: A Narrative History, New York, 1934, v. II, p. 581.)

55. Col. Theodoric Bland (1742-1790), who claimed to be a descendant of Pocahontas, escorted the Convention Army from Connecticut to Virginia, and commanded the barracks at Charlottesville until November 1779. At the surrender, the Convention Army included 4,991 men, 2,022 of them Germans; by war's end there were about 900 left, according to Otto Elster, p. 438.

56. Admiral Marriott Arbuthnot (ca. 1711-1794) had been commissioner of the Navy at Halifax between 1775 and 1778; he was made Rear Admiral in 1778, and Commander-in-chief on the American station in 1779.

57. The French and Spanish fleet, under Louis Guillomet, Comte d'Orvilliers, the French Admiral, was off Plymouth on August 16, 1779, and 31,000 French troops had gathered at Le Havre to invade England. Admiral Hardy did not do battle, but sailed back to Spithead. After a brief blockade, the French went to Brest in September, and the Spanish attacked Gibraltar, ending the invasion scare.

58. Lord George Sackville used that title until 1770 when he became Lord George Germain, to secure an inheritance, which title he used until 1782 when he became Viscount Sackville, the British Secretary of State for American Colonies. During the Seven Years War, he had been senior British officer in the Allied army under Prince Ferdinand of Braunschweig. At the Battle of Minden, August 1, 1759, he delayed following Ferdinand's orders to lead the British cavalry in action against the French, stopping instead to confer with the Commander-in-Chief. He was court-martialled and convicted of disobeying orders, separated from the army, and entered politics.

59. William Pitt, First Earl of Chatham (1708-1778), had opposed Britain's coercive measures towards the American colonies, and died on the floor of the House of Lords, while opposing the Duke of Richmond's proposal for making peace with America on any terms at all to avoid French reversal of the results of the Seven Years War.

60. John Montagu, 4th Earl of Sandwich (1718-1792), was the First Lord of the Admiralty from 1771 to 1782; he is also famous as the originator of the sandwich (a snack while gambling for 24 hours straight) and as the man after whom Captain Cook named the Sandwich (Hawaiian) Islands.

61. January 30, 1648 was the day that Charles I was executed by the victorious Parliamentary forces.

62. General Henry (Light Horse Harry) Lee (1756-1818), had led a surprise raid on the British garrison at Paulus Hook, across the Hudson from New York City on August 19, 1779.

63. This is a garbled account of the Penobscot expedition; Admiral Sir George Collier arrived with ten British ships on August 12; the Americans lost 474 men and all their ships, while the British had only 13 casualties.

64. The British still controlled Newport after Sullivan's abortive expedition in 1778, but evacuated the town in October 1779 as the focus of the war shifted to the South.

65. Admiral Robert Duff (?-1787) had become Vice Admiral in 1778. He had served with Rodney in Martinique in the Seven Years War, commanded in the Mediterranean in 1777, and defended Gibraltar in 1779.

66. Massachusetts militia Brigadier General Solomon Lovell [misspelled as Lowell in the text], whose attack on the British base in Penobscot Bay had recently failed, is here confused with James Lovell (1737-1814), who served in the Continental Congress from 1777 to 1782, and whose father, the Loyalist John Lovell (1710-1778), had been a teacher in the Boston Latin School, instructing Samuel Adams, John Hancock, Henry Knox, and other patriot leaders.

67. Continental Navy Commodore Dudley Saltonstall (1738-1796) was dismissed from the Navy after the failure of the Penobscot expedition and returned to privateering and the merchant marine, his career before the Revolution.

68. D'Estaing was in Georgia at the siege of Savannah from early September until October 20.

69. In fact, the Franco-American attack on Savannah had been a fiasco, and d'Estaing had retreated to Charleston on October 20, forcing Lincoln to retreat.

70. Peter Parker (1721-1811) eventually became Admiral of the Fleet, had participated in the 1776 Charleston campaign under Clinton, and was military commander at Jamaica from 1779 to 1781.

71. Unfortunately, Lincoln and d'Estaing had already failed at Savannah; Pensacola was held by the British until 1781.

72. Henry Laurens (1724-1792) was President of the Continental Congress in 1777 and 1778, and had helped to reject the Convention of Saratoga. Before the Revolution, he had been an important merchant in Charleston. He had resigned as President in December 1778, and had in November 1779

resigned from Congress to go to Holland to negotiate a treaty. British activities in the South kept him from leaving Charleston until the summer of 1780. (See below, note 51, 1780.) (Boatner, pp. 599-600.)

73. This is, of course, a reference to the Spanish Armada of 1588.

74. Casimir Pulaski (1748-1779), a Polish nobleman who served as a Continental cavalry leader, was killed in a cavalry charge on October 9 during the Savannah disaster.

75. The Combined Fleet, which had threatened to invade England all summer, had in fact dispersed in the autumn; this battle never took place.

76. Chevalier Anne-César de la Luzerne (1741-1791), the second French ambassador to the United States, arrived in Philadelphia in November 1779. He eventually became French ambassador to London.

77. Here is another report of an apparently imaginary naval battle.

78. Riedesel and Phillips set out for New York in late summer of 1779, even though Congress had not yet approved their release; en route, they received a letter from Washington ordering them to return to Virginia. They returned to Bethlehem, Pennsylvania, on October 10 and stayed for six weeks until their parole (not an exchange) was finally approved; they proceeded to New York, arriving on November 29, 1779. (Brown, pp. 88-95.)

79. The Sublime Porte was the Turkish government, so called because of the high gate of the building where the chief departments of state were located. The sultan or ruler of the Ottoman Empire was Abdul Hamid I, who ruled from 1773 to 1789; his grand vizier was his chief administrative officer, who in time of war was also a generalissimo. Russia and Turkey had fought the First War with Catherine of Russia from 1768 to 1774 over the declining Ottoman Empire's possessions in the Crimea and in Eastern Europe. That war had concluded with what was for the Turks a humiliating peace in July 1774, the treaty of Kuchuk Kainarji. In 1779, war was narrowly avoided by French mediation, and in March the Turks and Russians signed the Convention of Ainali Kavak, which made an ally of the Russians the Khan of Crimea and established Russian rights to intervene in the affairs of the Danube principalities. Russia and Turkey would go to war again in 1787, in the Second War with Catherine of Russia, which would last until 1792. (Encyclopedia Britannica, vol. 27-28, pp. 452-454; vol. 21- 22, p. 112.)

Royal Navy of Great Britain

No.		Cannon
	Of the First Rank	
1	Britannia - N.B.	110
2	Royal George	110
3	Royal Sovereign	110
4	Ville de Paris	110
5	Victory	100
	Of the Second Rank	
1	Atlas	98
2	Barfleur - N.B.	98
3	Blenheim	90
4	Dreadnought	98
5	Duke	90
6	Formidable	98
7	London	98
8	Namur	90
9	Neptune	98
10	Ocean	98
11	Prince	90
12	Prince George	98
13	Princess Royal	98
14	Queen	98
15	St. George	90
16	Sandwich	90
17	Union	90
	Of the Third Rank	
1	Africa	64
2	St. Albans	64
3	S. Antonio	64
4	Ardent	64
5	Asia	64
6	Ajax	74
7	Albion	74
8	Alexander	74
9	Alfred	74
10	America	64
11	Alcide	64
12	Agamemnon	74
13	Princess Amelia	80
14	Arrogant	74
15	Anson	64
16	Bedford	74
17	Belleisle	64
18	Belliquer	64
19	Bellona	74
20	Bellerophon	74
21	Berwick	74
22	Bienfaisant	64
23	Boyne	70
24	Barfort	64
25	Buckingham	70
26	Buffalo	64
27	Cambridge	80
28	Colossus	74
29	Canada	74
30	Captain	64
31	Centaur	74
32	Dublin	74
33	Chichester	70
34	Cornwal	74
35	Culloden	74
36	Courageux	74
37	Cumberland	74
38	Conquerer	74
39	Defence	64
40	Defiance	74
41	Devonshire	70
42	Dorsetshire	70
43	Dragon	74
44	Eagle	64
45	Egmont	74
46	Hector	74
47	Elizabeth	74
48	Essex	64
49	Exeter	64
50	Europa	64
51	Fama	74
52	Foudroyant	80
53	Grafton	74
54	Grampus	70
55	Hampton Court	64
56	Hector	74
57	Hercules	74
58	Hero	74
59	Infante	74
60	Invincible	74
61	Intrepid	64
62	Irresistible	74
63	Kent	74
64	Lancaster	70
65	Lennox	74
66	Leviathan	70
67	Lancaster	64
68	Lion	64
69	Magnanime	74
70	Magnificent	74
71	Marlborough	74
72	Mars	74
73	Modesta	64
74	Monarch	74
75	Monmouth	64
76	Montagu	74
77	Nonsuch	64
78	Norfolk	74
79	Oxford	74
80	Plantagenet	74
81	Princess George	80
82	Prudent	74
83	Polyphemus	74

84	Ramillies	74
85	Raisonable	64
86	Resolution	74
87	Revenge	64
88	Robust	74
89	Prince William	64
90	Protheus	64
91	Princessa	70
92	Russel	74
93	Repulse	64
94	Ruby	64
95	Royal Oak	74
96	Sulton	74
97	Shrewsbury	74
98	Sommerset	70
99	Shilling Castle	64
100	Suffolk	74
101	Superb	74
102	Temeraine	70
103	Terrible	74
104	Thunderer	74
105	Triumph	74
106	Torbay	74
107	Trident	64
108	Valliant	74
109	Vengeance	74
110	Vigilant	64
111	Prince of Wallis	74
112	Warrior	74
113	Warspite	74
114	Royal William	80
115	Warwick	74
116	Worcester	64
117	Yarmouth	74

Of the fourth rank

1	Achilles	60
2	Ste. Anne	60
3	Antelope	50
4	Assistance	50
5	Bristol	50
6	Centurion	50
7	Chatham	50
8	Colchester	50
9	Conquistador	60
10	Defiance	60
11	Dreadnaught	60
12	Dunkirk	60
13	Edgar	60
14	Experiment	50
15	Firme	60
16	Foway	60
17	Hampshire	50
18	Hannibal	60
19	Isis - N.B.	50
20	Jersey	60
21	Jupiter	50
22	Leopard	60

23	Medusa	50
24	Midway	60
25	Panther	60
26	Pembroke	60
27	Portland	50
28	Preston	50
29	Renown	50
30	Rippon	60
31	Romney	60
32	Salisbury	50
33	Swiftshire	60
34	Warwick	50
35	Windsor	60

Of the Fifth Rank

1	Action	44
2	Assurance	44
3	Active	28
4	Aelus	32
5	Alarm	28
6	Ambuscade	32
7	Aquillon	28
8	Arethusa	32
9	Apollo	32
10	Amazon - N.B.	32
11	Argo	28
12	Aurora	32
13	Blonde - N.B.	32
14	Blanche	36
15	Boulogne	32
16	Boston	32
17	Brilliant	36
18	Boreas	28
18	Brune	32
20	Camel	28
21	Carysfort - N.B.	28
22	Convert	32
23	Crescent	32
24	Coventry	28
25	Delaware	28
26	Diamond	32
27	Diane	32
28	Dolphin	44
29	Emerald	32
30	Enterprise	32
31	Fox	28
32	Garland - N.B.	28
33	Glory	32
34	Guadeloupe	28
35	Greyhound	28
36	Hector	40
37	Hussar	28
[sic]	Juno	32
38	Isis	28
39	Janus	44
40	Jason	32
41	Lancaster	44

42	Lioness	28	3	Ariadne	20
43	Levant	28	4	Ariel	20
44	Liverpool	32	5	Cormorant	20
45	Lizard	28	6	Camille	20
46	Coal	30	7	Crocodile	24
47	Ludlow Castle	30	8	Deal Castle	24
48	Lynx	44	9	Dolphin	20
49	Lowesstone	32	10	Daphne	20
50	Maidstone	28	11	Dromedary	26
51	Medea	32	12	Flamborough	20
52	Melampe	36	13	Forward	20
53	Milford	28	14	Gibraltar	20
54	Minerva	32	15	Glasgow	24
55	Montréal	32	16	Galathe	20
56	Neger	32	17	Hind	20
57	Pallas	36	18	Harpy	20
58	Pearl	32	19	Kensington	20
59	Phoenix	44	20	Mercury	20
60	Pandora - N.B.	36	21	Nightingale	20
61	Pool	40	22	Porcupine	20
62	Proserpina	28	23	Porpoise	24
63	Proteus	32	24	Port Mahon	24
64	Pelican	28	25	Proteus	20
65	Québec	32	26	Russ	20
66	Rainbow	44	27	Rye	20
67	Raleigh	32	28	Scarborough	20
68	Resource	28	29	Seaford	20
69	Richmond	32	30	Seahorse	20
70	Roebuck	44	31	Sybel	24
71	Romulus	44	32	Squirrel	20
72	Saphire	32	33	Success	20
73	Shannon	32	34	Sphynx	20
74	Southampton	32	35	Terpsichore	20
75	Solbay	32	36	Tortoise	20
76	Stag	32	37	Thomas	24
77	Surprise - N.B.	28	38	Trent	24
78	Tartar - N.B.	28	39	Titus	24
79	Thames	32	40	Trion	26
80	Thetar	32	41	Vigilant	24
81	Tortoise	28	42	Unicorn	20
82	Trien	28	43	Union	26
83	Twee	36	44	Warspite	26
84	Triton - N.B.	32	45	Warrior	26
85	Valeur	28	46	Wacke	24
86	Venus	36	47	Wagen	20
87	Vestal	32	48	Wasp	24
88	Vulture	28	49	Wier	24
89	Vution	36	50	Wolf	20
90	Vulcan	28			
91	?				
92	Volusia	32			
93	Winchester	32			

Of the Sixth Rank

1	Andromeda	24
2	Aleborough	20

Sloops of War

1	Albany	14
2	Aldernay	10
3	Ariadne	12
4	Atalanta	16
5	Badger	14
6	Beaver	14

7	Bonetta	10
8	Camilion	16
9	Carcass	8
10	Cherokee	10
11	Ceres	16
12	Cupid	14
13	Cygnet	18
14	Despatch	18
15	Dreadfull	18
16	Druid	16
17	Deceipt	10
18	Diligence	16
19	Dolphin	18
20	Dragon	16
21	Favorite	16
22	Ferret	18
23	Fly	14
24	Fortune	18
25	Fury	18
26	Grasshopper	16
27	Harpy	18
28	Hawk	18
29	Hazard	18
30	Hornet	16
31	Hunter	16
32	Hope	10
33	Halifax	12
34	Hound	16
35	Lynx	14
36	Martin	18
37	Nautilus	16
38	Nymph	14
39	Orter	10
40	Ostrich	18
41	Porcupine	16
42	Porpoise	16
43	Pegasus	12
44	Prince Edward	16
45	Ranger	8
46	Raven	14
47	Scorpion	12
48	Sharn	12
49	Spethwel	10
50	Swallow	18
51	Swann	18
52	Swift	16
53	Sylph	16
54	Savage	16
55	Sallash	16
56	Tamar	16
57	Trial	16
58	Viper	10
59	Vulture	18
60	Wadse	14
61	Weasel	16
62	Wolf	18
63	Zephyr	16
64	Yack	14

Recapitulation

First Rank
5 of 100 to 110 cannon

Second Rank
17 of 90 to 98 cannon

Third Rank
117 of 64, 74 to 80 cannon

Fourth Rank
35 of 50 to 60 cannon

Fifth Rank
93 of 28 to 44 cannon

Sixth Rank
50 of 20 to 26 cannon

64 Sloops of War
55 Armed Ships
 5 Bomb Ships
 4 Fire Ships

Total 445 Warships

N.B. - I know the ships, designated with N.B., rather well and have been on board them.

1780

The 1st   Today I wished I were in Wolfenbüttel; this is the fourth New Year's Day that I have wished this. -- For you, my friends and loved ones, I utter today the most ardent wishes for an everlasting and eternal well-being.   May God be your friend and benefactor. -- I have to do without you and cannot even draw on any news from you. No letters have come my way. How many may have come from Germany to me in these last 3 years! If I only received one single one to learn whether my folks were still alive and in good health.

Boston Monday paper [Independent Ledger], Jan. 3. *London, Oct. 1:*
A letter from Bridlington, Sept. 24, says:
Without a doubt, you will have heard the loud noise [alarming situation] that has been bothering us since Tuesday night. But - God be praised - it was nothing more than [this]: [the pirate] Paul Jones, who has seized 2 ships of ours not far from Flamborough Head.   He intended to land yesterday morning and burn Flamborough, Scarborough, Bridlington and Hull.[1] But luck was with us; the sea was so agitated that it was impossible for him to do so.
It is now certain that Admiral Rodney has been designated commander-in-chief of His Majesty's ships [sailing] to Jamaica. Moreover, we have a report out of The Hague, Sept. 24, that the present campaign will not end before the French have established themselves on British shores; all possible preparations have been made, the fleet is ready to sail and can do so at the first order. But other news from France says that Comte d'Orvilliers and the Spanish Admiral, Don Luis de Cordova,[2] had a very vehement dispute while riding at anchor before Plymouth Harbor because the former was not willing to burn the city of Plymouth. The Spanish Admiral thereupon left the fleet with his division. This, together with the report that there were 10,000 sick in the combined fleet and, moreover, the late season, will presumably prevent the intended landing. [summary]
*   Boston, Jan. 3. The latest news from Europe says that the British fleet under Sir Charles Hardy is at Spithead and that the combined fleet has been parading in the Channel for 3 weeks. Letters from Bordeaux say that 2 French*

frigates have seized the Engl. ship Jupiter of 50 cannon that intended to sail to Lisbon. The latest report from Martinique states that the Russel, a British ship of 70 [74] cannon, was wrecked at the Rock of Scylla.[3] [accurate]

How did the ship get there? Previously [p. 158] you have reported that she was riding off New York. The ship *Jupiter* of 50 cannon is said to take a large sum of money to New York.

Paris, Sept. 21. Because of his health, Comte d'Orvilliers is no longer able to command the combined fleet and has asked the King to be recalled. As his successor, His Majesty the King has appointed Comte du Chaffault Lieutenant General of the fleets; he has already departed. [accurate]

Paris, Sept. 28. We have news from Cadiz that because of the heat wave and in order to deceive the enemy, work at the siege of Gibraltar is done by night rather than by day. Four hundred cannon and mortars, 40,000 [25,000] bombs and bullets are behind the walls of San Roque and since there are no more than 1,000 small cannon [cannonines], His Catholic Majesty is said to have ordered some from France together with some engineers. The garrison consisting of 3,500 men will, in fact, be too small to man all the guards and posts and cover some 900 cannon. In spite of Don Barcelo's vigilance, some enemy ships, loaded with provisions of all kinds, have nevertheless found ways and means to enter Gibraltar. Several Portuguese ships, loaded with provision and intending to enter Gibraltar, have been seized. [accurate]

London, Oct. 9. It is said that Sir Henry Clinton will be recalled and Lord Cornwallis will in turn succeed him at the command. A new corps of Hessians and Hannoverians will presumably appear in America [in 1780] [next year] and supposedly disembark in New York.

A gentleman arriving here in a Dutch packet boat said that he has passed through a fleet of 12 [23] sails; it is believed that this fleet's sole purpose was to catch Paul Jones. [accurate]

London, Oct. 13. Through Sir Joseph Yorke, dispatches arrived from The Hague yesterday stating that the King was said to demand that the Dutch extradite Paul Jones so as to punish him in accordance with the law. Because of a crime, this Paul Jones deserted from English service; his [true] name is Jones Paul.[4] [accurate]

Since I treated the daughter of Major General Warner in Hardwick for jaundice [Gallenfarben], I was frequently in their house. Once, our conversation focussed on my having been taken prisoner of war. The general loved to hear that story because it was he who had captured us.[5] I told that I owned but the one shirt I was wearing and whenever it was being washed, I had to go without a shirt until it had dried. Since he had found me without a shirt, the general testified to that. When he brought me to his daughter, everyone in the house was weeping, the young as well as the old people. Yesterday, a servant of the general came bringing me a package containing 2 new shirts. With it came the following letter from the daughter, [quoted here in the original]:

"Sir! When I reflect on the many inconveniences you are subject to, I cannot forbear condoling with you in all the misfortunes your change of life exposeth you to and wishing it were in my power to extricate you therefrom. But however hard and difficult they would be to lesser minds, I please myself with the honor of your acquaintance which your good sense, patience, and fortitude will be a sufficient antidote against despair and support you under the heaviest trial. I have only to lament that you should dispel me from the number of your friends by not accepting when so often warned of the patronage of my friendship. I'll assure you, Sir, nothing will afford me more sensible pleasure than when I am instrumental in warding off the heavy and cruel hand of oppression. In token of which I beg leave to ask your acceptance of a couple new shirts, I know you want them. I hope shortly to have the pleasure of seeing you at our house. My sister presents her compliments to you and she would be much obliged to you, if you would send her by the bearer one portion of your physic pills. I remain your most affectionate friend. Hardwick, Jan. 12, 1780. Unity Warner"

[There follows a translation of the above letter into German.]

Here, in these regions, the snow is 3 foot deep in the plains and where the wind has drifted, there are mountains of snow 18 or 20 feet high. The road cannot be passed without snowshoes.

New York, City, Nov. 30. It is quite certain that Admiral Parker has seized 18 French ships of 24 to 40 cannon and taken them to Barbados and Antigua. They came from France and were intended for Martinique. They had all kinds of merchandise and goods as well as 9 months' provision for Comte d'Estaing's fleet on board. The Engl. frigate Hammond has seized a French scow coming from San Dominica, and loaded with 200 barrels of sugar, and taken her to Bermuda. [not found]

Boston, [Independent Ledger], Jan. 17. *The latest reports out of New York state that [on the 23rd of] last month, a fleet of 150 ships has set sail for Europe; it consisted of transports with invalids on board. Admiral Arbuthnot has departed from New York with a larger fleet [of 150 ships]. This fleet had General Clinton and General Cornwallis together with [8,000 to] 10,000 men on board. The enemy has made it known in New York that this fleet was assigned to attack South Carolina. The Skipper News assures that many [2] of these ships had capsized in a violent storm.* [accurate]

Rutland, Jan. 19. As I was in want of medicine, I was forced today to go to Worcester on snowshoes [raquets]. Since I had never walked on these before, these 15 miles became very trying.

20th   This noon, a man came from Rutland asking for me. He had arrived yesterday and was to take me to a sick woman in Upton, 15 miles away. Through him the commissary General Mercereau sent me the following letter:

Dear Doctor! The Bearer Mr. Walkow come for you to go to Upton to See a Seek Woman there. Should you incline to go, you have my Permission. I wish you may cure the Women, please to write me, Should You go. I am to Serve You so far as is Consistent With my Duty.
　　　　Your Most Humble Servant
　　　　Joshua Mercereau. Dep. Com. General of Prisoners.[6]

I was stiff from yesterday and neither could I nor did I want to go to Upton. The man begged me to come with him since he would not be allowed to come home without bringing me along. But I assured him that I would gladly come along if I could go on horseback. But since that was not possible, seeing the snow was 3 to 4 feet deep, he hired a sleigh with beds on it as well as 4 strong men who had to pull me on that sleigh to Upton. The men went on snowshoes. Never did I see such a vehicle.

As for the sick woman, see my remarks on New England sicknesses.[7]

In several places, especially in Cork in Ireland, much is being written about Paul Jones and his fleet. This consists of a new, Boston-built frigate of 32 cannon, one ship of 20 cannon, 2 brigantines of 18 cannon and two small tenders. This fleet cast anchor in the Bantry Bay on Sept. 12 having 5 prizes with them. Having lost all masts, the *Serapis* had to surrender to Paul Jones. Paul Jones' ship is said to have sunk.[8] A fleet of 16 warships is at sea to catch this pirate.

Massachusetts Spy, Jan. 20: *London, Oct. 1, 1779. Lord Sandwich has encouraged an older gentleman to be quite confident about Great Britain's defenses in claiming he would have 64 warships ready by April 15.* [accurate]

Worcester [Massachusetts Spy], Jan. 20: *An agent from Congress arrived in Havana on July 8 and presented the Spanish ambassador with plans prepared concerning the expedition against [West] Florida. As a present and as security for the 750,000 piasters advanced to the United States, the Provinces of East and West Florida are to be given to Spain. The plan has been accepted and two frigates, several privateers and armed vessels have already set sail to go there. An infantry regiment together with a great number of armed men have sailed to settle there.*[9] [accurate]

   Amsterdam, Oct. 7, 1779. The French frigate <u>Pallas</u> has just landed at Texel accompanied by the English warship <u>Serapis</u>, which had recently been seized by Paul Jones. The latter had transferred his command onto the <u>Serapis</u> because his own ship had sunk shortly after the action. Other ships also arrived, all forming part of Paul Jones' fleet; the rest are expected.

   According to all reports, a number of Hessians and Hannoverians are said to be sent to America next spring. [accurate]

   A letter from Portsmouth, Sept. 27.

   Our large fleet under Sir Charles Hardy keeps riding at anchor at Spithead waiting for a favorable wind.

   Two English squadrons of warships and frigates have been sent out, one to the north and one to the west, to capture Paul Jones and clear the Engl. and Irish coasts.

   A few days ago, several West Indian merchants paid a visit to Lord George Germain and reminded him of the miserable condition of the West Indian commerce and of the insecurity of the Jamaican fleet. This consisted of more than 100 merchant ships and was covered by only one warship and 2 frigates. His Lordship listened to them with the greatest patience and then declared that he very much regretted not to be able to support them with larger forces. He added that [England's] *supremacy on the great ocean was lost and it will not be easy to regain it. The daily increase of the naval powers of France and Spain are the reason that Comte d'Estaing could maintain the blockade at Martinique. These and other circumstances are the reasons for many revolts and, nevertheless, there are absolutely no means available against them at present.* [accurate]

My dear Thomas! These again are very ridiculous announcements, which no Englishman would admit even if they were true.

Philadelphia, Dec. 19 [15], 1779: Extract out of a letter from Alicante in Spain, Sept. 21, 1779.

   The combined French and Spanish fleet consisting of 66 warships excluding frigates, bomb and fire ships, is looking for the Engl. fleet under Sir Charles Hardy. This one consists - without frigates - of 41 ships and avoids any possibility of engaging in a battle with the combined fleet. Nevertheless, the latter has already seized 4 Engl. ships of 64 and 74 cannon. More than five hundred transport ships lie ready to put 60,000 elite troops on English soil.

   Gibraltar is being besieged by 20,000 elite Spanish troops and the harbor blockaded by a Spanish fleet so that neither succour nor provisions can get through. - - The English are being hard pressed from all sides. -- The Emperor of Morocco has absolutely refused to provide the English at Gibraltar with extra victuals; our people,

on the other hand, are being abundantly supplied from there with everything.
[accurate]

My dear Thomas! Here again are many falsehoods.

Rutland, Jan. 27. Yesterday, I was taken to Worcester on a sleigh and today I was brought here. It is very cold; the oldest people cannot remember so much snow or such slippery conditions.

[Continental Journal] Boston Saturday [Thursday] paper, Jan. 29 [27]: *We hear that Gen. Washington plans to seize Staten Island* [near New York] *For this purpose, he sent a corps of 18,000 [about 2,000] men [and several hundred flags] out of the Province of New Jersey across* [the ice] *on 200 sleds under the leadership of Lord Stirling. They landed successfully, took the entire English occupation force of 800 men prisoner,* [spiked all cannon] *and drove away with between 800 and 900 barrels of supplies.*
This effective coup de main was done without losing one single man.[10] [selective]

This was a great feat.

Extract out of a letter from Hannover. The number of troops, having now been levied from this Electorate since the beginning of the American war, is so large that it makes it exceedingly difficult for the recruiting officers to raise more recruits or to complement the existing regiments each year. Petitions have gone to the government that men who have wives and children be exempt from military service. Many have been expelled and have had to leave their families and country. All this has been reported to London and instructions are being anxiously awaited. [not found]

These again are falsehoods, for the Hannoverians are not in America but in Gibraltar.[11]

London, Sept. 21. The public can now be reasonably sure that one of the vacant blue ribbons is destined for the Honorable Lord Sandwich. Patriots may keep on complaining and call this pardon undeserved, nevertheless everyone believes that there are few in this Kingdom who have deserved a ribbon (rope) as much as this Lord Sandwich. [not found]

At the end of this month, the guinea is worth 180 Spanish piasters in paper money.

Month of February 1780

2nd   Today the news arrived here in Rutland that a corps of Tories, Canadians and Savages under the command of Brant and Butler have crossed Lake Champlain and invaded New Hampshire - another lie.

Boston Saturday paper, Febr. 5: *Letter from New Haven, Jan. 26:*
The oldest people cannot remember ever seeing so many fish in the sound. It is very cold. [not found]

Boston [Independent Ledger], Febr. 7: *From a gentleman who has recently arrived from Braunschweig, we hear that, of the fleet which had just sailed from New York, several ships have perished and most of the men drowned. We also received the report that the Ramillies, an English ship of 74 cannon, has been consumed by fire and all the men have lost their lives.*[12] [accurate]

Boston Thursday paper [Continental Journal], Febr. 17: *Fishkill, Febr. 3.*
We hear that the English, [our cruel enemy] have made an inroad into New Jersey with 2 divisions and assaulted our guards at Elizabethtown. They have also burned the church [meeting house], the schoolhouse and the jail there and led several inhabitants away as prisoners. At the same time, the enemy burned the Academy at Newark and took the judge and 25 prisoners along.[13] [accurate]

The judge had to march through the deep snow in his bare feet; this was somewhat barbaric.

Rutland, Febr. 22. The report reached us today that a general exchange of all the prisoners of war has been approved. Thus, if it is true, we will finally be exchanged and abandon our sweet captivity, but I repeat - if it is true.

At the end of this month, the guinea is worth 230 Spanish piasters in paper money.

Month of March 1780

Boston, Monday paper [Independent Ledger], Febr. 28: *Fishkill, Febr. 20 [10].*
We hear that last Thursday, the enemy with 100 horses and 300 men has assaulted one of our forts near White Plains close to Young's House, that was commanded by Colonel Thompson. Our men courageously defended themselves but were subdued by sheer numbers. Colonel Thompson was wounded and taken prisoner. -- Capt. Roberts, from the 15th Massachusetts Bay Regiment, was shot dead together with 14 men, 20 wounded and 50 [45] captured. The enemy burned Young's house and 5 of the wounded were consumed there by fire. They performed their usual cruelty on the prisoners of war, too horrible to tell. [accurate]

--but is it true?
N.B. I know this Colonel Thompson quite well. He is a native of Brimfield and a farrier by vocation. --

Worcester paper [Massachusetts Spy], March 2: *Boston, Febr. 27 [14]. [Extract of a letter dated Jan. 22, 1780.]*
A letter out of Charleston in South Carolina confirms that Pensacola is in Spanish hands; that 5 weeks ago, a fleet of 20 ships had sailed there; that the Spaniards have captured the 16th Regiment and several English troops near the Mississippi, totalling about 1,200 [1,100] men, and taken them to Havana. [accurate]
[Febr. 24] We also hear of an expedition by Butler and Brant, who are engaged in plundering, killing, and burning. [summary]
Through Capt. Sampson, who after an annoying journey of 89 days arrived from France last Tuesday, we have learned that the inhabitants of Ireland are afraid that our worthy allies, France and Spain, will undertake a landing in that Kingdom. They have therefore asked the English Court for help whereupon they were sent 40,000 guns together with ammunition, all the necessary pieces of armament and the order to watch over and defend the coast. Thereupon, the Irish formed an army which was commanded by the Earl of Shannon. These revolted and declared that they were resolved to become independent like the Americans. This was intimated to the

London Court and at the same time, the Court was asked to confirm their independence. In the event this should be refused, they were decided to reach their goal by the sword.[14] [accurate]

My dear Thomas, that again is nonsense.

Boston, Febr. 28. Extract from a letter from Nancy, Nov. 2, 1779. The latest in the English letters reads that the Irish Parliament have declared that until their independence and free trade are assured throughout the whole world, they would neither let any English merchandise into their harbors nor send anything there [to England]. [This intelligence may be depended upon.] [accurate]

It is likely that everybody will believe this report -- and yet it most certainly is a lie.

Letter from Charleston in South Carolina, Jan. 11.
We have reports that our enemies, the English, are building large batteaux and preparing all sorts of things for a second expedition against this town. This shall be undertaken as soon as the reinforcement from New York arrives [and then with a little more energy]. *-- If the enemy will truly make a second attempt on the fort, I believe that this undertaking will bring them as much dishonor and misfortune as their unjust actions deserve; our fort and river are and will be very strongly fortified.* [accurate]

Worcester, March 2.
On Monday, General Heath passed through this city. He came from headquarters and continued on his way to Roxbury.
Copies of the latest speech by the British King to his Parliament are said to have recently arrived in a ship from England [Europe] but they have as yet not been distributed. We know that much from it that the King has declared he would rather lay his crown at the feet of his enemies [meaning France and Spain] *before he would submit to the independence of the Americans.* [accurate]

-- Good old Thomas, he cannot stay away from it!

Massachusetts Spy, March 16: *Extract out of a letter from St. Eustatius, Jan. 18.*
News arrived here yesterday that the English fleet under Admiral Parker met a French merchant fleet destined for Martinique; part of the 14 or 15 ships were either seized or sunk. They are said to have also taken two or three French frigates. We also have the reliable report that Admiral Rodney has sailed from England with reinforcements; we are expecting him by the hour. [accurate]

Worcester paper [Massachusetts Spy], March 9: *Excerpt out of a letter from Lisbon, Sept. 28, 1779.*
France and Spain make every possible effort to draw Portugal into this war, and England makes the same effort to keep this power neutral, to which this power is anyway most inclined. We will soon see which side this power will take. [accurate]

Extract out of a letter from a highly placed gentleman in France, which was also brought to us through Capt. Sampson. The combined fleet is in the Portsmouth [Plymouth] Channel. Fear and horror are spreading throughout England. Our troops are ready to embark from our shores and take possession of England. Admiral Hardy avoids the fight [every chance of spotting the combined fleet] *and nobody knows where he may be now. Two English warships of 50 and 64 cannon have recently been seized. Many merchantmen and other ships fall into our hands daily. [Four of their East Indian merchant ships have also fallen into our power recently.] May God give His blessings to that future campaign that the war may be ended, and friendship, peace and unity be restored. May these last forever between America and France, and may these two powers defend each other against their enemies and render each other happy.* [accurate]

Philadelphia. Congress, on Jan. 13, decided that the names, ranks, and numbers of all the officers and privates among the prisoners of war in each Province [their resp. states] be sent to General Washington as soon as possible. Information should also be given as to the place where each of them is staying so that in the event it should come to a general exchange of the prisoners of war between us and the English, they could immediately be called. [accurate]

Massachusetts Spy, March 16, 1780: *London, Dec. 21, 1779.*
Since the dispatch has arrived bringing the good news of Comte d'Estaing's defeat, several different reports have been received here. One of these says that Comte d'Estaing has arrived in Brest with two ships of his fleet on the 9th. He had left a packet boat sailing near the American coasts under the command of Monsieur de la Motte Picquet and immediately after his arrival at Brest, continued his journey to Paris.[15] [accurate]

The good news, mentioned in the Gazette Extraordinaire, was made known to the public through firing the cannon from the park and from the towers and through a running fire [feu de joie] last night. We also have the pleasure of assuring our readers that General Prevost's reports have arrived, which confirm that Comte d'Estaing has been defeated and has left the American shores. [accurate]

We can likewise communicate the report that upon Comte d'Estaing's defeat at Savannah, the value of the American paper money has fallen by 40%. [accurate]

Lieut. Gen. Burgoyne has laid down his command in Scotland as well as the command of his regiment. It is quite certain that through the contagious disease, which spread through the French fleet off Brest last November, 12,000 Frenchmen have been taken from this world. [accurate]

Admiral Barrington is commanding a fleet to cover Gibraltar and to observe the Spanish in the Mediterranean. Admiral Rodney sailed to the West Indies from Spithead on Dec. 8. Maj. Gen. Vaughan will set sail with a corps in a few days and also proceed to the West Indies where he will take over the command of the English army.[16] [accurate]

Basseterre on the Island of St. Kitts in the West Indies, Dec. 28, 1779.
Admiral Parker's fleet seized a French frigate on which all the enemy signals of Comte d'Estaing's fleet were discovered as well as a report about the arrival of a supply fleet under the cover of a ship of 40 cannon and 2 frigates. The admiral immediately made his dispositions and seized the entire fleet. It then sailed under French flags to Port Royal [Fort de France] from whose shores his signals were being answered until he put 800 men ashore close to Point Negril. Some ships were brought very close to two forts and they silenced them in a very short period; the troops took possession of them [the forts], spiked all the cannon, [knocked off the trunnions], burned [the carriages] and all this in 45 minutes. Seventeen ships, full of supplies, etc., as well as 3 frigates [and one forty gun ship] taken as booty, 2 batteries ruined, and if 3,000 men could have been put ashore, the Island of Martinique would

undoubtedly have been seized. We lost the gallant Capt. Harmond on the Conqueror, who was killed while demolishing the forts. [accurate]

The arrival of the English fleet at St. Lucia is being confirmed; it consists of 1 ship of 98 [90] and 3 of 74 cannon as well as 7 frigates, all having the 19th Infantry Regiment on board [copper bottoms and 9 infantry regiments on board]. [accurate]

Boston [Independent Ledger], March 13. *A deserter from New York has told that a packet boat recently arrived from Falmouth with the news that 25,000 Frenchmen have marched into Hanau.* [accurate]

That again is a very stupid lie! What business would they have there?

Worcester paper [Massachusetts Spy], March 16.
English news out of the New York City paper:
London, Nov. 4, 1779: Lord Cornwallis definitely is commander-in-chief in North America to take the place of Sir Henry Clinton.[17]
His Excel. the Hessian minister paid his respects to the King at St. James yesterday and presented His Majesty with a contract in regard to subsidies; it concerns another 12,000 Hessians to enter into English military service. These are to open the campaign in North America under the command of Prinz Ernst von Mecklenburg, a brother of the Queen of England, next summer.[18] [accurate]

My dear Thomas, this is highly improbable!

From a letter from Braunschweig in Germany, Nov. 6, 1779, we have learned that 50,000 Prussians have received orders to march to the Lower Rhine. One believes that these, together with the Hannoverian troops and those that Hesse [Cassel] can provide, will [turn the balance] [counterbalance the French influence] and make it possible for the Dutch to declare themselves publicly for Great Britain. [accurate]

French news out of the West Indies from Martinique, Febr. 3, says that the siege of Gibraltar is being very seriously continued; that Don Barcelo has seized an English fleet of 42 ships with succour and victuals for the garrison of Gibraltar; that no ship has been able to escape except one frigate from the escort, which sailed all alone through the horrible fire of the Spanish fleet and finally succeeded in entering Gibraltar. [accurate]

News from Fort New York, Febr. 16:
The ship Apollo, having arrived here, has brought the news that, following a disastrous fire, the city of Savannah-le-Mar on the Island of Jamaica has been completely reduced to ashes. The captain spoke with a Royal ship at latitude 32 and longitude 73 and saw that Admiral Arbuthnot's fleet, having the Royal army on board, took its course toward South Carolina in the best order and in a favorable wind. [This fleet consisted of close to 300 sails.] [accurate]

Boston, March 9. Last Tuesday, a truce ship arrived from Bermuda bringing some 90 [30] American prisoners. We learned from their escort that one of our cruisers had come upon a large English ship on the ocean, which was in a most precarious situation. She belonged to the fleet which had sailed from New York. This ship carried on board the fourth part of the cannon, ammunition and other appurtenances belonging to the artillery, together with 82 officers and soldiers of the artillery. She had lost her masts and was close to sinking. She had gotten into this terrible situation through that same horrible gale that had surprised Admiral

Arbuthnot and has lost all hope of reaching a port. Our ship took the crew and supplies on board and soon thereafter, the ship capsized. These people, who had been rescued from certain death, were taken to Bermuda; there they gave the same report we already had heard, namely that the Arbuthnot fleet had been completely driven off course in an unusually bad gale and it is presumed that many ships had sunk. The 1,500 horses that had been put on board in New York had all been thrown overboard [none was supposed to be saved]; not one has remained alive. By the beginning of February, not a single ship of this fleet had arrived in Bermuda or any other harbor, although they had sailed from Sandy Hook on Dec. 26. Should most of this large enemy fleet be lost, which according to their own account had 10,000 of their best troops on board, and there is every reason to believe it, - then this would constitute the greatest loss that the enemy has suffered after Saratoga. -- Be that as it may, that much is certain that the ships of the enemy fleet were so scattered that to carry out their plan, the enemy had quickly to think of another reinforcement. All the reports are in agreement, that this fleet had but a 2 week supply of victuals on board. How terrible must have been that situation wherein the enemy found themselves after they had consumed all the provisions! [accurate]

That can well be possible. When we were sailing to America from Germany, we had 32 horses with our 1st Division that - as stated - were placed before Stade on board the ship *Martha*. Of these, 19 were thrown overboard; on the English fleet, the horses had probably been locked in more closely on the English fleet. Thus in our fleet, 4 men and 19 horses had died.

Boston, Thursday paper [Continental Journal], March 16: *Bilbao, Jan. 22.*
We have the report that Admiral Rodney has sailed to Gibraltar with 21 warships and 6,000 land forces. He will encounter the Spanish fleet of 20 warships and since 24 warships have been sent after him from Brest, he will certainly have great difficulties to overcome. [accurate]

Boston Friday paper, March 17: *London, Nov. 3.*
The Royal ship Janus and the brig Jamaica have seized 8 Dutch ships that came from Surinam and were loaded with goods for the Americans.
By the year 1780, our war power will be no less than 290,000 [390,000] men. [summary]

Rutland, March 20. Letters arrived here from our Maj. Gen. von Riedesel today, through which we learned that our baggage and some such pieces of regimentals as cloth et al. have been sent from New York and have arrived in Providence. Capt. von Bärtling sen. went there immediately to receive it all.
March 26. Capt. von Bärtling returned and has brought along some letters from Germany. I received one from the Municipal Physician Dr. Topp in Wolfenbüttel, dated Jan. 30, 1777. Although this letter was more than 3 years old, I nevertheless was happy [to know] that my family had been well at that time. We also learned that much baggage had either been lost or spoiled and that nothing of my baggage was there. That was a true message of doom and a greater loss than I can bear because with 250 piasters I cannot replace the loss. But that which I miss the most is my diary from Febr. 22, 1776, until the last of 1777, which I left behind in my valise at Fort Edward. I left my best things with the large baggage in my coffer at Trois-Rivières on the 1st of Jan. 1777, -- everything is lost. My collected coins, about 70 to 80 piasters, also the bark work made by some Canadian belles, -- which I had intended for my dear daughter Caroline, everything is lost! -- Let's wish the Canadians a good, cold but healthful winter!

Providence paper [The Providence Gazette], March 24 [25]:

From the camp at San Roque in Spain off Gibraltar, Oct. 8: Two sailors and one soldier from Hannover have deserted and come to us. They confirm the report that the enemy in Gibraltar receives no more than half their ration and that they are so much in want of firewood that they must cook their meals [dress their victuals] with cedarwood or peat. Their workmen do not receive more than two pounds of bread and one pound of meat in 3 days; their gunpowder is bad. [accurate]

Brest in France, Oct. 21. It is certain that if the wind becomes favorable, our fleet with 56 ships will set sail next Saturday or Sunday. The troops have embarked, and the order from the Court to set sail is definite. [accurate]

Brest, Nov. 5. The order from the Court to the fleet has been changed [thus it really was not definite]. *They have not departed as yet, but with the first favorable wind they are to set sail. The ships Solitaire, Indian, Cato and Actionaire are designated to go to East India.* [accurate]

[Massachusetts Spy, March 30], *Philadelphia, Febr. 29. We have news from London that Lord Sandwich shot himself.* [accurate]

Worcester paper [Massachusetts Spy], March 30: *Boston, March 23.*

From Capt. Babson and several others who have recently arrived here from Europe, we have received the following report. Admirals Rodney and Ross have sailed from England with 21 ships of the line as well as some transport ships with recruits, provisions and other necessities for the garrison of Gibraltar on Jan.7. Not far from Cap Finisterre, they encountered a Spanish fleet, loaded with all kinds of provisions. This fleet of 31 ships and 2 frigates came from San Sebastian and was intended for Cadiz. With the exception of 3 ships that saved themselves through flight, the entire fleet was seized by the English. Not far from Cape San Vincente [de la Barquera], *the Spanish Admiral de Langara* [19] *came upon them with 8 warships. In very hazy waters, the Spanish Admiral took the Engl. fleet for a fleet of transport ships and was just about to sail toward them, being in fact already among them, when he noticed his error. He immediately gave his fleet the signal to withdraw and to take to flight. The admiral was so closely involved that he could not take to flight. Two ships of his fleet, unwilling to abandon their admiral, stayed with him. They showed a glorious example of Spanish valour in that situation. -- Another Spanish ship of 74 cannon had been engaged with 2 English ships of 74 cannon for 4 hours, when finally the Spanish ship blew up into the air and all the men were buried in the ocean. The admiral and the other ships were near ruin when they surrendered; it is said that one or more [Engl.] ships have sunk. Thereupon, the English fleet safely entered Gibraltar with all their transports and delivered the garrison, locked in by sea and land, from the most horrible condition of what that place has ever lived through. There are added reports that a fleet of 36 French and Spanish warships have enclosed Admiral Rodney with his fleet at Gibraltar.* [summary]

Paul Jones, who is getting so much attention, has sailed from Holland, and entered La Coruña on the American frigate Alliance, which he is now commanding; he will sail to Philadelphia. He has 150 Americans on board who, from being prisoners of war in England, have deserted to Holland. Among these is the brave Captain Cunningham, who has lived in a jail in England [for many months], is considered a pirate and treated like one. Paul Jones seized a ship on his trip which, loaded with gunpowder, was destined for Gibraltar. [accurate]

Extract from a letter from Newburyport, March 17 [14].
According to a reliable report, we know that Gen. Lincoln has gathered an appreciable number of troops in South Carolina and that such preparations are being made for the defense of this province [that State] and especially of Charleston that, if the enemy should make another attempt on it, they would be most warmly received. [accurate]

We also know for certain that no news has reached New York by the 5th of this month about the fate of the fleet under Arbuthnot or of Generals Clinton and Cornwallis or of the arrival of any Engl. ship in any American or West Indian harbor. Gen. Knyphausen is commander at New York, Gen. Tryon is second -in - command and has the English under command. [accurate]

New York City, Febr. 11 [21]. We have a report that Admiral Rodney has arrived in the West Indies with 6 warships, 7 frigates, and 3,000 land forces on board. [accurate]

Poughkeepsie, March 13. Through several people from New York, we have gotten the following news, that is considered reliable. We do not wish, however, to transmit it to our readers as absolutely certain so that they will not flatter themselves too much in that the future campaign will end unsuccessfully for our enemy. [accurate]

An English ship under Captain Underhill was taken by the French but then retaken from the French by the English sailors on board. They arrived in New York with the news that Comte d'Estaing's fleet has encountered 3/4 of General Clinton's fleet as well as the Generals Clinton and Cornwallis and taken them prisoners; thus these are in the power of our allies. This same English fleet has suffered very great damage in a dreadful hurricane, and the dispersion of this large enemy fleet with its dismal consequences have [completely] spoiled the planned push toward the South. Following these reports, which must be very depressing for the British tyranny, their adherents have begun to sell their possessions and are preparing to go to England. One also believes that all English and foreign troops will soon be recalled from America because their help is needed to defend the West Indian Islands. [accurate]

My dear Thomas! You will soon hear that much to your surprise the Engl. fleet and army that were considered lost have reached their place of destination.

Worcester [Massachusetts Spy], March 30. *We have a report that Comte d'Estaing has arrived in France. We have also been informed that the enemy is preparing soon to leave New York. Everyone believes that the war will be waged in much earnest between the English and the French in the West Indies.* [accurate]

At the end of this month, the guinea is worth 260 specie in paper money.

Month of April 1780

Boston Monday paper [Independent Ledger], April 3: *Hanau in Germany, Nov. 27, 1779.*
We have received the report that the Hannoverian troops have gotten orders to keep their horses, tents and all necessities ready to march immediately in a campaign. Whether they are intended for America or somewhere else remains a secret. [accurate]

New York, March 14 [1]. The privateer <u>Shark</u> from London and a cutter from Guernsey have captured a Spanish ship and brought it into Falmouth. This ship of 900 tons came from the South Seas and had 3 trunks of doubloons on board; likewise 48 [47] trunks with 600,000 [200,000 dollars] piasters in silver, another trunk with 270 [white] silver marks, 9 small trunks full of gold, 400 tons of cacao, 15 bales of furs, 140 tons of copper, and a variety of other articles [of great worth]. [accurate]

This is a giant prize.

The following apparently is a correct calculation of English military power in all the parts of the globe: Great Britain 111,000 men; in North America, the West Indies, Gibraltar and Minorca 89,000 [79,000] [Provincials 8,000] men, the Irish Establishment 15,000. Irish Association 44,00 [42,000] men; East Indian Company troops 35,000 men. Naval power 96,000 men. Without the newly established corps, a total of 390,000 [386,000] men.[20] [accurate]

   Boston, April 3. *A London paper, not too outdated, gives the report that several English warships, destined for prisoners, have taken a strong fort away from the Spanish in South America. with all the ships in the harbor. These ships had such large amounts of gold and silver on board that each ship's captain expected a share of 70,000 pounds.* [accurate]

Worcester paper [Massachusetts Spy], April 6: *Rutland, March 23.*
Captain von Bärtling of the German Grenadiers, Capt. Fricke of the German Dragoons, [Quartermaster] Frede of the Hessian Jägers, and Ensign Rynd of the British troops request that all the prisoners of war immediately make their appearance in the barracks at Rutland to receive their regimentals and their pay because a general exchange of the prisoners of war is taking place. [accurate]
   London, Nov. 1. *As we can definitely assure you, the following are the main articles of the peace treaty that is to be concluded at the earliest time possible.*
 1. Each party will restore whatever they have conquered and seized.
 2. The 13 Provinces of North America are to be declared free and independent.
 3. England is to withdraw her armies and fleets from these 13 Provinces.
 4. Gibraltar is to be ceded to Spain [etc. etc]. [accurate]

My dear Thomas, Gen. Clinton has not even thought of it as yet.

   London, Dec. 2 [5], 1779. It is definitely true that most of the European powers have proposed to the Court of Great Britain to recognize North America's independence. This is the more credible as a recognition of this independence would most certainly have a special and great influence on these courts and on European countries [in general]. *-- This is the situation in which we Englishmen find ourselves! -- And what chance do we have in waging war against a superior power that has enormously enlarged our national debt and where could we turn for support; nobody is feeling sorry for us, it would be better to spring the mine!* [sic] *Our misfortune will perhaps bring us back to reason that we have been blinded by our previous bliss.* [accurate]

My dear Thomas! This again is nothing but nonsense!

   Charleston in South Carolina, Febr. 9. We have had several reports about the British fleet that had gathered at Sandy Hook last Dec. 24 and then left. In our opinion, the most reliable among these mentions altogether 140 [94] ships including warships, transports and merchant ships, which had taken their course toward the south with 10,000 [8,000] men on board under the command of Generals Clinton and Lord Cornwallis. In the event the fleet should be driven off course, the place of rendezvous was to be Tybee.[21] The ships that had lately been seized and brought here had this order. Two warships and one frigate have been seen off this bar. For one week now, many shots from heavy cannon have often been heard during the night, which - so they think - have been signals to gather the scattered ships. A fortnight ago Thursday, two American frigates, _Providence_ and _Ranger_, returned with the tender _Eagle_ from their trip to Tybee bar, where they discovered 5 English ships riding at anchor, which seemed to be warships. There were also another 8 ships ready to sail. Our 2 frigates have brought 2 enemy sloops in here, that had come from New York and been intended for Georgia. They had 14 officers and 32 [noncommissioned officers and] privates from Lord Cathcart's Light Dragoons as well as a large supply of saddlery on board; they too had become separated from the fleet. [accurate]

Baltimore, March 17 [7]. A gentleman arrived here on Sunday night, who had left Charleston on Febr. 10. He has told us that on that day alarm guns had been heard in the neighboring forts around the fortress that announced the long awaited English army and fleet. We have been assured that they had arrived 40 miles south of Charleston and that this army was commanded by Gen. Clinton and Lord Cornwallis. One corps of the enemy army has already advanced 25 miles to Wockmalaw Island toward Stono Ferry. General Lincoln has already sent a galley from Charleston, which is to hinder the enemy's march. The gentleman added that the garrison at Charleston is resolved to defend themselves to the last man and thus all the possible preparations are being made for a good defense on water and on land. Another 5,000 men stand ready at the first order to take their places in the lines.

Another gentleman, who arrived here from Petersburg in Virginia yesterday, has informed us that on Sunday, Febr. 27, an officer of Colonel Baylor's Dragoon Regiment had arrived there from Charleston in 2 weeks with orders to General Scott from Gen. Lincoln which state:

He should hasten as much as possible with the troops under his command to reach Charleston because [an army of English and Hessians] [very formidable body of the enemy] are on the march to besiege Charleston. He had also come upon General Hogun with his brigade 50 miles before Charleston.[22] [accurate]

Hartford [Connecticut Courant], March 28. A few days ago we have [learned] that an enemy corps, 600 men strong, has advanced to Skenesborough from St. Jean and destroyed the iron works and mills there. [We have also heard] that a number of militiamen under the command of Colonel Herrick has gone there to keep the enemy back. [accurate]

My dear Thomas, those are lies!

Boston, March 20: The latest European newspaper writes that the Spanish fleet has been parading in Brest harbor and that it was supposed to set sail under the command of Don Luis de Cordova, who gave the following speech to his officers [before-hand]:
'My children!

It is true that our friends and allies have almost always beaten their enemy with equal power and frequently forced them to retreat with superior power. Should we not be superior to our enemy now, then let us do everything possible to be equal to them in every respect. This is the 4th time that I am going to fight for my King and country and that must also convince you that we will not always lose our lives when we go into battle [etc., etc.] " *This admiral is 72 years old.*

Comte du Chaffault, a gallant and skillful admiral, commands the large French fleet in place of Comte d'Orvilliers, who for health reasons has returned and been favored by his king with a substantial pension.[23] [He wrote in a letter from Lisbon that Portugal does not want any longer to remain neutral]. [accurate]

Rutland, April 7. Today our baggage arrived. Much of it was rotted and much has been stolen.

Worcester paper [Massachusetts Spy], April 13: *Trenton, March 15.*
Last week, commissioners of the English and American armies assembled at Perth-Amboy to conclude a cartel or a general exchange of the prisoners of war. From our side, Maj. Gen. St. Clair and Lieut. Colonels Hamilton and Carrington were present; from the English side, Maj. Gen. Phillips, and the Lieut. Colonels Gordon and Norton; it is so far unknown, however, what has been accomplished. [accurate]

New York, April 25 [27]. Extract from a letter of an officer in Admiral Arbuthnot's fleet, dated Charleston Bar, March 9.
We are in sight of the Rebel fleet, which is riding at anchor near Sullivan's Island. Tomorrow, we will advance with the Royal ships <u>Renown</u>, [<u>Romulus</u>], <u>Roebuck</u>, <u>Raleigh</u>, <u>Blonde</u>, <u>Perseus</u>, <u>Camilla</u>, and <u>Germaine</u>. The Rebel fleet consists of the <u>Boston</u>, <u>Providence</u>, <u>Queen of France</u>, <u>Ranger</u> and <u>Notre Dame</u> with the <u>Pricole</u> of 20 cannon and another 2 ships of 20 cannon as well as the French frigate <u>Charnier</u> of 32 cannon. Our army has opened a battery of 40 cannon. In this very moment in which I am writing this, we are crossing the bar. [summary]
New York, April 8 [27].
Last night, various pieces of news have come in here from New Jersey and Connecticut. They say that Charleston was taken by Sir Henry Clinton on March 19, that the Rebel fleet was seized and the army scattered. [selective]

Worcester paper [Massachusetts Spy], April 20. *The latest news from South Carolina has been brought to us by a ship that had left Charleston on March 26. On that day, the fortress was still safe and in our hands. Our army is in good spirits.*
We have learned from Boston today that Charleston was still in our hands on April 1. [accurate]

Boston, Monday paper [Independent Ledger], April 24: *London, Jan. 25.*
From a letter from France that arrived here via Flanders yesterday, we have learned that 16 Dutch cargo ships, having on board hemp, pitch, tar, ropes, sails and many items needed for ship building, have arrived at Brest in France. [accurate]

Worcester paper [Massachusetts Spy], April 27: *From the St. Kitts paper in the West Indies, Nov. 28, 1779.*
Admiral Parker seized and partly demolished 13 [12] French ships on Nov. 17. On board these ships, he has taken 1,149 men prisoner. They had 8 [6] months' provisions on board for 15,000 men as well as 2,000 large hogsheads of [fine fresh]

Claret wine, 15,000 ton of wheat flour, 5,000 [500] large casks of pork, 1,500 barrels of beef, [several thousand tons] *of ship biscuit [bread], peas and sweetmeats, pastry, tomato, pomade for external use etc. in huge amounts.* [summary]

At the end of this month the guinea has a value of 290 piasters.

Month of May 1780

Boston Monday paper [Independent Ledger], May 1: *London, Jan. 11.*
As the latest news from Hannover tells us, rumors are circulating there that France plans to invade the Electorate of Hannover. For this purpose, the troops in Alsace and Lorraine have already been reinforced and everything has been prepared in said Electorate to receive [give them a warm reception] the monsieurs properly. [accurate]

Chatham, April 16. Last Friday morning, 600 enemy troops again came from Elizabethtown to Staten Island but the guards were vigilant so that they could not be overtaken but yet so weak that they could not resist. ·· The enemy is led by the well known General Skinner whose cruelty equals his noted timidity. ·· Women and children were completely undressed and all became victims of barbarism with words and whippings. ·· In the houses, the mirrors and all the rare things that could not be taken along, were smashed. ·· How often has this region already been plundered by the English!
This time, they did not show the least respect for widows and old people; a blind old woman was stripped of all her clothes and abused in the most abominable way. It seemed that this time they only intended to plunder in order to provide a little sustenance for poor Skinner and his wretched and cruel party.[24] [accurate]

Providence, April 29. The commissioners, who recently gathered in Amboy to settle a general exchange of the prisoners of war, have dispersed without accomplishing anything.
We have received a report from Cadiz that the Spanish fleet off Gibraltar has been totally defeated. [accurate]

Boston Monday paper [Independent Ledger], May 15: *Extract out of a letter from Ireland, Febr. 7.*
The British Ministry apparently continues to want to subdue the Americans, but how? ·· England can no longer send any troops from Europe, and the Americans are not willing to go over to the English. ·· Much is being said and written about the present situation of the British ·· how necessary and valuable a union between Great Britain and the American Colonies would be for the happiness of both nations.
This year, the war will cost 32 million pounds and will increase the national debt for far over 200 million pounds. [accurate]

Boston, May 15. Yesterday a truce ship arrived here [at Newport] from New York and brought several prisoners along. We learned from them that during the past 2 weeks, 9 American privateers have entered New York as prisoners. ·· News from the South tells that on April 20, no attack had yet been undertaken against Charleston. [accurate]

Rutland, May 18. This morning, we had a total lunar eclipse.

Rutland, May 19. This has been an unusually dark day. My room is a very bright corner room with big windows but it is so dark that I had to burn the light from 9 o'clock in the morning until 4 o'clock in the afternoon. Everything I saw seemed yellow, even the sheep. The following night was so dark that the animals were unable to see: the horses ran against houses and trees, the dogs howled terribly as soon as they left the house etc. Such darkness is surely very strange during a full moon.[25]

Worcester paper [Massachusetts Spy], May 18 [25]: *London, Jan. 18.*
Through the report we have received from Capt. Clarke in Kasmaskaska [Kamchatka?] of Capt. Cook's death we conclude that he [Cook] had intended to discover a road through the NW Passage. His attempt, however, must have failed, otherwise we would have had news from him long ago. The sad message about his death came by dispatch from Kamaskaska via [St.] Petersburg. [accurate][26]
London, Febr. 18. The victory of Admiral Rodney over the Spanish fleet has been made public here with thundering cannon. [accurate]
New London, May 19. A few days ago, a truce ship arrived with 110 American prisoners of war from whom we have learned that people in New York are living in the greatest fear and anxiety. Since they suspect a call from our allies at any moment, they have prepared 20 large ships loaded with stones. At the first report of the French fleet's arrival, these will be sunk in the most narrow passage of the port entrance. [summary]

My dear Thomas! New Yorkers can no longer frighten even their children with the French!

Extract of a letter from Charleston in South Carolina, March 20.
This morning, the tide brought 8 English warships across our bar; they are now riding in 5 fathoms of water. To our surprise, a warship and a frigate went across the bar tonight; I say to our surprise because we have been assured by our pilots and all those who know the bar, that it is impossible to render a warship so light as to cross this bank. But she has gone over and is now quietly riding at anchor.
Actually, the following have crossed the bar: one ship of 64, one of 50, one of 44 cannon, 5 frigates and other smaller warships. [inaccurate summary]

Boston Monday paper [Independent Ledger], May 22. *Out of Philadelphia, we have the report that Admiral Rodney has arrived in St. Lucia with 5 warships on April 24, and the English fleet there is 22 warships strong.* [accurate]

Worcester paper [Massachusetts Spy], May 25: *Boston from May 22.*
Extract out of a letter from Morristown, May 17.
Yesterday, a pilot boat with Captain Hallet came here from Alexandria, Virginia [Grenada] in 18 days. He told us that, before his departure, a dispatch had arrived there from Charlestown in South Carolina with the report that the enemy had undertaken an assault on this fortress but had been beaten back with the loss of 1,500 [150] dead but not many wounded and that General Clinton was among the dead. [selective]
Hartford, May 23. Last Friday, i.e., the 19th of this month, a great [very singular] darkness [of the visible heavens and atmosphere] reigned in this place, as far as we could ascertain, across the whole country [in the two neighboring towns from which we have heard.] [From 8 o'clock in the morning till 4 o'clock in the afternoon, it was so dark in the brightest room that without a light one could neither read nor write a letter. The following night, in spite of a full moon, there reigned darkness of

such density that it can only be compared to the Egyptian one.   Horses, dogs, and the like were unable to see.   The horses ran against houses, trees, and walls, the dogs were howling, etc.   Everything seemed to be yellow.]   *Our scientists and philosophers are herewith requested kindly to share with us their opinions about this darkness and about other particular phenomena in their special locations with a correct indication of the period of time, i.e., beginning, duration and end, about the hues of the colors in the clouds and about other visible, noteworthy objects.   It has, moreover, been reported that several persons have seen the solar disk in some places at the time of the greatest darkness.   We also wish to know this with [a reasonable degree of] certainty.* [selective]

At the end of this month, the guinea is worth 380 piasters in paper money.

Month of June 1780

Worcester paper [Massachusetts Spy], June 1: *[St.] Petersburg, Capital of Russia. [Jan. 20, 1780].*

A supplement to the geographical calendar in this city gives information about the appearance of a comet in the course of this year and the next, according to the table of Professor Lensel [?]. The table indicates the degrees of longitude and latitude it will cross. The comet will be visible from the month of May 1780 till the end of April 1781. If the calculation is correct, we will be able to see it during all that time. [accurate]

The following reports from London have been taken from the New York paper: London, Febr. 28.

Sir James Wallace was honorably acquitted by a court martial [at Portsmouth] for the loss of the warship Experiment. [accurate]

London, March 4. Yesterday, Sir James Wallace paid his respects to His Majesty the King and was most graciously received. [accurate]

London, March 7.   Admiral Digby has returned from his journey to Gibraltar and seized one ship of 64 cannon as well as 4 East Indian ships and taken them to Portsmouth [Plymouth]. [accurate]

London, March 10. When it was proposed in Parliament to raise a loan of 13 million, 20 million were immediately granted.

A few months ago, the Spanish naval power consisted of 46 warships, [since then] the Phoenix, Monarca, Diligente, Princesa and Guipuzcoana have been seized by us, the Domingo went up in flames and the San Eugenio and Julian were shattered against a rock; all this was brought about by Admiral Rodney; the Podagrosa capsized on her journey from Brest to Cadiz and two were demolished in the Bay of Cadiz. This mighty fleet was thus reduced to 35 warships and many of these 35 have been so damaged in the latest battle and by several gales that they are very much in need of repair.

All the reports agree that the combined French and Spanish fleet consists of 101 warships, and our fleet consists of 99 warships. But if one considers that many of ours are 3 stories high and almost all have copper bottoms and moreover so many of our fleet are ships of 74 cannon, one will immediately see the great difference. Moreover, we have 18 ships of 50 cannon, which we used to count among the warships in the last war, but which are no longer counted among these. We also have 10 of the most beautiful ships of 44 cannon, and a number of warships will be built this summer. When we add all these together, it must be obvious to everyone that we are able to continue ruling the oceans especially as we are still able to build new ships. We therefore can confront our enemies with a terrifying fleet, stronger than France and Spain will ever be able to have. [accurate]

Worcester paper [Massachusetts Spy], June 11 [8]. *We hear out of Providence [extract of a letter from Edenton, dated May 10] that a ship has arrived there from Edenton in North Carolina, bringing the news that the English have been defeated before Charleston and beaten back with a loss of 3,000 [300] men [killed and 250 taken prisoners]. [This report is believed all over Providence.]* [summary]

But my dear Thomas, it will not be believed all over Rutland![27]

The unusual phenomena in the atmosphere on Friday, the 19th of last month, were the same in New London, New Haven, Boston, and Hartford.

Rutland, June 6. Today, all the naval officers and merchants departed to Boston from here for the exchange. I accompanied them to Worcester.

Rutland, June 7. This morning, I heard in Worcester that last night the Hartford mail coach went to Boston with the message that Gen. Clinton had bombarded the fortress of Charleston from May 5 to 12. On that day, however, General Lincoln surrendered with his army, thus becoming prisoner of war.

Worcester paper [Massachusetts Spy], June 8. *Here the detailed report is given of the victory which Admiral Rodney had won over the Spanish fleet not far from Gibraltar. The following ships from the Spanish fleet, which were being commanded by Admiral Don Juan de Langara, have been brought into Gibraltar: Phoenix of 80 cannon and 700 men, San Julian, San Eugenio, Monarca, Princesa, Diligente, each of 70 cannon and 600 men.* [summary]
    Boston, June 6 [1]. Eight days ago, 2,000 Hessians embarked in New York and sailed toward the east or perhaps to Québec for they [the French there] are very worried. Others again say that they were returning to Europe because the Landgrave of Hesse-Cassel had recalled his troops, whom he had lent the British tyrants for a while and whose time of service had expired almost one year ago. [summary]
    From a letter from Edenton, we read that Charleston was still in our hands on May 10. This Edenton is noteworthy because as long as this town has existed, no man has yet been born there who has become more than 24 years old. It is said to be one of the most pleasant places in America. But when foreigners, especially Europeans, settle there, they have at times become 40 years old. This town lies between 2 rivers on a neck of land. [accurate]
    Fishkill, Jan. [June] 1. A party of enemy plunderers, commanded by Colonel DeLancey, landed at Horseneck last week where they did their King a questionable service in burning down 2 houses. In one of these was an old and deaf woman whom they let be consumed by the flames; they also murdered 5 militiamen.[28] [accurate]

Congress has taken a loan of 3 million piasters from France. I have already stated that one piaster is 1 schill. 8 groschen in Convention money.

The Province of Massachusetts Bay must send 5,000 men [of new troops] to the army; 15 men are going from Rutland. But they are having difficulties in bringing them together because each village here hires its own soldiers for a certain time. Some have been hired for 9 months, each [soldier] for 1,500 pounds in paper money, some also for 100 piasters in silver money; but it causes a great deal of trouble in each community to get the money together. [accurate]

Boston, June 12. A letter from the camp at Morristown, May 28, states:
We have the reliable report that His Excel. our Honorable Lieut. Gen. Washington has been graciously appointed Lieut. Gen. over the Royal French [troops] in North America and Vice Admiral of the white flag by His Most Christian Majesty, an honor never before bestowed on a foreigner. [accurate]

Worcester paper [Massachusetts Spy], June 15: *London, April 6.*
A number of Russian and Danish officers have recently arrived here to serve with the English fleet; they have high recommendations.
Parliament has received the confirmation of the revolt in Brest; here are the main reports about it. As soon as the order came for the troops to embark for North America, they all lost courage and were raving with discontent. One regiment stoutly and absolutely refused to embark; the garrison was immediately assembled and coercive measures taken. The revolt, however, got worse, even reaching a horrible pitch, until after many desperate scenes, and after the colonel of one regiment had been killed, it finally quieted down. The rebellious regiment was finally locked in, disarmed, brought into safety, and a report sent to the King. A few days thereafter, the following terrible judicial sentences from the King arrived, namely that 100 men [every 10th man belonging to this unhappy regiment was] were to be shot. This was carried out and frightened the rest so much that thereafter they embarked peaceably. It must be most unpleasant for this French fleet that Admiral Graves has been ordered to observe them with 9 warships and frigates.
In a Dutch ship, which has been brought into Yarmouth, 3 tons of sheet copper for the French fleet have been discovered. [accurate]
Parisian paper, March 4.
Contrary to all expectations, the English have called for reinforcement in Gibraltar and perhaps also in Port Mahon. A little refreshment for the English Ministry! But it contributes little or nothing at all to their power or benefit! At the same time and through a lucky coincidence, Rodney was hindered in his trip to the West Indies so that Comte de Guichen arrived before him. -- It is hoped that the large and appreciable force France entertains in America on water and on land this year will be of the greatest advantage to the Americans.
The war can be waged by France the more effectively and decisively since this power will find a lesser object. -- Their actions will be better carried out and the privateers will have more opportunity to do damage to their enemies. -- --Prenez garde vos [sic] monsieurs! [Pay attention, gentlemen!] [accurate]

Extract out of a letter from Paris, April 9.
In several of the coming months, a comet will be visible. It is the same wondrous apparition or the same light that was seen in the year 1680, thus one hundred years ago. It has been especially noted by Sir Isaac Newton that it was the same that appeared 43 years before the birth of Christ and in the same year in which Julius Caesar was murdered. Natural scientists have assured us that the course of this

extremely large fireball could not be measured at its last appearance in our air. Its course had gone beyond all calculation in numbers.[29] [accurate]

Worcester, June 15.
We are reliably informed that before May 2, the enemy threw no less than 10,000 [7,000] bombs into the fortress of Charleston and continually shot at this city from 800 [cannon] of the fleet and of their lines. [accurate]

Boston Monday paper [Independent Ledger], June 19: *Reports from Martinique from April 20 [23] state that 3 individual naval battles have occurred between the English and the French fleets in the West Indies. In the first two actions, the English fleet has taken flight but in the third it has been beaten and totally demolished.*
In one of these actions, Admiral Rodney was killed whereupon the flagship and the Sandwich, each of 98 cannon, lowered their sails and surrendered.[30]
Moreover, this newspaper is writing about several other places. Charleston had not yet surrendered on May 15 and the news being spread in New York by a handbill that Charleston had been taken by General Clinton [on May 12], was entirely false. [accurate]

Rutland. Next September, some new paper money will make its appearance, which is said to be equal [in value] to gold and silver. The old paper money will be exchanged for it and burned; Congress will give one [new] paper dollar for 40 old ones.

Boston Monday paper [Independent Ledger], June 26.
In this paper, the capture of Charleston is finally being announced and that on order of Congress.
It would be too lengthy to translate all the letters that had been exchanged between the commanding Generals Clinton and Lincoln before the capitulation; they are 24 in number.
The fortress was surrendered on May 12; thus the handbill given out in New York was not wrong. The garrison marched out with all the honors of war and was then made prisoner. [There were 7 generals, namely Major Gen. Lincoln, Brigade Generals Moultrie, McIntosh, Woodford, Scott, Du Portail and Hogun; 9 colonels, 14 lieut. colonels, 15 majors, 84 capt. and staff capts., 84 lieuts. and sec. lieuts., 32 ensigns, 209 noncommissioned officers, 140 fifers and drummers and 1,977 privates.] *During the siege, the following were killed: 1 colonel, 1 aide-de-camp, 8 [6] capts., 3 lieuts., 10 sergeants, 58 [68] privates. One major, 2 capts., 5 lieuts., 18 sergeants and 114 privates were wounded. All these were from the Continental troops without the militia, so says the report. The militia was so scattered about in the fortress that no list of their losses has come in as yet.* [selective]

N.B. Look back and read the article from Poughkeepsie quoted previously [on p. 189].

Worcester paper [Massachusetts Spy], June 29: *Trenton, June 10 [14].*
From here comes the report that the English and the Germans, under the command of Gen. [von] Knyphausen, have made inroads in New York as far as Elizabethtown Point on June 6 and penetrated up to the Connecticut Farms 2 miles from Springfield. As it is customary with the English, they burned 10 [20] of the best farms [about every building in the Connecticut Farms above]; to give another example of British inhumanity, they shot Mrs. Caldwell,[31] *one of the fairest in*

character and appearance, as she was holding her little child in her lap in her room [as she sat in her parlor, attended only by her maid and small child]. [summary]

My dear Thomas! This was certainly not done intentionally but by happenstance. -- In war, the most unforeseen things can happen.

They also announce from there that Gen. Clinton has arrived in Staten Island from South Carolina with a reinforcement; moreover, that 5 officers and 35 privates, who were American prisoners, have deserted from New York on the 4th of this month. [summary]

New York, June 10. From the latest news from England that we have received from the Royal ship Triton, we have learned that on Good Friday, Commodore Walsingham, who is about to sail to the West Indies, has left with a favorable wind. His fleet consists of 3,000 [300] transport and merchant ships, which have a few thousand troops on board, and [without frigates] are being covered by the following ships of 74 cannon: the Thunderer, Egmont, Berwick, Ramillies, and Torbay. When the French fleet departs from Brest, Admiral [Thomas] Graves has orders to go immediately after them with the following fleet which consists of beautiful, new ships, all provided with copper bottoms: London of 98 [90] [cannon], Resolution, Shrewsbury, Invincible Defence, Royal Oak, Marlborough, Monarque, [Bedford] each of 74 [cannon]; Prudent and America, each of 64. They will join up in Torbay with Commodore Walsingham, [and another 6 warships will be joining them.].[32] [accurate]

Extract from a letter from an officer of the prisoner ship Falmouth off New York, April 7.

'I only wanted to say that I am a prisoner here on the ship Falmouth, a most dismal prison where we have no room to lie down. When we go to bed, we have to lie down at the same time and whenever one of us wants to turn, all have to do so. This is a hellish, confounded hole, of which no one can form an idea. Never have people been locked in such an abominable hole, that can only be compared to hell. This is the British way of treating us." [accurate]

Now, something to remember, my dear Thomas!

After we had been captured not far from Bennington on Aug. 16, 1777, our officers and privates were taken on board a guard ship off Boston, also a dismal hole. They were treated there with unspeakable contempt and tyranny; the victuals they were given, were lying on deck and the sailors stepped on them with their feet. They had to lie way down in the ship on the bare floor where rats and mice were running over them to and fro and did not let them sleep. I have frequently heard this from many [people]; I myself have fortunately not been there.

At the end of this month, the guinea is worth 420 piasters in paper money.

Month of July 1780

Worcester paper [Massachusetts Spy], July 6.

After the surrender of Charleston, Admiral Arbuthnot summoned all the officers from our ships, paid them many fine compliments and made them great promises. He used all his eloquence to persuade them to enter the British service but they magnanimously refused to do so. Nevertheless he found occasion to persuade some of the foreigners. -- The English have now confessed on their own that they lost 1,700 men in the Charleston siege.[33] [accurate]

From the Hartford Post, Baltimore, June 20.
The very famous General Arnold, who is called the American Hannibal in England, left Philadelphia a few days ago and continued his journey to the army to take his command under His Excel. General Washington. [accurate]

Stop, my good Thomas! You have misspoken, you wanted to say Arnold, the American horse trader. Yes indeed, this had been his title before this war, because he used to trade horses selling those from New England to Canada and the Canadian horses back to New England. Many Canadians have told me this in the year 1776, and here in New England every farmer knows him and calls him Arnold, the horse trader. He has his home not far from Hartford in the Province of Connecticut.

Boston, June 30. News from headquarters on June 19 says that Gen. [von] Knyphausen continues to remain in Elizabethtown. General Clinton has actually arrived in New York with reinforcements and will apparently join up with Gen. [von] Knyphausen. [summary]
Charleston in South Carolina, June 8. Last Tuesday, the news came that Colonel Tarleton has won a major victory over the Rebels. Gen. Clinton had the pleasure of announcing it to the Royal army and navy as well as to the [loyal] inhabitants.[34] [accurate]
Headquarters at Charleston Neck, June 1, 1780.
[General Order]. *The gen.-in-chief congratulates the army on the victory that has been won over the enemy at the outer frontier of this Province by Lieut. Gen. Count Cornwallis. Lieut. Colonel Tarleton was commanded to pursue the enemy with a corps of cavalry, infantry and the British Legion. After a forced march of two days, in which they marched nearly 100 miles, they reached the Rebels. These rejected the conditions of surrender. One hundred and seventy of them were cut to pieces* [sic]: *cannon, flags, baggage etc. of the entire corps were captured.*
Our losses are small but are mentioned with greatest regret by His Excel.: two officers and 3 privates were killed, one officer and 16 privates wounded [20 officers, noncommissioned officers and privates wounded].
List of the killed, wounded, and captured Rebels: killed were 1 lieut. colonel, 8 captains, 14 noncommissioned officers, 1 adjutant, 1 reg. quartermaster and 293 privates dead and wounded. Captured were 50 men. Taken as booty were 2 metal 6 pound cannon, 2 howitzers, 3 flags, 2 ammunition wagons and 35 with baggage etc.
A ship from New Providence has brought the message that Admiral Rodney has seized 2 French warships in the West Indies and sent them to Antigua. [selective]

Boston Monday paper [Independent Ledger], July 20 [10]: *Philadelphia, June 24* [27].
Extract out of a letter from Morristown, June 23. Gen. Knyphausen set out from his camp this morning with 14 [13] regiments, which consisted of about 5,000 men as well as the new corps, and advanced toward our right wing, which was commanded by General Greene. They marched up to Springfield and after having burned the place, they withdrew again. [accurate]
June 24. We have been informed that Clinton has gone up the North [Hudson] *River with all the forces he has been able to assemble. He will apparently be joined by [von] Knyphausen.*

London, March 12. A gentleman who has recently left Paris says that it is absolutely certain that the Spanish fleet will be 42 warships strong this spring. They will unite with 72 French warships and thus will amount to a fleet of 114 warships without [counting] frigates etc. [accurate]

Worcester paper [Massachusetts Spy], July 13. *On the 22nd of last month, several transport ships left Sandy Hook; they had 3 Hessian Regiments about to sail to Québec on board.* [accurate]

Fishkill, June 29. Last week, 90 sails, large and small ships, appeared on the North River not far across from Colonel Phillips' House, and we surmised that Gen. Clinton intended an attack on West Point. But since our militia had quickly assembled, most went back down the river. This excursion may also have been made so as better to carry out their plan of burning and ravaging in New Jersey. -- To be sure, they had burned Springfield but had to pay dearly for it, for, according to the most reliable account, their loss amounted to about 700 [500] men. [summary]

New York paper, June 19: London, March 30.
Our latest news from Braunschweig indicate that when the last mail was sent, the ruling Duke was at his last gasp and it is believed that the next mail will bring the news of his death.[35] [accurate]

Out of Brest, we got the news of a horrible happening. On the 9th [of this month], a large Dutch ship was announced riding about off the harbor and, as far as one could judge, without pilots and sailors. As the sea was rather calm, 2 ships immediately set sail to see what the reason was. At their arrival, the men were not a little astonished to see a man hanging from the mainyard. When some of them immediately went aboard, they discovered that it was the captain and to their even greater surprise, they found all the crew lying dead on deck and it was even stranger yet that all these dead had been nailed down. The ship was taken into port and it was found out that none of the entire cargo was touched. This extraordinary incident raised everyone's curiosity. Several ships immediately set sail to see if anything could be found out or discovered by whom and how this brutal act of inhumanity had been carried out. [accurate]

My dear Thomas! This again is quite a strange lie. Those who had seized the ship would have rather taken her as a good prize and made the crew prisoners. For they could know in advance that such a deed could not be kept secret -- and sailors, who does not know their desire for money!

In a New York paper from July [June] 21, it is written that on every occasion, the Rebels declare their losses as being less than they really are. They have again done this before Charleston for the number of these Rebels imprisoned in this fortress is no less than 7,000 men.[36] [not found]

Worcester paper [Massachusetts Spy], July 21: *Boston, July 18.*
With the greatest pleasure, we can now inform our readers of the successful arrival of the fleet [armament] from Brest at Newport. The news of this great, happy event was yesterday sent to the High Council of this city by General Heath through a dispatch, and a number of private letters. [accurate]

Worcester, July 19 [21]. For the past 8 days, more than 3,000 men of the militia have gone through this Province [state] and New Hampshire and are continuing their march to the Province of New York. We can only hope for a good outcome of the preparations that are being made in several provinces. [accurate]

Paris, Febr. 19. Preparations being made in St. Malo and orders issued by the Ministry not to have the English prisoners of war who are to be exchanged embark, make us think that the project of a landing in one of the Kingdoms of His British Majesty has in no way been abandoned. The division, which Monsieur de Ternay will command, and which consists of 12 warships, is apparently destined for North America. [accurate]

Paris, Febr. 20. Everything is being prepared with the greatest zeal for an expedition. There is also talk everywhere that the fleet destined for America will take along a small army of about 12,000 men, who are to be put into action in that continent. [accurate]

March 2. Yesterday, Marquis de Lafayette had his farewell audience with His Majesty in Versailles. He is going back to America and will serve under Comte de Rochambeau, who will go there with 12,000 men [8 regiments] to give support to the United States. The fleet, accompanying these troops, is likewise destined for America and consists of 12 warships. The troops have received orders to march to Brest on the 15th of this month.[37] [selective]

From a London paper, March 26. All the Royal ships at Spithead gave the customary sign of mourning on the occasion of the death of Sir Charles Hardy.

From the same London paper comes the detailed description of the naval battle, which has taken place in the West Indies between Admiral Rodney and Comte de Guichen, in which the latter was beaten.

There is a report out of Providence that a Spanish fleet has arrived in the West Indies.

Extract out of a letter to the High Council in Boston, from Maj. Gen. Heath, dated Newport, July 21.[38]

'*On the 13th of this month, Admiral Graves arrived in New York with 6 warships. This afternoon 15 or 16 large Engl. warships appeared east of Block Island; Admiral Graves has presumably joined Admiral Arbuthnot, which makes the English stronger than the French. From some deserters from New York, we have learned that the arrival of the French fleet in Rhode Island has greatly terrified the occupation forces in New York. The inhabitants are also frightened and make plans for their own personal safety as well as that of their possessions.* [not found]

Worcester paper [Massachusetts Spy], July 27: *Madrid, Capital of Spain, March 27, from the camp at San Roque.*

The enemy is daily improving their fortifications, planting more cannon and exercising their troops. For several days, they have not fired a single shot in our direction at our men; they have returned 303 prisoners of war in exchange for an equal number [from our side]. [accurate]

Boston, July 21. The latest news we have from England tells that Parliament has forbidden trading with the American Colonies. This shows that they consider them lost. We also have reliable information that England finds herself in such [restrained] circumstances that she cannot send any recruits to the army in New York; because Ireland is lost, everything is in confusion in England and all of Europe has declared itself against England. Yet they do not want to give up their arrogance and stubbornness. [selective]

Extract out of a letter of a distinguished officer from Newport to his friends in this city, July 13.

I wish you were here. You would enjoy yourselves, our harbor is a splendid sight. The First French Division consisted of 7 warships of 64 to 88 cannon, a hospital ship of 64 cannon and a large number of transport ships.

You know that I have always been an admirer of our allies but I was never so happy about the naval and army officers as I am now. Last night, our city was illuminated and there was joy on all the faces. -- Everything seems favorable to our [great and] just cause.

The general and the commodore are the most affable men. They are playing officer and great lord. [accurate]

Philadelphia, July 18 [12]. Yesterday, Capt. McClanaghan came here after a short journey from S. Eustatius. We learned from him that without counting the frigates, the French and Spanish fleet in the West Indies was 36 warships strong; that in St. Lucia the English fleet had locked up part of them; that everyone there is of the opinion that all the Engl. islands in the West Indies will shortly be in the possession of our allies. [accurate]

Boston Monday paper [Independent Ledger], July 23: *Extract out of a letter from St. Pierre, July 8.*

A fleet of 23 French and 9 Spanish warships have sailed from Fort Royal to Grenada [Guadeloupe] with 2,000 land forces on board to unite there with 12,000 Spanish troops and then undertake a landing at St. Christopher. [accurate]

[in English]

An Infallible Cure for Love.

Take the Spirit of Indifference one Ounce, of the Powder of Disdain twelve Grains, of the oil of absence, and the Spice of Employment of each ten ounces with three ounces of good advice, and the same quantity of Sound Confederation, put them into a Small Sauce pan of Sound Reason with two quarts of best Hearts café Stir and boil them together with a Considerable Time, then strain them through a fine rag of Patience into a Vessel of Prudence and take half a pint of this mixture just going to Bed and lay upon You as many Coverlets as You can get or will be sufficient to give you a Sweet [sic], by Closely observing the above directions You'll certainly be cured.

To Maistre George the King! From the London General Advertiser.

Ha! Ho! So! You are comparing yourself to William, the Dutchman, do you not? And when your subjects leave you and do not want to submit to the present government of an impudent, villainous and unintelligent minister chosen by you, you say that you want to leave them and go to Germany, settling there in one of your provinces just as that other one once wanted to do when he was annoyed. May God be with you on your miserable, stupid and asinine journey, my dear George! William and you are as different from each other as an honest man is from a broom stick. The English found it necessary at that time to keep William and his Dutchmen in a good mood, but we do not care how malcontent you and your swine are. William was loved and you are despised. James, a tyrant and a blockhead, was chased out of the country and nevertheless kept on hoping to regain William's place. To lose William would indeed have meant a loss. To lose you cannot mean a loss; leave him behind who will rule after you. Reflect on what you are doing and quickly get rid of your infamous minister or your place will -- --. The longer you are playing the donkey, the greater will be your shame in the end. This is inevitable --.

Your wife is a good woman and your son a very promising fellow. With them but without you, we will be the happiest people on earth. I beg of you in God's name, leave, the sooner the better, and never to return; take along Boreas, Minden, Twitcher,[39] Sir Hugh and all your belligerent donkeys and swine. This will be a marvelous farewell!

Bon voyage! Adieu, soon, soon -- poor George!

-- signed Millions.

At the end of this month, the guinea is worth 390 piasters in paper money.

Month of August 1780

Boston Monday paper [Independent Ledger], Aug. 7: *Extract out of a letter from West Point, July 5.*

Captain Sacket was sent to White Plains with a small party, where he encountered a strong party of Royal British cattle thieves. He killed 16 [11] men and took 15 prisoner, seized 400 oxen and cows and brought all of them to Fishkill. [accurate]

[Boston, Aug. 7]. *Last Tuesday, the ship <u>Essex</u>, which was commanded by Captain Cathcart, arrived here after a short cruise. She had taken 4 rich prizes, loaded with dry goods and provisions, away from the English. These 4 ships had been destined for Québec. Two have already come in here and the others are expected by the hour.* [not found]

Boston [Independent Ledger], Aug. 7 [10]: *Philadelphia, July 25 [26]. On Thursday, the 19th of this month, the first and second Pennsylvania brigades set out from their [respective] camps under the command of Brig. Gen. Wayne with the order of taking [collecting and bringing off those] cattle in Bergen county, which was immediately exposed to the enemy. Having carried out the order, they visited a blockhouse on their way back, that was located in the vicinity of Bergen town. It had been built and garrisoned by a number of refugees, and that under duress, so that they would not to be forced into the British sea service. This building was found proof against light artillery. One part of these 2 Pennsylvanian regiments was ordered to take this blockhouse by assault. But having taken it and seized all the abatis and the pickets, it became absolutely necessary to withdraw. There was in fact no other entrance to the blockhouse but a subterranean passage that could be passed through by but one person at a time. Our loss consists of 69 men, dead and wounded, incl. three officers.[40]* [accurate]

N.B. I would have liked that blockhouse, it seems to have been similar to a rabbit's burrow?

Worcester, Aug. 10. We have been informed that 33 Engl. merchant ships destined for Québec have been seized in different latitudes by our allies and taken to several eastern ports. We can soon expect important news from the South because both armies are in motion. [summary]

Boston [Independent Ledger], Aug. 14: *New York, July 22 [24]*.

A large French ship called LeFarjes and coming from East India from the Island of Mauritius was brought here with 150 men last Friday. Admiral Graves had seized it. It is the richest ship that has ever been brought into a North American harbor; her cargo consists of silk, tea, coffee, pepper, spices etc. [accurate]

New Haven, Aug. 3. Several deserters who have sailed with the latest fleet to Huntington from New York, arrived here with the news that the Blonde, a British frigate of 32 cannon, has capsized in the sound [Hell Gate], but that all the men have been rescued. [accurate]

N.B. This was one of the most beautiful frigates ever built in England. It was she that had escorted us, the First Division of the Ducal Braunschweig troops, to America.

Worcester paper [Massachusetts Spy], Aug. 17: *Poughkeepsie, July 27*.

We hear from the lines of our army [in Westchester County] that a number of deserters daily come over to us from the enemy and that, at the same time, 30 [of them all well armed and equipped], [mostly Hessians], have arrived [came off in a body]. We also have a report that Lieut. Gen. Burgoyne's army is to be exchanged for the prisoners of war in Charleston and that there is hope for a general exchange of prisoners to come to pass. [accurate]

N.B. During the past 3 years, I have often read this paragraph in public papers but it has always been revoked. The general exchange will coincide with peace, my dear Thomas.

Boston paper [Independent Ledger], Aug. 21. *We have learned that a corps of Refugees, 1,000 men strong and serving with the British, has been captured, killed or scattered by our colonel and 400 men.* [summary]

N.B. Those fellows must indeed have been desperate but we first need a confirmation.

The Portland of 50 cannon and 4 frigates are in Newfoundland. This place is occupied by 1,500 men, who are afraid that the French naval power may pay them a visit. [accurate]

This paper gives a very detailed description of a revolt in England. Forty to fifty thousand rebels have been supported and led by Lord George Gordon; this Lord has been taken prisoner and put in the Tower. [41]

In the papers, much ado is being made about the fact that the fleet, consisting of 30 ships and destined for Québec, has been seized.

Each cargo is said to have a value of 20,000 pounds, but today we have learned from an English officer, who had come on said fleet as prisoner of war to Rutland from England, that the enemy has not kept more than 5 ships of this fleet. The rest has been retaken by the English sailors and now successfully brought in to Halifax and New York. This officer is Lieut. [*Colonel*] Hill from the 9th Regiment.

On Aug. 23, a package with letters arrived here from our Maj. Gen. von Riedesel from New York and I had the pleasure of receiving letters from my wife, son and daughter, dated Jan. 30, 1780.

I was greatly pleased about the good state of health of my wife and children at that time but deeply grieved about the news that my brother had died on April 10, 1779. Thus, the hope of seeing him again in this world has vanished.

Worcester paper [Massachusetts Spy], Aug. 31: *London, May 12 [11].*
Extract out of a letter from Portsmouth [Gosport], May 9 [19].
*Sir Charles Hardy, Admiral and Commodore of the grand Engl. fleet, died
yesterday morning when the podagra [gout] had entered his stomach. He had
arrived here [in Portsmouth] last Tuesday and was saluted by the fleet on
Wednesday morning. His flag is flying half-mast at present and will remain so
until after his burial. He will presumably be buried in Westminster Abbey. In the
present troubles, his death is considered a great loss. Capt. Kempenfelt had to
remain with him until his death, as he so desired. He was 67 years old and 58 years
in the service of the King. Without counting his jewelry [landed property], he left
140,000 pounds sterling in pure gold. It is said that he has bestowed an appreciable
sum to the school at Chelsea, where naval officers are being educated and trained.*
[accurate]

The Worcester paper [Massachusetts Spy], Aug. 31, *says that a rattlesnake was
killed in Petersham as big as has ever been seen there before. Twenty-two young
ones ran out of her throat when she was opened up, the smallest of whom was 7
inches long.* [She was 5 foot 6 inches long and the thread with which her length was
measured was 16 1/2 inches long. She had 14 bells on her tail.] [accurate]

N.B. This incident confirms that which I have already said on p. 118, i.e., that
whenever there is danger, the young snakes creep into the old one's throat -- behind a
fortification, as it were.[42]
As I visited some sick people in Petersham, I had the opportunity to see the skin of
the reptile that had by now been stuffed; it was beautifully marked. I asked the man to
sell me the skin. "No," he said, "I won't. But if you want to take it back to Germany
with you, I shall give it to you as a present." I have it with me and shall try to preserve
it.

From the New York Mercury, Aug. 4: *Charleston, South Carolina, July 13.*
*The sloop Industry arrived here yesterday, having come from [New] Providence
in 7 days. We have learned from her that on the day of her departure from there, the
Roebuck (Capt. Ross) of 44 cannon had arrived from S. Christopher with the glorious
news that Admiral Rowley has seized 25 Spanish transport ships with troops on
board, destined for Havana. He has sent these to St. Kitts and Barbados where they
all have safely arrived.* [accurate]

Boston [Continental Journal], Aug. 24. *Last night, a cartel ship entered the port
here from Newfoundland. She had 140 American prisoners of war on board, who
had been imprisoned there for some time and been uncommonly well treated during
their captivity.* [selective]

Poetry [in English H.D.]

I sing still of Fanny, sweet Fanny my fair,
Whose lips are like rubies, like down her soft hair.
Her cheeks like the morning when with blushes be spread
And her eyes like two planets they such influence shed.
I first loved my charmer for that she was neat,
Was lovely, was lively, was kind and complete,
Was the queen of all beauty, was my fancy, fair queen,
Was comely in feature, in shape, and in mien.

I next lov'd my fair one for the charms of her breast
None of which no fair female now even possess'd,
Wit, sense, and good humor have rooted this thane
And virtue, and truth and the fruit that they bane.
I now love my Fanny not alone for her charms,
Combined with such virtue as her chaste bosom warms,
Not because she's an angel if on earth such there be,
But my Fanny I love, because Fanny loves me.

At the end of this month, the guinea has a value of 350 piasters in paper money.

Month of Sept. 1780

Boston Monday paper [Independent Ledger], Sept. 4: *Providence, Aug. 24 [26]*.
Last Thursday afternoon, the general review of the French army took place at Newport. All the cannon of the fleet and all the batteries of the city were fired. This new, magnificent show, altogether unknown to us, which gave the multitude of spectators the greatest pleasure, cannot be praised enough. Everybody saw this as a good omen for future happy enterprises. [accurate]

Prenez garde, vous messieurs! [Be on your guard, gentlemen.]

News from Weston is that on the 1st of this month, 20 French warships were riding at anchor at Cap François and that the Spanish fleet sailed to the Island of Cuba.
In Jan. of this year, reports came from Russia and France that a comet would appear in the month of May, which would be visible until April 1781, i.e., an entire year. Did anybody in Germany see this comet? Here in America, nobody has seen or heard of it. Or perhaps they will see it later? The latest news from Europe tells that the English national debt amounts to 220 million pounds sterling.

From the Hartford Post [Connecticut Courant, Sept. 5]: *Philadelphia, Aug. 19 [23]*.
On the 17th of this month, the brig Bellona arrived here as a truce ship from Charleston, South Carolina with a number of ladies. These cannot sing praises enough about the courtesy with which they have been treated by the English officers on sea and on land. Moreover, we have learned that all the troops from Charleston have joined Lord Cornwallis except for 1 or 2 regiments of Hessians, who have remained behind as occupation forces. Lord Cornwallis, however, has withdrawn until Charleston. [We have also been informed] *that the Engl. Cavalry was almost cut off in an action, that Colonel Tarleton has been wounded and Lord Rawdon killed.* [selective]

Worcester [Massachusetts Spy], Sept. 7. *On Monday, Gen. Lincoln passed through this city to Elizabethtown in New Jersey to meet up with Gen. Phillips, who will get there from New York, to effect an exchange of the Convention troops.* [accurate]

Nothing but useless and vain attempts.

Baltimore, Aug. 8 [3]. The English papers say that 61 warships [from 110 to 14 guns] have been built in England, which had been ready in the beginning of June;

namely 25 warships, 7 [1] of 50 [52] cannon [6 of 50, 4 of 44 cannon]; 27 [23] frigates of 28 to 44 cannon and 2 sloops of war. [accurate]

    New York, Royalist paper, July 12.

    South America is now being attacked with force, especially by the successful Gen. Dalling, who has sailed there from Jamaica. The First Division under Colonel Polson and the 2nd under Brigadier Campbell have already reached the San Juan River and seized the castle by the same name [San Juan del Sur]. *This is 15 miles above Lake Nicaragua, on which stand the rugged fortresses [rich cities] of Granada and Leon. This undertaking will quite probably form the base for the sovereign authority [establishing a base] upon the great South Seas.*[43] [accurate]

    Rutland, Sept. 11. Today, Captain von Bärtling went to New York to get some money.

Anecdote

    A Scottish priest was studying the Revelation of St. John and now believed for sure that women had no souls and were therefore free from future rewards and punishments. But as soon as his doctrine had spread in the country, he was challenged by all his brethren, the priests, to receive the reward for all the errors he had committed during his time in office. When he had appeared, he was asked whether he really had such a poor opinion [of women]. *He answered* [with a quote] *from the Revelation of St. John. 'You will find this quote,' he said, 'in the 8th Chapter, Vers. 4, where it is written, 'And as he opened the seventh seal, there was a silence of half an hour in Heaven'? Now I challenge you all, my colleagues, to ask yourselves if this could have been possible if women had been present. Since then none have gotten there and the attraction to this sex leads us to believe that they are in an evil place. The consequence of this is that they possess no immortal parts and should consider themselves lucky that all the troubles and bad tricks they create in the world are our responsibility.'*

    Worcester paper [Massachusetts Spy], Sept. 14: *Boston, Sept. 7.*

    On the 16 [15]th of last month, the eternally memorable Aug. 16, 1777 was celebrated with all solemnity. [That was the day on which the Baum Corps and the Braunschweig Dragoon Regiment had been captured.] *Fourteen toasts were pronounced and 14 cannon fired. Bennington is in Vermont County in the Province of New Hampshire. As they have indicated with the 14 toasts, the inhabitants want to have their own Province, but Congress does not want to recognize them as yet.*

    Last Monday, the mighty Captain Sanford and the 2 Lieuts. Miller and Davis broke out of the jail at Concord. They had broken their parole and belonged to the infamous, bestial, and murderous Tarleton's Cavalry, who were serving the British tyrant and are at present in Charleston. There, they have daily given convincing samples of their unheard-of acts of inhumanity as e.g. in the massacre of the amiable, gallant Colonel Buford and 170 men in front of this man's [Buford] *Corps at Lynche's Creek in South Carolina. Mr. Clinton had wished his bandits luck for this cruel feat.*[44] [summary]

    N.B. See the paragraph from the Worcester paper, July 6. [p. 199]

    Worcester paper [Massachusetts Spy], Sept. 14. *We have the report from the Hartford Post that an aide-de-camp of Gen. Gates has arrived at Congress in Philadelphia with the news that this general and his army have been totally beaten* and dispersed [by Lord Cornwallis]. *Gen. Gates had scarcely been able to take to flight and was pursued for 60 miles by 380 [300] cavalrymen. We do not wish to state this as absolutely true and hope to give you a more detailed report in the next paper.*[45] [summary]

Boston Monday paper [Independent Ledger], September 18: *Baltimore, Aug. 25. The confirmation is herewith given that Gen. Gates has been totally beaten not far from Camden in South Carolina and that he had to flee to Hillsborough, 60 miles from the battlefield. He is now trying to reassemble his army to make another attempt.* [accurate]

N.B. I wished Lieut. Gen. Burgoyne had beaten Gen. Gates.

We have also been informed that 3 of our American privateers have been seized in the St. Lawrence River and taken to Québec.

N.B. Those were really a bit too bold.

At the end of this month, the guinea has the value of 350 piasters in paper money.

Month of October 1780

[In English]

Poetry: The Ladies' Generous Confession

Too plain dear Youth that telltale Egis -- my heart your own declare
For Heavens sake let it suffice -- you reign triumphant there,
Forbear your utmost skill to ley [sic] -- no farther urge your sway,
Press not for what I must deny -- for fear I should obey.

Could all your arts successful prove -- Would you a maid undo!
Whose only failing is her love -- And that her Love for you
Say would you use that very Power -- You from her Goodness claim:
Therein in one fatal Hour -- a life of spotless fame.

Desist my dear to do her ill -- because perhaps you may
But rather try your utmost skill -- to save me than betray
Be you yourself my virtuous Garde -- Defend and not pursue
Since t'is a Task for me too hard -- to strive with love and you.

Boston [Continental Journal] paper, Oct. 2 [5]: *Boston. We know that in spite of their boasting, the Royalists in New York have to live very thriftily because everything is so dreadfully expensive. For one pound of fresh meat, they have to pay 3 shill. sterl. or 21 groschen 6 cent. Last Saturday, a truce ship arrived from Halifax with 70 prisoners of war, who praise the good treatment* [they have received] *from the English.* [accurate]

Worcester paper [Massachusetts Spy], Oct. 5: *Hartford, Sept. 20. Yesterday, His Excel. General Washington, Governor Trumbull, Comte Rochambeau, Admiral Torbay, Marquis de Lafayette, Gen. Knox and several distinguished officers of our allies arrived here and were saluted by 10 cannon shots. They held a conference.* [accurate]

Fishkill, Sept. 28. Last Monday, His Excel. Gen. Washington, coming from Hartford, passed through this city and continued his march to West Point. On his arrival, one of the greatest treacheries that had been committed by the infamous General Arnold was discovered. The latter had presumably let himself be blinded by British gold to surrender West Point to the English. [accurate]

Arnold had sent John [Joshua] Smith from Haverstraw on board the enemy privateer Vulture, which was riding at anchor not far away, to take Colonel Robinson ashore because Arnold had something important to discuss with him. The colonel refused to go ashore but Major André, adjutant general of the Engl. army and first aide-de-camp of General Clinton, went ashore with Smith. Arnold talked with him in secret for awhile and then went with him to Smith's House. The following morning, Arnold asked for a different set of clothing for Major [John] André because he might be recognized in his regimentals. Smith provided him with such. The following day, André was prevented from going on board the Vulture because our cannonboat was in the river, whereupon they decided to go by land. Arnold gave our passports to André and Smith for getting through our lines. On Saturday morning, Smith successfully took André across the border and thinking him out of danger, left him. Thereupon, André came upon 3 of our militiamen, who asked André for some money for beer. Because he had no other money but gold on him and also wished to get rid of the fellows, he gave them a guinea. Since this was a very strange experience for the Americans, who were used to seeing nothing but paper money, these people surmised that he must be a spy and arrested him. He begged and promised them many thousands of guineas if they would let him go but these fellows assured him that they were native Americans, who would not let themselves be blinded by 100,000 guinea pieces and forget their duty. They took him to the headquarters fortress at West Point, where he was examined. In his boots, Arnold's passport from the fortress West Point was found and also the reliable report of the crews, ammunition, provisions etc., together with his plan of surrendering all this to General Clinton. André and Smith were both taken into custody, will have a hearing and receive their rewards. Upon learning of Gen. Washington's arrival as well as of the presence of a spy at headquarters and of Smith's arrest, Arnold became greatly confused, had his horse brought over to him, hastened away and got into his boat, that took him on board the Vulture. There he is now in safety. He has written a letter to Gen. Washington assuring him that neither his wife nor the officers of his suite had known anything of his undertaking. We will soon be able to report more.[46] [accurate]

Worcester, Oct. 9 [5]. Several very valuable prizes have lately been brought into Boston and Philadelphia. [accurate]

A letter from Weston has given us the news that 6,000 troops have embarked in New York, who have been intended for Virginia or Newport; they have taken many cannon and much ammunition along. [accurate]

Rutland, Oct. 8. General Lincoln has sent a very amicable letter to the officers in captivity at Rutland assuring them that a general exchange of prisoners of war will certainly come off etc., but when? -- Surely not before the end of the war.

New York [The Gazette and the Weekly Mercury], Sept. 4: *Extract out of a letter from London, July 5.*

The hearings concerning the insurgents in London have started, many of them will be executed. One believes that Lord Gordon will be one of them; his fate will be decided in 2 weeks.[47] [accurate]

[Massachusetts Spy, Oct. 12]: *Admiral Rodney has arrived at Sandy Hook with 10 warships and 2 frigates.* [accurate]

They are reporting a great deal in this paper from Boston about the cruelties of the Savages near the Mohawk River and the adjacent countryside. [*We have also been informed*] that General Clinton has written to Gen. Washington not to have Major André executed because he had gone ashore on a truce ship and could therefore not be considered a spy. But this would seem ridiculous to Gen. Washington etc.

Worcester paper [Massachusetts Spy], Oct. 12: *Fishkill, Oct. 5.*
Out of headquarters, we have the news that Major André received the deserved reward for his work, i.e., he adorned the gallows last Monday. The fate of this unhappy man is much deplored by his enemies but will be approved by the laws of all the nations. Judging by his comportment at the end, one can say that even if he did not die a good Christian, he surely died like a brave soldier! He died in the prime of life, Major André. The pride and the rose of the British army; -- the friend and confidant of Sir Henry Clinton.
Moreover, we have been informed that the truly infamous Arnold, through whom this unhappy André had lost his life, has betrayed many of our friends in New York who have remained faithful to our just cause, and that as many as 80 [50] of them have been thrown into jail. [accurate]

N.B. This is the same Arnold whom quite recently the Americans used to call the American Hannibal.

Boston Thursday paper [Independent Chronicle], Oct. 12.
The following is a letter that Major André had written to Gen. Washington.
Sir! Buoyed above the fear of Death by the Consciousness of a life Spent in the pursuit of Honor, and fully Sensible that it has at no Time been Stained by any Action which at this Serious Moment Could give me remorse, -- I have to Solicit your Excellency if there is anything in my Character which Excites Your Esteem, if ought in my Circumstances can impress you with Compassion, that I may be permitted to die the death [dead] of a Soldier. -- It is my last request, and I hope it will be granted. I have the Honor to be etc. [accurate] [A translation into German follows]

Chatham, Sept. 27. Gen. Phillips and Gen. Lincoln were both in Elizabethtown last week to effect the exchange of the prisoners of war, yet like all previous ones, this meeting turned out to be futile; they will soon reconvene on Long Island. [accurate]

Boston Monday paper [Independent Ledger], Oct. 16: *Boston. The following has been forgotten to be announced:*
A correspondent has expressed his admiration for the worthy inhabitants of Cambridge, who had to suffer so much from the prisoners of war and their connections in that place. It is quite true that they have asked to have them removed to another place but they are still in Cambridge. May God let us live in those happy times when our official laws were not being trampled on and an officer, not following the order to move the prisoners to another place, was immediately

dismissed. -- It was a noble word Peter spoke when Simon tried to bribe him: 'May your money perish with you,' he said. -- If only commissaries over the prisoners had a little of Peter's spirits. -- Would God they had! [accurate]

Worcester paper [Massachusetts Spy], Oct. 19: *Extract out of a letter from Toppan* [sic], *Oct. 2.*

Before you receive this, you will have heard of Arnold's infernal treachery. It is impossible for human nature per se to unfold from within a greater quantity of sins and treachery than he possesses all by himself. There is [perhaps] no obligation he owes God and nature that he has not violated. It has now been discovered that Hell itself had already claimed him its own when he was but a tender youth and infused him with all kinds of devilish and evil deeds. [accurate]

N.B. Poor Arnold! How would you fare if you had had the misfortune to fall into your own countrymen's power! You would nevertheless be rewarded according to your crime, for your crime will always remain abominable before the world! A traitor to his country!

Boston Monday paper [Independent Ledger], Oct. 23: *Chatham, Oct. 4.*

From New York, we have been informed that Arnold was saluted there at his arrival with 13 cannon shots and that he took his noon meal with the commander of the fortress that same day. [accurate]

Worcester paper [Massachusetts Spy], Oct. 26: *Philadelphia, Oct. 4.*

The following is a letter of the infamous Arnold to Gen. Washington on board the Vulture, Sept. 29 [25].

Sir!

My heart, which is absolutely convinced of its innermost sincerity, stands behind the step I have presently taken, however wrong the world may consider it. Since the beginning of this unhappy war between Great Britain and the Colonies, I have always had the love for my country as basis [for my actions], and it is just this very love for my country which is the motive for that which I have now undertaken. However inconsistent my behavior may appear to the eyes of the world, I also know that men should be capable of a sane judgment. I have nothing to ask for my person -- and -- probably nothing to expect. Since I have too often experienced the ingratitude of my country, I shall not attempt [asking] anything [of them]; but the world-renowned humanity of Your Excellency entices me to implore your gracious protection of Mrs. Arnold; to protect her from all evil treatments to which the ill-judged revenge of my countrymen could perhaps expose her. All that has happened, I did on my own. She is good, as innocent as an angel, and incapable of undertaking anything evil. I am therefore asking that she may be permitted to return to her friends in Philadelphia or if she so desired, to come to me. On the part of Your Excellency, I have no worry about anything concerning her but I am afraid she might be abused by the ill-advised fury of my countrymen. I would also beg of you that the included letter be transmitted to Mrs. Arnold and she may be permitted to write to me. Moreover, I wish that my baggage, which is of little consequence, be sent to me. The payment for it will follow on demand. I have the honor to remain with the deepest respect etc. Benedictus Arnold. [accurate]

P.S. I have to give the gentlemen of my suite their due, namely Colonel Varrick and Major Franks, and affirm on my honor that they as well as Joshua Smith, who as I know is under suspicion, are completely innocent and know nothing at all of the actions I have undertaken; neither have they ever been engaged in anything harmful to their country.[48]

Philadelphia. The following personage paraded through the streets of this city on Saturday. A stage was erected on a cart, on which General Arnold was sitting in effigy in his own regimentals. He had 2 faces, representing the treason. In the left hand, he held a marque, and in the right, a plan of Fortress West Point together with a letter to Beelzebub. In it, Beelzebub was informed that he [Arnold] had caused every misfortune possible in this world and would now have to hang himself. Behind the figure of the general was the shape of the devil, dressed in black. He was shaking a money bag before the general's ears and holding a pitchfork in the other hand, ready to drive him to Hell as a reward for all the evil deeds his gold-thirsty soul had committed. In front of the general was a large lantern, made of translucent paper, on which his evil deeds could be read. On the one side, General Arnold was kneeling before the devil, who was pulling him into the infernal fires. Out of Gen. Arnold's mouth came the following words, 'My dear Sir Devil, I have faithfully served you,' to which the Devil replied, 'And I shall give you your reward.' On the other side, 2 figures were hanging with the title 'The Traitor's Treachery.' These signified Adjutant General André from the British army and Joshua Smith, the former hanged as a spy and the latter as a traitor to his country. In front of the general's effigy, the following was written: Major General Benedictus Arnold, Commander of Fortress West Point. The crime of this man was high treason. He left the important post at West Point at the Hudson River, with which he had been entrusted by our great commander, His Excel. Gen. Washington, and went over to the enemy in New York. It was his intention to surrender the fortress into the enemy's power, but the omniscient Providence of our Creator graciously averted it, delivering the Adjutant General André into our hands; having received the infamous surname of a spy, he was hanged. With the deepest disgust, the treachery of this ingrate general is herewith being publicly presented and he himself declared infamous. At the same time, there are to be attestations of joy that the omniscient Providence has so graciously interceded. Thereupon, the likeness of his body was hanged as traitor to his country and transgressor of laws and honor. At 4 o'clock, the procession started in the following order: several gentlemen on horseback, a line of American officers, one line of gentlemen on foot, a guard from the garrison and closely ahead of the gentlemen, a fife and drum corps playing the Rogue's March. Many onlookers demonstrated their disgust with this treachery by throwing the figure, and thus the remembrance of this traitor to his country, into the flames, letting it sink into ashes and eternity. [accurate]

Boston, Oct. 19. Arnold, the infamous, is brigadier general in the English army and is said to have gotten his commission as early as 9 months ago.[49] [accurate]

From the north, we hear that a respectable corps of Englishmen, Tories, Canadians, and Savages has come from Canada across Lake Champlain, captured Fort St. George and Fort Ann, made the small garrisons prisoner and seized the forts. They are now murdering, burning, raping and plundering the region there. The inhabitants of Tryon County are likewise alarmed by this report and even more so that a considerable corps under the well-known Butler and Brant will arrive in that county; the militia is assembling to stop them.[50]

We have every reason to believe that the enemy's movements from Canada are part of the plans which had been made by our enemy and the traitor to our country, *of whom we are fortunately rid now. Without a doubt, he has worked on the destruction of his country to make it the home of tyrants and slaves.* [summary]

Worcester [Massachusetts Spy], Oct. 26. *We have reports that the combined French and Spanish fleet has seized a considerable number of Engl. merchant ships and Royal transports together with their crews; the ships were loaded with provisions and dry goods intended for America.*

We hope shortly to tell our readers in detail about this fortunate incident. [accurate]

At the end of this month, the guinea has the value of 326 piasters.

Month of November 1780

Worcester paper [Massachusetts Spy], *Nov. 2.*
In our previous issue, we wrote that the combined fleet had seized a number of Engl. ships. Since then, we have gathered several more detailed reports. This fleet set sail from England with 158 [58] sails incl. the 5 East Indian ships. Eleven transport ships had 1,500 [500] troops on board and were destined for America and the West Indies. The Ramillies of 74 cannon and the frigates Thetis and Southampton were covering them. The fleets came upon each other at midnight and that is why we cannot yet ascertain the exact number of the captured ships. We do know, however, that the Ramillies has arrived in Madeira and that in these 8 days, no more than 4 ships have gotten there. We must, therefore, assume that the rest have been seized. The combined fleet, 30 warships strong, had departed from Toulon and Cadiz and encountered the Engl. fleet at latitude 36 [long. 17].[51] [accurate]

New York, Oct. 11. Monday afternoon, the ship St. George arrived from London in Sandy Hook. Three weeks ago, this ship had left an Engl. fleet, 168 sails strong and under the cover of 2 warships and 4 frigates, and because there has been an almost continually favorable wind, we expect this fleet any day now. Last Monday, the brig Hope also arrived from Cork in Ireland in 8 weeks. We learned from her that on Aug. 14, the Irish fleet, 140 sails strong and destined for America, had departed from Cork under the cover of His Majesty's warships and frigates. Both fleets will unite at a certain latitude. [summary]

From a letter from Albany, Oct. 21, we see that our enemy, the English, have definitely seized Fort St. George and Fort Ann. These places had been occupied by Warner's Regiment, whom the enemy took prisoner. [summary]

Chatham, Oct. 18 [11]. Last Sunday, most of the Engl. and Irish fleets arrived at Sandy Hook. The rest are riding along the American coast and are expected by the hour. [selective]

Boston [Continental Journal], Nov. 6 [9]. *Today, the news came that a battle has occurred in the South, in which the Americans have been completely victorious. But we already know that it was nothing else but Colonel Ferguson's withdrawal from Kingsbury not far from Charlotte with his corps of 1,400 men, on which occasion the Americans took a few prisoners.* [selective]

Boston Monday paper, Nov. 12. *There is again mention of an immense victory which General Gates has won over Lord Cornwallis.* [summary]

But this needs first to be confirmed.

Worcester paper [Massachusetts Spy], Nov. 16: *New York, Oct. 21.*
It has pleased His Excel. General Clinton, our commander-in-chief, to appoint Benedictus Arnold, Esq. colonel of a regiment with the commission of brigadier general. [accurate]
We also give you the reliable report that all the ships of the English and Irish fleets have successfully arrived at Sandy Hook. [summary]

N.B. Mr. Thomas already had the combined fleet capture them.

Worcester paper [Massachusetts Spy], Nov. 20 [23]: *From the Hartford Post. Baltimore, Oct. 31.*
A New York paper, Oct. 13, gives the news that a packet boat from Philadelphia destined for Holland, on which the Honorable Henry Laurens was a passenger, has been seized at sea by the English frigate Vestal and taken to Newfoundland. Henry Laurens, President of the American Congress, who had been sent to England, as well as the letters which were all of the greatest importance, have fallen into enemy hands.[52] [accurate]

[Massachusetts Spy, Nov. 30], *Chatham, Nov. 8.*
Last week, 40 officers and 150 privates from among our countrymen, who had been exchanged, came to Elizabethtown from New York. [accurate]
We have also been reliably informed that a prisoner exchange has finally been agreed upon and will take place very soon. Everybody believes that but doubts a [general] *exchange! -- The Ship Brutus has arrived from Salem, Virginia with the news that Gen. Gates has encircled Lord Cornwallis and his army in South Carolina with superior forces and that this army will definitely be burgoyned [sic].*[53] [not found]

At the end of this month, the guinea has a value of 380 piasters.

Month of December 1780

Rutland, Dec. 6. Today, an American captain, by the name of Bliss, arrived here with the news that all our officers together with 100 of our dragoons and 46 Hessian Jäger are to be exchanged. The noncommissioned officers of our Dragoon Regiment immediately went into the countryside to get the dragoons. We were also told that commissary Mercereau has definitely been dismissed and in his stead, Major Hopkins, who is expected any day, has been reappointed commissary.

Worcester paper [Massachusetts Spy], Dec. 6: *Norwich, Nov. 14.*
We have learned that a great treachery has recently been discovered that was planned to liberate the Convention troops in Virginia. Someone by the name of Ross, a man of high repute, had gotten the commission of brigadier gen. for himself from the enemy as well as many other commissions presumably for his friends and partisans. It was his plan to provide the Convention troops with guns and ammunition so that they could cut their way through to Carolina. How lucky we are that this has been discovered beforehand and brought to naught! [accurate]
With the greatest pleasure, we can now give you the reliable news that after so many vain efforts, a general exchange of the prisoners of war has finally been

achieved and been concluded by the Generals Phillips and Lincoln. We will soon be able to give you the articles. [summary]

N.B. I still do not believe it, my dear Thomas, even if you assure me so persuasively; what I have said over and over again is still valid: the general exchange will be arranged together with peace!

We have received a report [from the Continental Journal, Dec. 8] on Nov. 12 [Dec. 1] that Admiral Rodney departed from Sandy Hook, presumably to the West Indies. We also know that an enemy frigate with a copper bottom has capsized in the sound at Hell Gate and is considered lost. [accurate]

Boston Monday paper [Independent Ledger], Dec. 11: *Philadelphia.*
Major General Lincoln as well as 3 brigadier generals, 3 colonels, 9 lieut. colonels, 11 majors and a great number of our officers have been exchanged and are finally set free. [accurate]

Boston [Continental Journal], Dec. 11 [14]. *Letters from Martinique report of a terrible hurricane that afflicted all the West Indian Islands on Oct. 12 and devastated the Island of Barbados. This island had never before felt anything, but this time all the houses have been swept away by the terrible wind and the high water. The jails were opened and the prisoners escaped onto the high mountain peaks. Six thousand white people and many more blacks have drowned or been killed in some other way. Almost all the ships riding at anchor there were grounded and all the men lost their lives.*[54] [selective]

Rutland, Dec. 13. Today, the new commissary Major Hopkins arrived here saying that as soon as 100 dragoons are assembled, they will march off together with the officers and jägers.
Captain von Bärtling, who departed for New York on Sept. 11, has not yet returned. Until his return, Ensign Specht shall stay with the rest of the prisoners of war. Major Hopkins visited me today and, to my greatest surprise, told me that he was sorry to inform me that I would not be exchanged with the regiment to which I belonged. He said that my name was not on the list. I told him that, according to our service [regulations], I was not counted among the officers and therefore my name did not belong on that list. "I have heard that from Captain of the Cavalry Fricke," he said, "and am very much astonished about it. At this moment, I have lost a great deal of the respect that I have had for the Germans since they degrade those to whom they entrust their lives and their health. Moreover, are you not on parole just like the officers? I remember having read your name when you gave your signature in Bennington and in Brimfield." I could not deny that, -- "but be that as it may," he said, "I cannot let you go. I shall, however, ask for an immediate report from the headquarters of General Washington because I cannot possibly believe that a man like you, who has always been in the company of officers and signed the parole with them, is at the rank of a corporal." As Major Hopkins was saying all this in public, it brought the hatred of all our officers upon me. Since Major Hopkins said that I was a CHIRURGUS, which neither I nor my countrymen could deny, I should be exchanged for another CHIRURGUM. The officers asked Major Hopkins to let me go along because I was the only CHIRURGUS with the regiment seeing that the others were all away. Major Hopkins said, "Don't beseech me, gentlemen, you cannot implore me more than Wasmus has already done. I am infinitely sorry not to be able to let him go because I know how much he would like to join you." -- All this did not help, the officers even blamed me saying that I did not want to be exchanged, that I had arranged it all with the commissary Major Hopkins and the like. Capt. Bliss had taken his noon meal at the house of the Captain of the Cavalry Fricke and in the presence of Major Hopkins told me, "Captain of the Cavalry Fricke says that you are no CHIRURGUS,

you had left Germany as corporal and only come along to clean the dragoons' beards and continue to be listed as corporal in the Captain of the Cavalry's Company. Now tell me," he continued, "if you are no CHIRURGUS but a corporal, what is the reason that everybody has been conferring the title of CHIRURGUS upon you or -- as we call it in our service -- Doctor? Everybody knows that you have done the work, that you have most diligently cared for and cured the sick in both Engl. and German corps. --" Major Hopkins finally added, "You may be considered a corporal by your countrymen, but we consider you a CHIRURGUS, a useful man, who has conducted himself very well among us and excelled in his art; you will simply have to be exchanged for one of our doctors!"

None of all the prisoners of war has rendered this service in captivity or been able to do so but I. I am the only CHIRURGUS, who has held out the whole time with the regiment, I know that each of my high-placed brethren has lauded me for it; but now that this is happening, that I am to stay behind without my fault, I am being charged, accused of not wanting to go along, wishing to remain in this happy country. Why did I need to give an exact account? I could say it is connected with the service, since no mortal could force me here.

Madrid, July 28. The siege of Gibraltar is now being continued in earnest.

Boston [Continental Journal], Dec. 14. *A New York paper reports on the horrible destruction which the hurricane has brought about in Jamaica. Twelve warships and all the transport and merchant ships have either been driven ashore or sunk and all the people on them have died. The sea had risen 6 feet higher than usual that day. Through the devastating storm, a ship of 90 cannon has been driven to the middle of town. About 30,000 people have lost their lives there.* [accurate]

The following was taken out of a Dutch paper.
London, Sept. 1. The privateer Alligator *of London has seized the Russian ship* Liberty, *destined for Nancy, that had 280 bales of hemp and 558 bars of iron on board, and taken it to Falmouth. This is the first Russian ship the English have taken away, and we are curious to learn what stirrings this incident will bring about at the Russian Court.*

Rutland, Dec. 24. Because the 100 dragoons and 46 Hessian Jägers have not yet been gathered, Major Hopkins said that he wanted to complete the number with the remaining prisoners and set out for New London with them the day after tomorrow. And so it was done. The fixed number set out for Rutland with their officers today, the 26th of Dec. I wrote the following letter to Maj. Gen. von Riedesel, which I gave to Capt. Rivers of the 60th Engl. Regiment. He promised to hand it himself to the General and tell him everything, also the behavior of Captain of the Cavalry Fricke.

Right Honorable Baron, Gracious Major General,
To my great sorrow I have to report that I have to stay behind here in captivity and what is the hardest to bear -- that I have been charged by those who should be convinced of my integrity that I myself am to blame for it. My difficulties are caused by the fact that I am a CHIRURGUS and therefore have to be exchanged for another CHIRURGUM. Captain of the Cavalry Fricke has done everything possible to have me come along but Major Hopkins cannot be moved to exchange me as corporal. -- And then it was said that I had arranged it with the commissary. I myself have beseeched the commissary to let me go along but to no avail. This decision and all that I have had to suffer through it, has almost robbed me of my senses. Only the thought of my having the support of my General's [*sense of*] justice and grace keeps up my courage and increasing my desire soon to be so fortunate as to be able to explain everything in detail to my gracious General. I am respectfully beseeching you, Right Honorable Sir, soon to effect my

exchange and reunite me with my Dragoon Regiment that to my great sorrow, I have now had to leave. I remain etc.

Worcester paper [Massachusetts Spy], Dec. 28: *Boston Dec. 21. From New York, we have received the report that 4,000 troops have embarked there, who are to invade Connecticut under the command of the infamous Arnold.*[55] [summary]
Baltimore, Nov. 21. We have the reliable news that the English frigate Hussar recently sank at Hell Gate in the sound.[56] [accurate]
London, Aug. 29. The ship Congress from Philadelphia, which was destined for Amsterdam, *has been seized by our frigate Vestal with all the mail from Laurens, his secretary and another Rebel gentleman and successfully taken into Portsmouth. They were assigned their lodging in the Tower of London.*
This Mr. Laurens, last President of the American Congress, had previously been a saddler in Charleston, South Carolina, and was now sent as ambassador to Holland from Congress. There, he was to borrow a sum of money and, as security, pawn the Province of New York. [summary]

N.B. Mr. Thomas took pleasure in putting "Lying Royal Gazette" under this paragraph.

Fishkill, Dec. 21. A messenger passing through here today has brought the news that a number of ships coming from New York have appeared not far from New Haven. They have 1,000 [4,000] men on board and are under the command of the traitor Arnold. [accurate]
Worcester, Dec. 28. Yesterday, a number of Engl., Braunschweig and Hessian officers [the Braunschweig Dragoon Regiment and the Hessian Jägers] *passed through this city to be exchanged.* [accurate]

Nothing has been seen here in New England of the big comet that in the course of this and the next year was to appear as was reported from [St.] Petersburg on Jan. 20 and from Paris on April 9 of this year.

How long Shall anxious Thoughts my soul and Grief my Heart Oppress?
How long my Enemy's insult and I have no Redress.

At the end of this year, the guinea has the value of 350 piasters in paper money.

Appendix[56]

Riedesel II 38, II 39, Part I, p. 59-60[57]

Right Honorable Baron,
Gracious Major General,

To you, Right Honorable Sir, I wish respectfully to report that the prisoners in the barracks here are now found to be in good physical condition. I have also had English and Hessians under my care whenever they were in need of medicine. During the 16 months that I have been here, I have had several men seriously ill, but except for one Hessian Jäger, who had been shot dead by the man on guard, none has died during this time right up to this day. I have set a complete fracture of the leg of an Englishman, cured several venereal diseases and other bad accidents. From the English, I have to request the payment of a medicine bill over 16 pounds which I advanced, and since I have incurred debts due to it and my salary hardly suffices to maintain myself here, I wish to be paid for it. I have had much trouble and work with the English but ask for nothing but the value of the medicine on the bill. [*The following 3 lines are badly marred by missing fragments. H.D.*] But I hope eventually to be exchanged [*and then live?*] of my   ?   ? [*as?*] it was customary in the last war in Germany   ?   ?   ?.

I have been most unhappy for not having received any of my baggage except a coffer, which I had left at Trois-Rivières, and a portmanteau I had left at Fort Edward. I believe that the Regimental Surgeon Vorbrodt took my coffer with him -- my loss at Bennington was 12 pounds. in cash, instruments and baggage. Since I have lost everything, I am poor and, in regard to pieces of clothing, particularly shirts, in the most miserable condition. Would that we will never be exchanged!

Should the position of Regimental Surgeon ever become vacant, I respectfully ask that you, Right Honorable Sir, will graciously think of me. You, Sir, could graciously improve my fortune and change my rank, in which case I would gladly sacrifice myself.

Persevering with the most obedient respect and reverence, Most Honorable Sir and Baron,

Major General of my Gracious Lord
Your respectful servant
J.F. Wasmus, Rutland June 5, 1780.

NOTES

1. John Paul Jones (1747-1792), sailing out of Brest in the *Ranger*, had attacked coastal shipping in the Irish sea and landed on St. Mary's Isle as part of a plan to hold the Earl of Selkirk hostage to bargain for the release of American prisoners in April and May of 1778. In 1779, due to the good offices of Franklin, Jones secured another ship, which he named *Bonhomme Richard* in honor of Franklin's Poor Richard's Almanac, and sailed from Lorient around Ireland and Scotland, capturing 17 ships in the process. On the 23rd of September 1779, Jones fought the *Serapis* (which was accompanied by the *Countess of Scarborough*) off Flamborough Head on the coast of York. (See below, notes 4 and 8.)

2. Don Luis de Cordoba was Admiral of the Spanish fleet which joined D'Orvilliers and the French in July 1779; the combined fleet anchored off Plymouth on August 16 during the invasion scare, but Hardy sailed the British back to Spithead and the combined fleet, low on provisions and weakened by a smallpox epidemic on the French vessels, was forced to return to port, ending the threat of invasion.

3. The *Russell* was refit at Antigua and fought with Rodney against de Grasse in April 1782, at the Battle of All Saints Passage.

4. Born in Scotland in 1747, he was the son and namesake of a Scottish gardener, John Paul. He went to sea in his teens and was accused of murder for flogging a ship's carpenter, who later died; cleared of this, he later killed a mutinous crewman in 1773 and was unemployed in America at the outbreak of the Revolution, assuming the name of Jones to hide his identity.

5. We are confused about this story; after his capture in 1777 at the Battle of Bennington, Wasmus refers to a Colonel Warner, who joins him for dinner and indicates that this man had commanded the American left wing in the battle--clearly this is Col. Seth Warner, Colonel of the Vermont Continental Regiment. Seth Warner had been born in Connecticut but moved to Bennington, Vermont as a young man; we can find no indication in the authorities we have consulted that he ever lived in Hardwick, Massachusetts, although the Vermont Republic did make him a general after the battle. There was, however, another General Warner who did live in Hardwick: this was Jonathan Warner, who, according to Charles Miner Thompson, was given overall command of the three-pronged raid launched at General Lincoln's behest against Ticonderoga, Skenesborough, and Lake George in September 1777, and who is best known for having commanded the Worcester County militia during Shays' Rebellion in 1786. We think it possible that Wasmus, perhaps due to the stress of capture and his unfamiliarity with the Americans, may have confused the two Warners. [MCL & HD] (Thompson, Independent Vermont, p. 327.)

6. This is Wasmus's copy of Mercereau's English letter.

7. cf. entry for May 12, 1781.

8. The *Serapis* had so damaged Jones' *Bonhomme Richard* that its captain, Richard Pearson, asked if Jones had asked for quarter, at which Jones shouted his immortal line, "I have not yet begun to fight." The *Serapis* eventually surrendered after an American grenade set off an explosion of its ammunition and the Americans boarded it in time to watch the *Bonhomme Richard* sink.

9. West Florida stretched from the Chattahoochee River, its boundary with Georgia, all the way to the Mississippi, and north as far as the Yazoo River, north of Natchez, according to the treaty ending the Seven Years War. Spanish rights to Florida had been confirmed by the Treaty of Utrecht, but were exchanged for the former French possessions west of the Mississippi (excluding Louisiana and New Orleans, which the French retained) by the Treaty of Paris. Recovering Florida was one of the Spanish war aims, and in 1779, the Spanish General Galvez captured Baton Rouge and Natchez, seizing Mobile in 1780 and Pensacola in 1781. (Boatner, 1042-1043.)

10. On January 14-15, 1780, General William Alexander had taken 3,000 troops across the ice from New Jersey to attack the British on Staten Island; the raid was unsuccessful and the British, in retaliation, burned buildings at Newark and Elizabethtown in New Jersey.

11. Wasmus is correct here; Hannover troops were not in America but they did reinforce Gibraltar. (Elster, p. 375.)

12. Since Mackesy notes that the *Ramillies* escorted a convoy to the West Indies in August 1780 (a convoy which was lost to Allied attacks), this report must be somewhat inaccurate. (Mackesy, The War for America, pp. 357, 359, 375.) The *Ramillies* was sunk in a gale off the Grand Banks in 1782. (Marcus, op.cit., p. 450.)

13. This was done in retaliation for the raid on Staten Island 10 days earlier.

14. In November, there had been free trade riots in Dublin, and Irish Volunteers organized and armed in response to the previous summer's invasion threat had demanded legislative independence, in striking parallel to the activities of the American patriots. The British concessions in December eased the economic crisis, and the unrest subsided.

15. D'Estaing had been wounded during the disastrous Franco-American attack on Savannah in October 1779 and returned to France, where he helped to influence the French to send Rochambeau's troops to America.

16. George Brydges Rodney (1719-1792) had entered the Navy at 13, became rear admiral during the Seven Years War, during which he was notably successful in the West Indies, and had moved to Paris in 1774 to escape his creditors, only returning to England on his promotion to Admiral in 1778. He was made Commander-in-Chief on the Leeward Islands station late in 1779.
John Vaughan (?-1795) had served with the 10th Dragoons in Germany and then led the 94th, Royal Welsh Volunteers in America during the Seven Years War. He had fought at Charleston and Long Island in 1776, captured Fort Montgomery during Clinton's effort at diversion in October 1777, and had returned to England in 1779 where he was made Commander-in-Chief of the Leeward Islands.

17. Charles Cornwallis (1738-1805) joined the Grenadier Guards at 18 and was at the Battle of Minden in 1759; he was elected to Parliament in 1760 and became Lt. Col. of the 12th Regiment in the same year, leading his troops into action in Germany, succeeding his father and becoming the 2nd Earl Cornwallis in 1762. He was promoted to major general in 1775 and commanded the British reserve at the Battle of Long Island; Clinton accused him of negligence in letting Washington escape total defeat at Trenton. He led the British at Brandywine in 1777 and later occupied Philadelphia; in 1778, he was made second-in-command to Clinton, returning to England when his wife died at the end of the year. At the end of 1779, it was thought Cornwallis would soon replace Clinton since the latter had asked the government to accept his resignation, but Clinton in fact continued in command in America. (Franklin and Mary Wickwire's excellent two volume biography, Cornwallis in America and Cornwallis, The Imperial Years, Boston, 1970 and Chapel Hill, 1980, places his American service in context.)

18. Prinz Ernst von Mecklenburg (1742-1814) was the brother of Queen Charlotte of England and was a cavalry officer in the service of Maria Theresa of Austria.

19. Admiral Juan de Langara y Huarte (1736-1806) had entered the Spanish navy at 14 and was noted for charting new maps for the China and Philippine seas. In this action he was trying to prevent

Rodney's relief of Gibraltar. Outnumbered, he was severely wounded, but celebrated in Spain for his heroic conduct.

20. Mackesy includes a chart of the strength and distribution of the British army, taken from Lord North's return books which, for March 1780, gives a total strength of 142,386 men, including 61,402 in South Britain, 5,651 in Scotland, North America 35,942; West Indies 8,119; Gibraltar 5,874, Minorca 2,134; This does not include the Navy or the Irish establishment; Mackesy was unable to find returns for the latter. (Mackesy, op. cit., pp. 524-5.)

21. This was Tybee Island off Savannah, Georgia.

22. James Hogun had been born in Ireland and settled in North Carolina in 1751. Involved in local politics and the militia, he was made Col. of the 7th North Carolina Continentals in November 1776, fighting at Brandywine and Germantown in 1777, and promoted by Congress to brigadier general in 1779. He commanded Philadelphia until November of that year and marched south for three months, in snow and cold to defend Charlestown, arriving in March 1780. He became a prisoner when the city fell in May and refused parole, staying with his men and dying in captivity in 1781. (Boatner, pp. 508-509.)

23. Count Louis-Charles du Chaffault (1708-1794) was indeed at the end of a long career in the navy, which would end in a Revolutionary prison.

24. This was the Tory Cortlandt Skinner (1728-1799), who had been Attorney General of New Jersey before the war. He was appointed Brigadier General of Provincials and raised a brigade late in 1776. Skinner's Brigade was stationed on Staten Island, participated in the Springfield, N.J. raid in June 1780, but spent much of its time reinforcing the New York City garrison. (Boatner 1012-13.)

25. May 19, 1780 was known as the "Dark Day" in the colonies. David Ludlum has called it the "most terrifying day in American history, psychometeorologically." Some Americans thought the phenomenon Wasmus describes was the Day of Judgment, but the real cause was trans-Allegheny forest fires whose smoke and ash were blown east by prevailing winds. (David Ludlum, "Almanac," Country Journal, May, 1988, p. 15.)

26. Captain James Cook (1728-1779), whose voyages of exploration had taken him a distance equal to thrice the earth's circumference, had discovered the Hawaiian Islands, but engaged in a fatal dispute with some of the inhabitants. One of the *Discovery's* boats was stolen and Cook seized a native leader as a hostage; on February 14, 1779, he was attacked and killed in a skirmish in the surf.

27. Wasmus was right; Charleston had surrendered to the British on May 12.

28. Oliver DeLancey the elder (1718-1785) was the senior Loyalist officer in America, had fought at Ticonderoga in 1758,and had led Loyalist faction in New York politics at the outbreak of the Revolution. He raised three battalions of "DeLancey's New York Volunteers," also known as the "Refugees," one of which was stationed in Queens, as was DeLancey, who was a brigadier general. In 1779 his property was confiscated, and he left New York for England in 1783.
His son, Oliver DeLancey (1749-1822) had been educated in England and entered the British Army in 1766, joining the 17th Dragoons in 1773. In 1779, he was a major, serving as Deputy Quartermaster General in Clinton's Charleston expedition, becoming Clinton's Adjutant General in 1780.

29. Sir Isaac Newton (1642-1727) had indeed observed the so-called Great Comet of 1680, arranging for the collection of many observations, defined its orbit as a parabola, and showed that comets orbit the sun. Sir Edmund Halley also observed this comet, but it was the comet of 1682 that he predicted to return 76 years later, in 1758, and which is now called Halley's comet. The Great Comet of 1680 has a period of 575 years and so could not have returned in 1780, but the writer of the Paris letter is obviously familiar with the notion of comet periodicity, established in 1758-59 by Comet Halley's return.

30. Rodney lived until 1792; this is one of many reports based on rumors which illustrate the difficulty of following the course of world events during the Revolution, when newspaper stories were often unreliable, being based on traveller's accounts, or the reports of biased observers.

31. Hannah Caldwell, wife of the Reverend James Caldwell who was minister of a Presbyterian church in Elizabethtown, New Jersey and chaplain of the New Jersey Brigade, had moved to Connecticut

Farms (now Union) with her nine children to escape the conflict. According to Joseph Tustin, editor of the Ewald journal, "her body was left exposed in the street in the hot sun." (Ewald, p. 418.)

32. Admiral Thomas Graves (1725?-1802) was sent to join Arbuthnot in New York as his second-in-command, arriving on the 13th of July shortly after the French force under Rochambeau reached Newport.

33. Clinton in fact reported that he had lost only 268 killed and wounded, a figure which seems to have been accepted by historians of the battle. (Boatner, p. 213.)

34. Banastre Tarleton (1754-1833), cavalry leader, was the commander of the Loyalist British Legion during the Charleston campaign. (see below, note 43.)

35. Duke Carl had suffered a stroke in 1776 and was succeeded by his son, the Crown Prince, Carl Wilhelm Ferdinand, in 1780.

36. The British claimed to have captured 5,500 Americans; some historians estimate the number to have been closer to 3,300, still the largest single capture of American prisoners in the Revolution. (Boatner, 212-213.)

37. Jean Baptiste Donatien de Vimeur, Comte de Rochambeau (1725- 1807), began his military career in the cavalry during the War of the Austrian Succession (1740-1748), and fought at Minorca and in Germany during the Seven Years War. Promoted to Lt. General in 1780, he commanded the expeditionary force sent to aid the Americans in that year, leaving Brest with 5,500 troops in May.

38. William Heath (1737-1814), a Roxbury, Mass.farmer, who had been a Massachusetts legislator before the Revolution, was active in the militia, although he had no combat experience until the Revolution. As commander of the Eastern Department, he had been in charge of the Convention Army in Boston.from 1777 to 1779. Between June and October 1780, he was stationed in Providence to receive Rochambeau.

39. Boreas is, of course, Lord North, the Prime Minister; Minden is Germain, the Secretary of State for American Colonies, whose insubordinate conduct at the Battle of Minden led to his separation from the army; Twitcher is an even more interesting insult, as it refers to Lord Sandwich, the First Lord of the Admiralty, who was compared to the character of Jeremy Twitcher in John Gay's Beggar's Opera, when he "peached" on his former friend John Wilkes (1727- 1797). Wilkes, a Member of Parliament, was brought to trial in 1763 over a scurrilous attack on the government in his paper, The North Briton. Before the House of Lords, Sandwich charged him with having written an obscene parody of Pope's "Essay on Man," called "Essay on Woman." Wilkes was expelled from Parliament and forced to flee the country.

40. This was the skirmish at Bull's Ferry, New Jersey, on July 20- 21, 1780. Washington had sent Wayne and the Pennsylvania Brigade to destroy a blockhouse just north of Hoboken, which was used as a Loyalist base for woodcutters. Wayne shelled the blockhouse and some of his troops, against the orders of the officers, rushed the fortification with the results described in the article.

41. Lord George Gordon, 1751-1793, the youngest son of the Duke of Gordon, was a Member of Parliament, who had organized and headed Protestant Associations to repeal the Catholic Relief Act of 1778 (which extended some political rights to Catholics). On June 2 1780, Gordon led a mob which marched on Parliament with an anti- Catholic petition, and subsequently rioted, destroying Catholic chapels, the homes of prominent Catholics, and even broke open the prisons. The military was called out to suppress the riot, 450 people were killed and wounded, and Gordon was charged with high treason but eventually acquitted. Convicted of libel in 1787, he spent five years in Newgate Prison (where he lived in luxurious private quarters and frequently entertained); he died shortly after he converted to Judaism and was circumcised.

42. Like some of the earlier tales about rattlesnakes, this charming folklore is not true.

43. In the 18th century, the San Juan River was deep enough to support shipping, and the British had tried before, during the Seven Years War, to sail up the river to Lake Nicaragua to capture the colonial capital of Granada, being blocked by the fort at El Castillo in 1762. In 1780, the Governor of Jamaica led a second British expedition, which included the youthful Horatio Nelson, and besieged the fort and captured it. But the tropical climate and local diseases took their toll leaving the survivors too weak

to bury their dead: of the 1,400 who had gone to Nicaragua, only 320 were still alive at the end of September. (Boatner, 802; Stephen Kinzer, "El Castillo Journal," New York Times, May 23, 1988.)

44. On May 12, 1780, Tarleton's cavalry caught up with Col. Abraham Buford's 3rd Virginia Continentals, the last organized American troops left in South Carolina after the surrender of Charleston. The Americans, who outnumbered the British, inexplicably held their fire until too late to stop Tarleton's cavalry charge, and Tarleton's sabres cut down the Americans even while the latter tried to surrender, especially after Tarleton's horse was killed and his men thought he was a casualty. One hundred thirteen Americans were killed, 203 captured, most of whom were badly wounded. Tarleton lost only 19 men killed or wounded, and became the object of American propaganda as "Tarleton's quarter" became defined as a massacre of surrendering men.

45. This was the Battle of Camden, August 16, 1780. Gates had embarked on a night march to attack the British under Cornwallis; his troops were half-starved and ill from their rations of molasses and corn-meal mush. Coincidentally, Cornwallis had left Camden at the same time, marching to attack Gates at dawn; the two forces met at 2:30 A.M. on the 16th. When the battle began at dawn, the British annihilated Gates' army. Gates fled all the way to Charlotte, North Carolina, a distance of 60 miles.

46. Benedict Arnold, whose accomplishments on the 1775 invasion of Canada, as well as what he had done at Valcour Island and at Saratoga, had been eventually rewarded with the command of Philadelphia when the British evacuated in June 1778, had been accused of corruption and cleared by Congress. More charges were made in 1779, and Arnold, feeling many grievances, offered his services to the British. He sent them information, for which he was paid 10,000 pounds, and, when he was appointed to command West Point, asked a price of 20,000 pounds for its surrender. Clinton agreed, and Arnold proceeded to weaken the defensive forces, neglect crucial repairs, and set up a network of spies, including Joshua Hett Smith. Smith was sent on board the *Vulture*, where he met John André, disguised as a merchant, since Tory leader Col. Beverly Robinson thought Arnold was anxious to meet André. Arnold and André held a woodland meeting, after which André hid in Smith's house; American troops attacked the *Vulture* driving her down the river, André was captured with incriminating documents in his stockings, and Arnold, aided by his wife's pretense of hysteria, successfully escaped.

47. Gordon was not executed but was acquitted of the treason charges.

48. Arnold had married Philadelphia belle Peggy Shippen in 1779; she was aware of the conspiracy and eventually joined her husband in exile in England; Smith was also a co-conspirator.

49. Arnold had indeed been given a brigadier general's commission by the British, and, in addition to his pension, received £6,315 for his losses; his wife also received a £500 annual pension.

50. In the fall of 1780, Sir John Johnson led an Indian and Tory raid through the Mohawk and Schoharie Valleys, burning and killing as they went, escaping to Oswego despite the efforts of the New York militia. At the same time British forces invaded from the North, raiding the upper Connecticut Valley, while another British force, led by Major Carleton, marched through Fort Edward, Fort George, Fort Ann, and attacked Ballston, just north of Schenectady.

51. The combined fleet had encountered a British convoy sailing for the Indies on August 9; its escort, including the *Ramillies,* fled in the face of the enemy's overwhelming superiority, and 61 ships were captured, carrying 3,000 men and £1 1/2 million in supplies. (Mackesy, p. 357.)

52. Travelling to Europe to negotiate a treaty with Holland, Laurens was captured off Newfoundland on September 3, 1780. The British used his captured documents as a reason to declare war on the Dutch. Laurens was kept a prisoner in the Tower under very harsh conditions and was eventually exchanged for Cornwallis in time to serve as one of the American commissioners at the peace negotiations.

53. This reads like a satirical reference to Gates' disastrous defeat at Camden the preceding summer.

54. Hurricanes at this time were especially deadly because they occurred without warning, often causing devastating loss of life. The Annual Register of Events for 1780 describes the terrible impact of a hurricane on Jamaica on October 3, unusual in that it was apparently accompanied by an earthquake. An even more violent storm hit Barbados on October 10, killing an estimated 9,000 people, many dying in the ruins of their houses and barracks. 800 prisoners of war were "liberated by the demolition of the

prisons," but "behaved tolerably well."   The same storm resulted in heavy damage at St. Lucia, Dominica, Martinique, and St. Eustatius. (London, 1788, pp. 292-294, 295-298.)

55. In December 1780, Arnold raided along the James River in Virginia. He did eventually raid in the north, attacking New London, Connecticut on September 6, 1781, and burning a number of buildings and several ships.

56. The New York Times, May 2, 1986, (II, 4:3) reports that salvage expert Barry Clifford planned to dive to the apparent site of the *Hussar*, using sidescan sonar to locate the wreck, which was believed to contain "a fortune in gold and silver."

57. Riedesel II 38, II 39, Part I, p. 59-6056

1781

Month of January 1781

1st   Today, I am once more stepping [sic] into a new year still in America, as yet a prisoner! - Alas, when will come the year, the month, the day for me to return to Germany, - to be so fortunate as to embrace my relatives and friends again. -- When will that happy day dawn for me?

> [in English]
> But since I can't rehearse the Will of Fate--
> Nor give my woes, nor give my Joys a date,
> I will at last suspend my present care --
> And for your safety offer up a Prayer.
> May friendly Angels their Soft Wings Display--
> And be Your Guard in every Dangerous Way
> May all your future life be blest with Peace --
> And every Day the Spring of Joy increase.
> In every State may you most Happy be--
> And when far Distant do but think on me.--

This shall be my wish for you, my friends and loved ones, that I am sending you today.

Worcester [Massachusetts Spy], Jan. 4: *London, Aug. 20*
When the King received the news that the fleets in the East and West Indies had been seized by the combined fleet, he was immediately stricken with paroxysms and he showed all those signs of frenzy that befall persons who have been bitten by a tarantula. Lord North, the chief physician in matters of politics, immediately sent for the band of state fiddlers, who by fiddling various delectable tunes, usually cheer up His Majesty's mind on such occasions. They were also successful this time and awoke the King from his stupor but unfortunately he immediately fell into it again. Lord North also caught the sickness and in the next moment the entire Court was overcome as in an epidemic by this infectious pestilence, a kind of lunatic mania. Her Majesty, the Queen, jumped naked out of bed and appeared as Venus. The Prince of Wales appeared stripped like Apollo of Delphi, the Queen's lady-in-waiting forgot her modesty, the Lords had forgotten to put on their trousers. And now a great tumult ensued. The Privy Councillors came with their secretaries, the

Royal Guards and all servants assembled in the big antichamber [sic] *all pell-mell dancing like some maniacs who do not know what they are doing. They were pushing each other, belly to belly, back to back, right and left, hands across etc.*

The DOCTORES of the clergy are making preparations to drive out his spirit of frenzy with powerful prayers.

The DOCTORES of jurisprudence have made their observations about it and written it down.

The DOCTORES of medicine are busy with preparing necessary emetics and clysters to drive this type of frenzy either up or down.

And the grave diggers in the Kingdom are ready to bury those who have been done away with by this pest. [accurate]

This is a burlesque, my dear Thomas! If it is your own, I assure you that it does not redound to your honor. -- --

There are no rough spiders (tarantulas) in New England: but [*they do exist*] in South America and the southern Provinces of North America as the Carolinas, Georgia and Florida, and also in the East Indies. It is said to be absolutely certain that whoever has been so unfortunate as to be bitten by a tarantula cannot be awakened from the coma except through music. The victim falls into a deadly coma a few minutes after being bitten or stung. If the MUSICUS is so lucky as to play a tune that entices the senses and awakens the person - which does usually happen - then one is cured. The person will, however, get up and feel quite drowsy, will begin to dance and chat in an unusual manner as if nature is eager to get rid of the spider poison. Many are saying this; whether it is true - I do not think so.[1] --

Boston Monday paper [Independent Ledger] Jan. 8. *Boston:*
We know for certain that the preparations made in New York have not been directed against some part of Connecticut but make up a reinforcement that went south [under the command of the infamous traitor Arnold]. [summary]

Rutland, Jan. 11. Since the time [of voluntary service] by most of the soldiers in the American army has been spent, the United States are obligated to raise a new army by next spring. The order had already been given to all the towns and villages in the previous year. Rutland, a village of 200 inhabitants, must furnish 25 men with all the necessities. The inhabitants hire their soldiers and, for 3 years of service, give each of them 100 pounds at the New England rate of exchange; this is 441 1/3 piasters in Conv. money, earnest in gold or silver. In addition, the community must provide each soldier with regimentals, give him a salary of 2 lbs. in gold or silver per month, help him maintain his regimentals for 3 years and pay for his subsistence in the army. These are expensive soldiers![2]

Worcester paper [Massachusetts Spy], Jan. 11: *New York, Dec. 25.*
Last Thursday, General Arnold with the corps under his command sailed from Sandy Hook for an expedition. [accurate]

Rutland, Jan. 13. Last night, Capt. von Bärtling sen. rather unexpectedly returned, bringing along money, pieces of regimentals and baggage that had arrived from Germany. I did not receive those items which my wife had sent me from Germany in the year 1777 including shirts, 2 pipes, shoes, stockings and 50 lancets, and I will probably never get them. Yet, this loss is small compared to the loss I have previously suffered. But I had the great satisfaction of receiving 12 letters from Germany, of which some were very old; the most recent was from April 15, 1780. One of these letters had been opened; these are the first sealed letters that have come to us in captivity. I was very happy!

Together with Capt. von Bärtling, Lieut. Gebhard[3] has also returned, who, on orders of our Maj. Gen. von Riedesel, is to stay behind here with the prisoners of war together with Ensign Specht.[4] Since Capt. von Bärtling has been exchanged, he will go back to New York.

Massachusetts Spy, Jan. 18, 1781. *From Philadelphia it is reported that, because of lack of victuals, Gibraltar will soon have to surrender.*[5] [selective]

Paris, Sept. 4. Letters from Marseille report that a ship from Smyrna [Izmir], heavily loaded with silk and cotton, has gotten away and escaped from the English in the following amusing manner. The ship was being pursued on her return trip by an English frigate. The French captain, having no hope of escape, ordered all his people below deck except an Italian, whom he allowed on deck instructing him how to behave toward the English. The latter had now come very close and fired a cannon whereupon the Italian immediately waved a white cloth signalling that he was in distress. The Englishmen came closer and called to him to strike the sails. The Italian pleaded that he was in distress adding that he was a passenger coming from Smyrna; that the captain of the ship and more than half of the crew had already died of pestilence and 5 or 6 lay dying below deck; that he believed for sure he would be the last victim of this lethal disease if he continued to remain on the ship. He begged him [the captain] to help him and take him on board his ship as quickly as possible, whereupon the Engl. capt. replied, 'Before I take one of you on board, you may all go to hell! No, by God! Even if you had all the riches of Peru on board, I would not invite any of you.' The Italian continued begging and said that he was not one of his [the English captain's] enemies, adding that all his enemies lay dead in the ship. If he did not want to take him aboard, he should at least have enough pity and compassion to supply him with some necessities. The Engl. capt. was finally induced to have him presented with some bottles of vinegar, tied to a pole. Then he quickly set sail and left the French.-- [accurate]

Boston Monday paper [Independent Ledger], Jan. 22: *Cadiz, Aug. 22. We know for sure that 30 [33] ships with a cargo of provisions, destined for Gibraltar, have been seized by the fleet under Don Barcelo and taken to Cartagena.*[6] *On several ships that the combined fleet had seized, as much copper has been found as is needed for the bottom of 5 warships.* [accurate]

Worcester paper [Massachusetts Spy], Jan. 25. *Fishkill, Jan. 18.*
General Clinton, who uses every opportunity to further the cause of his Master George, last week sent 2 spies to the Pennsylvania militia, which is well disposed toward us, with written assurances that if they laid down their arms and came into his camp, he would pay them the outstanding debt in gold and provide them with new clothing. However well disposed these fellows were toward us, they nevertheless handed the 2 spies together with their instructions over to General Wayne and both were hanged.

We wished Sir Henry Clinton would not burden us so much with hanging his spies -- *he could use his money more profitably to pay his own troops, who* [almost daily] *come over to us in considerable numbers. They complain violently that they are poorly paid, ill clothed, and,* [as we have known all along] *worse fed.* [accurate]

Boston, Jan. 18. During the latest hurricane on the Island of Jamaica, 3 cities have been swallowed up in earthquakes and inundations and more than 1,500 inhabitants [500 families] have lost their lives. [accurate]

Massachusetts Spy, Febr. 1:   *London, Sept. 16.*

Two men are now confined in the Tower, who not long ago were presidents, namely Lord George Gordon, President of the Protestant Association, and Henry Laurens, President of the American [Rebel] *Congress.* [accurate]

At the end of this month, the guinea has the value of 375 piasters in paper money.

Month of February 1781

Worcester paper [Massachusetts Spy], Febr. 1:   *London, Oct. 2.*

English letters assure us that the ministry is now firmly resolved to continue the war in America [in downright earnest]. *The King has designated 10,000 fresh troops to reinforce the army under Sir Henry Clinton and gives His Excel. absolute assurance of supporting these [troops] with all the necessities. The government now holds all the plans made by France and the Rebels against the British in America in its hands, incl. the one showing joint undertakings of the French and the Rebels against Canada. Fourteen regiments and part of the guard have been ordered to embark for America now.* [accurate]

Worcester, Febr. 1. It is now believed that the French Court has decided to send an adequate force over to America early in the spring. In conjunction with our army, they will starve out the English fleets and armies as well as their hirelings and drive them completely off the American shores. Nevertheless, it is most necessary that every city and village immediately furnish its quota of recruits so that they can join the army as quickly as possible. This will enable our great commanders to open a campaign that will doubtless be decisive. If we do this, we can flatter ourselves with the hope that God will bless us, establish our independence and give America peace and quiet. [7] [accurate]

Boston Monday paper [Independent Ledger], Febr. 5: *Philadelphia, Jan. 17.*

Extract out of a letter from Fredericksburg, Virginia, Jan. 8.

Last Friday noon, General Arnold landed with about 1,500 infantrymen and some cavalry 15 miles south of Richmond, where he arrived the following day. Westham with all its fortifications has been destroyed by this traitor, large supplies of rum have been emptied onto the streets, much sugar and other goods thrown into the water but no tobacco has been wasted. They withdrew that same day. It is certain that the traitor Arnold is holding the chief command although some have asserted that it was General Phillips, who was commanding this corps. [8] [summary]

Extract out of a letter from a distinguished gentleman of the Netherlands, Amsterdam, Sept. 20.

We have received your letter from July 10. Your news that the spirit of the Americans of 1775 and 1776 is beginning to awaken again has given us much pleasure. Our ladies of rank have immediately engaged themselves with fixing the date of your independence. This will certainly be definite for what gentleman would be so bold as to enter into a dispute with the fair sex or [even] *contradict them. The ill-bred fools at St. James will continue to fight against it [independence], however vainly, but we have been aware for a long time that they have absolutely no manners* [etc.] -- [accurate]

Rutland, Febr. 7. Captain von Bärtling sen. went to New York again. We could not persuade Major Hopkins to have me go along because he had to await orders from General Washington's Headquarters etc. I wrote Gen. von Riedesel the following letter:

Right Honorable Baron, Gracious Major General:
To you, Right Honorable Sir, I wish respectfully to report that although he has taken great pains and offered me his parole, I was not able to get out of captivity together with Captain von Bärtling. Major Hopkins said that he was not permitted to do anything about it because he had already written to General Washington and now had to await orders. However sad I view my present situation to be, I am nevertheless happy that I have never been guilty of that with which Captain of the Cavalry Fricke and others --- have charged me.[9] I am an honest man, and nothing is more precious to me than this my moral character. Let me add that the greatest fortune on earth will never have the power over me to disregard those duties to which I have solemnly committed myself. I am most respectfully asking you again, Right Honorable Sir, to advance my early exchange, etc., etc.

I also wrote letters to my wife and friends.

Worcester [Massachusetts Spy] Febr. 8. *The latest news read that Arnold is 10 miles south of Petersburg with his corps and that the Virginia militia is approaching in order to overtake and capture him.* [accurate]

Arnold, take care! --

Boston Monday paper [Independent Ledger], Febr. 12: *Baltimore, Jan. 16.*
A letter from the West Indies announces the arrival of 10 Engl. warships and 12 infantry regiments. The ships under the command of Sir Samuel Hood are the Barfleur, Monarch, Gibraltar, Princessa, Monarca, Alfred, Belliquer, Prince William, St. Albans, Panther etc. [accurate]
        Trenton, Jan. 17. The malcontented soldiers of the Pennsylvania Regiments, who had left the army, have now been paid the money due them and have quietly returned to the army and their duties. Taken as a whole, this situation at first appeared to have some import and gave us cause for alarm, but it now gives us added proof of the steadfastness, honor and faithfulness of our soldiers who are fighting for the freedom of their country, willingly sacrificing themselves. This must teach General Clinton that he can bribe a vile General Arnold, but that it is not within his power to corrupt an American soldier.[10] [accurate]
        Chatham, Febr. 24. Last week, a strong detachment of our army crossed over to Staten Island and there attacked an English picket; they killed 3 and took 2 prisoner. [accurate]

N.B. This was a most important affair.

Boston, Febr. 19. We learn from a letter from Martinque, Jan. 19, that Holland has declared the United States of America independent and that Spain has taken away East and West Florida from the English.[11] *During the last holy days, an attempt was made by persons in New York and Long Island to seize the person of Sir Henry Clinton and take him captive to General Washington. Unfortunately, it was discovered and his headquarters have since been covered by 2 cannon. Several persons under suspicion have been thrown in jail.* [summary]

Rutland, Febr. 20. A woman from Hardwick has had an open leg wound for many years and has been compelled to lie almost continuously in bed for the past 2 years. I was called to her and found the leg very swollen and full of abscesses. The least movement caused her great pain. Several physicians in New England had made attempts but were not able to cure the leg. It had already cost the man [her husband] a fair bloodletting. I had little hope of curing the leg because the patient did not have good humours. Tearfully, she asked me to help her. If I could not help her, she would have to die, she said in the presence of two American doctors, each of whom had already gotten more than 500 piasters for tending to the leg. First, I had her take an emetic-- this seemed ridiculous to the gentlemen -- after which I prescribed loosening, gentle purgatives. Thereupon I covered the abscesses with dry charpie [scraped lint] and wrapped the leg up to the body with a wet bandage that was moistened with T. Vegt. min. goul[ard's extract];[12] in 10 weeks, the leg was completely cured. She asserted that the fontanels [ulcers] on both legs were free from attacks. The man, who was not in the best of circumstances, frequently urged me to send him a bill supposing that it would at least amount to 50 or 60 piasters. I did not give him a bill but told him that he owed me 10 piasters, which he paid me with tears in his eyes. -- "What am I to do?" he exclaimed, "I cannot repay you the benefits you bestowed on me but the world will know it." He was a scholar, a Rebel and a poet and he wanted to put the following piece in the newspapers, which I, however, did not permit. This is the poem:

The overflowing of a Grateful Heart Humbly inscribed to the Respected Doctor Wasmus in Commemoration of favours received by his obliged friend and obedient Servant, who groans under the Pressure of a Burden of Benefits. Hardwick, Febr. 18, 1781.

> Awake, my muse inspire my Heart --
> Teach me to act a grateful Part
> Nor let the invenom'd cruel Dart --
> of base Ingratitude
> Admittance find within my Breast.
> But may I make it my request
> That those may be forever blest,
> That Seek to do me good.
>
> My thanks to Heav'n I'd first present
> For all its gracious favors lent
> Nor ever forget the Instrument
> By Providence employ'd
> Whose overflowing Generous Soul,
> No Stingy Principles infold
> Whose healing Hand has Blessings roll'd,
> By Worthless me employ'd.
>
> Directed by his friendly Heart
> He play'd the Skillful Surgeon's Part
> And cur'd the raging Ulcers Smart,
> which had for many years before
> Occasion'd bitter Groans and Sighs
> Lamenting Moans and Weeping Eyes.
> With all her friends did Sympathize,
> Such anguish had the Sore.
>
> But when the Cure his hand affray'd
> what Alteration was there made
> How soon the Swelling was Allay'd.
> The Inflammation gone.
> The cure assuay'd returning case
> Express'd in Smiles her friends did please,

The cure performed by Swift Degrees
Brought Consolation on.

How good was Heav'n thus to incline
the learned Stranger's Gen'rous mind
And blest the means by him design'd to Save
the needed Limb of her that is my loving mate
and helper in this trying State.
Surely the benefits are great,
we have received by him.

Say you who're active to Defray
the depths of natural Mystery.
And nice Distinction love to try.
Say which you most admire
His Skillful Hand or Gen'rous breast
which sordid avarice had supprest.
For when his Bill I did request
But Dollars Ten required.

Surely Such favours from his Hand
Enlarged Gratitude Demands
which makes me much indebted Stand
Such goodness he doth Show.
While my full heart for joy doth leap,
while tears of Gratitude I weep.
I'll wish my Patron he may reap
as liberal as he sow'd.

And Since he'll nothing more receive
my burdend bosom I'll relieve,
By wishing him a long reprieve
from all that may annoy.
May Peace and Health his Days attend
And when his mortal Scene shall end
With Rapture may his Soul ascend
to Boundless Realms of joy --

Ebenezer Washborn[13]

[Capitalizations and spelling in the original.] [There follows a German translation of the above poem.]

From the Worcester paper [Massachusetts Spy]. *Richmond, Virginia, Jan. 10:*
Copy of Arnold's letter, which he had sent at Burwel's Ferry to the commanding officer on shore.
'On board His Majesty's ship Hope, Jan. 2, 1781.
The corps of His Majesty's troops, which I have the honor of commanding, has been sent here solely to protect His Majesty's faithful subjects [in this colony]. I am somewhat astonished to see armed inhabitants appear on shore. Nevertheless, I am sending Lieut. White to you in a truce ship in order to be informed about your intentions and undertakings. -- Should the troops encounter resistance at their landing, then everybody must expect appropriate treatment. It is my duty to assure you that I do not have the intention of offending peaceful subjects much less of taking possession of their belongings. Everything furnished to my troops will immediately be paid here. Yours etc.
Benedictus Arnold, Brig. Gen.'

Chatham, Jan. 31.   Last Friday, Gen. Robertson arrived in New York from Staten Island with about 2,500 men. He is believed to have the intention of invading this Province, perhaps to carry out his filthy plan to poison the minds of our brave soldiers. -- Everything we can advise Sir Henry Clinton is that he satisfy his restive hirelings, the Hessians, to whom he owes 15 months pay, before trying to corrupt our soldiers [tempting them] *to betray [their country].* [accurate]

Boston, Febr. 25 [15].   We know from a Martinique paper that Comte d'Estaing has had an encounter at sea with Commodore Hood,[14] *who had been designated to go to St. Lucia with 16 warships and 100 transport ships carrying troops and provision. After brief resistance, Comte d'Estaing seized 6 of their warships and 95 transport ships.* [accurate]

N.B. Our Thomas did do some reading.

At the end of this month, the guinea has a value of 370 piasters.

Month of March 1781

[in English]

Acrostic

Exact in Shapes, how do her Charms engage!
Lowly in mind though of high Parentage,
Ingenious, Witty, active, Polite, Free
Sober and chaste Soft as the zephyr be
A Beauteous face, join'd with a Beauteous mind,
But rarely in one Woman can one find:
Exalted Virtue dwells in her fair Breast,
The Lodging worthy the illustrious guest .
Happy the man who shall the fair obtain
Rejoice he may to wear the silken chain.
Unto what wond'rous heights his pleasures rise,
Gazing with rapture on her brilliant Eyes,
Good Heav'ns how pleas'd to press her Snowy Breast,
Let warm imagination paint the rest.
Excuse the muse if she's approach'd too near
 Silence shall seal her lips t'offend the fear.

The following is a letter from a gentleman in Virginia.
When Judas Arnold landed in Virginia with the corps that Gen. Clinton had stooped so low as to entrust to him, he sent an officer on shore to Gen. Nelson to order him to surrender immediately with the troops under his command. Gen. Nelson replied, 'Return, give Arnold my regards and tell him that I will send him 100 barrels of tobacco.'. 'I don't understand what you mean,' said the officer. 'Arnold will immediately understand it,' shouted Gen. Nelson, 'with 100 barrels of tobacco, I can buy Arnold and his corps.'[15] *-- We have been informed from Boston that Congress has ordered new paper money to be printed and the old to be exchanged and burned.*

Worcester paper [Massachusetts Spy], March 1: *London, Nov. 2.*

The following - so we are told - are the Articles of Peace that have come from Madrid with the latest mail.[16]

In the name of - etc. - In order to prevent further desolation of war and to ward off the increase of misfortune for so many people [to stop the effusion of more Christian blood], we, the belligerent powers of Great Britain, France, Spain and the 13 United Provinces [States of North America], being by our plenipotentiaries assembled in Madrid, do hereby agree upon the following articles of pacification:

Art. I. That all hostilities shall cease in Europe on next Jan. 15 and all captures made in Europe after that day shall be restored. Likewise those having been captured in the American or African waters shall be free on March 15 and those in Asia on July 15.

Art. II. Great Britain shall withdraw her armies and fleets and shall forever renounce her rights as [and title of] sovereign[ty] of the 13 United Provinces [States of North America], i.e., from Georgia to New Hampshire, both inclusive, and [does and] will forever recognize the 13 United Provinces [acknowledge them in full sovereignty] as Free and Independent States.

Art. III. Great Britain must restore, to France, Pondichéry[17] *and whatever else she has conquered from her in Asia, also the Island of St. Lucia, in the West Indies; to give up the Island of Cap Breton, the Islands of St. Pierre and Miquelon, together with the right to fish on the coast of Newfoundland.*

Art. IV. Spain must withdraw her troops from West Florida, but remain in possession of New Orléans; and Great Britain must withdraw her forces from Nicaragua and every other part of the French and Spanish territories which they may have conquered in the course of this war.

Art. V. France, Spain and the 13 Provinces [United States] must forever guarantee sovereignty over Canada as well as over East and West Florida to Great Britain.

Art. VI. France must restore the Islands of the Grenades, the Grenadines, Dominica and St. Vincent to Great Britain with all their dependencies in the same condition in which they were when France had taken them over.

Art. VII. It has been unanimously decided by these powers that none of them should make demands [on their own to restore] *whatever this war may have ruined; on the contrary, they have bound themselves to live forever like friends and allies, that all their harbors be open to all these powers and that, in accordance with the rights and laws of all nations etc., they will support each other in case of need.*
[accurate]

N.B. The author of the above will have had fun producing this peace [sic] of amusement. Don't you think so, my dear Thomas?

Worcester paper [Massachusetts Spy], March 8. *The celebrated Capt. Paul Jones arrived in Philadelphia from Lorient on the ship Ariel on the 19th of last month.*
[accurate]

Boston Monday paper [Independent Ledger], March 12: *Chatham, Feb. 21.*

Last Monday, our men lost several whalers belonging to Brunswick [near Staten Island]; on the other hand, our men seized 3 sloops from the enemy, which were taken to Brunswick. [accurate]

Boston, March 12. Extract out of a letter from Nantes, dated Nov. 30.

Since the prospects of our enemy seem good in the South, the British Government is resolved to continue the war in America in greater earnest and is preparing to send no less than an additional 10,000 of their troops to America and the West Indies. I wished we would not flatter ourselves with false hope in America; not deceive ourselves with the dangerous idea that England is not able to do this or that and the like; believe that they have enough to do in Europe with resisting their enemies and thus preventing them from sending extra troops and provisions to America. These ideas have frequently given us a [dangerously] false sense of security and we have recognized our mistake too late. Penobscot is a case in point. -- In spite of this would-be weakness of the enemy, let us focus our attention on our own strength and no longer depend on what others should do for us. Perhaps we will then be better able to carry out our plans and surely work for our cause with more honor. -- [accurate]

Worcester paper [Massachusetts Spy], March 15. *We received the news that Admiral Rodney has entered the Dutch free port of St. Eustatius with his fleet and seized all the French, Spanish and American ships there. If this is true, it will probably induce Holland to declare war against England.*[18] [accurate]

N.B. This is of no great import, my dear Thomas, the Dutch are peace-loving and can stand a good push.

Boston Monday paper [Independent Ledger], March 19. *A ship loaded with wine has arrived here from Teneriffe. On his journey, the captain spoke on different days with 3 Dutch ships, whose crews unanimously stated that the war between Holland and England had already been declared. On board the Romulus, which has been brought into Newport, 10,000 guinea pieces have been discovered, with which the troops of the traitor Judas Arnold were to be paid.* [accurate]

Worcester [Continental Journal], March 22. *[Philadelphia, March 7]*
We have the confirmation from Philadelphia that the English have seized all the ships at St. Eustatius as well as the Dutch ships in all the other European harbors. [summary]

Boston Thursday paper [Continental Journal], March 25 [29]. *[Extract of a letter from a general officer, dated West Point, March 16, 1781.]*
The fleet which had set sail from New York with troops aboard last week, returned on Sunday. They had apparently received a report that the traitor Arnold has been captured with his corps, and that caused their return. Marquis de Lafayette, a brave and gallant officer, has landed in Virginia with 1,500 men of the [France's] elite troops. [accurate]

Independent Ledger, March 26: *New York, March 7.*
Last week, one of His Majesty's warships arrived here from Chesapeake in 4 days; in several letters, we have read the news that Brig. General Arnold has very much distinguished himself. His post has been considerably fortified with new defensive works and covered with many heavy cannon. Portsmouth, the main headquarters of this general, is safe from all attacks by the French and the Rebels. -- [summary]

Extract out of a letter from Philadelphia, Febr. 27.
Judas Arnold is in Portsmouth, Virginia, where he experienced a major exodus on the part of his troops. It is said that no less than 600 men have deserted him - and

that he is trapped there with 1,000 men. At the mouth of the Elizabeth River, where it joins the James River, one ship of 64 cannon, 2 frigates, and one ship of 28 [20] cannon are riding, which also blockade him. -- [accurate]

Worcester [Massachusetts Spy], March 9 [29].

From Boston we have received the news that the French fleet has seized a large part of the Cork fleet, destined for New York; moreover, that Arnold, the infidel, has been captured together with his troops. Because both pieces of news will first need confirmation, we do not wish to present them as truth.[19] [accurate]

This confirmation, my dear Thomas, will probably fail to appear for a long time. --
I had a cap made in Manchester as well as a pair of trousers. Incl. the work of making them, they cost 1,600 piasters in paper money. Even if the guinea has the value of 375 piasters, it is, nevertheless, incredibly expensive

End of this Month

Month of April 1781

1st   Since my practice is growing by the day and I am therefore never at home, I have no time to read the papers, much less translate them. I am therefore stopping the news that I used to take from the papers. --

3rd   While I was visiting patients in Brookfield today, I had the opportunity of being in the company of an American colonel. He assured me that our former Chief Clerk Senf from the Dragoon Regiment had been appointed colonel and commander of the American engineer corps and invested with a commission and that either he had already married the only daughter of General Greene or would shortly do so. After Gen. Washington, this Gen. Greene is the second-in-command and has large estates in Virginia and Pennsylvania. Thus, Senf will be sole heir there.[20]

7th   Today, I was riding through Hardwick in the warm sun. I saw a large couleuvre (adder) about 5 feet long and of very beautiful colors. I was surprised to see a snake so early in the year and made the effort of getting off my horse to kill it. All the people whom I told about it were very happy that I had killed the first snake I had seen. They said, "This is a good omen, you will be lucky this year and get the better of all your enemies." So superstitious are the New Englanders. --
My headquarters in Hardwick are at Major General Warner's. Here I have my own room, which during my absence is always locked. It is now called "his room," and I maintain here a kind of pharmacy. Because I frequently use up all the medicine I have with me, I refill my jars here without having to ride back to Rutland.
Miss Amity, the general's oldest daughter, who has taken it upon herself to care for my affairs and who calls me brother, will soon get married. She has already given orders to her sister Constance to take care of everything I need whenever I shall be in their house. I am supposed to come to the wedding and Miss Constance wants me to take her. I am making all possible remonstrations against it, also telling her that if she lets herself be taken by a prisoner of war to her sister's wedding, her many and devoted admirers will be jealous; that she is so fond of dancing and that I have no idea of how to perform these dances. "All right," she said, "if you can be so cruel as not to dance with me, we will sit way back in a corner and talk about your wife and children, is that what you want? Would that be all right with you?" "Of course, agreed! and we will drink a little glass with it." --
Hardwick lies 15 miles west of Rutland. This general has the largest manor in the County of Worcester. When he is not in service, namely during winter time, one sees the maj. gen. do all kind of farm labor and this is the way of life of all American officers. There is no pride in these rich people; they are diligent workers and make it their fondest

and most important business to be of use to their fellowmen, to console them in misfortune and to share their happiness.

End of this Month

Month of May 1781

1st   Today I travelled to the wedding in Hardwick. I had hardly stayed long enough to witness the actual ceremony when I was asked to go to a patient in Petersham. It was 7 o'clock at night when I left Hardwick. All the wedding guests were displeased at my departure, but I was happy to escape. I had to promise to come back that same night or the following morning. That was not possible, however, because I visited a patient in Barry through which I had to pass on the way back before returning to Rutland.

3rd   Today, I was back at Rutland and found letters and messages for me to go to Princeton and Holden. Thus, I took another horse and rode to Princeton.

4th   I rode to Holden. This village is located 10 miles east of Rutland. I have a pharmacy there similar to that in Hardwick, this one is at Mr. John Childroy's,[21] a IUSTITIARIUS [legal advisor], at whose house I also have my own room and feel at home. The room is solely for me and during my absence, nobody may enter. As in Hardwick, I do not pay any rent for it. I have fixed certain days in which I am to be in these places, and those wishing to consult me can come. When I arrive, I always find a few waiting because it [my practice] is not only known in the entire county but everywhere else too.

12th   Since some naval officers departed for New York today to be exchanged, I gave my treatise, written on 8 sheets, to Captain William Ross, who has promised on his honor to give it to the Hessian post in New York. This treatise deals with the diseases in Canada and New England and also with the herbs and roots which these provinces produce. I discovered these partly by myself, partly I learned about them from the inhabitants; I also studied them in English books. It is addressed to my friend, the Chancery Administrator Werner in Wolfenbüttel. I wish from the bottom of my heart that this work, which has cost me very great effort, will safely get into my friend's hands.[22]

20th   Today, the news arrived here in Rutland that our Convention troops have been marching to Rutland from Virginia. Is it true? I do not believe it.[23] --

At the end of this month, the guinea has the value of 390 piasters in paper money.

Month of June 1781

18th   So far, it has not been very hot here this year; on the contrary, it is so cold that in spite of the sun shining, one has to sit near the fireplace today. People fear that the cold may harm the grain. The wind is continually blowing from NNW.
The good slaves, who as Royalists have sought protection with the English at the beginning of this war, have been confiscated by Congress and will now be on public sale for the one offering the most. This is very hard![24] --

24th   Today, letters to Lieut. Gebhard from Maj. Gen. von Riedesel came from New York together with my exchange certificate. I had been exchanged for an American doctor by the name of Skinner, from the 2nd Virginian Regiment, as early as last March. At the same time, the dep. commissary general Major Hopkins sent me a pass to go to Halifax or New York by truce ship.

Boston, June 22, 1781.

[In English]: This may Certify that the Bearer Doctor Wasmus, former Prisoner of War to the United States of America, now being exchanged and having Permission to go from Rutland on the most direct Boat to New London and from thence to New York on a flag of Truce. He is Therefore to pass unmolested, while behaving himself as a Gentleman in his Situation ought to do.

John Hopkins
Dep. Com. Gen. of Prisoners.

As I have now been finally exchanged, I have to ride around collecting the money owed to me.

30th   The old paper money has been discontinued. New [paper money] has been substituted, but nobody is willing to accept it. The old can still be spent in contribution [sic] where a paper piaster is equal to a silver piaster. Whoever has no paper money must spend silver money. Eight days ago, I had as much as 100,000 paper piasters and was really in a dilemma. But now I wished I had 100 times as much; I exchanged 400 piasters today. Nothing but gold and silver is now coined. The French fleet and army on the coast of America are selling out all their provisions in New England; that brings much gold and silver into the country.

End of this Month

Month of July 1781

1st   The Convention troops do not want to come as yet. We have here several pieces of news from them: that they had recently been lévied by the English; that they had liberated themselves; that they had been moved farther inland to Virginia and so forth.--

24th   Today, the reliable news came that the Convention troops continue in Virginia and have been made prisoners of war; that all [their] officers, 118 in number, have been separated from them and taken to Hartford and East Windsor in the Province of Connecticut. This must be true for I have spoken to a man here who knew several of our officers by name, including Lieut. Colonel von Mengen. We probably will soon have more news.

I am daily awaiting news that a truce ship is to sail to New York or Halifax.

Wherever I go these days, the inhabitants do not want to believe that I am to leave them for I have more patients than any of their doctors in New England. But there is no way that I can remain here; I would be listed as a deserter. What shock would that cause in the hearts of my wife and children if they heard that I had deserted!--

Many of those reading this will answer me, "Why do you worry in New England about what they are saying about you in Germany?" Yes, [you are right] I would not hear it, that is true, but should a woman decide to submit to the terrible inconveniences of such a long journey? That is most terrifying for anyone and particularly difficult for a woman. The mere thought of it makes me shudder!

No, my friends, I have to leave you, I cannot stay with you. Two obligations are calling me back to my post, I may not forget these, I may not! For I have committed myself to both in the most solemn rite.--

And now the hope, the sweet thought of embracing my beloved and my friends in Germany once again, is completely revitalizing my soul. What warmth I am feeling in my heart while writing this! -- I will see you again, Providence will grant me this happiness! --

End of this Month

Month of August 1781

20th   Today, I found at Esq. Paine's in Worcester a letter to Lieut. Gebhard, which had come from New York. It was from Capt. von Bärtling sen., who wrote that on July 24, Maj. Gen. von Riedesel would set sail for Canada with all our troops, who had gathered in New York.[25] This was terrible news for me. The idea of making the dreadful journey over the ocean through the Gulf and the St. Lawrence River to Québec in the fall almost makes me think of remaining in New England. -- Nevertheless, I immediately wrote a letter to the commissary gen., Maj. Hopkins in Boston, that he should let me know whether a truce ship would soon depart from there. He answered that he would send a truce ship to Halifax in Nova Scotia in a fortnight. If I felt like going along, I would soon have to come to Boston. I, therefore, started getting ready for my journey, selling horses and surplus furniture. Everywhere, people expressed their bon voyage in peculiar ways; they especially wished that as soon as I got on the high seas, I would be captured again and brought back here. Because I have had a quiet life among them, have been lucky in all my undertakings, have been honored and loved by everyone and yet didn't want to stay with them, they prophesized that I would not fare well. Many said, "You will regret it when you are in miserable Canada and often wish you were with us; you will then not be able to see your wishes fulfilled. -- You are going to our cruel enemy, who are trying to destroy us; you will again join those who are making us slaves and want to ruin us. But we shall pray for you, bless you, and wish you good luck and godspeed; we pray to God that He be your protector, who fills your heart with compassion, so that cruelty will never enter it. -- May you be charitable and humane toward those who might come as prisoners into your power or into that of our tyrannical enemy so that you may be so fortunate as to be of service to your enemy. -- Alas, may you never forget how you have been taken in and treated by the inhabitants of New England, whom you had considered your enemy." -- I am often exposed to this preaching for hours whereby very many tears are forever being shed, especially by the fair sex. --

31st   Today, I came back to Rutland and took leave of all my friends here. Pastor Buckminster and his family were troubled by my departure.

End of this Month

Month of September 1781

2nd   I rode to Worcester from Rutland via Princeton, collected some more money owed to me and continued [riding] to Holden. At these 3 places I was offered 5 cows and 3 oxen to take along as presents if I consented to stay in New England. But it was of no use trying to persuade me. I was firmly resolved to return to my post. If I were not married, I would certainly remain in this fortunate country among these good people. Never will I find such good fortune again, -- when I return [to Germany]. And how easily could that [my staying here] have been realized if this evil war had been terminated and my wife had decided to come to me. --
Financially, I am in a very favorable situation. I have 99 portuguese, 96 guinea pieces and 285 piasters or specie in silver. If I could only substitute money for the sea journey to Canada, I would immediately give 100 specie. N.B. One portuguese is 8 specie, and 3 guineas are 14 specie.

3rd   I rode to Worcester and stayed with Mr. Paine, Esq. My horse was taken to a meadow and my portmanteau locked away because I was to stay 4 days with him. Before this war, this man used to be one of the King's first councillors; he has 3 sons in the English services and one of them is pharmacist general with the Engl. army in New York.

6th   I finally took my leave and rode to Shrewsbury today, where [on the]

7th,   I hurt my right arm by a fall down the stairs.

8th   I reached Weston. Because my shoulder was very swollen and hurt a great deal, I had to stay here and let my shoulder soak. This would have been a fine opportunity for remaining during the winter because I was incapacitated, but I had to follow my destiny. --

10th   The news came that General Arnold had arrived in New London with his fleet and his army on board and had plundered and burned the city on the 7th of this month.[26]

11th   I reached Boston. I had rushed my trip because I feared that the cartel ship might set sail before my arrival. I took my lodging in the inn "To the White Lamb" on Main Street. Boston lies under 42°20' of northern latitude on an island and is almost completely surrounded by water. It has but one entrance on land from the side of Roxbury, called Boston Neck, which has been artificially constructed. Boston has 17 churches; the main street is 3 Engl. miles long and the city as a whole is oblong in shape. The streets are well paved and very densely populated; it has a large port that is sown with islands, as it were. The largest ships can come so close to the city that one can enter them from the dockyard. All ships lie here very securely [anchored]. This Province of Massachusetts Bay borders 3 other Provinces, that are called New England; these are New Hampshire, Connecticut and Rhode Island. To be sure, it is not the largest Province of North America but it is better settled than the rest and, according to the latest register, it has more than 600,000 inhabitants.[27]   Boston is the capital and, regarding its commerce, industry and communication, the 2nd city in North America.[28]   It does not only entertain superior trade relations in New England but also with the other Provinces, the West Indies and other parts of the world. In addition to commerce, the inhabitants of Boston are occupied with wool and linen weaving, with distilling rum, shipbuilding and most of all with fishing at the promontory of Cape Cod, which got its name from the many stockfish and dried cod. For this fish is called codfish and more than 40,000 kilograms of these fish are caught annually.

Marblehead in Essex County, a beautiful little town, has the most extensive fishery of all the seaside towns there. The inhabitants usually take 5 trips to Nova Scotia [each year] and often bring back 20,000 to 25,000 kilograms of dried cod and stockfish. These New England fish, however, are not as good as those that are caught by the English on the banks of Newfoundland. The New England fish are too heavily salted. Because salt is generally rare in America, they take the concentrated salt of the Tortugas or from the Islands of Cap Verde for salting fish. The English, on the other hand, take their salt from Portugal or France.

Cambridge in Middle Essex County is the seat of a university or Harvard COLLEGIUM. There, as many as 300 to 400 students are usually [enrolled], who are instructed by 3 professors in the manner of English universities, namely in theology, oriental languages and mathematics. Falmouth, a commercial town at the southern coast of this Province, exports much wood for shipbuilding etc. In addition to these, a number of other towns are found here and there in this Province, but they are not as lively as the seaside towns; most of these are open cities where the houses do not stand in regular fashion as they do in the seaside towns. Many of them, such as Salem, Rehoboth, Goshen, Bethabora, seem to express with their names etc. a region of Palestine inhabited by the Europeans in North America. The whole Province is divided into 13 counties and each of these again in special city and village districts. As I have mentioned before, such a New England village usually has a tract of land measuring 7 English square miles. When 80 families have settled here or, according to a new regulation, 150 tax payers live here, they have the right to send one of their fellow citizens as deputy to the annual legislative assembly in Boston, thus taking part in public affairs. Together with the proceeds from farming and fishing, abundant cattle raising and forestry constitute the greatest wealth of the Province. Large quantities of logs, planks, even ready-made houses are exported from here, together with tar, pitch, turpentine and potash. A large amount of such salted provisions as beef and pork also go to the West Indian Islands every year. From the fishery alone, one can place the annual earnings at better than two million piasters. Two other Provinces also belong to Massachusetts Bay, namely Maine and Sagadahoc, which are located completely outside the district between New Hampshire and Nova Scotia. These are not permitted to send their deputies to the annual legislative assembly like the other Provinces. They have settled along the seacoast and inside the Bay of Fundy. Both of these Provinces have more than 20 seaports, large and deep enough for warships; they do not freeze in the winter. The ports most likely to be ice-bound are Falmouth, Townsend, Majabagaduce, Sheepscot, Penobscot etc. The first of these lies on the Penobscot River and is the most important. A very lively timber trade in white pine goes on there; masts of 72 and 80 feet are not rare at all. In the year 1722, one counted here between 16,000 and 17,000 souls who, like Vermont, have tried in vain to become a separate Province. The two islands, Nantucket and Martha's Vineyard, are mostly inhabited by Quakers and likewise belong to Massachusetts Bay. They support themselves with fishing, mostly whaling, which they pursue in the St. Lawrence Gulf and Davis Strait. The inhabitants multiply so fast that every year some have to emigrate to other provinces. Nantucket, a sandy rock of about 30,000 to 34,000 morgen, sends even more whalers out to sea than Great Britain and in the year 1778, it had 197 ships at sea with 2,200 sailors on board. Boston is the capital of the 4 Provinces that are called New England. The capitals of the other Provinces are Québec, Capital of Canada and Halifax, Capital of Nova Scotia.

Massachusetts Bay	-Boston
New Hampshire	-Portsmouth
Rhode Island	-Newport
Connecticut	-New Haven
New York	-New York
New Jersey	-Port Amboy
Pennsylvania	-Philadelphia
Delaware	-Newcastle
South Carolina	-Charleston
Maryland	-Annapolis
Virginia	-Williamsburg
North Carolina	-Wilmington
Georgia	-Savannah

I reported to Major Hopkins, the dep. commissary gen. of all the prisoners of war in this Province, and learned that a cartel ship would sail to Québec in a few days, on which I could embark if I so choose. --

12th   This morning, Major Hopkins introduced me to Governor Hancock,[29] who treated me with extraordinary friendliness, talking many things over with me. -- The English naval officers, Capt. Tonge's 2 lieuts. and doctor, and the Paymaster General of the Province of Canada, Mr. Winslow, were presented to the governor along with me. Like me, they have been exchanged and want to sail to Canada. The officers had all been taken prisoner on board a ship. Capt. Tonge had commanded the war sloop *Jack* of 18 cannon and, in company of the English warships *Charles Town* and *Vulture*, was to accompany 29 transport ships to Halifax. They were, however, attacked on their journey not far from the Spanish River [now Sydney River] on the coast of Cap Breton by 2 French frigates, *Astrée* and *Hermione*, each of 44 cannon. Capt. Tonge engaged both frigates and for more than 2 hours was exposed to the tiers [of cannon] of both frigates; his rigging and sails were so much damaged that he was compelled to strike his sails and surrender after the fleet was safely out of sight. Capt. Tonge had suffered no more than 2 dead and 3 wounded. According to their own account, the enemy frigates had had 56 dead and wounded. Such an advantage could a small ship gain over a large one in one engagement! They [the French] took the *Jack* to Boston.

16th   Colonel Skinner, the commissary general, arrived here from the headquarters of General Washington and we learned that the cartel ship was not to sail to Québec but that a French cartel ship was to go to Halifax with English sailors on board. If the French commodore on the frigate *Astrée* allowed it, we could all go along.

17th   Capt. Tonge and I went to the French frigate *Astrée* and asked the French Capt. Monsieur de la Peyeuse to allow us to join him on his journey to Halifax. He wrote down our names right then and there and sent one of his officers to the cartel ship with the order to take us along. With the first favorable wind, the cartel ship is to set sail. Mons. de la Peyeuse showed us great honor: we were to take the midday meal with him. The cleanliness on this ship was extraordinary and I do not know whether English ships are better in this regard. I also made the acquaintance of the ship's doctors. The first doctor persuaded me to buy some medicine from him, warning me that medicines were scarce and expensive in Canada. I knew that medicines had been scarce and expensive in Canada in the years 1776 and 1777, but how should I know if in the meantime many medicines had not come to Canada from Europe. Nevertheless, I took the risk and bought 400 pounds of rhubarb pills for 800 piasters. One piaster is 2 schill. 16 groschen in Conv. mintage. At my departure from Braunschweig I had to pay the same for 1 pound [of rhubarb pills]. Moreover, I bought china powder nitrum dept., tartar cream, ammoniac salt, gum arabic, ammonia, guajo [guaiac] liquid, various mercurials and more such items as Empl. Ungt. [unguent] etc. for as much as 745 piasters, i.e., for 1,545* piasters total. All this was packed in bales, sealed, signed with my name and taken to the French cartel ship. Since I was led to expect some profit from these medicines, everyone would easily conclude that I am ready to go to Canada. But this terrible journey will cause us many more anxious hours. If it were only one month earlier or if we could only depart immediately. Who knows how long we will have to stay here and moreover, will there be a ship in Halifax ready to take us along and set sail at once? All these thoughts worry me. But let us hope for the best. --
In Boston, the news is expected every day that Lord Cornwallis has been captured with his army, for he has been encircled by Gen. Greene and 10,000 French auxiliary troops.[30]

*according to Convention money 2,060 schillings.

20th   We received orders to embark tomorrow.

21st   Today, we embarked. Major Hopkins allowed me to take the Dragoon Rudolph Tacke along as servant. How happy I was to have someone to take care of my things! -- It was 10 o'clock in the morning when we went aboard the French ship. This cartel ship was a scow of 250 tons ballast, called the *Squirrel*. Besides us, she had 82 sailors for exchange on board. The wind was from the east and against us.

22nd   We had a favorable NW wind this morning, and 1 French ship with 50 cannon and 3 frigates of 36 to 44 cannon set sail. We were all on board and also had our pilot with us.
So that we might not learn which course the French ships had taken, we had orders to set sail. The wind was calm and the French capt. had orders from the governor not to sail farther than Castle William. We, therefore, cast anchor between this castle and Governor's Island. In the evening, we went to Boston by boat to see Polly Sullivan. She was -- the general's only child and was ---.

23rd   Toward evening, we received orders to set sail but since the port entrance was full of cliffs and sandbanks, the pilot considered it dangerous. We therefore were lying to.

24th   At 5 o'clock in the morning, we set sail. The wind came from NW and we took course toward NE. At 7 o'clock, we had passed the most perilous spots between the islands and the sandbanks as well as the lighthouse, and at 9 o'clock, we were across from Marblehead, which lay about 3 miles on the left. Soon afterwards, we had lost [sight of] all the land and at noon, we had Cape Cod on the right at a distance of about 40 miles and Cape Ann on the left at a distance of about 50 miles. The wind was abating.

25th   The wind continued blowing from NW. In the forenoon, the English warship *Chatham* of 50 cannon passed us and took 24 sailors from our ship. We informed the *Chatham* that 4 French warships had departed from Boston on the 22nd of this month. This is the same *Chatham* that 3 weeks ago seized the French frigate *Magicienne* of 36 cannon not far from the Boston lighthouse. Until noon, we attained a distance of ----------92 Latitude 42°39'.In the afternoon, a very strong wind blew from NW.

26th   In strong NW wind, we sailed until noon --156 Latitude 43°49'. We reached Brown's Bank in the afternoon and had [measured] 80 fathoms, toward evening 40 fathoms. We passed Cap Sable and before nightfall, we saw the shores of Nova Scotia.

27th   In continual strong NW wind, we advanced in 24 hours ------------------------144 Latitude 43°58'. In the afternoon, the wind changed to NE, becoming contrary. We passed Cap Negro [Island] about 6 miles to our right and toward evening, we were about 3 miles away from the left shore and had Cap La Have [Island] on our left. Three big ships could be seen in front of us, but on account of the distance, we could not tell if they were friend or foe. On our right, we saw an American privateer that did not come near us, however. At 6 o'clock in the evening, the 3 Engl. ships approached us so that we could recognize them. They were the *Assurance* of 44 cannon and the frigates *Charles Town* and *Vulture* that were to join the *Chatham*. Capt. Tonge went on board the *Assurance* and so did 22 sailors from our ship.

28th   Last night, we passed Cap La Have [Island]. The wind changed to NNW Course toward NE. Four Rebel privateers appeared, one of which came very close, fired a cannonball at us and immediately took flight. At noon, we saw the lighthouse of Halifax Harbor. At 3 o'clock in the afternoon, we passed it and Cap Sambro, which lay on our left, and then reached Halifax Harbor. The wind grew contrary. At sunset, we cast anchor one mile from Halifax while facing the city and George's Island.
Up to here we sailed --87

Total --479

Halifax lies under 44°40' of northern latitude.

29th   The wind continues to be contrary today and only by tacking could we advance a little; we again cast anchor and, having disembarked at noon, we went on a boat to Halifax. Together with several other regiments, the Hessian Infantry Reg.[von] Seitz lay here in garrison. We reported to Governor Sir Andrew Hamond and Brig. Gen. Campbell as well as to Colonel [von] Seitz[31] and learned that, 5 weeks ago, Major Gen. von Riedesel had arrived here from New York with a number of Braunschweig troops and had continued sailing from here to Québec. The worst news we heard was that no ship would sail to Québec this fall and that we would consequently have to remain here this winter. Capt. Tonge, his 2 lieuts., the doctor and I moved into the big coffeehouse, called "The Golden Ball," [32] [owned] by Mr. O'Brien.

30th   At the urgent request of Capt. Tonge, the governor promised to buy us one of the ships that had been seized and brought in; in it we were to ride to Québec.
How calm and contented I felt to be free once again! But what do I say? I had never been deprived of my freedom; I was just happy to be out of the region where I had been exposed to the envy, the hatred, the prejudices, lies and slander on the part of my countrymen. A region where the inhabitants, our enemy -- if I am entitled to call them

that -- had always treated us all in love and friendship. They had respected me particularly since I had done various things that many of my equals had not been able to do or to cure. But this had caused the envy and had been the reason why I was hated, despised and lied about by my countrymen. -- Every other nation would have been happy about it and would have sought to elevate their compatriot even higher in granting him the honor. Only my base-minded countrymen thought it did them credit to be contemptuous of their country and their compatriots. -- Nevertheless, I have been lucky enough to get to Halifax and hope to be just as lucky to get to Canada. There, my presence will refute my enemies' lies and prove the rightness of my just cause.[33]

The inhabitants here received us very amicably. They were astounded that I had been a prisoner for 4 years and felt sorry for those continuing to be in captivity in New England; but since they are living among good people, there is no need to pity them. Halifax lies on a height, almost 2 miles long, and has been constructed in oblong fashion. It has beautiful fortifications and one of the most attractive harbors, which is 20 miles long. The city itself has been badly built, the streets are not paved, a totally different nation seems to live here. New England merits our preference. -- Several Germans live in and around Halifax; some 17 [57] Engl. miles out of Halifax is a village called Lunenburg,[34] which is entirely inhabited by Germans. Anyway, the Germans are said to be the richest people in Nova Scotia. There are pigs in Halifax that are black and look misshapen; they are said to be African pigs.

From a friend in Worcester, by the name of Mr. Duncan, I carried a letter to a merchant in Halifax by the name of Achincloss. These two had come from Scotland to America at the same time. But Mr. Achincloss was no longer alive; 2 years ago, he had drowned in a storm at sea between New York and Halifax, together with his brothers. Nine ships had perished at that time. Reading the letter, the young wife, 24 years old, cried and her tears ran upon the paper.

"My husband lies buried in the ocean," she said. "He and Mr. Duncan had been true friends. The unfortunate war prevented me from reporting my husband's terrible death to Mr. Duncan. He [Duncan] writes in his letter that we should take you in as a friend. You will, therefore, be our friend, and I am herewith offering you a part of my house hoping you will immediately take possession of it and stay with us. My venerable old parents, my 2 sisters and I, whom you see gathered here, our servant and our maid are the family in this house. We will all make it our most important business to make life pleasant for you." I replied that I had already taken up quarters in the Coffeehouse in the company of 3 officers and, at the first opportunity and favorable wind, we would set sail for Canada. "Alas, my dear friend," the young widow continued, "my parents and I will do everything possible to prevent you from taking this dangerous journey at this time of year. It is too late to go there and very rarely does a ship arrive safely in Québec in the fall. You ought to stay with us this winter, and next spring you can sail to wherever you wish." I replied that as early as Boston, I had made a friendly agreement with the 3 officers mentioned above not to leave them before Québec and I could not break that. Should we, however, stay here in Halifax during the winter, I should consider myself most fortunate if she, her parents and sisters accepted me among their friends. I had to stay there the whole day and had innumerable questions to answer. The father of this widow, Mr. Fillis, had been a merchant in Boston; he had fled to Halifax with the British fleet and army under Gen. Howe in 1776 and reestablished himself here.[35]

End of this Month

Month of October 1781

1st   A sloop was sold at an auction and the governor ordered her purchased for 230 pounds sterling. He gave her to Capt. Tonge to sail to Québec. She had been an English packet boat, seized by the Americans, made into a privateer of 45 tons ballast and, carrying 8 cannon, she was called "The Greyhound." Capt. Tonge gave her the name *"Jack,"* and the 230 pounds paid for her were credited to the Canadian Government.

As soon as the *Jack* is equipped, we will set sail. I wish it would happen soon. Today, Capt. Tonge and I were guests at the young widow's.

3rd   The frigate *Charles Town* brought in the captured American ship *Polly* of 26 cannon, whose home base is in Salem; the ship is an invalid and in order to get her here, they had to throw all the cannon overboard. Our *Jack* will be ready to sail tomorrow. The Royal ships *Assurance* and *Vulture* arrived here in the afternoon and brought in the American privateer *Fair American* of 10 cannon, that has her home base in Newburyport.

5th   The news that we had already heard before our departure from Boston was repeated today by persons that had come here in the prize mentioned before; namely that Admiral Graves has come upon Monsieur [Comte] le Barras, who had set sail from Rhode Island with 8 warships to unite with Comte de Grasse. Admiral Graves had seized 7 of these warships.[36] I wished that it were so but the news appears too good to be true. --

In the afternoon, the Royal ships *Amphitrite, Vulture* and *Charles Town* departed from here. Capt. Tonge assures us that we will surely set sail tomorrow. All the people in Halifax tell us that it is dangerous to sail to Canada at this time of year and they do not believe that we will reach Québec this fall. Two years ago at the end of September, Colonel von Speth set sail from here to go to Québec. But because of an adverse wind, they could not enter the St. Lawrence River, and he returned in Nov.

Many of the victuals we had bought in Boston were left on the French cartel ship, for the Frenchmen on this ship had treated us very gallantly. Thus we did some shopping here: 10 stübchen [a liquid measure] each of Port wine, Porter beer, West Indian rum, 3 lbs. of green tea, 20 lbs. of coffee, 8 lbs. of chocolate, 40 lbs. of white sugar, 36 chickens, 3 sheep, 1 pig, 6 himten of potatoes, turnips and white cabbage. How much all this cost can be deduced from the fact that one chicken costs one guilder in Conv. money and for one lb. of tobacco (Petun) I paid here 3 1/2 shill. in Halifax currency; this amounts to 22 groschen and 6 pennies in Conv. money.

6th   This forenoon, all the baggage was brought on board. Capt. Tonge told me in confidence that because the ship drew so much water, he did not expect much from it. It had to be pumped out every 2 hours. This was terrible news and I began to regret that I had my medicine and baggage taken on board. Since a ship was going to England, I wrote to my wife in Wolfenbüttel.

In the afternoon, we embarked and at 4 o'clock, we weighed anchor. We sailed in calm NW wind, passed Cap Sambro at 7 o'clock, reached the ocean and took course toward SE. At the harbor entrance, we encountered the Spanish ship *Disdain* from Bilbao, which the *Chatham* had seized. The pleasant young widow, who had not been able to persuade me to spend this winter in her delightful company, cried when I bade her farewell for the last time. She stood on the shore with her sisters, and Capt. Tonge and I waved with our hats and kerchiefs, which they answered with their white kerchiefs until we had lost sight of them and it had become dark. Now, Capt. Tonge pointed to a basket saying, "Forgive me for not showing it to you earlier. But I was afraid you would go back on shore, wishing to thank the widow Achincloss for it and even let yourself be persuaded to remain in Halifax this winter. Yet, your company is so important to me that I had to prevent that at all cost." In the basket, I found 6 bottles of Port wine, 3 bottles of French brandy, a smoked ham, a mutton roast, 2 pieces of smoked salmon, green tea, coffee, chocolate, sugar and 1 1/2 dozen of lemons. A letter lay on top, which I translated from English. [Here follows the letter in German.]

"Dear Sir! I am taking the liberty of giving you some necessary victuals in this basket for the journey. Whenever you enjoy any of it, remember your sincere but also unhappy friend in Halifax, who not only wishes you a happy arrival in Canada, but also that you may enjoy all the happiness this world can offer until the end of your life. If you think me worthy of your friendship, you will make use of the first opportunity to let me know in a few lines that you are alive. When you write to Europe, do not forget to tell your dear wife of my love and friendship for her and to send regards to your dear children. My parents and sisters also send you cordial greetings and wish you bon voyage. Farewell, dear friend, I do not wish you to have any reason to regret your not wanting to stay with us this winter. I rather wish that Providence will forever watch over you and soon unite you with those who, without a doubt, are sighing for you on that other continent. This is the wish of your sincere friend,   Elisabeth Achincloss."

How did I feel reading this letter!
"Cruel creature! Barbarous woman!," I exclaimed, "I find all these gifts you have showered on me extremely difficult to bear because you have robbed me of the opportunity to thank you. And how did I ever deserve so much kindness and friendship!" -- Capt. Tonge laughed and danced all around me while I exclaimed, "With how much enjoyment would I share all this with you, my friends, if only these divine people knew that my heart is filled with the deepest gratitude!" -- Our kitchen and cellar were quite enriched by this gift. We immediately prepared a punch and until 12 o'clock we continually drank nothing but punch while remembering all our friends on both continents. --

7th   In favorable NW wind, we have sailed from Halifax until this noon -------------82
Latitude 45°11', course SEE. Toward evening, the wind changed to NE and blew so hard that it was impossible for us to keep our course. This night, our little ship was almost continually on the verge of sinking and was being pumped incessantly.

8th   With continual, storming NE wind during the past 24 hours, we did not advance any farther than   --- 22

Total   ---583

Latitude 45°30'. We saw land before us at a distance of about 20 miles to the NE: the shores of Nova Scotia.
In pleasant sunshine this afternoon, there was no wind at all (calm). Tonight the wind changed from the direction of SW to SE.

9th   Strong SW wind. We saw the shores of Nova Scotia at a distance of about 6 miles on our left. At 10 o'clock, we were opposite the Canso Harbor, and Capt. Tonge was intending to sail through the Strait of Canso, which is 400 miles nearer than going around Cape North. Around noon, we saw 2 American privateers that were pursuing us. Through the glass [telescope], we saw the American flags very distinctly. They were sailing much faster than we and consequently would soon catch up with us. At my suggestion, Capt. Tonge had bought quite beautiful charts in Halifax for 6 guineas. These charts indicated all the harbors one could enter on the shores of Nova Scotia and we were by a small harbor, Aylesbury Port [Petit-de-Grat Inlet], belonging to Cap Breton. As the chart very distinctly indicated the entrance between the cliffs and the sandbanks, Capt. Tonge decided to enter here. We arrived safely with the larger of the privateers closely behind us. We shot through its sail with a 9 lb. cannon and it turned around us perhaps to give us a broadside. Yet before they were able to turn the ship completely around, it ran aground. Upon seeing this, the second privateer sailed toward the left shore and 2 minutes later, it also ran aground. We sailed farther into the harbor and as the water [level] was falling -- it was ebb tide, -- we also ran aground. To the left of us was a very high hill onto which we hurriedly placed a cannon to cover our ship. Another 9 pound cannon was taken up a height on the right side. The larger privateer was cannonaded; after the 7th shot it struck its sails and surrendered. It was a 2-masted schooner of 50 tons of ballast having 10 cannon and 18 men aboard. It was commanded by a Capt. Würmstadt and 2 lieuts. Capt. Tonge had the prisoners taken on our ship and sent his First Lieut. Mr. Hutchinson with 15 sailors on board our captured prize. The ship's name was *Hope* and she had set sail from Marblehead as recently as 4 weeks ago. The captain had been captured in this war as many as 10 times and every time had lost a

ship. He was a young, pleasant man of 29 years, who showed a great deal of courage telling us right to our faces without any trace of inhibition that if he had known the entrance into the little harbor as well as Capt. Tonge, he would certainly have taken us captive. He added: "I don't want to be captured more than 4 more times since 14 [sic] is a baker's dozen. Now, since I ran out of luck, I wish to be on parole." Capt. Tonge settled the parole for him and his officers, which consisted of going to Boston with their sailors immediately and there reporting to Major Hopkins, dep. com. gen., as prisoners of war; that until a like number of English prisoners of similar rank were sent to Halifax, New York or Québec, they would not act against England in a hostile manner; that after our departure, they would stay in this harbor for 24 hours and not give any information to our enemy during this time. The American capt. hired a small boat from the inhabitants, which was to take them to Canso Harbor tomorrow. No more than 5 families, a mixture of Savages and white men, dwelt there in wretched quarters. They were French, who lived miserably on nothing but fishing. Around midnight when the flood was highest, we set sail to take also the 2nd privateer, but it had already bolted. Up to this harbor, we sailed --49
Latitude 45°50'.

Total --632

10th   Yesterday, we entered here without a pilot and today, we had to exert much effort to get out with a pilot. This time, we had escaped the danger of being captured; it would indeed have been [an] extraordinary [streak of bad luck] to have to return so quickly into captivity. The wishes of my friends in New England would have been fulfilled, however. How surprised they would have been to see me back so soon! The American captain told Capt. Tonge that if he [Tonge] did not want to be captured, he should not sail through the Strait of Canso, for the American brig Lion of 16 cannon and 2 privateers were cruising there. Capt. Tonge replied that in spite of everything, he was determined to sail through the Strait but told me in confidence, "Now we have to sail around Cape North so that we will not again fall into the hands of the Rebels." It was 4 o'clock in the afternoon when we set sail. The wind was from NW, course toward east

11th   Light W wind. In the early morning, we saw 3 large ships about 6 miles away on our right. Since they had taken a different course, they became more and more distant. Until noon, we advanced --58
Latitude 45° 55'. Course toward E. We are about 200 paces away from the former fortress of Louisbourg. We could very distinctly recognize the ruins of this fortress as well as the former great battery and the lighthouse. The wind is from WSW today but has changed last night, the

12th,   to SE so that we have advanced very little.
We continue having the shore of Cap Breton on our left; at noon we passed Scatarie Island. In 24 hours, we advanced but ---29
Latitude 46° 25', course toward E to the Spanish [Sydney] River, because Capt. Tonge believed he would still find the coal fleet of Québec there. About 5 miles behind us, we saw a ship in full sail. As far as we could recognize through the glass, it was a brig. We suspected that it was the brig Lion, of which Capt. Würmstadt had told us. She was probably pursuing us but could no longer catch up with us since the wind was calm and we were also too close to the Spanish River. It was 8 o'clock this evening that we entered here. The fleet from Québec had sailed away at least a fortnight ago but the coal fleet from Halifax was still here. Since so many privateers were cruising around and, moreover, since our ship was in such bad condition that it drew 9 to 12 tons of water every 3 hours, Dep. Paymaster Gen. Mr. Winslow doubted that we would safely reach Canada this year and decided to return with the coal fleet to Halifax. There are no other inhabitants but coal miners in this harbor but there is a battery with cannon and a small garrison. Up to here we have come closer to Canada by ---------------------------------------31

13th   This morning, Mr. Winslow went aboard another ship. The weather is rainy and foggy. At noon, we set sail in SW wind and our course was northeast.

14th   Early this morning, we passed Cap du Nord and the Ile St. Paul and took course toward NW. The wind continued blowing from SW and it was quite foggy. We heard a cannon shot very close by. Since we did not know whether the ship from which the shot had come was friend or foe, we kept very quiet and no one was allowed to say a loud word. We reached the Gulf of St. Lawrence and around noon, the fog had dissipated. We now saw a large 3-masted ship about one mile from us. Capt. Tonge said that we were quite close to the Iles-de-la-Madeleine (Vogel Inseln). Until this noon, we had sailed from the Spanish River   --88
Latitude 48° 23'. This evening, the wind became contrary changing to NW; there was a frightening storm, which also continued this morning the

15th.   Last night, our ship was almost continually under water and since, on account of the adverse wind, the ship could no longer be controlled, Capt. Tonge ordered the rudder to be tied on one side and all the sails to be struck. Eight men had to pump continuously; they were relieved every fifteen minutes. One officer was on guard so that the pumping would not slacken. Then, everybody [else] went to bed.

    Total   ---838

How was it possible for me to sleep in such weather and with such commotion! Capt. Tonge and his crew were [also] sleeping quite sweetly as if we had the most pleasant weather. At daybreak, we saw the shores of Newfoundland at a distance of about 15 miles NW from St. Georges Bay. We had not advanced at all during the past 24 hours. In the afternoon, the wind changed to SW but was rather calm. Course toward NW.

16th   Last night, we passed the Iles-de-la-Madeleine or Birds Islands and this morning, we saw the last of them behind us. In continuous SW wind, we advanced till noon------   --48
Latitude 48° 57'. Course toward NW. In the afternoon [we had] a violent storm from SW, which lasted all night, the

17th,   with the same violence. It seemed as if our little ship was at any moment to be swallowed by the waves. Everybody had to pump and so as to encourage the men, the capt. and I alternately joined in the pumping. Last night, we had taken our course too far toward the west and at daybreak, we were no more than about 50 paces away from the high, rocky shore of Bonaventure. We very nearly had our ship crash. Capt. Tonge's quick decisions saved us from this great danger. He himself steered the ship and we sailed safely through between Bonaventure and Rocher Percé, in English Split Rock. This Rocher Percé emerges about 40 to 50 ells[37] out of the water; there are 2 passages through it and a small sloop with spread sails used to pass through the larger opening, which is about 6 to 8 feet deep. This rock offers an extremely beautiful sight. Bonaventure in Canada has a very high, red-rocky shore and is also very pleasing to the eyes. About 100 ells from our ship, we saw 5 whales, one behind the other; one could often see half of their bodies from head to tail above the water. They were much longer than our ship; it looks very beautiful when they spout the water. Capt. Tonge said, "I do not like to see these gentlemen that close." We evaded them and took course toward NE. Around noon, we again took course toward NW and passed the Baie de Gaspé, Cap de Gaspé as well as Cap-des-Rosiers.
Until noon, we advanced   --79

    Total   ---965

Since we could not see the sun, no [measurement of] latitude was taken. In the afternoon, we had advanced quite a bit beyond Cap-des-Rosiers when the wind suddenly changed and stormed so violently from NW that it was impossible for us to keep our course. Capt. Tonge again ordered the rudder tied and we gave ourselves over to the waves. Alas, what pen could describe the terror, the horror of such a night! --

18th   This morning, we had the Ile d'Anticosti about 6 miles to the north. The storm continued; since the water rose very high, the ship could not be well controlled. We sailed back to the Baie de Gaspé, passed the Cap de Gaspé and a very high cliff called "The Old Woman." Since we could not enter the Baie de Gaspé, we finally went into the Baie de la Malbaie. Our prize *Hope* was with us and we learned that she was in just as bad condition as our *Jack* and had to be pumped almost continuously. After having cast anchor, Capt. Tonge, Lieut. Cox and I went ashore at Pointe St. Pierre where we had the midday meal in a house. Our landlord's name was James Pruce and he was born in New Jersey. The inhabitants here are French, English and Scots but also half Savages etc. and live under the Canadian government. We had come yesterday near Bonaventure and thus reached the St. Lawrence River, which is at least 70 miles wide here.

19th   Last night [*we had*] a terrible storm from NW. How happy we were not to be exposed to those terrible waves. We slept on shore. In order to offer our crew a change of meat, Capt. Tonge bought an elk from one of the inhabitants here. We also ate it roasted for breakfast: it is very coarsely striated but more tender than beef. The inhabitants, all new settlers, have very few pigs and sheep, which along with the cows and steers, they have to keep for breeding purposes.

20th   The storm from NW continued last night and even during this forenoon, but in the afternoon the wind changed to SE and we embarked. At 5 o'clock, everyone was on board. The sailors had great trouble winding the anchor. It may have gotten entangled with a rock. At 11 o'clock at night, it was cut off and we set sail. Around midnight, we heard a cannon shot from our prize *Hope*. We concluded that she too could not get her anchor loose. We replied with another cannon shot and in continuous SE wind, followed our course toward NNW.
The SE wind is so strong that we can sail 8 or 9 miles an hour. This noon, we had already advanced much farther than before. Now, the wind changed again to NW and blew more violently than ever. Capt. Tonge took course to NE, yet he could not keep it for long. The sails had to be struck again and the rudder tied lest the masts should break. Once more, we surrendered our destiny to the raging waves. It is very cold and much snow is falling.

22nd   This morning, we saw Anticosti about 10 miles east of us. The storm continued from NW the entire day. We again saw 3 whales very close to our ship. Capt. Tonge said, "I have so much respect for these gentlemen that I seek to avoid them."

23rd   Last night, our rudder had again been tied. The storm continues even today with the same violence. We had been driven closer to the north shore and saw Cap-des-Rosiers. We tried to take course toward SSW but since the storm was becoming more violent, we returned and entered the Rivière-du-Renard (Fox River). Two houses stood near the river and since we saw the chimneys smoking, we went ashore. The people who lived here were French.
From the Baie de la Malbaie, we had not advanced more than 33 miles in more than 3 days------ - --33
Since the Baie de la Malbaie we have not seen our prize *Hope* again.

24th   In the bay of this river, we saw a great many seals. Our landlord shot a number of wild pigeons for us. These agreed very well with us, as we were extremely hungry. The storm abated this forenoon. Last night, we slept on shore again and as we got thoroughly warmed up, we felt rather good. After 11 o'clock this morning, the wind changed to SE. We quickly embarked and set sail, for the wind was favorable. We sailed 9 miles in one hour.

25th   By noon, in SE wind, we have come closer to Québec by ----------------------137
But now the wind changed to NW again and blew so violently that Capt. Tonge said that in his whole life he had never seen such high water as this in the St. Lawrence River. We believed [*ourselves*] close to the south shore but discovered with horror that we were near the north shore and in danger of being wrecked, for the violent NW wind drove us forever closer to the cliffs. Capt. Tonge had the large sail spread and took course toward NE; with violent curses and some emotion he said, "This sail must either take us away from this damn shore or else [*take*] the ship into an abyss." But the mast held the sail until we had lost sight of the rocky shore. Much snow had fallen today and it is so cold that one can scarcely keep from freezing to death. Unfortunately, Capt. Tonge had been unwilling to take a stove along although he had been offered one in Halifax. Since we were now rid of the rocks, we fastened the rudder and gave ourselves over to the waves once again.

26th   This morning, the wind abated and the water was very calm. About 3 miles ahead of us, we saw a large ship. We thought it to be the same ship we had seen on the 14th, not far from the Iles-de-la-Madeleine, sailing to Québec. It could not possibly be an enemy ship since they would not dare to venture out this far at this time of year. The wind now changed to NE. We took course toward NW, passed Mont Louis as well as 3 rivers[38] at a distance of about 6 miles and by noon, we had advanced ------------------------25
We are under 49° 43' of northern latitude. We have not yet seen our prize *Hope* again. The cold is extraordinarily severe. One can hardly stand it!

27th   Course toward W and NW. With continual NE wind, we came closer to Québec this noon by --79

        Total --1,239

We passed Cap Chat and although the sky is overcast, we can see both shores. The large ship in front is afraid of us and in order to get away, has spread many sails. It even fired a cannon and we replied whereupon it fired another cannon and spread some additional sails. Toward evening, we had lost sight of it. Our pumps are continuously in action, day and night. Toward evening the wind changed to SW and we saw Mont Camille.

28th   The wind is NE, course toward W and SW. The weather is pleasant. What joy! Capt. Tonge said that if the wind continued in this way, we would cast anchor near the Ile-du-Bic this same night. Toward evening, we passed the Ile-de-St. Barnabé and at 7 o'clock this evening, we cast anchor at the Ile-du-Bic.
Up to here, we advanced ---87

        Total --1,326

The large fall fleet of more than 200 large ships from Québec was riding at anchor here, having assembled to sail to England. As protection, they had 6 frigates of 32 to 44 cannon.
At 10 o'clock this evening our prize *Hope* finally arrived.

29th   This morning, many English gentlemen came on board to get some news; they were surprised that we had started out from Halifax so late in the year. Capt. Tonge said that he would rather go twice to Europe than once to Québec from Halifax. I also learned that [Major] General von Riedesel held the post of commander at Sorel.[39] One of our passengers, by the name of Cox, an Engl. naval lieutenant, who had departed from Halifax with us, decided to sail to England this year with the fleet riding at anchor here. He therefore went on board the frigate *Hind* this morning and I gave him 17 sheets of my diary to take along together with letters to my wife and my friend. Mr. Cox promised on his honor to mail all these letters in England. I hope he will be more honorable than Mr. Hudson has been, who had promised me the same. Nevertheless, I do not wish to blame

Capt. Hudson and charge him with [*neglecting*] anything; for I cannot know in what situation fate had placed him that he was compelled to break his word of honor. In times of hostility and particularly in this unfortunate war in which one is also forced to fight battles against the elements, the most bizarre events often occur. -- The 10 sheets lost by Mr. Hudson have now been replaced, for they are included in the 17 sheets mentioned above. This afternoon, the wind blew strongly from NE. We weighed anchor and set sail. We were about 4 miles away from Bic when the ship *Mercury* passed us coming from Québec. Capt. Tonge knew this ship and had learned in Bic that Capt. Schanks, Commander of the fleet in Canada, was expected today at Bic on board the *Mercury*. Capt. Tonge had to speak to Capt. Schanks on important matters and we sailed straight toward the *Mercury*. Its commander, however, was so foolish as to take us for an enemy privateer; he fired at us with cannon and took to flight. This will strike the reader as strange indeed since we were sailing to Québec having a fleet of more than 200 ships behind us. How could a man with any common sense act this way and then take to flight? Capt. Tonge was terribly angry, but seeing that our ship was not equal to the sailing capacity of the *Mercury*, he gave a signal to our prize *Hope* to pursue it; thereupon the *Hope* arrived as quickly in Bic as the *Mercury*. We followed and finally arrived at Bic again but Capt. Schanks was not on board the *Mercury*. As it was almost 5 o'clock and began to snow and storm violently from the NE, everyone believed we would cast anchor and stay here until tomorrow. Capt. Tonge, however, set sail. In the absolute darkness, the pilot missed his course since - as he said - our compass was of no use; thus we went too far to the SW. It was past midnight when we struck some rocks. Oh God! What a noise! Our ship struck one rock after another and we all believed each moment to be the last of our lives. Because of the ship's violent motions, we could not sleep anyway, so Capt. Tonge and I were kept busy playing piquet. At first, he was completely silent but then called out to the helmsman to keep the powder dry.

Toward morning, the ship ran aground on a rock and lay on one side with the water running down it. From time to time water entered the ship through the holes made by the many blows which the ship had suffered. We were, however, saved this night from being shipwrecked. Because there were many men on board, the pumps operated continuously, and with the ebb tide - as stated before - the water continued to run off.

30th   After this horrible night, the day, so ardently desired, finally broke. The snow that had fallen last night must have been 3 feet deep. One rudder was broken and we lay among more than a thousand cliffs and rocks; among them were some too big to see over. Our prize *Hope* likewise lay on a rock but since the water was rising with the tide, it came afloat and set sail as early as 10 o'clock. Our ship did not move; it only straightened up because of the water coming in and the help of the sailors. But since the bottom was punctured, she stayed put. Now grapeshot was prepared and the 2 life boats we had on board were put in good repair so that they could immediately be dropped into the water. But these were in no way adequate to save even half the men from drowning. We saw houses standing on the SW shore and on our right, we had the large, deserted Ile Verte. "Without a doubt, there have to be people in these many houses," we said to each other. Capt. Tonge now ordered the loading of the 4 great cannon and immediately fired each, at two successive times. Capt. Tonge and I alternately looked through the telescope and to our satisfaction, recognized people busily running from one house to the next. The cannon were fired once more and white kerchiefs, bed sheets and the like were tied to the mast. With even greater satisfaction, we soon observed that these people put small canoes into the water in order to reach us. And now, I embraced Capt. Tonge and thanked him for his wise and providential care of the gunpowder last night, which now saved our lives. The water was rising in our ship by the minute and was rising in the cabin as well; everything in the ship was floating about and the sea water entered everywhere spoiling everything including my medicine. But I no longer thought of anything. The hope of being rescued revitalized my entire being. Happiness and relief could be seen on all faces; the sailors, who last night cried out "God, have mercy upon our souls," began cursing anew. It was past 10 o'clock when the Canadians surrounded our ship with many canoes (canots d'écorce). Our ship was yet one hand above the water, that is, it had a board one hand wide [*above the water line*] when it should have had 9 feet of board. Capt. Tonge and I climbed into one of these canoes, in which a Canadian was staying ready to row and at once, he started out toward the shore. We were not even halfway to shore when our ship went underwater and the sailors who could not be picked up so fast climbed up the mast. It was past 12 o'clock when we were all ashore. The parish (village) is called Cacouna and lies 7 leagues or 21 miles away from Bic; it is the first village in which Christians live. Many people live around here, probably Savages but no Christians. I never was more thankful to my Creator than on this day. -- We took quarters in the best house with a Canadian and remained this day. Capt. Tonge gave orders to the Canadians that, on the days when the ship is in low water, they should take baggage, coffers and the like, as well as cannon, bullets and cartridges ashore. For this, they would be well paid by Governor Haldimand. They should take as presents all such provisions they would find in the ship as salted meat, rum and whatever else they may discover. The baggage, cannon and the like would be taken by ship to Québec. I must mention something else about Capt. Tonge. In the greatest danger last night, he was continuously with his sailors and when they started to pray, he cursed them in horrible fashion. "You damn fools, now you want to pray even though you have probably not done so in all these years. This is not the time to pray, we must work so as not to go to hell." (The English call 'to perish at sea' 'to go to hell.') By his threats and curses, he succeeded in getting the sailors back to pumping and then he said, "Since I see you proving yourselves to be seamen and Englishmen, you shall have rum." A barrel of rum was hauled up on deck and now everything got into motion; everybody worked and drank. Capt. Tonge kept on singing vicious songs, drinking punch, cold punch, sometimes wine, sometimes rum and was, or at least seemed to be, so cheerful as if he was attending a comedy. --

31st   This afternoon we walked to the posthouse, which was 2 leagues away. But since we could not obtain a calash, we had to remain for another day. We were, however, promised a calash for tomorrow morning. The walk had been very trying for us today and since there are as many as 170 Engl. land miles from there to Québec, it would take very long to get there. Thus, it will be more reasonable to go by post, although, having lost all my possessions, I am now poor again. If I had only not bought the medicine! I would now own a small fortune! --yet-- although poor, I did save my life and I am in good health! What a blessing!

End of this Month

Month of November 1781

1st   This morning, Capt. Tonge and I drove to Rivière-du-Loup in a calash and had the pleasure of finding our prize *Hope* there. The ship's carpenter was making a new rudder. Capt. Tonge spoke of nothing but his wife and his 2 children, whom he hoped to find in Québec in good health. How fortunate for him to be so close to them! One could distinctly see the joyous anticipation on his face. He said that he had sent dispatches to Governor Haldimand from Halifax and although it was night, he continued on his way on horseback. I remained here since I did not wish to be exposed at night to the difficulties that such a season brought with it when it sometimes snowed, sometimes rained and the roads were generally bad. If I had entertained any hope, however, of finding my wife and children in Québec, with what pleasure would I have continued the journey together with Capt. Tonge. I slept soundly during the night and went in a calash this morning, the

2nd,   from here to Kamouraska where I lodged in the posthouse. The postmistress was 32 years old, had 16 children living and was pregnant with the 17th. The reason for this rapid population increase in Canada is that the women do not nurse their own children. This woman had no twins either. The Hesse-Hanau Regiment moved into winter cantonment here.

3rd   I drove to Ste. Anne [de la Pocatière] where I stayed overnight.

4th   I drove to St. Thomas. The Hesse-Cassel Regiment von Lossberg was in winter cantonment here.[40]

5th   I drove to St. Vallier and had the Ile-aux-Coudres [Ile-d'Orléans!] on my right.

6th   I had the Ile-d'Orléans and the famous Falls of Montmorency on my right, was at Pointe Lévi at 3 o'clock, crossed the St. Lawrence River at this point and came to Québec. From the Ile-du-Bic up to here is 180 [miles]. Our prize *Hope* had arrived by the day before yesterday at noon, and the capt. 2 hours later, having ridden day and night. Our Regiment Prinz Friedrich and the Anhalt-Zerbst Regiment were in winter cantonment here.[41] I reported to Lieut. Colonel Prätorius, Commander of the Reg. Prinz Friedrich, and learned that our Maj. Gen. von Riedesel together with the Dragoon Regiment were at Sorel. I met several good friends who were surprised by my presence here; for together with the Dragoon Regiment, the news had arrived that I had deserted. -- I was also handed several letters from Germany that had been sent from there 2 or 3 years ago. Although they were dated, I still enjoyed them and read them with great pleasure. Capt. Tonge promised to send my coffer to Sorel as soon as it arrived.

8th   I wrote to my friends and family in Germany.

Total of Engl. miles from Boston to Québec ----------------------------------1,506

9th   I drove in the post calash to St. Jean [de Boischatel] from Québec, where I stayed overnight.

10th   I passed Cap Santé and the church with 4 spires and arrived at La Croix, where I took my lodging.

11th   [*I went*] via Cap-de-la-Madeleine, Trois-Rivières to Grand [Ya]machiche, where I took my lodging. Many attractive barracks have been built here for the Royalists and those who have emigrated from the Colonies.

12th   Today via [La Seigneurie de la] Rivière-du-Loup, Maskinongé to Berthier. There, I crossed the St. Lawrence River to Sorel. It was 7 o'clock in the evening when I arrived here. I reported to Maj. Gen. von Riedesel and the other officers. Everyone seeing me was surprised and could not understand where I had come from. "Through the air," was my reply. Although the clear-headed might consider me half-witted deep down in their hearts, now that I was here-- nevertheless, no praise was given to me by ----------- ----. I hope my readers will understand me well because it is no small feat to be praised by that ------- bunch. --
Now, there was no longer any reason why I should incur suspicion since by my presence I have refuted the lies of my desertion. These short-sighted men never met with such good fortune [*and therefore*] they would never have done what I did. I did this for your sake, you who are so close to me! Nothing do I have more at heart than to make all 3 of you happy. Would that the dear Lord who created me hear my prayer that I may embrace you once again and press you to my heart that keeps on beating for you alone. Know my beloved that I am steadfast enough to see you again after surviving the terrible hardships of a long and frightful journey on the sea in order to burst forth with a happiness 3 times as great. -- From Québec to Sorel are 135 miles. I thus rode 308 Engl. miles from the Ile Verte to Sorel on the post calash.
From Captain of the Cavalry Fricke, I received the shirts, shoes, stockings and 2 pipe bowls and stems that had been sent to me from Germany in the year 1777. The Reg. CHIRURGUS Vorbrodt handed me a package of letters from my wife and my friends. He also had a coffer that I had left behind in Trois-Rivières on June 1, 1777, which had been opened, however; likewise one which I had left in Fort Edward in the portmanteau.

If I had not found the description of my journey from Europe to America in it, I would never have found either my coffer or my portmanteau. To the disgrace of my countrymen, I have to say that both, coffer and portmanteau, had been plundered; instead of my things, they contained among others, old musketeer trousers without seats and old musketeer stockings, whose feet had rotted. My collection of coins and my stored money were also gone, even such surgical instruments as pistuaries[?] lancets, syringes and the like had vanished. The cork work, made by Canadian belles, that I had designated for Caroline [his daughter], was also lost. Of 15 new shirts that I had ordered in Trois-Rivières, I found none, but instead 3 torn musketeer shirts. A pair of new boots, for which I had paid 8 piasters in Montréal, had also disappeared. In short, the baggage thieves must have thought that we would never return from captivity.

13th   Today, the 53rd and 84th Engl. Regiments went from here to Trois-Rivières in batteaux to their designated winter cantonments. The greatest Engl. hospital is in Trois-Rivières. I am still receiving letters from Germany, but most of them were mailed a few years ago. Much has changed here in Sorel during the past 5 years. Everybody is in the barracks together, officers and privates. More than 50 new barracks have been built. The garrison consists of our Dragoon Regiment and a detachment of Engl. Artillery with 120 men. About 60 Engl. tradesmen also live here as well as all persons belonging to our General Staff. Four redoubts and some blockhouses have likewise been constructed.

20th   Colonel von Bärner arrived and became commander at Sorel. Three companies of our Light Infantry Regiment were moved to the barracks here; the 4th company went to Yamaska and the Jäger Comp. to St. François into winter cantonments. Since sick Canadians are coming to me for help, I have sent for medicine from Montréal. But at what price! One lb. of rhubarb costs 16 piasters and in Québec they even ask 19 piasters. I now have every reason to regret the loss of my medicine and can say that I lost more than 6,000 piasters at Ile Verte. Moreover, the journey itself has cost me a small fortune since having bought the medicine I ate and spent more time than I would have if I had not purchased it; for in my own mind, I already imagined myself wealthy. But here too the saying is correct: HOMO PROPONET DEUS DISPONET [man proposes, God disposes]. When I left Rutland, I was in possession of a fortune of more than 1,300 piasters and when I came to Québec, Capt. Tonge had to advance me 3 guineas so that I could defray my travelling expenses to Sorel. The only thing I can still hope for is [the payment of] a medicine bill from the Engl. treasury and 3 years of forage and baggage money if that will be paid at all. -- Everything is very expensive here and I have to cut down considerably if I want to make it with my salary. We receive good bread and quite good provisions in general but who can eat salted meat and dry peas every day! Many with a far greater income than I can do so but I cannot. The salted pork is so delicate that I eat most of it raw instead of lard. --

Reg. CHIRURGUS Vorbrodt is staying on the other side of the Rivière Richelieu in a hospital. A ferry, which is pulled by 2 Englishmen, goes across this river. The King pays them provisions and 9 piasters per day.

23rd   Last night, the Richelieu froze. Yesterday evening, the ferry was still operating; today wagons and carts with hay and straw etc. are crossing over. The St. Lawrence River is only frozen at the edges. The Richelieu enters the St. Lawrence River about 200 paces from my barracks.

24th   A last ship arrived from Québec bringing my coffer for which I had to pay half a guinea freight. There still was sea water from Ile Verte in it; but what I had hoped for, only a few books had rotted -- among those still good was Thaddeus Commentaries. The news came that Lord Cornwallis with 9,000 men has been captured. I had already heard it in Boston but at that time, nobody really wanted to believe it.[42]

At times, I completely forget and am totally unaware of being in Canada again. I often imagine that an adverse fate has removed me to Siberia. -- But cannot Canada be [rightfully] called the American Siberia? -- Alas, my friends in New England, you are worrying about me. I know you want to find out whether I safely ended the horrible journey to Québec. Would that I were fortunate enough [*to be allowed to*] write you no more than these words, "I am alive and in good health." This I owe you for the many benefits you have bestowed upon me but I cannot, I may not do it. I have no opportunity and, moreover, I would not be allowed to do so and, without permission, I would not dare to do it at any price.

End of this Month.

Month of December 1781

1st   I received the prescribed medicine from Montréal.

17th   Last night, the St. Lawrence River froze solid and this morning, the peasants are driving across it.

20th   All through last night and even this morning, we have had one of the most terrible snow storms; there are huge snow drifts about.

22nd   Due to the wind, the snow drifts are 15 to 18 feet high in many spots; in the plains, the snow is 4 feet deep. --

25th   The cold increases and many people's hands and feet are frozen.

31st   Astonishing snow storm. We are completely snowed in and cannot get out of our stables and barracks. The dragoons have first to work themselves through [the snow] in order to reach their horses. Should it be the same in Siberia? It could surely not be worse. --

End of this Month

NOTES

1. Wasmus was of course correct in rejecting the notion that music or vigorous dancing (hence the tarantella) can counteract a tarantula bite. European tarantulas are members of the LYCOSA or wolf spider family, while the tarentulas of the American South are THERAPHOSIDAE.

2. The Continental Army had been reorganized in March 1779, into 80 Continental regiments; a number which was reduced in 1781. J. Warren Bigelow, writing the history of Rutland in 1879, states that the town's quota for 1777 was 36 men to serve for three years; each was given an additional 20 pounds bounty. In 1781, again according to Bigelow, the town's quota was 14, and each was given 90 pounds in hard currency or the property equivalent. ("Town of Rutland," in History of Worcester County, Massachusetts, Boston, 1879, Vol. II, p. 266.)

3. Lieutenant Theodor. Friedrich Gebhard, of the Braunschweig Grenadier Regiment, is recorded as having led a detachment back to Stade in October 1783; he was subsequently transferred to the newly formed Regiment von Riedesel. Elster, pp. 423, 440, 453,

4. Ensign Johann Julius Anton Specht of the Braunschweig Chasseur and Jäger Regiment; is recorded as having been taken prisoner at Bennington and later discharged from the service in America. Elster, pp. 423, 440.

5. The Great Siege of Gibraltar lasted from 1779 to 1783, when the Spanish tried to starve out the British. Despite their naval blockade, a few supply ships continued to enter the harbor, and in January 1780, Admiral Rodney defeated the Spanish Admiral De Langara and resupplied and reinforced the fortress. The English residents of the Barbary territory were expelled in January 1781, and the fortress was again threatened with starvation until Admiral Darby resupplied the fortress in April. Lord Howe led a successful third naval relief in 1782 and the siege was finally lifted in February 1783.

6. Don Antonio de Barcelo (1717-1797), who had gained fame by clearing the Mediterranean of pirates, had been appointed in 1779 as commander of the Spanish naval forces blockading Gibraltar.

7. The French Alliance of 1778 followed two years of secret aid and supplies to the Americans; the first concrete aid after the alliance was signed was d'Estaing's fleet, which left Toulon in April 1778. Rochambeau's expeditionary force in July 1780 was the beginning of more effective assistance and co-operation.

8. Arnold had left New York in December 1780 with 1,600 troops to prevent Virginia from supporting Greene in South Carolina by destroying military supplies; he also hoped to rally Loyalist support for the war effort. He occupied Richmond on January 5, 1781, burning stored tobacco and several buildings before withdrawing.

9. Captain Fricke had apparently charged Wasmus with desertion or fraternization with the enemy; he had denied his status as an officer and characterized him as one who had merely come along to clean the officers beards. The issue of surgeons' duties involving shaving the officers is mentioned in Gabriel Nadeau's 1945 article on Wasmus, which is based on Wasmus's letters to Riedesel and not on the journal, which Nadeau was unable to consult. Wasmus himself never mentions performing the functions of a barber, and reports Fricke's characterization of him as such as an insult. (See below, note 31 and the entry for December 13, 1780. See also "A German Military Surgeon in Rutland During the Revolution: Julius Friedrich Wasmus," Bulletin of the History of Medicine, vol. 18, 1945, pp. 243-300.)

10. This refers to the mutiny of the Pennsylvania Line, January 1-10, 1781. Due to grievances over conditions, pay, and terms of enlistment, 1,500 men mutinied and attempted to march away from their camp in New Jersey. General Wayne tried to stop them with arguments, but the mutineers wanted to present their grievances directly to Congress. After a brief skirmish, yielding two casualties, the mutineers marched to Princeton where they elected a Board of Sergeants to confer with Wayne, who negotiated. Congress appointed a committee to deal with the Council of Pennsylvania. At this point Clinton attempted to send emissaries who were empowered to offer cash payments and pardons to the mutineers; these two, John Mason and James Ogden, were arrested and hanged by the mutineers. A settlement was then negotiated under which those men whose enlistments had expired were freed, and most re-enlisted.

11. Holland had joined the League of Russia, Denmark, and Sweden in Armed Neutrality and had profitted from the contraband trade in the early years of the war. By 1780, Britain had activated the 1678 Anglo-Dutch Alliance, preventing the Dutch from trading with the enemy; the Dutch participation in Armed Neutrality was an effort at escaping this dilemma. (See below, note 18.)

12. Goulard's extract, a lead subacetate solution, was named for Thomas Goulard (1724-1784), French surgeon; T. vegt. refers to an alcoholic or hydoalcoholic solution prepared from vegetable drugs.

13. Ebenezer Washburn, according to Massachusetts records, was born in 1735 and died in 1795. He and his wife, Dorothy, had six children born between 1770 and 1784.

14. Samuel Hood (1724-1816) had joined the Navy in 1741 and served in North American waters between 1753 and 1756. After service in the Seven Years War, he became commissioner of the dockyard at Portsmouth in 1778, was knighted and promoted to Rear Admiral in 1780; and went to the West Indies as Rodney's second-in command.

15. General Thomas Nelson (1739-1789) had signed the Declaration of Independence and served in Congress as a representative of Virginia. He organized Virginia's local militia in response to Arnold's raids in the spring of 1781.

16. Although Congress had established peace demands, including British recognition of American independence, boundaries, fishing rights, rights of navigation on the Mississippi as well as withdrawal of British troops in August of 1780, and Adams and Jay had been named peace commissioners in 1779, peace negotiations were not serious until after Yorktown, beginning in Paris in April 1782.

17. Pondichéry had been seized from the French by British forces in July 1778 (see note 27, 1778.)

18. Rodney had captured St. Eustatius from the Dutch on February 3, 1781, taking possession of several million pounds worth of booty, which he did not realize actually belonged to British merchants. The British had declared war on Holland on December 20, 1780, using as their excuse the draft of a treaty

of commerce between the United States and Holland written by William Lee and found among the papers of Henry Laurens, who had been captured on his voyage to Holland, where he was to serve as ambassador. (Boatner, pp. 342- 43.)

19. Arnold had not in fact been captured; but the French had indeed captured a number of British victuallers sailing from Cork to the West Indies in July 1780, and they were to continue to prey on this traffic for the duration of hostilities.

20. There was a Colonel Christopher Senf, an engineer, present with Gates at Camden; his plan of the battle is in the Steuben papers at the New-York Historical Society. Greene had three daughters and two sons, all born after 1774, and thus could not have been Senf's father-in-law. Gates had no daughters. ("Plan of the Battle Near Camden, by Colonel Senf," Magazine of American History, vol. 5, October, 1880, pp. 275-278.)

21. John Child represented Holden in the first Provincial Congress, and had represented the town at a county-wide meeting of all the local Committees of Correspondence in 1774. (Nelson, p. 216, 225.)

22. Wasmus' treatise was apparently lost and has not survived to the present day. (Another German surgeon, Johann David Schoepff of the Ansbach-Bayreuth contingent, also wrote on The Climate and Diseases of America; his book was translated by James Read Chadwick and published in 1875.)

23. The Convention troops had been marched out of Virginia to prevent their liberation by Tarleton or Simcoe as Cornwallis approached Virginia. One group was marched to Easton, Pennsylvania, the other back to Rutland, Massachusetts.

24. The British had promised slaves their freedom for joining the Loyalist ranks, but some British commanders seized slaves of patriots as booty for profitable resale in the West Indies. At one point Virginia freed slaves who had served in the American Army, and Congress offered slave owners $1,000 per slave for slaves who would enlist in the Army.

25. Major General von Riedesel had been exchanged for General Benjamin Lincoln in 1780, and given the command of British troops on Long Island. He was ordered back to Canada in the summer of 1781.

26. Arnold landed in New London and plundered the city on September 6, 1781 to divert American troops from the Allied army marching to meet Cornwallis in Virginia. One hundred forty-three buildings were burned in fires which Arnold claimed were accidental.

27. Maine was part of Massachusetts until 1820; Historical Statistics of the United States includes estimates of the 1780 population of Massachusetts as 268,627, with Maine including an additional 49,133 people. (1960, series Z 1-19, "Estimated Population of American Colonies: 1610-1780.")

28. The first American census listed New York, with a population of 32,328, as the largest city in the United States, followed by Philadelphia at 28,522, and Boston with 18,038.

29. John Hancock (1737-1793) is probably best known for his signature on the Declaration of Independence. Nephew of the richest merchant in Boston, he graduated from Harvard in 1754 and inherited his uncle's business. He was elected to the General Court in 1769 and in 1770 headed the local committee to investigate the Boston Massacre. He served as President of the Massachusetts Provincial Congress, and represented Massachusetts in Congress from 1775 to 1780, being chosen as President between 1775 and 1777. He was elected the first governor of the state of Massachusetts in 1780, a position he occupied until his death (except for a brief interval between 1785 and 1787, due to ill health.)

30. In the spring of 1781, in defiance of Clinton's orders for him to secure the British conquest of the Carolinas, Cornwallis had marched to Virginia, reaching Williamsburg at the end of June. He established a base at Yorktown from which he was to harass American communications and destroy their supplies. De Grasse sailed to the Chesapeake, reaching it on August 26, and Washington began to concentrate his forces on the Yorktown Peninsula, marching south from New York. Washington reached Philadelphia on September 2 and Yorktown on September 14. Greene was in fact in the Carolinas, but Cornwallis was indeed outnumbered by the French and American forces.

31. Sir Andrew Snape Hamond (1738-1828), after a naval career in which he rose to the rank of commodore, served as lieutenant-governor of Nova Scotia from 1780 to 1782.

Col. von Seitz was in charge of the Hessian troops in Halifax until his death in March of 1783.

Brigadier General John Campbell commanded the British and German troops stationed in Penobscot. He and his wife were popular with the German officers for their hospitality; Campbell assisted Adjutant Cleve in procuring loans of money to pay the German soldiers. Campbell returned to his native Scotland in 1783. (Cleve to Riedesel, Suppl. I & II, taken from v. Riedesel II, 12 Part II, ROll 75, No. 166.)

32. The Inn of the Golden Ball stood at the corner of Prince and Hollis Streets in Halifax.

33. There is some evidence that Wasmus's fellow officers envied his popularity with the inhabitants, his acceptance by local "society," his intelligence, and the money he earned in his practice. Their prejudice may have had something to do with his history, i.e., his bloody encounter with an actor in Nicolini's theater troupe. Some of his countrymen had accused him of fraternization and attempted desertion; and Fricke had certainly attempted to prevent his exchange by deprecating his rank and his skill. (See above, note 9.)

34. Lunenburg had been settled in 1757 by Hannoverian immigrants (who named the town after Lüneburg in Germany); the Board of Trade had planned to settle French Protestants on the site (established as Fort Lawrence in 1750), but turned to Germans because of a shortage of suitable French emigrants. Winthrop Bell, The 'Foreign Protestants' and the Settlement of Nova Scotia. Toronto, 1961 provides an authoritative history of the settlement. Interestingly enough, there is a town by the same name in Worcester County, Massachusetts, close to the town where Wasmus spent much of his parole, which was "named by a party of King George's subjects who were travelling through the place, and gave it the name of Lunenburg in honor of his German possession." (Adin C. Estabrook, "Lunenburg," in History of Worcester County, Massachusetts, 1879, p. 30.)

35. The widow's marriage license issued by "Marriot Arbutnot, Esq., Governor and Commander-In-Chief in and over His Majesty's Province of Nova Scotia" May 13, 1777, lists her as Mary Fillis, to be married to Thomas Achincloss. Fillis's grave is still in the old St. Paul's cemetery in Halifax.

36. This is a reference to the Battle of the Chesapeake Capes, September 5, 1781. Admiral Thomas Graves (1725?-1802) had succeeded Arbutnot on July 4, 1781, in command of the fleet supporting Clinton. Graves found that de Grasse was blockading Cornwallis's transports and carrying French and American troops from Baltimore to Yorktown, and awaiting Admiral de Barras's French convoy carrying the French siege train. Graves's 19 ships attacked de Grasse's 24 vessels, and the resulting 2 1/2 hour action left the French with 220 killed and wounded, as opposed to the British casualties of 336. The British returned to New York, leaving de Grasse and Barras to continue blockading Cornwallis. (Boatner, p. 225-226.)

37. The English ell was 45 inches in length; in Scotland, 37 inches, while the Dutch or Flemish ell was only 27 inches long.

38. This is not to be confused with the town of Trois-Rivières, which lies on the north bank of the St. Lawrence between Québec and Montréal, and which had served as General von Riedesel's headquarters in 1776 and 1777.

39. Sorel, which lies at the confluence of the Richelieu and St. Lawrence Rivers, 29 miles north of Montréal, became General von Riedesel's headquarters from 1781 to 1783. Here, in a simple but beautiful house erected for the commander-in-chief by General Haldimand, the first Christmas tree on North American soil was lit in 1781.

40. There were two Lossberg regiments: the first, referred to here, was the Alt-Lossberg, whose chief was Lt. General Anton Heinrich von Lossberg, and whose commander, after 1778 was Col. Johann von Loos; it had fought at Long Island, White Plains, Fort Washington, Trenton, Brandywine, Germantown, Philadelphia, Monmouth and had been quartered in New York until June 1780 and thereafter in Canada. The second Lossberg regiment was called Mirbach's or Jung-Lossberg's; its chief was Major General Werner von Mirbach until 1780, and after that Lieutenant General Friedrich Wilhelm von Lossberg, a 62 year old soldier, who had previously commanded the Leib-Regiment and replaced Knyphausen in command of the Hessians in New York, successfully bringing them back to Hesse in 1783. The Jung-Lossberg regiment was commanded by Col. Johann von Loos through 1776, Lt. Col. von Schick until October 1777, and Col von Romrod after that, fighting at Long Island, White Plains, New York, Germantown, Redbank, Philadelphia and stationed at New York from 1778-1783. (Atwood, pp. 260-263.)

41. The principality of Anhalt-Zerbst had furnished 1,160 men to the British war effort.

42. Cornwallis had surrendered one-quarter of the British troops in America on October 20, essentially ending British efforts to suppress the American Revolution.

1782

Month of January 1782

Whosoever wishes to, may beg for the many gifts of the spirit
Great is the wish, small the enjoyment.
Fate shall have but this one request from me
To be equally free from want and from plenty.

1st   Each regiment has been provided with one pair of snowshoes (raquets) per man, on which the men are to learn how to walk. Each man is also to receive one pair of Indian shoes (moccasins).

On Jan. 19th, 1779, when I was still in captivity, the Battalion von Bärner was supposed to march from La Baie via Lac St. Pierre to [La Seigneurie de la] Rivière-du-Loup, a march of about one German mile. The strong NW wind produced such severe cold that 21 men of this Battalion fell and died on the march and some 50 lost fingers, ears and toes. And the men had been very well clothed. --

6th   Terrible snowstorms. We were again snowed into our barracks and [on the]

7th,   for a period of 12 hours, nobody could come in or go out. [A tunnel] was dug through the snow.

14th   Major General von Riedesel went to Québec this morning.

18th   The birthday of the Queen of Great Britain was celebrated. This morning, Sergeant Major Reinemund, brother-in-law of Lieut. Colonel Baum, who was perhaps tired of the comforts of Sorel, fell on the St. Lawrence River into a hole where water is drawn, and drowned. One does not receive any news here. In winter time, Canada has no communication with the rest of the world; it is as if this was the end of the world.

The rumor is spreading that a Congress in Vienna has determined that France and Spain ought to make peace with England and leave the hostilities in America to the King of England alone. On the other hand, England is to withdraw all the hired foreign troops from America.[1] But the question is this: Where did this news come from? Out of thin air? Our prize *Hope* was the last ship that arrived in Québec and it did not bring that kind of news. When I left Halifax on Oct. 6, I did not hear anything of the sort. The Boston papers used to write that sort of nonsense last summer.

Since I have brought the Boston and Worcester papers from last year to our Maj. General von Riedesel, who in turn sent them to Governor Gen. Haldimand in Québec, it is possible that the news mentioned above was taken from them. Several Royalists on snowshoes are said to have come through the wilderness from Albany. They have brought the news along that peace has actually been concluded. Would that it were true! We would perhaps then be so fortunate as to be rescued from this 2nd Siberia, but I do not believe this either. If there were inns in the wilderness, where they [the Royalists] could have stopped, we might believe it. But in such cold and in such deep snow it is not possible to march 500 miles on snowshoes, on which they cannot go farther than 20 to 25 miles a day; that would require almost one month's time. How would they transport their victuals and how would they be able to eat frozen bread? Fifty men of our regiment have to use snowshoes each day in order to learn [*how to walk in them*]. The winter continues to be most severe. The Canadians cannot remember such a hard winter or one in which so much snow has fallen.

End of this Month

Month of February 1782

1st   Our men keep [*practicing*] on raquets every day. It continues to be very cold and more snow is falling. The feet of a deserter by the name of Müller, from the Regiment Specht, were frostbitten; today, I amputated all 5 toes of his right foot. When he is well again, he will be hanged. Why not hang him right now? He would no longer have to suffer all that pain.

13th   Our Maj. Gen. von Riedesel returned from Québec again. Many more reports were received about Lord Cornwallis, and that the English had left New York and Charleston, and that Gen. Washington was shot dead and the like. All these are winter stories, invented by the perfidious Canadians. We will not be able to get any reliable information before next spring when ships start to arrive at Québec. Everything is being prepared for an imminent review; Vice Governor Maj. Gen. Clarke is expected here.[2] Great preparations are being made for this reception. Twenty-four dragoons shall constitute his bodyguard.

18th   Maj. Gen. von Riedesel departed for Montréal and St. Jean. Rumors or lies are being spread again: Gen. Clinton has left New York and moved to Halifax. On this journey, Colonel Leslie perished with his entire brigade and the like.[3]

End of this Month

Month of March 1782

1st   Our Maj. Gen. von Riedesel arrived here again and with him Maj. Gen. Clarke, who was honored by 1 capt., 1 subaltern officer and 30 dragoons in boots. The feet of a Canadian from Berthier were frostbitten; I amputated 3 of his toes today.

5th   Major Holland, having arrived last night, reviewed the garrison here in the usual fashion.
Maj. Gen. von Riedesel went to Trois-Rivières with Gen. Clark today.

7th   Maj. Gen. von Riedesel returned and the Engl. Colonel St. Leger as well as Brigadier Gen. Loos from the Hesse-Cassel corps arrived here.

30th   A truce ship arrived at St. Jean from the province of Vermont; therefore a courier went to Québec today. Governor Haldimand is expected here. Today, I amputated 2 toes of another Canadian.

The Lance-Corporal Lambrecht shot himself today.

End of this Month

Month of April 1782

1st   Gen. Haldimand arrived and on the

2nd,   departed from here for St. Jean.

3rd   One of our jägers was taken to the hospital here; he had wanted to shoot himself but had not aimed correctly.[4]

7th   Last night, the solid ice of the Rivière Richelieu broke up and one chunk of the ice broke up in the St. Lawrence River; it was 7 or 8 feet thick. Those dismal batteaux will soon be ready for action again.

17th   The ice in the St. Lawrence River broke up with a great crash today. Not far from our barracks (stables), icebergs are forming. The water is rising and threatens to flood [the country].

18th   Since the ice in Lac St. Pierre has not yet broken up, the water is overflowing the bank here.

19th   At the Leib Squadron, the water actually entered the barracks; on the

20th,   it climbed even higher.

21st   Since the ice in Lac St. Pierre has broken up, the water [level] is falling here.

24th   The water is below the banks.

A soldier of the Regt. von Rhetz came through the wilderness from Albany [reporting] that most of the French in Boston have embarked and sailed to the West Indies; that Gen. Greene has risked an attack on Charleston but was beaten back with losses; that New York continues to be occupied by the English.[5]

Would that we soon received letters from Germany, would that these announced peace to us!

End of this Month

Month of May 1782

1st   The weather continues to be cold and overcast and since there is still much snow [on the ground], nothing green can be seen as yet. There is not much evidence of spring and fall in Canada, nothing but summer and winter.

8th   I was summoned today to be present when 3 deserters were given the death sentence. Their names were Müller from Reg. Specht, who had lost all 5 toes on one foot, Schulze from the Reg. Riedesel and the porter Scott, a watchmaker. All three will be arrested and Pastor Milius is in charge of the business of conversion.

15th   Yesterday [*the body of*] Sergeant Corporal [sic] Reinemund, who had killed himself by drowning on Jan. 18, was found near an island in Lac St. Pierre by an English detachment and, after due inspection, was buried.

21st   Every day, the garrison here must drill on the large parade ground. The mosquitoes [manenguens] are increasing.

21st   Every soldier received 18 cartridges today.

22nd   Today 20 cartridges [*for every soldier*]. Last night I received many mosquito bites. These can rightfully be called a natural scourge, in which, in contrast to other good qualities, Canada surpasses all other countries in the whole world. --

24th   Today, the jäger who had wanted to shoot himself ran a gauntlet of 200 men 8 times.[6]

26th   The news came that the King has made peace with the Colonies and that we are to be relieved by a corps of Hannoverians; that twelve thousand Hannoverians are going to New York to relieve the Hessians; that all Engl. troops are to move to the West Indies because the French are enforcing their power in the West Indies and have already taken St. Eustatius, St. Kitts and a few others away from the English. The King is said to have dissolved the old Parliament and appointed a new one. Gen. Clinton and Gen. Arnold are said to have gone to England, and Gen. Carleton has taken the command over New York etc. All this news is supposed to have come from England with the ship *Bellona*; the ship, however, was wrecked on a cliff 20 leagues below Québec, and except for 4 men, all the people on it have drowned.[7]

28th   Our Maj. Gen. von Riedesel is holding a special review today. Another soldier, by the name of Weber from the Regiment von Riedesel, has been brought here from Montréal; he had been caught with the other three [deserters]. As he is of the Catholic faith, the priest from the Anhalt-Zerbst Regiment has been charged with the business of conversion.

Another 4 ships have arrived in Québec from England and one from New York but we have learned nothing new but that there is much talk of peace. Particularly those who desire peace speak a great deal about it and that means most of them. To be sure, many are wishing for ------, ------. Gen. Haldimand is expected here; perhaps we will learn something new; he has been absent from Québec for 9 months.

End of this Month

Month of June 1782

1st   Gov. Haldimand arrived here and after mustering the garrison, he took his midday meal at Maj. Gen. von Riedesel's and then went down the St. Lawrence River to Québec.

2nd   It seems that Governor Haldimand did not bring us any news. We are ready to march and whatever troops need in a campaign has been distributed among our men. I only wish with all my heart that we will hear more about peace.

4th   The King's birthday is being celebrated in the usual way today.

7th   Maj. Gen. von Riedesel went to Montréal with his suite.

10th   The outer troop detachments from all the regiments are arriving today so as to be present when the 4 offenders are executed.

11th   At 3 o'clock this morning, the garrison here was in arms and the capital criminal court began at the main guardhouse. Around 5 o'clock, the offenders were taken to the places where they were to be hanged. As soon as they entered the circle, a sealed order was opened and read aloud by Lieut. Colonel von Bärner. This was Maj. Gen. von Riedesel's order: that no one was to be hanged but that 2 of them were to be shot. Then, all 4 had to cast lots with 2 dice on a drum. The lots fell on Schulze and Weber to be shot. The two cripples, Scott with his crooked arm and Müller, who had lost almost all of his 5 toes on the right foot, remained and were condemned [to serve] as slaves on a frigate. -- Today, Maj. Gen. von Riedesel returned.

Last night, the news arrived that Admiral Rodney had beaten the French fleet under Comte de Grasse in the West Indies. Because of this, all the houses of the English here were lit, but the French acted as if they did not notice anything, although some of their windows had been smashed.[8]

Québec Gazette [Extraordinary], June 9 [11]. *This morning, the ship Cornwallis arrived here from Antigua and brought the following news from the Antigua Gazette in St. John's in Antigua, April 17, [1782].*

Last Friday the 12th, the Engl. and French fleets encountered each other at 7 o'clock in the morning; the former under the command of Admirals George Rodney and Samuel Hood, the latter under Admiral Comte de Grasse. It came to a bloody engagement between the Islands of Dominica and Guadeloupe. The glorious action lasted with unabating fury on both sides for a long time; both fleets were almost of equal strength but fortune bestowed total victory [with never fading laurels] upon the British fleet, whose thunder spread death and destruction among the French fleet. Without a doubt, this will discourage them from considering similar undertakings for some time to come. After an action of 3/4 hour, La Ville de Paris, capital ship of 120 [110] cannon that had Admiral de Grasse and 1,500 [1,300] men on board, surrendered to the brave Sir Samuel Hood on board the Barfleur [of 90 cannon]. The French ship had 500 dead and wounded by this time. La Glorieuse of 74 cannon and 900 men is captured; she suffered 235 dead and wounded. The Hector of 74 cannon and 900 men is captured. Le Caton [Caesar] of 74 cannon and 900 men is captured. We already had one lieut. and 30 [10] men on board when by some unfortunate accident the ship took fire and of all the [911] people, only 30 were rescued.

Le Ardent [sic] of 64 cannon and 800 [100] men is captured.

Le Diadème of 74 cannon and 900 men sank and all the men perished.

Our known losses are 230 dead and 759 wounded. Our fleet is pursuing the enemy fleet and we hope soon to hear of the conquest of several ships. Admiral Rodney writes that if the sun had offered 2 hours more of day [light], few of the French would have escaped. [accurate]

Oh, great Joshua! If you had been there, you could have bid the sun to stand still.[9] The French fleet was stronger than ours by 2 warships and had a greater number of cannon and men in their fleet. This superiority, however, could not prevent the engagement.

Admiral de Grasse has been captured and 2 other enemy admirals have been killed. After this engagement, the Engl. fleet met 2 other warships of which one, whose name is not yet known, has been seized, and the Saint Esprit of 90 cannon was sunk and all the people aboard lost their lives. -- [accurate]

Poetry
[in English]

<u>The British Muse on This Glorious Day.</u>

Bellona spreads her dire alarms
And calls the Britons forth to arms.
With eager haste behold them fly,
Resolv'd to conquer or to die.
With joy the glorious call obey;
For glory points to them the way.
Undaunted they their foes will meet
And triumph o'er the Goals [Gauls'] defeat.
Britannia raised her dropping head.
And smiling thus the goddess said,
"My sons, the glorious task pursue
Maintain your rights and France subdue."

The Québec paper of June 27 brings the news that an English fleet has dispersed a French fleet and taken several transport ships with troops as well as a ship of 74 cannon. [selective]

End of this Month

Month of July 1782

1st   We received reliable news that our officers from the Convention of Saratoga have been exchanged and are in New York; they will come here with the first fleet.[10] It is said that we are to camp. Thus, we must leave our beautiful gardens that have cost us so much effort and toil. --

7th   Québec paper, July 4. *The English have seized 10 French transport ships and taken them into Plymouth; among these are 2 of 900 tons. In all, they had 130 cannon and 1,012 men on board. We have additional reliable news from St. Lucia [Nevis] that another French warship of 50 [80] cannon has surrendered to an Engl. ship of 64 cannon. From several French islands, we received the report that on April 18, 17 French warships were missing. Another news item arrived in St. Lucia from Antigua that the <u>Sovereign</u>, a French warship [of 74 cannon], has been seized and [another one] sunk. [summary]*
From another letter, we have learned that 7 French warships were seized in the Caribbean Sea. [accurate]

N.B. If it is true. I wished it were true, I wished it had happened long ago, -- until now it seemed as if the English had not been really serious. "As a last hurrah," they apparently want to gain an advantage over the French in order to maintain their rule of the sea; I say "as a last hurrah," for everything will probably soon be over.

Québec paper, July 11: *Vienna, March 13. Last Friday, the Holy Father, Pope Pius [VI], arrived here to pay a visit to His Majesty our Emperor. [selective]*
Naples, March 4. Last Friday, 4 strong tremors from an earthquake were felt here; the inhabitants took to flight into the open fields. [accurate]

London, April 4. Brook Watson Esq. is going as commissary general to America with Sir Guy Carleton [to take] *the place of Commissary Gen. Mr. Wier, Esq. This Mr. Watson has attained a certain reputation because he saved himself from a shark in a sheerly incredible fashion. After the capture of Havana, he was bathing near that place when [on his leaping from the edge of a boat into the river], this fish bit off one of his legs. Through this, the monster was prevented from pursuing him under water and swallowing him IN TOTO.*[11] [summary]

April 13. Yesterday General Burgoyne was in the House of Commons in his uniform as commander-in-chief of the armed forces in Ireland. Maurice Morgan Esq. and William Pitt the Younger both will go as commissioners to America to begin peace negotiations; these two men are very popular with the Americans.[12] *According to the letters that have come here, the Provinces of Connecticut, Maryland, Pennsylvania and Virginia have given their delegates instructions to do everything in their power to effect a reunion with the mother country. Our fleet in the West Indies is 48 warships strong and will be adequate for opposing our enemies.* [summary]

April 15. Sir John Johnson is going to be superintendent general of all the Savage nations [Indian tribes] in [the Province of] Canada and Vice Admiral Campbell[13] *commander-in-chief of Newfoundland; both are departing for their designated places.* [accurate]

Sorel, July 12. Today one officer, 2 noncommissioned officers and 30 men from our regiment and the Battalion von Bärner went on a quick commando [raid] to Crown Point to wreck havoc there; each soldier received 30 cartridges.

17th   Our Dragoon Regiment and the Battalion von Bärner moved to a camp close to Fort No. 4. Maj. Gen. von Riedesel ordered every man to be given 1 lb. of fresh meat and he sent 2 bottles of Port wine for every 3 men of his own squadron. At sunset, the tents were struck and we again moved into our ----- barracks.

20th   Since I have applied several times to Maj. Gen. von Riedesel that through his intercession I might receive the payment for medicine the English paymaster has owed me since Rutland, I received permission today to go to Québec in a batteau. This batteau was to transport those condemned to the frigate. I was to look after my affairs on my own. At 7 o'clock this morning, we departed, passed Trois-Rivières in favorable wind and came to Batiscan in the evening.

21st   At 4 o'clock this afternoon, we reached Québec; we thus had covered more than 30 German miles since yesterday. My medicine bill listed the funds I had spent on medicine that was given to the Engl. prisoners of war in Rutland. With a letter from our general, I reported to His Excel. Governor Gen. Haldimand and presented my bill. This was examined by the physician general of the Province of Canada, Dr. Mabane. Thereupon I received from the governor a warrant for the value of the bills, which amounted to 62 guineas and which was to be paid to me by the Engl. paymaster. If Maj. Gen. Phillips had not died in Virginia, I would have received 1,000 specie more, for he had promised to pay me at least 1 specie per day, the same that an Engl. surgeon's mate received. I had been performing these duties for better than 3 years, yet Haldimand did not want to accord me anything. For his thriftiness, he is hated by the English. -- He is Swiss by birth. --

24th   One ship of 50 cannon and 2 frigates sailed down the St. Lawrence River to capture Paul Jones, said to cruise in the Gulf with a small fleet.

26th   Our batteau departed from here, but since the wind becomes contrary in the evening and the journey to Trois-Rivières is dangerous against the current, and also because of the many little sandbanks and rocks, I decided to go on land with the post calash.

27th   This morning, I departed with the post and reached Deschambault this evening.

28th   I arrived in Trois-Rivières today and visited all the old friends. Many people, whom I could not remember, still knew me; after all, I had not seen them since the month of May of 1777. The grandmother had died last year having become almost 99 years old.

31st   This noon, our batteau finally arrived here after having run the risk of being crushed against cliffs and boulders several times during the past 6 days. I said farewell and we went up to Pointe-du-Lac. The wind is from the NW and contrary. It is strange that this wind has already been blowing with the same violence for more than 4 weeks.

End of this Month

Month of August 1782

1st   In contrary wind, we rowed until [La Seigneurie de la] Rivière-du-Loup, where we stayed overnight.

2nd   With much effort and toil, we returned to Sorel.

3rd   The Québec paper [Aug. 1, 1782] *reports that General Carleton has written a letter to General Washington in which he announces his arrival and expresses his desire to reach an agreement between Great Britain and the Colonies. He therefore would send Mr. Morgan to him [General Washington] for the purpose of negotiation if he would first send the necessary passports for this man. General Washington's reply was that nothing was closer to his heart than that calm be restored and bloodshed terminated; that he would immediately write to Congress in Philadelphia and then let him [Carleton] know Congress' decision at once. Thereupon, the resolution of Congress soon followed that, in the name of Congress, General Washington should reject everything from Gen. Carleton and also refuse any passport for Morgan. This happened in the beginning of May. Thus, the Americans do not wish to make peace!* -- [summary]

5th   The NW wind continues to blow and both yesterday and today the storm has been terrible. Because of this, it is so cold that one must sit near the fireplace -- and there is again a rumor about camping.

11th   Orders were given to move back to camp tomorrow.

12th   At 5 o'clock this morning, we and the Battalion von Bärner moved to the old camp where we had been in July.

17th   The Light Company of the 53rd Regiment camped somewhat in front of our left wing.

18th   Maj. Gen. von Riedesel went to the Regiment von Rhetz at Nicolet.

23rd   The news came that a corps of Americans joined by Frenchmen have moved against Niagara. Another corps of Americans were camped at Fort Edward and patrolling the region as far as Crown Point, if it is true. --

24th   Early this morning, our Maj. Gen. von Riedesel arrived here again and there is now talk of marching. The Light Company of the 53rd Reg. marched to St. Jean this noon and in the afternoon we received orders to be ready to march at the first order. I have a beautiful cabin built for myself, which will be ready tomorrow; I should be annoyed if I had spent the guineas in vain.

27th   Last night I slept in my cabin for the first time and I was safe from insects. I was commanded by Maj. Gen. von Riedesel to stay in Sorel. -- Nothing could be more welcome to me since the corps will march to the Ile-aux-Noix to improve fortifications of that island. This corps consists of the English 29th, 34th and 53rd Regts. as well as our corps except for the Regt. Prinz Friedrich, that is stationed in Québec. The following stayed back here in garrison: Commander Lieut. Colonel von Bärner, 2 captains, 2 subalterns, a detachment of some 70 men; our Jäger Company and one company of the Hesse-Hanau Jäger Regiment as well as one detachment of English Artillery. The Reg. CHIRURGUS Vorbrodt remained in the hospital on the other side of the Richelieu and I stayed in the garrison.

28th   At 5 o'clock this morning, the general march was beaten, the Dragoon Regiment went up the Richelieu on batteaux and the Battalion von Bärner marched on land. I can truly say that I would have liked to march along if they had not gone to that cursed island where in the month of October 1776, I spent 14 sad days in distress. I now consider myself really fortunate to remain here. I leave my cabin with pleasure and move back to my Engl. merchant.

End of this Month

Month of September 1782

1st   Today I received a letter with the news that our corps had arrived in St. Jean the day before yesterday, i.e., the 30th of August, and that yesterday it was at the Ile-aux-Noix. We hear nothing new about peace, really not a blessed thing. This is because Canada has little contact with the rest of the world. Would that I had never seen Canada again! --

5th   The order came today that all the men who can possibly be spared by the garrison here be sent to the Ile-aux-Noix. Thus, 8 of our dragoons have departed. There continues to be much talk about peace; also that a French fleet has been locked in Boston harbor; if it is true. --

7th   Cornet Schönewald passed through on his way from the Ile-aux-Noix to Québec; he will go to Halifax or New York.

Québec paper, Sept. 12: *Paris, June 23.*
Monsieur le Comte d'Artois will go to the camp at San Roque on the 4th of next month. The siege will be continued in earnest and Gibraltar will perhaps be conquered before peace is established. That it may be soon in sight is everywhere expected and Lord Hertfort's arrival at Versailles confirms the opinion that the preliminaries will shortly be signed.[14] [not found]

15th   We received the news that Lieut. Gebhard and Ensign Specht are still in Rutland. The French disease is so common that one finds villages in which all the inhabitants, large and small, young and old, have been infected with it; thus they all have cankers in their throats.[15] The King and Parliament have been informed about it and it is expected that a radical cure may now be undertaken at Royal expense. This indeed is the only way.
General Haldimand will pass through here to go to the Ile-aux-Noix.

28th   A batteau went to Berthier to take General Haldimand there.

30th   The batteau returned here today, for Gen. Haldimand had received a message from Québec that 2 packet boats had arrived in Québec from England and the frigate *Hussar* from Halifax. Thus, His Excel. returned to Québec. We also heard that a fleet from New York was in the St. Lawrence River; it is said to have all our Convention troops and all our previously imprisoned Engl. and German officers on board. Moreover, there are presumably 2 ships with gifts for the Savages in Canada among them, their cargo estimated at 80,000 pounds sterling. These 2 ships were seized by the French and the English later recaptured them from the French. In addition, all the Hessian recruits who had come from Germany had been sent to this place. To get the dispatches from the homeland for our Maj. Gen. von Riedesel, Cornet Schönewald has been sent to Capt. Cleve and is expected to return this winter -------- he will then have to go through the wilderness on snowshoes; that will be a tough march for him.

End of this Month

Month of October 1782

4th   Last night, Cornet Gräfe passed through here with an express of Gov. Haldimand to our Gen. von Riedesel. Nothing is known of what the packet boats have brought from England. Everything is being kept quite secret. The news came that Engl. regiments in Canada are to be sent to New York or the West Indies; another blatant lie. If another dozen regiments came here, we could improve our defenses, but we can certainly not dispense with any. We are expecting our Maj. Gen. von Riedesel.

7th   Maj. Gen. von Riedesel arrived here from the Ile-aux-Noix and continued to Québec on the

8th.
The imprisoned officers from the Convention of Saratoga have finally been exchanged and they have arrived in Québec. Our Capt. von Wolzogen also arrived in Québec with recruits.[16]

22nd   Our formerly imprisoned officers arrived here as well as the recruits from Braunschweig.

23rd   Orders came today for our Dragoon Regiment to march to St. Antoine and St. Charles for winter quarters. The Regiment von Riedesel and 2 companies of the Regiment von Rhetz are to come to Sorel as occupation forces. The news that Engl. regts. are to be sent to the West Indies has its origin in the fact that more than 26 transport ships have had beds provided and installed for the transportation of troops; they are to sail to New York. The reason is that there is enough wood in Canada, while it is scarce and expensive in New York.
A soldier's life is peculiar. As soon as he has properly settled down in a place and is beginning to become known, he must move to another place. Sorel is not the best place in Canada, yet I have been here for one year and do not like leaving. But I must now do so just at a time when I have become known in and around Sorel and am a little in balance again ---- but c'est la guerre.

End of this Month

Month of November 1782

1st   The recruits for the Regiment von Riedesel arrived here and occupied the watchhouses.

3rd   We set out and went to St. Ours in batteaux.

4th   We reached St. Antoine, which lies 6 leagues from Sorel on the Rivière Richelieu. The Grenadier Battalion, which Lieut. Colonel von Mengen commands, went down the Richelieu to the St. Lawrence River and further to Berthier, where they took up their winter quarters.

5th and 6th were spent in assigning the quarters.

7th   Our Drag. Regiment arrived here and moved into their winter quarters. The men came one by one, and 1 or 2 men were assigned to each house. The landlord has to provide nothing but beds, a table, chairs, firewood and kitchen utensils. By the way, we are receiving royal provisions as good as any soldier has ever received on this earth. I am lodging with the amiable Mons. Deschambault.

End of this Month

Month of December 1782

1st   The snow lies 2 feet deep. The Rivière Richelieu is not yet frozen in the center.

23rd   At Beloeil, 4 dragoons in a sleigh drowned in the Richelieu today; they had gone after their provisions. Their names were Grupe, Tomme, Schmidt and Probst. How many are already buried in these evil Canadian rivers! --

25th   Today our Chief Paymaster Gödecke died in Trois-Rivières of dropsy in the chest.
At this year's end, it is my heartfelt wish that the news of peace, now being spread around more and more, may prove to be true so that we may once again be released from Canada.

End of this Year

NOTES

1. Both Austria and Russia had, for their own reasons, offered to mediate the conflict between Britain and her American colonies with their European allies. The Austrian mediation effort did involve an attempt to separate France and Spain from their American alliance, but in the end was unsuccessful. The authoritative work on the peace negotiations is Richard B. Morris, The Peacemakers: The Great Powers and American Independence, (New York, 1965). (See Morris, chapters 9 and 10 for a discussion of the mediation efforts and John Adams successful resistance to what would have resulted in the partition of America.)

2. This may be a reference to Sir Alured Clarke (1745?-1832), who had come to New York in 1776 as Lt. Col. of the 54th Regiment; he was transferred to the 7th Fusiliers in 1777 and eventually became "muster-master general of the Hessian troops in succession to John Burgoyne," being appointed Lieutenant-Governor of Jamaica in 1782. He was Major General in 1791 and in 1798 was Commander-in-Chief of British forces in India. (Dictionary of National Biography, Oxford, 1949-50, pp. 416-417.)

3. Wasmus was correct to suspect the veracity of this report: Clinton in fact remained in New York until Carleton arrived to replace him in May 1782. Colonel Leslie might be a reference to Alexander Leslie (c.1740-1794), who had begun the Revolution as Lt. Col. of the 64th Regiment at Halifax, but was Major General by 1780, having replaced Cornwallis as commander in the South after Yorktown; at this point he was still trying to hold Charleston and Savannah.

4. It is not surprising that the isolation and hardships of the Canadian winter led to low morale among the troops and even to suicide or self-mutilation; most of these men had been away from their homeland since 1776, and peace negotiations were still dragging on.

5. Greene had been given command of the Southern Department in December 1780, after Gates' disastrous tenure, and had successfully resisted Cornwallis' attempts to regain control of the South. By December of 1781, Charleston and Savannah were the only remaining British outposts in the South. British forces under Major James Henry Craig (1748-1812) had evacuated Wilmington in November and taken a position on Johns Island near Charleston, where they were unsuccessfully attacked by the Americans under General Henry ("Light-Horse Harry") Lee on the 28th and 29th of December 1781.

6. Typical penalties for errant Braunschweigers included: 80 blows on the shirt, for insubordination to a noncommissioned officer; running the gauntlet 10 times through 100 men, for getting drunk on outpost duty; running the gauntlet 32 times, over a two day period, for desertion. Other deserters were court-martialed and shot; in at least one instance 4 deserters were punished by drawing lots to select two for capital punishment, while the other two were condemned as galley slaves on a frigate. cf. p. 29, also note 60, 1776.)

7. Much of this paragraph is rumor: peace negotiations were finally underway, but agreement was not reached until November 1782; no Hannoverians were en route to New York; North's ministry had fallen on March 20, 1782 to be succeeded by Rockingham's, dedicated to ending the war in America; Clinton had indeed been replaced by Carleton in April, while Arnold had been in London since December 1781; St. Kitts had indeed fallen to the French in February 1782, while St. Eustatius had fallen the previous November; there had been discussions in London in which the plan of withdrawal to the West Indies had been considered, but evacuation would not occur for another year.

8. Admiral George Brydges Rodney (1712-1792) had indeed captured de Grasse in the Battle off Saints Passage, April 9-12, 1782, but had failed to follow through and defeat the rest of the French fleet. Rodney sailed to Jamaica, leaving the Bahamas vulnerable to the Spanish, whose expeditionary force soon captured the islands.

9. This is, of course, a reference to Joshua 10:12.

10. At the close of the year 1779, the majority of the officers of the Convention Army had been exchanged, leaving 23 officers with the 788 privates in Charlottesville. All but Lt. Col. von Mengen, one captain from each regiment, and one noncommissioned officer from each company were exchanged by early 1781. (Memoirs, Letters, and Journals of Major General Riedesel, William L. Stone, translator and editor, vol. II, Albany, 1868, pp. 81, 91.)

11. Sir Brook Watson (1735-1807), left an orphan in 1741, went to sea at a young age, and lost his leg to a shark off Havana when he was only fourteen. After serving as commissary under Wolfe at Louisbourg in 1758, he established himself as a merchant in London in 1759. He served as Commissary General to the British forces in Canada in 1782 and 1783 and was elected to Parliament in 1784, serving until 1794. (DNB, 912-913.) In 1778, the American painter John Singleton Copley (1737-1815) who had come to London in 1774, painted Watson's encounter with the shark; "Watson and the Shark" is in the National Gallery of Art in Washington, D.C.

12. Charles Watson-Wentworth, Marquess of Rockingham (1730-1782), had succeeded North when the latter resigned in March of 1782, but had died of influenza a few months later before he could carry out his policy of extricating Britain from the American War. He was succeeded by his Secretary of State, William Petty Fitzmaurice, Earl of Shelburne (1737-1805). Maurice Morgan (1726-1802) had been private secretary to Shelburne in 1766 and served in Québec in 1768-1770. An undersecretary of state in 1782, Morgan was secretary of the Peace Commission 1782-83. William Pitt the Younger (1759-1806), Chatham's second son, had entered Parliament at the age of 21 in 1780 and only two years later, in July 1782 became Chancellor of the Exchequer in Shelburne's ministry after July 1782.

13. John Johnson succeeded his brother-in-law Guy Johnson as Indian superintendent in March 1782; his appointment was renewed in 1791 and he was made colonel in the British army. Since the Americans had confiscated his land in New York, he was compensated, both with money and with a large tract of Canadian land.

John Campbell (1720?-1790) had served in the Seven Year's War, was flag-captain at Quiberon Bay in 1759, captain of the fleet under Keppel in 1779 and in 1782 a Vice Admiral, was made Governor of Newfoundland and Commander-in-Chief on that station until 1786.

14. Francis Seymour Conway, Marquess of Hertford (1719-1794), had been a privy councillor and ambassador extraordinary to France in 1762 had been Lord Chamberlain since 1766.

15. The French disease, or Morbus Gallicus, was a common name for syphilis (a term which was not commonly used until 1850, although it had been introduced by Fracaster in 1530, in a poem about a shepherd named Syphilis, who contracted the disease through blasphemy). Venereal disease was a constant problem for the armed forces on both sides in the Revolution; in 1778, Congress had introduced a bill to fine infected soldiers for the cost of their own treatment. One British surgeon estimated that " a regiment of four hundred men had an average of three hundred cases of venereal disease a year." (This includes many men who "were infected two or three times a quarter.") The British army also fined infected soldiers. (Theodore Rosebury, Microbes and Morals, New York, 1971, p. 29; William J. Brown, et al., Syphilis and Other Venereal Disease, Cambridge, 1970, p. 136; Sylvia R. Frey, The British Soldier in America, Austin,1981, p. 44.)

16. Captain Carl Ludwig von Wolzogen, in the 5th company of the 2nd Battalion of the Leib Regiment, did not return to Braunschweig, but asked to be discharged, in America, in 1784. Elster remarks that he had gone to America with the last transport of recruits and had not returned and that he seemed to be much in debt. (p. 450.) The Duke wrote to Riedesel on September 27, 1782 that von Wolzogen should ask for discharge if he was not to be dismissed; the Duke was willing to continue his pay for 6 months or a year and even pay his debts as long as he would arrange to leave his service, which he apparently did.

1783

Month of January 1783

15th   The order came for the general's Dragoon Squadron to march to Sorel and to parade there on the Queen's Birthday on the 18th.

16th   We marched to St. Ours and today, [*and on*] the

17th,   we came to Sorel.

18th   A feu de joie was made. Besides the garrison, the first company of the 31st Reg., one company of the Reg. Specht from Yamaska and our squadron had moved here from the Ile-Dupas. Together with the garrison, these were placed on the ice of the Richelieu in a row two men deep and made three running fires; thereupon they roared a frightful, throaty hurrah.

19th   We marched back to St. Ours and today, the

20th,   we moved back into our quarters at St. Antoine.

End of this Month

Month of February 1783

13th   Orders came that 2 squadrons of dragoons and 2 companies from the Reg. von Rhetz were to advance to Beloeil and Chambly so that in case of need they could quickly reinforce the garrison of St. Jean; a detachment of Rebels has been troubling our post at Pointe-au-Fer. It is perhaps their intention to burn our fleet at St. Jean but I do not yet believe any of this. For as long as I have been in captivity, men were summoned to such an undertaking every winter but nothing has ever come of it. As I mentioned before, the expedition of 1775 under Montgomery and Arnold will never be forgotten by the Americans. They will never again be so foolhardy as to undertake the like during the winter. It should be added that a combined French and American corps is not only fortifying Ticonderoga but also building ships at Skenesborough. This is probably all the winter news.[1]

15th   A detachment of 5 men per company, taken from all the German regiments, passed through here to St. Jean under the command and direction of our Captain von Girsewald.[2] A Light Infantry Company of the 31st Reg. and 50 Engl. Artillerymen also passed through our parish with several cannon on sleighs and likewise went to St. Jean. Our Leib Squadron is in Fort Chambly and Major von Meibom's[3] Squadron returned to Beloeil. We are still at rest.

20th   Three days of rain have almost melted the snow, and the ice of the Richelieu threatens to break. The inhabitants assure us that Lake Champlain must be open. The oldest inhabitants cannot remember such weather in Febr. and March. If the Americans wanted to start something against Canada, they would surely be totally out of luck. It would seem best for them just to seek to maintain their independence, which no one can possibly deny them any longer.

22nd   It is 7 years ago that we marched out of Wolfenbüttel and nevertheless, we are to be mustered for a future campaign this very day. The whole day, we have been waiting for Major Holland but he did not come. In the evening, a terrible snowstorm engulfed us. Thus, 7 years have passed! Who would have thought that this horrible war would last this long! And still there is no prospect that it could end in England's favor. -- Yet, you cannot always win in a game. You have also to get used to losing.

23rd   Major Holland does not want to see us this year. He will be content with the lists that were sent over to him this morning. That sounds good. -- --
In the wintry air, snow has been falling 2 feet deep since yesterday. Three captured Rebels are said to be in Chambly, one of whom is Captain Stone from Rutland. If I could only see him and with some luck be of use to him! If at all possible, I would gladly offer him some of my own to make his captivity more bearable. The poor man! How unhappy he must be as a prisoner of war in Canada. --And his amiable family in Rutland! If you [Stone's family] only knew how much all this friendship and human love you bestowed upon me is alive in me in ever so precious remembrance. My heart is so completely filled with gratitude that I will make it my duty to be of use to your husband and father and -- to pay my debts. --

24th   Last night, the order came for Major von Meibom and the Vacant Squadron to set out immediately and march to St. Jean. Ours, that is the General's Squadron, is to move to the quarters at St. Charles again. I also received orders to march with the 2nd Squadron although it was not my tour. Thus, I reached Beloeil this evening where I met the Vacant Squadron.

25th   We marched to St. Jean via Chambly, where we were placed in barracks at the small fort. I would never have believed it possible that such a deserted place, grown over with woods and brush, as St. Jean was in the year 1777, could have changed this much. Between Chambly and St. Jean, the right bank of the Richelieu has been quite attractively built up; the inhabitants are mostly English, who emigrated from the Colonies. St. Jean is a small fortress town; the fleet lies near the large fort and is still frozen in on the landward [settled] side, while the other side is free of ice. The ships here are the Commodore's ship, the *Royal George*, the *Inflexible*, the *Washington*, the *Maria*, the *Carleton*, the *Trumbull* and the *Canada* to say nothing of the small armed ships and cannon batteaux. The radeau or Floating Battery lies on the bank in ruins. Since it sailed so poorly, it was not worth much. This small fleet is commanded by Commodore William Chambers. The garrison at St. Jean consists of one detachment of Engl. Artillery, the 29th Reg., 2 comp. of Hesse-Hanau Jäger, 8 Dragoon Squadrons, 3 companies of the Reg. von Rhetz and Loyalists, whose numbers I cannot determine. Colonel von Creutzbourg, commander of the Hesse-Hanau Jäger Reg., is commander of St. Jean.[4] The Light Company from the 31st Reg., one company of Hesse-Hanau Jäger as well as the detachment under Capt. von Girsewald, that had marched ahead of us, are camping in the woods at Pointe-au-Fer.

26th   Maj. Gen. von Riedesel arrived and is lodging on board the *Royal George.*

28th   The Loyalists and Canadians have returned from the Ausable River; they had been detached to fell trees. These men had been provided with supplies until the month of May and did not know why they were recalled. The Ausable River is located 33 miles behind Cumberland Head on Lake Champlain. They assured us that no Rebel has been at Crown Point this winter, much less at Pointe-au-Fer. Thus, the report from Pointe-au-Fer,[5] which I had given on the 13th of this month, must be counted among the customary winter stories and -- what are we doing here? -- or better, why did we come here? -- What a question! It is the human predicament to suffer! ---
There is much talk of peace, it will eventually become true.-

End of this Month

Month of March 1783

From the 1st to the 5th, there was nothing new but today 3 Loyalists came through the wilderness. One of them told me a great deal about the terrible march through the wilderness and begged of me and everyone listening to him not to ask him anything. For he was not allowed to tell anyone but Governor General Haldimand all the news that he had brought from New York. From their faces, however, one could perceive that they had nothing to tell.

7th   We received orders to march back to our winter quarters tomorrow.

8th   We set out early in the morning and marched back to Beloeil. Since we made a rendezvous at Chambly, I had the opportunity to see the 3 prisoners of whom I had written on Febr. 23. It was not the capt. but another Stone from Rutland, who had never had anything to do with the war. This unhappy fellow with the rest had been trying to settle in Cohasset for 2 to 4 years. While they were clearing the land of wood, they were caught by a party of Savages and dragged to Canada. Cohasset lies near the New England border in the wilderness, about 150 Engl. miles away from Sorel. This Stone had already been imprisoned for more than 3 years. He and I knew each other quite well. "How different has my captivity been from yours," he said, weeping. Since I did not want to expose myself to the prejudice of the Englishmen present, I could not even say much to him. For he is called a Rebel and thus not worthy of our attention. But I showed him that I felt compassionate and friendly toward him and promised to visit him again soon. I took leave. How useless we are and how unworthy of human society when we do not share in the sufferings of our brethren and, although we do have the strength, not provide any comfort.

9th   Today, I reached St. Antoine and moved back into my quarters.

12th   Maj. Gen. von Riedesel returned from St. Jean; so did Captain von Girsewald. Thus, this campaign has ended rather quickly.--

23rd   The news reached us that Lieut. Colonel von Ehrenkrook died yesterday of dropsy in Trois-Rivières. Since there is so much talk of peace now, we should soon believe it, and at the very moment that I write this, I hear that our General von Riedesel himself has announced it at Sorel.

24th   Reports of peace increase; we soon ought to hear that they are definitely true.

30th   In the past ten days, I have received letters from Québec, Sorel and Montréal, which all say that there is peace. This news has produced great consternation among the merchants and among the peasants in the region of the Rivière Richelieu, who are also having great difficulties. They used to be able to sell their wheat at 8 livres per hdt. [hundredweight] but they want to get 10 livres. Now, as the news of peace is spreading, no one wants to offer more than 4 livres. That is a big difference. One livre is 6 groschen.

31st   Last night, the Rivière Richelieu broke up and is now almost free of ice. One still does not hear anything reliable about peace other than that the merchants in Montréal have received a newspaper from Boston, in which the articles of peace can be read. If only they are not the same as those that I have previously recorded in this book. Next month, we will hear more about it.

End of this Month

Month of April 1783

We also spent the month of April without learning anything more certain concerning peace. As it is customary with all peace treaties, there are two parties here in Canada: one wanting the war to continue and the other wanting peace. Many of our corps do not want peace, nor do the merchants and the Canadians in general as they continue flattering themselves with the hope that Canada will come again under French rule. This war has also made the Canadians wealthy. It would not be inappropriate for them now to contribute something more from their great abundance to the King --- ---- ----- ---- for at present they only give one shilling or 7 groschen a year for each morgen of land. -- Two Engl. naval officers, one of whom was Capt. Tonge, have come from New York on land bringing positive news of peace. They are said to have been but a few minutes in Sorel with our Maj. Gen. von Riedesel, for whom they had some letters and then hastened on their journey to Governor Haldimand at Québec. This is all we have learned of peace this month. We must conclude that this peace has not turned out to England's best interest since the English authorities are most reserved about making it known.

End of this Month

Month of May 1783

Oh you pleasant, superior man! [sic] Never have you been more dear to me than now when you announce peace to us. We have received the reliable report today that this evil war has finally ended, that peace has definitely been made. The 13 Provinces have been declared Independent and thus, their Unanimity, Perserverance and Fortitude have finally brought about their Independence. You good people, your wish has now been fulfilled. As it is written on your money "We are one," remain forever unified among yourselves. I would like to be in New England now for only a few days[6.]

7th   Today, peace was made public at the Dragoon Regiment through the following proclamation:
George III, King of Great Britain etc.
The preliminary articles have been signed in Paris on the 30th of November last between our commissioners for peace negotiations and the commissioners of the United States of America as well as the commissioners of the United Forces. It was their task to settle upon the succession of the articles of peace, which have been proposed between us and the United States. Peace will be concluded between us and His Most Christian Majesty, and the preliminary articles for the restoration of peace between us and His Most Christian Majesty at Versailles were signed last Jan. 20 between our minister and His Catholic Majesty and the preliminaries between us and the King of Spain likewise signed at Versailles on Jan. 20 by our and the Spanish ministers. In order to end the misery of war as soon as possible, we have agreed upon the following plans with His Majesty, the King of Spain, the Gen. States, the United Provinces, and the United States of America

namely: that all ships and merchandise which are seized in the Channel and the North Sea after a period of 12 days, counting from the signing of these preliminary articles, are to be returned by both the one as well as the other party. From the Channel and the North Sea to the Canary Islands, the time of one month has been determined; included is that which may have happened on the ocean or the Mediterranean during that period; two months from the Canary Islands to the Equinoctial Line or Equator and 5 months for all the other parts of the world without exception or other real description of place and time etc. Here, the Articles of Peace are following in order, which, however, are too lengthy, etc.

Given at our Court of St. James, Febr. 14, 1783, in the 25th Year of our Reign!

Long Live the King!

End of this Month

Month of June 1783

1st   Today I had the pleasure of receiving 3 letters from Wolfenbüttel, which had all been written last January. To my greatest sorrow, I learned that my good mother had died at Salzgitter on May 1, 1782. How much I would have liked seeing her once more!
--
Following yesterday's orders, we set out, embarked in our batteaux and rowed to Sorel. Here, each squadron was assigned 2 barns incl. the adjacent pigsty and other stables. I stayed in the hospital with the Regimental Surgeon Pralle,[7] who was so kind as to leave me part of his quarters so that I would not have to sleep in the barn.

3rd   Cornet Schönewald arrived back at Sorel. He had gone to Halifax in the frigate *Pandora*, from there to New York and then back to Québec. One day before his departure from New York, he had spoken to Major Hopkins and learned from him that Lieut. Gebhard and Ensign Specht were still in Rutland.

4th   The King's birthday was celebrated; as usual, cannon and small arms were fired.
Our entire Braunschweig corps is here in and around Sorel; only the Reg. Prinz Friedrich is still in Québec.
The Americans do not want to take back any of the Refugees, Loyalists, Tories or Provincials, as they are called, who had emigrated during the war and crossed over to the Royal settlements and armies; even though it had been established in the Articles of Peace and particularly mentioned by the King of England and especially been recommended to the American Congress that those having been exiled be readmitted and helped to their former estates. Nevertheless, one hears from some coming from the Province that several, having gone back to their families from Canada and New York, had been shot in a tumult that rose at their return or lost their lives in other ways. They were called infidels because they had not been faithful to their country and were not worthy to live among humans.[8]

12th   I heard that 2 strangers from the Colonies had arrived at Sorel last night; one of them was said to be a physician from Worcester in New England, who had very cautiously asked for me. I immediately traversed the Rivière Richelieu to Sorel, looked for him and was surprised at finding a good friend; at his parents' home, I had been honored as child and brother. His name was Jonas Moor, 26 years old. I was most happy to see him and he told me much from there. They had received the news of peace earlier than we here in Canada. His main concern had been to see me once more before my departure for Europe and he and his guide had marched 350 Engl. miles through the wilderness where they had not come upon a single human. They arrived on the 18th day at Sorel. This is more than can be expected from a friend. Could that kind of friend ever be found in Germany? Both their faces were so disfigured from mosquito bites that I

would not have recognized him if he had not told me his name. He tried everything to persuade me to return to New England with him and to send my baggage on a ship to Boston. But I could not do this as much as I would have liked living among these good people; I must go back to my wife and children. Would that they were here!--
There is drill here every day now. Orders have gone to all the commanders of our regiments that they should make known that everyone, whoever he may be, may ask to be discharged -- either to stay in this country or to go to the Colonies. But this order was not in the least carried out properly.

19th   For the past 4 days, there have been maneuvers and shooting with powder. Today was the largest and the last maneuver.

20th   The batteaux are going to get our large baggage.

23th   Several vessels, which came from Québec, arrived here to get our baggage. The regiments expect marching orders very soon because the transport ships which are to take us to Europe have already arrived at Québec. We have heard, however, that they are in need of major repair, which may take as long as a month's time. I wished we would not set sail before the Month of Sept. since the Equinoctial winds, namely those coming from the SW and NW, will then start to blow for up to 4 or 6 weeks.

24th   The discharges are continuing diligently; from our regiment, more than 70 dragoons have applied, but -- as I said before -- the order has been given -- but -- will it be followed? --
Our Captain Cleve, aide-de-camp of our general, will soon depart for Europe. Doctor Moor's face has regained its former natural shape. We received the news from New York and Long Island that about 18,000 Loyalist families will go from there to Nova Scotia and Canada. They had once emigrated and were now not allowed to return to their country and their estates, which had already been confiscated for a long time. Having been avowed Royalists for a long time, they had emigrated to please their King. Powerful men, who had hoped to play a powerful role in the future, had led the little people astray and they are now all unhappy. The King has granted them some land that they are to clear and cultivate; for a certain number of years, they will receive daily Royal provisions, etc.

30th   Since each day there is talk of marching, Doctor Moor has departed again. He will be walking from here to Carillon, will cross Lake Champlain and continue his journey via Bennington, Springfield and so on to Worcester. He now has company since many of those discharged are returning to the Colonies. As he was lodging with me, we were always together during the time he was here. He frequently dined at Captain of the Cavalry Fricke's since he [Fricke] knew his parents quite well. During that time that I have been so fortunate as to have this one true friend with me, I have generally tried everything possible to make his life comfortable. It would have been a great joy for both of us to continue our travels together ---- I gave him several letters to take along, particularly to Major Gen. Warner, to his parents, to commissary Mercereau, to Pastor Buckminster etc.
May God grant him a safe return.

End of this Month

Month of July 1783

3rd   Baroness von Riedesel, wife of our general, departed for Québec with her children.

7th   Maj. Gen. von Riedesel departed for Québec and Brigadier Colonel Specht took over the command.

8th   The large baggage of our Drag. Reg. was taken onto the ship *Providence* to be transported to Québec.

9th   Orders came from Gov. Gen. Haldimand that all the German troops are to have land provisions through the 24th of this month; on the 25th, ship provisions will begin. Thus, we will soon set out for Québec.

15th   We ate [*fresh*] green peas, carrots, and potatoes today, which for Canada is very early. Before our departure for Europe, what pleasure to enjoy something that our Kind Benefactor has again allowed to grow so abundantly this year. Would that in a few months we may taste the kind of produce which our Gracious God has offered the inhabitants of Germany.

16th   We received the order that, on the 18th, the First Division, consisting of the Drag. Reg., Grenadier Battalion and Reg. von Rhetz, is to set out on their march to Québec; the Second Division, consisting of the Reg. von Riedesel, Specht and von Bärner, will set out on the 19th; the Reg. Prinz Friedrich is still in Québec. Our baggage ships weighed anchor today and sailed out of the Richelieu into the St. Lawrence and cast anchor again.

17th   Our baggage ships set sail for Québec. Everybody is preparing for the journey to Europe. -- Our regiment will go to Québec on batteaux.

18th   Yesterday, Lieut. d'Aniers arrived from New York reporting that the Hessian corps in New York has not received marching orders as yet. We set out from Sorel today and rowed as far as St. Colbert.

19th   We rowed to [La Seigneurie de la] Rivière-du-Loup.

20th   We passed Grand [Ya]Machiche, Pointe-du-Lac, made a rendezvous at Trois-Rivières, and came to Cap-de-la-Madeleine where on the

21st,   we had a day of rest.

22nd   We rowed to Batiscan, where on the

23rd,   we again had a day of rest.

24th   In favorable NW wind, we rowed 18 leagues and although with all the cliffs and boulders, we were frequently in great danger, we arrived safely at Pointe-aux-Trembles. Some of us will have trembled today -- -- from taking money chests along on the batteaux. -- For it was once again our lot to battle against this terrible element [nature]. We can conquer everything except this one. -- --

25th   We stopped at Pointe-aux-Trembles; another day of rest.

26th   We rowed up to St. Augustin where on the

27th,   we had another day of rest.

28th   We were reviewed not far from Québec in Wolfe's Cove [now Anse-au-Foulon] in the usual fashion and our corps embarked on the following transport ships: *Québec*--general's ship; *Silver Eel*--Dragoon Regiment; *Jason*--Grenadier Battalion; *William and Mary*--Battalion von Bärner; *Betsy*--Regiment Prinz Friedrich; *English Hare*--Regiment von Riedesel; *Wier*--Regiment von Riedesel; *Resolution*--Regiment Specht; *Little William*--Reg. Specht; *Freedom, Dolphin*--the rest of Reg. Prinz Friedrich; *Providence, Ceres*--Regiment von Rhetz. Since the 13 ships above cannot be manned with the required number of crew from our corps, several men from the Anhalt-Zerbst Regt. will be transferred to us. Each bed is 7 feet square and 6 men are to lie in it, that is cruel! --

The Hesse-Cassel Reg. von Lossberg, Hesse-Hanau Regiment, the Hesse-Hanau Jäger Regiment and the rest of the Anhalt-Zerbst troops embarked on other transport ships. The 13 ships, mentioned above, have altogether 2,427 men on board. The fleet that is to accompany us consists of 28 ships incl. the frigate *Pandora* and they are to set sail for Europe with the first favorable wind. I was in Québec today and visited Capt. Tonge.

29th   I received the order from Maj. Gen. von Riedesel to sail with him on the ship *Québec* to Europe. "We came together on one ship and also want to go back together on one ship," the General said in an amicable tone of voice. That was a pleasant and auspicious order. Without a doubt, there will be more space than on the *Silver Eel* where 6 men have 7 feet square to lie in. --

30th   I ordered my baggage brought on board the *Québec* and spent this night and the next in Québec.

31st   I embarked on board the *Québec*. This ship was newly built in France 5 years ago. She was a frigate of 44 cannon. The English seized her from the French and she is now designated to transport our Major Gen. von Riedesel, his family and suite to Germany. She is as attractively furnished as the most beautiful private home. All the cannon have been taken off. Here I have enough room and a bed which is hanging from ropes. It is not a hammock but a bed which the English call a cot.

The pilot, who is to guide us to Bic, also came on board today.

I cannot end this month without mentioning the countryside which presents itself to the viewer from the Upper City of Québec. As for grandeur, beauty and variety, it excels everything I have seen in America so far. In its broad expanse lying open before us, our attention is drawn to immense cliffs, immeasurable rivers, pathless forests and settled plains, and then again to mountains, lakes, cities and villages; the senses almost lose themselves beholding the infinite dimension of this scene. Nature shows herself here in all her grandeur and our imagination is almost incapable of picturing anything more beautiful than the various scenes presenting themselves to the eyes of the beholder. From Cap Diamant, one thousand feet above the surface of the river and the highest part of the cliff on which the city has been built, the view is considered by many even more beautiful than from any other place. Yet it seems to me that the view from the Cap is far less beautiful than that from the Battery. For when one overlooks the different objects below, they lose their size, as it were, and it is as if one looks down upon a drawing of the land rather than upon the land itself. I am talking about the Upper Battery, leading to the bastion, which is about 300 feet above the surface of the water. Standing only a few feet away from the edge of the slope, one can suddenly look down the river and the ships sailing to the Lower City always appear to vanish underneath one's feet. The river itself, being here more than 4 miles wide, can be followed to the extreme tip of the Ile-d'Orléans where it loses itself between the mountains narrowing inward from both sides. It is one of the most beautiful of nature's creations and on a calm summer evening it often has the appearance of a large glassy surface where all the brilliant colors of the sky as well as the images of the various objects on shore are being reflected with indescribable beauty. The southern bank, variously alternating between bays and promontories, has almost remained in its original natural state and is covered with tall trees. The opposite side, however, is densely settled with houses that, as far as the eye reaches, expand to one apparently uninterrupted community. Before leaving this region, I must briefly mention two natural phenomena in the vicinity of Québec, that certainly deserve to be seen. The one is the Falls of the Montmorency, the other that of the Rivière Chaudière. About 6 or 7 miles below [NE of] Québec, the first river falls into the St. Lawrence River. At about the same distance above [SW of] the city, the other unites with the same [river]. The Rivière Montmorency flows through a wild and densely wooded area on an irregular course across a bed of broken rocks until it comes to the edge of an abyss from which it drops down in an uninterrupted and almost vertical fall of 240 feet. Except at flood time, the volume of water in this river is not extensive. But because of the force with which it rushes from the slope over the rocks, the water breaks into foam, and the river grows ever more expansive; thus the falls appear to be of considerable width. From bank to bank, the river itself is less than about 50 feet wide. Falling down, the water looks exactly like snow being swept down from the roofs of houses, it only appears to be moving much more slowly. The Falls create a considerable amount of spray and when the midday sun shines straight upon it, many colors emanate in great beauty. When one sails up or down the St. Lawrence River past the mouth of the Rivière Montmorency, the falls show themselves in the utmost splendour.

Near this waterfall, General Haldimand had a very beautiful private home built for himself[9].

The falls in the Rivière Chaudière do not have half the height of those of Montmorency but are at least 250 feet wide. The area around this waterfall is in every respect preferable to that of Montmorency.

End of this Month

Month of August 1783

Comp. CHIRURGUS Sandhagen has resigned his commission and will remain in Québec. From our Braunschweig corps, 19 Comp. CHIRURGI remain in America, most of them in Canada.

2nd   Our Maj. Gen. von Riedesel embarked with his suite.

3rd   One part of the fleet, including us, weighed anchor, sailed up to Paul's Hook and cast anchor at the Ile-d'Orléans. The wind was blowing strongly from SW.

4th   This noon, we set sail in a strong SW wind, passed the Ile-aux-Coudres, continued throughout the night of the

5th,   and cast anchor at the Ile-du-Bic at noon. Passing l'Ile Verte today, I saw, at a distance of 6 or 7 miles, the dismal spot where we collided with the rocks and where our ship became shipwrecked in Oct. 1781. We also met several ships coming from New York that had families of the unfortunate Loyalists on board.

6th   Last night, the frigate *Pandora* joined us. The news came that a ship with Hessians on board has run aground on a sandbank near the Ile-aux-Coudres. It was not possible to free it and so it had to be unloaded. We are having a very favorable SW wind; it is too bad, however, that we cannot make use of it. From Québec to the Ile-du-Bic, we sailed --180

7th   The SW wind continues and we are lying to. Our Gen. von Riedesel ate on board the frigate *Pandora* today and on departing he was saluted with 13 cannon shots. All the sailors hung in the rigging en parade. -- On board our *Québec*, he was received by our oboists with "God Bless [sic] the King". Transport in English miles --------------------180

8th   It is calm today.

9th   Contrary east winds.

10th   Contrary east winds.

11th   Capts. von Pöllniz and Gerlach, together with the Master Clerks Besson and Koch, came to our ship from Québec on the schooner *Mercury*. All are now accounted for. The wind continues to come from the east. As soon as it changes to our favor, we will set sail and wait no longer for the ships that are still missing.

12th   The wind continues contrary; it is foggy and it is raining.

16th   In these days, several other ships full of Loyalists came through here on their way to Québec.

17th   This afternoon the fog lifted and at noon, after the frigate *Pandora* had given the signals, our fleet weighed anchor; although some ships were still missing, we set sail in a favorable SW wind. --- At our departure, we were saluted from the Ile-du-Bic with several cannon shots. We passed the Ile-de-St. Barnabé and took course toward ESE.

18th   This noon, we passed Cap Chat and in the past 24 hours, we have sailed -----129
This afternoon, we passed Mont Louis and its 3 rivers. At 4 o'clock, the ship *Providence*, on which Major von Lucke has embarked, fired a cannon shot and hoisted the flag of distress. The frigate *Pandora* immediately turned and sailed toward it, at the same time giving the signal to the fleet to stop. We, on the *Québec*, continued our course alone and, losing sight of our fleet before nightfall, did not know what had happened on board the *Providence*.

19th   Last night, the wind changed to south; around noon, we saw our fleet sailing on our left at a distance of about 10 miles. We passed the Rivière-du-Renard and until noon, we advanced --137
Course toward EES. It is SSW wind. We passed Cap-des-Rosiers, Cap de Gaspé, Baie de Malbaie, the Ile-de-Bonaventure and reached the Gulf of St. Lawrence with Anticosti on our left. Today, the anchor ropes from below deck were also taken in.

20th   This morning, we saw no land. The SSW wind was so strong and the motions of the ship were so violent that almost all on board became seasick and, what struck me as most peculiar, the pigs and dogs were the first to become sick and to start vomiting. Until noon, we advanced --97
Course toward SE. Since the wind abated in the afternoon, our sailors caught 80 codfish of which the largest weighed 40 and the smallest 18 pounds. They were distributed as provision among the men, a fine meal.

21st   At daybreak, we passed the Iles-de-la-Madeleine or Birds Islands and until noon, we came closer to Europe by ---94
When evening came, we passed the Ile St. Paul and Cap du Nord on Cap Breton. It is raining, dark and very cold.

22nd   This morning, we saw the high mountains of Terre Neuve [Newfoundland] behind us on the left, the last land of America. I gave it my blessing! -- We have now reached the western ocean and further advanced --126
As there was clear sky today, our Captain Boyd observed the sun and [*said*] that we were below the 47°4' of northern latitude. Course toward ESE. We are having strong SW wind.

23rd   We advanced a good deal with it, approaching Europe during the past 24 hours by --226
Latitude 45° 30'. Course toward ESE. When evening came, the wind abated and has even turned to a contrary SSE.

24th   In this continuing contrary wind, we advanced with tacking ---------------------78
Latitude 49° 1'. Course toward ESE. In the afternoon, we reached the Great Bank of Terre Neuve or Newfoundland and measured a depth of 40 fathoms. The contrary wind was so violent that our *Québec* was in terrible motion this night of the

25th,   and nobody could sleep. Until this noon, we advanced ---------------------------98
A dark sky, a violent, unfavorable wind and the terrible agitation of the water [*made it necessary*] to nail shut the hatch of our ship when evening came; for the waves were rushing in with great force. Such precautions produce frightening thoughts in every person and no pen can describe the horror of such a night as [*the one of the*]

26th   was. Sleeping was out of the question. The wind has continued from SSE.
We advanced with it --102
Since in the afternoon the water frequently rushed into the cannon port holes, at the onset of evening, our hatch was nailed shut again. What preparations!

Total---1,267

27th   Last night was the third that we could not sleep. The only consolation in our misery is that we are rapidly advancing. The wind changed to NNW last night and it is raining and very warm. This convinces us that we have already reached another climate.
In the last 24 hours, we advanced --249
Course toward east. In the afternoon, all the portholes were again nailed shut since the waves have been sweeping over the deck. --

28th   Notwithstanding the terrible motion, I slept a little last night. The wind continues to be favorable to us and it is blowing from WSW. With it, we approached Germany till noon by --218
Latitude 45° 55'. Course toward east. The ship's rocking motion has never been stronger than today and till noon on the

29th,   with SSW wind, we did not advance more than --------------------------------178
Latitude 46° 29'. Course toward the east.
This afternoon, we saw a ship following the same course as we.

30th   The wind is the same. With it, we advanced in the past 24 hours ---------------176
Latitude 47° 15'. Course toward the east.

31st   The continuing strong SSW wind did not let us sleep much last night but it brought us closer to Germany by --193
Latitude 48° 7'. What joy! Our captain hopes to see the coast of England tomorrow.

Total--2,281

End of this Month

Month of September 1783

1st   Until this noon, the SWW wind has advanced us   -------------------------------126
Latitude 45° 8'. Course toward the east.

2nd   With continual SWW wind, we have advanced until this noon -------------------120
Latitude 48° 19'. Course toward the east.

3rd   Until this noon, the strong SW wind has brought us foward by -----------------220
Latitude 48° 41'. Course toward the east.

4th   Last night was again very troublesome. SW wind. With this, we advanced -186
Latitude 40° 6'. Tonight, we reached a depth of 60 fathoms and thus have reached the English Channel.

5th   With extraordinarily high seas, last night was the most troubling of the entire journey. The terrible motions of the ship were frightful. The ship frequently leaned so much to the side that one stood now on his head, now on his feet, and we believed we would surely be buried in the abyss. Advanced --190
The wind continues from SW. Latitude 49° 26'. Course toward the east. Being careful not to come too close to the English coast and so avoiding an accident, our Capt. Boyd had sailed too far toward the French coast; thus, we saw no land. This afternoon, the sailors brought the anchor ropes out again. What joy! We spoke with the crew of the merchant ship *Earl of Galloway* that, coming from London, was sailing to Charleston. From them, we learned that we had the Scilly Isles 9 or 10 leagues NW to the rear of us.

6th   With a calm sea, we slept quite well last night. With favorable NW wind, we advanced   --174
Latitude 50° 55'. Course toward the east. We spoke with a ship, coming from Portugal, that had seen the English coast only yesterday. Their capt. told us that we had passed Cap Lizard and Plymouth and had Stuart Point to the NW only 9 leagues to our rear. Although we did not yet see any land, our captain hopes to reach Portsmouth tonight. The terrible NW wind, however, that is beginning to storm frightfully, as well as the accompanying fog, is causing us great fear; for we are certain to be near the Engl. coast.

Total---3,303

Our course was at present directed toward the Engl. coast, but we were worried that, in order to avoid all danger, the capt. would be compelled to take a course back toward the coast of France at nightfall. Yet, Kind Providence that has bestowed so many undeserved favors upon us until now, that in so many sleepless nights inspired us with the consolation that we would not perish, suddenly tore down the curtain, offering us the pleasure of seeing land. The fog lifted and, to our great joy, we saw the famous Isle of Wight and at 6 o'clock this evening, we cast anchor at a depth of 9 fathoms not far from St. Helens. A number of ships were riding at anchor here, among them a Danish flagship. This Isle of Wight is a very fertile island, has 5 cities and 25 parishes. Its shores are mostly white as snow or chalk.

7th   Early this morning, we weighed anchor in order to reach Portsmouth, which is 3 miles away; but this storming NW wind almost drove us onto the sandbanks. Thus, we had to cast anchor again. Up to here, we advanced --58

Total---3,361

At Spithead, we saw a great number of ships riding at anchor. About 500 paces from us toward Portsmouth, we also saw the 3 masts of the *Royal George* of 110 cannon, that last year had sunk there.[10] Since we scarcely had 5 fathoms of water here, we moved a little farther away from the sandbanks into 10 fathoms of water this evening. Capt. Freemann, aide-de-camp of our Maj. Gen. von Riedesel, and our Capt. Boyd went to Portsmouth this evening in order to continue to London from there. A ship cast anchor not far from us; coming from New York, it had several companies of the Ansbach-Bayreuth Regt. on board. This ship must have been in great danger, for it had lost both its main and mizzenmasts.

8th   This morning, we were tacking to Stokes Bay since the NW wind continued to be very strong; we cast anchor there. From here, it is 3 miles on water and on land to Portsmouth. Maj. Gen. von Riedesel went to Portsmouth with his family and suite today and will continue from there to London in order to report our arrival in person to the King. --

9th   The NW wind is storming so violently that we are afraid we will be adrift. Our ship's lieutenant, therefore, ordered another anchor cast. The water is so agitated that no boat can be hoisted out. As soon as it is calmer, I shall go to Portsmouth.

10th   Although the water was still agitated this morning, we went ashore at 10 o'clock and went further to the Town of Stokes. From there, we went to Gosport on a very pleasant road. That avenue filled us with great admiration since by a combination of nature and art it had been rendered quite charming indeed. From Gosport, we crossed the Channel to Portsmouth. Having been here 8 years ago, we still remembered this beautiful city very well. We enjoyed ourselves to our hearts' content, went to see a comedy and some of us also visited the gallant houses. -- --

My friend Besson and I were lodging alone at the Inn of the Red Lion. The innkeeper and his wife still knew us from 8 years ago, assuring us that we had not changed at all, but [added] that they now liked us 10 times better than 8 years ago; for at that time we had not known any English, while they could now talk with us. -- Capt. Freemann returned from London last night, and this morning, our Maj. Gen. von Riedesel departed for London with his family. We also learned that our Capt. Cleve had arrived at Portsmouth on the 6th of this month, the same day on which we had cast anchor at St. Helens; he had continued his journey to London and had arrived there at almost the same time as Capt. Freeman.

11th   The NW wind is continuing to storm and the sea is in frightful motion.

12th   This morning signals were given to all transports to weigh anchor and sail to the Downs. This order was meant for us too but the water was so agitated that it was impossible to get aboard our ship. A large sloop, ordered to go with the flood tide at midnight to get the rest of our general's baggage and the like, was supposed to take us along. Notwithstanding the horribly agitated water, we departed at midnight and arrived on board our *Québec* on the

13th,   at 2 o'clock this morning.
The NW wind continues to storm without abating. Of the transport ships of our fleet having Braunschweig troops on board no more than 3 ships have arrived at Spithead. On these were the 3 commanders, Lieut. Colonel Prätorius on the *Freedom*, Lieut. Colonel von Hille on the *English Hare* and Lieut. Colonel von Mengen on the *Jason*. The rest have possibly sailed past here going straight ahead to the Downs. The ship, mentioned before, which arrived from New York without its masts, was the frigate *Sybil*; on board she had the troops mentioned above under the command of Colonel Voit von Salzburg. Two other dismasted ships also accompanied this frigate with other Bayreuth troops on board under the command of Colonel von Seybothen.

I regret that during the time we had been riding at anchor here, there was not one day of calm; otherwise the *Royal George*, a ship of 110 cannon, would have been hoisted out of the water. It should be mentioned that all skilled navigators have assured us that it was impossible to get this huge ship out although the English in particular have often been successful in this work. Nevertheless, a MECHANICUS has been found in Gosport who, although without experience on the sea, has promised to hoist the ship out of the water at his own expense. This was to be done on the first calm day and all preparations have been made accordingly. Two warships of 74 cannon each, that are to be used for this purpose, have already been unrigged. Everyone knows that this man possesses a fortune of about 2,000 pounds sterling. If he cannot raise the ship, his 2,000 pounds will not even suffice [to cover the expenses]; if he, however, carries out his proposed plan, he will have made his fortune. For he has asked for and been granted by the Admiralty half the value of the ship and half the value of the ship's contents as reward. What can be the value of a ship that has lain underneath the water for such a long time? To this I reply that if the man gets the ship out, the King will gladly give him 10,000 pounds, especially since this sum represents but the eleventh part of the ship's value. Such a ship costs the King 110,000 pounds at any time. Each cannon costs 1,000 pounds as Engl. captains have often assured me. The wealth remaining in the ship could consist of the following: first of all, Admiral Kempenfelt had received 30,000 guineas (in coins) that same morning to pay his officers and seamen, which was to be done that afternoon. In addition, there were many valuables belonging to the admiral and the other officers: silverware, many golden and silver watches, more than one hundred barrels of wine and rum - of all vintages; more than one hundred barrels of Engl. beer, syrup, etc.; between 200 and 300 tons of butter and more articles of value that water cannot spoil. [*When it sank*], the ship had been ready to sail and was supposed to set sail for the American coast the next day. It was noticed that, during the previous night, the ship must have sprung a leak somewhere. The captain, having the command of the ship under Admiral Kempenfelt that day, had ordered the carpenter to look for the spot where the ship was leaking. This carpenter ordered all ballast etc. to be moved to one side whereby the ship tilted to that side. These men had been so careless as to forget to secure the cannon portholes. Through these, water had entered the ship and sunk it in less than 2 minutes.

Including Admiral Kempenfelt, there were 1,500 people on board, among them 300 women. Of all these, about 150 incl. 3 women were rescued; but these had all been on deck. Those who had been down below in the ship are still there. The reason that so many women had been on board was that, since the ship was to set sail the next morning, the admiral had given permission that each sailor could have his wife or mistress with him that night. Thus, the day had been a festive occasion, as it were. In all corners of the ship there was music, dancing, drinking and singing; each one was in this or that way -- involved with his sweetheart, -- and in this situation, they suddenly went into eternity. It is said in Portsmouth that the admiral himself had locked himself in his cabin with his mistress at that very time. Forty Jews from Portsmouth, who had still been trading, calling in debts and the like on board ship, had also drowned.

One hundred guinea pieces have been offered [as reward] for the admiral's body, and great rewards for the bodies of several other officers who went down with the ship. For the English fleet, the year 1782 had been calamitous; not that they had suffered from the enemy, no, the ocean had caused the disasters. Besides this *Royal George* of 110 cannon, the *Ville de Paris* of 120 cannon, that had been seized by Admiral Rodney, had also sunk, together with 6 warships of 74 cannon; in addition, many transport, victual and merchant ships were sunk here and there.

The wind continues to storm violently from NW. That is why we cannot yet sail to the Downs where Maj. Gen. von Riedesel is expected to join us again.

14th   With SW wind, it is raining and quite stormy. At noon, it appeared to be clearing up, and at 2 o'clock this afternoon, we weighed anchor at the very moment that the flood tide was highest. At our departure, we had Spithead on our left and St. Helens on our right. Gusty SW wind. Course toward EES.

15th   Early this morning, we saw the Engl. coast on the left and the French coast on the right. Course toward ENE. Last night was the calmest of our whole journey. There was a gentle breeze, the sky was bright and our *Québec* was being softly driven forward with 18 sails spread. NE. She has the possibility of spreading 32 sails. At 10 o'clock, we were opposite the city of Dover, which was quite pleasant to look at. Dover has a fairly beautiful castle, on top of which stands a cannon, bearing the name "Queen Anne's Pocket Piece." This cannon shoots 12 pound balls and bears this inscription: "When You load me Well and Keep me Clean, I carry my Ball to Calais Green." This fable is still believed by many English. Calais in France lies across the Channel, 21 Engl. or 5 German miles from Dover. Probably no cannon will ever shoot that far. Before reaching the Downs, we had the displeasure of seeing several dead bodies, various hats and other things floating by our ship. It was noon when we reached the Downs. We cast anchor among more than 160 ships. All our transport ships are here and of the fleet that had left Canada, only one ship, having troops from Anhalt-Zerbst on board, is missing. It is a brig by the name of *The Earl of Abercorn*. Our Maj. Gen. von Riedesel will arrive here from London very soon and the order has already been given to all ships' captains by the commodore that we are to depart for the North Sea on the 18th of this month. The city of Deal lies one Engl. mile away from us and appears to be much less attractive than Portsmouth and other Engl. cities. Its inhabitants are mostly pilots living off capsized ships. Up to here, we approached Germany by --118

Total ---3,479

16th   This morning, the wind was blowing from the east; with it, some 80 ships set sail. Six Engl. and one American frigate were among them. There were ships of almost all nations that were taking course toward Portsmouth. It is warm and pleasant weather. If we only had a favorable wind at the time of our departure, we would quickly reach Germany's borders. We weighed anchor this afternoon and moved a little closer to the city of Deal. In the evening, we had a stormy east wind. Tonight, the uppermost, i.e., third mast of our ship was taken down since an even stronger wind was anticipated. We were lying at a dangerous spot where almost every year ships are wrecked. This is not a harbor where ships are protected; it is no better than the open sea. Two years ago, 29 transport ships were lost in this vicinity.

17th   Last night was very troubled. In strong wind, we had dense fog that continued throughout the following forenoon. At noon, the sun broke through and the sky was clearing. The wind continues from the east and the water is horribly agitated. The frigate *Pandora* left us and if the wind should change in our favor, we shall set sail tomorrow.

18th   The wind continues to storm like a gale from the east.

19th   Last night, the wind had changed to south! Early this morning, the commodore gave the fleet the signal to depart; we only had to wait for the arrival of our Maj. Gen. von Riedesel. Yet before our fleet had set sail, the report came that our gen. had arrived at Deal. It was noon when our fleet departed and one hour later, we had lost sight of them.

20th   Gusty SW wind and rain. *The Earl of Abercorn* came today and cast anchor near us. A Royal pilot, a burgher from London, came on board to guide us across the North Sea. A short time ago, he had piloted the Engl. Prince William Henry to Stade.[11]

21st   This morning, our Maj. Gen. von Riedesel came back on board. With continuing SW wind, now it is stormy, now the sun is shining, now it is raining. To all our satisfaction, we finally set sail at noon, taking our course toward ENE. *The Earl of Abercorn* being all by itself accompanied us.

22nd   The continual and strong wind has brought us a very troubled night, to be sure, but it also took us closer to Germany by ---219
Our course continues toward ENE.

23rd   This morning, the wind has almost completely abated and it is raining very hard. We have the rocky Island of Helgoland to our left. Up to here, we advanced ------130

Total ---3,828

The Earl of Abercorn is staying behind since it does not sail as well as we; it is taking its course toward the Weser. Toward evening, the wind changed to east, exactly counter to us. Since it was very foggy, we cast anchor one mile from Helgoland in 17 fathoms of water at 10 o'clock at night.

24th   It was 2 o'clock this morning when we weighed anchor, for the wind had changed to our advantage to the SW. We soon saw the burning lanterns of so-called Neuwerk[12] in front of us and those of Helgoland behind us. At 6 o'clock, we passed by the red barrel, entered the Elbe River and had lost sight of Helgoland. At the red barrel was a Hamburg guard ship and one of their pilots came on board. We now had the lighthouse of Neuwerk in front and to our right; at 7 o'clock, we had passed Neuwerk; at 9 o'clock, Cuxhaven and the beautiful village of Ritzebüttel. Here, our gen. went ashore and continued his journey on land. In the evening, the wind abated and we cast anchor at Freiburg.

25th   At 8 o'clock this morning, we weighed anchor. Since the wind had changed to the east, we sought to advance with the flood tide. The contrary wind wants to play its tricks on us until the very end when we are so close to Stade.

This part of the Elbe is safe. We are tacking here from one buoy to the other and everyone is happy to see the shores of Germany. -- Our fleet reached Stade as late as yesterday. We cast anchor opposite Glückstadt.

26th   At 11 o'clock this forenoon, we set sail and at 4 o'clock this afternoon with tacking and much effort, we finally arrived in the vicinity of Stade. But since the water was running off with the ebb tide, we could not disembark today. The Drag. Reg. has already marched off from Stade and as soon as the other regiments have disembarked and rested in Stade for one night, they are also to march off. From Helgoland until Stade, we advanced   --76

Total--3,904

27th   This noon, we disembarked and marched to Stade. On our ship, one detachment of each regiment has been present. They have each received orders to follow their own regiment. To transport my baggage, I was therefore compelled to take a post chaise. It was 9 o'clock this evening when I left Stade to arrive at Buxtehude at 1 o'clock in the morning. From here, the Dragoon Reg. has marched to Harburg this morning where they will have a day of rest tomorrow. Thus, I remained in the posthouse tonight.

28th   I rode in the post chaise almost to Harburg where I met up with the Drag. Reg.

29th   Today, many marched to Winsen on the Luhe.

30th   We marched to Lüneburg and had trouble getting through the gate since the crowd was unusually large. Everyone was curious to see our black drummers. We had 8 blacks (African) as drummers in the regiment. They drew many onlookers! --

End of this Month

Month of October 1783

1st   We had a day of rest in Lüneburg.

2nd   We marched to Bevensen in the territory of Medingen.

3rd   To Uelzen. Here, our black drummers again had the honor of being inspected.

4th   Day of rest.

5th   We marched to Flinten in the territory of Bodenteich.

6th   We marched to the small market town of Wittingen, in the district of Knesebeck. Our general went to Braunschweig today.

7th   We marched to Gifhorn, where we first encountered people looking for their relatives. --

8th   We marched to Weddel near Braunschweig in the district of Campen. Here, we witnessed other moving scenes of father and son, wife and husband, brother and sister meeting each other with tears of joy.

9th   Today, we marched via Mascherode through the Lechlum Woods to Wolfenbüttel. It took a long time before we were discovered by the inhabitants of Wolfenbüttel since they did not know on which way we were coming. But finally they met our Advance Guard in the little grove, not far from the avenue leading to Salzdahlum.[13] The closer we came, the more people we had around us. Everyone called to his relatives or friends and wherever I looked, I saw friendly people waving at me, even shouting my name, many of whom I did not know at all. Many had grown considerably in these 8 years; they had come of age and changed so much that I could not possibly have known them. I found my wife and children in good health; in almost 8 years, the latter had likewise grown so much and so tall and were so different that I could not possibly have recognized them. At our departure, my son had been 10 and my daughter 8 years old. The various and moving scenes that occurred right before our eyes cannot be described. From our corps that had come from America, no one was allowed to go to Braunschweig but all had first to come to Wolfenbüttel where everything was to be regulated. That was the strict order. --

Total of Engl. miles from Québec to Stade --3,904

12th   The Dragoon Regiment will continue with 4 companies; each comp. with 1 capt., 1 lieut., 1 sergeant major, 1 quartermaster, 1 trumpeter, 2 corporals and 36 privates. The black drummers, who have been drawing so much attention everywhere, are going to join the Regiment von Riedesel. Moreover, one battalion of 4 comps. is going to be formed out of the Artillery corps, each company being 36 men strong. The Leib Regiment will consist of 12 comps., each comp. of 60 privates, which in future shall be called Regiment Prinz Friedrich. Furthermore, another regiment of equal strength will be formed. This shall be called the Regiment von Riedesel since this general is to command it. Besides the Marching Regiment and Garrison Company, this will be the entire Braunschweig corps.
     Out of all the regiments coming from America, the best men shall be selected. Officers, over and above the required number, are to receive an allowance or a pension or will now and then be placed among the Marching Reg. or the Garrison Comp. or else are to become common constables; impecunious ones will receive a pension and many will be discharged. --
     All this is being decided by a commission meeting in daily sessions in the castle of Wolfenbüttel. The principal members of this commission are Maj. Gen. von Riedesel, Major Bethge[14] and Councilor of War Stricker.

18th   The Commission today decided that Regimental CHIRURGUS Müller would be placed with the Dragoon Regiment, Regimental CHIRURGUS Schrader with the Reg. Prinz Friedrich, and Reg. CHIRURGUS Bause with the Reg. von Riedesel as Regimental CHIRURGI. Thus, the four remaining Regimental CHIRURGI were being discharged.

20th   All the Company CHIRURGI had to go before the Commission. I was the only one to stay with the Dragoon Regiment and of the 40 Comp. CHIRURGI who during the American War had been in Braunschweig's service, only 19 will be continuing.

30th   The Dragoon Regiment and the Regiment von Riedesel will receive regimentals today and tomorrow. The regimentals are coming from the House of Prussia. The Drag. Reg. is to be mounted; each drag. has to give a security of 50 schillings.

End of this Month

Month of November 1783

1st   Today was review. His Serene Ducal Highness himself mustered us. Afterwards, both regiments had to form a circle and after hearing the Articles of War, they had to swear [*the oath of allegiance*]. That took place in front of the August Gate near the Treasure House to the left.

2nd   Today, we, i.e., the Drag. Reg. and 1 Battalion von Riedesel, marched to Braunschweig into garrison. The 2nd Battalion von Riedesel [*remained*] in garrison at Wolfenbüttel.

19th   My family came from Wolfenbüttel and I took lodging with the widow Schwalbe in the Sack.[15]

> Now, be quiet my heart, be quiet and
> content with your fate! And do not ever lose
> that! -- Let no violent passions rebel
> [*inspired by*] our hatred of injustice and vice ----
> Lord, you who have helped me bear the
> morning and the midday of my life, let the
> evening, approaching with rapid steps, alas,
> let it be fairer and calmer than the day! --
> And when it comes, do keep me in Your Holy
> Care. Amen.

NOTES

1. Wasmus uses "winter news" to refer to the frequent rumors spread through the British and German troops in Canada after communications with the outside world were cut off by the freezing of the St. Lawrence. See, for example, his entries for 1782.

2. Staff Captain Ernst Heinrich Wilhelm von Girsewald, of the Regiment von Riedesel, of the Convention army; he died in 1818 as a Braunschweig Major General. (Elster, pp. 453, 456, 461.)

3. Major Justus Christoph. von Meibom, of the Dragoon Regiment, had been captured at Bennington and was for a time commander of the Braunschweig troops in Westminster, Massachusetts. His 1778 reports to Riedesel survive. Eventually, the major and his son, Ensign Carl Chris. von Meibom, of the Regiment von Riedesel, left their captivity, apparently without permission of the Americans, and travelled to Flatbush. Riedesel, who had by 1780 been given the command in Long Island, gathered all the wayward Braunschweigers in the area and formed a new Dragoon Regiment. Major von Meibom and his son were recaptured by the Americans in Flatbush, but freed on parole to New York at Riedesel's request to George Washington. The major was sickly and had apparently taken to heavy drinking during his captivity. (Stone, Vol II, pp. 95, 97.)

4. Col. Carl Adolph Christoph von Creutzbourg was a Hesse-Hanau officer who eventually commanded a light infantry battalion. (Atwood, p. 247.)

5. Pointe-au-Fer, now Rouses Point.

6. The British and the Americans had agreed on preliminary peace articles on November 5, 1782. The British signed preliminary articles of peace with France and Spain on January 20, 1783, proclaiming an end to hostilities on February 4; Congress proclaimed an end to hostilities on April 11 and ratified the provisional peace treaty on the 15th. The final treaty was signed in Paris on September 3, 1783 and was ratified by Congress in January 1784.

7. Surgeon Julius Pralle, Regimental Surgeon of the Regiment von Riedesel, became County Surgeon at Jerxheim after the war. (Elster, p. 453.)

8. There are a number of excellent accounts of the experiences of those Americans who supported the King during the Revolution, including Wallace Brown, The Good Americans, New York, 1969; Robert M. Calhoon, The Loyalists in Revolutionary America, New York, 1968; Mary Beth Norton, The British-Americans, Boston, 1972; all of which consider the situation of Loyalist exiles and the harsh treatment meted out to those who tried to return. Catherine S. Crary's The Price of Loyalty (New York 1973), contains moving accounts by Loyalists of their persecution during and after the Revolution.

9. Haldimand's house is till standing today and is used as a senior citizen's clubhouse and restaurant.

10. Rear Admiral Richard Kempenfelt (1718-1782), whose career in the Navy had been capped by his brilliant victory southwest of Ushant in which he captured twenty prizes from de Guichen, was refitting at Plymouth in order to proceed with Howe to the relief of Gibraltar. On August 29, 1782, his ship, the *Royal George,* was careened or heeled over, by shifting the guns onto one side, in order to repair a leak just below the waterline. The ship was crowded with visitors: tradesmen, women and children. Although the Admiralty report stated that a breeze had overturned her, most authorities believe that the shift of weight placed undue stress on the rotten timbers of the old ship, causing a large section of the bottom to fall out, sending the ship with all aboard straight to the bottom. About 800 people, included Admiral Kempenfelt, drowned; Cowper's poem, "Loss of the *Royal George,*" memorializes the occasion.

11. Prince William Henry (1765-1835) was the 3rd son of King George III and Queen Charlotte. He was sent to sea as a midshipman in 1779 and sailed under Rodney at Cape St. Vincent in 1780. He was made Duke of Clarence in 1789 and succeeded his brother George IV, in 1830; King William IV was known to the people as the "Sailor King" because of his naval experience.

12. Neuwerk is a tiny island off the mouth of the Elbe River.

13. Lüneburg was the salt capital of Germany as early as the 11th century, providing salt for seasoning and food preservation throughout the Hanseatic League. Salzdahlum was one of several place names in the immediate vicinity reflecting this influence, including Salzgitter, Salzhausen, and Salzhemmendorf.

14. Major Bethge was administrator of the Braunschweig arsenal.

15. Im Sack is a street in the heart of the old city of Braunschweig; still in existence, the name means "Dead End Street."

Epilogue

There is an entry in the Brimfield, Massachusetts town register of births that reads: "Wasmus, Demus, s. Sarah Hitchcock,* May 23, 1779 (Demas Hitchcock, s. Sarah, C.R.)" [sic]

The name Demas can be found in the New Testament, Colossians, chapter 4, verse 14:
"Luke, the beloved physician, and Demas greet you."

*Sarah Hitchcock was the oldest daughter of Joseph and Mary Hitchcock (Wasmus' landlords in Brimfield), born October 3, 1751.

Bibliography

Anburey, Thomas. With Burgoyne From Quebec: An Account of the Life at Quebec and of the Famous Battle at Saratoga (vol. one of Travels Through the Interior Parts of North America). Toronto: Macmillan, 1963.

Andrews, Melodie. "Myrmidons From Abroad: The Role of the German Mercenary in the Coming of American Independence." Ph.D. dissertation, University of Houston, 1986.

Annual Register of Events. 1780. London: J. Dodsley, 1788.

Applebaum, Diana Karter. Thanksgiving:An American Holiday. New York: Facts on File, 1984.

Arndt, Karl J.R. "New Hampshire and the Battle of Bennington: Col. Baum's Mission and Bennington Defeat as Reported by a German Officer Under General Burgoyne's Command," Historical New Hampshire, 32, (1977) pp. 198-217.

Atwood, Rodney. The Hessians: Mercenaries from Hessen—Kassel in the American Revolution. Cambridge: Cambridge University Press, 1980.

Bailyn, Bernard, and Hench, John B. The Press and The American Revolution. Worcester: American Antiquarian Society, 1980.

Balderston, Marion, and Syrett, David. The Lost War: Letters from British Officers During the American Revolution. New York: Horizon Press, 1975.

Benecke, G. Society and Politics in Germany, 1500—1750. London: Routledge and Kegan Paul, 1974.

Berlin, Ira, and Hoffman, Ronald. Slavery and Freedom in the Age of the American Revolution. Charlottesville: University Press of Virginia, 1983.

Bigelow, J. Warren. "Rutland." History of Worcester County. Boston: C.F. Jewett, 1879.

Bird, Harrison. March to Saratoga: General Burgoyne and the American Campaign. New York: Oxford University Press, 1963.

Boatner, Mark Mayo, III. Encyclopedia of the American Revolution. New York: McKay, 1966.

Brandow, John Henry. The Story of Old Saratoga and History of Schuylerville. Albany: Fort Orange Press, 1900.

Brown, Marvin L., Jr., ed. Baroness von Riedesel and the American Revolution: Journal and Correspondence of a Tour of Duty, 1776—1783. Chapel Hill: University of North Carolina Press, 1965.

Brown, Richard D. Revolutionary Politics in Massachusetts: The Boston Committee of Correspondence and the Towns, 1772—1774 Cambridge: Harvard University Press, 1970.

Brown, Wallace. The Good Americans. New York: Morrow, 1969.

Brown, William J. et al. Syphilis and Other Venereal Diseases. Cambridge: Harvard University Press, 1970.

Burleigh, H.C. Captain MacKay and the Loyal Volunteers. Bloomfield, Ontario: Bayside Publishing Co., 1977.

Calhoon, Robert W. The Loyalists in Revolutionary America. New York: Harcourt Brace Jovanovich, 1968.

Campbell, William W. Annals of Tryon County. New York: Dodd, Mead, 1924.

Carrington, Henry B. Battles of the American Revolution: Battle Maps and Charts of the American Revolution. New York: Arno Press, reprint of 1877 and 1881 editions.

Carsten, F. L. Princes and Parliaments in Germany: From the Fifteenth to the Eighteenth Century. Oxford: Clarendon Press, 1959.

Crary, Catherine S. The Price of Loyalty. New York: McGraw-Hill, 1973.

Curtis, Edward E. The Organization of the British Army in the American Revolution. New Haven, Conn.:Yale University Press, 1926.

Dabney, W.H. After Saratoga:The Story of the Convention Army. Albuquerque: University of New Mexico Press, 1954

Digby, William. The British Invasion From the North. James Phinney Baxter, ed. Albany: J. Munsell's Sons, 1887.

Du Roi. Journal of Du Roi the Elder, 1776-1778. Charlotte S.J. Epping, tr. Philadelphia: University of Pennsylvania, 1911.

Eelking, Max von. The German Allied Troops in the North American War of Independence, 1776-1783. J.G. Rosengarten, tr. Albany: J. Munsell's Sons, 1893.

Elster, Otto. Geschichte der stehenden Truppen im Herzogtum Braunschweig-Wolfenbüttel, vol. II, 1714-1806. Leipzig: Heinsius Verlag, 1901.

Elting, John R. The Battles of Saratoga. Monmouth Beach, New Jersey: Philip Freneau Press, 1977.

Estabrook, Adin C. "Lunenburg," History of Worcester County. Boston: C.F. Jewett, 1879.

Frey, Sylvia R. The British Soldier in America: A Social History of Military Life in the Revolutionary Period. Austin: University of Texas Press, 1981.

Furneaux, Rupert. The Battle of Saratoga. New York: Stein & Day, 1971.

Glatfelter, Charles H. Pastors and People: German and Reformed Churches in the Pennsylvania Field, 1717-1793. Breinigsville, Pa.: Pennsylvania German Society, 1980.

Graymont, Barbara. The Iroquois in the American Revolution. Syracuse: Syracuse University Press, 1972.

Hawke, David Freeman. Everyday Life in Early America. New York: Harper and Row, 1988.

Hoffman, Eliot Wheelock. "The German Soldiers in the American Revolution." Ph.D. dissertation, University of New Hampshire, 1982.

Holborn, Hajo. A History of Modern Germany, 1648—1840. New York: Alfred A. Knopf, 1969

Hyde, Charles M. Historical Celebrations of the Town of Brimfield. Springfield, Mass.: C.W. Bryan, 1879.

Katcher, Philip R.N. Encyclopedia of British Provincial and German Army Units 1775-1783. Harrisburg: Stackpole Books, 1973.

Kellogg, Jefferson B. and Walker, Robert H. Sources for American Studies. Westport, Conn.: Greenwood Press, 1983.

Kemp, Peter, ed. The Oxford Companion to Ships and the Sea. New York: Oxford University Press, 1976.

Kinzer, Stephen, "El Castillo Journal," New York Times, May 23, 1988.

Lamb, R. An Original and Authentic Journal of Occurrences During the Late American War. Dublin: Wilkinson & Courtney, 1809.

Lancaster, Bruce. The American Heritage Book of the Revolution. New York: American Heritage Publishing Co., 1958.

Lanctot, Gustave. Canada and the American Revolution, 1774—1783. Margaret M. Cameron, tr. Cambridge: Harvard University Press, 1967.

Learned, Marion. Guide to the Manuscript Materials Relating to American History in the German State Archives. Washington, D.C.: Carnegie Institute, 1912.

Lemisch, Jesse, "Listening to the Inarticulate: William Widger's Dream and the Loyalties of American Revolutionary Seamen in British Prisons," Journal of Social History, 3, (1969) pp. 1-27.

Ludlum, David, "Almanac," Country Journal, May, 1988, p. 15.

Lumpkin, Henry. From Savannah to Yorktown: The American Revolution in the South. Columbia, S. C.: University of South Carolina Press, 1981.

Luzader, John F. Decision on the Hudson: The Saratoga Campaign of 1777. Washington, D.C.: National Park Service, 1975.

_____. Documentary Research Report on the Saratoga Campaign to September 19, 1777. Saratoga National Historical Park, January 8, 1960.

Mackesy, Piers. The War for America: 1775—1783. Cambridge: Harvard University Press, 1964.

McManus, Edgar J. A History of Negro Slavery in New York. Syracuse: Syracuse University Press, 1966.

Marcus, G.J. A Naval History of England, I, The Formative Centuries. Boston: Little Brown, 1961.

Marvin, Rev. Abijah. "Leicester, " History of Worcester County, Boston: C.F. Jewett, 1879.

Melsheimer, Friedrich Valentin. "Journal." Proceedings of the Literary and Historical Society of Quebec. 1891.

Moody, T.W. and Vaughn, eds. A New History of Ireland. vol. IV, 1691—1800. New York: Oxford University Press, 1986.

Morris, Richard B. The Peacemakers: The Great Powers and American Independence. New York: Harper & Row, 1965.

Nadeau, Gabriel. "A German Military Surgeon in Rutland, Massachusetts During the Revolution: Julius Friedrich Wasmus," Bulletin of the History of Medicine, vol. XVIII, no. 3 (October 1943), pp. 243—300.

Nelson, John. Worcester County: A Narrative History. New York: American Historical Society, 1934.

Newton, Earle. The Vermont Story: A History of the People of the Green Mountain State, 1749—1949. Montpelier: Vermont Historical Society, 1949.

Nickerson, Hoffman. The Turning Point of the Revolution or Burgoyne in America . Boston: Houghton Mifflin, 1928.

Norton, Mary Beth. The British—Americans. Boston: Little, Brown, 1972.

Perkins, James Breck. France in the American Revolution. Boston: Houghton Mifflin, 1911.

Pettingill, Ray W., tr. Letters From America, 1776—1779: Being Letters of Brunswick, Hessian, and Waldeck Officers with the British Armies During the Revolution. Boston: Houghton Mifflin, 1924.

Pope, Dudley. Life in Nelson's Navy. Annapolis: Naval Institute Press, 1981.

Riedesel, Friedrich Adolphus. Memoirs, and Letters and Journals of Major General Riedesel During His Residence in America. Max von Eelking, ed., William L. Stone, tr. 2 vol. Albany: J. Munsell, 1868.

Robson, Eric. The American Revolution: Its Political and Military Aspects, 1763—1783. New York: Norton, 1966.

Rosebury, Theodore. Microbes and Morals. New York: Viking Press, 1971.

Schoepff, Dr. Johann David. The Climate and Diseases of America. James Read Chadwick, tr. Boston: H.O. Houghton and Co., 1875.

Senff, Col. Christian. "Plan of the Battle Near Camden," (from the Steuben Papers, New - York Historical Society), Magazine of American History . vol. 5, October 1880, (p. 275.)

Shy, John. A People Numerous and Armed: Reflections on the Military Struggle for American Independence. New York: Oxford University Press, 1976.

Smith, Clifford Neal. Brunswick Deserter Immigrants of the American Revolution. McNeal, Arizona: Heritage House, 1973.

Snell, Charles W. A Report on the Strength of the British Army Under Lieutenant General John Burgoyne, July 1 to October 17, 1777, and on the Organization of the British Army on September 19 and October 7, 1777. Saratoga National Historical Park, February 28, 1951.

Symonds, Craig L. A Battlefield Atlas of the American Revolution. Annapolis, Md.:The Nautical and Aviation Publishing Company of America, 1986.

Taylor, Robert J. Western Massachusetts in the Revolution. Providence: Brown University Press, 1954.

Thomas, Isaiah. The History of Printing in America. Albany: J. Munsell, 1874.

Thompson, Charles Miner. Independent Vermont. Boston: Houghton Mifflin, 1942.

Toth, Charles W., ed. The American Revolution and the West Indies. Port Washington, N.Y.: Kennikat Press, 1975.

Valentine, Alan. The British Establishment, 1760—1784. Norman, Okla.: University of Oklahoma Press, 1970.

Van de Water, Frederic F. The Reluctant Republic: Vermont, 1724-1791. New York: John Day, 1941.

Von Papet, F.J. "The Brunswick Contingent in America," Pennsylvania Magazine of History and Biography, vol. 15, 1891, pp.218-224.

Wagner, W. "Erinnerungen eines Braunschweigers aus dem Siebenjährigen Kriege," Braunschweigisches Magazin, October 7, 1900, pp. 153-159.

Ward, Christopher. The War of the Revolution. (2 vol.) John Richard Alden, ed. New York: Macmillan, 1952.

White, Walter S. The Governor's Cottage. Sainte-Anne De Sorel, Quebec: Centennial Commission, 1967.

Wickwire, Franklin & Mary. Cornwallis: The Imperial Years. Chapel Hill: University of North Carolina Press, 1980.

Wood, William. The Father of British Canada: A Chronicle of Carleton. Toronto: Glasgow, Brook, and Co., 1922.

——————. The Passing of New France. Toronto: Glasgow, Brook, and Co., 1922.

Wrong, George M. Canada and the American Revolution: The Disruption of the First British Empire. New York: Macmillan, 1935.

Index of Names

General Index

About the Translator and Editor

HELGA DOBLIN is Professor Emerita of Foreign Languages at Skidmore College. Her articles and translations have appeared in the journals *New York History*, *Military Affairs*, and the *Bulletin of Fort Ticonderoga*, and she is currently translating other documentaries of Braunschweig troops in the American Revolution.

MARY C. LYNN is Associate Professor of American Studies at Skidmore College, where she specializes in American social and cultural history. Her work has appeared in *New York History*, *Tamkang Journal of American Studies*, and *Skidmore Voices*, and she is the author of the book *Women's Liberation in the Twentieth Century*.